At a first glance, it will appear as if Falola's new fascinating book simply illustrates the popular saying by George Orwell that "The best books... are those that tell you what you know already." However, and most significantly, what makes this particular work so insightful and unique is that one is able to learn about the history of West Africa through the prisms of Falola's multiple visits, interactions and researches conducted for several decades across the sub-region coupled with his long years of teaching, examining and writing about West Africa. This book is a quintessential primer for bringing the knowledge of West Africa to mature students and the general readers.

Koya Ogen, *Professor of History, Osun State University and former Provost, College of Education, Ondo*

This comprehensive textbook on West Africa offers a deep exploration of the region's history. With its engaging writing style, extensive research, and insightful analysis, it is an invaluable resource for students and educators alike, providing a window into the historical forces that have shaped the region and beyond. This teaching resource is a must-read for teachers interested in helping students obtain a deeper understanding of the region's cultures, economies, politics, and identities.

Henry Lovejoy, *Director of the Digital Slavery Research Lab, University of Colorado Boulder*

Scholars and students alike will actually enjoy reading this invaluable book and will keep returning to it as a deep well. Falola covers major ecological, economic, and political transformations over the longue durée in West Africa while also enlivening history with attention to people's daily lives, pastimes, and priorities—food, art, aging, schooling, and other topics. With a detailed timeline, a thoughtful structure, and spotlights on important West African thinkers, this book is an engaging and usable text that will serve generations to come.

Shobana Shankar, *Professor of History, Stony Brook University*

Professor Toyin Falola, the most prolific historian of our time, has brought a sublime finality to West African history text. Scholars in various fields of studying, teaching, and writing West Africa will find this a most useful book to adopt.

Kwabena Akurang-Parry, *PhD (Visiting Scholar) Professor of African History, Heritage Studies & World History, University of Ghana, Legon, Ghana*

A HISTORY OF WEST AFRICA

This book introduces readers to the rich and fascinating history of West Africa, stretching all the way back to the Stone Age, and right up to the modern day.

Over the course of 27 short and engaging chapters, the book delves into the social, cultural, economic, and political history of West Africa, through prehistory, revolutions, ancient empires, thriving trade networks, religious traditions, and then the devastating impact of the trans-Atlantic slave trade and colonial rule. The book reflects on the struggle for independence and examines how politics and economics developed in the postcolonial period. By the end of the book, readers will have a detailed understanding of the fascinating and diverse range of cultures to be found in West Africa, and of how the region relates to the rest of the world.

Drawing on decades of teaching and research experience, this book will serve as an excellent textbook for entry-level History and African Studies courses, as well as provide a rich general introduction to anyone interested in finding out about West Africa.

Toyin Falola is the Jacob and Frances Sanger Mossiker Chair in the Humanities and University Distinguished Teaching Professor, Department of History, The University of Texas at Austin. He is the recipient of many distinguished awards, including 18 honorary titles.

Routledge Global Africa Textbooks

Series Editor: Toyin Falola

A History of West Africa
Toyin Falola

A HISTORY OF WEST AFRICA

Toyin Falola

Routledge
Taylor & Francis Group

LONDON AND NEW YORK

Designed cover image: peeterv

First published 2024
by Routledge
4 Park Square, Milton Park, Abingdon, Oxon OX14 4RN

and by Routledge
605 Third Avenue, New York, NY 10158

Routledge is an imprint of the Taylor & Francis Group, an informa business

© 2024 Toyin Falola

The right of Toyin Falola to be identified as author of this work has been asserted in accordance with sections 77 and 78 of the Copyright, Designs and Patents Act 1988.

British Library Cataloguing-in-Publication Data
A catalogue record for this book is available from the British Library

Library of Congress Cataloging-in-Publication Data
Names: Falola, Toyin, author.
Title: A history of West Africa/Toyin Falola.
Description: Abingdon, Oxon; New York, NY: Routledge, 2024. |
Series: Routledge global Africa textbooks | Includes bibliographical
references and index.
Identifiers: LCCN 2023028202 (print) | LCCN 2023028203 (ebook) |
ISBN 9781032055961 (hardback) | ISBN 9781032055947 (paperback) |
ISBN 9781003198260 (ebook)
Subjects: LCSH: Africa, West–History. | Africa, West–Politics and government.
Classification: LCC DT475 .F35 2024 (print) | LCC DT475 (ebook) |
DDC 966–dc23/eng/20230620
LC record available at https://lccn.loc.gov/2023028202
LC ebook record available at https://lccn.loc.gov/2023028203

ISBN: 9781032055961 (Hbk)
ISBN: 9781032055947 (Pbk)
ISBN: 9781003198260 (Ebook)

DOI: 10.4324/9781003198260

Typeset in Sabon
by Deanta Global Publishing Services, Chennai, India

CONTENTS

To Funmilayo Frieson,
the face of Africa's future

ACKNOWLEDGMENTS

I have visited all the West African nations. I have interacted with people from all the major West African countries. I have conducted research in every one of them, most recently in the Sahel. I have done both policy and peacekeeping work in conflict areas. Of all the African regions, this is the best known to me. I am grateful to all those who have assisted me over the years. Without my contacts and a network of support systems, I would not be what I am today.

In my long years of teaching African history, West African history is what I have taught the most, beginning as a secondary school teacher in 1973. Then I became an examiner for the West African Examination Council (WAEC), setting questions on the subject for students across the entire region and grading their examination papers. Afterward, I began to write about the region, first for practice sessions in books such as *Islam and Christianity in West Africa*, *A Summary of West African History*, and later for full high school courses in Nigerian schools, notably *A History of West Africa, 1000 AD to 1984*. All these books followed examination councils' teaching and examination requirements, notably the WAEC and the London General Certificate of Education. I am grateful for the opportunities from collaborators, as well as examination and teacher networks. That era is long gone, as my career shifted to college and more advanced levels.

This current book, *A History of West Africa*, is motivated by my deep-seated desire to bring the knowledge of West Africa to mature students and general readers. To the best of my ability, I have tried to avoid ongoing and yet-to-be-resolved debates, if only to avoid unnecessary distractions. I have settled with the conventional. However, a future edition of this book will elaborate on some of the issues discussed here, introduce additional innovative topics that are now being carried to the classrooms, and update the currency of controversies in the literature.

I owe a debt of gratitude to many people, especially my students. I have also had the privilege of asking undergraduate students to read various chapters to determine accessibility. I thank Krosdot Consult, as well as John Kwame in Ghana, Damilola Osunlakin, and Daniel Eworo at Ahmadu Bello University for organizing the contacts with students to test-run the adequacy of the chapters. I owe the students the suggestion that I should treat each chapter as "independent," that is, not to assume that the book will be read from cover-to-cover. I am also grateful to Oluwafunminiyi Raheem, Sikiru Alimi, and Simi Hassam for reading various chapters. 'Tayo Keyede assisted with the final touches to bring the manuscript to production. Many thanks to Mike Efionayi, who worked with me on some of the illustrations, and to Sirah M. Diallo for sourcing the images. I appreciate all of their efforts and contributions.

FIGURES

FIGURE 0.1 Map of Modern West Africa. Author's collection.

West Africa

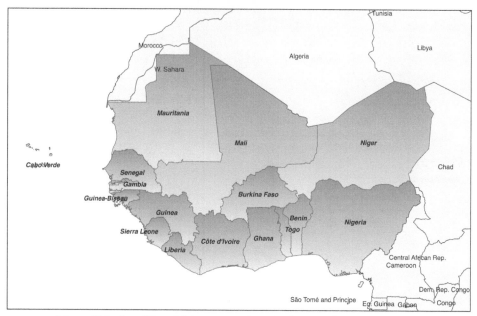

FIGURE 0.2 Map of Modern West Africa zoomed in. Author's collection.

PART I

Introduction

2

FIGURE 0.3 African regions color-coded on political map. Author's collection.

1

INTRODUCTION

Part I: Introduction

This book is divided into 27 chapters across five parts, each depicting various eras and their defining themes in the history of West Africa. In this introduction, which is Chapter 1, subsequent chapters will be examined using the approach and central theme of discussion to gain insights into what the chapters are about.

Chapter 2, "Writing West African History," reviews the controversies that greeted the emergence of African history as a credible discipline, as well as the integrity and acceptability of the sources of information on most of the countries in the West African region, most of which are backed up with evidence tinged with personal sentiment. This is understandable because scholars have had to draw from the information at hand due to a lack of attention. For this reason, this book is not overly troubled by the limitations of previous studies; instead, it employs a user-friendly approach to studying the available data on the history of West Africa by comparing it against the judgment of experts across various academic disciplines. This effort is necessary and timely, as national identity crises have become everyday realities in the region. Identity conflicts will likely continue to be enduring global challenges, if not impediments, to joint development and peace. The degree to which people desire to seek information about their roots demands an immediate reconsideration of our attitudes toward identity issues. This is hugely relevant in West Africa, given the region's particular challenges.

Chapter 3, "Geography, Landscape, and Composition," investigates the geographical landscape of the West African region. The physical representation of the African continent has been affected by the political intentions and questionable underlying motives of some accounts. According to some scholars, especially those who are experts in geography-related fields, the general map of the world is politically configured. For example, there has been difficulty in getting populations to agree on maps of territory and over boundaries. There are numerous maps that questionably describe the same world we all inhabit. The foundational interest is in exploring West African geography to determine

DOI: 10.4324/9781003198260-2

the process through which it has developed and its resulting accuracy or lack of it. By critically engaging with various experts, a scientifically informed conclusion can be reached about the subject.

After conveying a base knowledge on the region's natural compositions, the chapter discusses the available natural resources to provide an understanding of the region's attraction to the global community, especially to those who have embarked on countless exploitative expeditions throughout recorded history. Understanding the inventory of West Africa's natural resources will also help define how they contribute to the political conditions of the countries in the region. Additionally, the chapter investigates West African peoples and their cultures, and adopts information about linguistic heritage(s) to provide helpful evidence. Tracing linguistic ancestry has been identified as one of the most important ways to detail a people's beginnings. Although contiguous cultures and populations living in proximity are prone to pick up the language of their neighbors, this does not necessarily mean that neighboring communities share the essential linguistic elements that define a people's identity and history, allowing this process to analyze group-specific practices of engagement.

Part II: Early History, State Formation, and Societies

This part begins with Chapter 4, "Evolutions and Revolutions," which is designed to provide background information about the West African people. Using a multidisciplinary approach, it draws on anthropology and archaeology to speak to the origins and history of the inhabiting people. This chapter provides archaeological findings and other forms of evidence to establish a strong foundation for the region's history. As most humans have deep-seated connections with hunting and gathering at the beginning of their development, this chapter also examines the prehistoric hunting system(s) of the West African people. This understanding provides insight into the close relationship between the hunting system of a people and their technological development.

For the most part, it is understood that hunting was practiced even in the Iron Age era by individuals with higher technological knowledge. The Stone Age, the Neolithic Revolution, and the Iron Age, among other early eras, are also examined in this chapter. These periods are discussed with the consensus that the discovery and understanding of the development of civilizations that have occupied the region are rooted in concepts that have sustained themselves for long periods. From the Stone Age, there are critical sociological developments that, once redefined and reformed, enable us to trace the activities of local populations to understand their culture, economy, and philosophical thoughts. This chapter is also concerned with the agricultural systems and food chains that dominated the Neolithic Revolution, mainly how newly adopted agriculture techniques affected the forms of produce available. This is crucial because the available food varieties provide us with the information necessary to understand the quality of human nutrition during the period.

Chapter 5, "Societies and Cultures in the Iron Age," covers the Iron Age, which was one of the three most important stages (along with the Stone Age and the Neolithic Revolution) in the early trajectories of West Africa. The three periods are all part of humanity's shared history, and they form the basis for studying and understanding the evolution of different technological, sociopolitical, and economic developments around the world. Societies and people have undergone many changes because of evolving dynamics and external influences. The general improvement in the world's level of technological advancement throughout the Iron Age allowed for a group of people or a cultural identity to understand that they shared the world with a wide variety of other people; whereas, it was previously difficult to be knowledgeable and learn about the cultures of anyone that was not near them. The chapter shows that the exploration of the various cultures in the region provides meaningful information that can be used to reconstruct the events of the period. For instance, the Nok culture, located in Iron Age West Africa, is reported to have achieved a commendable level of creative skill, as shown in their sculptures and other recovered artifacts, demonstrating that theirs was a great culture and civilization. Believed to have been located mainly in present-day Nigeria, the Nok culture is acclaimed for its artistic competence and aesthetics, signs of intellectual evolution. Other notable materials that have been credited to the Nok include iron tools, axes, other stone tools, and stone ornaments and devices used to make work easier. The Nok society is also one of the few and earliest cultures in the West African region to develop iron-smelting technology (Figure 1.1).

Chapter 6, "The Trans-Saharan Trade," explores past economic trade exchanges between the peoples of sub-Saharan Africa and North Africa, whereby cultural and religious belief systems were exchanged, which has inevitably defined contemporary relationships, identities, and status. Establishing the foundation of trade between these geographically distant peoples and cultures enables an understanding of the migration and cultural assimilation dynamics that inevitably developed due to these relations. The cultural exchanges in the regions were enhanced by their proximity, and several historical sources have established the connection between these

FIGURE 1.1   The historically inhabited caves of Grottes de Nok in Northern Togo in Western Africa   https://www.shutterstock.com/image-photo/historically-inhabited-caves-grottes-de-nok-359932832.

regions that date back to antiquity. Recorded history also shows that trading relations have existed between them stretching to the seventeenth century. The spread of Islamic culture in the West African region was connected to the trade with North Africa, granting a reason for the exploration of the need to understand regional relations. However, the exchanges between the different civilizations were not limited to religious ideas; there were also instances of exchanging technological knowledge, political systems, and other essential values. This chapter further examines the effect of this trade in crafting the contemporary heterogeneous nature of West African countries, especially concerning their religious beliefs and cultural dispositions (Figure 1.2).

Chapter 7, "States and Empires," considers the historical rise of various West African civilizations and their sustenance. It cautions against the temptation to assign their greatness to the spread of Islam and Arabic civilization, which perforated the region as a result of the trans-Saharan trade discussed in the previous chapter. This would be misleading and limiting, as these people also had an intergroup trade record that covered areas with no Arabic influence. Thus, the chapter attempts to explore the beginning of the Empires in the region and the many ways they made significant efforts and decisions to organize themselves. For example, the Benin Empire and the Old Oyo Empire attained technological and political milestones in their evolutionary processes, and objects demonstrating their development are spread worldwide in contemporary times.

SLAVE GANG CROSSING THE AFRICAN DESERT.

FIGURE 1.2 Illustration of the trans-Saharan slave trade. Slaves forced to cross the desert, nineteenth century https://www.gettyimages.co.uk/detail/illustration/trans-saharan-slave-trade-slaves-forced-to-royalty-free-illustration/1301259006.

To know and understand the institutions and systems used to achieve these feats is to unravel the secrets behind their organization and philosophical leanings.

Learning about the past helps us place the philosophical focus of these people in the proper context, which can be challenging to ignore, regardless of distractions by current events. Culture has proven vital and pivotal to people's growth, indicating that detachment from their cultural history means that they are redirected but not necessarily lost. In every conceivable way, people try to portray their culture's long-held values, even unconsciously. It is essential to learn about these civilizations because the world is gravitating toward identity politics. Many African groups in this region could be exposed and become vulnerable to erasure or appropriation in the long run without an anchoring of cultural continuity and history. Importantly, knowing more about the Asante civilization in Ghana, or acquiring more information about the Senegambia civilization and Sahelian kingdoms, will encourage an appreciation of these respective cultures and their influence on the present.

Chapter 8, "Domestic Economies," explores West Africa's precolonial domestic history and its attendant constraints such as the paucity of source materials and chronology. The precolonial domestic economy was diversified and comprised agriculture, mining, manufacturing, and commerce, where specialists and professionals in various fields offered essential services. The chapter presents distinguishing features of the production and distributive systems, starting with the essential factors of production and exchange between land, labor, and capital. It examines how these factors contributed to growing the economies of the regions, including the production system, which was characterized by significant changes and innovations, regional diversities, and complex organizations, resulting in a complex range of goods. It highlights different production sectors that dominated the precolonial economy in Africa, such as gold mining, salt production, tin and ceramicware production, and manufacturing, among others. The chapter also analyzes the different currencies in the region before the colonial period, as well as how external and international trades operated in the regions.

Chapter 9, "Traditional Religions," focuses on the documentation of indigenous African religions. Before contact with the West and the Arab world, indigenous Africans had a wide variety of their own religious beliefs, designed per their cultural values and requirements. Some are expressed through Orisa worship among the Yoruba people, which has, surprisingly, gained recognition even in the contemporary world. It further addresses the patterns of worship and injunction of different religions, such as Akan, Odidani, Jola, and Serer, among others, by interrogating practitioners of the religion to gather vital information about their belief systems. While the forms of worship varied across groups, it is widely agreed that these modes of worship were aimed at a Supreme Being through proxies (deities). The worship systems, their doctrinal differences, their epistemological background, and the different features of African religions are the focus of the chapter (Figure 1.3).

Part III: West Africa in the Era of Atlantic Economies and Globalization Up Till the Nineteenth Century

Within the six chapters of this part, the socioeconomic and sociopolitical conditions of the states and societies in the region during this period are examined. First, Chapter 10,

FIGURE 1.3   The Orisa Eleggua, Afro-Cuban Yoruba religion https://www.shutterstock.com/ image-photo/photographic-image-orisha-eleggua-afrocuban-yoruba-2167047533.

"Islam," explores the activities carried out by the Africans who were converted to Islam in the region. It examines the growth of Islam before the nineteenth century and discusses the reasons for Islam's spread, as well as its influence on societies. Starting from North Africa and then across the Sahara, this chapter covers the circumstances that led to Islam's widespread influence in the region in connection with the trans-Saharan trade. As it was prevalent that people exchanged economic ideas and values, they similarly spread aspects of their religion and culture to the West African nations and their people.

In Chapter 11, Christianity's importance to West African history is underlined because the historical trajectory of the African people changed significantly with the advent of the missionaries. These missionaries intended to conquer the spiritual life of Africans through the replacement of their traditional religious identities. Also, during the final stage of slavery, when some of the enslaved Africans across the Atlantic were freed through injunctions, some Africans captured from different parts of the continent were stranded in Sierra Leone. While some remained, others, such as Bishop Ajayi Crowther and Samuel Johnson, went back to their homeland to establish and share Christianity. The historical presence of Christianity in Africa, dating back to antiquity, served as the foundation for establishing the practices of the faith and promoting its values and beliefs. This chapter will highlight how Christianity came into West Africa, tracing it from the precolonial days to pentecostalism in contemporary times. The impact of religion on education, health, and the economy will also be discussed.

In Chapter 12, "The Trans-Atlantic Slave Trade," the focus is on the tragedies that had troubling and disfiguring impacts on the people. In interrogating the experience of slavery, the research and its conclusions are not numb to the reality that digging into the histories of slavery comes with emotional baggage. This chapter examines the active players (the Portuguese, the Dutch, the French, the English, and the Spanish) during the trans-Atlantic slave trade experience and their different roles, including the economic, ecological, political, psychological, and social effects, among others, of the slave trade on the West African people and how it benefited the West. The chapter further analyzes the economic, ecological, psychological, and political impacts of the trans-Atlantic slave trade on the West and on West Africans.

Chapter 13, "Economy and Society: External Commerce," examines the precolonial economic culture of West Africa, which was largely defined by two significant factors: the trans-Atlantic slave trade (discussed in the previous chapter) and legitimate commerce. It analyzes the link between European contact with West Africa (and the rest of Africa) and the economic activities-cum-relationship from that period until colonialism. The trade in humans was dominant until the early nineteenth century when abolitionist activities yielded positive results and the slave trade declined in favor of the trade in raw materials—mostly agricultural produce—known as "legitimate trade" or commerce. The economic labor demands proved fatal for the indigenous Americans, and thus, Europeans turned to Africa. This marked the commencement of the trans-Atlantic trade, or triangular trade, as it is also known. Not only did this change the commercial relationship between Europeans and West Africans, but it also affected the culture of West Africa vis- à-vis practices, activities, and occupations. This chapter focuses on the "legitimate" commerce and other economic practices in West Africa, especially during the nineteenth century until the advent of colonialism, and the significant part it played in ushering in colonialism. It also aims to show that the West African economy was not always about the activities of the Europeans, even in the era of trans-Atlantic trade.

Chapter 14, "Transformations and Revolutions," interrogates the tensions that existed between different major precolonial West African civilizations. Most often, these conflicts arose out of the cyclical nature of contention for regional power and dominance. This topic is particularly important because the West African nations have long been caught in a web of conflict and strife in the context of state formation and expansion. Also, scholars consider this period revolutionary, given the complex web of global and local developments of the time. Political authority in West Africa had switched at the turn of the nineteenth century from filial privileges to military prowess and individual capacity. The abolition of the slave trade and the establishment of "legitimate" commerce, which in large part changed the social fabric of society, also contributed to this. This chapter looks at each of these, outlining the fundamentals of the many advancements and changes that took place throughout this period.

Chapter 15, "Nineteenth-Century Jihads in West Africa," examines the history of Islam's growth in West Africa, beginning in the seventh century and ending with the jihads in the nineteenth century. The precise date of Islam's entrance into West Africa is unknown because many earlier incidents of contact and conversion were not recorded by early Arab sources, except where they indicated the conversion of a respected figure (royalty), which was considered a victory for the faith. The chapter explores the ideological, social, and political backgrounds of the different jihads and their intellectual, social, and political contexts throughout the century and their effects on West Africa.

Part IV: The Colonial Era

This part contains discussions regarding the state of West Africa after the precolonial period. Chapter 16, "Colonial Rule and Its Impact," the first chapter in this part, examines the imposition of colonial authority and the administration of colonies through the indirect rule system, where French and Portuguese colonialists engaged the services of African chiefs directly in their colonies. These chiefs were incorporated and integrated into the administrative system according to convenience, the cost of administration in the colonies, the size of the colonies, and the availability of personnel. Also, the policy of assimilation and association, which was implemented in regions under the control of the French, is explored in this chapter. Undeniably, colonial rule came with measures of good and evil, encouraging development while accelerating people's degeneration. The idea of taxation, for example, albeit not alien to the majority of these West African countries and civilizations, although not at the level introduced during the period of colonization, was imposed to exploit people's financial resources. Despite the consensus that colonialism had destructive effects, there is also an understanding that its introduction necessitated a redefinition of African politics and economics and also affected other areas such as infrastructure development, education, and religion, among others.

Chapter 17, "West Africa and the World Wars," investigates the involvement of West African countries in the World Wars, examining how West Africans were drafted into what were originally European wars but were later said to have evolved into wars against racism and colonialism. The First World War changed West Africa's trajectory and laid the foundation for the independence struggles that came after the Second World War. This chapter discusses the role of West Africans in the World Wars, the colonial administration in the interwar years, and the impact and consequences of the wars on the region. Furthermore, this chapter explores the far-reaching consequences of the World Wars on the region's economy and politics.

Progressing further, Chapter 18, "Continentalism, Nationalism and Independence," considers the efforts of some African nationalists, the brains behind African political independence. The road to the independence of the West African region was, in fact, partly paved by the exposure of Africans who fought in the World Wars. Having stood shoulder to shoulder with the Europeans who were forcefully controlling their home countries' economic and political systems, their knowledge and perception gradually changed. They noticed that, contrary to the generally held misconception that these Europeans were devoid of human flaws, Europeans were as human as Africans. They also realized that these Europeans would find it difficult to challenge them in combat if they possessed similar sophisticated technology. These thoughts appeared to be commonplace among those Africans who fought during the period and would eventually be transformed into a nationalist drive to challenge the imperialists until they renounced power. The chapter focuses on Africa's resistance to colonialism, the notions of nationalism and Pan-Africanism, and the different expressions of nationalism through movements, political parties, and prominent nationalist leaders from various West African regions. It also explores women's contributions to independence struggles, nationalist movements, and the impact of radicalism and trade unionism on the West African independence movement.

Chapter 19, "The Road to Independence in West Africa," focuses on protests and demands before the Second World War. European colonists worked to increase their control over colonies and protectorates in Africa in the few decades following the scramble for Africa and before the First World War. They also devised social and economic policies during this time to direct the management of their African colonies. This chapter focuses on protests and demands before the Second World War and the attendant political radicalism that arose as a result of the war. It further explores constitutional reforms in British West Africa and the independence of the French colonies, where African political leaders engaged in the decolonization process.

Part V: The Postcolonial Era

The abolition of colonialism on paper was by no means the end of the story. Events surfaced in the postcolonial period in the region that demonstrated that it, in many ways, had merely been redefined, making the postcolonial history of West Africa as revealing as the earlier eras. Chapter 20, "Postcolonial Politics," explores the main issues that have emerged in West African politics, especially regarding instability, militarization, and the quest for democracy since independence. Upon attaining independence, West Africa was soon embroiled in coup after coup, the cycle lasting about three decades in some countries. With limited requisite knowledge of leadership in running a modern nation—unlike leadership within the precolonial political structures—these groups and their compatriots seized power aggressively. Consequently, the chapter looks at alternating cycles of military and democratic leadership of states in the region, including the fact that as Europeans ended formal colonialism, certain countries considered doing away with the identities thrust on them by the colonial authorities through the drafting of the colonial borderlines.

Chapter 21, "Economies and Development," is dedicated to interrogating the economic imperialism that occurred in the countries within the region after the end of colonization. Although postcolonialism has a significant impact on a wide range of disciplines, including the social sciences, cultural studies, geography, and anthropology, economists have avoided discussing it as if it does not impact the human experience within their field of study. This chapter discusses economic imperialism in Africa and its postcolonial impact on the region, including how West African countries were transformed through regional integration, agriculture, industrial revolution, and women empowerment.

Chapter 22, "Postcolonial Cultures," explores the vibrant cultures of the people within the region. There is no contention that Africa is home to many beautiful cultures and that the western region of the continent contains many practices and sights. Every society across the world has cultural traditions that serve as the building blocks of its identity. Although West African cultures and their custodians have been introduced to centuries of denigration and despoliation, their adaptability remains phenomenal, making studying them both fascinating and essential. These cultures express themselves through their arts, religions, crafts, clothing, architecture, cuisine, music, folklore, and other practices. With the range of these materials available to study, it is believed that this exercise will bring great intellectual value and understanding to the means of survival of these traditions.

In Chapter 23, "Cultural Changes and Popular Cultures," the uniqueness of West African cultures in their manner of growth and relatedness is highlighted. Cultures are a set of conscious or unconscious attitudes unique to a people, each with its language, norms, rituals, values, ethics, and artifacts, among others. Popular culture is generally observed beliefs, lifestyles, and practices sustained through history or in contemporary society. The chapter examines ancient cultures, cultural changes, and contemporary cultures, as well as different types of festivals in the West African region and their transformative influence on language, entertainment, fashion, and women.

Chapter 24, "Religions and Religious Changes," focuses on the theorization of different scholars to understand the essence of religion and its sociological relevance. These theories–wishful thinking, symbolism, and intellectualism–are each explored in this chapter. It discusses traditional religions in West African societies and how they influenced all aspects of society, including agricultural practices and political systems. The rapid growth of Christianity and Islam in contemporary West Africa is also explored in this chapter, and how contemporary religious practices are gaining hold, causing a radical and intensive religious revolution within African societies.

Chapter 25, "Contemporary West African Identities," examines modern West African identities, their social contours and ramifications, and the historical events that have shaped them. It also looks at the origins of West African identities, including indigenous, Islamic, slave, and colonial identities, and globalization. Africans have continued to contend with identity-based crises as a major bane of positive development in the region. The enthusiasm with which Africans have embraced Western culture demonstrated in their preference for Western languages, names, food, music, and religion, has further confirmed their role as enablers in their own contemporary enslavement. This chapter aims to enlighten readers about African identity, especially the different types of West African identities. The chapter concludes that West Africa is a kaleidoscope of multiple identities at various levels, all with the potential for unity in diversity. The region must rise above its differences and social ills and, as it did with Pan-Africanism, reclaim pride in African culture and establish the African agency's capacity for development.

Chapter 26, "West Africa and the Wider World," seeks to unravel the relationship between West African countries and the rest of the world at the current moment. It is inevitably difficult for the continent, much more the region, to act in a manner separate from the current world order. Multiculturalism has necessitated this reality and makes it crucial that we study the current relationship of the region with the world so that it will be easier to predict what the future will bring. To negotiate the well-being of the region's people, it has become necessary that West African countries organize themselves into units to enable them to voice their perspectives, especially when their region is exposed to challenges. For this reason, the Economic Community of West African

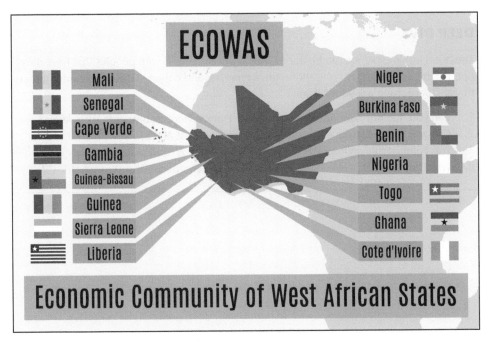

FIGURE 1.4   Map of the Economic Community of West African States (ECOWAS) https://www.gettyimages.co.uk/detail/illustration/vector-map-and-flag-of-the-economic-royalty-free-illustration/1203547728.

States (ECOWAS) was formed. The organization is responsible for coordinating joint economic systems for the common advantage of various nations. The pretext remains that most of these countries continue to carry debts they have had since colonialism. This chapter will explore the existing relationship between countries in the West Africa region and between the region and the world, as well as those countries' involvement in international organizations and their dependence on world powers since the postcolonial time (Figure 1.4).

Chapter 27, the last chapter in the book, titled "Trajectories and Projections on the Future of West Africa," analyzes the current trajectories of development in West Africa, evidenced by its multifaceted sociocultural leanings. With over 700 distinct languages and diversity in culture, religious, and ethnic attributions, the region is unarguably one of the most diverse in the world. Though colonialism and neocolonialism have impacted the sociocultural life of the people and cultural symbols such as food, music, and economic and religious activities have succumbed to Western influences, there is an observable trend whereby most West African countries are standing up against imposed external infiltration. This chapter concludes that drastic action must be taken to achieve the prospective future envisaged for the continent. For West Africa to take its rightful and top position in the global scheme of things, policies that promote diversification of economies, foster entrepreneurship and innovation, as well as on climate change and corruption eradication must all be put in place.

DEEP DIVE

The history of West Africa can be traced from a distant period with peoples that have developed highly sophisticated civilizations, great empires, and nation-states up to contemporary times. Questions to ask yourself are:

1. Can you mention four Anglophone and six Francophone countries in West Africa?
2. Can you locate Portuguese-speaking countries in West Africa?
3. Was colonial rule an important contribution to West African civilization?
4. Why is the period between the 1950s and 1960s regarded as the "Year of Africa"?

2

WRITING WEST AFRICAN HISTORY

Introduction

Although the use of the methodological approach of oral evidence and traditions in the reconstruction of African history has substantial values of its own, there are still problems encountered that have been addressed to validate this approach. This is so in West African history as it is in other parts of the world. Being aware of this fact, scholars have combined a medley of other methods in their organization and narration of historical events of the subregion. In analyzing the sources of historical study, the shortcomings and limitations of the various sources of history make it imperative that they complement and cross-check against each other as much as possible if they are to be regarded as reasonably admissible materials for historical reconstruction.[1] West African historians are interested in a vast array of information and facts to produce a record of the past, especially to counter the arguments of imperial and colonial historians and anthropologists.

One of the foremost and important sources for the reconstruction of the history of West African societies has been practical and unwritten sources of history, such as oral and material evidence, as well as oral traditions.[2] Oral sources include historical materials passed down from generation to generation by word of mouth. Other unwritten sources are evidence from auxiliary sources such as archeological excavations, linguistic affinities, ethnography and culture, botany, and paleontology. As historical study grew and advanced, unwritten sources, such as oral evidence, were crucial to the study of preliterate societies.[3] Even in the modern and contemporary era, many societies' lives can be reconstructed by adopting and using oral evidence.

Although historical research seeks wider and more comprehensive source materials to meet the goals of accuracy and objectivity, oral evidence and traditions in West Africa may remain the originator from which the written accounts can be made. However, the search for credibility in the modern world confers on the historian the responsibility to adopt a complementary strategy for the research, writing, and reconstruction of West

DOI: 10.4324/9781003198260-3

African history. This chapter seeks to illuminate the above with clarification and definition of the key concepts, an analysis of the oral evidence source and historical research, an outline of the strategy of complementarity in historical reconstruction that historians have adopted, as well as a conclusion that stresses the need for the effective harnessing of all source materials for history, research, and writing.

Oral Evidence and Other Unwritten Sources

The major concepts imperative for clarification in this chapter, such as oral evidence and archeological and other unwritten sources, are intertwined with the definition and conceptualization of history itself. According to Charles Firth, "History is the record of the life of societies of men [and women], of the changes which those societies have gone through, of the ideas which have determined the actions of those societies and the material conditions which have helped or hindered their development."[4]

Other scholars, such as Edward Carr, have defined history as "a continuous process of interaction between the historian and his facts, an unending dialogue between the present and the past."[5] The unwritten sources are the oral, archeological, and material records and evidence of people and society's past activities especially adapted to reconstruct the history of various preliterate West African societies. They include oral evidence and traditions,[6] natural objects or features such as forests, streams, rivers, hills, valleys, and artificial equipment or artistic objects like shrines, cutlery, pottery engravings, carvings, sculpture, and entertainment instruments. These unwritten sources are also tapped from other auxiliary sources such as archeological excavations, linguistics, anthropology, ethnography, botany, social biology, zoology, paleontology, or fossil remains.[7] Oral evidence refers to historical material sources handed down to an individual, family, community, society, or nation by word of mouth from generation to generation.[8]

Historians affirm that even in the modern and contemporary times of human development, the abundance of written sources coexists effectively with the indispensable aspect of historical reconstruction, such as oral evidence and other unwritten sources. In sum, oral evidence also involves the historical materials evident in human memory, traditions, culture, physical structures, artistic works, languages, and folklore used for the historical reconstruction of the lives of human societies in many parts of West Africa.[9]

Colonial Misconceptions and Arguments about West African History

Colonial historiography was founded on shaky ground. It utilized the early European accounts written before the nineteenth century, returning to European contacts and encounters in the fourteenth and fifteenth centuries. This early contact by Europeans was wholly devoted to economic and commercial interests, and the information kept by the traders related especially to trade with West Africans in gold, ivory, textiles, spices, and slaves.[10] Sometimes, the traders used the availability of these commodities to identify the continent, such as the Gold Coast, Ivory Coast, and The Gambia. Most of the writings of the traders were not explicit and were wholly concerned with economic activities, covering only the coastal areas of Africa, and any information about the interior of the continent was second-hand.

The later European accounts that colonial historiography adopted were generated in the eighteenth century by explorers, expeditions, and missionaries and the records of officials of colonial administrations across West Africa with the direct colonization of the entire African continent by the beginning of the twentieth century. But these accounts, records, and diaries kept by the Europeans were highly subjective as they were products of the European worldview and saw Africa in the light of European values.[11] The collected information was weak as it was second-hand and came from cooks, stewards, and other associates who were mostly ignorant of what they were reporting. In their writings, they paid close attention to "exotic" West African practices, as they saw them, without an attempt to comprehend the essence of such practices.[12]

The main assumption of colonial historiography was the ideological weapon adopted to justify the European conquest of Africa. Therefore, historians such as David Hume and Hugh Trevor-Roper believe that the entire African continent did not enter modern history until contact with Europe.[13] It was also their belief that the continent lacked any development of civilization and must, therefore, undergo the process of pacification; it had become the white man's burden to bring enlightenment to the continent.[14] Colonial historiography equated history only with written records, rejected African societies' rich historical heritage of oral traditions and literature, and ignored the earlier written materials and sources of Africa's history such as *Ajami*, Arabic, Ge'ez, and hieroglyphics.[15] Under this Eurocentric writing, Africans were degraded and presented as higher beastly animals.[16]

Also, historical studies were sponsored for administrative purposes and were included in the colonial records. These colonial administrative records were replete with anthropological analyses, as well as oral traditions that contained historical data. Before the end of colonial rule, a large percentage of the historical records acquired by European explorers, missionaries, and colonial administrators were based on oral data. Abubakar Ibrahim maintains that though these may have been insufficient in volume and depth, like the travelogues of Hugh Clapperton and Heinrich Barth, they included major and important events.[17] The writings of colonial historiography were essentially a justification of slavery and imperialism under which the West African subregion was to be subjugated permanently and made subordinate to their European masters.[18] Thus, the "Hamitic hypothesis" was developed to show that West Africans could not function independently without external stimuli from Europeans or elsewhere.[19]

According to Ibrahim, citing Fage, since 1949, West African historiography has become increasingly similar to that in other parts of the world. He admits that there have been instances of challenges due to the relative lack of early documented materials and the ensuing need to establish other sources such as oral history, linguistics, and archeology.[20] Colonial historiography did not see African studies as the task of the historian but as that of the anthropologists. Therefore, much effort was channeled toward the conduct of what was termed "tribal studies," as Africans were seen as "primitive tribes," "noble savages," the people of the "dark continent," and many other negative stereotypes and depersonalizations. Another notable feature of colonial historiography was the influence of evolutionism in their writings.[21] The idea of the European master's race and supremacy loomed large in their presentation of Africa. Their accounts were, thus, laced with bias, racism, and various prejudices.

Even though European scholars and philosophers such as Georg W. F. Hegel,[22] Arthur P. Newton,[23] and others have attempted to denigrate Africa's civilization and past, historical evidence in Africa has proven otherwise. Walter Rodney's seminal work in this area showed concrete examples of civilization, dynamism, and development from ancient Egypt, Ethiopia, Nubia, the Maghrib, Western Sudan, Zimbabwe, and others.[24] In fact, in West Africa, the empire of Ghana flourished at a time when Europe was in the "Dark Ages." According to Rodney, it was actually "European colonial bourgeois anthropologists whose philosophical outlook on 'primitive societies' caused them to separate African society from its historical context."[25] Thus, the nature of their studies and work was subjective.

Oral traditions and literature were significant parts of history on the African continent, a factor disputed and rejected by colonial historiography. So, the West African historical reality, preserved through narrative oral traditions, folklore, songs and chants, rituals, proverbs and wise sayings, poems, carvings and paintings, scarification, and several indigenous forms of writings, such as Nsibidi in the Ibibioland of Nigeria, cannot be ignored in African historical reconstruction. This was the rich West African historical heritage and evidence jettisoned by colonial historiography. Even where they were recognized, modifications were made to fit in with the colonial accounts (Figure 2.1).

Colonial historiography presented the notion of a pre-colonial African society in constant instability, with a lack of social harmony, and morally inferior to Europeans.[26] But African history has demonstrated that through the slave raids and liberation struggles on the continent, it was contact with European imperialists and colonizers, especially those with authoritarian or totalitarian ideologies, that led to destruction, instability, disharmony, and misery in Africa. So, on that premise, Africa held and stood on higher moral ground and could be described in the period as morally superior to the European colonial order.[27]

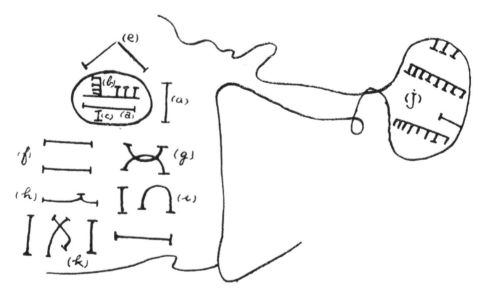

FIGURE 2.1 Nsibidi characters for an "Ikpe" judgment as recorded by J. K. Macgregor https://commons.wikimedia.org/wiki/File:Ikpe_nsibidi.jpg.

The Hamitic hypothesis and a host of condemnations were a blatant move to deny the West African peoples their measure of freedom, self-determination, and independence and permanently subjugate them to the vagaries of colonialism and imperialism. However, West African societies had functioned with dynamism, movement, progress, and development at their own pace for several millennia before contact with Europeans.[28] Furthermore, colonial historiography remains an inadequate guide in the study of West African history as part of its assumptions was colored by the theory of evolution. Adopted into practice on the continent, it led to the system of apartheid in South Africa, which was resented by the international community.[29] Thus, the series of prejudices, biases, distortions, and stereotyping of Africans posed a real challenge in adopting colonial accounts, records, and methods to carry out the objective reconstruction of African history.[30]

To this end, the preliterate societies of West Africa did not receive the desired attention in the colonial accounts and records as they were often regarded as "tribal societies" in their primordial stages, with a backward culture.[31] Therefore, West African history continued to suffer under European imperialist-colonialist perspectives, even up to the second half of the twentieth century.

Oral Evidence, Historical Research, and Writing

As recently as the mid-twentieth century, historians of the Western tradition continued to treat African historiography as an ethnohistory of folk history relevant only to anthropological studies and not a serious enterprise worthy of any historical engagement by any professional at all. This erroneous belief is anchored on the premise that the African continent is not rooted in prehistoric character, lacking in writing, civilization, and a proper sense of history worthy of study. This consideration was misrepresented and misinterpreted in African history predominantly because of the culture of an oral tradition linked with folklore, concluding that Africans lack consciousness in terms of history. Undoubtedly, sources of African history are drawn from the oral tradition of the people and reported through time as knowledge, literature, and cultural identity. This is especially true in the community from which it was drawn, while other oral traditions are transmitted as part of the individual experiences of people who are part of a particular generation. Usually, oral sources represent the baseline through which information about ideology, history, philosophy, and community worldview is represented.[32]

Oral traditions may have their weaknesses, but so too do written sources; thus, the oral tradition cannot be dismissed based on its weakness of not being a reliable source for historical reconstruction. Ajayi and Alagoa argue that the limitations recognizable by historians working on oral tradition do not invalidate African historiography as a scientific enterprise.[33] Even more relevant when dealing with oral tradition is recognizing its limitations and correlating it with other sources to achieve balance. While contributing to the relevance of oral tradition, Jan Vansina maintains that:

> With all practitioners in the field, we can re-affirm that oral traditions are a legitimate and valuable source for … historians – sources which admittedly are usually difficult to handle, but which can yield information about past events and past trends. They

are indispensable if we hope to arrive at a genuine understanding of what happened in Africa.[34]

Although it took some time to convince historians trained in the Western tradition, who are used to written sources, to accept unwritten sources of history such as oral evidence, those sources remain the pivot for the beginning of any meaningful form of historical research and writing. They also provide great evidence of immense contributions to the writing of the history of many societies.[35] These societies include Africa, Latin America, the Caribbean, the Middle and Near East, and even Western societies, where relics, dated stelae, carvings and drawings, ruins, and the activities of court historians, griots, oral artists, and poets have been utilized in the reconstruction of history (Figure 2.2).

Effectively harnessing the advantages inherent in oral evidence helped the work of scholars such as Joseph Greenberg in his study of Africa, Charles K. Meek's ethnographical work, Henry Barth's historical research in Nigeria and elsewhere, and the writings of anthropologists that all stem from the usage of the rich material sources in oral evidence. Rupert East and Daniel Akiga's reconstruction of the early history, culture, and society of the Tiv of Central Nigeria[36] was also hugely based upon oral evidence and unwritten sources, as was Saburi O. Biobaku's work on the Yoruba of southwest Nigeria.[37]

The historian's foremost methods of research into the past involved the use of oral evidence and traditions, asking questions, interactions with members of the society in question, and taking note of evidence from auxiliary sources.[38] What may later be acclaimed as written and documented history is collected from these oral and physical materials of society. West African history is a notable example of the vitality of oral evidence and other unwritten sources, and the chapter-based system of historical documentation, according to Western standards, also started early on the continent. Most of

FIGURE 2.2 A griot woman https://commons.wikimedia.org/wiki/File:P2000360_Trio_Da _Kali_(Klangkosmos_-_Weltmusik).jpg.

the early historical developments that have been recorded were generated from oral traditions and other unwritten sources. These are evidenced by the works of the renowned Egyptologist Cheikh Anta Diop, Africanist historians such as Kenneth Dike, Yusufu Bala Usman, Jacob F. Ade Ajayi, Elizabeth Isichei, John D. Fage, Abdullahi Smith, Jan Vansina, and others.[39]

In most cases, the already documented histories of many West African societies are heavily laced with biases. Therefore, by using corroborative evidence from the rich reservoir of oral evidence, a more meaningful and objective account of a society's history can be reconstructed by also considering the views and observations of the common people. In addition, the overall records of the life of societies have not been exhaustively written, and available oral sources can help historians in their craft of developing the history of such societies for their entrance into the realm of historical and intellectual study. In this case, the production of history through oral evidence and other unwritten sources becomes not only possible and essential but also imperative to the needs of human development.[40]

The Methodology of West African History

Over the years, archeologists have used data from other fields of research that explore the study of human communities and their importance in understanding modes of transition and developmental continuity.[41] Data from ethnography and anthropology has so far proven useful in the development of archeological interpretations. Researchers from the region, and often archeologists, collect data from these fields to enrich their method's content. Paul J. Lane noted that archeologists had used analogical modeling, which has since become part of archeological study and analysis.[42] By so doing, archeologists have used ethnography to transform their discipline and engage the past from a different perspective than that which their discipline offers. They are also momentarily and spatially separated from either Western or other cultures in an attempt to improve research methods in archeology. One strand that has proven counterproductive is the inclination to categorize human cultures from the point of view of evolutionary structure and to further establish or perpetuate the idea that past societies left something behind and, thus, excluded from certain developments. This reconstruction approach is not only unphilosophic; it is also unscientific.

Scholars in the field have long presented the evolutionary categories governing the use of analogs in archeological study; therefore, ethnographic analogs considered for analysis were also driven by selecting and considering the evolutionary process. With this, archeological interpretations drew their comparisons, which were important in the methodology of archeological study. Studies on Paleolithic sites in Europe used ethnographic extrapolations from African hunter-gatherers, particularly the Kalahari San, to show the similarities between communities that reflect a timeless history, while issues such as the division of labor and concepts of social organization and rituals became difficult to infer. Such comparisons were incorrect; there is no proper analogy between how early human beings lived in the ancient ice age and modern societies, equated with capitalist economy and democracy and living in a humid, semi-arid nation-state. European scholars' misrepresentation of African history is opposed to cultural and physical differences, especially those between dark-skinned Africans and Europeans.

It was not just in this way that such comparisons were erroneously made. In the mid-nineteenth century, European scholars depicted Africans as primitive and wild people.[43] This categorization was used to distinguish fundamentally non-Western societies, their cultures and practices, but as research emerged, both Western and non-Western societies seem to complement each other on a comparative basis. Therefore, ideas such as living modern savages and barbarians laid the grounds for comparison in the field of archeology, other than for past civilizations that share similar technology in terms of the practice of survival. While such colonial and racist conceptions of research methods may have modified their ethnographic comparisons, it cannot be said that the discipline has rid itself of such stereotypes.

Analogy as a mechanism relies primarily on the inductive style of reasoning. The analogy model for research believes that if two objects have common observable similarities, they are likely to share other similarities that are less observable. When the proportion of measurable similarities between objects is greater than that of peoples and cultures, there is a propensity for other variables to be normal. However, this is not the case in West Africa since the presence or absence of other typical characteristics hypothesized might not be related to such measurable similarities. Ethnographic deductions often turn out to be quite common based on the principles that similar cultural conditions could produce similar cultural conditions with the development of methods in archeology, and cultural phenomenon is simply an ethnographic parallel. In Western archeological studies, the pursuit of this methodology made West African societies become models of comparison. This is also because prehistoric European archeology coincided with the West African era of colonial anthropology, and colonial domination was central to the business of recording the history and cultures of diverse groups.

In terms of archeological methods, what was obtainable in the West African region as inferences drawn from excavations, especially from the residents' material culture, vis-à-viz what was observable from the practices in areas where studies were carried out? The method limited comparisons from one geographical space to another and provided continuity between past and present communities. For example, this approach also influenced studies in other parts of Africa. Lane argues that Caton-Thomson used such analogies to make deductions from her observation of the characteristics of Shona houses that were identical to those she had excavated in Zimbabwe and prove continuity from the points of material culture to elements of similarities in methods and architecture.[44] The use of comparison, on the whole, seems controversial since archeologists were projecting the present into the past, so it became impossible to draw conclusions from past social formations and objects that have no connection with the present. This also calls for caution in the reconstruction of African history using an ethnographic analogy.

Despite its oddities, the growth of archeological and functional disciplines in the West African region has helped to understand societies' history and development patterns in the subregion.[45] For instance, historical archeology has helped unravel other aspects of African archeology. Historical and archeological sources for the reconstruction of African history include oral and material records that demonstrate the evidence of people and society's past activities, specially adapted to reconstruct the history of preliterate society. Other auxiliary materials for reconstructing West African history from various sources such as archeological excavations, linguistics, anthropology, ethnography, botany, social biology, zoology, paleontology, or fossil remains are also useful.

Historians believe that in modern and contemporary periods of human development, the proliferation of written sources coexists successfully with the indispensable element of historical reconstruction, unwritten sources, and archeological evidence. The historical material evident in customs and culture, particularly those of West Africa, physical structures, artistic work, languages, and folklore, was deployed and used for the historical reconstruction of the lives of human societies in these archeological and unwritten sources. Also, the overall record of social life has not been written extensively, and archeological sources may assist the historian's ability to establish the history of those societies for their entry into the field of historical and intellectual research. In this case, the processing of history through archeological sources is not only feasible and crucial but also completely essential for human growth (Figure 2.3).

Oral traditions have been identified in different forms, including narrations by eyewitnesses, myths, legends, poems, music, and commentaries. Among the Nigerian cultural groups, the oral sources commonly available are titles and names, poetry, lists containing genealogies, legends, commentaries, precedents in law, and personal narratives. The use of oral tradition is particularly important because many African history writers were not educated but were able to use oral tradition to write the history of the

FIGURE 2.3   A script for the Vai language which was invented in Liberia in the early nineteenth century https://commons.m.wikimedia.org/wiki/File:West_Africa_Vai_Document _Lores.jpg.

people, thus validating the need to use oral tradition to reconstruct West Africa's past. Over the years, African archeologists have recognized the need to decolonize their methodologies to allow Africa to move closer to its goal of decolonizing its people, memory, and institutions. Archeology has contributed insight into West African history by using a multidisciplinary approach that deploys multiple sources such as written sources and oral tradition.

It is important to be cautious about how other disciplines, such as historical archeology, are used in the reconstruction of African history. Augustin Holl had earlier warned that the way historical archeology is used in the study of African history suggests that the field of study is aimed at establishing models of "control," "subjugation," and spoliation of Africa and Africans.[46] Holl's position reflects the problems of imperial domination of the system of knowledge production and the individuals responsible for it and engaging in its teaching and learning. In this vein, scholars such as Akin Ogundiran and Toyin Falola, among others, have advocated for the decolonization of historical studies, especially in a way that will improve the understanding of African history globally.[47] Sadly, even far into the twentieth century, the Eurocentric understanding of African history dominated global perspectives on Africa. In addition, scholarship in archeology's teaching methods usually does not aim to dismantle Western ideas about African heritage, encouraging the next generation of archeologists to hold on to the same inherently problematic Western misconceptions.

Oral tradition is one of the sources used in writing African history. It is also a reliable source of historical reconstruction, especially for preliterate African societies that did not develop the art of writing.[48] Oral tradition is used to pass on history, customs, traditions, and folklore from one generation to the next. As an integral part of the transmission system of communication, oral tradition is one of the valued ways African cultural heritage is stimulated and promoted in society. Several works of literature have served many purposes in West Africa and many other societies on the African continent. For example, the Tiv-speaking people of the central Nigeria area used satirical plays by humans and puppets to reassert social control over people who do not conform to certain cultural principles.[49] The *Oriki* or praise name, a tradition among the Yoruba people of West Africa, has continued to serve as an important historical information source.[50] Proverbs are essential methods of communication that guide, rebuke, admonish and encourage.[51] Myths are authorities that emphasize supernatural powers and are believed to have solutions to supernatural problems. They are also institutionalized authority with social and political power over people and are defined as culture. Thus, myths have served as a medium through which the African people are socioculturally organized.[52]

Though there are many other sources for the reconstruction of African history, the historian's primary interest in oral sources, as with other historical sources, is to understand the system that produces knowledge. This knowledge is often regarded as the culture of the people, along with various events that have characterized the history of society and whose sources may not be available for study; thus, oral tradition helps in scrutinizing events. Usually, this historical reconstruction method is employed because those involved or those who witnessed past events, are no longer present. As a result, anything linked with and bearing witness to historical events is essential in reconstructing history.

Oral sources in the form of myths began to develop in many communities that had no written history but had some individuals from their populations whose duty was to keep track of their rulers and maintain their history. Thus, for instance, an oral historian in a Yoruba court was employed to memorize dynastic lists.[53] When people came into contact with the art of writing in the Nigerian region, such as the *Ajami* and Arabic manuscripts, at some point of transformation, oral traditions of ancient times were translated into writing and later became historical plays, ballads, or sagas. This may have started around the tenth century AD when the groups around Borno and Hausaland, through the Sanhaja Berbers, the Tukrur, the Malinke, the Saifawa, and other North-East African nomads, were believed to have come in contact with the Arabic literature that came with Islam. Ibrahim states that the earliest type of history-writing in West Africa was done by Islamic scholars. This predated the Sokoto Caliphate's literature and that done by Western-educated Nigerians who wrote about their different communities[54] (Figure 2.4).

Oral tradition and archeology have been extremely useful in the reconstruction of African history, but in addition to these two, Muslim scholars constitute one of the significant sources of reconstructing Africa's past, particularly West African history.[55] Arabic writing provides valuable materials that contribute to our understanding of Africa's past. For example, it has been observed that geographers and historians before Leo Africanus were not knowledgeable about Kanem. Thus, what they disseminated came largely from what was learned from the Arab scholars and merchant groups who moved to places such as Marrakesh, Tunis, and Cairo in search of knowledge. Tadeusz Lewicki submits that some information about Africa, especially from the ninth century,

FIGURE 2.4 Arabic script from Timbuktu https://commons.wikimedia.org/wiki/File:Folio
_Quran_Maghrebi_script_Mamma_Haidara_Library_34119.jpeg.

continued to emerge in distorted forms in Arabic sources until the thirteenth or fourteenth centuries.[56] African students, unfamiliar with the Arabic language and issues connected with Arabic sources, appeared skeptical of that category of sources.

Although what was documented in most Arabic writings was not essential for historical documentation, it was for political and economic relations, especially between Arab and non-Arab worlds. The quest to improve geographical knowledge in the ninth century was because of the need for the Muslim aristocracy to obtain relevant information that would enable them to manage commercial and political relationships in the vast Muslim territories they had acquired and in which they had established their presence and dominance. In the Abbasid era, Sahib al-Barid was responsible for posts, and his duties included the keeping of information with regard to route distances, method of transportation and the economic and political conditions within the province of the empire.[57]

In West Africa, Islamic scholars and educated Western elites had a written history before the 1950s. According to Ibrahim, Waziri Junaidu bin Muhammad Buhari of Sokoto, Adamu al-Ilori, and Ibrahim Madauci of Zaria, among others, had written histories of individuals in the Nigerian region before this period. There was also a large body of literature from the writers of *Iwe Itan Oyo*, the Chamba of the Adamawa region, and the history of Lafiya. Though such history may be uncommon among some non-monarchical Igbo communities, it is estimated to have impacted about 80 percent of the country's recorded history in the twentieth century.[58] As a primary methodological approach, this demonstrates the importance of oral sources in analyzing and writing West African history during the study period. The second part of the growth of techniques saw the:

> Continuation of non-academic writing of history, from the Islamic scholars and Western-educated Nigerians, and the emergence of the academic writing of history by trained historians from various universities within and outside Nigeria. The activity brought the emergence and intellectual use of oral source for scientific historical studies.[59]

Ibrahim's work shows that the pioneers in this area were Kenneth Dike and Saburi Biobaku, who first promoted the use of oral practices. In the 1950s, Dike also pointed to the deficiencies of relying on written records for historical reconstruction. Appeals concerning the limitations of historiography's exogenous viewpoint emerged and, therefore, the need for internal sources of historical reconstruction from within.

To demonstrate the strength of oral sources, Biobaku's *The Egba and Their Neighbours*, written in 1957, made extensive use of oral traditions in addition to materials from the British Public Records Office in London.[60] In Benin and Yoruba's historical research schemes, Dike and Biobaku later led schemes by an interdisciplinary study to recover local history. According to Ibrahim:

> The study and use of oral traditions received uplift with the coming of Jan Vansina. His contributions first came to the public notice with his article in the first volume of the *Journal of African History* in 1960, "Recording of the oral history of the Bakuba". In it, he made a brief statement of the merits of oral tradition and the need for its systematic recording and analysis. This was followed by an account of his work

among the Kuba people of Congo. His seminal theoretical work on the subject was, however, published in French in 1961 and was translated into English and published in 1965 in Chicago as *Oral Tradition: A Study in Historical Methodology.*[61]

Following the publication of books to reconstruct various African groups' histories using oral sources, scholars in Africa began to focus on the usefulness of oral tradition as an important historical reconstruction source. Vansina contributed a lot by teaching the topic in various universities in the development of oral tradition studies. His works played a significant role in the development of the Africanist method of studying history and historical reconstruction. Also, his work was considered relevant for the enterprise by using oral sources and customs and became one of the most important works on African historiography. Although there have been arguments on the use of oral sources in historical reconstruction since the emergence of African history as a formal discipline in the mid-twentieth century, Ibrahim posits that

> African historians like J. Vansina and Alagoa have worked tirelessly to develop a rigorous approach to the use of oral sources to recover the histories of many non-literate peoples. They proved that oral sources consisted of, at least in part, orally transmitted memories of actual past events.[62]

Furthermore, several writers had no formal training in using other sources, so they could only use oral traditions as their means of telling the African story. But in the second half of the twentieth century, notably from the 1950s, when scientific study started, the insufficiency of linguistic, written, anthropological, archeological, and other source materials for Nigeria's historical reconstruction became apparent. Philips O. Curtin states that "the decades of the 1960s begin with the publication of the oral traditions of Jan Vansina demonstrating the critical control that was necessary if oral histories were to become a reliable source."[63]

A Multidisciplinary Approach in the Reconstruction of West African History

The limitations of unwritten sources, such as archeological and oral evidence and traditions, have not gone unnoticed by historians, and for purposes of objectivity and credibility, the comprehensive and complimentary usage of all available sources has been the most scientific approach in the annals of West African historiography. In the case of oral evidence and traditions, the problem of time and chronology has remained a teething challenge for historical research and writing. This has been the same with archeological sources, especially in Africa, where large areas are yet to be covered by its work. The oral evidence and traditions of societies such as those in West Africa are also based on human memory and subject to failure in the long run.[64] The historian adopts concepts and theories to understand society better and place it in its proper perspective. Writing and documentation also become necessary so that this systematic approach to the study of history can be easily referred to periodically.

The essence of modern and contemporary history has been to produce a record of society that would have permanence and transcend itself; therefore, oral evidence alone may not completely fulfill this objective. Jan Vansina has also noted what he described as "the vague and generalized nature of (oral evidence) and oral poetry."[65] This is because some of the oral evidence and sources fall into categories of fairy tales, legends, and fables, and a historian will need care in handling them for the reconstruction of the past.[66] Despite the argument against the use of oral sources, they have remained essential sources for writing African history. A historian needs to use oral sources to exercise caution in different ways. The historian should understand that precision in dates is rare and oral tradition is liable to distortion for politics and the quest to over-glamorize certain individuals in the society, families, or even clans.

Often, the process through which information is transmitted from one generation to another makes it complex and susceptible to certain inaccuracies. Thus, the historian must be clear whenever deploying any of the strands of the oral source. Phillips Stevens maintains that:

> It is the job of the historian to discover which elements in [the] oral tradition are reliable as [a] source of data, which are reliable, and which can provide clues to the locations of reliable sources elsewhere, and this task can be so frustrating as to cause the researcher to reject oral sources altogether.[67]

Similarly, perseverance is essential while using oral sources to get to a genuine and valuable finding. The patience required to deal with oral sources enables the researcher to unravel elements of truth and falsehood in exaggerated narratives meant to satisfy and promote individual or group interests. As a historical study method, one of the ways oral sources can be evaluated is through the use of an interdisciplinary approach. This implies that oral sources should be backed by other sources to establish internal consistency and draw meaningful conclusions.

As society advances more toward Westernization, traditional African institutions, values, and custodians erode and pass away, rather like the wisdom of old age. Thus, new and advancing generations do not take oral evidence as history in their knowledge of the past, which constitutes a major problem. Moreover, the method of adopting oral evidence and other unwritten sources is restricted to specific areas, communities, cultures, traditions, and societies and cannot be universally adopted for historical research and writing.[68] Therefore, the historiographical approach and strategy or method of complementarity in using source materials have been an invaluable asset to the historian's craft, especially regarding the reconstruction of West African history. For example, written sources are a greater form of communication that progresses from generation to generation, covering a much broader scope and outreach over large geographical areas. It also complements or finishes the work of the oral evidence, traditions, and even other unwritten and auxiliary sources restricted to particular areas, cultures, and societies.[69]

Conclusion

This chapter has observed that despite the relative primacy and importance of archeological and other unwritten and auxiliary sources, they cannot be used in isolation without other sources, especially the written sources of historical reconstruction for the continuous development of the study of West African history. The contemporary world's advances in communications, technology, and universality call for complementarity and the comprehensive usage of all source materials in writing societies' history.

Furthermore, significant past events in most societies have been written down and documented as such societies' historical development. Thus, in the reconstruction of West African history, the researcher combines these written events with archeological and other unwritten sources to produce a more balanced, comprehensive, objective, and acceptable history. So, in the contemporary period of the development of West Africa, and even world history, studies of history can still be produced from unwritten sources as the starting point for continuous refinement and development. However, for a true and universally acceptable reconstruction of the history of the lives of families, communities, societies, and nations, historians have recommended that all sources must be considered in historical research and reconstruction to achieve the ultimate goals of credibility and objectivity that are so crucial to the life and work of the historian.

DEEP DIVE

Use an African myth or proverb of your choice to explore how sayings explain African beliefs or worldviews.

Questions to ask:

1. What does this saying/story teach me about the people it describes?
2. How does this saying influence the people who would grow up listening to it?
3. Is this similar or different to the worldview I am used to? If yes, how so?
4. In what way is the saying applicable to everyday life?

Assignment 1

Objective

The objective of this assignment is to ensure that students complete reading the chapter and to get them to understand that the use of oral evidence and traditions may have their underlying weaknesses yet are highly effective primary source tools in reconstructing West Africa's history and, thus, accurately represent the nature of history in the subregion.

Method

Students will be expected to write a short note in response to the question.

Reading Comprehension

What are the sources that could be used for the reconstruction of West African History?

Assignment 2

Objective

The objective of this assignment is to ensure that students complete reading the chapter and to get them to think about the many ways in which West African history could be reconstructed through oral traditions, oral evidence, and other unwritten sources. In addition, students will be expected to identify the methodology of West African history and the limitations contained therein.

Method

Students will be expected to write a short note in response to the question.

Reading Comprehension

Discuss the role a multidisciplinary approach can play in the reconstruction of West African history.

Notes

1 Gabriel Eluwa, *Introduction to Historical Research and Writing* (Ibadan: Africana-FEP Publishers, 1988), 3.
2 Daniel F. McCall, *Africa in Time-Perspective: A Discussion of Historical Reconstruction from Unwritten Sources* (Boston: Boston University Press, 1964).
3 Joseph Ki-Zerbo, "The Oral Tradition as a Source of African History," *Diogenes* 17, no. 67 (1969): 110–124.
4 Cited in Eluwa, *Introduction to Historical Research*, 14–19.
5 Eluwa, *Introduction to Historical Research*, 1. See also Edward Carr, *What Is History?* (London: Penguin Books Limited, 1987), 30.
6 Olukoya Ogen, "Exploring the Potential of Praise Poems for Historical Reconstruction among the Idepe-Ikale in Southeastern Yorubaland," *History in Africa* 39 (2012): 77–96.
7 See, for instance, Carlos Magnavita, "Contributions of Archaeological Geophysics to Field Research in Sub-Saharan Africa: Past, Present, Future," *Azania: Archaeological Research in Africa* 51, no. 1 (2016): 115–141.
8 Jan Vansina, *Oral Tradition as History* (Madison: University of Wisconsin Press, 1985).
9 Funso Afolayan, "Historiography and Methods of African History" (Oxford: Oxford Bibliographies Online in African Studies, 2012), https://www.oxfordbibliographies.com/view /document/obo-9780199846733/obo-9780199846733-0011.xml.
10 Michał Tymowski, *Europeans and Africans* (Leiden: Brill, 2020).
11 Klas Rönnbäck, "The Idle and the Industrious – European Ideas about the African Work Ethic in Precolonial West Africa," *History in Africa* 41 (2014): 117–145.
12 Adiele Afigbo, "A Re-Assessment of the Historiography of the Period," in *A Thousand Years of West African History*, eds. Jacob F. Ade Ajayi and Ian Espie (Ibadan: Ibadan University Press, 1965), 419–430.
13 Hugh Trevor-Roper, *The Rise of Christian Europe* (New York: Harcourt, Brace & World, 1965).
14 See the contrast in Basil Davidson, *The African Past: Chronicles from Antiquity to Modern Times* (London: Longman Group Limited, 1964), 3–7.
15 Clarence G. Contee, "Current Problems of African Historiography," *Negro History Bulletin* 30, no. 4 (1967): 5–10.

16 Okpe T. Adie and Joseph S. Effenji, "The Issue of Rationality in the History of African Philosophy," *GNOSI: An Interdisciplinary Journal of Human Theory and Praxis* 1, no. 1 (2018): 95–106.

17 Abubakar Z. Ibrahim, "The Significance of Oral Sources in the Reconstruction of Nigerian History in the 20th and 21st Centuries," *Zaria Journal of Liberal Arts* 3, no. 1 (2009): 399–407.

18 David Olusoga, "The Roots of European Racism lie in the Slave Trade, Colonialism – and Edward Long," *The Guardian*, September 8, 2015, https://www.theguardian.com/comment-isfree/2015/sep/08/european-racism-africa-slavery.

19 St. Clair Drake, "The Responsibility of Men of Culture for Destroying the Hamitic Myth," *Presence Africaine* 24, no. 25 (1959): 228–243.

20 Ibrahim, "The Significance of Oral Sources."

21 Ray H. Byrd, "Social Darwinism and British Imperialism, 1870–1900" (MA diss. Texas Tech University, 1971).

22 Omotade Adegbindin, "Critical Notes on Hegel's Treatment of Africa," *Ogirisi: A New Journal of African Studies* 11 (2015): 19–43.

23 Arthur P. Newton and J. Ewing, *The British Empire Since 1783: Its Political and Economic Development* (London: Methuen, 1929).

24 Walter Rodney, *How Europe Underdeveloped Africa* (London: Bogle-L'Ouverture Publications, 1972).

25 Rodney, *How Europe Underdeveloped Africa*, 85.

26 Chinua Achebe, "An Image of Africa: Racism in Conrad's Heart of Darkness," *Massachusetts Review* 18, no. 4 (1977): 782–794.

27 Rodney, *How Europe Underdeveloped Africa*, 108–112.

28 Adiele Afigbo, "Igboland before 1800," in *Groundwork of Nigerian History*, ed. Obaro Ikime (Ibadan: Heinemann Educational Books, 1980), 73–82.

29 Lea Ypi, "What's Wrong with Colonialism?" *Philosophy & Public Affairs* 41, no. 2 (2013): 163.

30 Yirga G. Woldeyes, "Colonial Rewriting of African History: Misinterpretations and Distortions in Belcher and Kleiner's Life and Struggles of Walatta Petros," *Journal of Afroasiatic Languages, History and Culture* 9, no. 2 (2020): 133–220.

31 Joseph Conrad, *Heart of Darkness* (California: Coyote Canyon Press, 2007).

32 Amy Starecheski, "Squatting History: The Power of Oral History as a History-Making Practice," *The Oral History Review* 41, no. 2 (2014): 187–216.

33 Ebiegberi Alagoa, *Oral Tradition and Oral History in Africa and the Diaspora: Theory and Practice* (Lagos: Centre for Black and African Arts and Civilization, 1990). See also Ebiegberi Alagoa, "Oral Tradition among the Ijo of the Niger Delta," *Journal of African History* 2, no. 3 (1966): 405–419.

34 Vansina, *Oral Tradition*.

35 Monika Glowacka-Musial, "The Hidden Power of Oral Histories," *The Journal of Academic Librarianship* 46, no. 1 (2020): 1–10.

36 Rupert East, *Akiga's Story: The Tiv Tribe as Seen by One of Its Members* (trans.) (London: Oxford University Press, 1965).

37 Saburi O. Biobaku, *Sources of Yoruba History* (London: Clarendon Press, 1973).

38 Gerald Nelms, "The Case for Oral Evidence in Composition Historiography," *Written Communication* 9, no. 3 (1992): 356–384.

39 Isaac Yongo and Moses T. Tsenongo, "The Oral Artist as Historian," *Journal of the Historical Society of Nigeria* 1, no. 1 (2004): 73.

40 Osakwe C. C. Chukwuma, Echum T. Ojong and Okene A. Adam, *The Nigerian Civil War Oral History Project* (Kaduna: Nigerian Defence Academy, 2017), 27–46.

41 See, for instance, Martins O. Olorunfemi, Benjamin A. Ogunfolakan and Ademakinwa G. Oni, "Geophysical and Archaeological Survey in Igbo Oritaa (Iwo), Southwest Nigeria," *Africa Archaeological Review* 36 (2019): 535–552.

42 Paul J. Lane, "Barbarous Tribes and Unrewarding Gyrations? The Changing Role of Ethnographic Imagination in African Archaeology," in *African Archaeology: A Critical Introduction*, ed. Ann B. Stahl (Oxford: Blackwell Publishing, 2005), 24–31.

43 Ebere Nwaubani, "Kenneth Onwuka Dike, Trade and Politics, and the Restoration of the African in History," *History in Africa* 27 (2014): 229–248.

44 Lane, "Barbarous Tribes."

45 Kehinde D. Oyeyemi, Michael A. Oladunjoye, Ahzegbobor P. Aizebeokhai, Philip G. Ajekigbe and Benjamin A. Ogunfolakan, "Integrated Geophysical Investigations for Imaging Archaeological Structure in Ancient Town of Ile-Ife, Nigeria," *Asian Journal of Information Technology* 4, no. 7 (2015): 246–252.

46 Augustin F. C. Holl, "Review of African Historical Archaeologies," *GEFAME Journal of African Studies* 1, no. 1 (2004). http://hdl.handle.net/2027/spo.4761563.0001.106.

47 Akinwunmi Ogundiran and Toyin Falola, eds. *Archaeology of Atlantic Africa and the African Diaspora* (Indianapolis: Indiana University Press, 2007).

48 Monica D. King, "The Role of Oral Traditions in African History," *The Dyke* 2, no. 2 (2006): 42–52.

49 Iyorwuese H. Hagher, *The Kwagh-hir Theatre: A Metaphor of Resistance* (Ibadan: Caltop Publishers, 2003).

50 Bolanle Awe, "Praise Poems as Historical Data: The Example of the Yoruba Oriki," *Africa* 44, no. 4 (1974): 331–349.

51 George E. Onwudiwe, "Proverbs: A Veritable Language Ingredient in Communication in Igbo," *Unizik Journal of Arts and Humanities* 8, no. 2 (2006): 14–33.

52 Isidore Okpewho, *Myth in Africa: A Study of its Aesthetic and Cultural Relevance* (Cambridge: Cambridge University Press, 1983).

53 'Bayo Ogunyemi, "Analysis of Musical Forms in Yorùbá Court Music: A Study of Ìgà Ìdúnùngánrán of Lagos State," *Ihafa: A Journal of African Studies* 9, no. 1 (2018): 160–181.

54 Ibrahim, "The Significance of Oral Sources," 401.

55 Louis Brenner, *Controlling Knowledge: Religion, Power, and Schooling in a West African Muslim Society* (Bloomington: Indiana University Press, 2001).

56 Tadeusz Lewicki, *Arabic External Sources for the History of Africa to the South of Sahara* (London: Curzon, 1969), 8.

57 Thomas Hodgkin, *Nigerian Perspectives: An Historical Anthology* (London: Oxford University Press, 1975), 9.

58 Ibrahim, "The Significance of Oral Sources," 402.

59 Ibrahim, "The Significance of Oral Sources."

60 Ibrahim, "The Significance of Oral Sources."

61 Ibrahim, "The Significance of Oral Sources."

62 Ibrahim, "The Significance of Oral Sources."

63 Ibrahim, "The Significance of Oral Sources," 403.

64 Eluwa, *Historical Research*, 71–74.

65 Vansina, *Oral Tradition as History*.

66 Yongo and Tsenongo, "The Oral Artist as Historian," 72–73.

67 Phillips Stevens, Jr., "The Uses of Oral Tradition in Writing of African History," *Tarikh* 6, no. 1 (1978): 21–30.

68 Eluwa, *Historical Research*, 25.

69 Cited in Eluwa, *Historical Research*, 71–73.

3

GEOGRAPHY, LANDSCAPE, AND COMPOSITION

The Geographical Location of West Africa

The geography, landscape, and composition of the West African subregion have attracted the envious attention of various other countries and continents, with the European imperialists at the forefront of the scramble for its subjugation and exploitation. A variety of work has been done to represent West Africa's position on the world map,[1] indicating how the West African subregion is strategically placed in the central and western savannah belt and the sub-Saharan area of the African continent.[2] The subregion is bordered to the south by the vast Atlantic Ocean, and across a distance of 580 miles, extends from the Bimbia Peninsula East of the Bimbia Creek (latitude 2° 45'55") to the east and its western parts. This point also covers the vast Sahara region and down to the Meridian of the Ajara Creek between Badagry in Lagos and Porto Novo in the Benin Republic. In the eastern part of the West African state of Nigeria lies the vast Niger Delta region, which is bordered mostly by the Gulf of Guinea and the Southern part of the Republic of Cameroon, which point also reaches the coast of Senegal.[3] Inland of this West African region is the former French colony of the Benin Republic, while the northern part of Nigeria is bordered chiefly by the Republics of Niger and Chad.[4]

However, West Africa's borderlands and boundaries are colonial creations of the British and the French through conquest and spoils of war.[5] Considering the position of a nation like Nigeria, the sub-location region might be regarded as the westernmost section of Africa and a part of Africa's heartland. West Africa is situated on the African continent between longitudes 2^0 2' and 14^0 30' east and between latitudes 4^0 to 14^0 north. The subregion has a North–South area and length of about 5,112,903 kilometers, making up the equivalent of about 1,974,103 square miles. The Atlantic Ocean, at sea level, is the lowest point in West Africa's geography.[6]

DOI: 10.4324/9781003198260-4

The West African Climate

In West Africa, temperatures vary from season to season and region to region. The high African plateau, the lowlands, the coastal areas, and the interior have unique features. On the high plateau, the average annual temperature ranges between 21°C and 27°C. In many of the areas, temperatures range from 20°C to 25°C, whereas the typical annual temperature in the lowlands, such as the Sokoto plains, the Chad Basin, and the Niger-Benue, is 27°C.[7] The coastal margins of the West African subregion, particularly those along the Niger Delta to Senegal and The Gambia, have lower means than the rest of the subregion. The distribution of temperature in West Africa is primarily determined by altitude and proximity to the sea. However, due to its tropical location, West Africa experiences high temperatures. Depending on the area, the mean monthly temperature might rise over 27°C, while daily maximum temperatures could range from 35°C to 38°C and even higher (Figure 3.1).[8]

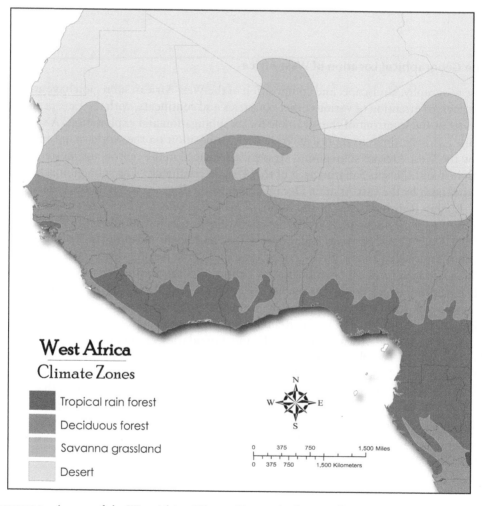

FIGURE 3.1 A map of the West Africa Climate Zones. Author's collection.

According to a study by Victor Oyenuga, West Africa has a warm tropical climate with high temperatures all year.[9] The rainy season lasts from mid-March to November in the south and north-central areas and from May or June to October in the northern parts of West Africa. The interplay of two air masses, the comparatively warm and wet tropical marine mass and the relatively cold, dry, and stable tropical continental air mass, influences the climate of West Africa. The first rises over the Atlantic Ocean and is related to the southwest winds, while the second begins in the Sahara Desert and is connected with the harmattan, which is dry, chilly, and dusty. Temperatures in West Africa "do not fluctuate regularly; constant elements such as relative humidity and rainfall are heavily relied on to differentiate between the season and climatic zones."[10]

In the southern parts of the West African subregion and the central Sudanese zone, the long wet season witnesses heavy rains, high humidity, and the blossoming of plants, with fresh and greenish pasture and rapid growth of grasses and weeds. This wet season, which is the major period for planting crops, is usually accompanied by frequent storms. In the northern parts of West Africa, the long dry season starts earlier and ends later with no break in between, thus merging the two seasons into one. Two other seasons— the long dry season, from October to April and in some areas up to June or July, and the wet season for the remaining few months—also stand out. During this period, there is no rainfall, and the dry conditions crack the soil.

The short dry season lasts for about one month, between July and August, followed by the short wet season from September to October, when there is a decrease in rainfall. The lengthy dry harmattan season is chilly and misty from November to mid-March, with foggy and dusty days blown in by winds from North Africa. This causes grasses to whither, and tree leaves become brownish before falling (Figure 3.2). Annual rainfall totals in West Africa range from 2,500mm in the south, north, and central zones to less than 400mm in other parts of the subregion.[11] The Sahara and the southern and central zones of the subregion have double peak rainfall, while the northern part has a single peak rainfall comparable to North Africa.

Temperature, rainfall, and humidity control the natural vegetation and growth of indigenous and exotic plant types in West Africa. As a result, staple crops such as cassava, yam, cocoyam, melon, sweet potatoes, maize, peanuts, rice, cowpeas, and cashew, and some vegetation and plantations such as cocoa, oil palm, rubber, coffee, and cotton thrive in humid tropical forest zones and central midlands with prolonged rainfall. The savannah region, which represents one of the country's vegetation zones and is the natural habitat for grazing livestock such as cattle, goats, sheep, horses, camels, and donkeys, has lower rainfall and a shorter rainy season than the rest of the country. However, excessive rainfall in some parts of the subregion and many regions along the coast, particularly in the Niger Delta and sections of coastal Guinea-Bissau, has resulted in severely leached soil and significant soil erosion, making the land unfit for long-term vegetation.

Also, natural vegetation zones result from the interaction of soil types. According to Geographer Nwadilibe Iloeje, West Africa is divided into two primary vegetation zones— the forest and the savannah. The forest zone is further sub-divided into three zones each— freshwater swamp, saltwater swamp, and high forest—while the savannah zone comprises the Sudan Savannah, Guinea Savannah, and Sahel Savannah.[12] The saltwater swamp forest vegetation includes tidal swamps, rivers, and lagoons with mangrove tree species. It is

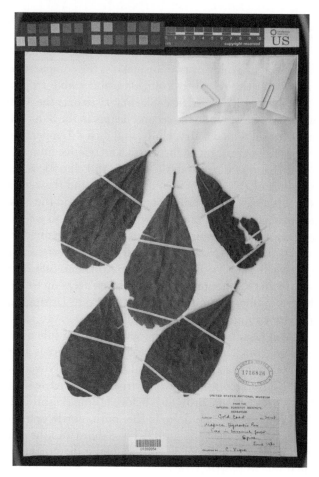

FIGURE 3.2   Uapaca togoensis, Gold Coast, Ghana https://commons.m.wikimedia.org/wiki/
File:Uapaca_togoensis-NMNH-11531747.jpg.

not a widely cultivated area except for swamp rice in stable areas of the vegetation zone. Freshwater swamp forest vegetation lies inland and on higher ground, and because the area is a low-lying zone, the lagoons and rivers overflow during the wet season, providing the swamp forest vegetation with fresh water for eight or nine months of the year.

The most significant vegetation species are found in the high forest vegetation zone. There are a variety of palm and fiber plants, like the wine and roof-mat palm used for thatching roofs (Figure 3.3) and providing rafters, poles, and stiff piassava fiber to make brooms, sleeping mats, and baskets. It is the major source of timber for large constructions and cabinet making. It also includes commercial cash crops such as cocoa, oil palm, plantain, rubber, banana, plantain, and kola nuts. Also, some fruits and major staple food crops like maize, yam, sweet potato, rice, cocoyam, beans, groundnut, and cashew are mainly found in the Guinea Savannah. The subregion also has timber trees such as the scented Sapele wood, the African Mahogany, and Iroko trees (Figure 3.4).

Furthermore, the Guinea Savannah zone is the most extensive vegetation zone in the subregion. It is located in the center of Nigeria, expands south to Southern Nigeria, and

FIGURE 3.3   Thatching with palm leaf mats among the Igbo people https://commons.wikime-dia.org/wiki/File:Igbo_palm_thatch.jpg.

pushes north to the Zaria area, with an annual rainfall of 100 to 150cm. The rainy season in West Africa appears for about six to eight months. Among the plants identified were false balsam (Copaiba), used to carve mortars and pestles for pounding yam, and poor mahogany. The prominent species in the northern part of the Guinea Savannah are the locust bean tree, shea butter tree, and mangoes, with fewer and shorter trees in the northern part of the savannah than in the southern part. In the rainy season, the region is lush and grassy, but the tough and fibrous vegetation dies in the dry season.[13]

Groundnuts, sorghum, and millet are the most common crops grown in the West African Sudanese Savannah zone. Grasses in this zone are shorter, coarser, and thicker than those in the Guinea savannah zone, making cultivation difficult without irrigation systems. However, the grass cover is short and fluffy, which may be seen on a vast scale, with dense bush trees such as shea butter, acacia, locust bean, tamarind, and mango trees intermingled. This zone is also part of the tsetse fly–free belt that runs through West Africa, making it ideal for rearing and breeding ruminant livestock such as cattle, goats, sheep, donkeys, horses, and camels, giving them an abundance of feed and water. The West African Sahel Savannah zone is the last Savannah-type vegetation zone between the Sahara and the Sudanese Savannah's northern border, and it goes southward, encompassing around 18,130km of Nigeria's extreme northeast corner. Annual rainfall is low as the rainy season only lasts three to four months, resulting in sparse vegetation and producing very short grasses. The few kinds of grass found in the zone are preserved as the only pasture available for livestock grazing.[14] Plants such as Acacia raddiana and a variety of shrubs, such as African myrrh and others, characterize the zone.

According to Louis Bonaparte, "The foreign policy of a particular nation depends upon its geography."[15] West Africa's geographical location and its great population are

FIGURE 3.4 An Iroko tree (Chlorophora excelsa), native to the west coast of Africa https://www.shutterstock.com/image-photo/iroko-tree-chlorophora-excelsa-native-west-2229533103.

important instruments of influence in the African region and the international community. This factor is based on its vast terrain, topography, landscape, and climate. The geographical location of the continent also determines the nature and character of its international history. Other geographical factors that have helped the subregion's conduct in Africa and international affairs are the size, length, and width of the landmass, which are strategic assets of any geopolitical region, especially in times of war or invasion by enemy nations or a war situation where more troops can be deployed. The climate in West Africa, particularly the subregion's temperature, relief, seasons, and so on, has influenced its power in the international community due to its development of an agricultural base and the thriving of human and natural resources. With a corresponding development of the agricultural and other vital natural resources and their grouping into sectors, the West African subregion is well equipped to accomplish significant gains in Africa and internationally.[16]

Physical Conditions in West Africa

Studies by scholars such as Iloeje, Sobule, and Rene Pelissier have shown that the geography of West Africa reveals a rich array and wide range of topographical features, soil types, and other physical conditions and features. The most notable physical, geographical, and topographical features in West Africa include the major rivers of Senegal, The Gambia, Benue, and the Niger in Nigeria, and other landscape features such as the Sahara Desert, mountains and plains, highlands, and lowlands. In the eastern and central parts of the subregion, thick forests can be envisaged as a major physical and topographical feature, a situation almost similar to the plantations and the forest region of the southwestern parts of Nigeria. Benue and the Niger valleys form a confluence at Lokoja, while plains with enough trees, vegetation, and grassland are found north of the confluence. Highlands, hills, and mountains extend from the confluence, especially from the southeastern Benue region to the communities on the border with the Cameroon Republic. From the River Niger, highlands also extend to the southwestern Nigerian area. These physical features are characteristic of the geography of the West African subregion.[17]

Another major area of note in the topography and physical condition of West Africa is the oil-rich Niger Delta region of Nigeria and the creeks and islands of countries such as Guinea-Bissau. There are vast regions with swamps, rivers, and creeks, including the Cross River deltas, that connect with various rivers (Figure 3.5). A great forest belt also exists in the western and central Sudanese parts of West Africa. There are lagoons in the coastal areas, while the core subregional features are attracted to desert plains, especially in Nigeria, Guinea-Conakry, Niger, Chad, Senegal, and others. Geographically, sedimentary rocks cover the Lake Chad Basin and coastal regions, including the Niger River delta and the western parts of Sokoto and the Benin Republic. These rocks are endowed with peak elevations and other high altitudes of the mountainous regions of varying degrees, which rise above the plains at 300 meters and more.[18]

Nigeria can be classified into highlands and lowlands, the high plateau, and the lowlands. The high plateau includes the north-central plateau, the eastern and northeastern highlands, and the western uplands. The lowlands consist of the Sokoto plains, the Niger and Benue trough, the Chad Basin, the inner coastal lowlands of western Nigeria, the lowlands and Scarp lands of eastern Nigeria, and the coastlands. These, with some exceptions, are also characteristic of other West African states.[19] However, the most mountainous area lies along the southeastern borderland between Nigeria and Cameroon, and it has the highest points in Nigeria, over 2,000 meters.

Soil types in West Africa are influenced by certain climatic and vegetational zones within the subregion. They can be classified into four climatic soil zones: the northern sandy soil, the interior zone of literate soil, the southern belt of forest soil, and the alluvial soil. The northern sandy soil is found in the subregion's central and northern parts. In the Sahel Savannah belt of West Africa, this soil is formed under aridity by the depositions of sand by the wind and the encroaching Sahara Desert. These areas include Mali, Senegal, and states such as Borno, Sokoto, Zamfara, Katsina, and Kano in Nigeria. Again, in Nigeria, the soil also includes the Zaria loam, which is suitable for cultivating cotton, groundnut, millet, sorghum, and cowpeas.[20] The southern humid tropical forest climatic zones are represented by the forest soil subregional belt, which has a long rainy

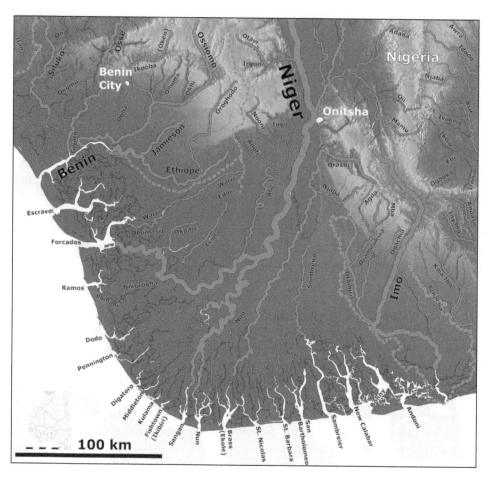

FIGURE 3.5 The Niger Delta https://commons.wikimedia.org/wiki/File:Niger_Delta_OSM .png.

season, a short harmattan phase, and dense forest cover. The soil transforms into a fertile clay loam that produces crops like cocoa, oil palm, and rubber, which are essential to Ghanaian and Nigerian agriculture.

Sands and clay make up the interior zone of laterite soils. They are drained and seasonally flooded to form the fadama, which is deeply corroded, sticky, and impervious to water, with low fertility and little agricultural value. Research shows that when this soil is exposed to the surface, it becomes as hard as brick and can be used for road paving and wall construction as is done in countries such as Nigeria, especially in Katsina, Kano, Sokoto, and the other West African states of Benin Republic, Togo, and Ghana. Again, in Nigeria, an exception is the Biu Plateau, which has rich soil that is productive with prospects for the expansion of cotton farming in the area.[21] The alluvial soil zone can be found throughout West Africa in the flooded plains of rivers or deltas, as well as along the coastal flats of countries like Nigeria. The zone here stretches from the seashore to the inland valleys of the Niger and Benue Rivers. The soil within this subregional zone does not depend highly on climate or vegetation but on the underlying parent rock, characterized by "freshwater soil of grey to white sand, grey clay, and sandy clay with humid topsoil. Another group consists of brownish to black saline mangrove soils with a mat of rootlets."[22]

Studies in the geographical relief features of West Africa show changes in elevation over given areas of land, aspect, shape, and slope of certain areas in the subregion. In Nigeria, for instance, the valleys of the Niger and Benue rivers area are the most expansive region and terrain in the country. In the north of the valleys lie plains, and to the southwest of the River Niger stand rugged highlands, while in the southeast of Benue State can be found hills and mountains on the borderlands with Niger, Chad, and Cameroon. Such highlands along the Nigeria-Cameroon border include the Obudu Plateau, which is above 1,584 meters (5,197 feet), the Mambilla Plateau, above 1,524 meters (5,000 feet), and Mount Chappal Waddi, which is above 2,000 meters (6,562 feet). The next area is the Niger Delta region which geographers and scientists have described as the world's largest acuate fan-shaped river delta. It is mostly a coastal belt of swamps of vegetated tidal flatlands and lowlands varying from 10 to 60 miles in width, composed of a network of rivers and creeks and bordered by dense vegetation, with virgin forest covering the intervening stretches of dry ground.[23]

In studying the relief features of West Africa, it is necessary to identify the extreme ends and points of the subregion. These are the subregional points further north, east, west, and south. The northernmost point is located on the border with Niger and Chad immediately northeast of countries such as Mauritania. The easternmost point is located on the border with Cameroon, directly east of Munyego in Borno State. The headland south of the town of Egeregere in Bayelsa State of Nigeria has been identified as the southernmost point, while the westernmost point is on the border between the Benin Republic and Oyo State, immediately east, in the direction of Jabata, a Beninoise town, and other strategic coastlines from the Gulf of Guinea to the coast of Senegal.[24]

The main drainage areas in West Africa are made up of four major networks: the Niger-Benue basin and the Lake Chad basin in Nigeria, the Volta Rivers, the Senegal River, and the short coastal strips bordering lakes such as Lake Volta. The River Niger and its primary tributary, the River Benue, are major rivers in Nigeria. River Niger has multiple rapids and waterfalls, but the River Benue has none and is passable throughout its length save during the dry season. The tributaries such as the Sokoto, Kaduna, Taraba, Katsina-Ala, and Yobe are among the rivers that drain into the Lake Chad. The Volta and Senegal rivers and other West African coastal locations are drained by small rivers that run into the Volta and the Atlantic Ocean.[25]

Artificial lakes also contribute to this effective network of drainage systems in West Africa, such as the Akosombo Dam in Ghana (Figure 3.6). Among these is Lake Kainji on the Niger and Lake Bakolori on the Rimi River; the waters of the River Niger flow into the Gulf of Guinea through Nigeria's huge Niger Delta area. Within Nigeria, this system involves the Benin and Forcados rivers, the Cross rivers, the Escravos, Opobo, and the broad bay into which the Calabar and the Bonny rivers flow. The Lagos harbor also forms a major outlet for drainage to the sea from the series of lagoons entering parallel to the coast and from the various rivers draining into them. Interestingly, this process begins from the Niamey River in Niger and connects to the Volta River in Burkina Faso. The Oxbow Lake, river meander belts, freshwater swamps, and levees in the great

FIGURE 3.6 Akosombo Dam in Ghana https://www.gettyimages.co.uk/detail/photo/hydroelectric-power-station-royalty-free-image/494265361.

Niger Delta area and other coastal strips in West Africa also contribute significantly to the drainage system to the Atlantic Ocean and the Gulf of Guinea.[26] These topographical and soil types, as well as physical conditions and features, make for a humid and tropical area and climate in this westernmost part of the African continent.

The Natural Resources of West Africa

West Africa is blessed with a wide variety of natural resources like crude oil, diamonds, gold, aluminum, bauxite, uranium, tin, iron ore, manganese, and columbite. Diamonds are abundant in West African nations such as Liberia, Sierra Leone, and Côte d'Ivoire, while Nigeria and Ghana are famous for gold and crude oil. Natural resources and minerals such as bauxite and iron ore have also contributed significantly to the resource richness of Guinea-Conakry, Guinea-Bissau, Sierra Leone, and Liberia. Senegal, Mali, Guinea-Bissau, Togo, and some other West African countries are also rich in phosphates. Oil resources have been discovered in Côte d'Ivoire, Liberia, and Sierra Leone, paving the way for these countries to enter the list of oil-producing areas and nations.[27]

Some West African states, like Sierra Leone, are vastly rich in some of the world's greatest natural resources (Figure 3.7). For instance, Sierra Leone is rich in solid diamond and gold deposits and natural resources such as rutile, platinum, chromite, and lignite. Various types of clay and base metals such as copper, nickel, molybdenum, lead, and zinc count among its long list of natural resource endowments; thus, in its economic policy development, the mining sector occupies the center stage. Guinea-Conakry is reputed for its rich natural resources. In addition to diamonds, gold, and other metals,

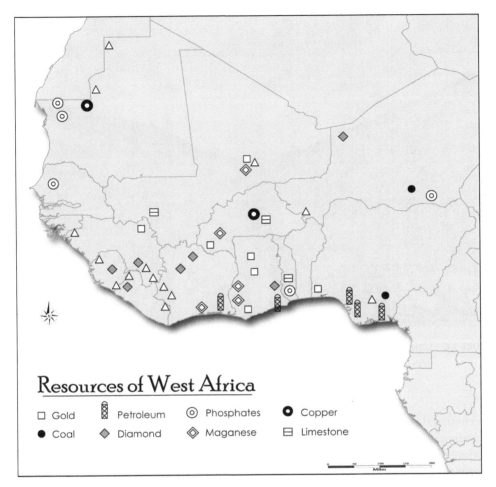

FIGURE 3.7   A map of Resources in West Africa. Author's collection.

the country also holds about 50 percent of the world's bauxite reserves. Diamond, bauxite, aluminum, gold, salt, and iron ore are among the country's solid minerals, including
graphite, limestone, manganese, nickel, and uranium. Guinea-Conakry has continued
to rank among the world's top five producers of bauxite. In Mali, the natural resources
sector is dominated by gold mining, as the country is the third largest producer of gold
on the African continent. Among Mali's other mineral resources are diamond, bauxite,
limestone, iron ore, nickel, manganese, petroleum, tin, phosphates, and uranium. The
Republic of Niger also has significant deposits of uranium (Figure 3.8).

Another major instrument in the archaeological and historical development of West
Africa is the availability of the highest quality of natural resources and the potential
for the adoption of these for a sound economic policy in the interest of progress and
development. West Africa's ability to harness the vast potentials that the subregion possesses has, to some extent, determined its power and influence within the international
community throughout its history. This has helped the subregion achieve its state-building and national development objectives across various areas, including domestic and

FIGURE 3.8 Open-pit gold mine in Ghana, Africa https://www.gettyimages.co.uk/detail/photo /open-pit-gold-mine-africa-royalty-free-image/489587485.

international policy, as well as the national interests of its many states. Like any other subregion or geopolitical zone, West Africa's resources and economy are based upon the production, exchange, and distribution of goods and services, as well as the efforts to improve the sharing of the international wealth of the subregion.

Due to their natural resource endowments, West African governments have tried to create a strong and competitive economic basis and a living space for their continuously surging population both at home and abroad.[28] This has improved the subregion's status in power relations in Africa and the world. The subregion's resources are predominantly occupied with oil and gas production and other mineral resources, which remain a source of strength in its domestic and foreign relations.[29] Oil production and sales have contributed greatly to determining the power and capabilities of West African countries like Nigeria within the international community. The subregion's adoption of an economic policy that expands markets at home and abroad develops technology that encourages the growth and expansion of direct foreign investment, and international trade has also cut business deals in specific sectors in various world regions.

In 2003, Niger was named the world's fourth-largest producer of uranium. In Burkina Faso, gold mining has played a significant role in its economy and society. According to the *EITI 2010 Report*, Burkina Faso also has significant reserves of manganese and phosphates.[30] Thus, the West African subregion is rich in natural resource allocation and reserves, making the development and advancement of a sound economic policy an absolute necessity for its growth and progress.

West African Peoples and Culture

In Nigeria alone, there are over 300 ethnic groups and nationalities, of which the three largest are the Hausa in the north, the Igbo in the southeast, and the Yoruba in the southwest of Nigeria. Other major groups include, but are not limited to, the Tiv, Ijo, Fulani, Edo, Efik, Idoma, Igede, Kanuri, Itsekiri, Urhobo, Isoko, Nupe, Igala, Ibibio, Ebira, Gwari, Birom, Marghi, Jukun, Katab, Chamba, Kuteb, Alago, Eggon, Etulo, and many others. In the northern part of the country, Hausa is generally and predominantly spoken, while the northeastern parts and the north-central areas interchange the Hausa language with their local dialects and languages. The language spoken in the southeast part of the country is predominantly Igbo, and in the southwest, the spoken language is essentially Yoruba. The south-south or Niger Delta region hosts a variety of languages ranging from Ibibio, Bekwarra, Ikwerre, Efik, Ijo, Ika-Igbo, Urhobo, Ishan, Edo, Ososo, and a host of others.[31] But because of people's colonial experience under Great Britain, Nigeria's official language is English. For general conversations, business or trade, and other social engagements and interactions, broken or pidgin English is commonly used across the country's geopolitical zones.[32] However, human interactions through pidgin also cut across other West African countries like Ghana, Benin Republic, Liberia, and Sierra Leone, and a blend of Creole is used in many parts of Guinea-Bissau.[33]

As a multiethnic composition of peoples in the West African subregion, the people of West Africa have a wide variety of cultures. But these cultures identify mostly as African and have been united, especially beginning with the anti-imperialism struggles of the 1960s and the early 1970s. Thus, the subregion provides a common platform for the expression of different cultures by the people in customs and traditions, food, medicine, clothing styles, dance, folk songs, literature, rituals, marriage, family and inheritance, kinship, and etiquette (Figure 3.9).[34] A few examples include greetings and respect for the aged and the elderly, social stratification, and several other aspects of culture and tradition, preeminently African in nature and character. A major way of life of the West African people is seen in their religious beliefs.[35] Islam is the dominant religion in the subregion, while large numbers of other peoples and groups profess the Christian religion, and about 20 percent of the population of the West African peoples are engaged in traditional and indigenous religions. In West African countries such as Nigeria, Muslims are most predominant in the core northern part of the country, while Christians are mostly found in the north-central areas and the southern part of Nigeria. Islam also has a strong foothold in the southwest of Nigeria, chiefly among the Yoruba, and also in northern Nigeria. Practitioners of indigenous or traditional religions are mostly found in the south, but they also cut across several regions and communities in Nigeria.[36]

Social and cultural instruments are among the tangible elements of power West African states possess for state-building and domestic and foreign-policy projection. Diverse social and cultural groups that comprise the subregion unite to form a strong international community and union, and project such a power and image in the world system. These social and cultural units are a source of strength and powerful public

FIGURE 3.9   Hausa culture https://commons.wikimedia.org/wiki/File:HAUSA.jpg.

opinion for the galvanization of ideas and as the basis for domestic and foreign-policy decision-making for the countries in this part of Africa. More so, the West African subregion has experienced several origins of migration and settlement and the forging and formation of states within the area over many centuries. Thus, in the contemporary period, the 2017 population estimate gave the people of West Africa a numerical strength of 381,202,440, making the subregion one of Africa's most populous areas and one of the most populous subregions in the world.[37] Of this number, 189,672,000 were estimated to be female, while 192,309,000 were counted as male, with vast numbers of ethnic groups.[38]

However, the different ethnic groups, creeds, cultures, and faiths share geopolitical and territorial locations and owe their sociopolitical loyalty and identity to West Africa. Scholars like Kenneth O. Dike, A. Adu Boahen, Yusufu Bala Usman, and the Sierra Leonean historian, Ibrahim Abdullahi, have shown in their works that the people of the West African subregion have long mingled together, interconnected, and intermeshed into each other at various levels. This could be seen through intergroup relations, trade relations, intermarriage, sociocultural integration, regional contiguity, and other factors that render the people non-monolithic in their historical development and transformation.[39]

Over the years, the people of West Africa have engaged in various occupations. Agricultural activities are common everywhere and cut across all regions of the countries within this great part of Africa.[40] Hunting is also a feature of the occupation of the people, especially in the rural areas that are mostly in the sub-Saharan regions, the central and western Sudanese regions, and the areas of the Niger Delta region in Nigeria and the other coastal strips of West Africa that host dense forests. In Nigeria, fishing is a major occupation in communities such as the Niger Delta,[41] the north-central areas, especially the Benue region, and some parts of the north.[42]

In many communities across West Africa, people engage in small-scale private mining activities and theft.[43] This involves digging up huge stones and precious rock deposits and breaking them up for building and construction work. This is done through manual and communal labor in Nigeria, especially in the Plateau and Nasarawa areas, many parts of the Benue region, and other areas of the north-central zone. Similar interests are carried out in other mining complexes in the West African states of Guinea-Conakry, Mali, Sierra Leone, and Ghana, among others. The West African people are also occupied in several trading and business interests and concerns, such as wholesale and retail trade of several products and services, with the southeasterners of Nigeria dominating several facets of trading activities in the country and elsewhere, such as in the Benin Republic and Ghana. West Africans are engaged in all sectors of the economy, including education, medicine, oil and gas, banking, shipping, manufacturing, transport and communications, aviation, and several other means of livelihood.

In this strategic position, various instruments are employed by the West African countries to project the subregion in the international system to gain added advantages. The instruments are also important components of the lives of these nations, which they could fall back upon, unleashed in policy formulation and implementation in many sectors to earn respect and to take their pride of place in the comity of nations. In West Africa, therefore, these instruments, which are the powerful ingredients for a strong position in foreign affairs, include the social and cultural instrument, the geographic and population instrument, natural resources and economic policy, and the instrument of ideology and propaganda.[44] Through the principle of national interest, Nigeria, along with other West African states, seeks to strike a co-relationship and cooperation with the rest of the world. Therefore, West African foreign relations are conducted to expand the developmental goals within the subregion to ensure the sociopolitical and economic growth and development of human and material resources and the spread of peace and prosperity.[45]

Nigeria's and other West African countries' Africanist ideologies have played a major role in domestic and foreign interactions. These instruments have promoted the ideology of Pan-Africanism, African unity, and development.[46] The above can be classified under the tangible elements of the West African peoples' power and capability to project themselves internationally. Under their immediate international community, the Economic Community of West African States, the West African peoples also project and promote a strong national character, morale, and will. They also do this through dynamic leadership and excellent appreciation of power politics, effective use of skilled diplomacy, an organized array of pressure groups, and informed public opinion, among other things.[47]

The Language Families of the West African Subregion

Joseph H. Greenberg's classification of language groups and families in Africa identifies the Niger-Congo family.[48] According to him, this language family can be further divided into the Kwa, such as the Yoruba, Edo, Ibibio, Kalabari, Okrika, and Nembe, with the Twi of Ghana and the Wolof of Senegal being some of the most influential speakers within the group. Others identified include the Benue-Congo and Cross River groups or families such as the Efik, Tiv, Idoma, Igede, Alago, and others in central Nigeria. The eastern Adamawa sub-family group was also listed in his classification and included groups such as the Fulani and other smaller groups around the Nigeria-Cameroon border with Adamawa State and Futa Djallon in Guinea. Greenberg also came up with the Nilo-Saharan family. Greenberg states that this has been spoken by Nigerians in the northeast, particularly the Fulani, Kanuri, Dinka, and Lou, in Taraba State and several states of sub-Saharan western parts of Africa.[49]

In addition to this classification, Greenberg discusses the Afro-Asiatic language family, which he explains has been sub-divided into the Chadic group, such as the Hausa in West Africa, the Semitic group of languages identified with Arabic and Hebrew, and the Berber, spoken in some Tuareg and other communities of the Northeast in Nigeria and other neighboring West African states such as Chad, Niger, and Guinea. In the central Sahara, the dominant language family groups include the Mandinka or Mande. Among the Chadic family groups are the Hausa, nearest to the Sahara, and other Nilo-Saharan communities such as the Songhai, Kanuri, and Zarma, who live in the eastern parts of West Africa on the borderlands of Central Africa. Within Mali, Niger, and Burkina Faso, the nomadic groups of the Tuaregs speak the Tuareg language, which is a division of the Berber language. In West Africa, for historical reasons connected with the colonial experience, western European languages such as French and English have predominated many aspects of human interactions in the coastal cities and areas. But in the inland and core northern parts of West Africa, the Arabic language has had a foothold as a result of Islamic influence.[50]

Conclusion

This chapter has been an effort to present the features of the land and people of West Africa in its natural and physical characteristics. Attempts have been made to identify the location of the subregion, its topography and soil types and physical conditions, relief and drainage, climate and vegetation. Also discussed are their ethnicity, language families, culture and traditions, faiths and creeds, their means of sustenance, population status in Africa and the world, their long intergroup relations, and their efforts at sociocultural integration and interactions in the subregion. All of these are examined before the advent of European imperial and colonial domination. The study also shows that for centuries, the people of West Africa organized and developed themselves in the social, economic, and natural habitat and their environmental spheres and spaces in several sectors of their various precolonial polities.[51]

European explorers, missionaries, and traders met flourishing empires and states with vast amounts and reserves of natural resources before their government's imperialist conquest and domination of this vast westernmost part of Africa.[52] The knowledge of the geography, landscape, composition, languages, and peoples of West Africa has helped the understanding of the fact that the subregion is endowed and equipped with enormous geographic, demographic, economic, political, human, natural, and material resources well enough to project its image, power, and influence in the international system, and to achieve its objectives in terms of growth, progress, and development.

DEEP DIVE

Pick a traditional practice performed by a people group, like facial markings among the Yoruba of Nigeria, and look for one or two other countries or people groups where this practice is done.

Questions to ask:

1. Are the reasons for this practice different between the groups, or are they similar?
2. What does this tell you about the differences or similarities between people in West Africa?
3. Mention five places you would like to visit in Africa. Give your reasons.
4. Are traditional practices as relevant today as they were many centuries ago?

Assignment 1

Objective

The objective of this assignment is to ensure that students complete the reading of Chapter 3 and to get them to understand how the composition of the various peoples of West Africa and its abundant natural resources and endowments were potent factors that created viable potentials in the socioeconomic growth and development of the subregion.

Method

Students will be expected to write a short note in response to the question.

Reading Comprehension

Why has the geography, landscape, and composition of the West African subregion attracted the attention of foreign countries and continents, particularly the European powers, which led the way for the scramble for its subjugation and exploitation?

Assignment 2

Reading Comprehension

Pick a traditional practice performed by a people group, for example, cuisines among the Asante of Ghana, and look for one or two other groups where this practice is done.

Objective

The objective of this assignment is to ensure that students complete the reading of Chapter 3 and to get them to account for the reasons why there are differences and similarities in the practice of facial markings between the various groups in West Africa.

Method

Students will be expected to write a short note in response to the question.

Notes

1 See Emmanuel K. Akyeampong, ed. *Themes in West Africa's History* (Ohio: Ohio University Press, 2006); Basil Davidson, *West Africa Before the Colonial Era: A History to 1850* (London: Routledge, 1998); and F. K. Buah, *West Africa Since A.D. 1000: The People and Outsiders* (London: Macmillan Publishers, 1977).

2 Harold R. Jarrett, *A Geography of West Africa, Including the French Territories, Portuguese Guinea, and Liberia* (London: Dent, 1961).

3 Jarrett, *A Geography of West Africa.*

4 Nwadilibe P. Iloeje, *A New Geography of Nigeria* [New Revised Edition] (Lagos: Longman Nigeria Publishers, 2001), 200–203.

5 Anthony I. Asiwaju and Paul Nugent, eds. *African Boundaries: Barriers, Conduits and Opportunities* (London: Pinter, 1996).

6 William Adams, Andrew S. Goudie and Antony R. Orme, eds. *The Physical Geography of Africa* (Oxford: Oxford University Press, 1999).

7 Derek F. Hayward and Julius S. Oguntoyinbo, *Climatology of West Africa* (New Jersey: Barnes and Noble Books, 1987).

8 Hayward and Oguntoyinbo, *Climatology of West Africa.*

9 Victor A. Oyenuga, *Agriculture in Nigeria* (Rome: Food and Agriculture Organization of the United Nations, 1967), 308.

10 Eroarome Aregheore, *Country Pasture/Forage Resource Profiles: Nigeria* (Rome: Food and Agriculture Organization of the United Nations, 2009), 14.

11 J. K. Loosli, Victor A. Oyenuga and Gabriel M. Babatunde, *Animal Production in the Tropics: Proceedings of the International Symposium on Animal Production in the Tropics* (Ibadan: Heinemann Educational Books, 1974), 148–151.

12 Iloeje, *A New Geography of Nigeria*, 201. See also, Anthony M. A. Imevbore, "Floating Vegetation of Lake Kainji," *Nature* 230, nos. 599–600 (1989): 24–36.

13 A. A. Ademosun, "Utilization of Poor Quality Roughages in the Derived Savannah Zone," in *Animal Production in the Tropics*, eds. J. K. Loosli, Victor A. Oyenuga and Gabriel M. Babatunde (Nigeria: Heinemann Educational Books Ltd., 1974), 152–166.

14 Lloyd Clyburn, *Grazing Patterns of Sahel Sudan* (Washington: U.S. AID Technical Staff Paper, 1974).

15 Cited in John T. Rourke, *International Politics on the World Stage*, 4th ed. (Connecticut: Dushkin Publishing Group, 1993), 19.

16 Jonah Onuoha, *Beyond Diplomacy: Contemporary Issues in International Relations* (Nsukka: Great AP Express Publishers Limited, 2008), 51.

17 R. A. Sobulo, "Soil Fertility and Management in Nigeria," in *Proceedings of Nigeria-Australia Seminar on Collaborative Agricultural Research*, eds. Saka Nuru and R. G. Ryan (Shika: ACIAR Proceedings Series 4, 1983), 33–37.

18 Rene Pelissier, *Africa South of the Sahara* (London: Faber and Faber, 1991), 558.

19 Pelissier, *Africa South of the Sahara*, 553–556.

20 Pelissier, *Africa South of the Sahara*, 557–559.

21 S. A. Adegbola, *An Agricultural Atlas of Nigeria* (Oxford: Oxford University Press, 1979), 73.

22 Aregheore, *Country Pasture*, 13.
23 Iloeje, *A New Geography of Nigeria*, 199–201.
24 The World Fact Book, "About the World Factbook: The World Factbook Archives (July 2006 Report)," accessed August 20, 2022, https://www.cia.gov/the-world-factbook/about/archives, 27.
25 The World Fact Book, "About the World Factbook," 28–29.
26 Adegbola, *An Agricultural Atlas of Nigeria*, 28–30.
27 Mohammed Jalioh, "Natural Resources Endowment and Economic Growth: The West African Experience," *Journal of Natural Resources Development* 3 (2013): 66–84.
28 The World Fact Book, "About the World Factbook," 62. See also the editorial in *Daily Trust*, July 2, 2010, 8.
29 The World Fact Book, "About the World Factbook," 27.
30 EITI 2010 Report, 71–76.
31 Imelda I. L. Udoh, ed. *The Languages of the South-South Zone of Nigeria: A Geo-political Profile* (Lagos: Concept Publications, 2003).
32 Marc Kemper, *Beyond Barriers – Nigerian Pidgin Climbing the Ladder of Prestige* (Germany: GRIN Verlag, 2008).
33 Gilbert D. Schneider, *West African Pidgin-English: An Historical Over-view* (Ohio University: Center for International Studies, 1967).
34 Roy R. Grinker, Stephen C. Lubkemann and Christopher B. Steiner, eds. *Perspectives on Africa: A Reader in Culture, History and Representation* (Massachusetts: Wiley-Blackwell, 2012).
35 Geoffrey E. Parrinder, *West African Religion: A Study of the Beliefs and Practices of Akan, Ewe, Yoruba, Ibo, and Kindred Peoples* (London: Epworth Press, 1961).
36 David D. Laitin, *Hegemony and Culture: Politics and Religious Change Among the Yoruba* (Chicago: University of Chicago Press, 1986), 111.
37 The World Fact Book, "About the World Factbook," 31.
38 The World Fact Book, "About the World Factbook," 31.
39 Paul E. Lovejoy, "The Role of the Wangara in the Economic Transformation of the Central Sudan in the Fifteenth and Sixteenth Centuries," *Journal of African History* 19, no. 2 (1978): 173–193; Peter Morton-Williams, "The Influence of Habitat and Trade on the Polities of Oyo and Ashanti," in *Man in Africa*, eds. Mary Douglas, Phyllis M. Kaberry and Daryll Forde (London: Tavistock Publications, 1969), 80–99; and Isaac A. Akinjogbin, *Dahomey and Its Neighbours 1708–1818* (London: Cambridge University Press, 1967).
40 M. A. Havinden, "The History of Crop Cultivation in West Africa: A Bibliographical Guide," *The Economic History Review* 23, no. 3 (1970): 532–555.
41 'Gbade Ikuejube, *Ilaje: The Yoruba Fishing People of the Niger Delta* (Ondo: Novec'kol, 2005).
42 David H. L. Thomas, "Artisanal Fishing and Environmental Change in a Nigerian Floodplain Wetland," *Environmental Conservation* 22, no. 2 (1995): 117–126.
43 Kenneth Swindell, "Iron Ore Mining in West Africa: Some Recent Developments in Guinea, Sierra Leone, and Liberia," *Economic Geography* 43, no. 4 (1967): 333–346.
44 Alan Tonelson, "The Real National Interest," *Foreign Policy* 61 (1985–1986): 49.
45 Gilbert M. Khadiagala and Terrence Lyons, eds. *African Foreign Policies: Power and Process* (Colorado: Lynne Rienner Publishers, 2001), 15–66.
46 Guy Martin, *African Political Thought* (New York: Palgrave Macmillan, 2012), 55–70.
47 Victor Adetula, Redie Bereketeab and Cyril Obi, *Regional Economic Communities and Peacebuilding in Africa: Lessons from ECOWAS and IGAD* (New York: Routledge, 2021).
48 Joseph H. Greenberg, "The Classification of African Languages," *American Anthropologist* 50, no. 1 (1948): 24–30.
49 Cited in John E. Agaba and Chris S. Orngu, eds. *Perspectives on Nigerian Peoples and Culture* (Makurdi: Benue State University Press, 2016), 17–38.
50 Ousmane O. Kane, *Beyond Timbuktu: An Intellectual History of Muslim West Africa* (Cambridge: Harvard University Press, 2016).
51 Jacob F. Ade Ajayi and Ian Espie, *A Thousand Years of West African History* (Ibadan: Ibadan University Press, 1965).
52 Malyn Newitt, *The Portuguese in West Africa, 1415–1670: A Documentary History* (Cambridge: Cambridge University Press, 2010).

PART II

Early History, State Formation, and Societies

4
EVOLUTIONS AND REVOLUTIONS

Introduction

According to prehistorical narratives, human development took place over several centuries, resulting in the gradual evolution of humans' ability to control their environment and create a living space for both humans and animals.[1] In Western social and political thought, this line of development has given rise to the thinking about a single hierarchical or structural order of human society characterized by the stages of savagery, barbarism, and the final stage of civilization. These views were promoted in Western scholarship, especially in the nineteenth century.[2] It must be noted that during this ancient period, simple and natural ways of life and technological development and organization began to acquire dynamism, leading to progressive and complex forms of social, economic, scientific, and technological being in the modern period.[3] It is important to stress that this knowledge of early humans is at the core of the foundations of the archaeological and historical study of human society at the global level.[4]

The Prehistoric Development of Groups and Societies

Many bands of people and groups lived together and organized themselves while developing the means to harness and conquer their environment. This gave rise to early forms of technological development that defined their particular ages. These were not confined to a single area of the world, although the domestication of social and technological growth was more significant and renowned in certain areas than others. In the study of the prehistoric period, scholars have noted various groups and stages, including hunting and gathering societies, the period of the Stone Age, the Neolithic Revolution, and the advent of the Iron Age.[5]

Although Christian Thomsen invented the three-age system as a framework for ordering archaeological artifacts and historical epochs, these included the Stone Age, the Neolithic Revolution, and the Iron Age.[6] Sadly, while this formulation was

DOI: 10.4324/9781003198260-6

advanced to understand the origin and progress of human development, nineteenth-century European scholarship used these classifications as a model to redefine human technological development in other parts of the world as inferior or, at best, as a diffused version of the European "original version."[7] But what is even more dangerous in the adoption of this formulation and its misrepresentation is how it was transformed into an interpretive model for deepening the Eurocentric conception of Africa's history for which colonial archaeology and other subjective studies on African history are known.[8]

In early human history, these periods have been characterized by various shapes and sizes of stone carvings and rudimentary implements. The Neolithic or New Stone Age was marked by the advent of polished stone carvings and technologies, and this gave way to a period of successive ages of metal, such as the use of copper and gold, and the Bronze and later the Iron Age.[9] They were initially defined and identified based on European archaeological materials and artifacts, but later, this development was applied as a universal sequence of human technological advancement. This advancement was also a result of the socioeconomic basis of the mode of production at the time, which was predicated on hunting and gathering food for individuals, bands, and groups of humans living around the world. It must be emphasized that this level of socioeconomic and political development formed the structure of world prehistory in the period. With advancements in the study of archaeology, it was discovered that this development of societies was universal.[10]

It is important to note that sources used for the reconstruction of African history and the history of humanity, in general, are not exclusive and restrictive in understanding the history of a particular race against others. This is because archaeology has made significant progress in reconstructing the human past.[11] Thus, it is rather curious that colonial/imperial archaeology denied progress recorded by humans that occupied Africa, Asia, and other parts of the world through pretexts and ever-expanding political influence across these areas.[12] Bonnie Efros and Guolong Lai maintain that:

> Popular sentiments in the West have tended to embrace the adventure rather than ponder the legacy of archaeological explorers: allegations by imperial powers of "discovering" archaeological sites or "saving" world heritage from neglect or destruction have often provided the pretext for expanding political influence. Consequently, citizens have often fallen victim to [the] imperial war machine[s], seeing their lands confiscated, their artifacts looted, and ancient remains in their midst commercialized.[13]

For many years, this has been the trend in the European practice of archaeology in Africa and other parts of the world. The foundation of such "archaeological practice" has its origin from the earliest times, especially among European scholars who conceived Africa as a "dark continent" and the conjuring of the so-called Hamitic hypothesis. This became a theory of analysis that justified imperial domination and defined international power relations between Africa and other parts of the world. Rather than universalizing the objective practice of archaeology, some scholars have, over the years, worked toward universalizing wrong ideas and subjective "archaeological" practices. This places Africa at the lower rung of human civilization despite available evidence of human activities on the continent, especially using the three-age system as a method for ordering human activities over time.

PRODUCING FIRE BY FRICTION.

FIGURE 4.1   An artistic impression of a caveman producing fire by friction in the Stone Age. Location, ethnicity, and nationality unknown https://www.gettyimages.co.uk/ detail/illustration/caveman-producing-fire-by-friction-royalty-free-illustration /1073934574.

As discussed in Chapter 2, it must be emphasized that the study of early societies has been premised upon various sources, mostly unwritten, such as those inherent in oral, archaeological, and material records. These include oral evidence and traditions, natural objects or features such as forests, streams, rivers, hills, and valleys. Others include human-made equipment or artistic objects like shrines, cutlery, pottery, engravings, carvings, sculpture, and entertainment instruments. Archaeologists and other scholars garner auxiliary sources such as archaeological excavations, linguistics, anthropology, ethnography, botany, social biology, zoology, paleontology or fossil remains, and others. Oral evidence refers to historical material sources handed down to an individual, family, community, society, or nation by word of mouth from generation to generation. These have been used along with various material and physical remains of the societies to reconstruct the past, especially as regards hunting and gathering societies, the Stone Age, the Neolithic revolution, and the advent of the Iron Age[14] (Figures 4.1 and 4.2)

Hunting and Gathering Societies

Hunting and gathering societies developed out of the need for survival through natural resources available for sustenance, such as food. In the early period, hunters and

FIGURE 4.2 Iron Age protohistoric artifacts from northeastern Sierra Leone (West Africa) https://commons.wikimedia.org/wiki/File:Iron_Age_Protohistoric_artefacts_from _Northeastern_Sierra_Leone_(West_Africa)_(1764315079).jpg.

gatherers of the various regions of the world faced a system with unpredictable rainfall and short-term climatic fluctuations.[15] This was challenging for those societies, not in terms of the seeming abundance of food and avenues for gathering food, but in whether or not food could be available at given periods. In such a setting, observation was made as to whether plants were available in abundance to adjust to particular types of favored food in given periods, such as during arid seasons. In other circumstances, local hunters and gatherers intensified their use of wild animal herds rather than harvesting wild plants, as the productivity of plants became vulnerable to the changing variation in rainfall.[16]

During droughts, the consumption of ungulates was intensified as these were a more reliable resource than plants because their populations were maintained through movements that exploited local differences in topography, vegetation, and rainfall.[17] Wild ungulates became the means through which the hunter-gatherers increased their mobility, with the general use of plants to support forage efficiency and improve the plant components of their diet. The appearance of ungulates in some parts of the world was significant to the development of human history based on time and location. This is because the time factor was considered essential in evaluating the different stages of progress made in different human societies of the world and determining which group attained a particular type of civilization before others. This model was important because of the way the study of prehistory was organized by some scholars on what transpired in human societies and at what periods. This was intended to sideline Africans and confine them to the backwaters of world development.[18]

The complex nature of innovation and invention preoccupied the origin and development of hunter-gatherer societies. The invention of social and political units was a manifestation of unique interactions, especially between people's environment and their concerns about self-preservation. Thus, the invention of technology for group and individual self-sustenance resulted in simple social systems. Most bands were organized based on kinship, especially through the male line.[19] This arrangement was flexible and was the means through which the bands organized supporting cooperative activities with extended kinship without specific roles. Though some were known as arrow-makers or other types of labor, there was no specialized occupation capable of earning any complete form of living among bands.

Physically fit individuals combined the responsibility to hunt and the responsibility to gather. Societies varied from one to another depending on the various stages of the attainment of civilization. Thus, societies that created wealth became rich and advanced in terms of the division of labor and occupational roles, such as canoe-builders, band chiefs, and others. For group preservation, one of the most powerful instruments for division of labor was gender. Women gathered while men hunted. This division was not rigid, as women and men could do both; however, women were often confined to caring for children, and childcare and hunting were largely incompatible. This does not erase the fact that women foraged plant resources and hunted nearby game alongside childcare. In most cases, distant hunting and other very far occupational activities were done by men. The hunter-gatherer societies that preceded agricultural ones were organized in small groups of nomadic families similar to those of primate bands. The Khoisan of the Kalahari Desert[20] and indigenous Australians[21] are typical examples of hunter-gatherer societies in our contemporary time. The evolution of such forms of organization is responsible for the development of other complex forms of social, economic, and political orders.

Though Fukuyama alludes to Jean Jacques Rosseau's position on the origin of inequality as being traceable to the development of agriculture, he noted that band-level societies in pre-agricultural societies had no concept of private property in the sense that is conceived today. Like primates, however, hunter-gatherers occupied territories that they protected from intruders. Unlike agriculturalists who parcelled out land to designate it for production, the hunter-gatherer societies had less need to privatize property (land) as a form of incentive for groups and individuals. Thus, whenever society was under siege by predators, the band-level society moved to other places with low-density populations. Modern economic development in terms of exchange was not visible; therefore, the quest for investment, such as cleared land and houses, was also insignificant. Also, social and political development was based on human experience rather than a formal and organized state principle of government.

Fukuyama cited social anthropologist Ernest Geller, who referred to such relations as the "tyranny of cousins"[22] in the absence of state tyranny. This also means that the social world of the band in hunting and gathering society was limited to the circles of relatives surrounding them, who determined what they did, whom they married, how they worshipped, and just about everything else in life. Hunting and gathering was the group's occupation, sometimes organized along family lines.[23] The technology for preservation was limited, so hunted animals were shared among members and immediately consumed to avoid spoilage. Light weapons for killing animals, such as bows and arrows, spears, choppers, and knives used for butchering meat, were essentially the tools for hunting.[24]

Food gathering was carried out by using digging sticks and simple wooden bowls.[25] Processing of foods was elementary, and animal preparation for consumption was mainly done by roasting over a fire. Communal living was an essential feature of society, and everything was shared among members.[26] Evolutionary psychologists attribute this characteristic to the concept of modern-day Thanksgiving, Passover, and the sharing of meals during Christmas.[27] The process through which moral principles were cultivated in those societies largely depended on the need to share. Sharing in such societies was important because it preserved the people during times of scarcity. The principle was held with the commitment to function as a group and protect one another from lack.

Social formation was based on the group and the family, but there were distinctions based on gender which also helped in the division of labor. In terms of leadership and hierarchy of operation for the band level, no one was designated as leader, as is done today in centralized political systems with tenured leaders. Fukuyama maintains that strength, intelligence, and trustworthiness were important criteria for whoever led, but this was only a temporary position.[28] It is imperative to understand that hunter-gatherer societies consisted of a small number of nucleated families related by kinship. According to Fried, the band rarely exceeded 50 persons, and this was the basic unit that other foraging groups also assumed, and this occurred until they became sedentarized for more developed agricultural production.[29] The bands were usually spread across relatively vast territories. Steward states that every five square miles or more were allocated to or owned by one person.[30] Learning was done in the open, as everyone had information on what was happening to the other people in the band. In this social structure, few individuals were respected above their peers.

According to Fried, these individuals were referred to as headmen and had no significant authority to enforce rules because bands were largely governed by norms;[31] therefore, it was difficult to compel members to a task by any form of authority.[32] Band members were socially connected to the group, and women could marry outside the band. The practice established relationships and consolidated one group or another such that they could forge alliances to further protect each other and increase genetic multiplicity. Intermarriages across bands promoted peace and reduced hostility against one another.

The Stone Age

The Stone Age is one of the periods in prehistoric development that defined the capacity of humans in their evolutionary process as they grappled with the challenges of their environment and organized themselves.[33] Humans evolved in their cognitive capacity to fashion stone tools to overcome the challenges of time. The Stone Age was not the starting point of human evolution or technology; however, it is one of the stages of human evolution that defined human advancement in technology. The Stone Age started about 2.6 million years ago and developed many industries.[34] In this age, humans lived in small groups that were always moving from one location to another in search of water

FIGURE 4.3   Prehistoric Stone Age tools from Sierra Leone https://commons.m.wikimedia
.org/wiki/File:Prehistoric_stone_artefacts_from_Sierra_Leone_(West_Africa)_
(2532076540).jpg.

and food. Stones were sharpened for extracting animal meat, crushing, and pounding. Hammerstones were used to chip other stones made into sharp objects to process clay into a pigment by crushing it with stones and to break nuts, bones, seeds, and other useful materials[35] (Figure 4.3).

The Stone Age witnessed diversity in the ways humans approached their environment. For example, Hayden et al. maintain that as more animals were exploited, mortars and pestles became essential tools for processing foods, and techniques for making fishing tools were also improved; from the stone tool assemblage, there were records of tools such as leister, gorges, harpoons, and fishhooks.[36] Other technology included improved bows and arrows. The domestication of dogs also contributed to hunting.[37] These improvements show that humans increased their capability to conquer their environment and to further sedentarize.

The Neolithic Revolution

The term "Neolithic Age" was coined in the late nineteenth century by scholars, and it covers three different periods—the Paleolithic, Mesolithic, and Neolithic.[38] In this revolutionary period, societies acquired significance through the development of megalithic architecture, the expansion and spread of agriculture and its practices, and the adoption and usage of polished stone tools.[39] This period is sometimes referred to by the term "New Stone Age," which has been frequently used in connection with the expansion of agricultural practices among the societies of the world.[40] In connection with agricultural development, cereal cultivation and animal domestication were introduced, although these were developed at different times and places by different societies. As a result, scholars have been unable to establish a specific period for the commencement of the Neolithic period in ancient history.

Interest in the Neolithic revolution was sparked during the colonial and post-colonial periods in Africa. This was generally in the 1960s when decolonization and the attainment of political independence inspired interest in Africa's pre-colonial history. The aim was to repudiate the idea that Africa was outside history and that no historical part of the world system existed until the advent of European imperialism.[41] Thus, archaeology and multidisciplinary studies became vital in overcoming the limitations of evidence or sources for the illumination of pre-colonial Africa. However, coordination was difficult among scholars and this effort was compromised because the various scholars involved insisted on working separately and only within the accepted standards of their various individual disciplines. Even when archaeological work on the Neolithic or the New Stone Age started, archaeologists and other scholars did not situate it properly within the context of any contribution to progress and development on the part of Africa.[42]

Over time, archaeologists seemed to dwell so much on societies and sites that had attributes of technological development that they began to use this from a neo-evolutionist point of view against historical contingency.[43] This view persisted even into the 1970s when there was a shift in understanding the impact of colonial domination on societies and as a yardstick for understanding change and continuity in Africa, Asia, and Latin America. Archaeologists continued the use of cultural evolution as a principle and practice for investigating progress in human societies, especially making references from farming to metallurgy.[44] The Neolithic stage marks the last phase of the Stone Age.

As earlier indicated, there seems to be no single date ascribed to the beginning of the Neolithic era; however, available information on the period holds that it began in the present Middle Eastern region, where agricultural development was revolutionized around 9000 BCE, and in the southeastern parts of Europe around 7000 BCE.[45] Agriculture and its practices developed differently and at different times depending on the part of the world. Examples show that agriculture first developed in southeastern Europe at about 7000 BCE, in the central parts of Europe at about 5500 BCE, and in northern Europe at about 4000 BCE. In eastern Asia, the Neolithic period dates back from 6000 to 2000 BCE.[46] It has been suggested that the development of a Neolithic culture was a gradual and not a sudden change.[47]

Several factors have contributed to the difficulty of dating the Neolithic period. One of these was the development of pottery. The advent of pottery has sometimes been associated with the Neolithic period, although it did not occur after the growth and development of agriculture.[48] This is evident in the history of many cultures around the world. For example, in Japan, the adoption and usage of pottery predated the advent of agricultural practices, while elsewhere in the transcontinental areas of Western Asia, Lebanon, Turkey, and Egypt, agriculture predated the production of pottery and the development of such cultures, which contributed to making the clear dating of the Neolithic period confusing or contradictory. Scholars have also clearly shown that the term "Neolithic" was a nineteenth-century classification system of the phenomenon, which was not perfect but useful and appropriate.

Also, there is the question of whether the Neolithic age or period was a revolution in the annals of ancient history. The term "revolution" was used in the 1940s by Australian archaeologist Gordon Childe to express the high level of significance of agriculture in the lives of people, families, communities, and nations. However, recent scholarship has been of the view that the contribution of agriculture and its innovative practices in human societies has been exaggerated. Since revolutions deal with studies of changes in society happening abruptly, and seeing that the Neolithic period was of long duration, some have disputed that this may not have been a revolution.[49] It has been established that before the growth and expansion of agriculture, archeological evidence showed that human societies across the world lived a semi-nomadic life. These pre-agricultural human societies had a network of campsites and lived in different locations depending on the availability of resources and the variation in seasons and times. In certain periods, some of these campsites were adopted as the base of the particular group; thus, time may have been spent in the area exploiting the resources of those base camps. Some of these exploited resources included the consumption of wild plants, which has been regarded by many scholars as an aspect of agriculture.

Therefore, in this period, agricultural practices and foraging were not incompatible with humans. It has been acknowledged that a particular human group in the period may perform the role of hunter-gatherers and its activities in most parts of the year while performing farming activities during the rest of the year, sometimes on a small scale. Nevertheless, the division was striking as a major aspect of the semi-nomadic lives of ancient humans. Therefore, rather than concluding that this was a period of revolution, scholars have reckoned that it was a period that saw slow and gradual changes and processes.[50] Other developments during the Neolithic period involved the spread of agricultural economies, which led to the reduction of hunting and gathering activities. It also led to the widespread adoption of a sedentary way of life by peoples and societies around the world, increasing the awareness of domestication and the claim to ownership over vast territories. There were also in this period innovations in the construction of arrowheads and the need for defense and protection over certain areas. This was achieved by building and constructing massive walls around cities, which escalated conflicts and even warfare.

Conclusion

This chapter has observed that the study of archaeology remains at the root of the development process of the history of all societies, including in Africa. This has been seen in the three stages or ages of prehistoric development. In other words, archaeological sources can be the dominant evidence for writing early African history, as are narrative accounts of the history of other parts of the world. But colonial historiography was essentially anthropological, and this anthropology was made a tool of colonialism and the capitalist-imperialist system, which attempted to impose itself on the narrative of African historical developments. Therefore, this historiography was highly subjective rather than objective.

The ideologies, philosophical ideas, and theories about Africa from European imperialists interfered significantly with their judgment of historical events and developments in Africa. Thus, African societies were presented as static while ignoring the proliferation and diversity of state systems, complex forms of exchange and social stratification, and evidence of advanced forms of material art. It was, therefore, true that the European idea of causation in history about the element of selection of the most important facts of history and their interpretation was prejudiced and biased against Africa. Africanist and nationalist historiography emerged as a counter-ideology in the attempt to restore Africa's historical past, dignity, and glory.[51]

As the chapter has demonstrated, from the period of nationalist struggle to the attainment of independence by most African countries in the second half of the twentieth century, the stage was set, and the era became crucial to the success of this new historiographical method. This chapter has observed that despite the relative primacy and the importance of archaeological sources, they cannot be used in isolation from other sources, especially written sources of historical reconstruction. The contemporary world's advances in communications, technology, and universality necessarily call for complementarity and the comprehensive usage of all source materials in writing history. Furthermore, events of the past that were of great significance in most societies have been written and documented as the historical development of such societies. Thus, the researcher combines these with the archaeological and other unwritten sources to produce a more balanced, comprehensive, objective, and acceptable history.

Even in the contemporary period of the development of world history, studies of history can still be produced from archaeological sources as the starting point of their continuous refinement and development. But for a true and universally acceptable reconstruction of the history of the lives of families, communities, societies, nations, and historians have recommended that all sources must be considered in historical research and reconstruction to achieve the ultimate goals of credibility and objectivity that are so crucial to the life and work of the historian, especially in the attempt to debunk the claims of Eurocentric writers and scholars. This was championed by Edward Blyden, J. E. Casely-Hayford, Kenneth Onwuka Dike, J. F. Ade Ajayi, Saburi Biobaku, A. B. Horton, Walter Rodney, and Ali A. Mazrui. The period of nationalist struggle for the attainment of independence by most African countries in the second half of the twentieth century was crucial to the success of this new historiographical order, and the freedom of the continent became its crowning glory.

DEEP DIVE

Visit a museum or archaeological site near you. Choose any object of your choice and reflect on its cultural and historical meanings.

Assignment 1

Objective

The objective of this assignment is to ensure that students complete reading Chapter 4 and that they understand the role of objects in the interpretation of the past.

Method

Students will be expected to write a short answer in response to the question.

Reading Comprehension

Compare and contrast societies in different evolutionary stages.

Assignment 2

Objective

The objective of this assignment is to ensure that students complete the reading and to make them understand the extent to which the management of environmental elements encourages the implementation of political systems.

Method

Students will be expected to write a short note in response to the question.

Reading Comprehension

How did environmental factors contribute to the economic and commercial success of empires, civilization, and kingdoms and their need to implement formal political institutions?

Notes

1 Jeffrey K. McKee, Frank E. Poirier and Scott W. Mcgraw, *Understanding Human Evolution* (London: Routledge, 2016).
2 Johan Goudsblom, David M. Jones and Stephen Mennell, *The Course of Human History: Economic Growth, Social Process, and Civilization* (London: Routledge, 1996).
3 Reza A. Kohan, ed. *The Human Experience* (Columbus: Merrill Publishing Company, 1977), 1–3.
4 Kohan, *The Human Experience*, 3–11.
5 In this chapter, the intention is only to present brief or short notes and analysis concerning these archaeological and historical ages. This is especially true with regard to the place of Africa in the developments of these periods.
6 For details on Christian Jurgensen Thomsen three age system, see Peter Rowley-Conwy, "The Three Age System in English: New Translations of the Founding Documents," *Bulletin of the History of Archaeology* 14, no. 1 (2004): 4–15.
7 Until recently, iron and other cultures of technological advancement in Africa were seen by Western scholars as a false phenomenon that can only be achieved through diffusion. See, for instance, Leo Frobenius, *Voice of Africa: Being an Account of the Travels of the German Inner Africa Exploration Expedition in the Years 1910–1912*, Vol. 1 (London: Hutchinson & Co., 1913).
8 Charles Orser Jr., "An Archaeology of Eurocentrism," *American Antiquity* 77, no. 4 (2012): 737–755.
9 Susan Meyer, *The Neolithic Revolution* (New York: The Rosen Publishing Group, 2017); and George G. MacCurdy, *The New Stone Age and the Ages of Bronze and Iron* (London: Johnson Reprint Corporation, 1965).
10 Basil Davidson, *The African Past: Chronicles from Antiquity to Modern Times* (London: Longman Group Limited, 1964), 3–7.
11 This is not to denigrate the contribution of other disciplines; however, the way archaeology and anthropology were deployed in studying Africa's past made it compelling to question the rationale behind the adoption of the tools they used in studying human progress in Africa as against the way this is being studied in Europe. The three-age system, for example,

was formulated with the view to give proper ordering in the archaeological categorization of epochs. Unfortunately, in Africa, progress made during these periods were denied and termed as dependent on foreign agency.

12 Bonnie Effros and Guolong Lai, *Unmasking Ideology in Imperial and Colonial Archaeology: Vocabulary, Symbols, and Legacy* (California: The Costen Institute of Archaeology Press, 2018).

13 Effros and Lai, *Unmasking Ideology.*

14 Francis Fukuyama, *The Origins of Political Order: From Pre-human Times to the French Revolution* (London: Profile Books Limited, 2011), 43–51. The work has consulted an enormous amount of auxiliary sources for this seminal study. See 31–48.

15 John Gowdy, "Our Hunter-gatherer Future: Climate Change Agriculture and Uncivilization," *Futures* 115 (2019). See also Ofer Bar-Yosef, "Climatic Fluctuations and Early Farming in West and East Asia," *Current Anthropology* 52, no. S4 (2011): S175–S193.

16 Gowdy, "Our Hunter-gatherer Future."

17 J. O. Ogutu, H. P. Piepho, H. T. Dublin, N. Bhola and R. S. Reid, "Rainfall Influences on Ungulate Population Abundance in the Mara-Serengeti Ecosystem," *Journal of Animal Ecology* 77, no. 4 (2008): 814–829.

18 Mohammed Jalioh, "Natural Resources Endowment and Economic Growth: The West African Experience," *Journal of Natural Resources and Development* 3 (2013): 66–84. See also Paul J. Lane, "Barbarous Tribes and Unrewarding Gyrations?: The Changing Role of Ethnographic Imagination in African Archaeology," in *African Archaeology: A Critical Introduction, Blackwell Studies in Global Archaeology,* ed. Ann B. Stahl (Oxford: Blackwell Publishing, 2005), 24–31.

19 Laura Fortunato, "Lineal Kinship Organization in Cross-specific Perspective," *Philosophical Transactions of the Royal Society B* 374 (2019): 1–9.

20 Bruno David, Bryce Barker and Ian J. McNiven, *The Social Archaeology of Australian Indigenous Societies* (Canberra: Aboriginal Studies Press, 2006).

21 Alan Barnard, *Hunters and Herders of Southern Africa: A Comparative Ethnography of the Khoisan Peoples* (Cambridge: Cambridge University Press, 1992).

22 Fukuyama, *The Origins of Political Order*, 44–45. See also, Frans De Waal, *Good Natured: The Origins of Right and Wrong in Humans and Other Animals* (Massachusetts: Harvard University Press, 1997), 83–107.

23 Kristen Hawkes, James F. O'Connell and Nicholas G. Blurton Jones, "Hunting and Nuclear Families: Some Lessons from the Hadza about Men's Work," *Current Anthropology* 42, no. 5 (2001): 681–709.

24 Brian Hayden, "Insights into Early Lithic Technologies from Ethnography," *Philosophical Transactions of the Royal Society B* 370, no. 1682 (2015). Hayden's study was drawn from Namibia and central Australia deserts, which are semi-arid and similar to those of South and East Africa. See also www.des.ucdavis.edu.

25 Hayden, "Insights into Early Lithic Technologies," 4.

26 Hawkes, O'Connell and Jones, "Hunting and Nuclear Families."

27 De Waal, "Good Natured," 107–117.

28 Fukuyama, *The Origins of Political Order*, 45–48.

29 Morton H. Fried, *The Evolution of Political Society: An Essay in Political Anthropology* (New York: Random House, 1967), 83. See also, Julian Steward, *Theory of Culture Change: The Methodology of Multilinear Evolution* (Urbana: University of Illinois Press, 1972), 125; and Steven A. LeBlanc and Katherine E. Register, *Constant Battles: The Myth of the Peaceful, Noble Savage* (New York: St. Martins Griffin, 2004), 83–92.

30 Steward, *Theory of Culture Change.* See also Richard Lee, "Work Effort, Group Structure and Land-Use in Contemporary Hunter-Gatherers" in *Man, Settlement and Urbanism*, eds. Peter J. Ucko, Ruth Tringham and G. W. Dimbleby (Cambridge: Schenkman, 1972), 175–185; and Richard Lee, "Power and Property in Twenty-first Century Foragers: A Critical Examination," in *Power and Equality: Encapsulation, Commercialization, Discrimination,* eds. Thomas Widlok and Tadesse Wolde (Oxford: Berg Publishing, 2004), 19.

31 Sheina Lew-Levy, Noa Lavi, Rachel Reckin, Jurgi Cristóbal-Azkarate and Kate Ellis-Davies, "How do Hunter-gatherer Children Learn Social and Gender Norms? A Meta-Ethnographic Review," *Cross-Cultural Research* 2, no. 2 (2017): 213–255.

32 Fried, *The Evolution of Political Society*, 83. See also Steward, *Theory of Culture Change*, 125 and LeBlanc and Register, *Constant Battles*, 83–92.

33 William Allman, *The Stone Age Present: How Evolution Has Shaped Modern Life – From Sex, Violence and Language to Emotions, Morals and Communities* (New York: Simon and Schuster, 1994).

34 Ignacio de la Torre, "The Origins of Stone Technology in Africa: A Historical Perspective," *Philosophical Transactions of the Royal Society B Biological Sciences* 366, no. 1567 (2011): 1028–1037.

35 R. J. Blumenschine and M. M. Selvaggio, "On the Marks of Marrow Bone Processing by Hammerstones and Hyenas: Their Anatomical Patterning and Archaeological Implications," in *Cultural Beginnings: Approaches to Understanding Early Hominid Lifeways in the African Savannah*, ed. J. D. Clark (Mainz: Romisch-Germanisches Zentralmuseum, 1991), 17–32.

36 Brian Hayden, "Research and Development in the Stone Age: Technological Transitions among Hunter-Gatherers," *Current Anthropology* 22, no. 5 (1981): 519–548.

37 Hayden, "Research and Development."

38 Bill Finlayson, *The First Villages. The Neolithic Period (10,000-4500 BC)* (Bayreuth: Presses de l'Ifpo, 2013).

39 Anna and Mathew observed in their study in Eastern Africa that the stone tools, such as grinding stone tools found in the region, are closely related to the cultivation of cereals in and particularly related to the pastoral Neolithic archaeological context. For details, see Anna Shoemaker and Mathew I. J. Davies, "Grinding Stones Implements in the Eastern African Pastoral Neolithic," *Azania: Archaeological Research in Africa* 54, no. 2 (2019): 203–220.

40 Cristian Violatti, "Neolithic Period," *World History Encyclopedia*, April 2, 2018, https://www.worldhistory.org/Neolithic/.

41 It is widely acknowledged in Western scholarship that Africa had no history, except the history of European imperial activities in Africa.

42 Davidson, *The African Past*, 27–38.

43 While archaeological principles and practice are relevant in the reconstruction of past societies and historical epochs, it is equally important to be cautious in universalizing approaches toward understanding specific historical events and seeking comparative generalization. Events in history should be accorded their relevance in time and space. See Innocent Pikirayi, "The Future of Archaeology in Africa," *Antiquity* 89, no. 345 (2015): 531–541.

44 See Peter Schmidt, "Using Archaeology to Remake African History," in *Making Alternative Histories*, eds. Peter Schmidt and Thomas Patterson (Santa Fe: School of American Research, 1995), 118–147. See also Pikirayi, "The Future of Archaeology," 531.

45 Violatti, "Neolithic Period."

46 Violatti, "Neolithic Period."

47 Violatti, "Neolithic Period."

48 Violatti, "Neolithic Period."

49 Barry Cunliffe, *The Oxford Illustrated History of Pre-historic Europe* (Oxford: Oxford University Press, 2001), 47–65.

50 Violatti, "Neolithic Period."

51 Adiele Afigbo, *The Poverty of African Historiography* (Lagos: Afrografika Publishers, Lagos), 1977.

5

SOCIETIES AND CULTURES IN THE IRON AGE

Introduction

Social, political, and economic thinkers have categorized human evolution and development based on modes of production. Karl Marx examined the stages of human development, tracing them from simple hunter-gatherer bands to communalist groups that collectively owned property for the common good of all.[1] Slavery was another stage of human development; the human drive to conquer the surrounding environment extended to domination within the family, to overwhelm and control others physically.[2] Feudalism followed slavery, and agriculture was the main focus of production.[3]

Agricultural production, one of the greatest technological advancements in human evolutionary history, transformed societies in the Neolithic era.[4] The evolution of agriculture allowed sedentary humans to establish social and cultural patterns that can be traced to the present day. Deliberate attempts were made to cultivate and harvest surplus food during this period. The practice developed into an economic system of production that was relevant for managing resources. Agriculture enabled societies to support more people than in previous hunter-gatherer societies.

With hunter-gatherer societies, humanity developed into an epoch known as the Stone Age.[5] The continued development of human cranial capacity allowed for the production of superior tools. In the early Paleolithic Age, humans manufactured simple tools by shaping rock flakes and sticks for hunting and warfare. Tools were also used for extracting meat, and hammerstones were used to chip other stones into sharp objects for crushing or breaking nuts, bones, and seeds. Humans exploited their environment in more diverse ways, hunting animals for other purposes besides food.

Mortars and pestles were used for processing materials, and fishing techniques were improved with leisters, gorges, harpoons, and fishhooks. Bows and arrows were used for hunting, and dogs became domesticated as humans developed into sedentary groups. Improved tools increased the means of production, and agricultural advances led to dietary improvements and better fertility rates, leading to population growth. Humans

DOI: 10.4324/9781003198260-7

developed speech and language for communication during the Paleolithic Age,[6] which aided technological growth and development. Many groups remained nomadic during this period, and the human species spread across the globe. Increasing numbers of humans spread beyond their initial environments to disseminate ideas and knowledge about the environment. The late Stone Age, described as the Neolithic Revolution, contributed to the emergence of a broader, more diverse culture of production, and humans developed livelihoods distinct from their hunter-gatherer origins.[7]

Societies developed economic systems and material cultures to support their continued existence, creating their history and civilization through this process. The drive to conquer nature and the environment became very important because nature provided materials necessary for human survival. Humans engaged in these activities that supported their existence, and through this process, took control of their destiny and developed new tools for more efficient production. Human consciousness began to value land as a commodity and for its role as the means of production. Lands were owned by a small number of people, and they created wealth by using slaves to work the lands for food. This stage also marked the beginning of private property as a concept, which became more widely recognized under capitalism.[8] In the capitalist mode of production, human creativity developed machines to replace human labor, and wealth creation diversified into other sectors beyond agriculture. Private property was valued for its role in production, and humans focused primarily on increasing wealth. Human creativity and ingenuity remained significant in every stage of human evolution, along with an awareness of the surrounding environment.

The Development of Prehistoric Cultures and Societies before the Iron Age

Archaeologists and other scholars in various academic fields have studied the different epochs of human evolution. These periods are the hunter-gatherer society, Stone Age society, Neolithic society, and Iron Age society.[9] The hunter-gatherer society, which marks the evolutionary beginning of human societies, was largely characterized by the key occupations of hunting, gathering, fishing, fowling, and collecting. The human species demonstrated characteristics that are distinct from other creatures. For instance, people manipulated objects more easily than other mammals, which allowed them to craft complex tools that supported human systems of production. Their omnivorous nature enabled them to survive in virtually every climate, devising methods to exist in challenging environments. Scientific studies of human evolutionary history, culture, and society suggest that hunter-gatherer societies evolved before other production cultures. During this period, human society was organized into simple groups for subsistence production.

Human history depended largely on the creative ingenuity applied to communicate, process ideas, and fashion tools. Much of humanity's early evolutionary phase was characterized by food production, but people's needs became more diverse over time. Early social formations led to the development of cultures of domestication for social and technological growth. Although this development did not occur simultaneously across the world, social formation and the domestication of knowledge were essential features of early societies. The domestication process occurred through interactions between humans and their physical environment—humans began to develop production techniques to support themselves more effectively. Tools were developed to compensate for environmental variations, such as erratic rainfall or irregular climate conditions. It was necessary to develop knowledge and improve production methods to address uncertainty and ensure a reliable food supply in variable climates.

Humanity faced significant challenges in hunter-gatherer societies, which are significant for understanding the trajectory of human technological development. Societies that hunted food and gathered nuts and berries could not support a large population, and their small numbers could not produce tools efficiently. This culture was that of hunting and gathering at a subsistence level.[10] Hunting and gathering were the principal modes of production until the Neolithic era when pastoralism and agricultural production developed. As the cranial capacity of humans developed over time, they could understand their environment and harness its potential. This understanding improved the human species, increasing their proficiency in techniques and methods of production. Wooden and stone tools gave them new advantages. According to Feary and his co-authors,

> Human relationship with nature was so close that survival depended on intimate knowledge and manipulation of the natural world, understood through a cosmological lens. Localized adaptations led to distinctive morphological types, technologies, cultural traditions and languages and by 11,000 years ago, hunter-gatherer populations had spread across the Earth.[11]

The development of speech allowed these bands to communicate, cooperate, and transmit technical knowledge that continues to develop into the present day.

The Advent of the Iron Age

The Iron Age was one of the periods in human evolutionary history defined by increased human ingenuity in developing iron tools. The period saw the emergence of the efficient use of iron tools in conquering the human environment.[12] The coming of the Iron Age signaled the gradual waning and modification of the culture of technological development and production of tools made with either wood, stone, or other materials used before the emergence of metal, as well as a decline in values, which gave way to a new form of age characterized with iron tools. The Iron Age marked a significant change in the development of the human capacity to manipulate the environment and become more efficient.[13] Steel and other metal components were fashioned into tools via heating with carbon materials. Humans around the Mediterranean created iron tools, especially the people of the Mycenaean civilization in Greece and the Hittite Empire in Turkey. This emerged shortly after the Bronze Age.[14]

The emergence of the Iron Age varied throughout the world from one location to another.[15] Human ingenuity and improving production techniques were responsible for manipulating iron rather than bronze when it was discovered that iron tools were much stronger and superior weapons. Many archaeologists and prehistorians argued that the end of the Iron Age coincided with the beginning of the historiographical period or the beginning of the historical record.[16] Sub-Saharan Africa had no real, continent-wide Bronze Age; thus, the Iron Age immediately followed the Stone Age in many of these places.

Contentious Archaeological Issues Regarding the Iron Age in Africa

Africa's iron technology has been the subject of debate among scholars. Some believe that ironworking technology did not exist in prehistoric African societies.[17] Others have suggested that the existence of iron technology in prehistoric Africa means it was brought to the continent from outside sources.[18] However, evidence suggests that iron technology in Africa developed independently as a local initiative that occurred without external influence.[19] Although a significant number of earlier Eurocentric arguments regarding iron technology have been dismissed, a brief reflection on this discourse will allow a better understanding of ironworking societies in Africa.

The diffusionist explanation for the presence of iron technology in Africa is built on two main assumptions. Although iron was one of the first metals produced in Africa, along with copper and gold, diffusionists argue that it is not clear whether these minerals were worked locally. They claim that no available evidence supports the idea of indigenous ironworking in Africa.[20] This premise rests on the assumption that all societies developed copper technology before iron technology. West Africa had no evidence of furnaces that could be used for smelting, capable of heating minerals to high temperatures, predating the advent of iron.[21] Diffusionists further argue that iron technology is a more recent phenomenon in Africa than in other parts of the world. Their explanation suggests that iron technology diffused into the continent from the Near East, where knowledge of iron technology flourished during the second millennium BC.[22] The geographical proximity and possible cultural contact between the two regions may have made such diffusion possible. It has been suggested that the Phoenicians improved their knowledge of ironworking after contact with Egypt, and it transferred to Meroe in the eighth century BC.[23] From there, the technology would spread to Sudan, West Africa, the sub-Saharan region, and other parts of Africa.[24]

Contact between the Berbers has also been suggested as a method for spreading ironworking technology to West Africa. Van Der Merwe posits that trade settlements established by Phoenicians were important contact points, and the knowledge may have passed to the Berbers, who introduced it to West Africa and the rest of the sub-Saharan region.[25] There is also a suggestion that iron technology was transferred to different parts of the sub-Saharan African region through the Bantu migration,[26] a theory asserting that sub-Saharan Africa witnessed a population movement between 1000 BC and 1000 AD when the Bantu-speaking group moved to the southern part of Africa. The iron technology allegedly passed down to the Bantu group was acquired through interaction with other North African cultures, and this information would have been passed down to groups in the south as well.[27]

The arguments that Africa did not develop its iron technology independently have been countered with evidence from Africanist archaeologists.[28] These archaeologists noted that little is known about North Africa's evidence of iron technology. There is no evidence of iron technology practiced among the Berbers before that technology appeared in West Africa.[29] These archaeologists further argue that West Africa's distribution of iron ore suggests that the technology would have been more of an indigenous phenomenon than an external development.[30] In one explanation, the iron smelting technique that developed in West Africa is said to be a different technique, unlike the methods used among other cultures. The iron ore in the West African region does not

FIGURE 5.1   Metal work in contemporary Ghana https://commons.m.wikimedia.org/wiki/File
                :Wala_Man_Making_Iron_Pot_27.jpg.

require a complex smelting method. It is immaterial, therefore, to argue that the technology should have emerged from preexisting copper or bronze metallurgy[31] (Figure 5.1).

For Vansina, language could spread through contact and not necessarily through mass migration.[32] This has implications for the Bantu migration as a phenomenon responsible for transferring technology to Southern Africa. Robertson and Bradley posit that there is little evidence, if any, of migration in precolonial Africa.[33] It is difficult to prove that such a population movement, especially involving the Bantu language, was significant enough to be responsible for the spread of iron technology. African archaeological studies have uncovered evidence to suggest that iron production in West Africa was a local initiative developed indigenously.[34] The earliest forms of iron technology identified in Africa predated the suggestions made by diffusionist arguments.[35]

Ironworks in Africa

Iron metallurgy was a phase in sub-Saharan Africa's technological development. Well-preserved iron metallurgy in Africa is part of the archaeological evidence supporting the investigation of ironworking technology, serving as a valuable research object for technological change.[36] The construction of clay materials and fuel extraction are important components of iron production. Although these activities are not solely for working with iron, they can also be used to produce ceramic vessels and figurines. Early iron production in Africa required knowledge of and control over iron ore, slag, and bloom properties. These need careful manipulation of temperature and rationing of gas during smelting, along with other techniques.[37] Many of the processes involved in iron production were familiar to early African societies, despite the arguments made by those who would claim that iron technology was introduced from elsewhere.[38]

In Khatt Lamaiteg, southwestern Mauritania, and Agadez, Niger, evidence of ironworking technology dates back to 1890–1390 BC.[39] Copper was mined and smelted in Akjoujt from the ninth to the sixth centuries BC, while some similarities exist between copper working in Agadez and Akjoujt. Although one scholar used these similarities to support the diffusionist theory of Africa's ironworking technology, this position has since been dismissed. No adequate evidence supports the claim that ironworking technology in sub-Saharan Africa can be traced to North Africa.[40] The practice of iron smelting in Do Dimmi at Agadez in Niger seems to have occurred in the same period as the oldest smelting furnaces in Taruga and Nsukka in Nigeria during the sixth century BC.[41] In Central Africa, evidence of ironworking technology exists in Cameroon and the Central African Republic. Okolo, Doulo, and Obogobo contain evidence dating back to 800–200 BC and 790–530 BC.[42]

In East Africa, ironworks in Rwiyange and Mbuga in Rwanda date back to 1450 BC and 1430 BC.[43] West African evidence of ironworking technology exists in Daboya, Atwetwebooso, Ghana, dating back to the middle of the first millennium BC and continuing to the middle of the first millennium AD.[44] A study conducted at Dekpassanware in Togo found evidence of early iron smelting sites measuring up to 30 ha in size, with cultural deposits of laterite gravel and iron smelting slag waste that are 1.80–2.10m thick.[45] The site's pre–Late Iron Age deposit dates to 800–400 BC, and its late Iron Age deposit dates to 1300–1600 AD. Iron technology may have developed in this area from 400 BC to AD 100 or 1000. In Walalde, middle Senegal valley, a tradition of iron smelting dates from c. 800–550 BC. Although no furnace was recovered, 47 fragments of tuyere were found, and 19kg of slag were collected. It is approximated that the furnace temperature could reach 1,200–1,300 degrees Celsius.[46]

Like other regions, West Africa transitioned from a Stone Age economy to an economy that depended on iron. Jenne-Jeno, in Mali, for example, has ironworking evidence along with Diama and Nok in Nigeria. Nok is one of the earliest cultures found using iron technology in West Africa.[47] Nok culture emphasized the production of terracotta figurines, and its iron smelting activity dates back to 900 BC.[48] Material evidence retrieved from these sites includes tuyeres, furnace equipment, and charcoal remains recovered from the Nok valley. Other Nok cultural areas in Nigeria include Taruga, Samun Dukiya, and the Nsukka area around the equatorial rainforest's fringes. Ironworks in this area date to around 750 BC[49] (Figure 5.2).

Nsukka evidence of early ironworking phases has been recorded at Opi, Lejja, and Aku. In these sites, iron ore was smelted in naturally drafted furnaces, and molten slag was drained through a conduit collection pit that formed huge, heavy slags weighing up to 43–47kg. The temperature for iron smelting at these sites varied and is estimated to have been between 1,155 and 1,450 degrees Celsius.[50] Furnaces and slabs retrieved from the Nok sites are made of hard clay.[51] Materials found at the site include "iron axe blades, lip plugs, knife blades, fragments of arrows, spearheads, hooks, bracelets, and beads."[52] They also show impressions of cording related to daub construction materials and wattle. Furthermore, evidence of iron production exists across Southern Africa.

FIGURE 5.2   Nigerian Nok terracotta figurine https://commons.wikimedia.org/wiki/File:Male
_Head,_Nok_culture,_Kaduna,_Plateau,_or_Nassarawa_state,_Nigeria,_550-50
_BC,_terracotta_-_Brooklyn_Museum_-_Brooklyn,_NY_-_DSC08511.JPG.

Copper and iron smelting appear to have been simultaneous with sedentism and agriculture for the first millennium AD, precipitating an Iron Age that lasted for 2,000
years.[53]

Southern Africa's Iron Age is divided into three periods: the Early Iron Age, Middle
Iron Age, and the Late Iron Age. The Early Iron Age is associated with ceramic units
found in at least three locations: Mzonjani in KwaZulu-Natal, Gokomere-Ziwa in
Zimbabwe (Nkope), and Happy Rest (Kalundu) in Northern South Africa and eastern
Botswana. The culture evolved and developed in the first millennium AD at Kadzi in
Zimbabwe and Schroda in Shashi-Limpopo valley. The Middle Iron Age also saw the
production of ceramic units such as those found at the Leopard's Kopje site, which began
in the second millennium and continued into the Late Stone Age around the fourteenth
century AD.[54] Other societies in Southern Africa developed iron technology that formed
part of their industrial activity and provided an outlet for their creativity, allowing them
to fashion different kinds of tools.

Culture and Societies of Iron Age Africa

Archaeological research has shown that Africa's inhabitants used mineral resources
for centuries, manufacturing stone and metal tools and pottery across the continent.

This exploitation of natural resources has continued through the twenty-first century. Although some scholars have cast doubt on the origins of iron technology in Africa, it marks an important transition in human history.[55] Iron technology allowed humans to shape their environment with metal tools; they were able to change their settlement patterns, political institutions, modes of economic production, and methods of warfare.

Early African metal workers reduced iron and copper oxides (ores) to purified metals through smelting. Ores were heated in an enclosed earthen chamber, called a furnace, using charcoal. Archaeological evidence in Nigeria has identified three distinct types of furnaces: pit or bowl, dome, and shaft.[56] Smelting furnaces observed in various parts of Africa show a gradual progression of technique that culminates in the slag-tapping shaft furnaces observed during the colonial intervention in Nigeria and Africa.

In some iron smelting societies, cultural rituals were associated with ironworkers and workshops, and craftsmen who worked with iron were particularly prominent. The production and distribution of metal was a source of perceived and actual influence. Items such as hoes were critical not only for agriculture but also for negotiating social relationships and amassing wealth in the form of cattle.[57] Iron hoes could be traded for wives, horses, and exotic products, which linked iron access with social prominence.[58] In Ihube, Okigwe, an earthen pot called Ogadazu was used in rituals. According to local belief, water in the Ogadazu pot could heal ailments such as sores and swollen legs.[59] The bellows used in ironworking are also an important cultural aspect of iron technology. As production techniques evolved, different bellows were used—those covered in animal skins, rubber, and the more recent invention of motorized bellows.

The abundance of potsherds at smelting sites across Africa suggests that pottery must have played a major role in ironworking. Rulers of West African states used metal artifacts to expand and defend their territorial spaces. Akinjogbin asserts that Oduduwa's use of iron was a decisive factor in his war to consolidate control over Yorubaland.[60] There is also evidence that metal artifacts were used for ceremonial purposes in different parts of West Africa, including Yorubaland, Kanuriland, and Igboland, all in Nigeria, as well as in Boboland in Burkina Faso. Okpoko has identified various figurines cast and placed in royal ancestral shrines in Benin City.[61] Iron affected political and ideological development and the evolution of agriculture, resulting in rapid population growth in Yorubaland. Metal implements revolutionized agriculture—iron cutlasses and hoes allowed larger swaths of land to be cultivated more effectively.[62]

Specialization, a general term that refers to a form of economic organization, is one of many organizational structures for manufacturing. Specialist production, which entails processing materials that are not destined for the home or surrounding community, can be carried out on a part-time or full-time basis.[63] The low demand for specialists in many precolonial African communities meant that they often worked seasonally, farming during the rainy season and making crafts after the harvest.[64] Seasonal specialization is not suitable for every culture. Some craft development structures like Togo's Bassar,[65] Cameroon's Babungo, and South Africa's Nkandla were active throughout the year.[66] Stein maintains that this form of specialization, which might occur by household, village, or region, corresponds with the degree of political centralization in a society.[67]

Specialization occurs for several reasons, depending on a culture's background and stage of development. Leaders might use political tactics to cement their supremacy over environmental influences, and the availability of different resources influenced the types of specialization that took place.[68] In Southern Africa, issues such as gender dynamics, belief systems, and the amount of production involved were critical to a society's culture.[69] This significance stems from their association with the ideology that legitimized specialist roles in society. Historically, women were barred from performing tasks directly related to smelting, while iron smelting was often conducted at sites removed from residential areas.[70]

In Southern Africa, Zulu kings exploited production dynamics to exact tribute from specialists.[71] Some kings exercised tight control over the works of blacksmiths through regulation. It is suggested that specialization culture may have performed extremely well in Southern Africa, where tribute-paying processes were associated with historical state structures.[72] Kingships and blacksmiths were connected in many cultures, including Mali.[73] Smelters exercised both symbolic and real authority in areas like northern Cameroon. In theory, these blacksmith-kings possessed authority over smelters and blacksmiths within their domain, which entitled them to exact homage. This bound the majority of blacksmiths with their kings ideologically, although the latter were functionally autonomous[74] (Figures 5.3 and 5.4).

Eine Zulufamilie. (Nach Photographie.)

FIGURE 5.3   The Zulu people: African Bantu ethnic group in South Africa https://www.getty-images.co.uk/detail/illustration/zulu-people-wood-engraving-published-in-1891-royalty-free-illustration/1243619277.

FIGURE 5.4   Disused iron smelter south of Kamabai, Sierra Leone (West Africa) https://commons.m.wikimedia.org/wiki/File:Disused_iron_smelter_south_of_Kamabai,_Sierra_Leone_(West_Africa)_(2071810345).jpg.

Mackenzie asserts that the Njanja's transformation in Zimbabwe from a kin-based group to a stratified society in the late nineteenth century was driven by the economic influence gained from increasing their iron production.[75] Njanja's famous industry relied on raw materials from outside their territory, such as iron ores from the Wedza Mountains, which were controlled by the Mbire.[76] The Njanja initially acquired their ore illegally, returning to their villages for the smelting process. As their industry grew in the 1830s, they established diplomatic alliances with the Mbire to access greater quantities of ore. Njanja ironworking differed from other sites, such as the Bassar in Togo and Babungo in Cameroon, where iron was smelted on-site and taken to market processing.

The Bassar and Babungo groups regulated access to iron ore. The unregulated activities of the Njanja were largely constrained within their regional sphere of power.[77] Even after their metalworking activities increased, the Njanja did not establish distinct groups of smelters and smiths seen among the Bassar or Babungo.[78] Bassar smelters traded blooms with an independent group of specialist blacksmiths. Shona metalsmiths were experts in their craft, and their social standing was determined by the quality of their products. Smelter-blacksmiths typically enjoyed extreme wealth, with many wives and large herds of cattle[79] (Figure 5.5).

FIGURE 5.5   Blacksmiths in African Iron Age https://www.shutterstock.com/image-photo/old
-illustration-blacksmith-workers-tribe-unyamwezi-76215904.

Conclusion

The historiography of iron technology in Africa has focused overwhelmingly on whether the technology was developed locally or diffused into the continent. This chapter examines the nature and character of archaeological discourse regarding Africa's iron technology's origins and cultural development. The transition of African societies from the Stone Age to the Iron Age marked a significant turning point in human history, as human ingenuity provided control over the environment. Material evidence found across various African sites provides insight into the social, political, and economic organization of societies, showing how humans in this part of the world harnessed the inherent potential of their environment. This potential influenced the emergence and subsequent development of material and non-material cultures. Some of the conjectural histories surrounding the origin and development of iron technology have been debunked by efforts to reconstruct Africa's metallurgical history.

Iron technology led to a specialization in the social structure of societies. In Southern Africa and Central Africa, blacksmiths were recognized as significant members of the community, often holding titles as royalty. In some cases, they became regional leaders who controlled and commanded substantial political and military power. In some parts of West Africa, rituals developed around iron technology, such as with the Igbo people of Nigeria. Iron tools also became an economic commodity that was traded with other societies for increased agricultural production and aesthetic purposes.

DEEP DIVE

Collect mythologies and stories on fire from people and books. Reflect on the significance of the stories.

Assignment 1

Objective

The objective of this assignment is to ensure that students complete the reading of Chapter 5 and to get them to provide evidence supporting the claim that iron smelting and the advent of the African Iron Age were endemic to the continent.

Method

Students will be expected to write a short note in response to the question.

Reading Comprehension

Why did European scholars believe that Africa's iron age was ushered in by external forces? Discuss how Africanist archaeologists have attempted to dispute these claims.

Assignment 2

Objective

The objective of this assignment is to encourage students to think about how tools indicate human progress and make evident their ability to conquer and transform their environment.

Method

Students will be expected to have a group discussion (either in person or on the online discussion forum) to talk to their peers about the topic. Each student would be expected to create a post and respond to at least one other student. If this were to take place in person, then it would simply be a class-wide discussion.

Discussion

How is the presence and advancement of human-made tools an indicator of human progress and development?

Notes

1 Ratan Lal Basu, "Human Development According to Adam Smith and Karl Marx," *Culture Mandala: The Bulletin of the Centre for East-West Cultural and Economic Studies* 7, no. 2 (2007): 1–12.

2 David Neilson and Michael A. Peters, "Capitalism's Slavery," *Educational Philosophy and Theory* 52, no. 5 (2020): 475–484.

3 Pierre Bonnassie, *From Slavery to Feudalism in South-western Europe* (Cambridge: Cambridge University Press, 1991).

4 Graeme Barker, *The Agricultural Revolution in Prehistory: Why Did Foragers Become Farmers?* (Oxford: Oxford University Press, 2006).

5 Stanley H. Ambrose, "Chronology of the Later Stone Age and Food Production in East Africa," *Journal of Archaeological Science* 25, no. 4 (1998): 377–392.

6 Dana M. Cataldo, Andrea B. Migliano and Lucio Vinicius, "Speech, Stone Tool-making and the Evolution of Language," *PLoS ONE* 13, no. 1 (2018): 1–10.

7 Christopher Scarre, *The Human Past: World Prehistory and the Development of Human Societies* (London: Thames and Hudson, 2013), 176–199.

8 Ilia Murtazashvili and Jennifer Murtazashvili, "The Origins of Private Property Rights: States or Customary Organizations?" *Journal of Institutional Economics* 12, no. 1 (2016): 105–128.

9 Rusty Huddle, *Human Evolution* (New York: The Rosen Publishing Group, 2016).

10 Robert L. Kelly, *The Foraging Spectrum: Diversity in Hunter-gatherer Lifeways* (Washington, DC: Smithsonian Institution Press, 1995).

11 Sue Feary, Steve Brown, Duncan Marshall, Ian Lilley, Robert McKinnon, Bas Verschuuren and Robert Wild, "Earth's Cultural Heritage," in *Protected Area Governance and Management*, eds. Graeme L. Worboys, Michael Lockwood, Ashish Kothari, Sue Feary and Ian Pulsford (Canberra: ANU Press, 2015), 84.

12 Theodore A. Wertime and James D. Muhly, eds. *The Coming of the Age of Iron* (New Haven: Yale University Press, 1980).

13 P. de Barros, "Societal Repercussions of the Rise of Large-scale Traditional Iron Production: A West African Example," *African Archaeological Review* 6 (1988): 91–113.

14 History, "Bronze Age," *History*, accessed August 20, 2022, https://www.history.com/topics/pre-history/bronze-age.

15 See, for instance, Sarah Taylor, "The Introduction and Development of Iron Production in Korea," *World Archaeology* 20, no. 3 (1989): 422–431; Manfred Eggert, "Early Iron in West and Central Africa," in *Nok: African Sculpture in Archaeological Context*, ed. Peter Breunig (Frankfurt: Africa Magna Verlag Press, 2014), 51–59; and Jana Souckova-Siegolová, "Treatment and Usage of Iron in the Hittite Empire in the 2nd Millennium BC," *Mediterranean Archaeology* 14 (2001): 189–193.

16 History, "Bronze Age."

17 Stanley B. Alpern, "Did they or didn't they Invent it? Iron in Sub-Saharan Africa," *History in Africa* 32 (2005): 41–94.

18 Nikolaas J. van der Merwe. "The Advent of Iron in Africa," in *The Coming of the Age of Iron*, eds. Theodore A. Wertime and James D. Muhly (New Haven: Yale University Press, 1980), 463–506.

19 John A. Rustad, "The Emergence of Iron Technology in West Africa, with Special Emphasis on the Nok Culture of Nigeria," in *West African Culture Dynamics: Archaeological and Historical Perspectives*, eds. B. K. Swartz and Raymond E. Dumett (Berlin: De Gruyter Mouton, 2011), 227–246.

20 Francoise J. Kense and John A. Okoro, "Changing Perspectives on Traditional Iron Production in West Africa," in *The Archaeology of Africa: Food, Metals and Towns*, eds. Bassey Andah, Alex Okpoko, Thurstan Shaw and Paul Sinclair (London: Routledge, 1993), 449–458.

21 Ronald F. Tylecote, "The Origin of Iron Smelting in Africa," *West African Journal of Archaeology* 5 (1975): 1–9.

22 James D. Muhly, "The Bronze Age Setting," in *The Coming of the Age of Iron*, eds. Theodore A. Wertime and James D. Muhly (New Haven: Yale University Press, 1980), 25–67.

23 Francois Kense, "The Initial Diffusion of Iron in Africa," in *African Iron Working*, Ancient and Traditional, eds. Randi Haalaand and Peter L. Shinnie (New York: Norwegian University Press, 1985), 16.

24 A. J Arkell, "The Valley of the Nile," in *The Dawn of African History*, ed. Roland Oliver (Oxford: Oxford University Press, 1968), 7–12. See also van der Merwe, "The Advent of Iron in Africa," 463–506.

25 van der Merwe, "The Advent of Iron."

26 John H. Robertson and Rebecca Bradley, "A New Paradigm: The African Early Iron Age Without Bantu Migrations," *History in Africa* 27 (2000): 287–323.

27 Robertson and Bradley, "A New Paradigm."

28 Peter R. Schmidt, ed., *The Culture and Technology of African Iron Production* (Gainesville: University of Florida Press, 1996).

29 Kense, "The Initial Diffusion," 16.

30 Edwin E. Okafor, "New Evidence on Early Iron-Smelting from Southeastern Nigeria," in *The Archaeology of Africa: Food, Metals and Towns*, eds. Bassey Andah, Alex Okpoko, Thurstan Shaw and Paul Sinclair (London: Routledge, 1993), 432–448.

31 Robertson and Bradley, "A New Paradigm."

32 Jan Vansina, "The Western Bantu Expansion," *Journal of African History* 25, no. 2 (1984): 129–145.

33 Robertson and Bradley, "A New Paradigm."

34 Kola Adekola, "Dynamics of Metal Working Traditions in West Africa," *African Diaspora Archaeology Newsletter* 9, no. 1 (2006): 1–9.

35 Hamady Bocoum, ed., *The Origins of Iron Metallurgy in Africa: New Light on Its Antiquity – West and Central Africa* (Paris: UNESCO, 2004).

36 David Killick, "Invention and Innovation in African Iron Smelting Technologies," *Cambridge Archaeological Journal* 25, no. 1 (2015): 307–319.

37 Alpern, "Did they or didn't they," 41–94.

38 Leonard M. Pole, "Iron Working Apparatus and Techniques: Upper Region of Ghana," *West Africa Journal of Archaeology* 5 (1975): 11–39.

39 Cited in Emmanuel Kassey, "The Relationship Between Later Stone Age and Iron Age Culture of Central Tanzania" (Ph.D. diss., Simon Frazer University, 2005).

40 Okafor, "New Evidence."

41 Okafor, "New Evidence."

42 Augustin F. C. Holl, "Metals and Pre-Colonial African Society," in *Ancient African Metallurgy: The Socio-Cultural Context*, eds. Michael S. Bisson, Terry S. Childs, Philip de Barros and Augustin F. C. Holl (Oxford: Altamira Press, 2000), 116–138.

43 Marie-Claude Van Grunderbeek, "The Iron Age in Rwanda and Burundi: Archaeological Studies During 1978, 1979 and 1980," *Nyame Akuma* 18 (1981): 26–31.

44 Kense, "The Initial Diffusion," 16.

45 Philip de Barros, "Recent Early Iron Age Research in Bassar, Togo," *Nyame Akuma* 59 (2003): 76–78. See also Philip de Barros, "The Surprising Early Iron Age Site of Dekpassanware (Togo)" (Paper delivered at the Society of Africanist Archaeologists, Calgary, Canada, June 22–26, 2006).

46 Alioune Deme and Susan McIntosh, "Excavations at Walalde: New Light on the Settlement of the Middle Senegal Valley by Iron-Using Peoples," *Journal of African Archaeology* 4, no. 2 (2006): 317–347. See also Alioune Deme, "Archaeological Investigations of Settlement and Emerging Complexity in the Middle Senegal Valley" (Ph.D. thesis, Rice University, 2003).

47 Angela F. Rackham, Gabriele Franke, Henrik Junius, Tanja M. Männel and Christina Beck, "Early West African Iron Smelting: The Legacy of Taruga in Light of Recent Nok Research," *African Archaeological Review* 34 (2017): 321–343.

48 Rackham, Franke, Junius, Männel and Beck, "Early West African Iron Smelting."

49 Okafor, "New Evidence."

50 Okafor, "New Evidence."

51 Cited in Kola Adekola, "Dynamics of Metal Working Traditions in West Africa," *African Diaspora Archaeology Newsletter* 9, no. 1 (2011): 3.

52 Bernard E. B. Fagg, "Recent Work in West Africa," *World Archaeology* 1 (1969). See also Rackham, Franke, Junius, Männel and Beck, "Early West African Iron Smelting."

53 Peter Mitchell, *Southern African Archaeology* (Cambridge: Cambridge University Press, 2001).

54 Cited in Shadreck Chirikure, "Metals in Society: Iron Production and its Position in Iron Age Communities of Southern Africa," *Journal of Social Archaeology* 7, no. 1 (2007): 72–100.

55 Roland Oliver and Brian M. Fagan, *Africa in the Iron Age ca. 500 BC to AD 1400* (New York: Cambridge University Press, 1975).

56 Anselm M. Ibeanu and Ikechukwu Okpoko, "Ethnoarchaeological Investigations in Ihube, Okigwe Local Government Area, Imo State, Nigeria," *West African Journal of Archaeology* 24 (1994): 94–102.

57 Chirikure, "Metals in Society."

58 Terry Childs, "Style, Technology, and Iron Smelting Furnaces in Bantu-Speaking Africa," *Journal of Anthropological Archaeology* 10, no. 4 (1991): 332–359.

59 Ibeanu and Okpoko, "Ethnoarchaeological Investigations."

60 Adeagbo I. Akinjogbin, "The Impact of Iron in Yorubaland," in *The Origins of Iron Metallurgy in Africa: New Light on Its Antiquity – West and Central Africa*, ed. Hamady Bocoum (Paris: UNESCO, 2004), 55–59. Oduduwa is the mythical founder of the Yoruba people.

61 A. L. Okpoko, "Early Metal Using Communities in West Africa," *West Africa Journal of Archaeology* 17 (1987): 205–227.

62 Adekola, "Dynamics of Metal Working Traditions," 2.

63 Cathy L. Costin, "Craft Economies of Ancient Andean States," in *Archaeological Perspectives on Political Economies*, eds. Gary M. Feinman and Linda M. Nicholas (Salt Lake City: University of Utah Press, 2004), 189–221.

64 Chirikure, "Metals in Society."

65 Candice Goucher and Eugenia W. Herbert, "The Blooms of Banjeli: Technology and Gender in West African Iron Making," in *The Culture and Technology of African Iron Production*, ed. Peter Schmidt (Gainesville: University of Florida Press, 1996), 40–57.

66 Tim Maggs, "Mabhija: Pre-Colonial Industry in the Tugela Basin," *Annals of the Natal Museum* 25 (1982): 43–123.

67 Gill J. Stein, "Heterogeneity, Power and Political Economy: Some Current Research Issues in the Archaeology of Old World Complex Societies," *Journal of Archaeological Research* 6, no. 1 (1998): 1–44.

68 Peter Peregrine, "Some Political Aspects of Craft Specialization," *World Archaeology* 23, no. 1 (1991): 1–11.

69 Chirikure, "Metals in Society."

70 Terry Childs, "Traditional Iron Working: A Narrated Ethnoarchaeological Example," in *Ancient African Metallurgy: The Socio-Cultural Context*, eds. Michael S. Bisson, Terry S. Childs, Philip De Barros and Augustin F. C. Holl (Oxford: Altamira Press, 2000), 199–255.

71 Tim O'C. Maggs, "'My Father's Hammer Never Ceased Its Song Day and Night': The Zulu Ferrous Metalworking Industry," *Natal Museum Journal of Humanities* 4 (1992): 65–87.

72 Chirikure, "Metals in Society."

73 Tal Tamari, "The Development of Caste Systems in West Africa," *Journal of African History* 32, no. 2 (1991): 221–250.

74 Pierre de Maret, "The Power of Symbols and the Symbols of Power Through Time: Probing the Luba Past," in *Beyond Chiefdoms: Rethinking Complexity in Africa*, ed. Susan McIntosh (Cambridge: Cambridge University Press, 1999), 38.

75 John Mackenzie, "Pre-Colonial Industry: The Njanja and the Iron Trade," *NADA* 11 (1975): 200–220.

76 Mackenzie, "Pre-Colonial Industry."

77 Philip de Barros, "The Early Iron Metallurgy of Bassar, Togo: Furnaces, Metallurgical Remans and Iron Objects," *Azania Archaeological Research in Africa* 55, no. 1 (2020): 3–43.

78 Tamari, "The Development of Caste Systems."

79 Chirikure, "Metals in Society."

6

THE TRANS-SAHARAN TRADE

Introduction

On account of the Sahara Desert as a "natural barrier"—expansive, arid, "impassable," and "inhospitable"—and the paucity in written historical sources from West African societies, the region was, for a time, excluded from the story of the development of human civilizations, thus denying the cultural and political agency of its peoples.[1] When the contribution of West Africa to international developments was eventually recognized, its participation was limited to the period from its encounter with the Arab (Muslim) world.[2] Many of the social and political feats achieved were attributed to these foreign elements as part of a "Hamitic hypothesis."[3] However, further innovations in the methods of historical research—particularly the introduction of the fields of archaeology, economic history, and the adoption of oral traditions—yielded new information from North and West Africa.[4] This has altered earlier (erroneous) assumptions and necessitated the revision of many "facts," which have yielded better representative results.

The redesignation of the Sahara Desert from "desert barrier to global highway,"[5] denoting the volume of (commercial) traffic that developed across the region between the seventh and twenty-first century of trans-Saharan exchange, is the result of years of adept research and new discoveries. This has confirmed the place of sub-Saharan Africa as an active participant in the development of human civilization. Serving as a conduit between the region and the Mediterranean world, the trans-Saharan trade facilitated the exchange of cultural ideas and economic wealth between the peoples of West Africa, North Africa, and the wider world—Europe and Asia.[6]

On the continent, the activity and items—gold, ivory, leather, slaves—of this trade across the Sahara stimulated transformative social and political developments along its various alternating routes, leading in some places to the development of rich commercial centers, centralized political systems—states and empires—and the introduction of Islam.[7] Whereas the wealth from this trade facilitated the development of impressive empires such as Ghana, Mali, Songhai, and Kanem-Borno,[8] the introduction of Islam

DOI: 10.4324/9781003198260-8

had a more extensive and enduring impact in the region. Not only was Islam the basis for many a diplomatic tie between the principalities within the region and at both ends of the Sahara Desert, but the Islamist reformist movements (jihads) of the eighteenth and nineteenth centuries produced extensive political and cultural transformations across the region. This commenced from the Sahel, through the forest to the sea. As Ralph Austen explains:

> This faith played various roles throughout the region, as a legal system for regulating trade, an inspiration for reformist religious- political movements, and a vehicle of literacy and cosmopolitan knowledge that inspired creativity—often of a very unorthodox kind—within the various ethnolinguistic communities of the region: Arab, Berber, and Sudanic (Mande, Fulani, Hausa, Kanuri, and others).[9]

Critical to the expansion of this trans-Saharan trade was a set of preexisting internal short and long-distance trading systems that ensured intergroup relations before the seventh century. As J. Devisse points out, it is important to keep in mind that the existence of "a long-distance trade economy involving merchants rested on the existence of a demand for certain rare and costly products (such as salt, kola, gold, wheat, fabrics and copper) which had to come from elsewhere."[10] In the regions south of the Sahara, this demand for exotic goods was maintained—before the establishment of trans-Saharan trade connections—by preexisting local short and long-distance trading systems to which the trans-Saharan trade provided an international dimension.

Origin of the Trans-Saharan Trade in West Africa

Although no precise date is agreed upon as marking the beginning of interactions between West and North Africa, it is believed that trade between the peoples of both regions (across the Sahara Desert) began as early as 1000BC,[11] on a much more limited scale than from the eighth century. Hopkins asserts that the Carthaginians pioneered trans-Saharan trade in the fifth century BC and that the Romans promoted it three centuries later when they expanded into North Africa. However, it declined significantly, if not completely, after their defeat in the fourth century AD until it was revived following the Byzantine re-conquest of North Africa in 533–555. The consensus appears to be that, though the trans-Saharan trade predated the Islamic era, the continuous expansion of the desert over time made it increasingly difficult to cross, deterring traffic along that axis until the arrival of the camel and the gold incentive.[12] By the eighth century, however, conditions favoring regular (annual) trans-Saharan caravan crossings converged to introduce an era of great commercial traffic that lasted over a thousand years till around 1875.[13] This transformation was due to two critical factors: the availability and use of camels—best suited for such terrain—and the development of demand for coinage in the Maghrib and the Western world. The latter made such an arduous and dangerous journey across the Sahara a worthwhile endeavor.

Gold was central to the northern interests in the trans-Saharan trade.[14] Stories of the king of Mali's wealth and his inexhaustible supply of gold drew North African interests to West Africa. Even when other commodities were later added, including ivory, leather, and slaves, West African gold (highly sought after for its high purity) continued to be a valuable commodity throughout this trade,[15] only to be challenged subsequently by rising demand for slaves. It remained undisputed until the thirteenth century. Not only was gold easier to transport across the desert (compared to other food products), its weight-to-value scale gave it a greater economic advantage over other commodities.[16] Driving the value of gold from the ninth century was:

> the annual currency requirements ... of the gold-minting dynasties in North Africa and in Spain (the Aghlabid governors of Ifrïkiya in the ninth century; the Fâtimids of Ifrïkiya in the tenth century; the Umayyads of Spain in the tenth century; the Fâtimids of Egypt after 970; the Zîrïds of Ifrïkiya, and then the Almoravids).[17]

The vitality of the trans-Saharan trade increased in response to this demand, especially from the Fâtimids, the Umayyads, and the Almoravids, who undertook coinage at levels "unprecedented" in the Muslim West.[18] Other less important trade items included slaves, ivory, leather, and kola nuts.

For the societies south of the Sahara (in West Africa), salt was originally the most sought-after commodity from the north.[19] This is not to say that the South depended on the Sahara trade for all of its salt needs—as the South is known to have engaged in some salt production and collection activity,[20] which was reinforced by the Sahara trade. However, as the trade expanded to accommodate more people from even more remote locations, so did the variety in trade goods. Soon enough, humans, copper, metal and glass wares, horses, books, and even dates were added to the list of goods imported from the north.[21] Further, the trade across the Sahara relied on preexisting short and long-distance trade networks in the savannah and forest regions of West Africa, which had ensured intergroup relations before the era of regular desert crossings,[22] to deliver forest products like kola nuts, ivory, and fish to markets in the savannah and Sahel and vice-versa.

Nature and Organization of the Trade

The sheer expanse of the Sahara Desert—covering an area greater than the continental USA[23]—made the trade between West and North Africa a complex affair and necessitated some level of organization and planning to mitigate the difficulties and dangers of traveling across such a long distance. A journey that took between 70 and 90 days,[24]—depending on the point of embarkation and termination, across a harsh and difficult terrain ridden with marauders—required adequate preparations and astute economic decision-making; because added to the issue of safety was the matter of trade profitability—the economic incentive for such a dangerous journey—which determined the type of commodities ferried across the desert, all of which must be accounted for in the planning and organization processes.

Termini and Intermediate Locations

During the growth of this trade, caravanners developed certain practices to improve their chances of a successful desert crossing and trading venture. As Hopkins notes, "the organisational needs of trans-Saharan trade encouraged the development from very early times of centres which were designed to minimise the difficulties of desert trade and to increase the efficiency of the distributive system."[25] These centers can be split into termini and intermediate locations. Located at the southern and northern ends of the trans-Saharan traffic, termini cities were locations where caravans converged to load and unload goods for further dispersal to other far-flung locations. The great northern termini centers "stretched along the entire North African coast and included some inland capitals such as Cairo, Tlemcen in Algeria, and Marrakesh and Fez in Morocco like Fez, Mogador, Algiers."[26] These were entrepots located near or on the Northern African coast, where goods collected from the southern trade were dispatched to Europe and the Middle East. The southern termini locations included Awdaghust, Gao, Walata, Timbuktu, as well as Kano and Kukawa from the sixteenth century, where goods from the south are loaded and those from the north are unloaded and broken down into smaller caravans to be dispersed in the forest and coastal regions.[27]

Situated in scattered locations within the desert, intermediate settlements (halfway stops) reduced the hardship of a long and arduous journey across the Sahara. This mid-way oasis settlement included locations on the northern fringes of the desert like Sijilmasa (before it was destroyed in the eighteenth century) and Wargla.[28] These were locations where northbound caravans unloaded their goods and southbound caravans gathered before departure. Other southern desert locations such as Teghaza, Ghat, Wadan, Murzuk, Tuwat, and Asyut, Tawdeni, Ghadames, Agades (which was later replaced by Iferuan sometime in the nineteenth century) were where caravans stopped for water, provisions, and available trade goods, like dates and salt before moving on to the southern termini towns.

Traders and Trading Caravans

In the course of the trans-Saharan trade between North and West Africa, a variety of people specialized in the activities of long-distance trading, including the Wangara, the desert groups (Berbers and Jews)[29] and the Hausa. Whereas the Tuareg and Jewish traders operated in the northern regions and the southern Sahara edges, the Wangara and Hausa traders specialized in long-distance trade into the southern regions of West Africa.

Wangara (Dyula/Wangarawa)

Foremost and more widespread among these groups were the Wangara or Dyula, Jula, and Wangarawa[30] (as they are variously known) of Mali. They were Soninke speakers of Mande origin—though their identity often shifted over time and place—whose involvement in long-distance trading predated the conquest and spread of Islam in West Africa.[31] Known to sometimes traverse large expanses of the northern half of the continent, they mainly circulated between the southern edges of the desert and the eastern Hausa region, where they acted as middlemen in the gold trade.

Credited as "one of the earliest trade networks in western Africa,"[32] the Wangara specialized in the trade of highly valued commodities such as gold, salt, and kola nuts. Their role as one of the earliest southern participants in the trans-Saharan trade, the extent of whose trading activity—stretching from Gao to the Bariba and Hausa states—and expertise is extensively reported, made the title "Wangara" become synonymous with "trader," just as "Jula" would be in a later period. However, upon conversion to Islam—at least by the fifteenth century[33]—some Wangara families transitioned to a religious vocation. Still self-identifying as Wangara, they became full-time Islamic scholars and teachers, hence, their identification in the *Kano Chronicles* as the harbingers of the Islamic faith in northern Nigeria.[34] However, following the Moroccan conquest of Songhai in the 1590s,[35] many of the Wangara gradually resettled in areas to the south and southeast, which make up parts of present-day Nigeria. As settled people, they dominated markets like Borgu (Bénin), as well as those of northern Kogbaye, (near Igboho in Yorubaland) in areas of modern western Nigeria,[36] where their descendants can be found even today.[37]

Tuareg and Jewish Traders

Among the desert dwellers were the Tuareg and Jewish groups who also took part in, and prospered from, the trade across the Sahara in what was known as the Wād Nūn Trade Network.[38] The Wād Nūn trade network was "a commercial coalition operated by the Tikna and their allies, namely Maghribi Jews and members of the Awlā Bū al-Sibā."[39] They were a band of long-distance traders who were experts in camel caravanning spanning a wide territory, including modern-day Mauritania and the areas bordering western Mali, northern Senegal, and southern Morocco.[40]

The Tuareg are especially famous for their role as camel breeders, doubling as desert guides, traders, and marauders.[41] Prominent among these Tuareg groups were the Masufa of the *Ibadiya* sect, who became dominant players in the western crossing from as early as the seventh and eighth centuries.[42] In addition to owning large stocks of camels and a caravan guiding outfit, they were also known to impose levies on every camel load belonging to traders making their way to and from Western Sudan. For several centuries, they remained the leaders of this caravan trade in the desert, operating as camel ranchers and expert guides.

The presence of the Jews in early and medieval West Africa and their participation in the trans-Saharan trade, both on the north coast and across the Sahara, is reported severally in the texts on the trans-Saharan trade and medieval West Africa[43] (Figure 6.1). Like their Muslim counterparts, the lure of gold and the desire for slaves drove the Jews to follow the trans-Saharan trade routes into the West African interior before the ninth century.[44] In their centuries of participating in the caravan trade, Maghribi Jews served in royal courts, worked as artisans in the production of crafts, leatherwork, and blacksmithing and provided credit and other accounting services to merchants and the desert groups.[45] Gradually, this Jewish group grew into a prosperous community that thrived until they had a falling-out with the local desert population over what the latter considered an undue influence of the former over the trade in gold and silver.[46] Michael Gomez comments on the establishment of a Jewish settlement (Tendirma) in southwest Timbuktu, which became "a critical site of power under *Askia al-ḥājj* Muḥammad in the early tenth/sixteenth century."[47] Describing the extent of Jewish participation in the medieval trade of West Africa, Lyon submits that:

In the late twelfth and thirteenth centuries Genoese ships even entered the Atlantic coast for direct access to western African goods. By at least the twelfth century, and possibly centuries before that, Maghribi Jews resided in western African markets. In the fifteenth century, a handful of Jews were settled in Wālata, frequented Timbuktu and Gao, and formed a small quarter in the once prosperous oasis of Wādān.[48]

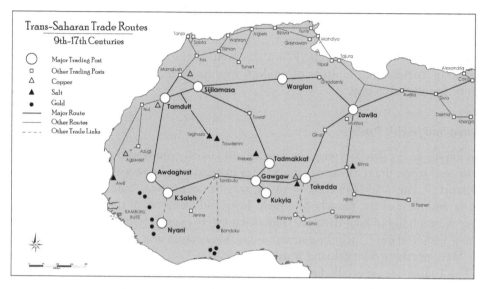

FIGURE 6.1   Map of the trans-Saharan trade routes. Author's collection.

Hausa Traders

From the sixteenth century—after the Moroccan invasion of Songhai (the 1590s), which moved major trade traffic eastwards—Hausa traders from Kano, Katsina, Sokoto, Gobir, and Kanuri traders from Kanem-Borno in the eastern regions of West Africa became another dominant force in the trade across the Sahara, especially in long-distance trade to the south. They exchanged salt, cloth, livestock, and leather goods for gold, kola nuts, ivory, and slaves.[49] Commercially skilled and highly organized, they established trading networks (including diaspora settlements) from as far north as Timbuktu to as far south as the forest regions of Nigeria and the coastal region of Ghana. Abner Cohen provides a concise description of this local, long-distance trade as follows:

> By long-distance trade, I mean the purchase or sale and the transfer of goods, mostly of perishable nature, across a distance of several hundred miles, principally between the savanna and the forest belt of West Africa ... The trade is organized on centuries-old lines. Long before the Europeans appeared on the scene, the West Africans had operated truly international trade, with developed systems of credit, insurance, brokerage, exchange of business information, transport and arbitration in business disputes. Law and order were normally maintained and strangers honoured their business obligations and deferred to the pressures of moral values and of moral relations of all sorts.[50]

Types of Caravans

Two types of trading caravans were involved in the trans-Saharan trade: one heading north across the Sahara Desert to Northern Africa and another (conducting the local long-distance trade) heading south into the interior of West Africa. Like their counterparts in the camel-driven northbound caravans, the southern interior-bound caravans comprised traders from different locations banded together to exploit their strength in numbers. Unlike the latter, however, the southern-bound caravans used donkeys and oxen rather than the camel, which preferred the "poorer" desert fodder and was susceptible to diseases.[51] Organized like armed convoys, they consisted of guards, drovers and porters, a guide, a quartermaster, a treasurer, and a leader.[52] A description given by Hopkins of such Hausa caravans in the nineteenth century reads thus:

> Hausa caravans in the nineteenth century consisted of 1,000 to 2,000 people, most of whom were armed, and an equal number of donkeys. They travelled for five or six hours each day on well-established routes, where water and food were known to be available, and sent out scouts to search for brigands and to negotiate for supplies. The round trip from Sokoto to Ashanti (a total of about 1,200 miles) took between six months and one year. Caravans were like slowly moving markets, selling some of their goods on the route and paying for foodstuffs and services as they went. Without them, long-distance trade would have been impossible.[53]

Although the size of such trading parties was diminished in the colonial period owing to the relative security of routes and the availability of secure markets, long-distance trading in the region has survived into the twenty-first century, reorganizing into systems that are not readily identifiable.[54]

The northbound trans-Saharan trade traffic featured two types of camel caravans: the "heavy" and "light convoys."[55] The "heavy" or large caravan convoy (*qāfila*; plur. *qawāfil*), mostly an aggregation of caravans from multiple locations, tended to be organized annually. It consisted of a large convoy of travelers made up of hundreds of men with several thousands of camels. The second "light" individual caravan (*mufrāda*) was typically made up of less than one hundred camels and a few teams of men. Both caravans moved around West Africa, traveling routes linking Sijilmasa in the north to Awdaghust in the south.[56]

Trade Routes

After securing the service of the naturally adapted camel, another important factor potential travelers across the Sahara Desert had to consider when making such a long and unpredictable journey was choosing routes with limited risks. And this is where the "Berber" speaking peoples (or "Tuaregs" as they came to be popularly known), who had settled both at the northern fringes of the Sahara Desert and around the scattered oases within it from at least the fourth century CE,[57] proved their indispensability. Having lived and engaged in some economic activities within the desert and its northern fringes[58] for a considerable period before the eighth century, these—mainly nomadic (herding)—"Berber" speaking groups were the best positioned to attempt a successful

FIGURE 6.2 Tuareg a camello, moro a pie, tuareg a caballo, tuareg a pie, ribera del Níger 1896 https://commons.wikimedia.org/wiki/File:Tuareg_a_camello,_moro_a_pie, _tuareg_a_caballo,_tuareg_a_pie,_ribera_del_N%C3%ADger_1896.jpg.

crossing to the south. They were to establish the "first systematically maintained caravan trade routes of the Muslim period"[59] (Figure 6.2). As John Wright postulates:

> Trade is likely to have developed through contacts made during nomads' seasonal migrations and predatory visits to oases and desert fringe communities. Regular markets and yearly fairs grew up where different peoples came together. Trading middlemen started by supplying goods and, with their nomadic associates, ancillary services to transhumant tribes-people, oasis-dwellers and settled communities within or on either side of the desert.[60]

As with other aspects of the trade, the formidability of the Sahara Desert also determined the routes taken and the societies that were impacted as a result. Just as this factor accounted for the significance of the Sahara dwelling groups, whose indispensability lay in their function as halfway stops (oases towns) and as guides to "safe" desert trails/ routes, the location of trans-Saharan trade routes was determined by three main concerns. These include the proximity of termini cities at the northern and southern fringes of the Sahara, the possibility of finding water en route, and the location of the trade commodity of interest. Even so, important trade routes were known to change (shift) in reaction to the "changing political and social conditions in the terminal cities themselves, as well as the tribal territories and oases along the way."[61]

As the trade expanded with the introduction of the Sahara-crossing camel, a complex web of routes developed across the desert linking West and North Africa. Three of these clusters of routes stood out as prominent. They included a group of westerly routes that linked Morocco with markets in West Africa, along the Senegal River and the upper ranges of the Niger River; another (central) group of routes that connected Algeria with West African markets like Jenne and Timbuktu along the middle ranges of the Niger River; and the third group of routes (more to the east) that linked Tunisia and the Fezzan with markets in Kano and Kanem-Bornu. Other less popular eastern routes linked Libya and Egypt with the states of Eastern Sudan and Kanem-Borno to Darfur, continuing up the Nile.[62]

The first sets of routes to attain prominence were those that linked (ancient) Ghana to Fez via Awdaghust. This route from ancient Ghana led until about the thirteenth century when it declined with the empire and was replaced from the fourteenth century by those from Mali and Songhai through Timbuktu to North Africa. By the seventeenth century, another set of routes in the eastern parts of West Africa, from Kano and Kanem-Borno, grew to surpass the others in importance, with the one from Kano enjoying greater prominence in the nineteenth century.[63]

Approaching from the north, merchants traveled from Europe and the Middle East to northern African termini cities like Fez, Algiers, and Tripoli. From then, those who intended on braving the journey to the West African markets proceeded to the settlements at the northern fringes of the desert, like Sijilmasa, one of the greatest market centers on the northern side of the Sahara.[64] Here they picked up necessary provisions, gathered some trade goods and sought the services of guides before embarking as part of a *qāfīla* (caravan of many other traders). The next stops were the "oases ports" within the desert, where merchants stopped to rest, drink, water their animals, and collect more provisions and some articles of trade before continuing on their journey south. There were other known stops at the salt-mining centers of the desert, the Sahel, and North Africa[65] before arriving at the final destination where gold was acquired. And because the merchants from the north could not travel into the forest areas directly to the source of the materials they sought, they had to rely on intermediaries. This was either because of the sheer distance to be covered, the threat of sickness and attack, or simply because the sovereigns of the countries where they traded forbade it.[66] These factors all contributed to the location and structure of the trade routes and many of the settlements that developed alongside them.

Trade Commodities

The commodities traded across the Sahara can be split into two broad categories: the state necessities, which comprised gold and slaves sent north and the salt, cowries and weapons that went south; and luxury goods, which included items such as kola nuts, expensive cloth, ivory, leather goods, pepper, and ostrich feathers that went north, and the copper, high-quality textiles (particularly those dyed with colors not accessible locally), glassware, beads, preserved foodstuffs, gum Arabic, spices and other assorted fancy goods that went south.[67]

Between these items of trade, the state's necessities were particularly vital to the buyers and the traders' economic and political institutions in all the trade's geographical spaces. Whereas gold and cowries served as major currencies, slaves constituted a

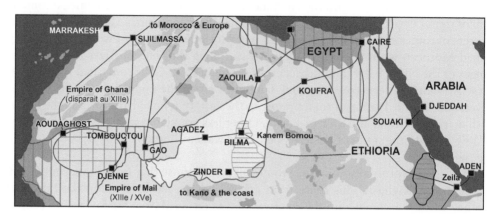

FIGURE 6.3 Niger saharan medieval trade routes https://commons.wikimedia.org/wiki/File :Niger_saharan_medieval_trade_routes.PNG.

substantial amount of the labor and military force in particular areas; salt was a dietary requirement; and military paraphernalia, including weapons and cavalry horses, was vital to the preservation and extension of many a political dominion. Even among these "vital" trade items, gold and slaves stood out and require further comments as to the extent of their implications for the global economy of the medieval period (Figure 6.3).

Gold

Although it is still unknown when the trans-Saharan trade in West African gold began, the region was the main source of precious metals for the global economy between the eleventh and seventeenth centuries. This resource flooded into Cairo and the Middle East from West Africa, helping to maintain Arab dominance until the end of the thirteenth century when silver took the place of gold as the primary currency. In the fifteenth and sixteenth centuries, West African gold helped Europe's domestic economy run smoothly, helped Spain and Portugal grow, and was used to settle international trade accounts. In Africa, the gold trade contributed to the rise of parts of North Africa and the wealth of the great West African states. A sizable amount of West African gold also found its way to India and China, where they were used to purchase spices and highly valued textiles (silk).[68] Gold maintained its position as the most important commodity of trans-Saharan trade until the fifteenth century when European competition started to draw the available supply to the Atlantic shipping routes.[69]

Slaves

Like the gold trade, the origin of the capture and sale of West Africans to North Africa as slaves is not yet ascertained. However, the expansion of Arab power from the seventh century saw a gradual increase in demand for slaves in North Africa and the Middle East, where they were to serve as soldiers and laborers. Nevertheless, as Devisse posits, by the ninth and tenth centuries, slaves were yet to become the main objects of the

FIGURE 6.4   Photo of cowries spent during the slave trade found in the slave museum in Badagry https://commons.m.wikimedia.org/wiki/File:Photo_of_cowries.jpg.

trans-Saharan trade, as were food products.[70] This position was still occupied by the gold and salt trade. Even so, when the trade in slaves expanded from about the eleventh and twelfth centuries, it continued unabated until the nineteenth century when it was outlawed.[71]

The figure of slaves exported across the Sahara Desert to North Africa and the Middle East between the eighth and nineteenth centuries has been highly controversial, as contending positions give very different figures. It appears that those who hold the view that the trans-Atlantic version of the trans-Saharan slave trade was more damaging to the region have provided the more conservative figures. The other group that aimed to establish that Africans did greater harm to each other than the West did in the trade of humans provided more liberal figures. Hence, while the former camp, represented here by Adu Boahen's study of early nineteenth-century slave exports,[72] placed the figure of slave exports across the Sahara at 10,000 per annum as compared to the 70,000 across the Atlantic, the latter camp—represented by Mauny,[73] who put the figures at two million every century since the late Middle Ages and Lewicki—suggested an outrageous 12 to 15 million in the sixteenth century alone.[74] However, what is hardly disputed is the impact African slave populations had on Western and Middle Eastern societies (Figure 6.4).

The Political, Economic, and Social Impact

Perhaps the most important individual stimulator of socioeconomic activity in West Africa between the eighth and fifteenth centuries, the trans-Saharan trade had far-reaching implications for the societies in the region, both directly and indirectly.[75] Societies affected directly included those with territories along the (major) trade routes; others whose locations contained one or two important trade commodities, the importance of which, like the trade routes, shifted with time; and those who served as market centers. As such, political units like ancient (Soninke) Ghana, Mali, Songhai, and Kano, which, at one time or the other, were strategically located on or along the major trade routes or were the source of one or more important commodities of the trade—gold, salt, and slaves—were noticeably transformed. The wealth from the trade transformed them into powerful and popular empires, states, and trading centers, as well as sources of cultural diffusion.

As for those areas indirectly impacted by the trade across the Sahara Desert, these covered societies, which, for not being located near any important trade routes or market centers, went into the production of trade goods to tap into the wealth of the trade. They came to rely on the goods of the trade for sustenance or were part of the vast majority who came under the (cultural) influence of Islam or were dislodged by the revolutionary movements of the sixteenth- and nineteenth-century Islamic reformist movements (jihads). Among these were some societies of the savannah and forest regions of West Africa, like the "lesser" Hausa states, the Ilorin emirate, the Jukun, Igala, Tiv, Igbo, and Ibibio.

Politico-Economic Impact

Politically, the wealth from the trans-Saharan trade enabled the emergence of powerful and expansive empires transforming, the history of several individual states and stateless societies. The emergence of these impressive political edifices followed the pattern of development of the trade, whose importance shifted gradually from the northwestern regions of West Africa to the central region and then to the eastern regions. For the convenience of study, Davidson provides a breakdown of polities and their location within the subregion accordingly:

> The 'western region', lying mainly between the Senegal and Gambia Rivers, may also be called *Senegambia*. The 'central region' consists of the Middle Niger country of the *Western Sudan,* together with the forest lands of Ivory Coast and Ghana. The 'eastern region' includes the *Central Sudan,* together with southern Nigeria, the Niger Delta, and neighbouring countries.[76]

It is important to note, however, that some of these states mentioned have not remained in the same location over the centuries. While some have seen their territorial reach diminish, others have relocated to the new locations that now bear the same name, while some are symbolic postcolonial adoptions. Also pertinent to note is that, throughout these periods, the peoples of these regions remained in contact with each other.

Ghana

Different in location and demographic composition from modern Ghana, Ancient Ghana—one of West Africa's great empires—whose origin is put at about AD 300, was built by the Soninke.[77] By the eighth century, the kingdom had grown to become a powerful trading state, named after the title of its king *ghana* (meaning "war chief").[78] It was located at the southern end of the trade routes from the north across the Sahara and at the northern end of the trade routes from the gold-producing country of West Africa. Given its strategic location, Ghana developed market centers that became a source of great wealth to the kingdom. Combining the wealth generated from taxing (import, export, and production tax) with that made from trading gold, Ghana could afford an army—necessary to defend its enviable position from covetous others. It also expanded its territories over other gold-producing areas (Baure and Bambuk) outside its dominion.

At the peak of its power in the tenth century, Ghana was a large empire with many provinces. By this time, the western route from Sijilmasa, through Awdaghust to Ghana, had become the most important in the trade across the Sahara. The quality of its gold and its famed reserves made the kingdom a choice destination for prospective traders. And for a time, the bulk of West Africa's gold came from this region. However, after it collapsed from an Almoravid invasion in the eleventh century (1077),[79] another empire (Mali) in the central region rose to take its place.

Mali

Located in the central region of West Africa, Mali became an empire in the thirteenth century (1235–1260) under the leadership of Sundiata /Sunjata after uniting the independent Mande-speaking groups in the upper Niger region, formerly under the overlordship of the old Ghana empire.[80] However, under subsequent kings, the Mali empire grew to surpass the old Ghana empire, conquering regions beyond the latter's territorial reach. By the fourteenth century, Mali had become the greatest empire in the region, and many who visited were in awe of it.[81] Its wealth came from the taxes derived from trade within its expansive territory and the tributes from its many provinces and tributaries. By the time of the reign of Mansa Kakan Musa (1312–1337), Mali had already taken control of the trade routes leading south to the land of gold and north to the land of salt, including Gao and Timbuktu.[82] His famous pilgrimage through North Africa to Mecca in the fourteenth century (1324) is a testament to the extent of the wealth and recognition of the empire in that period.[83] It even boasted ambassadors in Egypt, Morocco, and other places.

The fall of the empire of Mali, which began as a series of rebellions from its vassal states, has been attributed to factors including poor leadership, the inability to maintain control over its vast territory and the envy of other ambitious groups who wanted to appropriate the wealth of the important trade routes under its control.[84] Subsequently, Gao, Takrur, and the Wollof and Mossi people rebelled, while the desert Tuaregs seized the important market cities of Timbuktu and Walata. And so began Mali's gradual decline to a position of relative insignificance.

Songhai

The Songhai Empire was established by the people of the Middle Niger who lived in the ancient city of Gao.[85] As enterprising traders, the people of Songhai were able to attract some of the caravan traffic of the Adrar oases to the north of them. By the fifteenth and sixteenth centuries, Songhai controlled the major "trans-Saharan trade routes between

Air and the Mauritania Adrar."[86] Given that slaves had become an important item of the trans-Saharan trade by this period, Songhai, alongside its trade in gold and salt, imported, domiciled, and exported substantial numbers of slaves to North Africa and the Middle East.[87] By the sixteenth century, the empire had reached its peak, having conquered and reduced to vassalage many of the peoples to the north and south of it, including the Mossi of Yatenga, Deninke of Futa Toro, Borgu, and other eastern Hausa states.[88] Additionally, it had the important trading cities of Gao, Timbuktu, and Jenne within its domains, which became a great wealth source for the empire.

The knowledge of the wealth and influence of the Songhai Empire spread far and wide. In fact, by the sixteenth century, it was the largest empire in the West African region. Beyond its famed riches, however, Songhai's control of important northern trans-Saharan routes attracted the envy and ambitions of rulers as far as North Africa. Soon enough, the ruler of Morocco, Mulay Mohammed, dispatched an expeditionary force of 4,600 "handpicked men" armed with modern weaponry, who eventually captured Songhai in 1591.[89]

Kanem-Borno and the Hausa States

After the collapse of the Songhai empire, another empire, Kanem-Borno, became famous in the seventeenth century; located next to the eastern Hausa states.[90] And, as its predecessor states to the west, it conquered vast territories and established control over important trans-Saharan trade routes, which it wrestled from other contending parties, like Songhai and Kebbi. Dominated by the Kanuri,[91] the Kanem-Borno empire also conquered and reduced many of its neighbors to vassalage. At the peak of its power, the empire maintained diplomatic ties with the Ottoman conquerors of Egypt.[92] Commenting on the impact of the Kanem-Borno empire on the societies of West Africa, Davidson explains that:

> What the Kanuri and their allies and subjects were able to do, over a very long period and in a region of great importance, was to bring the advantages of a single system of law and order to a great many different peoples. And it was through this large empire that West Africa kept in regular touch with vital centres of civilisation beyond the Sahara, especially Egypt. It was through Kanem-Bornu that the goods of Egypt and other northern lands; horses and fine metalware, salt and copper, came into West Africa by way of the eastern Sahara; and it was often by the same route that the goods of West Africa, notably kola and ivory, were taken in exchange to those northern lands. In this respect, the markets of Bornu and Kanem were as important as the markets of Hausaland, or as those of the central and western regions of the Western Sudan.[93]

In the case of the Hausa states, their prowess lay in their position as producers of trade goods (including manufactured goods like cotton cloth and leather).[94] Kano was prominent among these states by the eighteenth century, which had developed into a bustling center of commerce, attracting trade and visitors from as far away as Morocco and Algeria.[95] In fact, by the nineteenth century, Kano was referred to as the Manchester of West Africa for its high industrial activity. Describing the extent of Kano's economic reach, Barth makes the following statement:

> There is really something grand in this kind of industry, which spreads to the north as far as Murzuk, Ghat, and even Tripoli; to the west not only to Timbuctu, but in some degree even as far as the shores of the Atlantic, the very inhabitants of Arguin [an island off the West African coast] dressing in the cloth woven and dyed in Kano; to the east all over Bornu, although there it comes into contact with the native industry of the country; and to the south it maintains a rivalry with the native industry of the Igbira and Igbo, while toward the southeast it invades the whole of Adamawa, and is only limited by the nakedness of the pagan sansculottes, who do not wear clothing.[96]

As a melting point of peoples and ideas, Kano, through its traders who traveled the length and breadth of the southern forest regions, spread its cultural influence into these regions as they went about the business of trade.[97] Perhaps even more consequential were the eighteenth- and nineteenth-century Fulani jihads, which had far-reaching social and political consequences on the region throughout the trade.[98]

Conclusion

There is no doubt about the remarkable significance of the trans-Saharan trade for the region of West Africa. From the eighth century, when regular traffic developed across the Sahara Desert, trade transformed the region into a beehive of socioeconomic activities. Not only did the trade open West Africa up further to the wider world, but it also became a catalyst for the development of more elaborate systems of political organizations, namely the rise of expansive empires. Underlying these political expressions, however, was Islam, the driving force behind many of the developments witnessed in the region between the eighth and nineteenth centuries. Even though economic incentives stand prominent among the factors that vitalized the trade, Islam served as the basis of political mobilization, cultural organization and as an economic facilitator.

DEEP DIVE

Assignment 1

Objective

The objective of this assignment is to ensure that students complete the reading of Chapter 6 and to get them to understand the diverse trade networks that developed among peoples of West Africa and beyond through the trans-Saharan trade, which connected them to other cultures where diffusion of civilization emerged.

Method

Students will be expected to write a short note in response to the question.

Reading Comprehension

What role did the three empires—Ghana, Mali, and Songhai—play in the development of trade and trade networks in West Africa and across Africa?

Assignment 2

Objective

The objective of this assignment is to ensure that students complete the reading of Chapter 6 and to get them to think about the sociocultural and environmental factors that forced the need for constant mobility from West Africa to other parts of the continent and beyond.

Method

Students will be expected to write a short note in response to the question.

Reading Comprehension

Examine some of the underlying factors that created the need for mobility and migration of West African peoples that would eventually open the way for the trans-Saharan trade and the spread of Islam in the region.

Notes

1 See Ghyslaine Lydon, *On Trans-Saharan Trails: Islamic Law, Trade Networks and Cross-Cultural Exchange in Nineteenth Century Western Africa* (New York: Cambridge University Press, 2008), 50; and Michael A. Gomez, *African Dominion: A New History of Empire in Early and Medieval West Africa* (New Jersey: Princeton University Press, 2018), 12.
2 The seventh century Arab conquest of parts of modern-day Spain and northern Africa, which saw an increased influx—into the region—of Arab merchants and missionaries who produced the "earliest" most detailed written accounts of the cultural life and political organizations of the people.
3 Robin Law, "The 'Hamitic Hypothesis' in Indigenous West African Historical Thought," *History in Africa* 36 (2009): 293–314.
4 For a more detailed explanation on how new research innovations and important archaeological discoveries have impacted conventional knowledge on the antiquity of West African civilizations and the trans-Saharan trade, see Jean Devisse, "Trade and Trade Routes in West Africa," in *UNESCO General History of Africa, Vol. III: Africa from the Seventh to the Eleventh Century*, eds. Mohammed El Fasi and Ivan Hrbek (California: Heinemann, 1988), 376–367; and Sam Nixon, "Trans-Saharan Gold Trade in Pre-modern Times: Available Evidence and Research Agendas," in *Trade in the Ancient Sahara and Beyond*, eds. David J. Mattingly, Victoria Leitch, Chloë N. Duckworth, Aurélie Cuénod, Martin Sterry and Franca Cole (New York: Cambridge University Press, 2017), 158–161.
5 Ralph A. Austen, *Trans-Saharan Africa in World History* (New York: Oxford University Press, 2010), 1.

6   David J. Mattingly, Victoria Leitch, Chloe N. Duckworth, Aurelie Cuénod, Martin Sterry and Franca Cole, eds., *Trade in the Ancient Sahara and Beyond* (New York: Cambridge University Press, 2017).

7   See, for instance, Klaus Braun and Jacqueline Passon, eds., *Across the Sahara: Tracks, Trade and Cross-Cultural Exchange in Libya* (Cham: Springer, 2020).

8   David C. Conrad, *Empires of Medieval West Africa: Ghana, Mali, and Songhay* (New York: Chelsea House, 2010).

9   Ralph, *Trans-Saharan Africa in World History*, iii.

10 Devisse, "Trade and Trade Routes in West Africa," 367.

11 Ralph, *Trans-Saharan Africa in World History*, 10; and Lydon, *On Trans-Saharan Trails*, 52–54.

12 Anthony G. Hopkins, *An Economic History of West Africa* (London: Routledge, 2020), 126, 129–130.

13 Hopkins, *An Economic History of West Africa*, 127; and Lydon, *On Trans-Saharan Trails*, 57.

14 Devisse, "Trade and Trade Routes in West Africa," 371.

15 Fathi Habashi, "Gold in the Ancient African Kingdoms," *De Re Metallica* 12 (2009): 65–69.

16 Ronald A. Messier, "The Almoravids: West African Gold and the Gold Currency of the Mediterranean Basin," *Journal of the Economic and Social History of the Orient* 17 (1974): 31–47.

17 Devisse, *"Trade and Trade Routes in West Africa,"* 387.

18 Devisse, *"Trade and Trade Routes in West Africa."*

19 Basil Davidson, *A History of West Africa 1000–1800* (England: Longman, 1977), 30.

20 Devisse, "Trade and Trade Routes in West Africa," 381.

21 Lydon, *On Trans-Saharan Trails*, 58.

22 Just as in the desert, where the Beber settlements had developed trading networks prior to the upsurge in trans-Saharan trade traffic—the same trade which enhanced their knowledge of desert tails—the south also featured a local, long-distance trading network which ensured that goods from across the Sahara got as far as the Western Atlantic coast. For more on the development and organization of local short and long-distance trade in West Africa, see Hopkins, *An Economic History of West Africa*, 99–105.

23 John Wright, *The Trans-Saharan Slave Trade* (New York: Routledge, 2007), 9.

24 Toyin Falola and Matthew M. Heaton, *A History of Nigeria* (Cambridge: Cambridge University Press, 2008), 33.

25 Hopkins, *An Economic History of West Africa*, 131.

26 Ralph, *Trans-Saharan Africa in World History*, 26.

27 Hopkins, *An Economic History of West Africa*, 131.

28 Hopkins, *An Economic History of West Africa*, 131; and Austen, *Trans-Saharan Africa in World History*, 26.

29 Hopkins, *An Economic History of West Africa*, 131.

30 Davidson, *A History of West Africa*, 46; Gomez, *African Dominion*, 32; and Nixon, "Trans-Saharan Gold Trade in Pre-Modern Times," 171.

31 Lydon, *On Trans-Saharan Trails*, 65; and Davidson, *A History of West Africa* 50.

32 Lydon, *On Trans-Saharan Trails*, 65.

33 Conrad, *Empires of Medieval West Africa*, 112.

34 Muhammad Al-Hajj, "A Seventeenth Century Chronicle of the Origins and Missionary Activities of the Wangarawa," *Kano Studies* 1, no. 4 (1968): 7–42.

35 Lydon, *On Trans-Saharan Trails*, 65.

36 Stephan Reichmuth, "Literary Culture and Arabic Manuscripts in 19th-Century Ilorin," in *The Trans-Saharan Book Trade*, eds. Graziano Krätli and Ghislaine Lydon (Leiden: Brill, 2011), 235.

37 Lydon, *On Trans-Saharan Trails*, 65–66.

38 Ali A. Ahmida, ed., *Bridges across the Sahara: Social, Economic, and Cultural Impact of the Trans-Sahara Trade during the 19th and 20th Centuries* (Newcastle upon Tyne: Cambridge Scholars Publishing, 2011), 39.

39 Lydon, *On Trans-Saharan Trails*, 4, 160.

40 Lydon, *On Trans-Saharan Trails*, 4.

41 Hopkins, *An Economic History of West Africa*, 118, 133.

42 Lydon, *On Trans-Saharan Trails*, 62.

43 Lydon, *On Trans-Saharan Trails*; Mark and Jose da Silva Herta, *The Forgotten Diaspora: Jewish Communities in West Africa and the Making of the Atlantic World* (Cambridge: Cambridge University Press, 2011); and John Hunwick, *Jews of a Sahara Oasis: Elimination of the Tamantit Community* (Princeton: Markus Wiener, 2006).

44 Lydon, *On Trans-Saharan Trails*, 66.

45 Lydon, *On Trans-Saharan Trails*, 68.

46 Lydon, *On Trans-Saharan Trails*, 68.

47 Gomez, *African Dominion*, 176.

48 Lydon, *On Trans-Saharan Trails*, 67.

49 Hopkins, *An Economic History of West Africa*, 107.

50 Abner Cohen, *Custom and Politics in Urban Africa: A Study of Hausa Migrants in Yoruba Towns* (Los Angeles: University of California Press, 1969), 6–7.

51 Hopkins, *An Economic History of West Africa*, 118.

52 Hopkins, *An Economic History of West Africa*, 108.

53 Hopkins, *An Economic History of West Africa*, 108.

54 Hopkins, *An Economic History of West Africa*.

55 Lydon, *On Trans-Saharan Trails*, 61.

56 Lydon, *On Trans-Saharan Trails*.

57 Devisse, "Trade and Trade Routes in West Africa," 371; and Davidson, *A History of West Africa 1000–1800*, 9, 34.

58 Eric Ross, "A Historical Geography of the Trans-Saharan Trade," in *The Trans-Saharan Book Trade: Manuscript Culture, Arabic Literacy and Intellectual History in Muslim Africa*, eds. Graziano Krätli and Ghislaine Lydon (Leiden: Brill, 2011), 13.

59 Ross, "A Historical Geography of the Trans-Saharan Trade."

60 Wright, *The Trans-Saharan Slave Trade*, 12.

61 Ross, "A Historical Geography of the Trans-Saharan Trade," 11.

62 Davidson, *A History of West Africa*, 33. See also Hopkins, *An Economic History of West Africa*, 130.

63 Hopkins, *An Economic History of West Africa*.

64 Davidson, *A History of West Africa*, 31.

65 Devisse, "Trade and Trade Routes in West Africa," 775–776.

66 See Nixon, "Trans-Saharan Gold Trade in Pre-modern Times," 174.

67 Hopkins, *An Economic History of West Africa*, 128–129; and Ralph, *Trans-Saharan Africa in World History*, 27.

68 Austen, *Trans-Saharan Africa in World History*, 30.

69 Austen, *Trans-Saharan Africa in World History*, 27; and Lydon, *On Trans-Saharan Trails*, 65.

70 Devisse, "Trade and Trade Routes in West Africa," 382–383.

71 Hopkins, *An Economic History of West Africa*, 130; and Ralph, *Trans-Saharan Africa in World History*, 31.

72 Adu Boahen, *Britain, the Sahara, and the Western Sudan, 1788–1861* (London: Oxford University Press, 1964), 127.

73 Raymond Mauny, *Tableau Géographique de L'ouest Africain au Moyen Age, D'apreS des Sources Écrites, la Tradition et L'archéologie* (Dakar: IFAN, 1961), 379.

74 Hopkins, *An Economic History of West Africa*, 130.

75 Wright, *The Trans-Saharan Slave Trade*.

76 Davidson, *A History of West Africa*, 27.

77 Davidson, *A History of West Africa*, 35.

78 Robert Z. Cohen, *Discovering the Empire of Ghana* (New York: Rosen Publishing, 2014).

79 A. J. H. Goodwin, "The Medieval Empire of Ghana," *The South African Archaeological Bulletin* 12, no. 47 (1957): 108–112.

80 John O. Hunwick, "The Mid-fourteenth Century Capital of Mali," *Journal of African History* 14, no. 2 (1973): 195–206.

81 Nawal M. Bell, "The Age of Mansa Musa of Mali: Problems in Succession and Chronology," *The International Journal of African Historical Studies* 5, no. 2 (1972): 221–234.

82 Davidson, *A History of West Africa*, 50.

83 Warren Schultz, "Mansa Mūsā's Gold in Mamluk Cairo: A Reappraisal of a World Civilizations Anecdote," in *History and Historiography of Post-Mongol Central Asia and the Middle East: Studies in Honor of John E. Woods*, eds. Judith Pfeiffer and Sholeh Quinn (Wiesbaden: Harrassowitz Verlag, 2006), 428–447.

84 M. Ly-Tall, "The Decline of the Mali Empire," in *General History of Africa: Africa from the Twelfth to the Sixteenth Century, Volume IV*, ed. Djibril T. Niane (Paris: UNESCO, 1984), 172–186.

85 Elizabeth Isichei, *A History of African Societies to 1870* (Cambridge: Cambridge University Press, 1997).

86 Ross, "A Historical Geography of the Trans-Saharan Trade," 21; and Wright, *The Trans-Saharan Slave Trade*, 49.

87 Ibiang O. Ewa, "Pre-colonial West Africa: The Fall of Songhai Empire Revisited," *Journal of the Historical Society of Nigeria* 26 (2017): 1–24.

88 Davidson, *A History of West Africa*, 77.

89 Ewa, "*Pre-colonial West Africa*."

90 Nura Alkali and Yusufu B. Usman, eds. *Studies in the History of Pre-Colonial Borno* (Zaria: Northern Nigerian Publishing, 1983).

91 Ronald Cohen, *The Kanuri of Bornu* (New York: Holt, Rinehart and Winston, 1967).

92 Rémi Dewière, "'Peace Be upon Those Who Follow the Right Way': Diplomatic Practices between Mamluk Cairo and the Borno Sultanate at the End of the Eighth/Fourteenth Century," in *Mamluk Cairo, a Crossroads for Embassies: Studies on Diplomacy and Diplomatics*, eds. Frédéric Bauden and Malika Dekkiche (Leiden: Brill, 2019), 658–682.

93 Davidson, *A History of West Africa*, 105.

94 Michael G. Smith, *The Affairs of Daura: History and Change in a Hausa State, 1800–1958* (Los Angeles: University of California, 1978).

95 Mahdi Adamu, *The Hausa Factor in West African History* (Zaria: Ahmadu Bello University Press, 1978).

96 Heinrich Barth, *Travels and Discoveries in North and Central* Africa (London: Longman, Brown, Green, Longmans, & Roberts, 1857), quoted in Hopkins, *An Economic History of West Africa*, 94.

97 Bawuro M. Barkindo, ed., *Kano and Some of Her Neighbours* (Bayero: Ahmadu Bello University Press, 1989).

98 John N. Panden, *Religion and Political Culture in Kano* (Berkeley: University of California Press, 2020), 432–435.

7

STATES AND EMPIRES

Introduction

Right from its earliest origins, the development of human civilization/society has been driven by the insatiable needs of humans, which in the beginning consisted of a basic desire for survival: the search for food, shelter, and warmth. In this original quest for survival, humans, whose greatest obstacle was the environment, fashioned tools and pooled together into groups, establishing various modes of social (intra- and intergroup) interactions—kinship, citizenship, trade, and other forms of social partnerships—to improve their chances at an easier existence. With an ever-growing capacity to subdue and adapt to the environment to meet immediate needs, population expansions were recorded, which produced tensions and competition to acquire and control access to increasingly scarce resources.

The next stage in political development in West Africa was sponsored by the availability and use of iron tools, which added another important dimension to social interaction. As certain groups acquired the capacity to compel others to do their bidding, society developed more complex forms of social organization and interaction, producing structures determined by individual capacities and the varying types of social contracts that emerged.

The history of the evolution of human society is perhaps more a description of developments in West Africa than in many other places, situated in a continent distinguished as the birthplace of mankind.[1] Beyond the archaeological evidence available to support the chronology of events are insights provided by European and medieval Arabic sources on the region,[2] substantiating the belief that this part of the world experienced the various stages of human social development. Contained in these sources are descriptions of West African societies at varying stages of social development—from decentralized village-group units to centralized kingship structures and expansive empires, consisting of several kingdoms/chiefdoms under one central leadership—engaged in various forms of social interaction, significant among which were trade and warfare that provided the momentum for a spectrum of socioeconomic and political developments (Figure 7.1).

DOI: 10.4324/9781003198260-9

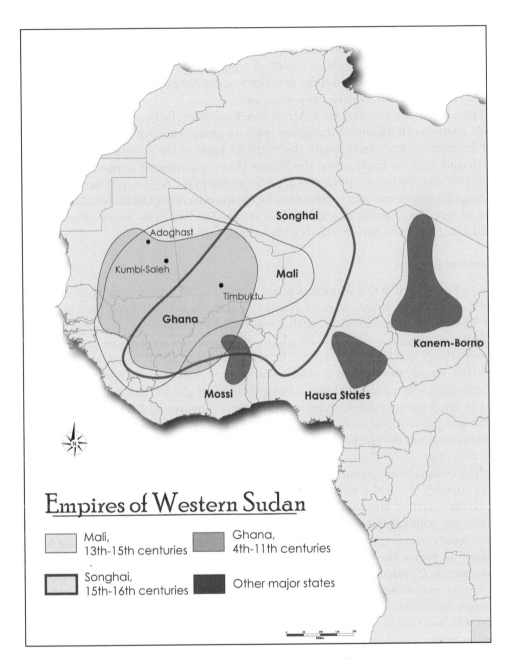

FIGURE 7.1   Map of the Empires of Western Sudan. Author's collection.

Although trade in West Africa developed from a basic need to supplement the limited provisions of varying environments, with a growing division of labor (arising from improved technical ability and agricultural surplus), the activity soon grew to command great socioeconomic and political relevance in the region. Socially, not only did trade connect many erstwhile isolated communities, but the interactions it encouraged also contributed to the development of extensive kinship ties and cultural exchanges. Politically, trade carried with it prospects of wealth and power, arising from the volume, variety, and value of commodities traded, the opportunities it presented for maintaining huge standing armies that aided the development of expansive political domains, as well as the maintenance of valuable diplomatic ties.

From the eighth century, West Africa benefited from the existence of such extensive trade relations—both within the region (with an internal long-distance trade) and without (in international trade)—with the northern parts of the continent and beyond. Its participation in the trade across the Sahara Desert contributed important transformations to social, economic, and political organization in the region, as it not only exposed the populations to new ideas epitomized by the introduction of Islam but also spread the idea of centralized political organizations (states and empires)—many of which developed along the trans-Saharan trade's alternating routes.

Sudanese Empires

The region covered in this segment, known as the "Sudan," comprising Western, Central and Eastern Sudan, stretches over a distance of more than 2,000 miles, from present-day north of Dakar to Lake Chad.[3] With a relatively limited amount of rainfall—between May and September—in the savannah, its geography comprised vast grasslands with scattered trees that were well watered by the River Niger and its many tributaries. Also relatively free of the menace of disease-carrying vectors like the mosquito and tsetse fly, especially when compared to the forest (Guinea) regions to the south of it, the Sahel was an attractive location for human settlement. From around 2000 BC,[4] the savannah witnessed gradual migrations into it by populations moving away from the drying-out Sahara regions to the north. Combined with the local populations, the savannah became one area of extensive human settlements and activity, featuring farming, pastoral, and trading communities organized into varying political structures, from very simple to more complex political organizations (Figure 7.2).

Accommodating large and diverse populations, the Sudanese region produced many centralized political systems. At least from the third century,[5] conditions had converged in the westernmost regions (from the west of Lake Chad all the way down to the Atlantic Ocean)[6] to enable the establishment of large states and empires. Earliest among these was Ancient (Soninke) Ghana, which, although its origins preceded the eighth century, came into some recognition in that period owing to encounters with North Africa through trade. The Mali Empire succeeded the Empire of Ghana by the thirteenth century, which in turn was replaced by the Songhai Empire after Mali declined in the fourteenth century.

The Ghana Empire

The Ghana Empire began in the first millennium and extended its reign until the second, with massive political and economic outreach that made it distinct from many other empires in the West African region.[7] Its geographical outreach stretched from what is currently known as southern Mauritania to Western Mali, and it equally covered the ground of the eastern part of Senegal as it is today.[8] Historical evidence established the

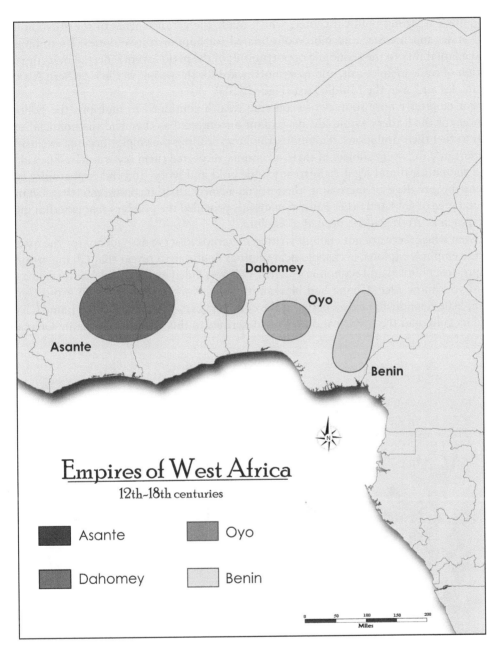

FIGURE 7.2   Approximate location of West African "Forest Empires". Author's collection.

time of dominance of this empire around the fourth to the eighth century, up to the eleventh century. The historical exploits of the empire, together with all its achievements during its time of dominance, qualify it to be one of the earliest empires that Africa had and certainly one of the most successful.[9] The empire's political embryo was formed when the Sahel's resources matured for exploitation. The originators of the empire organized a strong political center, which made the arrangements of the surrounding city-states much easier and more coordinated for administrative duties. Its suitability and adaptability to the economic opportunities of the period were reflected in its organization of trade in gold, salt, and ivory northward for the people in the Northern African countries and even the Middle East (Figure 7.3).[10]

For empires whose sources of economic wealth continued to multiply, the political powers of the leaders would always remain uncontested as they had the financial oxygen to fuel their ambitions. Therefore, the kings leading the empire became exclusively important, and every subject of their suzerainty respected them accordingly. They alone had the political and legal right to stockpile gold and ivory, and the opportunity gave them the privilege of increasing their social respect. It is incontestable that Ghana's abundance of gold and other natural materials provided the pointers that external interests, such as Arab traders, needed to explore.[11]

Even when there are not enough written materials to serve as evidence for the history of the empire's exploits, archaeological findings continue to reveal that Ghana attained impressive political and economic growth. This was aided by the people's informed technological knowledge. Ghana had blacksmiths who worked on metals. To avoid confusion, little relationship exists between the contemporary realization of the name Ghana and its gold, and the historical one being described in this chapter. The name Ghana in

FIGURE 7.3   Native people of Upper Senegal: Peuls and Malinkes. https://commons.wikimedia
.org/wiki/File:Le_Tour_du_monde-03-p020.jpg.

modern Africa, originally called the Gold Coast, was adopted in 1957 after the country gained political independence from the British.[12]

The Ghana Empire comprised the Soninke people, whose language was Mande. According to some accounts, Koumbi Saleh was the empire's historical center and was large enough to contain more than 50,000 people.[13] It was considered the central city-state that took control of all the neighboring ones and managed them in the matter of wars, politics, and economy so that they paid tributes and accepted the supremacy of Ghana's power. The empire was ruled by a king supported by well-organized cavalry units that ensured that external aggressors were kept at bay and managed internal complications and differing opinions that could serve as fertile ground for chaotic struggles.

One of the main reasons why Ghana commanded such respect was that it used its forces to further its political agenda by defeating opponents and making them vassals. The empire began to crumble when the Almoravids of North Africa invaded in the eleventh century.[14] In the following century, however, its decline was brought by natural and human factors.

The Mali Empire

The next notable political entity in the Western Sudan was the Empire of Mali that grew into prominence in the first half of the thirteenth century.[15] Its boundaries were large, including Kaoga (Gao), parts of the Atlantic, the Sahara and the tropical forested areas.[16] The historiography of empires like Mali was not much handed down by written history but primarily through oral accounts. Different sources establish that the sovereignty of the Mali Empire was widely extended within the region, with Mansa Musa, a historically powerful ruler, wielding strong political dominance.[17] Mansa Musa was cognizant of his region's political development, and he was able to galvanize part of the region's submission, owing to a well-developed political and economic system.[18]

Mansa Musa was aware of his political opponents' capabilities, whose strength could be consolidated in the quest for an integrated economy. He used this vast knowledge as a vista for the reconfiguration of his empire's economic infrastructure. For example, Musa understood that the Berbers were a great people who established an economically viable society and politically vibrant space. Apart from these, the knowledge with which Musa structured his empire was founded on information about politics and conflicts in the region.[19] This informed his formation of a sturdy and resilient military capable of ensuring his victory.

Musa was a great history student who connected disparate events and epochs to make projections and construct a philosophical foundation for the exploration of his immediate societies and suzerainty. For instance, the stories that impressed Sundiata, the creator of the Mali Empire that flourished between the seventh century and before his emergence to power, were about myth-making and military strength.[20] Al-Maghrib, a notable scholar, had reasonably influenced how Musa would approach the maintenance of the Mali Empire during his reign. Musa's greatness was partially revealed by Ibn Khaldun's account, which stated that during the period of his supreme dominance, his influence was felt across places in the Middle East, so much so that Arab neighbors approached him for a military alliance where the former would provide maximum military protection to him and his people (Figure 7.4).[21]

FIGURE 7.4   An artist's impression of Emperor Sundiata https://commons.wikimedia.org/wiki/
File:Emperor_Sundiata.png.

The period was a time of dominance and political relevance, structured on the eruption of interregional violence masterminded by stronger groups. Knowing this largely determined how people in charge of these empires instigated the processes that brought success. Mali, under Musa, became ambitious and sought direct access to distant places beyond its shores, especially to access economic and political opportunities.[22] The Mali Empire occupied a very strong position, with impressive accomplishments in philosophy, indigenous knowledge systems, and political management. The empire was structured to lean on spiritual and Islamic beliefs, with an economic system that brought about the class stratification of those who were higher in social status and those who were lower. Power relations between genders constituted another integral part of their political system, and there were stipulated etiquettes that governed political participation and power distribution in society. The Mali Empire asserted a great deal of political power exercised by the center, which superseded all subsidiary units.

The Songhai Empire

The third and last of the major Western Sudanese empires was the Songhai Empire, which succeeded Mali by the fourteenth century. The dominance of empires rarely went unchallenged, going by the reality that a highly centralized government was always prone to intermittent internal and external aggressions. This occurred especially when the political drivers maintaining its existence were conquered or dead. Even if the former was impossible, perhaps because of the military infrastructure in place, the latter was inevitable as successful kings would not live forever. As Mali expanded geographically and became politically impenetrable, other emerging groups sought available opportunities to overtake it and become the new center of power.

Here was the Songhai Empire, which rose to prominence as soon as Mali's sovereignty was challenged and its political pride severely wounded. As Mali faltered nearly half a decade before Mansa Sulaymān's reign ended,[23] it paved the way for a strong Songhai Empire to take over.[24] Perhaps because this newly fledgling empire had consciously learned from the downfall of the previous rulers, critically studying the reason for their eventual weakness, Songhai decided on a different approach to systematize its relationship with its subsidiaries. Power distribution in the Songhai Empire was different because it was a heterogeneous society reflective of plural identities and societies.[25]

The diversity in the Songhai Empire was institutionalized by a political system that enabled representation to break the walls of ethnic affiliation. It bolstered a system where political participation transcended familial loyalties, evoking what Francis Fukuyama referred to as "natural sociability."[26] This means that the empire was symbolic and can be linked to some ideas in a modern democracy, in which heterogeneity was well managed to recognize different identities. From the tenth century until circa 1591, Songhai had an imposing political dynasty that was able to manage resources and people.[27] According to Diop's narrative, Songhai's geographical reach extended from the east of the River Niger bank to as far as the Atlantic Ocean, and from the frontiers of the land of the Bindoko to the Taghezza and its dependencies under Askia Mohammed.

The beginning of the Songhai Empire started with Sunni Ali, who made incredible efforts to expand its political and geographical outreach.[28] Sunni Ali was known as a fierce warrior who controlled the sovereignty of his people and consolidated his military power with political and economic policies that transformed the empire, making it stronger. Sunni Ali was popular for his impartial treatment of religious leaders, with whom he related in ways that suggested a lack of reverence for their religious essence. The elites were subjected to control, but his leadership style and personality were resented.[29] Sunni Ali succeeded Sulaymān Dāma, who ruled the Empire for about 27 years.

Central and Eastern Sudanese Empires

Emerging in the central and eastern regions of the great West African savannah from the fifteenth century were the Empires of Kanem-Borno and the Hausa states/kingdoms, which were brought under the Sokoto (Fulani) Empire in the nineteenth century.[30] Occupying a similar geographical environment as their neighbors to the west, the region also developed similar forms of socioeconomic and political organizations, taking advantage of the same trans-Saharan trade and coming under similar influences from the north. Unlike the westernmost regions of the Western Sudan, which experienced a regional succession of empires, the Kanuri and Hausa states of the Eastern and

Central regions developed in parallel, even if the former (Kanuri) had an earlier start with ties to the trans-Saharan trade.[31]

The Kanem-Borno Empire

The Kanem-Borno Empire holds the record of having one of the longest-surviving dynasties in human history. It was documented to have started in the ninth century and lasted until the nineteenth century.[32] The empire captured regions that are today located in Cameroon, Chad, Nigeria, and Niger, and was established by individuals identified as competent horse riders and users, named the Zaghawa.[33] Kanem-Borno began its political engagements in modern-day Lake Chad of Njimi. After about 200 years of dominance, the leadership of the Kanem-Borno attracted a foreign religion, Islam, in the eleventh century, after which their empire became Islamic in orientation and principles. The suzerainty of the empire flourished for so long partly because of its proximity to the North African region, which came with the advantages of commerce, religion and knowledge (Figure 7.5).

Although the Zaghawa people began the process of state-building right at the start of the ninth century, they were overpowered during the period of religious conversion of the leadership that occurred in the eleventh century.[34] This drove them out of Njimi, which was subsequently taken over by Humai ibn Salamna, who eventually relocated the empire's political center. During this period of political modifications, the Saifawa dynasty was created, and it ruled for a substantial length of time, for about 771 years,

GROUP OF KANEM-BU WARRIORS.

FIGURE 7.5 Group of Kanem-Bu Warriors https://commons.wikimedia.org/wiki/File:Group _of_Kanem-Bu_warriors.jpg.

the longest in Africa.[35] Due to the realization that the Zaghawa people had been displaced from power, the Saifawa leadership claimed they were descendants of Arab civilization in order to lay claim to what they considered an advanced civilization.[36]

As a result of this close relationship with the Islamic world, it was possible for them to administer their socioeconomic affairs through the lens of Islamic philosophy and culture.[37] They flourished in trade, with their specific objects of trade being agricultural and fish products. What almost separated the empire from others was its high propensity for expansionism.[38] It exploited the interregional trade opportunities, obtaining firearms and weapons that could be used to engage in wars. Due to their established military power, they could desecrate existing religious practices that were deemed un-Islamic. They were usually victorious because of the numerical strength of the Mai groups, the ethnic identity of the conquerors of the Zaghawa. However, the main source of problems was the ambition for power among competing individuals.

The expansion of the Kanem-Borno Empire recorded success in trade and politics way into the nineteenth century before the collision with the Fulani jihadists, who also nursed ambitions of conquest.[39] Some factors rendered the Kanem-Borno Empire vulnerable to external aggressions. These included ecological challenges resulting in land desertification and increased drought challenges. As a result of the incessant challenges, the Fulani jihad created opportunities for the emergence of another dynasty.[40]

Despite carrying the glory and name of the Kanem-Borno Empire,[41] the new dynasty was considered a threat. Muhammad Al-Amin Al-Kanemi challenged the Fulani invaders, brought their threats under decisive control, and ended the Saifawa dynasty. The empire came to an end in the early twentieth century, following European conquest.

The Hausa States

The beginning of the Hausa states dates back more than a millennium, to circa 1000.[42] The kingdoms shared a reasonable level of organizational efficiency built on a heterogeneous foundation. All the Hausa states later came under the Sokoto Caliphate in the nineteenth century.[43] The Hausa states occupied the area of modern-day Nigér and Nigeria. The Hausa states were geographically located between the Western Sudanic kingdoms that stretched from ancient Ghana and Mali to the Eastern Sudanic kingdoms of Kanem-Borno.[44] They spoke the same language and shared a similar culture, which made it possible to create a long-lasting identity.

The conglomeration of these city-states was supported by advanced economic systems that traded predominantly in leather, gold, cloth, salt, and kola nuts, among other things. They experienced an all-time boom because they were helped by the geographical proximity to North Africa and the much wider West African region.[45] The Hausa conducted economic transactions with the rainforest region to the south and used the proceeds to consolidate their political and economic interest.

There are no contentions in their oral traditions that a certain Bayajidda, a migrant from Baghdad of a royal lineage, arrived in Daura, one of the oldest Hausa city-states, after which he married the town's queen.[46] According to the legend, their marriage was fruitful, producing children who created city-states such as Gobir, Zazzau, Rano, Biram, and then Kano. Because they occupied a geographically advantageous location that reasonably enhanced trade expansion, they became a center of economic activities in the region and began to experience an influx of Muslim traders.[47] This continued for a considerable period. As their trade was also affected by Islamic traders and scholars, many Hausa leaders converted to Islam before the end of the thirteenth century. As most of them now shared a common religion, it became easier to incorporate Islam and culture into state affairs.[48] As such, Hausaland came under the influence of Islamic culture, which continued for a very long time. Even though these city-states used the same language, subgroups such as the Fulbe, Tuareg, and Zarbama were part of Hausaland.

Hausa legends enable the understanding of the history of state formation. For example, legends that establish the ancestral foundations of the place of Bayajidda have some difficulties. This is because the ascension of this progenitor occurred during a sixteenth-century timeline, which, therefore, betrays the historical fact that the beginning of Hausaland can be traced to the previous millennium, 1000 CE. Some histories, for example, establish that the migration of the Hausa people to the region was inspired by drastic climatic or environmental changes in another location. Another argues that the Hausa were indigenous to the area, therefore casting strong doubt on the history of migration from another place. An enduring legacy of the Hausa states is that they reigned and prospered. They had very successful trading organizations that established a relationship between them and their neighbors.

Forest Empires: Oyo, Benin, Dahomey, and Asante

Situated in the southern regions of West Africa, the forest (Guinea) zones—which spread from the shifting savannah terminal to the Atlantic Ocean—are noted for the difficulty of their terrain, vegetation, and climate. Also, they were scenes of the development of large states and empires such as Oyo, Benin, Dahomey, and Asante. Marked by heavy rainfall (averaging over 100 inches every year), the region is characterized by dense vegetation, with scattered hills, mountains, and valleys, characteristics that attracted populations who mostly were fleeing the effects of population expansion and political conflicts.[49] Notwithstanding the environmental encumbrances, which included the menace of disease-carrying vectors like the mosquito and tsetse fly that inflicted malaria and limited livestock production, the people of the region managed to adapt to their environment. They produced the surpluses and technical know-how to support large states and empires, and played an active role in regional trade and connections to the Atlantic world.

The Oyo Empire

One of the largest political entities to develop in the forest region was the Oyo Empire, which started as an average savannah kingdom. Like many other historical experiences, the beginning of the Oyo Empire remains debated because expansive works of literature usually disagree in their analyses of the events around the emergence and fall of the Old Oyo Empire. Some historical accounts establish that the Yoruba people, from which the Oyo Empire was developed, migrated from places that continue to attract debates. According to oral sources, the Yoruba became the occupants of different locations during the eighth century CE.[50] Among all the Yoruba city-states, Oyo was positioned geographically for external exchanges, and this perhaps contributed to its immediate emergence as a strong power in the region. It engaged in extensive commerce, and the people were industrious in agriculture production.[51]

During the early period of the sixteenth century, Oyo was relatively stronger against its opponents, who also were empire builders. As a result of their military advantage, Oyo constituted a threat to smaller neighbors and remained a source of worry to them on many occasions. The northern neighbors, Borgu[52] and Nupe,[53] were so powerful that the realization of Oyo's potential depended on its ability to build political alliances and military force. The political leaders of Oyo updated their military strategies, systems, and knowledge. This was, perhaps, because they were able to build extensive commercial relationships that brought them the privilege of procuring horses, firearms, goods, and services from people they came in contact with.[54] Alaafin Orompoto[55] consolidated Oyo's power and influence by establishing a royal force that was consistently trained in military tactics to increase its professionalism. The fact that Oyo had improved during the seventeenth century made it extremely difficult to subdue, and, therefore, its hitherto powerful neighbors, the Nupe and Borgu, became fearful of Oyo's influence as they were no match for them in military strength.[56] Not long after Oyo emerged as a force to be reckoned with, it displayed its power by conquering its neighbor, Dahomey, in two historical wars between 1724–1730 and 1738–1748.[57]

Oyo maintained a constitutional monarchical system of government, which was reinforced by the fact that the Oyo king (the Alaafin) was chosen by the council of Oyomesi, which consisted of seven influential leaders who represented seven wards.[58] Typically, the selection of these leaders was outside the king's political influence, and they wielded so much power that they could oust the king if he failed in his political representation. This could manifest in different forms. For example, when the king abused his power, he would be indicted. Apart from these internal political arrangements, Oyo was a success in its economic and political expansion.[59]

Oyo's transformation generated internal and external crises that brought about the death or displacement of different leaders and created serious troubles. Alaafin Abiodun ascended the throne around 1754 and succeeded in expanding the empire's economic and diplomatic ties and maintaining political stability.[60] A contested succession gave way to the emergence of Alaafin Aole, who took over from him, though with a dwindling military power. Oyo entered the nineteenth century as a weak empire, dealing with internal power struggles and pressures from the Fulani jihad. Oyo's dominance was eventually brought to an end in the 1830s.[61]

The Benin Empire

A reputed forest empire was Benin, which, even as a contemporary of Ile-Ife, was younger, going by the traditions that it owed its ascendency to princely elements that migrated into the area from Ile-Ife. The Benin Empire was located in what is today identified as Edo State, domiciled in southern Nigeria. It probably began in the early thirteenth century and made considerable progress in establishing its redoubtable sovereignty in the area.[62] The history of Benin is sparse, with different stories, as there are claims that the indigenous people of Benin were once displeased with the leadership of the central city-state, headed by the Ogiso. This was when Oranmiyan, a popular Yoruba descendant of Oduduwa, founder of Ile-Ife in present-day southwest Nigeria, was on his expansionist voyage to understand, study, and perhaps conquer his immediate surroundings.[63] Oranmiyan soon established himself very quickly and created the impression that he had the intellectual capacity and emotional intelligence to organize the region into a powerful state that would become economically successful and extend its dominance to various settlements. Through practical demonstrations of his capacity, he won the hearts of these indigenous people, who, in a way, continued to show their interest in him, but not to the level of immediately transferring their leadership to him.[64] Over some more years, they trusted him and made his son, Eweka, a king but still selected their chiefs in line with established systems[65] (Figure 7.6).

However, with the ascension of King Ewuare, who reigned between circa 1440 and 1480, the internal politics of the Benin Empire changed, and he was described as a powerful leader with an unyielding capacity for military competence.[66] Being a warrior himself and a fearless man with powers, he extended the kingdom's popularity and made it the center of attention. Benin's influence expanded under his leadership, from the Niger Delta in the eastern area of the country far to the exterior of Lagos.[67] Over some years of ceaseless penetration, Lagos became a partial suzerainty of the Benin Empire in the nineteenth century as they paid tributes to the Oba of Benin.[68] Benin was known for its versatility. Its people were competent makers of ivory, and their craft ideas enabled them to become some of the most successful contemporary African woodcarvers.[69] Its brass smiths and bronze casters were exceptionally successful at making naturalistic heads, bas-reliefs, and other sculptures. [70]

One of the most important historical records of the Benin people was their well-developed architecture, which was used as an instrument against external aggressors and invaders.[71] They built their historic walls during the reign of King Ewuare, who shielded them from occasional wars mounted by external enemies. He was succeeded

FIGURE 7.6   An artist's impression of Oba of Benin https://commons.wikimedia.org/wiki/File
:Oba_of_Benin_1600s.jpg.

by Ozolua, who ascended the throne in 1481 and ruled until 1504.[72] From this period, the Benin Empire made substantial economic leaps by successfully trading resources to their potential buyers through the trade routes and joint arrangements they had masterfully established. A commercial deal in palm oil, pepper, and ivory created a pleasant relationship with their Dutch and Portuguese allies from whom they recorded massive patronage.[73]

Also, the Benin Empire profited maximally from the slave trade as they used their military might to increase the number of slaves in their custody, whom they exchanged with their business associates, the European traders.[74] The empire's emasculation came from familiar experiences. Princes and others developed an interest in power, igniting internal complications. Benin fell to the British in the nineteenth century.[75]

The Asante Empire

Extant literature establishes that Asante came into existence in the eighteenth century and successfully traded with neighboring states.[76] The geographical reach of the Asante started from modern-day Ghana, and it extended from there to the present Comeo River on their western boundaries and to current Togo on their eastern side. Interestingly, the development of the Asante Empire was linked to the time when the Europeans were already setting out for their imperialist voyages targeted at exploiting African resources. Therefore, it is a matter of coincidence that they knew that the region had a large deposit of gold, which could be traded to boost the European economy or give them maximum gain. It became evident that the empire's transformation during this period reflected their flexibility or openness to the European business associates who made incredible efforts to partner with them to benefit maximally from their natural resources. Trading went on unhindered for years under the control of the Asante[77] (Figure 7.7).

However, the situation changed drastically with the ascension of Osei Tutu, the Asantehene or paramount king. He used his political experience and knowledge to harmonize the Akan-speaking people to pursue their collective agenda against the seemingly tireless explorers from different geographical settings.[78] In around the 1670s, he had the opportunity for unification because he was singularly instrumental in dislocating nearby settlers who had posed a significant threat to his people.[79] Immediately after gaining the confidence of his people, expressed in their unanimous decision to crown him the king, he started by relocating their central government to Kumasi. From here, political authority and activities were distributed to the subregions. He introduced a royal stool that symbolized their ancestral authority and lineage, which became cardinal to the installation of kings and rulers, even after his demise.[80] The Asante Empire was a success for its immediate commercial transformation, and the people under its suzerainty did not doubt its power (Figure 7.8).

Gold was important as the most profitable economic item of trade, but the demand for slaves became stronger.[81] The demand for slaves was high, forcing them to consider engaging in the business to reap more benefits from the Atlantic market.[82] The arrival of the British and Dutch in the early eighteenth century reconfigured their market behavior as the people were now also involved in raiding slaves to enhance their economic opportunities. The rulers lacked access to adequate military weapons to defend themselves against their enemies, thus exchanging slaves for firearms and other weapons

FIGURE 7.7 An artist's impression of Asantehene figure, Asante people, Kingdom of Asante, Ghana https://commons.m.wikimedia.org/wiki/File:Asantehene_figure,_Asante_people,_Kingdom_of_Ashanti_-_Naturhistorisches_Museum_N%C3%BCrnberg_-_Nuremberg,_Germany_-_DSC03984.jpg.

from their European collaborators. Several kings ascended the throne and substantially contributed to expanding the empire.[83] The Asante continued to challenge and engage Europeans from time to time. At the conquest of Elmina in 1869, they realized they needed a more sophisticated approach to combat their existential threat, the British.[84]

The Dahomey Empire

Another great empire was Dahomey, which came into existence in the early seventeenth century and did not make many historical leaps until the succeeding century.[85] Some oral traditions established that the beginning of the empire was instigated by three brothers who contested the kingdom of Allada. Subsequently, one winner emerged and displaced the other two, who predictably ran for their safety. However, fleeing did not mean they reneged on their expansionist idea or intention. They alternatively established some settlements, one of which is identified as Porto-Novo,[86] and the other is called the

INTÉRIEUR D'UN KEST (cour de case).   Page 163.

FIGURE 7.8   An artist's impression of an Asante Compound, Ghana. https://commons.wikimedia.org/wiki/File:Bonnat_Aschantidorf.jpg.

kingdom of Abomey,[87] which incidentally would become the major centrifugal force in the creation of the Dahomey Empire itself. Although the one who created the latter was not as powerful as the neighboring kingdoms or empires, their continuous payment of tributes to the Oyo Empire indicated their comparatively weaker military prowess. Do-Aklin became helplessly submissive and subservient, devising schemes by which he would excuse his kingdom from Oyo's intractable dominance.[88]

However, the political tide changed with a series of events, including but not limited to the ascension of his grandson, Wegbaja, who immediately galvanized the people's existing goodwill, which he used to create a strong military front capable of challenging external aggressors.[89] In very quick succession, the lines of kings taking over increased, with each of them making significant contributions to the advancement of their political sovereignty and the attainment of autonomy devoid of tributes to surrounding enemies. It reached an important point where they achieved an unprecedented leap. This happened during the reign of Agaja, who ascended the throne in 1708 and immediately made significant progress. He made strenuous efforts to conquer Allada in 1724,[90] and three years later he also brought Whydah under his reign. The importance of these places can be underscored by the fact that European slave traders had already converted them into economic centers with military support (Figure 7.9).

The successful capture of these areas allowed the king to establish greater control.[91] The central state was called Dahomey, and it had provinces like Abomey, Allada, and

KING OF DAHOMEY GUARD

FIGURE 7.9 King of Dahomey Guard https://www.gettyimages.co.uk/detail/illustration/king
-of-dahomey-guard-royalty-free-illustration/1152439835?phrase=King%20of
%20Dahomey%20Guard%20&adppopup=true.

Whydah, which were all created by ancestral lineages under different intentions and
motivations. However, the expansionist dream was always in the thoughts of individuals who wanted to extend their economic and political power. This, therefore, led to
the advancement of the Dahomey Empire by kings, notably Tegbesu in 1732, Kpengla
in 1774, and Agonglo in 1789.[92] The kingdom was especially popular because of its
strong monarchical system. This system was different from many other states in the
region because it shared some characteristics with capitalist ethos, where the aristocrats were economically separated from the "middle class," the workforce, and the
lowly in society. The subordinated people were unable to challenge the authority of
the monarchs who ruled absolutely from the seat of power. Thus, a king was able to
consolidate his political power by making conscious efforts to capture as many slaves
as possible.[93]

Factors Responsible for the Rise of the Empires

Beyond the expression that "empires rise and fall," as the natural order of things is to
"peak and decline," there are factors that have contributed to the rise and fall of most

empires. In the case of the West African empires, some of these factors were common, while some were peculiar.

The rise of the empires (either to the west, center, or east of the region) rested on the agency of its peoples and the extent of their ability to subdue and adapt the environment to meet their needs, either as a matter of sheer survival or simple ambition. In this regard, widespread innovations in agriculture, technology, and political organization were crucial to positioning the people to take advantage of opportunities whenever and wherever they presented themselves. The Oyo Empire, for example, took advantage of its strategic location along the long-distance trade routes between the south and the Hausa states in the north (acting as middlemen), using the wealth generated to buy horses from the north, with which it built a cavalry to aid its expansion.[94] The Ghana Empire also benefited from its strategic location at the southern terminal of the trans-Saharan trade route from the north.

Another factor was the nature of the environment that the people occupied, as observed in the tendency to migrate to more economically viable locations. This determined the materials at their disposal—gold, slaves, ivory, kola nuts, leather, cotton—and, to some extent, the nature of their socioeconomic and political endeavors. This environmental influence was also evident in the skill of the people of the region as agriculturalists, pastoralists, miners, workers of gold and other valuable metals, ceramic, fabric and leather manufacturers, and, infamously, slave traders—activities that constituted a broad base for further sociopolitical advancement. In the forest areas, the Asante created a political entity that used its wealth in gold to build an impressive empire. With the army it built from the wealth generated in the sale of gold, Asante was able to conquer and subjugate its neighboring kingdoms and build a notable empire. In the savannah, similar feats were achieved by the Ghana Empire, which was famous for its gold deposits, and the Hausa States, whose trade goods spread as far as Fez (Morocco) in the north and Asante in the south.[95]

Trade was another crucial factor that contributed to the success of the vast and influential empires, and this can be said of both the savannah and the forest empires, including Ghana, Mali, Songhai, as well as Hausaland, Oyo, Benin, Asante and Dahomey. However, unlike the savannah empires, which relied chiefly on the trade across the Sahara Desert to consume its commodities—including gold and slaves—and supplied the wealth and diplomatic alliances necessary to build and maintain them, the forest areas had the trade across the Atlantic as another outlet for their commodities from the fifteenth century onward.

The importance of trade in the region across the Sahara Desert is not only evident in the fact that large states and empires rose along the routes but also in the class of professional traders that developed, particularly among the Dyula, Wangara, and Hausa. It is also pertinent to mention that beyond the value of gold and slaves, which brought much wealth to the region, trade also provided an avenue for the transfer of ideas like Islam, which came with its Arabic literacy and facilitated complex economic and political (administrative) functions.[96]

Islam was also an important factor behind the rise of states and empires. Introduced by missionaries and traders from North Africa from about the eighth century onward,[97] its impact was widely felt in the Western, Central, and Eastern Sudan, where it contributed to legal and administrative services. Of particular import, however, was the rise of Islamic revivalist movements later in the eighteenth and nineteenth centuries, which led to transformations in the socioeconomic and political institutions. In Hausaland, for instance, the Fulani jihad movement of the nineteenth century successfully brought all the major Hausa kingdoms under one Islamic Caliphate, with a central government at Sokoto. In this area, as in other forest areas where Islam held some sway, the faith (in whatever forms it was practiced) provided some basis for a political organization.

In summary, the factors responsible for the rise of empires (with reference to our areas of interest) can be listed as the environment, successful agriculture, trade, local agency, control of important trade routes, the conquest and establishment of tributary relationships, and the introduction of Islam.

Factors Responsible for the Fall of Empires

Many of the factors responsible for the collapse of the empires included internal cohesion problems, the emergence of weak (or less ambitious) rulers, over-expansion of territories, attacks from other states, and a decline in trade opportunities. In Ghana, apart from the cohesion challenges (internal wrangling among the ruling class), foreign invasion, and other challenges like over-expansion, the empire grew to become very expansive and increasingly difficult to administer effectively. However, over-expansion was not the biggest blow the empire suffered, as its final fall came from invasions from its Almoravid trade partners and Susu detractors in the eleventh century, which sacked the capital at Kumbi Saleh.[98]

In the case of the Mali Empire, it suffered rebellions from its vassal states—those of the Wollof, Tuareg, and Mossi—who took advantage of weak rulers and the loose administrative presence in the outlying regions of the empire—owing to its expansive size[99]—to strike out on their own. In this regard, the biggest blow to the empire was the loss of two of its important market cities, Timbuktu and Walata. As for Songhai, the most significant factor behind its decline was an attack from the Sultan of Morocco, Ahmad al-Mansur, who invaded the empire in 1591.[100]

Coming to the empires of the Central and Eastern Sudan, Kanem-Borno and the Sokoto Caliphate continued to thrive until the beginning of the twentieth century when they succumbed to pressures from the European influences coming from the Atlantic coast. Initially, these empires withstood the pressures of the trans-Atlantic trade as it continued into the twentieth century, notwithstanding the diversion of some of its traffic to the south. Hausaland fared relatively well, considering it had already established extensive trade relations down to the coast. However, these empires eventually fell in the battle against European conquest in the early years of the twentieth century.[101]

The forest empires of Oyo, Asante, Benin, and Dahomey suffered a decline for varying reasons, including colonial annexation. In Oyo, internal wrangling combined with provincial contests and attacks from jihadist elements from Ilorin eventually led to the decline and fall of the empire in the nineteenth century.[102] In Dahomey, it was a combination of the abolition of the slave trade, its main source of wealth, and the eventual colonial annexation of the territory. The Asante and Benin Empires were also afflicted by similar circumstances of European conquest.

The Significance of the Empires

As expansive political dominions made up of a centralized system of government with a cluster of outlying provincial regions, an empire represented the apex of pre-modern political organization and the height of economic development. The presence of empires in West Africa speaks to the social, economic, and political sophistication of the region's peoples, and is a sign of sociopolitical coming of age. For the people of West Africa, these empires brought order and stability.[103] Speaking of the empires' impact, Basil Davidson used the example of Kanem-Borno to reach the final conclusion:

> What the Kanuri and their allies and subjects were able to do, over a very long period and in a region of great importance, was to bring the advantages of a single system of law and order to a great many different peoples. And it was through this large empire that West Africa kept in regular touch with vital centres of civilisation beyond the Sahara, especially Egypt.[104]

DEEP DIVE

Assignment 1

Objective

The objective of this assignment is to ensure that students complete the reading of Chapter 7 and to get them to consider the elements necessary to have a politically and economically sound West African empire.

Method

Students will be expected to write a short note in response to the question.

Reading Comprehension

How are politics, economics, international relations, religions, and the environment related to having a successful empire? Provide at least two specific examples.

Assignment 2

Discussion

How do modern connotations of the word "empire" differ from traditional ones?

Objective

The objective of this assignment is to get students to consider how the concept of empires has evolved throughout history.

Methods

Students will be expected to have a group discussion (either in person or on the online discussion forum) to talk to their peers about the question. Each student would be expected to create a post and respond to at least one other student. If this were to take place in person, then it would simply be a class-wide discussion.

Notes

1 Basil Davidson, *A History of West Africa 1000–1800* (England: Longman, 1985), 7.
2 Outside archaeological findings were the (early) accounts provided by European classical historians like Herodotus, the Elder Pliny, Manetheon, and Strabo; and their Arab counterparts from the medieval period such as al-Masudi, al-Bakri, Ibn Battuta and others. See John D. Fage, "The Development of African Historiography," in *General History of Africa* 1, ed. Joseph Ki-Zebro (Paris:UNESCO, 1981), 26–27.
3 Anthony G. Hopkins, *An Economic History of West Africa* (New York: Routledge, 2020), 55.
4 Davidson, *A History of West Africa*, 9.
5 Davidson, *A History of West Africa*, 68.
6 Davidson, *A History of West Africa*, 28.
7 Patrick J. Munson, "Archaeology and the Prehistoric Origins of the Ghana Empire," *The Journal of African History* 21, no. 4 (1980): 457–466.
8 Robert Cornevin, "Ghana," in *Encyclopaedia of Islam* Vol. 2 (2nd ed.), eds. Bernard Lewis, Charles Pellat and Joseph Schacht (Leiden: Brill, 1965), 1001–1002.
9 A. J. H. Goodwin, "The Medieval Empire of Ghana," *The South African Archaeological Bulletin* 12, no. 47 (1957): 108–112.
10 John Reader, *Africa: A Biography of the Continent* (New York: Vintage Books, 1999), 286.
11 Robert Z. Cohen, *Discovering the Empire of Ghana* (New York: The Rosen Publishing Group, 2014).
12 Cohen, *Discovering the Empire*, 6.
13 Desmond Clark, ed., *The Cambridge History of Africa*, Vol. 1 (Cambridge: Cambridge University Press, 2001).
14 Nehemia Levtzion, *Ancient Ghana and Mali* (London: Methuen and Company, 1973).
15 David C. Conrad, *Empires of Medieval West Africa* (New York: Chelsea House Publishers, 2010), 17.
16 Cheik Anta Diop, *Precolonial Black Africa* (Connecticut: Lawrence Hill & Company, 1987).
17 Nawal M. Bell, "The Age of Mansa Musa of Mali: Problems in Succession and Chronology," *The International Journal of African Historical Studies* 5, no. 2 (1972): 221–234.
18 Michael Gomez, *African Dominion: A New History of Empire in Early and Medieval West Africa* (Princeton: Princeton University Press, 2018), 92–143.
19 James P. Oliver, *Mansa Musa and the Empire of Mali* (California: CreateSpace Independent, 2013).
20 Ralph Austen, ed., *In Search of Sunjata: The Mande Oral Epic as History, Literature and Performance* (Indiana: Indiana University Press, 1999).
21 Diop, *Precolonial Black Africa*.
22 Jan Jansen, "In Defense of Mali's Gold: The Political and Military Organization of the Northern Upper Niger, c. 1650–c. 1850," *Journal of West African History* 1, no. 1 (2015): 1–36.
23 M. Ly-Tall, "The Decline of the Mali Empire," in *Africa from the Twelfth to the Sixteenth Century*, ed. D. T. Niane (Paris: UNESCO, 1984).
24 Sékéné M. Cissoko, "The Songhay from the 12th to the 16th Century," in *General History of Africa*, 4, ed. D. T. Niane (Paris: UNESCO, 1984), 187–210.
25 Cissoko, "The Songhay," 187–210.
26 Francis Fukuyama, *Political Order and Political Decay* (London: Library of Congress Cataloging-in-Publication, 2014).
27 Nehemia Levtzion, "The Hegemony of Songhay," in *Cambridge History of Africa*, 3, ed. Roland Oliver (London: Cambridge University Press, 1977), 415–462.
28 Julianna Tesfu, "Songhai Empire (ca. 1375–1591)," *Black Past*, June 29, 2008, https://www.blackpast.org/global-african-history/songhai-empire-ca-1375-1591/.
29 Elias N. Saad, *Social History of Timbuktu: The Role of Muslim Scholars and Notables 1400–1900* (Cambridge: Cambridge University Press, 1983), 41–45.
30 Davidson, *A History of West Africa*, 28.
31 Ralph A. Austen, *Trans Saharan Africa in World History* (New York: Oxford University Press, 2010), 62.

32 Dierk Lange, "An Introduction to the History of Kanem-Borno: The Prologue of the Dīwān," *Bornu Museum Society Newsletter* 76, no. 84 (2010): 79–103.

33 Bawuro Barkindo, "The Early States of the Central Sudan: Kanem, Borno and some of their Neighbours to c. 1500 AD," in *History of West Africa I*, eds. Jacob F. A. Ajayi and Michael Crowder (Harlow and Essex: Longman, 1985), 225–254.

34 Humphrey J. Fisher, "The Eastern Maghrib and the Central Sudan," in *The Cambridge History of Africa: From c. 500 B.C. to A.D. 1050*, ed. Roland A. Oliver (Cambridge: Cambridge University Press, 1977), 288.

35 Muhammad Nur Alkali, *Kanem-Borno under the Sayfawa: A Study of the Origin, Growth, and Collapse of a Dynasty (891–1846)* (Maiduguri: University of Maiduguri, 2013).

36 Zacharias Pierri and Fr. Atta Barkindo, "Muslims in Northern Nigeria: Between Challenge and Opportunity," in *Muslim Minority-State Relations: Violence, Integration, and Policy*, ed. Robert Mason (London: Palgrave Macmillan, 2016), 135.

37 Muhammad Nur Alkali, "Kanem Borno Under the Sayfawa Dynasty: A Study of Origin, Growth and Collapse of Dynasty" (Ph.D. diss., Ahmadu Bello University, Zaria, 1978).

38 John Wright, "Kanem: Slavery and Trans-Saharan Trade," in *Encyclopedia of African History*, vol. 2, ed. Kevin Shillington (New York: Fitzroy Dearborn, 2005), 734–735.

39 Thomas Hodgkin, *Nigerian Perspectives: An Historical Anthology* (London: Oxford University Press, 1960).

40 Hamza M. Maishanu and Isa M. Maishanu, "The Jihad and the Formation of the Sokoto Caliphate," *Islamic Studies* 38, no. 1 (1999): 119–131.

41 Philip Koslow, *Kanem-Borno: 1,000 Years of Splendor* (New York: Chelsea House Publishers, 1995).

42 Ira M. Lapidus, *A History of Islamic Societies*, 3rd ed. (New York: Cambridge University Press, 2014), 458–459.

43 Mahdi Adamu, *The Major Landmarks in the History of Hausaland* (Sokoto: Central Coordinating Committee for University Inaugural Lectures and Seminars, 2010).

44 Adamu, *The Major Landmarks*.

45 Mahdi Adamu, *The Hausa Factor in West African History* (Zaria: Ahmadu Bello University Press, 1978).

46 Frank A. Salamone, *The Hausa of Nigeria* (Maryland: University Press of America, 2010).

47 Salamone, *The Hausa of Nigeria*.

48 Ahmad M. Gada, *A Short History of Early Islamic Scholarship in Hausaland* (Sokoto: Usmano Danfodiyo University, 2010).

49 Hopkins, *An Economic History of West Africa*, 64.

50 Robin Law, "A West African Cavalry State: The Kingdom of Oyo," *The Journal of African History* 16, no. 1 (1975): 1–15.

51 Law, "A West African Cavalry State."

52 Julius Adekunle, *Politics and Society in Nigeria's Middlebelt: Borgu and the Emergence of a Political Identity* (New Jersey: Africa World Press, 2004), 207–230.

53 Idris Sha'aba Jimada, *The Nupe and the Origins and Evolution of the Yoruba, C. 1275–1897* (Zaria: Abdullahi Smith Centre for Historical Research, 2005), 43–45.

54 Robin Law, *The Ọyọ Empire, C.1600-c.1836: A West African Imperialism in the Era of the Atlantic Slave Trade* (Oxford: Clarendon Press, 1977).

55 Islam Ali, "Gender Equality and Political Participation: A Review of 2003 Nigerian Election," in *Studies in World Affairs*, Vol. 1, ed. Kulwant R. Gupta (New Delhi: Atlantic Publishers & Distributors, 2006), 101.

56 Samuel Johnson, *The History of the Yorubas from the Earliest of Times to the Beginning of the British Protectorate* (Lagos: CMS, 1921), 161.

57 Femi J. A. Adegbulu, "Oyo from the Sixteenth to the Nineteenth Century: A Study in External Relations of An African State" (Ph.D. diss., University of Lagos, 2005).

58 Robin Law, "Making Sense of a Traditional Narrative: Political Disintegration in the Kingdom of Oyo," *Cahiers d'études africaines* 22, nos. 87–88 (1982): 387–401.

59 Peter Morton-Williams, "The Influence of Habitat and Trade on the Polities of Oyo and Ashanti," in *Man in Africa*, eds. Mary Douglas and Phyllis M. Kaberry (London: Tavistock Publications, 1969), 79–98.

60 David D. Laitin, *Hegemony and Culture: Politics and Religious Change among the Yoruba* (Chicago: University of Chicago Press, 1986), 113.

61 Joseph A. Atanda, "The Fall of the Old Oyǫ Empire: A Re-consideration of its Cause," *Journal of the Historical Society of Nigeria* 5, no. 4 (1971): 477–490.

62 Dmitri M. Bondarenko, "The Benin Kingdom (13th-19th Centuries) as a Megacommunity," *Social Evolution & History* 14, no. 2 (2015): 46–76.

63 Jacob U. Egharevba, *A Short History of Benin* (Ibadan: Ibadan University Press, 1968).

64 Egharevba, *A Short History of Benin.*

65 Goke A. Akinola, "The Origin of the Eweka Dynasty of Benin: A Study in the Use and Abuse of Oral Traditions," *Journal of the Historical Society of Nigeria* 8, no. 3 (1976): 21–36.

66 Stefan Eisenhofer and Jacob Egharevba, "The Origins of the Benin Kingship in the Works of Jacob Egharevba," *History in Africa* 22 (1995): 141–163.

67 Robert E. Bradbury, "Patrimonialism and Gerontocracy in Benin Political Culture," in *Man in Africa*, eds. Mary Douglas and Phyllis M. Kaberry (London: Tavistock, 1969), 17–36.

68 Bashir O. Animashaun, "Benin Imperialism and the Transformation of Idejo Chieftaincy Institution in Lagos, 1603–1850," *Journal of the Historical Society of Nigeria* 25 (2016): 37–52.

69 Philip J. C. Dark, *An Introduction to Benin Art and Technology* (Oxford: Clarendon Press, 1973).

70 Frank Willett, Ben Torsney and Mark Ritchie, "Composition and Style: An Examination of the Benin 'Bronze' Heads," *African Arts* 27, no. 3 (1994): 61–67.

71 Joseph Nevadomsky, Natalie Lawson and Ken Hazlett, "An Ethnographic and Space Syntax Analysis of Benin Kingdom Nobility Architecture," *African Archaeological Review* 31 (2014): 59–85.

72 Robert E. Bradbury, *The Benin Kingdom and the Edo Speaking Peoples of South-Western Nigeria* (London: Routledge, 1957).

73 Ebiuwa Aisien and Felix O. U. Oriakhi, "Great Benin On The World Stage: Re-Assessing Portugal-Benin Diplomacy in the 15th and 16th Centuries," *IOSR Journal of Humanities and Social Science* 11, no. 1 (2013): 107–115.

74 Philip A. Igbafe, "Slavery and Emancipation in Benin, 1897–1945," *The Journal of African History* 16, no. 3 (1975): 409–429.

75 Philip A. Igbafe, "The Fall of Benin: A Reassessment," *The Journal of African History* 11, no. 3 (1970): 385–400.

76 Ivor Wilks, *Asante in the Nineteenth Century: The Structure and Evolution of a Political Order* (Cambridge: Cambridge University Press, 1989).

77 Thomas C. McCaskie, *State and Society in Pre-colonial Asante* (Cambridge: Cambridge University Press, 2003).

78 Kwame Y. Daaku, *Osei Tutu of Asante* (London: Heinemann Educational, 1976).

79 John K. Fynn, *Asante and its Neighbours 1700–1807* (Evanston: Northwestern University Press, 1971).

80 Ivor Wilks, "The Golden Stool and the Elephant Tail: An Essay on Wealth in Asante," *Research in Economic Anthropology* 2 (1979): 1–36.

81 Kwame Arhin, "Trade, Accumulation and the State in Asante in the Nineteenth Century," *Africa* 60, no. 4 (1990): 524–537.

82 Agnes A. Aidoo, "Order and Conflict in the Asante Empire: A Study in Interest Group Relations," *African Studies Review* 20, no. 1 (1977): 12.

83 Margaret Priestley and Ivor Wilks, "The Ashanti Kings in the Eighteenth Century. A Revised Chronology," *The Journal of African History* 1, no. 1 (1960): 83–96.

84 Robert B. Edgerton, *The Fall of the Asante Empire: The Hundred-year War for Africa's Gold Coast* (New York: The Free Press, 1995).

85 Melville J. Herskovits, *Dahomey: An Ancient West African Kingdom* (Evanston: Northwestern University Press, 1967).

86 Stuart Butler, *Benin* (England: Bradt Travel Guides, 2019), 137.

87 Sheila S. Walker, "The History of an African Kingdom in Symbols," *Current Bibliography on African Affairs* 9, no. 2 (1976): 130–139.

88 Natalie Sandomirsky, "Dahomey: Eighteenth Century," in *Encyclopedia of African History*, ed. Kevin Shillington (New York: Fitzroy Dearborn, 2005), 333–334.

89 Elizabeth M. Halcrow, *Canes and Chains: A Study of Sugar and Slavery* (Oxford: Heinemann Educational Publishing, 1982).
90 Isaac A. Akinjogbin, "Agaja and the Conquest of the Coastal Aja States 1724–30," *Journal of the Historical Society of Nigeria* 2, no. 4 (1963): 545–566.
91 Dosu Alfonse, *Benin Republic and Dahomey Kingdom: History of Dahomey, Queen Mother, and the Ruling Environment* (South Carolina: CreateSpace, 2017).
92 Alfonse, *Benin Republic, and Dahomey.*
93 Patrick Manning, *Slavery, Colonialism and Economic Growth in Dahomey, 1640–1960* (Cambridge: Cambridge University Press, 2004).
94 Davidson, *A History of West Africa 1000–1800*, 66.
95 Hopkins, *An Economic History of West Africa*, 94.
96 Austen, ed., *Trans Saharan Africa in World History*, 76.
97 Basil Davidson, *A History of West Africa* (England: Longman, 1977), 36.
98 Michael A. Gomez, *African Dominion: A New History of Empire in Early and Medieval West Africa* (New Jersey: Princeton University Press, 2018), 41–68.
99 Austen, ed., *Trans Saharan Africa in World History*, 57.
100 Austen, ed., *Trans Saharan Africa in World History*, 58.
101 Toyin Falola and Matthew M. Heaton, *A History of Nigeria* (New York: Cambridge University Press, 2008), 106.
102 Falola and Heaton, *A History of Nigeria*, 74.
103 Gomez, *African Dominion*, 68.
104 Davidson, *A History of West Africa 1000–1800*, 105.

8

DOMESTIC ECONOMIES

Introduction

West Africa boasts of an extensive history of human habitation—going back five thousand years to (at least) the Late Stone Age (LSA)—as evidenced by related archaeological finds in the area.[1] Famed for its environmental encumbrances, the region is marked by a geographical diversity that not only features some moderate and extreme climatic and topographical conditions but also, in the course of many centuries, became the basis for the emergence of a multiplicity of societies/cultures in the area. Naturally, social evolution in West Africa—as in other regions of the globe—was significantly influenced by the nature of the area's geography, which comprises several belts of varying land and climate that can be broadly classified into two contrasting environments: forest (Guinea) and savannah (Central and Western Sudan), with other (sea and Sahara) zones at both extremes.[2] This marked ecological disparity between the forest and savannah zones of West Africa was to have far-reaching implications on the nature of political and economic developments in the region, most significant amongst which is (arguably) the regional division of labor it encouraged.[3]

Marked by an abundance of rain, dense vegetation, uneven terrain, and a plethora of disease-carrying vectors like the mosquito and tsetse fly, the Guinea environment placed restrictions on a spectrum of social and economic activity, proving relatively less suitable to support large populations. Owing mostly to the tsetse fly menace, the forest economy was centered on agricultural production.[4] However, notwithstanding the challenges—including communication and transportation difficulties owing to rough/uneven terrain, soils frequently lacking in nutrients (especially phosphorous), meager labor reserves, and the menace of tsetse fly and mosquitoes—to social and economic development posed by these environmental encumbrances, the inhabitants of the forest region, over time, adapted their environment and utilized forest resources to meet their needs, which resulted in the development of regional staples (forest commodities).[5] In situations where the available resources in the environment could not provide enough

DOI: 10.4324/9781003198260-10

sustenance, more resources were sourced via trade, either within the forest vicinity or outside the savanna regions (Figure 8.1).

With lesser rainfall and relatively sparse vegetation, the savannah—characterized by long stretches of grasslands and water bodies like the Rivers Niger, Senegal, and Gambia, whose courses aided transportation and communication—was the locus of a concentration of populations, pooling together to take advantage of an open area that was also relatively free of the mosquito and tsetse fly hazard.[6] Like their counterparts in the forest zones, the inhabitants of this area were mostly agriculturalists who produced (mainly grain) crops that were best suited to their environment. Outside agriculture, which was practiced across geographical divisions, the geographical milieu of the savannah also encouraged long-distance trading and extensive livestock production. The products from this were combined with the mining of iron, gold, and salt to create an economic mainstay that supported local populations in intra-regional trade and supplied international demands northwards to North Africa, the Middle East, Asia, and Europe.

Acknowledging the role of geography in the development and structure of West Africa's domestic economy is not to infer the immutability of the environment or a lack of agency amongst the regions' peoples. In the course of their interaction with the environment, the latter was much transformed as it influenced the day-to-day activity of populations. Areas once dense and inhospitable became locations of expansive settlements engaged in more remarkable socioeconomic activities than were previously possible. Forests were cleared and new patterns of cultivation and migration developed

FIGURE 8.1   (Gambia) Wallia Creek at the Senegal River, Nyani Kingdom https://commons
.wikimedia.org/wiki/File:GRAY(1825)_p106_(GAMBIA)_NYANI_KINGDOM,
_Wallia_Creek_at_the_Senegal_River,_a_caine_Bridge_over_the_creek.jpg.

to accommodate expanding populations.[7] This way, the frontiers of the savannah were extended into erstwhile forest areas, resulting in regional overlaps (where cereal and root crops were jointly produced) and local variations within the two main regions.[8] Thus, the domestic economy of West Africa featured regional variations in commodity production, which largely reflected the physical requirements of the crops and the environmental particularities of the various geographical zones. With this, a symbiotic relationship developed between the geographically disparate regions, which went a long way in serving the dietary needs of local populations, as well as offering opportunities for trade in "regional goods" within and outside West Africa.

Factors of Production

As with many other studies carried out into the internal economic activities of peoples and regions elsewhere around the globe, the subject of West Africa's domestic economy has, as a matter of unspoken intellectual convention, been approached from the viewpoint of progress or decline, using Western originated economic concepts, and done mostly in comparison to perceived superior Western examples. Nonetheless, except for the obnoxious predisposition elected by many an earlier researcher—from this Eurocentric tradition—to the object of their study, which has yielded many unrepresentative narratives, the option of a comparative study of periods and experiences has proven useful in demonstrating chronology (especially in non-literate societies), and the inadequacies of foreign concepts and theories do not eliminate their potential in studying the West African milieu if judiciously utilized. In that regard, the concept of factors of production will be applied here to explain socioeconomic experiences in West Africa—conscious of their limitations as ideas, which in the precolonial period, had little bearing on local sensibilities as in the areas of their fabrication—to provide some structure and direction to what would have been an amorphous and aimless account of events.

By the first century AD, when most West African communities had established an agricultural and commercial economy, three factors of production and exchange—land, labor, and capital—had become distinct. The most important was the land, which was jointly owned, although administered by the lineages, community leaders, or rulers who defended and upheld the people's rights to their lands, imposing bylaws and norms that governed land organization for economic activities.[9] Though these laws differed from region to region, they also had some features in common.

Furthermore, despite the infiltration of Islamic and Western ideas, corporate land ownership remained unthreatened throughout most of the precolonial period. Though there were areas with poor soil conditions or not enough land to accommodate large populations, as on the edges of the Sahara, land was generally not scarce, and all descent groups in the community had land rights.[10] As long as they were members of a descent group, everyone had the right to use the land for any legitimate economic activity. These rights were constant and unaffected, except during external invasion. However, visitors could also have access to land after meeting certain criteria, including giving symbolic gifts such as nuts and livestock or getting land from their hosts or the community. Whether in cash or material form, these gifts were not considered payment for the land but rather as confirmation that the guests honored the rights of their hosts who had granted them the land to use.[11] For example, among some groups, the visitor would work for the ruler or the leader of the descent group who gave them the land. Eventually, the land may become the permanent property of the visitor, who could then pass it on to their children.

Almost every community that practiced traditional religions revered the land and regarded the earth as the guardian of public morality and the source of human and agricultural vitality. They believed that land belonged to the living and the unborn offspring who could only live and survive in the world if there was land, as well as to the ancestors whose wrath may be incurred if the land were sold. Thus, members of the descent group, the individuals, and the outsiders were forbidden from alienating the land, a rule backed up by strong religious beliefs and consequences.[12]

Capital, another factor of production, was organized on an individual basis by those who needed it for economic or other reasons. It was funded through gifts, loans, savings, and earnings from the sales of goods. Many precolonial states had indigenous credit and banking institutions that were barely acknowledged.[13] In many communities, they had the cooperative savings clubs where members agreed on how much money to save over a set period, including rules and regulations that would govern loans and withdrawals.[14] Among the Yoruba existed small credit associations known as the *esusu*, which were mainly organizations of kinsmen or groups of friends providing credit services to members.[15] Moreover, despite religious rules that forbade the operations of money lenders, they existed in many communities.

Another sector of the domestic economy where the need for capital was greatly felt was trade. In existence was a "commercial capital market which served economic needs at local and inter-regional levels."[16] Locally, poorer members of society were known to have been indebted to wealthier ones, for which pawning was adopted as a system of guaranteeing payment. Also, at the inter-regional levels, professional traders were often in need of credit facilities to finance their economic activities, mainly because initial investments tended to be substantial while returns were delayed owing to complexities in the organization of trade in the period. In such instances, commercial capital was obtained either from fellow merchants or specialized money lenders. Such credit arrangements involved witnesses and guarantors depositing bonds or collateral in the form of land, houses, or livestock.[17]

The last factor of production was labor, centered on the extended family unit as the main economic entity and provider of labor.[18] People engaged their family members on the land to provide labor for their intended economic activities, making the job competent, effective, productive, cost-effective, and well-organized. Those usually involved in this engagement on the land were the head of the family, his wife or wives, his unmarried children, and other relatives living with him.[19] He would not pay the laborers any wages, but he would be fully responsible for their basic needs, including food, clothing, and shelter. And because the family size largely determined the volume of goods that could be produced, men married many wives and had lots of children, thus making large families the norm in most African communities.

However, there were alternative methods of securing more labor, suggesting that the African labor supply was more diverse than generally assumed. The cooperative groups employed able-bodied men (and sometimes women) within a community for specific tasks, and though the recipients of their services may not pay wages, they provided food and drink for the laborers. Peonage, or the patron-client relationship, was another source of labor supply. In this, a debtor would work for his lender or allow his son or relative to do so until the loan was paid off,[20] and the collateral security and interest on the loan were represented by labor. Among the Kanuri, there was a patron-client relationship between the nobility and the commoners.[21]

Also, out of the desire to solve the challenge of socioeconomic inequalities and the shortage of a labor market in a booming economy, domestic slavery started in precolonial communities.[22] The slaves provided the chiefs, warriors, and wealthy traders with labor for different economic activities, especially those considered odious by the freeborn. To ensure their loyalty and maximize their labor, slaves were often integrated into their owners' families and, thus, into the community. They were usually promised redemption as soon as they could buy their freedom, which was difficult because many slaves had little or no time to work for themselves. In most centralized states, using slaves on a large scale gave rise to an embryonic slave mode of production, which created a few rich slave owners as entrepreneurs and slaves as the labor force.[23] This occurred in parts of West Africa during the nineteenth century, including the Sokoto Caliphate, Borno, Ibadan, and Dahomey, where rulers had large farms worked by slaves who had the right to only a small part of the harvests to keep them alive.[24]

Production of Goods and Services

Though it has not been possible to document all the significant phases, the history of agriculture has been one of monumental transformation.[25] The production system was characterized by remarkable changes and innovations, regional diversities, and complex organizations, all of which resulted in a very diverse range of goods. The sectors in the production system comprised agriculture, mining, manufacturing, and the provision of essential services. Agriculture, which included farming, animal husbandry, and fishing, was the leading sector of the economy.[26]

In the Stone Age period (c. 3m BC–5000 BC), human communities in Africa went through a very long and slow pace of economic development.[27] Progress was slowest during the Early and Middle Stone Ages (c. 3m BC–15000 BC) when the communities mainly lived a migratory life, gathering fruits and hunting wild animals with crude stone tools. From 15000 BC, which marked the beginning of the later Stone Age, improvement became more noticeable and remarkable. Climate changes led to vegetational differentiation between the grasslands and forests. By 7000 BC, human fishing communities had emerged at Baringo on Lake Turkana, Ishango on Lake Mobutu, and later among the Zambezi River at Diama in Nigeria, using the barbed harpoon, net weights, and other fishing gear. Production of surplus food led to more permanent human settlements, which changed sociopolitical structures that eventually ended in the evolution of full-fledged descent groups and succession laws.[28]

Also, human communities who inhabited the grasslands and forests continued their migratory lives as hunters and gatherers but used refined stone tools. The Gwisho hunters near the Kafue River in Zambia typified the height of this development. By 2300 BC, these hunters led a communal life and hunted with dogs, bows and arrows. Like the fishing groups, they now produced enough food for larger populations, culminating in similar sociopolitical development. The relics of the hunting and gathering of groups are the San in Southwest Africa, the pigmies in the Zaire basin, the Ndorobo of Kenya, and the Mahalbi between Chad and the Nile.[29] All these groups, except the San and the *Gorate* (Ted-Danza) hunters in northern Chad, lived harmoniously with their agricultural or pastoral neighbors.

Therefore, the evolution of human settlements and descent groups occurred before the domestication of animals and crops, both being important phases in the agricultural revolution. Between 6000 BC and 5000 BC, human communities in the Sahara, then a grassland area, kept cattle, sheep, and goats. By 5000 BC, they had begun experimenting with various crops. As barley and wheat were not ecologically suitable for the soil, new crops were domesticated in the tropical and subtropical regions north of the equator between 500 BC and 5000 BC—sorghum (guinea corn) between the Sahara and Western Sudan, pearl and finger millet in the Sahara (from where they diffused to Ethiopia and the Horn of Africa), the *ansete* (banana family) and cowpea in the Ethiopian highlands, rice in the inland delta region of the Niger river, and yam varieties and the oil palm in the forest region of West Africa.[30] The desiccation of the Sahara from about 2000 BC compelled the diffusion of some of the crops to Egypt and subtropical Africa, north of the equator. Early farming communities existed from 1100 BC to the first century AD at Dartichitt in Southern Mauritania, Karusakata and Diama in Borno, Kintampo in modern Ghana, and Jenne.

The diffusion of domesticated crops was associated with the Bantu migrations. From their homeland in the Cameroons, the Bantu migrated, in about 500 BC, north of the Zaire Forest to the Lake Victoria region, where they introduced finger millet, yams, and herded cattle and goats.[31] Another Bantu group also migrated into the forest region between Zaire and Angola and introduced yams. The Bantu migrated from these two subsidiary centers into East and South Africa, introducing crops and animals as they went. Between the first and the eighth centuries AD, bananas, cocoyam, and plantain were adopted from Asia. After the fifteenth century, cassava, maize, groundnuts, tobacco, and a variety of fruits were adopted from South America, and in the nineteenth century, cocoa was also introduced from South America.

By the first century AD, a virile agricultural system adapted to the people's environment had emerged in most parts of Africa. The agricultural year followed a regular pattern—the bush was cleared in the dry season, ridging and planting were done during the earliest rains, weeding at intervals, and harvesting. The crops grown depended largely on the suitability of the soil. The harvest, a time of plenty, was usually a season of festivities and religious ceremonies during which sacrifices were offered to the gods of fertility for good harvests. In the tropical rain forest, stable root crops, varieties of yams, melon, pumpkin, and cowpeas were cultivated, while tree crops like oil and raffia palms, kola nuts, bitter kola, locust beans, and *akee* (apple) were domesticated. In the savannah, emphasis was on cereals (rice, millet, sorghum) and cotton, indigo, and groundnuts. The introduction of Asiatic and South American crops enriched the agricultural economy.[32] Each African community integrated the crops into its domestic economy at different periods, especially as the new crops could solve the problem of food shortages because of their high yields. As a result, the introduction of crops diversified the agricultural sector, improved nutrition, facilitated the support of large populations, and reduced the risk of famine.

Irrigation, shifting cultivation, permanent cultivation, mixed cropping, and rotational bush fallow were the major cultivation systems. The decision on which system to employ usually depends on physiographical factors, the tenure system, and land availability. Shifting cultivation was the most common method as it helped to reduce the spread and danger caused by weeds and insects while also boosting the fertility of the farmland without using fertilizers. It was effective in places with sufficient land since it required the temporary abandonment of overused land to reclaim its fertility. Although the instruments utilized were simple, farming was extensive. It was highly efficient as production met local demands while a sizable surplus could be exchanged for other goods and services. More specifically, agriculture was ritualized, with sacrifices offered at the start and end of the farming calendar to pacify the gods, spirits, or forces thought to influence agricultural fertility.[33] Pastoralists who lived in grassland and savannah areas, where there were no tsetse flies that posed a threat to livestock, practiced animal husbandry. They migrated in search of water and pasture for their herds, as well as to sell and exchange their products for foodstuff with farmers for sustenance.

Another major sector in precolonial West Africa was fishing, which was done using different traps, hooks, and nets. Fishing and related activities like canoe construction, ferrying, and the maintenance of fishing equipment dominated the economy of the riverine and coastal areas.[34] Like cattle-rearers, fishers also migrated in search of fish, the availability of which depended on floods and tidal movements. For example, the Sorkawa and Bozo of the middle Niger journeyed hundreds of kilometers along the River Niger each year to fish.[35] Likewise, the Fante of Ghana periodically traveled to the west, as far as Ivory Coast, and to the east, as far as Nigeria. The fishers also engaged in trade with inland groups, bartering fish for other items. By transporting their fish from one area to another, they established links between different hinterland settlements and contributed to the spread of knowledge, ideas, and modernization. During their migrations, the fishers often established fishing settlements that subsequently evolved into large cities like Lagos, Nigeria.[36]

Likewise, hunting was an ancient occupation that was important in the region where meat was in short supply.[37] Hunters used traps, bows and arrows, clubs, and guns. Hunting expeditions were more popular during the dry season when the workload on farmlands was lighter, and the bush was dry and could be easily burnt. The occupation was mainly restricted to professionals, who were men believed to possess the necessary charms to conquer spiritual and physical obstacles.[38]

Mining and manufacturing were the second significant sectors in the production processes.[39] Among the minerals mined were iron, gold, silver, tin, salt, and copper, with the working of iron being the most prominent. Ironworking was part of a larger and integrated system of miners, smiths, and smelters. Smelters were primarily miners, although smiths who shaped the iron into various tools and implements might also be smelters. Ironworking was popular by the first millennium BC (iron was wrought in Nok about 500 BC) and, by the fourth century AD, it had spread to most parts of Africa. Iron was smelted, split into smaller sizes, and processed into cutlasses, hoes, adzes, javelins, arrows, sickles, hairpins, knives, daggers, and various types of swords, which revolutionized trade, agriculture, and warfare. Notably, the smithing process was ritualized to preserve occupational secrecy.[40]

Some other sectors that dominated the precolonial economy in Africa included gold mining, salt production, tin mining and manufacturing (processing end products from plants, animals, and other local raw materials). Gold mining in Africa began post-500 BC, but large-scale production, especially in West Africa, did not start until the seventh century AD, when North Africa, Asia, and Europe had a high demand for gold.[41] Gold was a major article of trade and, like smithing, it was dignified and profitable, and also a source of wealth for leaders in gold-producing nations like Bambouk, Noure, Lobi, and Asante, all in West Africa, the Ethiopian foothills in Eastern Sudan, and the Zimbabwean plateau below the Zambezi River.[42] Salt was produced for domestic consumption and export in the Sahelian region by mining and along the coast by boiling seawater or letting seawater evaporate in the sun.

Nigeria and Chad were two of the few tin-producing countries in precolonial Africa. Tin was discovered in shallow terrace deposits in the Jos and Bauchi plateaus in Nigeria and was normally covered by different depths of barren land known as the "overburden."[43] Pickaxes and hoes were used to manually clear the "overburden." Afterward, the tin-bearing ground was washed in a river or stream to extract raw tin, which was then smelted using an iron-like process. Tin smiths then combined the melted tin with copper or lead to make alloys used to make cooking utensils, plates, and bronze sculptures.

The production of ceramicware was an important aspect of local manufacturing activity, owing largely to its common use as household utensils, ritual vessels, and ornaments.[44] The craft was also widespread because the materials required for its production were relatively readily available, less capital intensive (as it could be managed without special equipment like the potter's wheel), and transportation was both difficult (owing to the high risk of breakages) and cumbersome. However, owing to the labor demands of farm work, in the mainly agricultural economy, pottery tended to be a part-time occupation that reached its peak during the dry seasons when labor demands on the farm were low and weather conditions were most favorable for its production (firing).[45]

In West Africa, the textile industry was one of the oldest and most extensive manufacturing activities—next perhaps only to gold and salt in importance and reach, employing a significant number of people in the production of threads, yarns, dyestuff, and cotton. At its earliest development stages, raffia and the bark of trees were used before the discovery of cotton. However, by 1000 AD, the crop (cotton) was widely grown in the region.[46] Cotton technology quickly revolutionized the weaving industry, spreading it to other cotton-producing areas.[47] One of such great centers of cotton and cloth manufacture in West Africa by the fifteenth century was Kano, touted as the "Manchester of West Africa."[48] The Kano cloth industry had a wide market both locally and internationally. Its popularity in the region depended on its distinctive qualities (based on color and pattern) and the distributive networks established by adept Hausa traders, which ensured its widespread presence as far as Morocco and Mauritania.[49]

One of the most defining features of manufacturing in precolonial Africa is that it relied primarily on local raw materials supplemented with imported products. Although the production of various goods was restricted to certain households, children from other families were occasionally recruited as apprentices and fully trained. In addition, miners and manufacturers in other areas formed themselves into highly organized guilds, while some other communities only had loose associations. Manufacturing was a more varied industry than mining. Plants, animal products, and minerals were used to make manufactured materials such as processed foods, leather, fabric, porcelain, and wood. Manufactured goods were made from plants, minerals, and animal products in the form of processed foodstuff, cloth, leather, wood, and ceramic. Leather was made by a vast number of specialists who cured, tanned, and colored animal skins used to make bags, saddles, aprons, cushions, and other products. On a part-time or full-time basis, various professions, such as physicians, masons, vocalists, diviners, barbers, drummers, and other artists, provided specialized services.

Exchange of Goods and Services

In precolonial societies, several factors contributed to and facilitated the exchange of goods and services.[50] Firstly, the surpluses had to be disposed of because the production of goods had gone above the subsistence level. Secondly, economic activities were specialized in every society, and one occupational group frequently required products from another group. For instance, artisans and farmers mutually traded their products to meet their requirements.[51] Many African communities were not self-sufficient, and physiographic factors, levels of specialization, and skill acquisition differed from state to state, thereby promoting economic interdependence. For example, the savannah area of West Africa has been classified into three separate vegetations: the Sahel to the north, Sudan in the middle, and Guinea to the south.

The tropical rain forest continues south, merging with freshwater and mangrove swamps to the coasts. The implication of this geographical variation on trade becomes clear when it is realized that some crops thrived only in certain conditions of rainfall, humidity, and soil fertility. Kola nuts and yam grew well in the forest region, but tsetse flies made pastoralism impossible. As a result, millet, upland rice, and cattle, which were the products of the savannah, had to be traded for palm products and kola nuts from the forest zone. Even within the same geographical zone, there were evident variations, such as sub-zonal specializations in hunting, fishing, and manufacturing.

Routine supply of goods and other commodities by the head of households to their members, including gifts, inheritance, bride-wealth, and payment of tributes and taxes, was probably the first non-market institution of exchange. Thus, large quantities of goods were exchanged in all communities without money and often validated an existing social relationship.[52] Exchanges based on social relations limited the flow of goods to a few people and a few areas, eventually leading to exchanges based on rudimentary market principles. For a long time in some ancient societies, exchange by barter predominated, but it resulted in imbalance and inequality in exchange and, to a great extent, restricted trade to a small area. The shortcomings of the barter system partly facilitated the development of commerce infrastructures such as currencies, markets, trading conventions, communication language(s), trade routes, and professional traders.[53]

Periodic markets attracted more people from two or more communities, had a larger volume of trade, and served as distribution centers for raw materials, processed food items, imported goods, and craft industry products (Figure 8.2).[54] They were often held at locations convenient for people in different communities to attend, and they were scheduled on different days of the week to avoid clashes and ensure maximum participation. When market days overlapped, traders went to the nearest ones or those that had special goods in which they were interested. Also, the commercial system had some common salient features. Trade operated at two main levels: internal and external. The internal or local trade operated within the community, while all towns and big villages had daily or periodic markets, which served as the local exchange point

FIGURE 8.2   Ibadan market. Author's collection.

where producers, traders, and consumers met to transact business.[55] One characteristic of these markets is that they were often sited in open spaces, with trees, stalls, or tents providing shade, close to residences of the leading members of the community.[56] Sellers of similar commodities sat in groups, making it easier for buyers to easily find the items they wanted (Figure 8.3). The markets served as a central place for artisans, barbers, and other occupational groups rendering services to their customers.[57] Singers, poets, and drummers also used marketplaces as entertainment centers and performed there, and political and judicial activities were occasionally held there.[58] Markets were also venues for rapidly disseminating information and circulating news and rumors about current happenings in society.[59] The markets were well-organized, and trading went on peacefully. This order was maintained by market authorities, trade guilds, and customary regulations that prohibited attacks on helpless market traders. Outside of the marketplaces, trading also took place in private homes of chiefs and brokers, compounds, farms, and along pathways. For example, in Muslim areas, women in purdah

FIGURE 8.3   Roadside market. Author's collection.

conducted a lot of business in their compounds. There were also itinerant traders and hawkers.

Currencies

Before the colonial period, about three types of currencies were used in commercial transactions.[60] Produce currency, the first type, was a unit of exchange based on the key products of the region. These products included slaves, cloth, cows, horses, and salt. Cows were used as a unit of exchange in parts of East Africa and salt in the Sahara and parts of North Africa. Cotton strips were used in Borno, Sudan, Senegambia, and the areas now known as Central African Republic. In the Niger-Benue area, an *agi*, a standard calabash of corn, was considered the normal value, comparable to a large manilla equivalent to the measure of five cups of salt. The second type was metal currency, which consisted of gold, iron, brass objects, and copper. Iron plates were used in Nigeria, Niger, and the Cameroons. Manilla was used along the West African Coast and gold in Asante and Western Sudan. Gold currency was either in gold dust in small bags or in coins known in West Africa as *mithgal* or *dinars*.[61]

Cowry (*cryprae moneta*), the third type of currency, was more widespread than the others.[62] Imported from the Maldives, it first reached North Africa and the Middle East before 1000 AD, from where it spread to and remained in circulation till the early twentieth century in other parts of Africa. From the sixteenth century onwards, European traders imported huge quantities of cowries to Africa, further spreading their circulation and importance.[63] The cowry had some advantages, which accounted for its wide acceptability. Its units of counting were uniform in many areas and were usually counted singly or in multiples of tens and twenties. Also, it was suitable and efficient for small transactions and could not be counterfeited (Figure 8.4).

Like modern and general-purpose currencies, precolonial currencies acted as a medium of exchange, a common measure of value, a store of wealth, and a recognized

FIGURE 8.4   Cowries, small shells used as currency for the Atlantic slave trade https://commons
.wikimedia.org/wiki/File:Mus%C3%A9e_d%27histoire_de_Nantes_-_177_-
_Cauris.jpg.

standard of deferred payment.[64] Most African currencies shared the characteristics of
a general-purpose money, contrary to the views that they were primitive and special-
purpose currencies that failed to assist liquidity and could not be exchanged for other
goods and services. The sale of many commodities in most markets was usually arrived
at by haggling.[65] The seller would fix the highest price possible, stressing the quality and
scarcity of the goods. While decrying the merchandise, the buyer would offer a very low
price. To get a good deal, the buyer must be very skillful at haggling and bargaining.
Both of them would eventually agree on a price up to 2,000 percent lower than the price
originally quoted. However, some goods such as pepper, vegetables, and drinks measured in pots, calabashes, and skin containers could have fixed prices.

External trade was operated at two levels. The first was regional, involving societies
within the same geographical region. The second was international, linking one state
with others far away. Egypt, for instance, had commercial contacts with many other
regions within Africa. The trade could also be between two or more subregions, the
trans-Saharan trade between West Africa and North Africa being an example. From
the sixteenth century onward, international trade also linked Africa with other continents, notably Asia, southern Europe, and the Americas.[66] External trade organizations called for a complex network of routes, a well-developed transport system, highly
organized merchant groups, efficient credit institutions, and languages of commerce.
Transportation by land and water was well-developed and was essentially through
human porterage, pack animals, and canoes. The trade routes linked villages and towns
in the same locality, states, and regions.[67]

The various societies also had long-distance traders who specialized in carrying goods
from one market to another. They comprised the target traders who traded beyond

their states during the dry seasons and regular traders who sold what they produced. Professional and specialized traders such as the Dyula, Hausa, and Arabs dealt in high-value goods that they did not produce on their own, and official traders transacted business on behalf of rulers. Long-distance trade was organized in caravans, some of which could involve as many as 1,000 traders with guards, porters, guides, and leaders.[68] Traveling in caravans enlivened the journey and reduced the risk of missing the routes and being attacked by marauders. It was usually a slow journey, lasting five or more hours daily, with rest and sleep in places set up along the routes. The traders paid tolls or customs duties to state officials at different borders they passed through. The amount paid depended on the state's policy, the commodities involved (slaves, cloths, and horses attracted more duties than foodstuff), and the whims and caprices of toll collectors. External trade ensured the distribution of goods between areas of surplus production and places of scarcity among states and regions. As a result, trade became an essential factor in interstate relations in Africa,[69] so much so that trade relations were often maintained even in times of war. Importantly, external trade encouraged regional specialization and consequent large-scale production of goods.[70]

Conclusion

The precolonial domestic economy was diversified and comprised agriculture, mining, manufacturing, and commerce.[71] Specialists and professionals in various fields offered essential services. Farm and industrial products were produced in large quantities, well above the subsistence level, and local and long-distance traders distributed the surpluses. The domestic economy developed over time and always responded to internal and external changes.[72] Among the internal dynamics of change were population increase, occasional technical innovations, and expansion in the market. Among the external factors were contacts with the Middle East, Europe, and America. Finally, the economy provided the necessary basis for the political system and the emergence and survival of states.

DEEP DIVE

The four factors of production are key indicators of the precolonial African economy. Identify any of the factors of production of your choice and reflect on the importance of each in the survival of precolonial communities.

Assignment 1

Objective

The objective of this assignment is to ensure that students complete the reading of Chapter 8 and that they have a full grasp of how precolonial societies developed a domestic economy that thrived on indigenous technology, intra- and inter-group trade, and modes of commercial transactions. Additionally, students will be expected to provide evidence to support the claim that West Africans had currencies used to transact commerce at the regional and international levels.

Method

Students will be expected to write a short answer in response to the question.

Reading Comprehension

What types of products were exchanged between West Africa and North Africa? Discuss the extent to which the introduction of these products in both regions enhanced the agricultural development of their respective societies.

Assignment 2

Objective

The objective of this assignment is to ensure that students complete the reading of Chapter 8 and to make them understand the extent to which the exchange of goods and services encouraged external trade and large-scale production of goods.

Method

Students will be expected to write a short note in response to the question.

Reading Comprehension

Highlight some factors that contributed to and facilitated the exchange of goods and services in precolonial West Africa. What were the major characteristics of the periodic markets that made them unique markers in West Africa's precolonial domestic economy?

Notes

1 C. T. Shaw, "The Prehistory of West Africa," in *UNESCO General History of Africa Vol. I: Methodology and African Prehistory*, ed. J. Ki-Zerbo (California: University of California Press, 1981), 613. See also Basil Davidson, *A History of West Africa 1000–1800* (England: Longman, 1977), 10–15.
2 Though the sea and Sahara fringes represented other environmental/economic contexts, the economic activities of these areas—fishery, salt production, and animal husbandry—became aspects of the two broad economies of the Guinea and savannah regions.
3 Keith Hart, *The Political Economy of West African Agriculture* (London: Cambridge University Press, 1982), 29.
4 Elizabeth Isichei, *History of West Africa Since 1800* (New York: African Publishing Company, 1977), 1.
5 These include root (manioc) crops like cocoyam, yam, and cassava, and tree crops like kola nuts, palm fruits, plantains and cocoa, which reflect the physical conditions of the region. See Anthony G. Hopkins, *An Economic History of West Africa* (New York: Routledge, 2020), 72.
6 Another source of attraction was the opportunities offered by the existence of this extensive network of communication that traversed the area—along watercourses and overland—even beyond the Sahara Desert to the Middle East.
7 Hopkins, *An Economic History of West Africa*, 57.
8 Hopkins, *An Economic History of West Africa*, 72.

9 W. J. du Plessis, "African Indigenous Land Rights in a Private Ownership Paradigm," *Potchefstroom Electronic Law Journal* 14, no. 7 (2021): 45–69.
10 Parker Shipton and Mitzi Goheen, "Introduction: Understanding African Land-Holding: Power, Wealth, and Meaning," *Africa: Journal of the International African Institute* 62, no. 3 (1992): 307–325.
11 Muhammadu M. Gwadabe, "The Administration of Land and Labour in Pre-colonial Kano," *Journal of the Historical Society of Nigeria* 19 (2010): 23–38.
12 Aphu E. Selase, Li F. Jiang and Adator S. Worlanyo, "Land Tenure System in the Pre-Colonial Era: Ghana as the Insight," *International Journal of African and Asian Studies* 14 (2015): 92.
13 Akanmu G. Adebayo, "Money, Credit, and Banking in Precolonial Africa: The Yoruba Experience," *Anthropos* 89, no. 4/6 (1994): 379–400.
14 Rowland A. Effiom, "Impact of Cooperative Societies in National Development and the Nigerian Economy," *Global Journal of Social Sciences* 13 (2014): 19–29.
15 Hopkins, *An Economic History of West Africa*, 116.
16 Hopkins, *An Economic History of West Africa*, 117.
17 Hopkins, *An Economic History of West Africa*, 117.
18 Klas Rönnbäck, *Labour and Living Standards in Pre-Colonial West Africa: The Case of the Gold Coast* (New York: Routledge, 2016).
19 Rönnbäck, *Labour and Living Standards*, 73–92.
20 Robin Law, "On Pawning and Enslavement for Debt in the Precolonial Slave Coast," in *Pawnship in Africa: Debt Bondage in Historical Perspective*, eds. Toyin Falola and Paul E. Lovejoy (Boulder: Westview Press, 1994), 53–69.
21 Esther N. Goody, "Dynamics of the Emergence of Sociocultural Institutional Practices," in *Technology, Literacy, and the Evolution of Society: Implications of the Work of Jack Goody*, eds. David R. Olson and Michael Cole (New Jersey: Lawrence Erlbaum Associates, 2006), 257.
22 Akosua A. Perbi, *A History of the Indigenous Slavery in Ghana: From the 15th to the 19th Century* (Accra: Sub-Saharan Publishers, 2004).
23 Roberta W. Kilkenny, "The Slave Mode of Production: Precolonial Dahomey," in *Modes of Production in Africa: The Pre-colonial Era*, eds. Donald Crummey and Charles. C. Stewart (Beverly Hills: Sage, 1981).
24 Paul E. Lovejoy, *Transformations in Slavery: A History of Slavery in Africa* (Cambridge: Cambridge University Press, 2000).
25 Marcel Mazoyer and Laurence Roudart, *A History of World Agriculture: From the Neolithic Age to the Current Crisis* (New York: Monthly Review Press, 2006).
26 Ellen Hillbom and Patrick Svensson, eds., *Agricultural Transformation in a Global History Perspective* (New York: Routledge, 2013).
27 Grant S. McCall and Rebecca Taylor-Perryman, "African Stone Age," in *Encyclopedia of Global Archaeology*, ed. Claire Smith (Cham: Springer, 2020).
28 Lawrence Barham and Peter Mitchell, *The First Africans: African Archaeology from the Earliest Toolmakers to most Recent Foragers* (Cambridge: Cambridge University Press, 2008).
29 Pamela R. Willoughby, *The Evolution of Modern Humans in Africa: A Comprehensive Guide* (Maryland: Altamira Press, 2007).
30 Barham and Mitchell, *The First Africans*.
31 Jia Liu, "The Impact of Bantu Migration on Agriculture in Sub-Saharan Africa," *International Journal of New Developments in Engineering and Society* 3, no. 2 (2019): 28–34.
32 Robert C. Power, Tom Güldemann, Alison Crowther and Nicole Boivin, "Asian Crop Dispersal in Africa and Late Holocene Human Adaptation to Tropical Environments," *Journal of World Prehistory* 32 (2019): 353–392.
33 Michael K. Lang, "The Role of Religion in Agriculture: Reflections from the Bamenda Grassfields of Cameroon since Pre-colonial Times," *Mgbakoigba: Journal of African Studies* 7, no. 2 (2018): 54–73.
34 Paul Opondo, "Fisheries as Heritage: Indigenous Methods of Fishing and Conservation among the Luo Fishers of Lake Victoria, Kenya," in *Conservation of Natural and Cultural*

Heritage in Kenya: A Cross-Disciplinary Approach, eds. Anne-Marie Deisser and Mugwima Njuguna (London: University College London, 2016), 200–211.

35 Hopkins, *An Economic History of West Africa*, 43.
36 Pierre Failler and Gianluca Ferraro, "Fishermen Migration in Africa: A Historical Perspective and some Introductory Notes," *African Identities* 19, no. 3 (2021): 245–252.
37 Susan Kent, ed., *Farmers as Hunters: The Implications of Sedentism* (Cambridge: Cambridge University Press, 1989).
38 Kathryn M. de Luna, "Hunting Reputations: Talent, Individuals, and Community in Precolonial South Central Africa," *The Journal of African History* 53, no. 3 (2012): 279–299.
39 Siyan Oyeweso, "Mining and Manufacturing in Pre-Colonial West Africa," *Economic History Review* 1, no. 1 (1993): 16–25.
40 Onwuka N. Njoku, "Magic, Religion and Iron Technology in Precolonial North-Western Igboland," *Journal of Religion in Africa* 21, no. 3 (1991): 202.
41 Mark Cartwright, "The Gold Trade of Ancient & Medieval West Africa," *World History Encyclopedia*, May 13, 2019, https://www.worldhistory.org/article/1383/the-gold-trade-of -ancient--medieval-west-africa/.
42 C. Liesegang, "Gold Mining at the Coast of Guinea in Old Times and the First German Miners in the Colony Gross-Friedrichsburg of the Brandenburg-Prussians," *Koloniale Rundschau* 34, no. 2 (1943): 57–72.
43 David Tambo, "The Pre-colonial Tin Industry in Northern Nigeria," *Jos Oral History and Literature Texts* 2 (1981): 1–15.
44 Anne Mayor, "Ceramic Traditions and Ethnicity in the Niger Bend, West Africa," *Journal of Archaeological, Ethnographic and Experimental Studies* 2, no. 1 (2010): 5–48.
45 Hopkins, *An Economic History of West Africa*, 96.
46 Davidson, *A History of West Africa 1000–1800*, 152.
47 Colleen E. Kriger, "Mapping the History of Cotton Textile Production in Precolonial West Africa," *African Economic History* no. 33 (2005): 87–116.
48 Ghyslaine Lydon, *On Trans-Saharan Trails: Islamic Law, Trade Networks and Cross-Cultural Exchange in Nineteenth Century Western Africa* (New York: Cambridge University Press, 2008), 77.
49 Davidson, *A History of West Africa 1000–1800*, 152.
50 Ikechukwu R. Amadi, "Society, Production and Distribution in Precolonial Southeastern Nigeria," *Africa: Rivista trimestrale di studi e documentazione dell'Istituto italiano per l'Africa e l'Oriente* 55, no. 3 (2000): 398–406.
51 Paulo F. de Moraes Farias, "Silent Trade: Myth and Historical Evidence," *History in Africa* 1 (1974): 9–24.
52 Lars Sundström, *The Exchange Economy of Pre-Colonial Tropical Africa* (London: C. Hurst, 1974).
53 Caroline Humphrey, "Barter and Economic Disintegration," *Man* 20, no. 1 (1985): 48–72.
54 Polly Hill, "Notes on Traditional Market Authority and Market Periodicity in West Africa," *The Journal of African History* 7, no. 2 (1966): 295–311.
55 B. W. Hodder, "Rural Periodic Day Markets in Part of Yorubaland," *Transactions of the Institute of British Geographers* 29 (1961): 149–159.
56 B. W. Hodder, "The Yoruba Rural Market," in *Markets in Africa*, eds. Paul Bohannan and George Dalton (Evanston: Northwestern University Press, 1965).
57 Hodder, *"The Yoruba Rural Market."*
58 Adeyinka T. Ajayi, "Dynamics of Trade and Market Management in Pre-Colonial West Africa: A Survey Research in Indigenous Economy," *American Journal of Humanities and Social Sciences Research* 2, no. 6 (2018): 53–58.
59 Olufemi B. Olaoba and Oluranti E. Ojo, "Influence of British Economic Activities on Lagos Traditional Markets, 1900–1960," *Journal of the Historical Society of Nigeria* 23 (2014): 111–130.
60 Okafor O. Samuel, "The Colonialists and Indigenous Exchange Currency: Tracing the Genesis of Socioeconomic Woes in Postcolonial Nigeria," *International Journal of Sustainable Development and World Policy* 8, no. 1 (2019): 37–50.

61 Jan S. Hogendorn and Henry A. Gemery, "Continuity in West African Monetary History? An Outline of Monetary Development," *African Economic History* 17 (1988): 127–146.

62 Jan Hogendorn and Marion Johnson, *The Shell Money of the Slave Trade* (Cambridge: Cambridge University Press, 1986).

63 Toby Green, *A Fistful of Shells: West Africa from the Rise of the Slave Trade to the Age of Revolution* (Chicago: University of Chicago Press, 2019).

64 Endre Stiansen and Jane I. Guyer, eds., *Credit, Currencies, and Culture: African Financial Institutions in Historical Perspective* (Uppsala: Nordic Africa Institute, 1999).

65 Wilfred T. Uji, "Migrant Group and the Development of Market in Tiv Society of Central Nigeria: Pre-Colonial Period to Post Colonial Era," *Polac Historical Review* 1, no. 1 (2015): 218.

66 David Eltis and Lawrence C. Jennings, "Trade between Western Africa and the Atlantic World in the Pre-Colonial Era," *The American Historical Review* 93, no. 4 (1988): 936–959.

67 Alberta O. Akrong, "Trade, Routes Trade, and Commerce in Pre-colonial Africa," in *Gender, Democracy and Institutional Development in Africa*, ed. Njoki N. Wane (Switzerland: Palgrave Macmillan, 2019), 67–98.

68 Amady A. Dieng, *Social Formations and Long Distance Trade in West Africa* (Dakar: African Institute for Economic Development and Planning, 1975).

69 Peter Morton-Williams, "The Influence of Habitat and Trade on the Polities of Oyo and Ashanti," in *Man in Africa*, eds. Mary Douglas and Phyllis Mary Kaberry (London: Routledge, 2003), 80–98.

70 Ghislaine Lydon, *On Trans-Saharan Trails: Islamic Law, Trade Networks, and Cross-Cultural Exchange in 19th Century Western Africa* (Cambridge: Cambridge University Press, 2009).

71 Donald Crummey, *Modes of Production in Africa: The Precolonial Era* (New York: SAGE Publications, 1981).

72 Sundström, *The Exchange Economy*.

9

TRADITIONAL RELIGIONS

Introduction

Until the ascension of Islam and Christianity, religion in West Africa was not a source of controversy or internal conflict because of the understanding that humans were free to conduct their spiritual business as it pleased them.[1] Traditional religions represented belief systems that varied according to ethnic identities. They were a set of highly diverse, yet developed, religious inclinations with different initiation and indoctrination processes from many other religions of the world. Because of their nature, they were predominantly oral and not scriptural, and they were passed down from one generation to another using the same oral method. Due to the diversity of these religions, several critics concluded that Africans were polytheistic and seemed to recognize god(s) of lesser quality because of their polytheistic appeal.[2] Some views on African religions saw Africans from a socially and religiously underprivileged perspective, generating unsolicited pity or condescending responses.

From a careful examination of their indigenous religious systems, West Africans were described as practicing a form of multiple systems and a diffused form of monotheism.[3] To come to this conclusion meant that one understood what and how the people thought about their cosmic existence. Many practitioners believed that a Supreme Being was in charge of all earthly matters. A nod to the pervasive monotheistic ideologies, though its existence with the simultaneous veneration of other deities, called for classification as the practicing of multiple systems.

Efik Mythology

The Efik people are domiciled in Nigeria, with a proportion of them having settled in Cameroon.[4] Their traditional religion recognized a Supreme Being called Abasi, and they have continued to identify with principles and philosophies associated with the indigenous belief structure.[5] Abasi did not have children, as all humans were considered

DOI: 10.4324/9781003198260-11

his family. The belief system created no special boundaries between sexes or genders, and everyone was given an equal appeal before their God. Efik mythology stipulated that Abasi had a wife, Atai, who served as the mediator between Abasi and the people on many occasions. According to this religious belief, the creation of the human race was founded on the advice offered to Abasi by Atai (Figure 9.1).[6]

However, this creation story became complicated because humans violated some divine regulations. The mythology established that Abasi conceded to Atai's prescriptions about creating humans but decided to go about it on his terms. He agreed to create both a male and a female on the condition that they would be forbidden from procreation. Some oral sources believed that this injunction was given to prevent humans from being likely to overestimate their social importance. However, a couple violated this stipulation, and Abasi unleashed his anger on them. He killed both of them and created chaos and death for their offspring.[7]

Some other oral sources have established that the two created individuals, the man and woman, were actual children of Abasi and Atai, and the reason for chastising them was to ensure that they did not overtake Abasi in matters of creation and creativity. It was also to disallow them from providing for themselves, even in matters of security and other human welfare services. Initially, these two children observed the rules and acted in obedience to them. On one occasion, however, they became curious during their visit to heaven in their quest for sustenance. They suddenly became voyeuristic and engaged in the exploration of things like musical instruments. They learned how to sing and even developed the ability to make food independently of Abasi, who always determined

FIGURE 9.1   Efik, double-sided crest https://commons.wikimedia.org/wiki/File:Nigeria,_efik,
_cimiero_a_doppia_faccia,_1900-15_ca.jpg.

what and when they would eat.[8] According to Efik mythology, this marked another episode in the history of the creation of the world.

Their deliberate challenge of Abasi's authority or their failure to observe the basic injunctions required of them was a source of worry and Abasi immediately became angry, and he sought the best ways to rebuke them for their misdemeanors. Atai, having understood the gravity of Abasi's annoyance and grave actions, made strenuous efforts to ensure that the children did not overtake their parents to prevent Abasi's reactionary actions. Atai's love superseded their misdeeds, and she sought to protect them at all costs despite their unyielding nature.[9]

Since Abasi's children dared to challenge his authority, they were evicted from heaven along with their mother. The children were ejected because of their intransigence, and their mother because she could not bear her children being tortured by their angry father. Unknown to the children, they had only acquired a very minimal amount of the knowledge they needed for their advancement on earth. Their limited knowledge constrained them from reaching their full potential and, in most cases, brought about unanticipated frustrations for the people. Subsequently, it created a complex web of human experiences that inevitably caused a very serious crisis.[10] These factors contributed to Abasi's distance from human affairs and caused the Efik people to venerate their elders and the dead as they sought their assistance in running their human affairs. They understood that the invocation of the dead would provoke some spiritual presence that would cause their experiences to change from bad to good.[11] They also believed that their forebears' misdemeanor incurred Abasi's annoyance, which could not be revoked.

The Akan Religion

The Akan religion has been practiced by the inhabitants of Ghana[12] and some eastern parts of Côte d'Ivoire, who shared many cultural traditions for much of their history. Different religio-cultural connections bound these people, and it must be clarified as this has served as the foundation of the exploration of this religion. Linguistically, Akan represented several subcultures or subgroups whose differences at the linguistic level were linked to the changes in the settler communities, distance from the center of their origin, and some additional factors. Their dialectical variations notwithstanding, the Akan people have been keenly united and respected their indigenous belief systems, despite the infiltration of their religious spaces by the Abrahamic religions—Christianity and Islam. The Akan identity comprised the Asante, Fante, Akuapem, Kwahu, Akyem (Abuakwa, Bosome, Kotoku), Brong-Ahafo, and Nze.[13] They were believed to have a common ancestry that underscored their shared religious identity. They identified their God by different names, such as Nyankopon, Nyam, Brekyirihunuade (Almighty), Odomankoma (infinite inventor), and Anansi Kokuroko.[14] However, Nyame has been the most preferred by a considerable number of the Akan people when they address their God.[15]

According to some oral traditions, Nyame used to cohabit the world with humans, occupying a satellite position that was not geographically too distant from them. Indeed, the picture of proximity is painted in the narrative that reports a woman to have deliberately defied the instructions of this God as she raised her pestle high when pounding *fufu*, a traditional delicacy. Even though the old woman was on Earth, her pestle disturbed Nyame's privacy so much that he became threatened by such habitual intransigence as time went on. He was neither infuriated nor unhappy with the woman, but the development provoked him into deciding to move far away from them into the sky, where he believed they would be unable to reach him.[16]

Disturbed by the development, the woman thought of redemption. She was determined to regain favor with Nyame so that he would return closer to her, allowing them to cultivate their relationship as they had before. Thus, she instructed her children to arrange vertical piles of mortars to enable them to reach the heavens where their God dwelled. The myth explained that they were one mortar short to attain this, and as a response, the old woman ordered that they remove the bottom mortar to place it on top of the others.[17] They followed this instruction, but were unable to reach Nyame because removing one of the mortars brought about their unforeseen destruction.

Although the mythical narratives offered a human explanation of cosmogonic existence, they also came with a package of moral training. For one thing, it taught humans, in particular the Akan people, about the act and the art of obedience. Apart from their conventional belief in God, they also engaged in the veneration of their ancestors and deities. In fact, in the hierarchical arrangement of these events, the deities were placed above the ancestors. Their deities, generally referred to as Abosom, were viewed as human helpers on Earth as they have always been available during emergencies. These deities attained their power and energy from the power source Nyame and engaged in human interference in the physical sense. Priests served as the mediators, or go-betweens, between the deities and the people.[18] They offered prayer in anticipation that they would be accepted by these deities, and they poured libations as signs of reverence. The last leg of a triadic arrangement was made up of their ancestors, known as Nsamanfo.[19] They were recognized as those who transformed into spirits and were equally recognized in the Akan religion.

Asaase Yaa

The beauty of indigenous African religions was reflected in the reality that diversity in spirituality was considered an advantage.[20] Within the same family structure, there could have existed an unlimited diversity of religious practices. An example of this religious democracy was found in the accommodation of multiple practices by the Akan people of Ghana, despite their group identity. Many believed that a relationship with God was a personal experience, they created a social system where everyone was appreciated and accepted for the religion they chose to participate in. This other expression of religion among the Bono people, a subgroup of the Akan people, was called Asaase Yaa.[21]

This belief system was considered somewhat complementary to that of the other Akan peoples. Thus, in the Asaase Yaa's religion, Nyame's wife was considered important in the Akan cosmological understanding. She had good spirits, and her femininity was one of the rallying points for its adherents. They believed that because of this attribute, Asaase Yaa would be reasonably productive and support sustenance, as it has been cardinal to all humans to desire productivity in whatever they embark on. Strangely, however, this idea developed into a full-blown philosophical carving when a set of people in their society created a model figure of cosmic intelligence who was believed to answer their fertility questions and protect them against external negative energies that foiled their work. The idea that the power of intergenerational connections dwelled in women's ability to reproduce was inherent in her feminine composure, and, for this reason, the female god used her power of reconnection to join those spiritually disconnected people (Figure 9.2).[22]

For example, the dead were considered part of the human community whose presence was required for consolidation and consultation. This was difficult to enhance in the absence of a strong linkage between these individuals. But with the invocation of Asaase Yaa, the Akan people were confident that their departed ancestors were easily connected, after which they would make their familial requests and rituals.[23] Importantly, it was Nyame's wife who pleaded with him when his anger was provoked.[24] Therefore, to an extent, her role in the altercation between Nyame and the humans won her their trust, and they created more social positions for her to help in the enhancement of peace and the restoration of their social glories. The adherents invoked the presence of Asaase Yaa using libations, especially the ceremonial pouring of liquid, another symbol for the veneration of the spirit after they worshipped Nyame. Their perception of cosmic intelligence followed a hierarchical sequence where the male was recognized first, followed by the appreciation of the female god. As soon as Asaase Yaa's spirit was invoked and properly propitiated, the following entities in the hierarchy were the ancestors, and their acknowledgment was usually corroborative of those above.

From a closer observation, it was apparent that the adherents of the religion understood the importance of gender balance in the construction of their spiritual principles. They recognized that the workings of the universe were not unilaterally assigned to a single individual, believing that such spiritual behavior was a recipe for social degeneration. Unlike some other religions, Asaase Yaa adherents comprehended that the failure to represent the female sex in the spiritual world held the potential for the breakdown of social life. Therefore, the regard offered to Asaase Yaa manifested in different forms.

FIGURE 9.2   Asase Ye Duru https://commons.wikimedia.org/wiki/File:Asase_Ye_Duru.svg.

For example, she was always recognized whenever people in the community had social engagements like naming ceremonies.

The Dogon Religion

The Dogon religion, another West African indigenous religion, is associated with the people of Mali, whose linguistic identity was Dogon.[25] This traditional religion shared multiple characteristics with other indigenous African religions because it was deep-rooted in natural philosophy and embraced many aspects of human nature. According to some anthropologists who studied the Dogon religion and people, their ancestral beginning was difficult to trace because of the absence of corresponding oral materials to establish a foundation for the people. However, historical arguments located their history of migration to Mali and some parts of the Burkina Faso region. These anthropological accounts established that the Dogon religion was a triumvirate as it has been mapped out in three cults, which had been organized hierarchically, with the Supreme Being, called Amma, who was culturally believed to have created the universe at the zenith. This Supreme Being was considered the foundation of all energies whose position radiated all the forces involved in creating, shaping, and sustaining the cosmological existence. Amma occupied this position alone as the people never opposed a power or being of equal measure.[26] Religious devotion among the people was expressed outwardly as people observed rituals in the propitiation of their God (Figure 9.3).

Following a hierarchical sequence, the spiritual beings that occupied the next rank after Amma were the primordial beings traditionally called Nommo.[27] These were identified as the first celestial beings created by the Supreme Amma. Because of their early status, they internalized some natural laws and ideas that could influence or direct people's activities, not because they were awarded the power by Amma, but because they earned it.[28] The Dogon religion was neatly woven into daily experience. The adherents found expressions of their Supreme Being in virtually all their engagements. Their alignment of these ideas with their spiritual life was evident in their social and political views, and their food, art, politics, and other engagements were woven in ways that enhanced their religious convictions. This meant that their religion shared a reasonable bond with their cultural traditions, making it difficult for them to detach themselves from either.

Occupying the last space in the spiritual hierarchy were the eight Dogon ancestors believed to have physically contributed to the advancement of their collective direction. These ancestors were believed to constitute the genetic beginning of the people from which all the Dogon people descended. As a result of the disposition of Africans to their ancestral sources, these individuals were always revered at every given opportunity. However, the reverence accorded to them has been misinterpreted by some non-African observers of their religion because the idea of venerating the dead meant little to people who shared no emotional ties to the culture.

Regardless of their minor variations and reservations, the four subgroups in Dogon were united in their understanding of these spiritual beliefs and did not betray the status and hierarchies of these religious lines. As Amma is considered to occupy the apex position in the spiritual hierarchy, Nommo was viewed as the immediate product of Amma's creativity, while the ancestors at the lower side of the pyramid were accorded

FIGURE 9.3   Dogon people, Mali https://commons.wikimedia.org/wiki/File:Dogon12.jpg.

corresponding social and spiritual reverence. Contrary to the misconception that these indigenous adherents had a faulty notion of the Supreme Being, their structured religion proved that they understood the sequential process of natural events.[29]

The Igbo Religion

Cosmologically, the Igbo people believed that two asymmetrical worlds existed: the physical and the spiritual worlds.[30] The two worlds, although divergent, were deeply connected at the spiritual level. The activities of the living, that is, the physical world, were believed to be controlled by the spiritual world. As such, the spiritual world was occupied by a network of powerful stakeholders.[31] Mostly, the occupants of this status were categorized into four distinctive roles. In Igbo cosmology, Chukwu was regarded as the Supreme Being because of his association with the power of creation.[32] Notably, the Igbo religion did not constrain their conception of God with gender. All matters, both in the seen and the unseen worlds, were accepted as the manifestation of Chukwu's creativity and its unending capacity. Much reverence was offered to Chukwu because it determined everything in the world of the living, even though it was eternally unseen.[33] The organizational structure of the religion indicated their sequential placement of hierarchies, even for spiritual beings. At the top of the pyramid was Chukwu, who related with people through other socially recognized intermediaries that mediated between Chukwu and the other spiritual beings.

The word "Chineke" signaled the individualism of the creative force among the Igbo people because it represented a compound signification.[34] "Chi" has been interpreted as personal guidance, while "eke" is "to create."[35] This meant that each individual had a guardian who created and regulated affairs that especially concerned the person. Having divided the entire world into two opposing categories—the physical and the spiritual worlds—the Igbo believed that no less than four sets of entities occupied the spiritual world. The first were the spirits who manifested in physical form but detached themselves from the physicality of the human body because of the happenstance of death. The second was the personal Chi, which has been passively mentioned and was responsible for the in-life activities of an individual to determine such things as their destinies and source of life, from conception to death. The third were creatures that did not manifest human qualities, as they did not possess attributes associated with the human body. Called Alusi, they were equally considered living organisms whose lifespan was way beyond that of an average human (Figure 9.4). Examples include entities such as the sun, the earth, water, and the sky, among others.[36] These entities were also seen as creatures that manifested in different forms from humans. The fourth and final entity was the evil spirit called Ula Chi, which was culturally seen as negative energy constantly in opposition to the Chi (one's guidance angel).[37]

FIGURE 9.4   Female deity figure (Alusi or Agbara) https://commons.wikimedia.org/wiki/File :Standing_Female_Deity_Figure_(Alusi_or_Agbara)_Northern_Igbo_people _Nigeria_Wood_Dallas_Museum_of_Art.jpg.

In the spiritual perception or understanding of believers, evil existed because there was a force committed to that assignment. However, humans were constantly in pursuit of fulfillment and wanted to achieve their dream lifestyle, irrespective of the growing challenges. This, therefore, necessitated the involvement of spiritual beings, especially Chukwu, to meddle in their affairs for positive intervention so that it would be compara-tively easier to face the challenges posed by the negative energies discussed above. But to do this required observing some spiritual arrangements as Chukwu was so distanced and respected that it was not personally related with unless aided by some entities of lesser hierarchies, the ancestors, or the creatures that manifested in the varied forms.

It was believed that once a Chi was assigned to an individual, all issues related to their safety and welfare were handled by the personal Chi, known as Mmuo. This did not negate the fact that the negative force of Alusi could also be used to topple all the efforts of one's Chi and make a mockery of their struggles.

The Jola Religion

The Jola religion was a dominant pre-Islamic practice among the people of Senegal, Gambia, Mali, Casamance, and Guinea Bissau. The ferocious influence of Islam was so overwhelming that one might easily conclude that they had no indigenous religion in the past. Contrary to this sentiment, however, they were grounded in their indigenous wor-ship system before the incursion of Islam.[38] The Jola religion was practiced by those who culturally identified as Jola, some of whom have been found in Casamance, Gambia, Senegal, and some parts of Nigeria.[39] They were chiefly agrarian, which meant that their society was supported by developed agriculture.[40] In addition to cultivating items like rice and millet, they also engaged in other activities like palm-wine tapping, groundnut farming, and palm-oil processing. These people believed that Emit or Ata Emit was the brain behind the germination of their seeds and the force supporting their economic buoyance.[41] They believed that Emit was the occupant of the sky and could observe and follow all the events of those on Earth because of that vantage position.

Before the coming of Islam, they were united in the worship of their god. Further to the understanding that Emit was responsible for the creation of heaven and Earth, they believed that their Supreme Being understood every expression of human culture and, as such, created suitable religious practices and systems for them to avoid needless rancor inspired by differences in religion. Therefore, their orientation was that humans were free to worship any religious identity they considered helpful for obtaining and maintaining their peace of mind and spirit. The worshippers believed that the creation of spiritual entities had not ended and that their God, Emit, continued to ensure that people had additional freedom to pursue tasks that fit their purposes. They believed that Emit created these spiritual shrines called *ukine*[42] as representatives of the Supreme Being who was worshipped through them.

Some scholars argued that religion in Africa was not a distant enterprise where events were disconnected and disjointed. Instead, everything was interrelated; religion, law, social theory, medicine, marriage, and culture, among others, were intricately con-nected.[43] This made it difficult to separate these interrelated realities despite having accepted foreign religions. People who worshipped Emit were conscious of this real-ity and have shown that their social organization followed the path laid by it. It was difficult to establish the aspect of human activity that occupied the central position among the people, as they did not give special consideration to one above the other. Individual families had their different shrines called *bekin* or *enaati*, depending on the region, and they were recognized as efficient intermediaries.

The Serer Religion

The Serer religion has been interpreted as "the way of the Divine"[44] by its adherents. The root of this religion was planted deeply into the fabric of their religious practices. They believed in a Supreme Being called Roog, and this Being was understood to have used its creative ingenuity to organize the universe as we know it.[45] Before their conversion to Islam, many people in Senegal identified with the religion and considered it as one that represented their spiritual wishes. God was conceived as a Being with the expanding capacity to show mercy as it was responsible for the various dimensions of life, from birth, death, space, time, and the seasons.

The cosmological designs and essence were Roog's exclusive concerns because of the understanding that the power to control these only resided with the Supreme Being. The explanation that Serer worshippers offered for the existence of experiences, such as struggles between and among individuals or communities, relationships, and land issues, amidst other human experiences,[46] was their belief that humans, particularly the ancestors, had the power to determine what happened within the human experience. This meant that while Roog was considered the Supreme cosmic intelligence, there were roles appointed to stakeholders in the spiritual world.

They all believed that it was beyond human capacity to give life or take it; thus, Roog was exclusively linked to the issues of life and death. However, they believed that the existence of war, violence, and other human experiences could not be separated from humans, who were, in most cases, the masterminds behind their existence. For this, while they venerated their Supreme Deity and offered religious rites as conventionally accepted among the people, the ancestors were equally pleaded with so that issues that brought self-inflictions were carefully avoided or even prevented.[47] Although their sturdy religious foundations and beliefs repelled external religious practices for a long time, caused by their deep rootedness in their indigenous religious practices, they gave in in the long run. This was because of pressures associated with internal persuasion from their members who had embraced a new religion.

When observed intimately, there were some instances of connection between this religion and other African religions. For example, the burial rites of the Serer people had some deep interconnection with those of Ghana and Egypt.[48] This indicated that ancestors were considered sacred and deserved their religious veneration. They believed that once the ancestors were well appeased, their lives would experience a sudden transformation. As such, up until the fourteenth century, they carved pestles used as altars of veneration. These were called "dek-kur," representing a social signification that they held their ancestors in a good position. Like the Egyptian practice, they buried their dead with luxurious items to ensure a desirable afterlife.[49] The physical body was not seen as the only manifestation of human nature, as there were other phases of the human journey, including being an ancestor. Therefore, the ancestors deserved necessary religious veneration and reverence.

The Yoruba Religion

The Yoruba religion was another important indigenous religion. The Yoruba evolved a cosmology whose transformation within and outside its cultural reach was descriptive of its organized nature. The religion has existed throughout modern-day Nigeria, Ghana, Togo, and the Benin Republic, as sizable numbers of Yoruba people have been found in these locations.[50] The religion expanded so much that it garnered enough attention to receive global recognition. A significant number of practitioners exist in South America, the Caribbean, and other international communities. The Yoruba religion recognized Olodumare's supremacy as the foundational force behind the existence of every universal entity, inclusive of deities such as Oya, Ogun, and others (Figure 9.5).[51]

While Olodumare was identified as the most Supreme Being, the Yoruba religion also cosmologically explained the fundamental place of humans in the designation of their earthly experiences, termed *ayanmo*.[52] *Ayanmo* loosely described what was known as fate in other religions, but it was more than that. While fate was descriptive of divine enforcement, *ayanmo* highlighted the importance of humans in deciding for themselves, even when the recollection of what they chose in the non-human and non-physical state was impossible. In the Yoruba religion, nothing existed in isolation: stones, trees, oceans, rivers, oxygen, sky, planets and other natural occurrences were all expressions of life in different dimensions. According to the Yoruba religion, all humans interacted with these different dimensions of beings in their physical manifestation. In essence, they were persuaded to do good things so that their actions would not negatively influence entities that they were ignorant of.

FIGURE 9.5   Ogun shrine, Ketu. Author's collection.

Although the Yoruba religion believed in the supremacy of Olodumare, they did not believe that human pleas should be directly directed to It, especially when the focus was on individuals or single entities.[53] They knew that the construction of the universe was perfected and managed by some natural laws that were unexplainable to humans and, therefore, the constant invocation of Olodumare for one's personal life was inconsiderate or insensitive to the complex intricacies of the universe that humans inhabited. The Yoruba also believed in Ori, a religio-cultural entity that, though unseen, manifested in present status.[54] They recognized that Ori was powerful and, in some cases, could contest with other Ori in the struggle for the wishes of the people because the composition of the universe implied the presence of competition. Therefore, it was religiously preferable to invoke one's Ori as opposed to calling Olodumare because the Ori fought for an individual if such a fellow had *iwa pele* (good character) and appeased Esu, the spiritual conveyor who carried the contents of demand to the spiritual world.[55] Esu transmitted the prayer to the necessary and appropriate quarters without interfering, and then Ori pleaded with Olodumare, who granted *àṣẹ* (the performative force) to the prayers.

The Yoruba religion, having identified Olodumare as the Supreme Being, also recognized the places of *Orisa*, the different entities who did exceptionally well during their time of cosmogonic existence and in the execution of their duties. The different *Orisa* among the Yoruba were Orunmila, Esu, Obatala, Iyemoja, Ogun, Osun, Olokun, and Sango. Additionally, there were other beings known as *irunmole* sent to the planet to ensure that the works of Olodumare followed Its planned arrangements (Figure 9.6).[56]

FIGURE 9.6 Osun Osogbo. Author's collection.

Features of African Religions

The general impression that West Africa was one monolithic civilization implied that everything was similar from east to west, and north to south. Aspects of culture in the region are misrepresented to the world.[57] In fact, West Africa is a massive region with diverse cultural traditions and religious philosophies. Even though a handful of aspects of its cultures shared significant features and attributes in terms of beliefs and practices, this has not justified amalgamating the cultures as African religions varied from one group to another. Although it has been emphasized that they stressed different things regarding nature, cosmic existence, and supernatural forces, they communicated some important ideas and characteristics in common.[58]

The first was that irrespective of their cultural traditions, moral background, or geographical boundaries, they expressed a belief in God and gods. A common belief in the existence of a "Cosmic Originator" reverberated through African engagements across the continent and was founded on the understanding that the forces of nature were centrally controlled by a Supreme force in charge of the running of the seen or unseen activities inherent in the universe.[59] This Supreme power was conceived not as a distant concept removed from all the forces of the world but whose existence and characteristics were reflected in everything that had a marker of existence. As such, the concept of God implied that the entity was not a physical being with merely concrete or material manifestation. This immateriality of existence gave the impression that God was truly everywhere because the duty of overseeing the universe required omnipresent capabilities. In essence, God did not sit in a permanent chair (throne) or in one place remotely looking at the affairs of human beings who were the occupants of the different planes of existence. This belief has been the dominant theme in the general understanding of the world. For this, God has been revered and accorded the respect which complements Its universal significance.

Alongside this belief in God was the belief in gods. The African people believed that some beings, not necessarily humans, had the mandate to demonstrate the inelastic capacity of the cosmic body through other lesser creatures who interacted with supernatural forces to produce energies. Among humans, some beings possessed supernatural or superhuman qualities, and because they demonstrated that they were better than others, they were exalted to a divinity status, venerated, and honored for the immeasurable things they did in the course of their existence. In different civilizations in Africa, it was observed that among humans, for example, there were unique creatures associated with supernatural powers and given exalted positions in their various cultures. Across the continent, those who influenced the advancement of their people, either because they were extremely powerful or were gifted to the point that their mental capacity became a drive for their collective development, were simply given reverence and not worshipped. They were venerated as a sign of honor and appreciation for the things they brought during their existence. And because there was a general belief that people of these qualities were not ordinary, they decided to reach the Supreme God through them in their veneration process.

The practice of divination was a corollary of the belief in God as the foundation of universal energies.[60] This has been the meeting point between the two since God was believed to have an immaterial realization. Those who were given the extraordinary spiritual power to undertake actions not unconnected to supernatural prowess and proficiency were consulted for intervention on issues that appeared difficult to ascribe meaning to. As a result, diviners were to be found in many areas, irrespective of cultural differences.[61] They were those in whom the people placed their confidence, with the assumption that they could relate with God so that some important things would be revealed about their future or past activities. Diviners have been, therefore, the custodians of cultural science or knowledge deployed to attract supernatural forces so that they could be consulted for important issues. Diviners were not expected to have solutions to the problems they faced all the time. However, they were believed to have the capacity to initiate communication with the unseen forces as they sought their knowledge about things that happened to them in the material world.[62] Divination also did not necessarily imply that they were seeking interventions from supernatural forces, but rather, many sought divination to venerate the gods.

The action or the divination process varied according to the culture involved. The common thing that united them was that they expressed their feelings to the omnipresent forces in the universe. Diviners were conceived as the links between humans and the unseen forces who helped to understand the issues of the material world after consultations and to seek the knowledge of their gods. Divination was developed from the understanding that nature was controlled by forces everywhere, irrespective of location. The events in the material universe were triggered by the forces that existed in the domain of immaterial existence. By the universe's design, humans, animals, and plants were given limitations to their knowledge and capacity. However, among these categories of beings were those with excellent qualities. These qualities helped them to interpret the things of nature, and they made accurate predictions about the world, individuals, or society. The knowledge informed their position as the go-to sources in each of the communities, which they could consult the unseen forces, interact with them, and read the forces in some cases to understand what was happening or would happen to individuals or other creatures. In such a situation, their efforts warned people when the forces were negative or enhanced them when they were positive.

In addition to the practice of divination was the belief in making sacrifices. Sacrifices provided the avenue to manipulate existence-bound events, especially because they penetrated the world of the unseen, where forces interacted for various purposes.[63] The practice of offering sacrifices has been condemned by outsiders who have not understood the spiritual necessity for its practice. Sacrifices have had both spiritual and philosophical importance. The spiritual angle to the practice of sacrifice was underscored by the belief that the cosmic originator already programmed the forces of nature, and any attempt to rearrange these activities required a price to pay. Offering sacrifice did not rearrange the activities already programmed by God, but because it mandated the ones who offered to give out something to the universe, the program changed for them in some ways. The sacrifice, therefore, was seen as an expression of propitiation to the forces that would be rearranged in the course of things.[64] This meant that the understanding behind sacrifice as a spiritual engagement was that anyone who intended to rearrange the events of the universe for their advantage offered significant collateral in return.

Meanwhile, sacrifices have had their philosophical sides too. They were a phenomenon that helped the people to understand that they must offer something in return for what they were seeking. In other words, any individual who wanted to achieve success or perfection had to make some sacrifices in the form of dedication, persistence, and determination and continued practice to attain the goals or achievements they desired.[65] Where they accepted sacrifice as a (pre-)condition for living, it was evident that they had a dual understanding of sacrifice, as it was central to everything. The individual who wanted to achieve beyond their contemporaries, positively or negatively, had to bear the pains of doing what others did not, a sacrifice of their time, their energy, and/or dedication so that their desire would be met. Even in the spiritual sense, offering sacrifices meant that the individual was not doing as well as others, and when they were not giving what others who offered sacrifices as a way of achieving their potential were, they repaid in unpredicted measures.

Another central theme in these indigenous religions was the belief in ancestral existence.[66] Humans have constituted a chain of existence connected to different phases of life. Most religions understood that there were three different phases of existence: the living, the dead, and the unborn. The unborn are believed to await their opportunity to come to the physical world and begin their journey to complete the circle of existence. At this level, there has been a consensus that some individuals are reincarnated and await another turn; they were believed to revisit the world with the same energies but in different bodies.[67] The living were understood to lead their lives for a designated period, after which they transitioned to another phase of human existence. The world was believed to be constructed in this cyclical form so that the rotation of the events of the world would be conducive for all.

During people's physical existence, they are believed to be associated with kith and kin with whom they share numerous ties and things. Their genetic affiliation connected them in unexplainable ways. Because their genetic system has been extended to the succeeding generations, the living are understood to reduplicate themselves in others who will continue their work and expand their family achievements. As the living were recognized to impact the dead by building upon their legacies, the dead have impacted the living in positive and/or negative ways and were usually invoked when spiritually required.

Moreover, ancestor reverence did not come without its socio-spiritual significance. The dead members of a society were considered distant relatives who operated in the immaterial world where it was not only possible to have access to their living relatives but also affected the energies around them as they were believed to be capable of changing some things about their lives. Therefore, ancestors were seen as members of their family, society, and group, whose relationship with them was nourished and consciously maintained. Giving reverence to the ancestors did not translate to them being worshipped. Ancestors were recognized for the numerous things they did in the course of their existence. People indulged in ancestral veneration because it would help them rekindle their spirit and remind them that their existence transcends the physical world as they assumed the responsibility of an ancestor whenever their life was terminated. The understanding that the traits of these past humans were found in the living relatives strengthened the belief that they continued to exist in different forms other than the ones known to humans.

Among the Yoruba, ancestor veneration usually came in the form of *egungun* (masquerade). Ancestors contributed to the development of their society and performed their duties based on what was demanded of them by their living relatives. There was a consensus that their spirits overtook the *egungun* cult, and they prayed for the people during their engagements. They intervened in matters of conflict that led to separation and distance. The veneration of the ancestors served numerous purposes, some of which included their invitation to issues and areas where humans identified their limitations. In the phase of existence where ancestors dwelled, they manifested in immaterial forms and, for this reason, had the possibility of knowledge beyond that of ordinary people. For this reason, they were invoked by their relatives to influence a level of transformation or change in their own lives. When remembering their ancestors, some societies prepared sacrifices to propitiate the dead so that they incurred their compassion and love. In some African cultural traditions, the invocation of the spirit of their ancestors was common, where they designated specific spiritual assignments to them. The understanding that the dead and the living were connected was mutual knowledge because several modes of communication existed between the living and the dead.

Keenly associated with the theme of ancestors that dominate African religions was that of the afterlife. Except for the newly developed groups of atheists who ideologically protest their cultural traditions, many people believe in the afterlife. This sprouted from the thinking that the human body was a mere container of the soul. Everyone was believed to possess a soul trapped in their physical body, although with the capacity to receive messages from the forces outside them. The brilliance and agility of the human body were determined not to continue forever, and when the expiry time came, the soul would escape its trap and evaporate into the expanse of the universe where it roamed free. Some cultural traditions believed that on the occasion that the human body was terminated abruptly by forces that were not accounted for, and the time of the individual had not naturally elapsed, their soul freely roamed until it found another body that it would occupy for the continuation of its journey. The afterlife was then understood to begin from the individual's transition into the unseen world after they lost their life—[68] their breathing stopped and they could not be said to operate any longer in the realm of the living, where they drew breath and performed other activities associated with those on the physical plane of existence.

However, there was a division of space even in the afterlife. For those whose journey remained to be completed, they came around or were poised to reincarnate in different bodies so that they could continue with their cosmic assignment. Those who finished their assignment dwelled in the invisible world where they mingled with others of the same status and functioned as ancestors. In some African cultures, the afterlife of some individuals was marred by different scenarios because not only were they denied the opportunity to be integrated into the world of their ancestors, but they were also forced to roam in the expanse of the universe. This was why some Africans wished their departed members a peaceful transition and afterlife because, at this phase, humans were meant to experience a different kind of tranquility. When this was not the case, it indicated that they did not belong to the group of people with morally acceptable behavior. The general idea that essentialized the belief in the afterlife in Africa was that humans were not meant to stop existing at the termination of their breath in the physical form.[69] They were understood to be forces themselves but were given the mandate to function in physical form for a specific period.

What remained constant was that veneration was underscored by the awareness that there was a world that transcends the physical one. The people used veneration as a method of reaching out to their departed ancestors because they continued to influence the actions of those left behind. Also, the gods and God were venerated for purposes that ranged from mere exaltation to a demonstration of their intentions to honor the supernatural forces. To control the activities of the world, there was the need to propitiate the unseen forces of the universe so that the right energies took over their engagements and enabled them to achieve their objectives.

Religions did not always emphasize punitive measures for people because of their deeds. They did not use the afterlife as the basis for being held accountable for actions that were associated with them. To communicate with the unseen world, spiritually inclined people were required, allowing the priest to function in their socio-spiritual world. The diviners were considered priests because they communicated with the world beyond and carried the message of the invisible beings to the world. Serving as their intermediary helped to prove further that the essence of religion in Africa was to deepen people's spiritual understanding and draw them closer to the other beings with which they occupied the world. As such, a constant belief attached to African religions was that humans, animals, and plants were not the only occupants of the universe, and they needed to align with supernatural forces so that they were in tune with the world as organized by the Cosmic Originator.

DEEP DIVE

Assignment 1

Reading Comprehension

How do traditional African religions differ from religions brought by foreign influences? How were they similar?

Objective

The objective of this assignment is to ensure that students complete the reading of Chapter 9 and consider the commonalities and differences between non-African and African religions. Students are expected to address how many African religions overlapped or had similar philosophies.

Method

Students are expected to write a short essay in response to the question.

Assignment 2

Reading Comprehension

Define diffused monotheism. How does it differ from polytheism? Why were Africans classified as either monotheistic or polytheistic?

Objective

The objective of this assignment is to ensure that students complete the reading of Chapter 9 and understand the difference between monotheism and polytheism.

Method

Students are expected to write a short essay in response to the question.

Notes

1 Dmitry Usenco, *African Traditional Religion Versus Christianity: Some Semiotic Observations* (Oregon: Resource Publications, 2020), 121.
2 Offiong O. Asukwo, Sunday S. Adaka, and Esowe D. Dimgba, "The Need to Re-Conceptualise African 'Traditional' Religion," *African Research Review* 7, no. 3 (2013): 232–246.
3 John S. Mbiti, *African Religions and Philosophy* (Oxford: Heinemann, 1969).
4 Donald C. Simmons, "An Ethnographic Sketch of the Efik People," in *Efik Traders of Old Calabar*, ed. Daryll Forde (London: Dawsons of Pall Mall, 1968).
5 Harold Scheub, *A Dictionary of African Mythology: The Mythmaker as Storyteller* (Oxford: Oxford University Press, 2000), 3.
6 Douglas H. Thomas and Temilola Alanamu, eds. *African Religions: Beliefs and Practices Through History* (Santa Barbara: ABC-CLIO, 2019), 104.
7 Molefi Kete Asante, "Abasi," in *Encyclopedia of African Religion*, Volume 1, eds., Molefi Kete Asante and Ama Mazama (California: Sage, 2009), 2.
8 Asante, "Abasi."
9 Asante, "Abasi."
10 Asante, "Abasi."
11 Smith, *African Ideas of God.*
12 Edwin W. Smith, "Religious Beliefs of the Akan," *Africa: Journal of the International African Institute* 15, no. 1 (1945): 23–29.
13 Joseph B. Danquah, *Gold Coast: Akan Laws and Customs: And the Akim Abuakwa Constitution* (London: Routledge, 1928).
14 Joseph B. Danquah, "The Culture of Akan," *Africa: Journal of the International African Institute* 22, no. 4 (1952): 360.
15 Hasskei M. Majeed, "On the Rationality of Traditional Akan Religion: Analyzing the Concept of God," *Legon Journal of the Humanities* 25 (2014): 127–141.
16 Joseph B. Danquah, *The Akan Doctrine of God: A Fragment of Gold Coast Ethics and Religion* (London: Frank Cass, 1968).
17 Yaba A. Blay, "Akan," in *Encyclopedia of African Religion*, Volume 1, eds., Molefi Kete Asante and Ama Mazama (California: Sage, 2009), 24–25.
18 Danquah, *The Akan Doctrine of God.*
19 Anthony Ephirim-Donkor, *African Religion Defined: A Systematic Study of Ancestor Worship Among the Akan* (Maryland: University Press of America, 2010).
20 Irene N. Osemeka, "The Management of Religious Diversity in West Africa: The Exceptionalism of the Wolof and Yoruba in the Post-Independence Period," *Historia Actual Online* no. 33 (2014): 61–75.
21 Eva Lewin-Richter Meyerowitz, *The Akan of Ghana: Their Ancient Beliefs* (London: Faber and Faber, 1958), 31.
22 Georgina Kwanima Boateng, Molly Manyonganise, and Nobuntu Penxa Matholeni, eds. *Mother Earth, Mother Africa & African Indigenous Religions* (South Africa: African Sun Media, 2020), 41.

23 Peter K. Sarpong, "Asante Religion," in *Encyclopedia of Religion and Nature*, ed. Bron Taylor (London: Continuum Publishing, 2008), 119.

24 Kofi Opoku, *West African Traditional Religion* (Accra: FEP International Private Limited, 1978).

25 Huib Blom, *Dogon: Images & Traditions* (Paris: Bernard Dulon, 2010).

26 Marcel Griaule, *Conversations with Ogotemmêli: An Introduction to Dogon Religious Ideas* (London: Oxford University Press, 1965).

27 Dorothea Schulz, *Culture and Customs of Mali* (California: ABC-CLIO, 2012), 68.

28 Laura K. Grillo, "Dogon Divination as an Ethic of Nature," *The Journal of Religious Ethics* 20, no. 2 (1992): 309–330.

29 Griaule, *Conversations with Ogotemmêli*.

30 Chinwe M. A. Nwoye, "Igbo Cultural and Religious Worldview: An Insider's Perspective," *International Journal of Sociology and Anthropology* 3, no. 9 (2011): 307.

31 Nwoye, "Igbo Cultural and Religious Worldview."

32 Evaristus C. Ezeugwu and Gregory E. Chinweuba, "The Supreme Being in Igbo Thought: A Reappraisal," *Philosophia* 21 (2018): 26–47.

33 Christopher Ezekwugo, *Chi The Supreme God in Igbo Religion* (Kerala: Pontifical Institute, 1987).

34 Elochukwu E. Uzukwu, "Igbo World and Ultimate Reality and Meaning," *Ultimate Reality and Meaning* 5, no. 3 (1982): 195–196.

35 M. O. Ene, "The Fundamentals of Odinani," *KWENU: Our Culture, Our Future*, https://web.archive.org/web/20020819010001/http://www.kwenu.com/odinani/odinani.htm.

36 Marcel I. S. Onyibor, "Igbo Cosmology in Chinua Achebe's Arrow of God: An Evaluative Analysis," *Open Journal of Philosophy* 6 (2016): 116.

37 Ene, "The Fundamentals of Odidani."

38 Dean S. Gilliland, "Religious Change among the Hausa, 1000–1800," *Journal of Asian and African Studies* 14, no. 3–4 (1979): 241–257.

39 James S. Olson and Charles Meur, *The Peoples of Africa: An Ethnohistorical Dictionary* (Westport: Greenwood Publishing Group, 1996), 255–256.

40 Tidiane Sané, Catherine Mering, Marie-Christine, Cormier-Salem, Ibrahima Diédhiou, Boubacar Demba Ba, Amadou Tahirou Diaw, and Alfred Kouly Tine, "Permanences et mutations dans les terroirs rizicoles de Basse-Casamance (Sénégal)," *Espace Géographique* 47, no. 3 (2018): 201.

41 Timothy L. Gall and Jeneen Hobby, eds., *Worldmark Encyclopedia of Cultures and Daily Life: Africa* (Michigan: Gale, 1998), 301.

42 Olga Linares, "Cash Crops and Gender Constructs: The Jola of Senegal," *Ethnology* 24, no. 2 (1985): 83–93.

43 Ibigbolade S. Aderibigbe, "Religious Traditions in Africa: An Overview of Origins, Basic Beliefs, and Practices," in *Contemporary Perspectives on Religions in Africa and the African Diaspora*, eds. Ibigbolade S. Aderibigbe and Carolyn M. J. Medine (New York: Palgrave Macmillan, 2015), 7–29.

44 Cheik Anta Diop, *Precolonial Black Africa* (Rocky Hill: Lawrence Hill & Company, 1987).

45 Molefi Kete Asante, "Serer," in *Encyclopedia of African Religion, Volume 1*, eds. Molefi Kete Asante and Ama Mazama (California: Sage, 2009), 606.

46 Diop, *Precolonial Black Africa*.

47 Oscar Sundara, *Serer Religion* (United Kingdom: Lightning Source, 2012).

48 Abraham Adeleke, *Introduction to Yoruba: Language, Culture, Literature and Religious Beliefs* (Victoria: Trafford, 2007).

49 Akan Takruri, *Egyptian Language Connections to other African Tribes* (lulu.com, 2017), 32.

50 Jacob Olupona, "The Study of Yoruba Religious Tradition in Historical Perspective," *Numen* 40, no. 3 (1993): 240–273.

51 Bolaji E. Idowu, *Olódùmarè: God in Yoruba Belief* (London: Longmans, 1962).

52 Abiola Dopamu, "Predestination, Destiny and Faith in Yorubaland: Any Meeting Point?" *Global Journal of Humanities* 7, no. 1&2 (2008): 27–39.

53 Idowu, *Olódùmarè*.

54 Adebola B. Ekanola, "A Naturalistic Interpretation of the Yoruba Concepts of Ori," *Philosophia Africana* 9, no. 1 (2006): 41–48.

55 Toyin Falola, *Èṣù: Yoruba God, Power, and the Imaginative Frontiers* (Durham: Carolina Academic Press, 2013).
56 Obafemi Origunwa, *Fundamentals of Òrìṣà Lifestyle: Live the Medicine* (California: Orisa Lifestyle Academy, 2015), 113.
57 Aylward Shorter, "African Traditional Religion: Its Relevance in the Contemporary World," *CrossCurrents* 28, no. 4 (1978–9): 421.
58 See the comprehensive study on African religions in Ibigbolade S. Aderibigbe and Toyin Falola, eds., *Palgrave Handbook of African Traditional Religion* (Cham: Palgrave, 2022).
59 Francis F. Edet, "The Concept of God in African Traditional Religion," *Sophia: An African Journal of Philosophy* 12, no. 1 (2009): 127–135.
60 Evan M. Zuesse, "Divination and Deity in African Religions," *History of Religions* 15, no. 2 (1975): 158–182.
61 David M. Anderson and Douglas H. Johnson, "Diviners, Seers and Spirits in Eastern Africa: Towards an Historical Anthropology," *Africa: Journal of the International African Institute* 61, no. 3 (1991): 293–298.
62 Walter E. A. van Beek and Philip M. Peek, *Reviewing Reality: Dynamics of African Divination* (Zurich: Lit VERLAG, 2013).
63 Theo Sundermeier, "Sacrifice in African Traditional Religions," in *Sacrifice in Religious Experience*, ed. Albert I. Baumgartner (Netherlands: Brill, 2002), 1–12.
64 Francis A. Arinze, *Sacrifice in Ibo Religion* (Ibadan: Ibadan University Press, 1970).
65 Oluwafunminiyi Raheem, "Folk Liturgies and Narratives of Holy Wells among the Yoruba (Southwest Nigeria)," *Ethnological Tribune: Journal of Croatian Ethnological Society* 51, no. 44 (2021): 116–120.
66 Chinelo Eze, "West African Ancestral Cults Shows the Belief in Life after Death," *The Guardian*, October 18, 2020.
67 Ephirim-Donkor, *African Religion Defined.*
68 Kosmas B. Asenga, *African Traditional Religion's "Afterlife Belief" and Christian "Faith on Afterlife": Critical Study of the Chagga Christians of Rombo-Kilimanjaro, Tanzania* (Universidad San Dámaso: Faculty of Theology, 2020).
69 Anthony Ephirim-Donkor, *African Spirituality: On Becoming Ancestors* (New Jersey: African World Press Inc, 1998).

PART III

West Africa in the Era of Atlantic Economies and Globalization up till the Nineteenth Century

10
ISLAM

Introduction

Extensive contacts between West and North Africa date way back to the first millennium.[1] The rise of Islam occurred after the seventh century AD when factors conducive to its proliferation converged. Foremost among these factors was the Arab expansion into North Africa, which provided the social conditions and economic incentives for Islamic proliferation.[2] The Arab incursion of the seventh century set off a chain of actions and reactions, including the conquest of the Maghrib—beginning in the same century—and an expansion in the trade across the Sahara Desert, both of which set the stage for the introduction of Islam into West Africa.[3]

Once introduced, Islam—over a period that spanned centuries (between the seventh and nineteenth centuries)—gradually grew in coverage and appeal among the populations of West African states.[4] The religion's growing popularity was encouraged by the opportunities it held for trade, literacy, and other judicial and social values identified within its tenets. The account provided by Ibn Battuta gives the impression that the people accepted Islam (and some aspects of Arabic culture) to the extent that many African families, in Mali especially, considered the knowledge of the Qur'an virtuous and desirable.[5] These African families were devoted to studying the Qur'an and committing the verses to heart. However, this does not suggest that the dissemination activity was always seamless. The many occasions of Islamic reformist action (jihads) in the area embody the reluctance and outright resistance that often met attempts at (coercive) conversions and subsequent insistence on strict adherence to Islamic orthodoxy. This history of the struggle between Islam, particularly its orthodox practice, and indigenous cultural traditions represents another important aspect in the proliferation of the religion in West Africa.

DOI: 10.4324/9781003198260-13

The Growth of Islam Before the Nineteenth Century

The actual date of the introduction of Islam in West Africa is uncertain, not least because the earliest recorded cases of contact and conversion in the region were limited to individuals of great repute (royalty), whose conversions were considered a victory for the faith.[6] However, the religion was brought by Berber traders of the Lamtuna group, who had been converted via Arab conquest and trade relations by the second decade of the eighth century.[7] By the eleventh century, the Arab/Muslim world, which stretched from the Middle East over parts of Europe and Asia, had expanded to include Egypt and other parts of North Africa. The Arab conquest of the desert Berber groups, which began in the final quarter of the seventh century (682 AD), is suggested to have produced Muslim adherents among its major groups, at least from the end of the same century. However, accounts by Ibn Khaldun and al-Zuhri put the period of conversion at about the second decade of the eighth century (724 AD), suggesting an extended period of conquest, resistance, and conversion.[8] However, the infiltration of the continent by Islam and its believers occurred from the seventh century onward, starting with North Africa.

Contrary to some historical conjectures by revisionists, the spread of Islam was not solely marked by the conquest of the people. Its institutionalization was partly a product of a successful interrelationship founded on the intention of trading between and among people of different cultural and religious backgrounds in North and West Africa. At the time of the conversion of the Berbers, a thriving trade network already existed in the North African region[9] as part of a larger Mediterranean economy. It featured important trading centers like Sijilmasa and Tahert, which not only attracted a large number of North African and Arab merchants but also had routes linking Ghana and Gao by the tenth century. From this trade, individual Berbers were also known to have been converted through their interaction with Arab/Muslim merchants from Sijilmasa—one of the stations of a caravan route connecting North Africa to ancient Ghana—whom they served as guides and escorts. Islam began to find its way into West Africa through the activities of these merchants, especially the Berbers, whose desert environment and vocation as camel breeders made them best equipped to attempt the hazardous desert-crossing to the south.

Two important developments facilitated the trade across the Sahara Desert and, as a result, the spread of Islam to the regions south of it. These were the introduction of the desert-crossing camel by the eighth century and the switch to the use of gold currency by the Muslim (Fatimid, Zirid, and Almoravid) dynasties in North Africa and the Umayyad in Spain between the ninth and eleventh centuries.[10] Combining the high demand for gold in northern Africa with the availability of the naturally adapted camel to ease desert crossings resulted in an increase in the trade across the Sahara Desert to the ancient kingdom of Ghana, which was famed for the abundance and purity of its gold. Thus, the penetration of Islam into West Africa was precipitated by its established presence in Ghana, Kanem-Borno, and Chad regions—three places that were exposed to and had embraced the religion by the eleventh century.

Arab merchants/missionaries, seeing North Africa as a virgin religious site with only indigenous religious cultures and systems, maximized the potential and encouraged the spread of Islam. However, unlike in North Africa, where the strategy was to take over states and Islamize them by converting nobles and people of higher rank to Islam, the subject of political overthrow was not pursued immediately in West Africa. This is not-withstanding that conversions within the courts of West African rulers were still considered advantageous to the growth of the body of Islam.[11] Hence, among the earliest recorded converts in West Africa were kings who were viewed as possessing the political power to influence social decisions or instigate their direction, though this was not always the case.

Spreading a new ideology, especially one associated with a new faith, requires remarkable planning. The introduction of Islam—particularly as a religion whose obligations went beyond a basic profession of monotheism to encompass the entire spectrum of human endeavor—to areas with long religious traditions deeply woven into the fabric of society was bound to present some entanglements, no matter how appealing its prospects were. Politically, even where they truly converted, the rulers of most West African territories could not abandon the same traditional beliefs that gave them their legitimacy. Moreso, notwithstanding the various administrative and trade opportunities a relationship with Islam offered, West African rulers were wary of its "concept of a loyalty overriding the ordinary duties of a citizen towards his state."[12] As such, they were mostly constrained from demanding a blanket conversion of their subjects as this might also compromise the loyalty of their non-Muslim population. On the part of the citizenry who were wary of offending indigenous traditional sensibilities, the merchant and missionary elements who led the Islamic advance into West Africa maintained a measured approach to their proselytization activities in the earlier periods, choosing instead to focus on emphasizing the value in belonging to the Muslim community/brotherhood. For these main reasons, the approach to Islamization was generally gradual and measured.

Nevertheless, after a considerable period of interaction, the values of Islamic culture began to impress themselves upon local populations, leading to some adoptions and adaptations, which became the foundation for further expansion in the region. The cultural miscegenation that developed from this extended period of interaction with Islam and its culture produced among the people a system of mixed Islam that developed as a sort of compromise between Islam and the traditional religious belief system. This became a popular practice in the region until the seventeenth century, when it started to serve as the basis for Islamic militancy in expressing the same fundamentalist Islamist ideologies that produced the nineteenth-century reformist movements.

Although some historical reports convincingly registered the impression that the spread of Islam was not chiefly because of the mutual respect between the African converts and the Arab traders nor because of the profundity of the religion itself, it remains clear that African converts helped in the spread of the religion to the heart of West Africa. These include states such as Senegal, Senegambia, Niger, Nigeria, and Ghana, among others. Dependent chiefly on merchant dispersions, Islam followed the path of trade, establishing settlements along major trans-Saharan trade routes and pooling at the major trade centers, the locations of which differed with time. In this sense, the spread of the religion was not spontaneous but steady, and it followed an adaptive path. Since Ghana was one of the prominent West African states to adopt Islamic culture and influence, it played a vital role in spreading the religion's popularity in the heart of the region.[13]

Early Organization of Islam in West African Societies

According to some historical accounts provided by Al-Bakr, segregated Muslim communities linked to the trans-Saharan trade recorded a high presence of Muslims who were simultaneously taught Arabic literacy and culture.[14] Though missionaries did not always modify Islamic values to accommodate indigenous participation, they offered irresistible opportunities. These included the provision of information networks that allowed access to a more powerful knowledge base and enabled long-distance trade deals that benefited the ruling and merchant classes. This was enhanced through the provision of merchant tools such as granting credits to financially weak co-merchants and offering contract laws, among other things, to struggling political establishments. The sequestered Muslims who acquired a reasonable level of education and literacy in the Arabic culture became instrumental in creating social codes and moral principles.

With their proven intellectual capacity, Islamic clerics and missionaries became useful tools in the hands of the indigenous administrators, who eventually became interested in the religion and converted without reservations. As has already been established, a political leader's conviction has benefits for every idea marketed to the people. Apart from having the orientation that a leader was the natural model of moral and spiritual philosophy, they also wielded some social and political power to enforce their wishes in society. This explains why it was relatively easier to categorize people's social or religious positions based on what their leaders identified with during the time. The unique thing about these Arabic scholars is that they were, in earlier cases, merchant scholars who made economic gains while simultaneously spreading their religion. The merchants were instrumental in establishing an Islamic presence in Mali, Hausaland, and some other parts of the Sahel.

Clarifying that the modern political referent, Ghana, shares little relationship with the older Ghana Empire is vital to establishing that the success of Islam was related to the geographical and political connections brought by the trans-Saharan trade. The ancient referent had physical boundaries with the Middle Niger Delta region, consisting of parts of modern-day Mauritania, Senegal, and Mali. The Wangari, the Soninke, Malinke, and the Wa'kuri people were once the original inhabitants of these places. The fact, therefore, remains that the early people who accepted the Islamic culture never shared ancestral roots with those of contemporary Ghana. Even when substantial pieces of information associated the adoption of Islamic culture with coercion or the fecundity of the religion, the fact and significance of trade in this decision-making cannot be underrated. Kings within the societies of what was then Ghana, Mali, and other West African polities strengthened their external connections with the spread of Islam. They were inundated by an entirely new cultural spectrum that catered to their spiritual existence and the promise to improve their economic and political conditions.

Furthermore, this situation, which explains the likelihood of kings adopting or embracing the religion, is considered to be related to the opportunity to trade. They were more enthused by the realization that these Arabic merchants, starting from the eighth century, had relocated to many African places that they believed could serve their political interests. To a considerable extent, they became more persuaded and voluntarily helped spread Islamic culture. Following their settlements, people from different cultures and economic peculiarities began to mix. As they began to intermarry, they shared cultural ideas, values, and the basic principles of life over time. In this sense, the spread of Islam suggests the framework of modifications identified at the beginning of this chapter. Early converts, most of whom were kings who possessed the political power to influence social decisions or instigate its direction, consciously blended Islamic culture with African ones in the mixing aspect of Islamic exchange. As such, the relationship between Islamic scholars and local rulers was capitalized upon to ensure mutual dependency. The proliferation of Islam was also based on some modifications to existing social, political, and philosophical understanding. This was because it was difficult to resist the ideas and organizational structure of the religion, as its philosophies were responses to different parts of human existence.

From the twelfth century onward, Islam was established among the people, and the issue of its spread was later collectively pursued in the nineteenth century. In what would reflect the intricate connection between Islam and West Africans, the indices of identity later encompassed being a Muslim in many places in the savannah belt. With the rise of the Swahili culture, one noticed this kind of identity in East Africa.[15] In North Africa, the spread of Islam was notably successful, which dictated the relative success recorded in the Sahara Desert and the Sahel region of West Africa. A reasonable number of the converts in West Africa were influenced by proselytization, which reinforces the argument that tracing the beginning of Islamic culture in the West African countries must be linked to the exploration of Islamic activities in the North.

As for Islam in West Africa, the transformation of the religion hinged on some very important factors, some of which have been discussed here. Although there is a paucity of evidence that established that the rulers of the then Ghana Empire embraced Islam, there remains a consensus that it was received by traders and merchants whose connections helped spread the religion to people of similar social status. Hence, the notable factor was the centrality of the role of the masses or the peasants at the heart of Islam. Perhaps Islam found its greatest appeal in the checks it provided to the absolute power of their sovereigns and the protection against enslavement by co-adherents. Further propagation among the masses came with the jihads of the nineteenth century, where—stirred by a wave of Islamist fundamentalist fervor emanating from northern Africa—it became easier for them to identify with the idea, or perhaps simply because it appeared that their interest was being catered for. This enabled the root to be planted deeply into the fabric of their societies. Even more importantly, the critical mass of converts among the people would then consider it their social and moral duty to, in turn, contribute to the spread of such religious beliefs so that their chances of getting maximum benefits from the faith would increase.

Besides recognizing Islamic values and culture, many people in Mali also identified with Islam through conversion. Kings in the Mali Empire adopted Islam and encouraged the nobles to participate. One compelling instance of the Islamic impact was Mansa Uli Musa, who went on a pilgrimage to Mecca in the thirteenth century.[16] His historical religious tourism of Mecca led to the recognition of Mali by those in Cairo and elsewhere, who were awed by his wealth and generosity. Westward and southward of the Mali Empire encountered the infiltration of the Arabic scholars who continued with their proselytization into the heart of the savannah. Many more Islamic scholars came into the Mali Empire, which saw the establishment of Islamic schools and libraries after Mansa Musa's return from his journey to Mecca. Since converts studied and understood

Islamic literacy, they became the willing tool for the spread of the religion in West Africa.

Islam could accommodate millions of people so that as individuals of different faiths from other places were recruited, the numerical capacity of the religion was strengthened. The indiscriminate acceptance of the religion in the north and in some parts of West African states contributed significantly to its enhanced popularity and sustained it till the present moment. As more African people converted, they provided the force of attraction for foreign Arabic merchants and scholars to thrive in their places. Many of them became the internal compasses of such places and also volunteered their social participation for Islam to spread, and the flexibility of Islam to positional status reinforced its African domestication. Having realized that they could rise to clerical positions and make important decisions in the religion, people became committed to its course.

In many places, the Islamic crusaders became socially active by voluntarily involving themselves in social services such as performing administrative tasks, using inherent Islamic philosophy as a guide to their actions and engagement, giving educative opportunities to non-literate members, and volunteering to train them pro bono. They became equally useful for their spiritual existence by assisting in interpreting dreams, giving prayers on request, and doing so willingly. It is, therefore, arguable that the spread of the religion in West Africa had to do with the commitment of its missionaries. Making themselves useful in practical and community services essentially paved the way for the growth of Islam.

Factors Contributing to the Spread of Islam

There are inherent challenges in introducing a new idea, philosophy, or belief, especially when this new idea is to be shared with people through a different language. Despite the gradual introduction of Islam into the West African region, certain factors encouraged its spread, first among the ruling class and then to the general population. Islam became widespread in West Africa due to the persistence and pressure from those considered merchants and, at the same time, itinerant scholars and students. More importantly, it shows the incredible dedication of the carriers of the faith by penetrating the West African geographical boundaries. It is relatively possible to extend a faith or belief system, especially if people are not already occupied by a certain common belief system. However, it can be difficult, if not impossible, when people are deep-rooted in an indigenous worship system woven around their life aspirations and collective progression.

Before their contact with the world of Islam, West African countries were energetic believers in their religious systems.[17] Indeed, Ghana's nobles' indifference (alternatively, rejection) of the Islamic religion between the ninth and eleventh centuries was predicated on the internalized belief system they found conflicting with other forms of worship(s). Having observed the pattern of growth of the religion and analyzed the sequence, the following factors made it easier to penetrate the heart of the region.

Entrenched Scholarship

Before contact with other civilizations, Africans were exposed to indices of knowledge of their indigenous roots, including knowledge systems that were solely recognized and valued among themselves.[18] Therefore, the nature of this knowledge was reserved exclusively to a select few. One of the fundamental factors guiding the possession of knowledge during this period was secrecy. Perhaps because their knowledge systems were associated with other parts of life, such as business, security (safety), and spirituality, they centralized the systems and made them available only to a select few. This meant alienating some members of society whose exclusion from the knowledge sphere was either explained away as fate, or they were dismissed outright as unsuitable candidates for a society's secret knowledge infrastructure.

Automatically, knowledge seekers were willing candidates for any available belief system that favored and considered them viable in the acquisition of new and privileged knowledge. Islam conditioned itself to integrate these cultural agents into vibrant scholars with social importance. Perhaps Islam was looking for more converts who would understandably continue to extend the faith to the interior of African societies, so it was a tactical advantage to accommodate people and show readiness to convert them.

In addition, people were bolstered by the understanding that the acquisition of Islamic culture and religion would attract anticipated support from the influential leaders of the religion and, in the process, earn the support needed to become privileged members of society. Here, the Kanem-Borno case comes readily to mind. Their proximity to North Africa gave its leaders the geographical advantage to acquire Islamic scholarship and benefit greatly from the acquired knowledge.[19] This exposed them to new people and cultural traditions, and created a network of strong alliances in and outside their cultural boundaries. The adoption of Islam necessitated the exchange of diplomatic ties and embassies with the North African states, opening them to the global community through the Mediterranean countries. All this increased the popularity of the people in the region as they had unalloyed support from a bloc of followers of the same faith, which strengthened their economic bonds and increased their mutual respect. Apart from creating the possibility of the instant creation of wealth, it also gave them the necessary social regard to pursue their society's intended political and economic goals.[20] Therefore, scholarship became a very potent reason for the spread of Islam in the West African region.

The Emergence of an Indigenous Clerical Class

Another factor critical to Islam's advancement in West Africa was the development of an indigenous clerical class.[21] Before the Sudan region developed its indigenous clerical class, it depended on "North African coreligionists" to meet its developing religious needs. And, just as the value in trade commodities (particularly gold) from the region had attracted Muslim merchants to the area, so did the growing demand for Islamic teachers, scribes, diviners, and healers attract groups devoted to the provision of such spiritual needs, which easily translated to political relevance for the *ulama* (Figure 10.1).

Religious clerics were soon scattered around the region, finding their way into the courts of important rulers, where their services as scribes, religious instructors, and administrative advisers were welcomed and rewarded.[22] The expansion of Islam in the region, however, witnessed a remarkable leap in reaction to the development of indigenous clerical classes, not least because it toned down—in the eyes of the local peoples—the expatriate character of the religion and made it an African religion, which facilitated acceptance. More so, armed with a better grasp of local languages, traditions, and

FIGURE 10.1   Qur'an in two volumes with leather pouches https://commons.wikimedia.org
/wiki/File:Nigerian_-_Qur%27an_in_Two_Volumes_with_Leather_Pouches_-
_Walters_W853_-_Detail_A.jpg.

beliefs, this local clerical class was inclined to make a deeper impression on their people.
One of such (Fulani) clerical clans, the Torodbe, from Tarkrur, would play a decisive
role in the development of Islam in West Africa, especially from the sixteenth century.[23]

The Flexibility of Islam

One of the fundamental principles of Islam is its susceptibility to change. To say Islam
can change does not create the impression that Islam changes its core values to accommodate current trends in religious circles. It is mostly the opposite; instead, contextual
claims are made that border on African values. Islamic religion and culture carefully
address virtually all aspects of human experience and give judgment, advice, or recom-
mendations on the best approach. This is made possible by the availability of sufficient
intellectual materials attached to the Qur'an. These texts are called *hadiths* and represent the words and deeds of the Prophet of Islam during his existence on earth (Figure
10.2).[24]

Appropriating credibility to these two texts—the Qur'an and the *hadiths*—has helped
to circulate the religion to people of different creeds and beliefs. Islam was flexible to
African customs and traditions to a considerable extent. For example, Islam did not

FIGURE 10.2   Text from Hadith https://commons.wikimedia.org/wiki/File:Hadith_Al-Nabawi.jpg.

prohibit the popular polygamy marriage culture already rife in many societies. West African societies were peopled by individuals who supported their agricultural system and culture with the accumulation of many wives, leading to the birth of more children. They used their numerical strength to increase their farm sizes and businesses, and Islam did not condemn this practice. In the same vein, Islam was receptive to the leadership structure available in many places.

Being a patriarchal and monarchical society, the realization that Islam recognized a leadership structure that followed that design was key in accepting the religion. After their conviction that their positions were not threatened, the kings opened their arms wider to the religion. The fact that Islam protected the existing social order and leadership structure, the realization that the indigenous worship system was not threatened paved the path for Islamic growth. This situation, it must be pointed out, applied mostly to periods when Islam was entering a new domain and the number of Muslim converts was not enough to demand a change to/threaten the traditional status quo. However, the trend changed with the introduction of the spirit of Islamic revivalism and its fundamentalism from North Africa in the eighteenth century (from c.1747–1812).

The Jihads (Holy War)

The success story of Islam in West Africa is incomplete without the jihads.[25] Although the initial spread of the religion demonstrated peaceful exchange to a large extent, this is not to mask the roles played by the radical Islamic movements in spreading the religion. Islamic fundamentalism is not new to West Africa. Beyond its premise in the *hadith*, the jihad had found expression on many occasions in West Africa, famous among which were that of the seventeenth century (by Nasir al-Din) and in the eighteenth century (among the Torodbe in the regions of Futa Jallon and Futa Torro).[26]

However, early in the eleventh century, there was a preface to these "holy wars" in Western Sudan. Circa 1023, Tarsina launched aggressive attacks on the Sudanese people not long after returning from his pilgrimage to Mecca.[27] Unfortunately, he could not preserve his life. Succeeding this holy war was another brutal and bloody one in the fourth decade of the same century, circa 1040, during which the king of Takrur, War-Ajabbi, unleashed wars in his method of religious proselytization.[28] Between this time and the next decade, the Almoravid movement activated another holy war that ensured that the people of Ghana and Sijilmasa came under the control of Islam.[29]

Yet another development that stirred the spirit of Islamic revivalism in West Africa was the Wahhabi movement, "an angry surge of Islamic fundamentalism that swept the slothful Turk out of Arabia and established its first, puritanical regime there from c. 1747 to 1812."[30] In maintaining a constant stream of interaction with the outside world—North Africa and the Middle East—through the trans-Saharan trade and acts of pilgrimage, Muslims in West Africa had kept abreast with developments in the wider Muslim world. This, in turn, maintained some influence on the area as part of *Dar al Islam* (Islamic world). Thus, the "Wahhabi's revolt against Islam's lethargy and its otiose way of life"[31] and, perhaps even more importantly, the Sufi reactions to the movement contributed to enflaming an Islamic fervor that was already brewing underneath in Western Sudan.[32] The Sufi revival, "which reached a climax during the second half of the eighteenth century in the mosque of al-Azhar in Cairo,"[33] led to the founding of the Tijjaniya order.[34] Its influence on the nineteenth-century Islamic reform movements in West Africa is evident in the strategic role of the al-Azhar mosque—as the

FIGURE 10.3   Tombouctou-Mosquée of Djingerey-ber https://commons.wikimedia.org/wiki/File:Tombouctou-Mosqu%C3%A9e_de_Djingerey-ber_(AOF).jpg.

locus of ideological affirmation and dissemination—in Cairo, and also the impact of the Napoleonic conquest and occupation of Cairo on attitudes in the rest of the Islamic world (Figures 10.3 and 10.4).[35]

As the number of adherents exposed to the fundamentalist currents emanating from northern Africa grew among the populations of West African states, so did the sentiment that the societies in which they lived fell behind Islamic standards. This created a split between converts into rigorists (those against syncretism, who called for strict adherence to Islamic tenets/orthodoxy) and quietists (others who were for maintaining the status quo and mixed practice and religious coexistence). They intended to overshadow the so-called paganistic religious inclinations because of an inherent (though erroneous) belief that Islam was the only acceptable religion. Therefore, the militant ones accepted the responsibility to wage wars on those whose religions were considered paganistic, animistic, or outright impure to Allah. The association of spiritual credibility to other expressions of God was considered un-Islamic, and individuals convinced of Islamic supremacy could attempt to disallow the sustenance of "paganism." In a period culminating into the nineteenth century in Western Sudan, Central

FIGURE 10.4   Djinguereber Mosque, Timbuktu, Mali https://commons.wikimedia.org/wiki/File :Djinguereber_Mosque.jpg.

and Eastern Sudan, the historic jihads influenced the spread of the religion in West Africa.[36]

Trade

As early as the twelfth century, Muslim traders and scholars settled in various parts of the Sudan. They maximized this opportunity by settling in some of the market centers in the Sahel and later stretched it to the savannah environment. As identified by Ibn Battuta, Islamic merchants had no problem converting the nobles because of their positional advantage. There was equally corroborating evidence in Hausaland that during the fourteenth century, the Wangarawa people from Welle simultaneously exported their goods and religion, which was considered advantageous, and there were significant trade exchanges that predated these.[37] For example, from the mid-eighth century, Arabic merchants and scholars took the trade routes to penetrate parts of East and West Africa. Soon, they mingled with the locals and began to intermarry in the process. With trading as their reason for such interrelationship and miscegenation, these religious carriers continued to establish roots for Islam to thrive. Intermarriage usually compelled the exchange of cultural and religious philosophies; therefore, the established relationship between these Islamic merchants and the locals thrived and created new cultures.

The economic advantage brought by the introduction of Islamic culture was cashed in because of the availability of consolidating structures. Several West African countries were areas with developed agriculture-supported social and economic institutions. The fact that they had established agricultural products influenced many of these kings' decisions. Apart from making maximum use of the opportunity made available with the emergence of interregional trade, they could also place levies on individuals who engaged in the trading business. It was natural that the empires needed stronger security networks whose foundation could only be laid through an efficient military presence. However, this would be impossible without economic strength; therefore, the opportunity to tax trade and levy tributes through their satellite or proxy leadership structure validated their acceptance of Islam. And since Islam did not threaten their existing practices or challenge their supremacy, it was politically expedient to accommodate a religious inclination that could improve their economic conditions. As such, trade aided the Islamic culture and was instrumental in its eventual spread and awareness.[38]

The Impact of Islam on West African Societies

Culture

Islam brought about economic development, especially considering the transformation of the West African economy since its contact with Arabic merchants and missionaries. Another advantage is that it introduced the people to Islamic literacy and other habits.[39] Notwithstanding the introduction of Islam, all these additions that were ushered into West African politics came with some downsides. The first identified area of Islamic impact was the spread of Arabic culture with Islam. Arabs did not always separate religion from culture.[40] Everything was tied to Islam—from culture to economy, social

THE MOSQUE OF SANKORÉ

FIGURE 10.5   The Grand Mosque or Djingareyber Mosque in Timbuktu, Mali https://commons.
wikimedia.org/wiki/File:Dubois_1896_p300_Timbuktu_Grand_Mosque.jpg.

to political behavior and systems—and it was hard to separate these boundaries in the
Islamic culture.

Also, Islam was a threat to the survival of the indigenous religions in some areas.
West African cultures and traditions became immediate victims of the spread of Islam
as many Islamic scholars considered them anathema to the worship of Allah. Except for
certain locations where Islamic culture and indigenous cultural traditions converged,
some regions were separated by different beliefs. For example, the indigenous people
were accustomed to the veneration of the aged and the dead as an expression of reverence for individuals who had passed away.[41] This was considered irreligious and at most
sacrilegious in Islamic culture. It was believed that the only figure deserving of human
veneration in Islam was The Almighty Allah, and practicing otherwise suggests dual
loyalty, which received a ferocious condemnation (Figures 10.5 and 10.6).[42]

This orientation affected indigenous cultural traditions and systems the moment individuals were well-grounded in Islamic values. They immediately became loud crusaders
of Islam, to the detriment of their indigenous systems. Gradually but steadily, they demonstrated a higher commitment to the religion by avoiding indigenous practices that,
perhaps, could default on their usefulness in the new religion. The culture of reverence
for elders based on indigenous religion waned, and the corresponding veneration of the
aged and the dead had to be abandoned.

Cracked Unity

No matter how persuasive a philosophy appears, it cannot have a 100 percent record
of human patronage. People would always escape the participation of a belief system
or philosophy of ideas because of their ability to identify inherent loopholes and sometimes they might be unpersuaded. This exemplifies the situation of the then Ghana
Empire where, according to the reports of Al-Bakr, "the capital of ancient Ghana was
already divided into two parts; about six miles apart, the Muslim traders' part which

THE GRAND MOSQUE OF TIMBUCTOO

FIGURE 10.6   Timbuktu Sankore Mosque https://commons.wikimedia.org/wiki/File:Dubois
_1896_p279_Timbuktu_Sankore_Mosque.jpg.

had as many as twelve mosques and the King's part had one mosque for the use of the
king's Muslim visitors."[43] These two opposing parts comprised individuals of similar
indigenous knowledge systems that had been changed because of the circumstances of
conversion. These individuals were usually antagonistic toward the others because of
the inherent mutual suspicion that had been encouraged by the introduction of an alien
belief system.

   As the survival of religion usually demanded a reasonable political power, occasional
clashes often arose between relatives to upstage the other from the political seat for their
individual or parochial advantage. Such a scenario played out in Hausaland in the early
nineteenth century. The jihadists, led by Uthman dan Fodio, sought and successfully
established the Islamic political system as the "only" way to protect and uphold the
Islamic faith against degradation and usurpation.[44] Due to this, tensions were always
emerging within, and it unmistakably gave room for further divisions that made attaining
development difficult. In modern-day Nigeria, for example, the emasculation of the Old
Oyo Empire in the nineteenth century was characteristic of religious proselytization.[45]
Afonja, who had wanted the consolidation of satellite power in Ilorin and, perhaps, to
overcome the political and military base in Oyo, sought the alliance of the Fulani jihadists
in Ilorin, a garrison of the Old Oyo Empire. He used religious identity to seek external

coalition for the achievement of his provincial and ambitious agenda. Eventually, he was successful with that ambition, but the aftermath effects were equally consuming.[46]

Besides breaking the umbilical cord that connected him with the Oyo people in the process of seeking religious rescue from Muslim communities, Afonja also successfully created an acrimonious atmosphere. After the termination of his political opponents, those who provided him with political support turned against him and unleashed more havoc.[47] Therefore, the downside of the introduction of Islam was that it broke familial boundaries and undermined aspects of previous political control. Even among individuals from the same social backgrounds or networks, adopting Islam could have serious consequences on their relationship. The union was strained, making it impossible to create a united front in their process of political or social reformation or rehabilitation.

Religious Wars

One source of the problem was the understanding that people could be coerced to accept Islam. The fact that alternative African religions were unrecognized or not accorded enough respect created the basis for the extermination of indigenous practices and the subjection of the adherents to forceful conversion. While it was undeniable that pre-Islamic West African countries were not alien to intermittent wars or rivalries, there could be no contention about the disconnection of these wars from religious sentiments. Prevalent wars were inspired by economic emergencies and, sometimes, social exigencies. The older wars were not structured on differences in religious inclinations. However, the emergence of Islam in the region came with a culture of conversion inscribed in the religion's notion of jihad.

Islam accepted that one could fight for the establishment of religious principles. Wars created precedence and were used as the foundation to promote enforced conversions. For example, the incessant wars that dominated the Sudanese environment in the eighteenth and nineteenth centuries were justified on the basis of religious expansion.[48] People believed they were fighting the cause of religious proselytization, and, as such, they created an acrimonious atmosphere that impacted peace and stability.

Conclusion

From the preceding analyses, it has been established that the firm foundation of Islamic culture and religion followed a historical trajectory. The North African zone maintained culpable proximity to the Middle Eastern countries where Islam started. This proximity, however, was explored based on trade and education, giving primacy to the infiltration of the region by foreign merchants who simultaneously served as traders and missionaries. In the same way, the religion spread into the West African region due to commerce and diplomacy, among other things. However, getting into the region came with compelling realities, which have been explored in the body of this chapter.

Consequently, Islam brought an incredible trading opportunity, which reasonably boosted the region's economic growth. Scholars who were literate in the Arabic language and education gained influence, and there were Islamic schools to serve the needs of a new elite. Despite all these advantages, Islam came with immense consequences, including undermining the indigenous belief system, widening (dis)unity among the people, and introducing wars to win converts.

DEEP DIVE

Assignment 1

Objective

The objective of this assignment is to ensure that students complete the reading of Chapter 10 and to get them to understand how Islam spread and was largely accepted in Africa.

Method

Students will be expected to write a short answer in response to the question.

Reading Comprehension

Why was Islam an existential threat to African religions and traditions?

Assignment 2

Objective

The objective of this assignment is to ensure that students complete the reading of Chapter 10 and to get them to think about the various manners in which Islam reshaped religious, social, economic, and political life on the continent.

Method

Students will be expected to write a short answer in response to the question.

Reading Comprehension

Discuss the impact of Islam on West Africa in terms of trade, religion, politics, language, and education.

Notes

1 Ralph A. Austen, *Trans Saharan Africa in World History* (New York: Oxford University Press, 2010), 10; Ghyslaine Lydon, *On Trans-Saharan Trails* (Cambridge: Cambridge University Press, 2009), 52–54; and Anthony G. Hopkins, *An Economic History of West Africa* (London: Routledge, 2020), 129–130.
2 Corisande Fenwick, *Early Islamic North Africa: A New Perspective* (London: Bloomsbury Publishing, 2020).
3 Jamil M. Abun-Nasr, *A History of the Maghrib in the Islamic Period* (Cambridge: Cambridge University Press, 1987).
4 John S. Trimingham, *A History of Islam in West Africa* (London: Oxford University Press, 1968).
5 Ibn Battuta, "Audiences of the Sultan of Mali," in *Documents from the African Past*, ed. Robert O. Collins (Princeton: Markus Wiener, 2009), 15.
6 Peter B. Clarke, *West Africa and Islam: A Study of Religious Development from the 8th to the 20th Century* (London: Edward Arnold, 1982).

7 Mohammed El Fasi and Ivan Herbek, "Stages in the Development of Islam and its Dissemination in Africa," in *UNESCO General History of Africa, Vol III: Africa from the Seventh to Eleventh Century*, eds. M. El Fasi and Ivan Herbek (Paris: UNESCO, 1988), 68.

8 It is perhaps important to note that when Islam first found its way to the ancient kingdom of Ghana, many of the Berber groups were yet to convert to Islam.

9 Nehemia Levtzion, "Islam in Bilad al-Sudan to 1800," in *The History of Islam in Africa*, eds. Nehemia Levtzion and Randall L. Pouwels (Athens: Ohio University Press, 2000), 63.

10 Department of the Arts of Africa, Oceania, and the Americas, "The Trans-Saharan Gold Trade (7th–14th Century Century)," in *Heilbrunn Timeline of Art History* (New York: The Metropolitan Museum of Art, 2000).

11 This is because, in their experience, it was easier to change a people's position or orientation when the members of the authority that they emulated embraced a religion, a philosophy, or a new idea.

12 Humphrey J. Fisher, "The Central Sudan and Sahara," in *The Cambridge History of Africa Vol. 4: From 1600–1790*, ed. Richard Gray (New York: Cambridge University Press, 1975), 65. "The Fulani jihad was to prove the outstanding instance of the way in which the sword of faith might turn in the hands of those traditional rulers who had sought to brandish it to their own advantage."

13 Kazeem A. Adegoke, "Critical Appraisal of the Advent and Impact of Islam in West African States," in *Dynamics of Islamic Studies among World Disciplines: A Festschrift in Honour of Professor Ishaq Lakin Akintola*, eds. Taiwo M. Salisu and Kabir O. Paramole (Ogba: M-Class Publishers, 2018), 84–92.

14 Kane Ousmane, *Beyond Timbuktu: An Intellectual History of Muslim West Africa* (London: Harvard University Press, 2016).

15 Philip Curtin, Steven Feierman, Leonard Thompson and Jan Vansina, *African History from Earliest Times to Independence* (New York: Pearson, 1995).

16 Rene Bravmann, *Islam and Tribal Art in West Africa* (Cambridge: Cambridge University Press, 1974).

17 Jacob K. Olupona, *African Religions: A Very Short Introduction* (Oxford: Oxford University Press, 2014).

18 S. Muya, "The Efficacy of Traditional Knowledge in African Education," Paper Presented at the *Conference on Education and Indigenous Knowledge Systems in Africa*, College of Business Education, Dar es Salaam, Tanzania, August 2–3, 2007.

19 Nura Alkali and Bala Usman, eds., *Studies in the History of Pre-colonial Borno* (Zaria: Northern Nigerian Publishing, 1983).

20 Vincent Hiribarren, "Kanem-Bornu Empire," in *The Encyclopedia of Empire*, ed. John M. MacKenzie (Chichester: John Wiley & Sons, 2016), 1–6.

21 Lamin Sanneh, "The Origins of Clericalism in West African Islam," *The Journal of African History* 17, no. 1 (1976): 49–72.

22 Nehemia Levtzion, "Sociopolitical Roles of Muslim Clerics and Scholars in West Africa," in *Comparative Social Dynamics: Essays in Honor of S.N. Eisenstadt*, eds. Erik Cohen, Moshe Lissak and Uri Almagor (New York: Routledge, 1985).

23 John R. Willis, "The Torodbe Clerisy: A Social View," *The Journal of African History* 19, no. 2 (1978): 195–212.

24 Ram Swarup, *Understanding Islam Through Hadis* (New Delhi: Voice of India, 1983).

25 Philip D. Curtin, "Jihad in West Africa: Early Phases and Inter-relations in Mauritania and Senegal," *The Journal of African History* 12, no. 1 (1971): 11–24.

26 Aziz Batran, "The Nineteenth-Century Islamic Revolutions in West Africa," in *UNESCO General History of Africa, Vol. VI: Africa in the Nineteenth Century Until the 1880s*, ed. Jacob F. A. Ajayi (California: Heinemann, 1989), 540.

27 Ikenga R. A. Ozigboh, *An Introduction to the Religion and History of Islam* (Enugu: Fourth Dimension Publishing Company, 1988), 104.

28 Lucie G. Colvin, *Historical Dictionary of Senegal* (New Jersey: Scare Crow Press Inc., 1981), 18.

29 Mark Cartwright, "The Spread of Islam in Africa," *Ancient History Encyclopedia*, May 10, 2019, https://www.ancient.eu/article/1382/the-spread-of-islam-africa/.

30 Mervyn Hisket, "The Nineteenth-Century Jihads in West Africa," in *The Cambridge History of Africa, Vol. 5: From 1790–1870*, ed. John E. Flint (New York: Cambridge University Press, 1975), 126.
31 Hisket, "The Nineteenth-Century Jihads in West Africa," 126.
32 Batran, "The Nineteenth-Century Islamic Revolutions in West Africa," 543.
33 Hisket, "The Nineteenth-Century Jihads in West Africa," 126.
34 Batran, "The Nineteenth-Century Islamic Revolutions in West Africa," 543; and Hisket, "The Nineteenth-Century Jihads in West Africa," 126.
35 Bayard Dodge, "Al-Azhar," *World Affairs* 123, no. 2 (1960): 44–46.
36 Hisket, "The Nineteenth-Century Jihads in West Africa."
37 Paul E. Lovejoy, "The Role of the Wangara in the Economic Transformation of the Central Sudan in the Fifteenth and Sixteenth Centuries," *The Journal of African History* 19, no. 2 (1978): 173–193.
38 Stelios Michalopoulos, Alireza Naghavi and Giovanni Prarolo, "Trade and Geography in the Spread of Islam," *The Economic Journal* 128, no. 616 (2018): 3210–3241.
39 Ibrahima Diallo, "Qur'anic and Ajami Literacies in Pre-colonial West Africa," *Current Issues in Language Planning* 13, no. 2 (2012): 91–104.
40 Jeanette S. Jouili, "Islam and Culture: Dis/junctures in a Modern Conceptual Terrain," *Comparative Studies in Society and History* 61, no. 1 (2019): 207–237.
41 Igor Kopytoff, "Ancestors as Elders in Africa," *Africa: Journal of the International African Institute* 41, no. 2 (1971): 129–142.
42 Imad N. Shehadeh, *God With Us and Without Us: Oneness in Trinity Versus Absolute Oneness* (Cumbria: Langham Global Library, 2018).
43 Cartwright, "The Spread of Islam."
44 Hamza M. Maishanu and Isa Muhammad Maishanu, "The Jihad and the Formation of the Sokoto Caliphate," *Islamic Studies* 38, no. 1 (1999): 119–131.
45 Joseph A. Atanda, "The Fall of the old Oyo Empire: A Re-consideration of its Cause," *Journal of the Historical Society of Nigeria* 5, no. 4 (1971): 477–490.
46 Stephen A. Akintoye, *Revolution and Power Politics in Yorubaland 1840–1893* (London: Longman, 1971).
47 Samuel Johnson, *The History of the Yorubas from the Earliest Times to the Beginning of the British Protectorate* (Lagos: CMS, 1921).
48 Paul Lovejoy, *Jihad in West Africa During the Age of Revolutions* (Athens: Ohio University Press, 2016).

11

CHRISTIANITY

Introduction

The inability of the Christian religion to break meaningful ground within African society for a long time was due to the social and political distance between missionaries, the locals, and the "Gentiles."[1] For years, this disconnect hindered the spread of Christianity as the expansion of religion, even of culture, required the numerical strength of people who shared different cultural and religious values to allow for the proselytization of a newly found faith and the spread of its influence in an exponential capacity. However, the marginal size of this Christian community changed significantly during the second century when, under the reign of the Roman Emperor Trajan, the Jews of Cyrenaica and Egypt experienced a crisis, leading to complications of unimaginable proportions.[2] As a result of the conflict, the Alexandria church dwindled in social status, and as soon as they foresaw the possible extermination of the Christian faith, the Christian Church consciously began the induction of new individuals into the religion in the Greek-speaking population of Lower Egypt.[3] Christianity continued to penetrate various communities throughout various demographic areas as centuries passed.

The subsequent century brought about the success of religion in another dimension. For example, the Coptic-speaking Egyptians were attracted to the religion by factors related to the fervor of its crusaders.[4] Their reception of Christianity was also underscored by the previous efforts to translate the bible into the Coptic language. Language variations were considered in translating the Bible to the people's dialects, as individual linguistic differences were carefully catered for. The occupants of these geographical locations were included in the practices of the religion, whereas they were otherwise required to learn (to possibly understand) the Hebrew language. In the century that followed, the religion was also reported to have made significant progress in its intentions for wider numerical and geographical spread.[5] Though Christianity's growth during this period focused on communities of non-indigenous Africans, there would have been no

DOI: 10.4324/9781003198260-14

transformation, spread, or influence of the religion on the native Africans without these events and history.

The Spread of Christianity to West Africa

The proximity of North African countries has long been considered an influential factor in attracting external impact.[6] West Africa was known to those in the Middle East and Europe. North Africa was also perpetually invaded or systematically infiltrated by external civilizations with their expansionist agenda.[7] In the process, North Africa was exposed to and participated in the rise of Christianity up until the founding of Islam and its rapid spread.

In areas with a minority of Latin speakers, an African Church was established and presided over by the Archbishop of Carthage, the capital of the Roman province of Africa.[8] For centuries, attempts failed at exporting Christianity to most of North Africa, which probably explains why it did not spread across the Sahara as well. One challenge was the separation in language and culture between the different regions and a lack of the bible translated into the local languages. Thus, unlike Islam, Christianity could not have taken the North African routes to West Africa.

The initial introduction of Christianity to West Africa via the sea was initiated by the Portuguese.[9] Aware that the Muslims had recorded considerable progress in converting Africans to Islam, the Portuguese were motivated to take a similar, if not more effective, measure in their determination to spread the Christian faith. Upon realizing that their goal of maximizing the spread of Christianity could be achieved through a more inclusive approach, the Portuguese sent missions to West Africa to communicate with the "lost souls."[10] An outstanding aspect of this venture was the understanding that religious conversion could go along with trade. Along with other European missionary agents, the Portuguese understood that minds could be converted by obtaining slaves and other commodities. As a result, they pursued evangelization and enslavement simultaneously as measures of expansion and control.

The use of slaves in Europe, as early as the fifteenth century and perhaps prior, inspired Spain and Portugal to expand into the African continent to secure labor for agriculture and advance their missionary objectives.[11] Despite the Europeans' belief in the system's mutual benefit, an irony was the simultaneous enslavement of Africans and the projection of the Christian faith. The Portuguese, who introduced Christianity to the West African coastal areas, believed that by bringing enslaved Africans to Europe and other places to develop their agriculture, they were also salvaging or redeeming "lost souls." Regardless of the moral question that has remained unanswered about the tenability of the engagement in slavery, those who introduced Christianity, especially the Portuguese, dismissed the idea that enslaving Africans betrayed their religious claims.[12] The debasement that Africans experienced under the enslavement system calls into question evangelization's objectives.

The concurrent engagement in slavery and proselytization was legitimized by the legal backing of those in power who approved Portuguese traders and missionaries to go to West Africa. According to Adrian Hastings, "The Portuguese Padroado Real was effectively granted by Pope Leo X in his 1514 brief Praecelsae Devotionis, a control over the Church overseas almost greater than that exercised by the king at home."[13]

These documents served to solidify the determination of the Portuguese and other Europeans to engage in crusades in the name of the Church. For example, around 1483, the Portuguese established their presence on the Gold Coast, where they were asked by the local authorities to seek alternative places for settlement. They declined the request and insisted on "saving the lost soul of the King to prevent an inevitable doom from befalling him."[14] Though the king disagreed, their insistence on staying set the foundation for a conflictual relationship.

PART A

Early Contacts with European Explorers

The introduction of Christianity to West Africa can be traced back to the early contact between European explorers—Portuguese navigators in the fifteenth century, and the indigenous peoples of West Africa. These first contacts created the foundation for future missionary endeavors. Portuguese missionaries' innovative efforts in the fifteenth century led to the introduction of Christianity to some coastal parts of West Africa. In around 1415, the Portuguese invaded a part of Africa, capturing Ceuta. Prince Henry the Navigator organized these expeditions.[15] As the Portuguese looked for a sea path around Africa to the East, they were the first European explorers on the west coast of Africa. They aimed to end Arab control over the commercial route to the East via the Mediterranean and overland to the Red Sea and the Indian Ocean with succeeding expeditions.

The Portuguese exploration of Africa was partially attributed to the search for the Canary Islands and Cape Bojador. With this journey, they aimed to understand the strength of the Muslim Moors, who were considered the enemies of Portugal. Another explanation for the search was to find Africans who could help them fight against their Muslim rivals and another to spread the gospel to Africans. Until he died in 1460, Prince Henry sent explorers to sail to Cape Bojador to accomplish these goals. Through his efforts, some coasts of Africa were visited, and the Cape of Good Hope was also explored. After his death, several expeditions were launched; one landed at Elmina in the Gold Coast (now Ghana), the Coast of Sierra Leone, and Cabo Mesurado in modern Monrovia. Later, Fernando Gomez explored the coast of the Kingdom of Congo, the Islands of *São Tomé*, the Island of the Gulf of Guinea, and Senegal.[16] From here, exploration and missionary activities spread to other regions of West Africa.[17] Subsequently, the Church was established in West Africa in the fifteenth century, and the first missionary work was done on an island off the Atlantic coast. Pope Pius II designated a Portuguese Franciscan as Guinea's prefect in 1462; four bigger Islands were later converted in 1472.[18]

The early Portuguese explorers who brought Christianity into West Africa rarely did so beyond the trading posts on the coast. In some cases of their failed trials into the hinterlands in places like Benin and Warri in Nigeria, they were not able to do much until the nineteenth century when more missionaries took over the spread of the gospel.[19] When the missionaries and explorers numbering up to six hundred landed in Elmina, Gold Coast, in 1482, this marked another landmark in introducing Christianity into West Africa. After their arrival, they visited the Elmina Chief (Kwamena Ansa) to seek his alliance to strengthen and establish a profitable trade relationship and asked him to convert to Christianity. The Chief cooperated and gifted them a piece of land to build a Chapel and Fort. Similarly, in 1489, Behenti, the chief of Wolof (in Senegambia), and twenty-five people converted to Christianity.[20] Baptism was even performed four years later, largely due to political motivations. Having gained incursion into the Gold Coast, the missionaries by 1485 got to the capital of Mandingo in the interior, after which the King of Benin asked for the missionaries to be sent to his kingdom. Those sent in response initially failed to convert the king to support the religion because the king's real motive was military help, not Christianity. However, the king of Benin was baptized six years later and another a century later.[21]

Role of Missionaries

Missionaries, explorers, traders, and benefactors traveled to West Africa in large numbers through the efforts of European countries like France, Germany, and Britain. However, the primary agents of introducing Christianity to West Africa were European missionaries from various Christian denominations, including the Catholic Church, Protestant denominations like the Anglicans and Methodists, ex-slaves of African descent, and later, African-initiated churches. These missionaries greatly aided the spread of the Christian faith.

Catholic Missions

The Catholic Church was one of the first Christian denominations to establish missions in West Africa. Prominent missionaries like Father Théophile Ribot and Father Francisco Fernandez were instrumental in establishing Catholic missions in regions like Benin, Ghana, and Nigeria in the sixteenth century. The Roman Catholic Mission introduced Western education alongside Christianity to the Oba of Benin and chiefs around 1515. They built a school in the Oba's palace for his children and other chiefs' children. They instilled in the children Western education and Bible reading. Between 1515 and 1522, Portuguese traders arrived in Lagos, Nigeria, scrambling for raw materials and markets.[22] They won many converts, and Spanish Friars went to Benin around 1655. Spanish Jesuits attempted to spread Christianity to Sierra Leone in the late sixteenth century, but political unrest ended their efforts. Africans had little contact with European priests, who focused their ministry on European traders. However, the effort led to the conversion of a Sierra Leonean chief named Philip, who was baptized in the early seventeenth century.[23]

As a result, the missionaries were encouraged by the king and local Roman Catholic Church authorities to attempt to convert their African trading partners so that they could be recruited as allies in the fight against Islam. However, due to the prevailing commercial curiosity in the trade of slaves and pepper, which had become prevalent, missionary work was less common in the fifteenth century.[24] However, the Portuguese showed a noticeable interest in missionary work during the sixteenth century. For instance, in 1514, the Oba of Benin sent a diplomatic mission to King Manuel of Portugal, and in 1515, Christian priests arrived in Benin. Churches were constructed, a prince and some chiefs were baptized, and they started learning to read and write.

Due to the establishment of the Society of the African Mission to spread the Roman Catholic faith, Christianity was planted. In 1819, a young French woman from the town of Lyon founded the Associations for the Propagation of the Faith, which included organizations like the Society of African Missions and the Holy Ghost Fathers. From the eighteenth century onward, these new Roman Catholic missionaries made a significant contribution to the return of Christianity to West Africa. Sierra Leone and Liberia were transformed into the birthplaces of modern missions in Africa once the slave trade was abolished; although the society had attempted to spread Christianity in Sierra Leone in 1860, it was unsuccessful. The Roman Catholic faith was transplanted from Sierra Leone to Dahomey.

Nevertheless, Father Borghero established the Roman Catholic religion in Dahomey, present-day Republic of Benin, with the help of two other missionaries. Father Borghero, an Italian Roman Catholic priest in Dahomey's Whydah, visited Abeokuta and Lagos in 1860.[25] He returned to visit Lagos in 1862. But when he got to Lagos, he encountered several Catholic freed slaves from Brazil who had made a home there. Father Borghero was additionally taken aback when he encountered Brazilians residing in Lagos who had been baptized in the Roman Catholic Church. When Father Borghero met some people in Lagos who practiced Roman Catholicism, he was inspired to start a mission station there, but it did not have a regular priest. By 1862, Father Borghero had established Lagos as one of Ouidah's outposts in Dahomey and had dispatched a catechist there named Padre Antonio, a liberated slave from *São Tomé* Island.[26] While stationed there, Nigerians and other nationalities who resided in Lagos were taught the Roman Catholic faith by Catechist Padre; he performed various Christian activities. In 1868, the Catholic Mission changed Father Pierre Bouche's position as the resident Priest in Nigeria and relocated him to Lagos. The following year, the Roman Catholic Mission constructed a chapel in Lagos along with a primary school.

Protestant Missions

Protestant missionaries came to the subregion only after 1617.[27] Reverend Melville Horne, an Anglican Priest, went to Sierra Leone, attempting to evangelize. He emphasized the importance of missionaries learning the local languages of their potential converts and joined the Church Missionary Society (CMS) as an advisor.[28] Later, after the Dutch defeated the Portuguese in 1637, missionaries from the Dutch Reformed Church joined them. Methodist influence started with settlers from Nova Scotia in Freetown in 1792. The most prosperous Protestant missionaries were Presbyterian and Methodist.

The Protestant Evangelical spirit and enthusiasm inspired the Roman Catholic Church to establish Catholic Missionary Societies in France and other European nations, free from secular authority and political or commercial goals.[29] Due to political pressure, the Basel Presbyterians left Christiansborg in 1918 after arriving in 1828. The Wesleyan/Methodist missions came in 1835. Through Captain Potter, William de Graft's "Bible Band," also known as the "Meeting," a group he founded in the Gold Coast, asked the WMMS for Bibles, and on January 1, 1835, a missionary and copies of Bibles were sent to the Gold Coast to spread Christianity. Meanwhile, the North German missionaries from Bremen arrived in Cape Coast on May 5th, 1847. They started work at Peki on the

14th of November 1847 and penetrated mainly German Togoland among the Ewe until World War I forced them out in 1919.[30]

Through the efforts of missionary organizations like the Basel Missionary and the Church Missionary Society (CMS), Christianity was also propagated in Ghana, Nigeria, and Sierra Leone. Protestant missions gained prominence in West Africa. During the nineteenth century, the Christian societies that sent their missionaries to Africa included the Wesleyan Methodist Missionary (WMMS), the British-based Anglican Church Missionary Society (CMS), the London Missionary Society (LMS), the Protestant Missions (PM) from France, Germany, Holland, and the United States of America. The French Catholic Mission (FCM) came after the Protestant Mission (PM). Missionaries like J. T. Van der Kemp, John Philip, Thomas Birch Freeman, and Mary Slessor (a Scottish Presbyterian missionary in Nigeria) not only spread Christianity but also advocated the abolition of the slave trade in West Africa.[31]

The societies of these missionaries had a duty to abolish the slave trade and promote "legitimate trade" between Africans and Europeans. The missionaries built Fourah Bay in early 1827 in Sierra Leone and introduced Elementary Schools in the Gold Coast and Nigeria by the 1870s. In 1876, they opened their first secondary school, the Wesleyan High School, named Mfantsipim School in Ghana. Bishop Ajayi Crowther (c. 1806-1891),

FIGURE 11.1   Religious image with Virgin Mary blessing African children https://commons.m
.wikimedia.org/wiki/File:Mary_blessing_Africa.jpg.

who was converted to Christianity, was a pioneer student of Fourah Bay College and later translated the Bible into the Yoruba Language.[32] The Protestants stressed the value of studying and comprehending the Bible and the necessity of translating it into African languages. Students who attended mission schools took on Christian names, European attire, and Christian ways and attitudes of living to further accommodate Africans into Church-based lifestyles (Figure 11.1).

Roles of African Freed-slaves

The British Mission and other Christians, such as William Wilberforce, were partly instrumental in abolishing the slave trade. Missions preached the abolition of the slave trade based on God's love. However, scholars have pointed out that it was found that some European merchants continued to engage secretly in this trade after the abolition in 1807. As a result, the British government used its navy as a coast guard to check the nefarious activities of slave traders in the British colonies. The British designated Freedom Town in Sierra Leone to be inhabited by recaptured slaves. The missionaries further emphasized the biblical teaching that all human beings are created in the image of God (Genesis 1:27), and the biblical instruction of Exodus 21:16 proved that the slave trade was anti-Christian.[33]

Many areas of Africa saw the start of new missionary groups, including the LMS, CMS, Holy Ghost Fathers, White Fathers, etc. In 1804, the CMS and 1811, the Methodists started their work in the villages of Sierra Leone's liberated slaves. The missionaries had early success in places like Freetown and the nearby settlements. The Liberian coast, where Afro-Americans and former slaves were converted, was one early success story. Additional locations included the French outposts in Assinie, Grand Bassam (Ivory Coast), and Libreville (Gabon).[34] Missionary organizations founded in Europe and America around the eighteenth century were successful around 1840 in converting the people to Christianity and establishing long-lasting mission stations among the populace in West Africa. This was immediately after the end of the slave trade, which inspired new religious interests among Europeans and Americans. The emancipated slaves in areas like Sierra Leone and Abeokuta supported missionary endeavors with the help of missionary organizations. The Presbyterians sent Rev. Hope Masterton Wadded, Mr. and Mrs. Edgerl A. Chishalm, and E. Miller, who arrived in Calabar in April 1846, to establish the church of Scotland Mission in Cross River, a former slave-trading town of Calabar.[35] Their labor flourished because a Presbytery—the Presbytery of Biafra—was established in 1858. The Pioneer Missionary, Rev. Thomas J. Bowen, established missions in Ijaiye and Ogbomoso before traveling to Badagry due to the operations of the American Baptist Mission that began in Nigeria in 1850.

The freed slaves who had settled in Badagry and Abeokuta got the help of the Wesleyan Methodist, who sent a missionary named Thomas Birch Freeman, an assistant called William de Craft, and his wife from the Gold Coast to Badagry, in the same vein the Wesleyan Methodist sent Henry Townsend to Abeokuta. As ex-slaves were structured and stations opened in Lagos and Abeokuta, significant social, cultural, and religious transformation in Africa was mostly influenced by freed slaves. Former slaves in Britain and America gave most of the impetus for missionary engagement with Africa in the nineteenth century, and some later returned to Africa as missionaries, motivated by Christian providentialism and personal ties to their African ancestry.[36] Significantly, huge conversion movements that swept through Africa in the late 19th and early 20th centuries were heavily influenced by Christianized ex-slaves. In West Africa, where the Royal Navy released more than 70,000 slaves in Sierra Leone after the British abolished the slave trade in 1807, the influence of former slaves was especially notable. Many of those scattered into Christian villages around Freetown converted to Christianity before returning home to the coast of West Africa as representatives of Christian modernity.[37]

The gospel spread into the interior of the continent partly due to the involvement of former slaves in missionary activity, as many more African people were converted and trained by these freed slaves. They represented the European missionaries, most of whom had already departed West Africa and now served as the heads of various missionary organizations. They included Garrick Braide, a catechist in the Niger Delta region of Nigeria and a pastor for the Church Missionary Society (CMS), and Cyprian I. Tansi, a priest in the Roman Catholic Church. The former slaves were crucial in persuading and converting their people. Some native converts later worked for the European missionaries as priests and agents.[38] The recruitment and use of former slaves native to the area were necessary for the gospel to reach the interior territories. According to Deanville (1942), several Yoruba ex-slaves in Freetown, Sierra Leone, asked that missionaries be sent to Badagry to teach the Gospel, among other things, and so the Methodists sent missionaries to Badagry in the beginning in answer to their plea.[39]

Andrew Wilhelm, John McCormack, and Henry Townsend of the C.M.S., two ex-slaves of Egba from Sierra Leone, came to Abeokuta in 1843. A Yoruba freed slave named Samuel Ajayi Crowther joined the C.M.S team to spread the gospel in remote locations. Additionally, the Brazilian ex-slaves who had relocated to Lagos asked RCM to bolster the Catholic religion there and elsewhere, which prompted the establishment of RCM in Yoruba in 1886. By 1879, in northeastern Nigeria, W. Allakurah Sharpe, one of the Wesleyan agents who had been captured in Kanuri, begged for missionaries of the Wesleyan to be sent to Kanuri.[40]

Some former slaves, including the Rev. Thomas Birch Freeman (an ex-slave of an English mother) and William de Graft (an educated Ghanaian), made the indigenous people joyously receive the Gospel, and they did not hesitate to utilize other humanitarian services.

Role of African-initiated Churches in the Spread of Christianity in West Africa

During the colonial period, African Independent churches also arose. These churches opposed European missionaries' control of the Church and emphasized Africans' right to find their indigenous forms of Christianity that would incorporate aspects of traditional African culture that Christianity had previously rejected, like polygamy and syncretic practices.[41] With the emergence of an African Independent Church (AIC) in Sierra Leone in 1821, there were indications that African Christians were unhappy with how white missionaries conducted their work. The 1890s saw the formation of independent churches in Nigeria.[42] By the nineteenth century, African-initiated churches began to emerge, with some being headed by prophetic movements led by charismatic leaders. Prominent figures like William Wade Harris in Liberia and Simon Kimbangu in the Congo provided spiritual leadership that resonated with Africans seeking an alternative to Western missionary Christianity. These were often syncretic, blending traditional

African religious beliefs with Christianity. Examples include the Kimbanguist Church in Congo and the Aladura churches in Nigeria. They often incorporated elements of traditional African spirituality into their religious practices, making Christianity more culturally relevant to local populations. This syncretism helped bridge the gap between African traditions and Christian beliefs, typically led by African pastors and leaders, fostering a sense of autonomy and self-determination among African Christians.[43]

In Lagos, Nigeria, the United Native African Church was founded in 1891 as a break away from the Anglican Church; this has also shown improvement in the numbers of new, independent churches, each of these churches with a special goal and aim to uphold the African model free from the ideologies of the European missions, to represent a truly African church opposed to the ones established by Europeans. The African-initiated churches adopted aspects of African religious ethos, such as healing, spontaneous displays of worship, and ancestor veneration, while establishing their ecclesiology and polity. Though all of these places of worship condemned witchcraft, many accepted the practice of polygamy. Africans' love of rhythm, music, dance, and singing was taken seriously, which helped spread Christianity over the region. Whereas mission churches avoided faith healing due to concerns about syncretism, it was vigorously practiced by African-initiated Churches. The desire of African-initiated Churches to use the church to achieve spiritual and physical healing for everyone—not just the person but also the entire community—led to a growth in the expansion of the religion infused with African cultural and political values in West Africa.

Challenges and Resistance

Missionaries often sought the conversion of local rulers and elites, recognizing their influential role in their societies. The conversion of rulers had a cascading effect, leading to the conversion of their subjects, though the introduction of Christianity in West Africa was not without challenges. Many Africans resisted the new religion, viewing it as a threat to their traditional beliefs and practices, while missionaries often faced hostility and suspicion, considering that missionaries sought to convert Africans on both a spiritual and cultural level. Christianity and Westernization were mutually exclusive (if not synonymous) in this sense. If Africans did not assimilate into Western culture and civilization, they were still considered "pagans."[44] To this end, European churches stood against key African social institutions like gender roles, polygamy, festivals, funeral ceremonies, and worldviews. Africans were to be converted to Christianity to acclimate to Western Civilization; this view and its corresponding actions led to suspicions and resistance from Africans. Some missions used tactics like bans on polygamy, ancestral cults, and food rituals.[45] These acts of outlawing African culture led to many misunderstandings and diverse interpretations of biblical texts. For example, the missionaries' staunch opposition to polygamy, a prevalent African tradition that involves marrying many wives, was interpreted differently by Africans within the Christian context than by the missionaries. For many Africans, polygamy—and the numerous babies that came with it—was a godsend since it allowed for large-scale cultivation. A prosperous polygamist who cared for his wife and kids had high prestige. Additionally, polygamy was viewed as a guarantee of women's protection and was the cornerstone of the extended family, clan, and ethnic group.[46]

One of the most notable forms of resistance was the practice of syncretism, where traditional African religious beliefs and practices were merged with Christian elements.[47] For instance, in Nigeria, the Yoruba people combined their traditional deities (Orisa) with Christian saints, creating a unique religious blend that allowed them to preserve their cultural identity while outwardly appearing to embrace Christianity. However, certain elements of people's lifestyles could not be hidden, such as their marriages; missionaries of all denominations adviced their converts to divorce all but one of their spouses in order to be approved by the church. They could not be baptized until this was done, along with their families, and men with many wives could be excommunicated.

However, few white missionaries baptized first-generation believers. The inability of Europeans to survive in the tropical region of West Africa presented a difficulty for the missions in their endeavors to spread Christianity across the region. The environment also posed a significant obstacle to their efforts. They could not do so since they were unfamiliar with the area's tropical environment. For example, malaria was another illness that hindered the spread of Christianity in many areas of the hinterlands, and other missionaries suffered from heatstroke. The abundance of harmful insects (mosquitoes and the tsetse flies), the humid and unfamiliar climate, the absence of good harbors, the unfriendliness of the natives, the slave trade, and the Sahara Desert barrier were all cumbersome challenges to missionary enterprises in Africa.

The early missionaries also had challenges spreading Christianity because insufficient Christian material was available. The missionaries had to learn the local languages to translate the Bible and write several grammar books because neither Bibles nor grammar books were available in the area. For instance, the Rev. Johannes Zimmermann translated the complete Bible and a history of the Bible into the Ga language in Ghana in 1858. He additionally developed the Ga language's grammar. Rev. John G. Christaller, known as the "Father of Twi Literature," in 1874 also produced Twi grammar and vocabulary as a collection of Twi proverbs, a Twi translation of the Bible, prayers, and hymns.[48] The missionaries and the natives initially encountered a language barrier. The missionaries proposed that an interpreter be used for the native people to converse with them properly. However, in certain instances, missionaries spent a lot of time trying to learn African languages (e.g., the missionaries in Southwestern Nigeria spent time learning the Yoruba language[49]) or teaching the natives their European languages to convert people to Christianity.

Nearly every mission in West Africa experienced financial difficulties at the beginning of their missionary career. They were heavily reliant on the financial support of their local churches. However, even when money and other resources were available, they could not reach their destination in time. This was because all ships arriving at the coast at the time belonged to trading corporations and businesses whose primary focus was on trade. In this situation, supplies and other items had to be sent to different places, though not in the vast amounts that the missionaries would have preferred; the situation was only exacerbated by the lack of transportation the missionaries and their supplies faced from the coast to the land's interior.

African Agency, Independent African Churches, and Pentecostalism

Africa is part of the story of Christianity. The areas of Ethiopia and the Horn of Africa were connected to the Middle East from ancient times. Christianity spread to North

Africa. As pointed out above, initial attempts to spread the religion after the fifteenth century did not succeed. During the nineteenth century, African converts became the very agents that spread the religion. Indeed, the spread and dominance of Christianity in West Africa were made possible by Africans.

From the 1880s onward, Africans transformed Christianity in various ways. The rise of African Independent Churches created local missions controlled by Africans who interpreted the Bible and Christianity in ways most suited to them. Known as "inculturation," the Gospel became adapted to African culture. Thus, for example, "Yoruba Christianity" has emerged, accepting the core values in Yoruba culture as part of being a Christian. By the time we entered the twentieth century, the process of "inculturation" had produced the Aladura, hundreds of local churches known for their emphasis on praying. While the older mission churches, such as the Anglican, Baptist and Roman Catholic, remained, over the years, many churches were created in West Africa, with origins and leadership specifically African. Today, the most widespread is known as Pentecostalism.

Pentecostalism shares many things in common with the ideas of enculturation expressed in the late nineteenth century. The brand of Christianity developed from the thinking that spiritual life requires human consciousness, which would be reflected in the deliberate conversion of energy to facilitate the Holy Spirit. It is an offshoot of the religion that emphasizes a personal relationship with God, demonstrated in the dissipation of one's energy when in the presence of God.[50] It is important to state that this form of Christianity is now widespread in West Africa, most especially in Nigeria.[51] What fundamentally differentiates the Aladura and Pentecostal churches from the earlier white missions and Western-derived denominations is the understanding that Christians should always experience true conversion through baptism rather than mere declaration or proclamation.

Furthermore, Pentecostalism pursues an individual, dynamic relationship with God, which may manifest in speaking in tongues, healing, or the gift of accurate prophecy. This relationship and its resulting gifts are all known tenets of African-derived-churches and contemporary Pentecostals.[52] Although there have been controversies about some of the beliefs expressed by Africans in the nineteenth century and beyond (such as practicing polygamy or joining secret societies), the support of multiple Biblical passages is promoted by the African-derived churches.

The West African Pentecostal movements always receive a favorable appraisal among the global contemporary Christian community.[53] Their deeply embedded roots in the community allow them to command more worshippers. Mensa Otabil of the International Central Gospel Church, Enoch A. Adeboye of the Redeemed Christian Church of God, Joseph Ayo Babalola of Christ Apostolic Church, David O. Oyedepo of the Living Faith Church Worldwide a.k.a. Winners Chapel International, and Benson A. Idahosa of the Church of God Mission International, are very important names in the construction of the identity of the Pentecostal faith in West Africa.[54] In their efforts to adapt the Pentecostal religion to indigenous African practices and cultures, these leaders have made large sociological and political impacts connected with some developments during the nineteenth century.

Most of these Pentecostal churches are domiciled in Nigeria, which by no means dwarfs the reality that they have made equally significant leaps in other West African countries.[55] The massive turnout of the participants in the religious denomination attests to Ghana and Togo, two other West African countries, having a major presence of Pentecostal followers. Their redefinition of Christianity and the vibrant ways of portraying it appear to easily guide believers to remain committed and hopeful, adding hope and faith to conspicuous materialism.[56] Since the nineteenth century, the success of African-derived churches is a combination of what they initially received and their brilliant adaptation to African culture and fresh interpretations of the scripture.[57]

PART B
The Rise of Independent African Churches in the Nineteenth Century

Introduction

Africa's tapestry of belief systems shapes how people see life, interpret it, and relate to it. Religion in Africa has been at the core of the relative perception and descriptions of the fundamental characteristics of the continent. Embedded so much in the identities, traditions, and ideas of the continent, the question could be asked, would Africanism mean as much without the highly sophisticated religious and cultural attributes it has? These religious characteristics have endured from the pre-colonial ages of the continent through to contemporary African societies, manifested in the invigorated cultural enactments in seemingly eluding cultural values.

Taking this as a basis to understand the remote consciousness in the minds of Africans, one would partly understand the reason behind the continent gradually becoming the headquarters of Christianity and taking a position in the global politics of religion. Having received Christianity for over 500 years at different intervals, Africa has influenced the practice of the religion through syncretic results as practiced in the continent. Many practices in the world have been influenced by what could be well described as African Christianity. There is evidence of Africanness and African cultural subscriptions in the Christian practices in many places across the globe, as those in the diaspora have carried around these specific practices. Although the influence is seen in all types of Christian practices, Pentecostalism is one of the most evidently influenced branches by African Christianity.

Because of its popularity, Pentecostalism has grown to have different missions worldwide and becoming important in the global-trend-change in the practices.[58] It seems Africa caught the fire of the Azusa Street Revival of 1906 and, rather than let it die, spread it so strongly that it is often considered the starting point.[59] Now, several Pentecostal churches in Africa have global standings, having different branches across the globe and continuing in their expansions. For instance, the Redeemed Christian Church of God (RCCG) has been said to have foreign missions in about 160 countries across the globe, with more than 732 branches only in the United Kingdom.[60] The Living Faith Church (Winners Chapel) has branches in about 147 countries as of 2014.[61] Continentally, the fast growth of Christianity and the proportion of Christians on the continent is remarkable. For instance, 95.5% of Zambians are Christians, while 94.7%, 93.6%, 92%, and 90.7% of Africans in Seychelles, Rwanda, DR Congo, and the Republic of Congo respectively are Christians.[62]

This significant growth did not start in recent times or even with the establishment of many of these common churches in Africa, but rather, the potential of the spread and strength of African churches could be seen in how African Independent Churches had risen from the nineteenth century to earlier parts of the twentieth century; providing different options of Christianity to Africans.

The nineteenth century saw different religious movements by Africans, especially during the process of the consolidation of colonial rule on the continent. These were also partly in response to several issues, developments, and dissatisfactions that pricked the people's hearts during that period. Some were dissatisfied with the distance the early practices had from African cultures and believed that basic convictions could not practically allow for more engagement of the people. Hence, they outgrew the European religious practices and religious approaches for more relatable practices and what they saw as purpose and spirit-driven Christianity. The need to keep in touch with cultural practices that had heavily defined the people and the convinced syncretic importations into Christianity also made the creation of African Independent Churches necessary.[63] This included the conviction in healing and deliverance ministries triggered by pre-existing metaphysical understandings.[64]

More so, the reputable leaders at that time had been able to see beyond the antics of what was introduced to them by Europeans, and some either claimed to have received revelations from God or saw the need to break away from the limitations set by the European churches or factors that were seen to be a bar to free spiritual manifestation in the church.[65] So, to some extent, there was a need for the autonomous and independent practice of Christianity in Africa, particularly during colonization, because of the perceived peculiarities of the people.[66]

The Emergence of African Independent Churches

As expected, African Independent Churches did not emerge on their own. The nexus of their birth and prosperity is largely credited to multifaceted factors inherent during pre-colonial times and the early stages of colonialism. The Early Christian missions introduced the religion into the African community through various means that proved irresistible for Africans at those times. The emergence of African Independent Churches can be traced to efforts to resist White Christians' political, historical, and sociocultural views on Africans.[67] The African worshippers faced heavy biases in all aspects of their lives, and through the superiority of whiteness and Europeans in the church, Black Africans were being robbed of their Africaness as everything European was deemed greater and more spiritual.[68]

On the other hand, African dressing styles, names, and musical instruments were systematically unaccommodated in the Church as to the extent of original faith. This depicts that one could not become a proper Christian without being an African. Early European missionaries' perceived lack of interest in learning and embracing African ways gave way to discrepancies in the order. Apart from this, the Christianization of Africa held more weight for the foreigners than the indigenous. This was because Christianity, at that time, was enshrined in commerce, regional trade, colonization, and access to natural resources to the detriment of Africans who were disadvantaged in these practices. The resulting de-Africanisation of African values questioned the sanctity of the Church as an encompassing religion. Though Africans accepted the new order, they continued to hold onto their values and beliefs outside the boundaries of the Church. For instance, witchcraft and superterrestrial powers were strong beliefs in African societies, and the metaphysical appreciation of them could not be easily foregone. However, these beliefs were watered down in orthodox Christian practices and termed superstitious or barbaric, leading to fallouts at various phases.

As the need for African Independent Churches grew, notable figures in various locations rose to champion the separation and legitimate establishment of African Christianity. The impacts and popularity amongst the populace were seen in the followership they enjoyed. This was further evident in the followership of the likes of Wade Harris, Samuel Jackson, and Oshitelu among the leaders of Independent African Churches.[69] Their approach included addressing African beliefs of supernatural powers, the realization of the greater power of God, and the need to rely solely upon him with faith. These allowed Africans to have a Christianity they could picture through the lenses of their Africanness.

The establishment of the Church Missionary Society (CMS) in April 1799 brought about 17 clergymen and nine laymen to England. The committee that saw these movements' establishment had Williams Wilberforce, a strong voice against the slave trade, and Reverend John Venn and Charles Simon as pioneer members. Their resolve was to take the gospel of Jesus into the World of nonbelievers, with Evangelists being sent to faraway lands, especially where the emancipation of slaves was ongoing (e.g., Freetown, Sierra Leone).

This continued for years until a founding pioneer of the mission, Mr. Fowell Buxton, opined that Africans should be out to work in promoting the gospel for the redemption of Africa.[70] He offered that only then could modern civilization come to place Christianity as a catalyst of growth at the center. This vision resulted in the missionary expedition that came to Niger in 1841.[71] This expedition, which was comprised of Anglican and Methodist priests, having suffered setbacks, found its way to Badagry in 1842 at the behest of the Aku from Freetown, who made the frequent call to have missionaries there through meetups with Trinidad-Hausas.[72]

The CMS aimed to ensure an independent African Church was in order. Its churches were to be self-sustaining, self-supporting, and propagating. These saw the rigorous training of Africans in administration and skills acquisitions that would enable them to run effectively. Christianity had spread to Abeokuta during this period and was in Lagos by 1852.[73] These efforts saw the training of notable African clergymen like Bishop Ajayi Crowther, James Johnson, and others. One good attribute of this was that Africans quickly learned and grasped the teachings quickly enough to become well-versed individuals in Bible knowledge. They quickly expanded their knowledge base by training others to become assistant African bishops, catechists, and schoolmasters.

Such progress came at a cost as European missionaries started displaying hate for the successes achieved by the Africans. While Africans continued to gather educational qualifications and training in their numbers, many less-educated Europeans feared being outshined. To mitigate this crisis, the Church bestowed honorary degrees to foreigners in Africa to ensure their expertise and power remained over the natives. This act alone brought to light their contemptuous behavior towards African clerics, further paving the way for autonomy.

The reasons behind the development and rise of African Independent churches are many and not restricted to the desire to create a church that enjoys autonomy from the orthodox churches. One of the reasons was that Africans were not properly acknowledged or trusted with responsibilities that were core to the faith at that time. Hence, as a form of revolt, some Africans broke away to enjoy more autonomy and freedom in the practices of their faith. The case of the establishment of the CMS in Nyanza demonstrates this unequal relationship, as its refusal to give spiritual leadership duties to Africans and African clergy led to the establishment of the Church of Christ in Africa.[74]

African Independent Churches were not exempt from having their own political motivations and foundations. Many of them developed as political expressions and inciters of movements against colonial governments and authorities. The political motivations and directions of the churches were often imputed through their interactions with the sovereign properties of colonial governments. For instance, before his repatriation from Ivory Coast, Prophet William Wade Harris treated the Liberian flag with disdain and frustration from political build-ups.[75] Prophet Harris and other clergymen were tainted with politically motivated intentions in their movements outside the Orthodox churches. Harris and his likes were alleged to have been recruiting African clergymen to resist, including efforts towards the reduction of capitalist tendencies as well as the reduction of tax rates.[76]

Their motivations have also been expanded to include formulating economic gains by forming revolts based on economic deprivations. The sociological context of their movements varied from region to region and by country, based on collective experience. Olowola explains:

> These can be viewed in three areas: in South Africa, it is a reaction against apartheid; in East and Central Africa, it is a reaction against the land occupation of the white settlers and in other areas, it is a reaction against the social injustice of different types.[77]

As far back as 1967, Independent African Churches existed in various African countries.[78] These churches can be found in about thirty-two out of Africa's forty-one nations and colonies.

Separatists' movement of Independent Churches saw the establishment of popular churches in Africa. These movements had distinct modes of worship as Christian organizations; their activities were embedded in Africanness to suit the needs of adherents. These movements experienced developments based on their immediate societies. For instance, the development of African Independent Churches in Eastern Africa varied in theological virtues. One example was the Akurinu Church movement, which dates back to 1926[79] in Kenya. To a large extent, the Church movement addressed the country's sociocultural, political, and economic instability around 1830-1930. This coincided with the return of World War I veterans who told tales of the violence and harsh realities of who the Europeans were. At this time, Kenyans had begun to stir their national consciousness, and any efforts that helped to end white supremacy were welcomed. The Akurinu movement gained momentum in the late 1920s when four prophets from Murang'a claimed to have heard God's voice directing them to a worship retreat at Mount Kenya.[80]

This revelation came with the gathering of adherents to the Holy Mountain to attain spirituality. As the movement became a household name, the colonialist administration became wary and sought to end what they termed a "likable rebellion group" due to its large size. These brought about a series of persecutions and sanctions. Eventually, on the 2nd of February 1934, a notable Akurinu figure, Joseph Nganga, and his two assistants were shot dead by colonial soldiers.[81] Despite this, the adherents refused to falter; they became stronger and even earned the respect of the colonialists in the long run.

To attain the recognition they deserved, the group applied for official registration with the government, and consequently, the movement was registered under the name Holy Ghost Church of Kenya in 1959. This act was part of the body's steps to build permanent churches throughout Kenya after Independence. Steps to building independent bodies and institutions were also found in other countries in East Africa, particularly Ethiopia. Ethiopian Independent Churches stood out from the masses in their attempts to merge African lifestyles with Christianity in easily understood ways. This included the integration of the clamor for African self-improvement and leadership in the church as opposed to the European traditions, which preached a reliance on the Holy Spirit. These groups emphasized that God was not distinctly European but for all and did not condone colonization, with the understanding that salvation was not race or country-centered. These claims were more proliferated and digested by the nation's population, given that Ethiopia remained its own country as those territories surrounding it were under colonial rule. Reinforced by its early contact with Christianity since the time of evangelists like Philips, Ethiopia maintained its position as a model to other African Independent Churches and as an example of the ability of Africans to be in power without white interference.

The development of African independent churches in Ethiopia could be traced to the gradual prevalence of the concept of Ethiopianism, which saw the birth of several churches that tried to accommodate the cultural uniqueness of Ethiopians. Similar ideas of cultural relevance, social freedoms, and political independence were filtered into independent all-African churches by South African mission workers, highlighted by the movement in the 1880s.[82] Churches like the Tembu church, established in 1884, and the Church of Africa, established in 1892, were other examples of gravitation towards Africanism in Christianity.[83]

The Ethiopian church was also established in 1892, and Mangena Mokone, the founder, clearly indicated the church's intention to accommodate Ethiopian values.[84] The challenge in the Orthodox churches that led to these different establishments was the missionary churches' refusal to allow Africans to hold sensitive positions in the church and the importance that Ethiopia had as a symbol for African Christianity among the people. Their mentality regarding the land and its uniqueness was further strengthened by their references to Bible verses, such as, "Let Ethiopia hasten to stretch out its hands to God" (Psalm 68:31). This protracted scriptural relevance placed churches as "African Zions."[85] The African pride found in Ethiopianism was drawn largely from the long links the country had with Christianity on its own without the interference of Europeans, and as such, originality was one of the ideals sought to be projected.

One of the highlights of the Ethiopian African Independent Church's development was the movement by Simon Kimbangu, who was often regarded as a semi-literate who had claimed to receive directions from the Lord through visions. He was once converted by the missionaries and carried on his course until he claimed to have received a vision directing him to take on the duty of a healer and a prophet in line with the bible. This was one of the evidential proofs of the existence of a messianic approach in the African Independent Churches. He first tried to run from the divine responsibilities vested in him and looked for a job elsewhere. This was his story until he retired in 1921 to continue providing preaching and healing services to his people. He later started the Kimbanguist church, a separatist church distinct from the religious styles hitherto received.

Most West African countries like Nigeria saw the establishment of African Independent Churches in their communities through the activities of several religious movements. West African countries represented some of the most phenomenal Christian nations at the early point of the importation of the faith into the continent. Nigeria was one of the frontrunners in developing African Independent Churches; it started as a protest movement of the people against the exclusion of the African indigenes from the affairs of the churches and the missionaries. African churches functioned as reflections of the nationalism that was gradually making strides, especially among the traditional and the early nationalists in the country. The religious elites in West Africa, including figures like James Johnson and Edward W. Blyden, championed different demonstrations of displeasure at the colonial government and the discrimination against African clergymen in Nigeria, culminating in the establishment of the United African Church in September of 1891.[86]

The United African Church was the first indigenous African church in Nigeria and the beginning of other African independent churches, a position debated with respect to the Native Baptist church. The contraction was that the African Baptist Church, established in 1888, was only African in its leadership while retaining foreign attributes and practices.[87] The Native Baptist Church was established to address some early protests within the church and not to have an African tradition or distinction from the European Orthodox churches. Later, in 1894, the Native Baptist Church was brought back into the fold of the American Baptist Church, finalizing its distinction from a proper African Independent Church for this discourse.[88]

Nevertheless, 1901 saw the establishment of the African Bethel Incorporated at Ebute Meta. The church was established by Africans dissatisfied with how they were treated at St. Paul's Breadfruit Church. This was also the case in establishing the United African Methodist Church (Eleja) in 1917 after the Africans became aggrieved about the operations at the Methodist Church, Ereko, in Lagos.[89]

The developments continued, and the Aladura churches, which translates loosely in Yoruba as "The Prayerfuls," became a rallying point for the hundreds of thousands who sought a break from the mundane Western idea of Christianity. The Aladura Movement began in 1918[90] as a dissenting voice to the lack of spirituality and the religious forms of Western Christianity. The movement arguably was an offshoot of the Faith Tabernacle Church in Philadelphia, as the former influenced the latter through a literature publication.[91] Apart from this, the beliefs in divine healing and protection and moral codes based on puritanical virtues resulting from the 1918 influenza epidemic led to the creation of a prayer group by laymen members of the Anglican church.[92] The evident departure of many adherents in their folds in 1922 led to the creation of a new Christian order, the Faith Tabernacle, with diverse congregations.[93]

With time, the separatist movement gained momentum and expanded, owing to the divine healings of the renowned prophet Ayo Babalola,[94] whose healing abilities drew a mammoth audience to his prayer session. This was a trying moment for Yoruba religious adherents. There was low patronage and regard for the deities, and thus, traditional rulers were forced to mount suppressive pressures on the infant church. The coordinated persecutions from the traditional rulers, mission churches, and government forced the Aladura Movement to seek aid from the Pentecostal Apostolic Church in Great Britain. As one would expect, the union didn't last. Efforts by the missionaries from Britain to promote monogamous marriages, the reliance on medicine, and the exertion of full authority over the movement led to internal crises, which resulted in the establishment of the Christ Apostolic Church in the 1960s. By this time, the movement had gained many followers and extended to Ghana (Figure 11.2).

The Kimbaguist Church in Belgium Congo was the major face of the Independent Church in Central Africa.[95] It was the first and largest independent church accepted into the World Council of Churches in 1969. The church movement derived its name from its founder, a Baptist-trained catechist from the Lower Congo who drew attention to his movement through mass healings and biblical teachings in April 1921. Prophet Simon Kimbagu,[96] who trained in a British-run Baptist Missionary School, greatly impacted people across the Belgian Congo, French Congo, and Angola. He was called "Ngunza," which means prophet in the Kikongo language.[97]

The church was famous for its distaste for politics and violence, magic and witchcraft, dancing, the use of alcohol and polygyny. Despite the display of zero tolerance

FIGURE 11.2 Missionaries of the Basel Mission in Christiansborg (Accra-Osu) https://commons .wikimedia.org/wiki/File:Missionaries_Christiansborg_around1860_B002a.jpg.

for violence through advocacy for peace and community development, evident in the humanitarian and social services carried out in its early days, Prophet Simon was arrested and sentenced to life imprisonment for insurrection by Belgian authorities in 1921. The clampdown and persecutions that followed his arrest had no impact on the growth of the church. The church waxed stronger as it could preach the doctrines to neighboring communities, transcending natural limitations, class systems, and hierarchies. The growth continued until 1959, when the government officially recognized the main group. This move brought to life smaller groups who also regarded Kimbagu as God's special prophet and continued the religion's path.

Down in Southern Africa, the Zionist Churches took the attention in heralding African independent churches in the region. Like other AICs, they were significant for their subscription to the healing progression of the church, and Africans took the important role of championing the course of the movement. The church was motivated by the 1896 Chicago churches of the Christian Catholic Apostolic Church in Zion that spread its mission to South Africa before the end of 1904.[98] The theologies of the church were also accommodative of the healing roles of churches and the preponderance of the flow of the holy spirit in the church. The Pentecostal Zion Apostolic Church also developed from this philosophy, with the view of adding the second baptism to the core tenets of the church, something they considered to be lacking in other churches. These new churches adopted nomenclatures that would suggest the radiation or presence of the holy spirit in the church; hence, their descriptions as Spirit or Zion Churches. In the 1920s, the Zimbabweans opened the doors of their faiths to the Zion churches after the introduction of some workers from South Africa.[99] Beyond that, the Zionist Churches have been developing rapidly and have a large bearing on discussions on Christianity.

Syncretic, Theological, and Ritual Characteristics

Several theories have been developed on how the motivations behind the creation of every African Independent Church have caused distinctions between them and the conventional missionaries and European churches. Scholars like Kombo have also distinguished the ideological foundations of the churches from the perspective of how and why they were created.[100]

Some churches were established based on the belief in the reception of divine visions of the leaders and the mission that had led their leaders to their establishment. They were referred to as Messianic African Independent Churches.[101] The leaders were treated as messiahs whom God called out to push the movement for different purposes as the spirit might have led.[102] This could be seen as the basis of the celebrity preachers that have manifested in contemporary Christian practices in the continent. These churches took the concepts of healing and spiritual powers important in contra-distinction from the dogmas of the traditional or missionary Christologies. This brought them to a direct clash with the belief systems of the Orthodox churches and doctrines.

The ideology of these newly formed groups could have risen from the overbearing issues and the preponderance of African Traditional Religious beliefs on the influence of extraterrestrial forces on human nature. This was quite manifest during the 1918 influenza pandemic and the growth of African Independent Churches.[103] Some examples of these churches include the South African church called Nazareth Baptist Church (the Shembe Church) and Nigeria's Cherubim and Seraphim Church. Isaiah Shembe, who established the Nazareth Baptist Church,[104] Moses Orimolade Tunolase of the Cherubim and Seraphim Church,[105] and Kimbanguist Church's Simon Kimbangu in DR Congo were examples of those who were in the messianic position within their respective churches.[106]

The Ethiopian African Independent Churches, as a class of the AICs, also had distinctive characteristics in the phenomenal developments of African churches.[107] It should be noted, however, that these churches were not exclusively different, as the ethos of other churches could characterize a church. One of the major theological characteristics of the class was its different perception of the Old Testament in the bible.[108] This class believed that they had a direct link to the Old Testament Israelites and, as such, welcomed and used Jewish doctrines in their practices.[109] The Hebrew bible, therefore, had great bearing on their liturgy and doctrines.[110] It was also characteristic of the church to emphasize the importance of prophecy, healing, and miracles, following their manifestations and waves in the Old and even the New Testaments.[111]

These theologies have a link to the story of the Eunuch in Acts Chapter 8 of the Bible, from which they ascribed the basis of the trace of their faith.[112] Their support for prophecy and healing could have been heavily informed by preexisting traditional religious practices, just like the messianic class of the churches. The African Israel Church Nineveh and Ethiopian Orthodox Church were in the spotlight of these beliefs.[113] Abuna Yesehaq Mandefro, who founded the Ethiopian Orthodox Church in the Western Hemisphere, Archbishop[114] Enoch Mgijima of the Israelite Church of God in Jesus Christ in South Africa, and Rabbi Wentworth Arthur Matthew, who founded the Jamaican Ethiopian Hebrew Congregation also featured in this category.

Another class was the Zionist Churches, which characterized why many classes were linked to prophecies as one of their values; the Zionists took it as a primary and core foundation of their faith.[115] The Zionists were seen as one of the important classes of the movements of the twentieth century and also attracted traditional belief systems like others. They were important in the social structures of their communities as social justice and community participation were central to their beliefs. These churches included the Celestial Church of Christ in Nigeria and Zion Christian Church in South Africa.[116] Samuel Bilewu Joseph Oshoffa of the Celestial Church of Christ in Nigeria, Frederick Modise of the International Pentecostal Holiness Church in South Africa, and Engenas Lekganyane of the Zion Christian Church in South Africa were some of the leaders of the Zionists Church class.[117]

The difference between these churches and the Orthodox churches could be seen as a manifestation of syncretic changes and acclimation in Christianity, a phenomenon that continued radically to the contemporary practice of Christianity on the continent. The African Traditional Religious practices and beliefs served as the major sources of the adopted syncretic practices that characterize pillars of African Independent Churches.

First, the practice of ancestor veneration, which was particular to African Traditional Religious practices, was imported into the African Independent Churches at a considerable measure.[118] At some point, the Zion Christian Church and the Aladura had a special regard for the ancestors, whom Africans assume to be intercessors to God.[119] These practices received early criticism with an accusation of being capable of promoting idolatry and witchcraft in the name of flexibility of practices. Appealing to the ancestral spirits for guidance allowed Christians to relate Christianity to their cultures.

The Bible was deployed to reinterpret and reconceptualize divination in the new churches.[120] This was for the benefit of healing and the divination of problems and information; to be valid, clergy sought to provide biblical justifications. This helped extend practices and education to understanding African myths and legends and the relationships between the physical and spiritual planes.[121]

The Orthodox churches were largely seen as lacking charisma in their processions and manner of practice.[122] The adoption of charismatic postures by African churches distinguished them from the Orthodox. It became the basis of African Pentecostalism and was further encouraged by the Azusa Street movements in 1906. The churches believed in allowing the Holy Spirit to flow freely in the church and to be led by its spiritual direction.[123]

African religious beliefs are quite established on the strength of spiritual consultations, and the importation of these offered religious comfort zones to Africans. Hence, prophecy, speaking in tongues, and healing were perceived to be pillars of every church, conceptions that they felt were not properly propelled in the Orthodox churches. The syncretic attributes of the churches are beyond the bounds of African Traditional Religions. This is because, at that time, Africa was becoming a religious hot zone and a lab for religious solidification and missionary responsibilities. Hence, the co-existence of other religions also impacted the metamorphic transformation of Christianity in Africa. So, the preponderance of Islamic practices and Hinduism provided syncretic options for the churches. Hinduism and Zulu African cultures could be traced in the Shembe Church, and the combination of Islamic and African Traditional Religions was manifest in the practices of the Celestial Churches and Aladura churches in Nigeria. More so, the naming system practiced in these churches created a peculiar link with the rites of passage evident in African cultures.[124]

In Nigeria, the period of the development of the churches saw the adoption of several Yoruba ethnic beliefs, both religious and merely cultural.[125] Peel tried to distinguish this from syncretism by stating this:

> Can these churches be called syncretists? Not if we mean by that a desire to unite in one system what they saw as valuable in Christianity with what they identified as traditional Yoruba religion. Rather the opposite, for they justified their innovations on the grounds that the non-religious aspects of Christianity, which were owed to European culture, were being replaced by Yoruba non-religious elements.[126]

The distinction suggests that syncretism should be the adoption of religious materials and not mere cultural materials. While Peel has established this rightly, it is important to understand that separating religious values from culture is tricky in Africa since many cultural values are established from religious epistemology and metaphysical appreciations. Hence, using Yoruba music, songs, and other materials is distinctive because they are not limited to expressing religious attributes. More evidently, religious rituals in many of these churches were becoming similar to what was obtainable in the traditional practices.[127]

AICs and African Identities

The intention of creating African Independent Churches at the inception was not solely geared towards promoting Africanism or preserving cultures as a primary goal. It was mainly for the relatability of Africans, who were long immersed in the cultural and traditional materials of the continent with the new religion. More so, the readiness of the people, as well as their reception of the ideas, have shown that the churches were there to stay and, as such, could be used to acclimatize the convictions of people. With these needs for religious comfort, African identities were gradually preserved through what should have ordinarily been a murder of their cultures and religions.

The introduction of African cultural values in the practices of Christianity by the early members of African Independent Churches acted as measures of preservation of the cultural values of Africans within the ethos of Christianity. This helped them develop their liturgy, healing cultures, and church structures in such ways that connected the church to African identities. Singing cultural songs that aligned with or were amended to conform with Christianity were styles of the conceptions of African cultures, promoting African identities. The quest for the expression of faith practically provided a secondary achievement of having the church serve as an institution that mirrored the understanding of the people and a window to their identities. It turned the foreign, ambiguous influences around them into practices, ideas, and segments of their lives they could recognize as "African Christianity," which could be distinguished from the rest of the world's Christianity.

Today, Christian prayers, songs, creeds, and other religious materials have been made to adjust to traditional alternatives. This is better seen in the development of religious linguistics that has embraced African languages for several religious activities. The Bible has been interpreted into African languages to allow people a deeper understanding of the scriptures. The use of African languages for conducting services has become a standard practice. It is a common scene to see a preacher who preaches in English or a European language and has an interpreter beside him to consider those who do not understand English or French or any language used in the introduction of the religion.

In addition, the worship styles and practices in African independent churches were influenced by those that came from pre-colonial cultures and religions. Continuing these traditions was believed to open the door for originality and genuine worship, allowing people to feel God in what they saw as their original forms. These include the rituals performed in church, vibrant music, and even dances. Moreover, the elements of spirituality directly reflect African identities and belief systems, given that the people are well subscribed to human interactions with the spirit.[128]

However, there continues the presence of churches engaged in battles against sorcery, witchcraft, and ancestor worship that have now attained automatic assumptions of their negative significance because of the seed of hatred planted by the frontrunners of the colonial religions in Africa.[129] While these African cultures were put to use and adopted by the early Christians and members of the African Independent Churches, they also saw the need for the purification of African cultures and convictions in such a way that their practices in the church would not be adverse to the ultimate teachings of the Bible as well as question the supremacy of the Lord and Christ over the church as foregrounded by the Bible.

The African Independent Churches created a platform for overcoming religious hypocrisy, being that it gave Africans the opportunity to be genuine Christians, as well as genuine Africans without the threat of spiritual cobwebs that demanded the abandonment of all cultural values that were not of the Europeans or seen in the Bible.[130] Clifford sees the churches as a balance between the concepts of universalism and syncretism and recommends that the continuous development of the practices in contemporary Africa should reflect the same when he says:

> The importance of maintaining a balance between being genuinely African and genuinely biblical in the process of enculturation and the need to avoid syncretism or universalism cannot be overemphasized. African Christians must be discerning in their approach to enculturation, ensuring that they do not compromise the essential tenets of the Christian faith while also being sensitive to their cultural context. By avoiding syncretism and universalism, African Christians can maintain a balance between being genuinely African and genuinely biblical, and ensure that their faith remains faithful to the biblical message.[131]

To create a culturally sensitive and relevant environment for Africans that would allow them to worship in the manners they understood, the churches needed to assert their independence from the Orthodox churches and the colonial governments. The emphasis was on the religious autonomy of the churches and the core administration and leadership of the churches led and guided by African spiritual leaders. From this angle, there was a reflection of the desire for self-determination that made the churches form the basis for actualizing and promoting African agency and identities.

The adoption of practices like polygamy and respect for traditional institutions in the conceptualization and indoctrination of the churches allowed them to have a reflection of Africanism. The Zion Christian Church, Apostolic Faith Mission, Celestial Church of Christ, Aladura Churches, and other churches at the time either allowed the practice of polygamy in the church, with some of the religious leaders or stakeholders having more than one wife or were indifferent about the practices. The intention at the time could have been to make the church wide open to everyone, despite their ideological foundations. The reflection of these elements of African identities at the early stage often brought the churches against Orthodox and Western Christianity. The Western churches or Orthodox churches did not entirely come to Africa independent of the colonial agenda of European empires. Hence, the creation of the churches also acted as a response to the instrumentality of the church as propagation of the colonial agenda in their respective colonies. In this way, the idealists of the churches were breakaways from cultural imperialism being made solid in the minds of Africans and instead used the churches as agencies of African identities.

Moreso, the doctrinal and theological differences portrayed the members on the verge of possible Christian abuses that were termed indirect paganism at the time. Hence, accusations of paganism and heathenism expanded doctrinal tensions as the new practices were strange to the Orthodox churches. More importantly, the churches became a direct and worthy competition to the missionary spread of the Western and Orthodox churches at the time. From the preceding, it could be seen that the portrayal of African identities, intentionally or not, created a new light for those under the oppression of colonialism and restrictive European Christianity, though it created new challenges for these institutions, which continue to plague their existence.

The development of the African Independent Churches has shown to be a religious force of nationalism. It aimed to take Africa to Christianity and not just Christianity to Africa. The concept grew from this dissatisfaction towards the treatment of the Africans to properly restructuring the church liturgy and dogmas to make the religion comfortable for Africans and allow it to accommodate African idiosyncrasies. Hence, the churches are evidence of the role of the church in the re-establishment of Pan-African ideology and solidification of the African image. This is seen in how they have developed into global religions, positioning the continent in a lucrative and precarious location in the religious politics of the world.

PART C

Impact of Christianity

Education

Christianity has brought many positive and negative consequences to the West African people in different ways.[132] One advantage of Christianity's influence in Africa was the institutionalization of a more standardized education system.[133] Education was not alien to the people or structured by how missionaries organized their religious teaching methodologies. The missionaries were responsible for the form of educational system available in the region today, which has resulted in the codification of different languages and the acquisition of literacy skills. Whereas previously, and in many areas currently, the extant education did not emphasize literacy, it centralized society's survival skills and the necessary cognitive development of its students. The missionary education initiatives revolutionized West African countries and repositioned their role in the global culture and economy.[134]

Health

Another aspect where missionaries have contributed significantly to the available institutions in West Africa is health services, redefining medical practices and systems.[135] The Europeans undertook this initiative because many parts of West African countries posed health challenges, leading them to contract diseases that sometimes claimed their lives. Their intentions to "win souls" were sometimes sabotaged by being surrounded by hot weather, insects, and unfamiliar environments. However, rather than withdrawing their stake in the land and its people, they built medical centers to address emerging health challenges.[136] Even though these services were intended to meet their needs, missionaries sincerely spread the benefits to Africans.

Economy

The economic effects of Christianity can be seen as twofold. On the one hand, bringing religion to the continent facilitated trade through colonialism and enslavement. There was no place where the missionaries settled where trade was not permitted. The establishment of missionary centers was influenced by evaluating the proximity to coastal communities.[137] Thus, missionary activities were impacted by the economic value they provided for the people. During the period of the slave trade, the trafficking of slaves was permitted by the missionaries.[138]

Evaluating the Legacy

Introducing Christianity has impacted the region's socio-cultural and evolving dynamics of religious pluralism. During the transatlantic slave trade, Christianity was wielded as a means to justify the subjugation of Africans. European colonial powers employed religious rhetoric to dehumanize Africans. However, it also sowed the seeds of a unique syncretism between African traditional beliefs and Christianity among the indigenes and enslaved African populations in the Americas, a phenomenon known as African diasporic religions. Christianity has greatly influenced African culture over the years and is still being influenced by it today. In light of this, Ugwu Ibenwa stated that "although the imported world religions have brought in some positive influences or possible effects on West African communities, they have dealt a staggering blow on the social, economic, religious, and political systems in Africa."[139] Christianity and Islam have served as social revolutionaries in African societies. For instance, West Africa's emergence as a religiously pluralistic region coincided with the arrival of Islam and Christianity in various West African societies.[140] However, the introduction of Christianity did not lead to the complete eradication of indigenous African religious practices. Instead, West Africa became a crucible of religious pluralism, where multiple faiths coexist, often syncretizing elements of Christianity with traditional beliefs. This syncretism is particularly evident in the emergence of African Indigenous Churches (AICs), which blend Christian doctrines with local customs and practices. These African Indigenous Churches have millions of followers across West Africa and reflect the adaptability and resilience of religious traditions.

Furthermore, Western ideas of rationalism and individualism were introduced to Africa through Western education by these missionaries.[141] African secularism developed when many people questioned their religious beliefs and ultimately decided to live without them. Children learned a vast array of new concepts in school that touched on every facet of human existence, all of which were publicly and widely promoted as antagonistic to the African way of life; Africa was weaned by Western education. The development of schools, frequently overseen by Christian missionaries, is one of Christianity's most enduring legacy in West Africa.[142] These institutions were pivotal in advancing education and literacy across the region, laying the foundation for modern educational systems. However, the Christian missionary educational system is still criticized and blamed for the development of the influx of religious denominationalism into the educational system, literary education, inadequate educational services, the replacement of science and technical education with literary and religious languages, and subpar educational facilities.[143]

Beyond general education, one of the missions' greatest accomplishments was women's liberation, aided by education. The school helped girls develop a new sense of self and gave them the tools they needed to support themselves as teachers, nurses, etc. This liberated many from societal constraints and enabled them to make independent decisions about their husbands, jobs, and family lives. Additionally, professional training was justified by education. In addition to general schooling, this allowed educated

Africans to secure white-collar positions, and great, specialized schools created prospects for professional development.[144]

Christian missionaries were also instrumental in establishing healthcare facilities and promoting modern medicine in West Africa. Today, many of the region's prominent hospitals and healthcare systems have Christian origins. The genuine gospel message was the primary focus of the pioneering Christian Missions; the provision of medical services followed this. They claimed that in the same way that Christ was motivated to heal the ill primarily by true compassion, so too were they (missionaries) who traveled in Christ's name motivated not only to preach the gospel orally but also to cure the sick.[145]

As a result of the spread of Christianity across the region and the subsequent establishment of indigenous churches, which were formed in response to the needs and understanding of African people, together with the extensive movement characterized by passion, thousands of Sub-Saharan Africans now practice the faith in a variety of churches that are unrelated to foreign church traditions, structures, leaders, doctrine, or discipline. Additionally, the Church in Africa expands daily and rapidly reaches most other parts of the region through Pentecostalism's evangelistic campaigns. West African Pentecostal Churches, particularly in Nigeria, have created such outstanding missionary institutions that they have changed Africa. Through the successful establishment of missionary stations outside of Africa by churches like Deeper Life Bible Church, Reformed Christian Church of God, and others, Africans have transformed into agents of revival in the nations that first introduced them to the gospel.[146]

Conclusion

In 2020, Christians accounted for up to 49 percent of the continent's population, compared to 42 percent of Muslims. Africa has quickly changed from a continent where indigenous and traditional religions predominated to where Christians and Muslims now form the majority. Before the arrival of Christianity, West Africa was a continent dominated by indigenous, traditional religions, with lesser populations of Christians and Muslims. This chapter has explored early Christian missionaries in Benin, Warri, The Gambia, and Ghana, as well as the foundation of the nineteenth-century success in Sierra Leone. Beginning in the nineteenth century, the success of Christianity in West Africa was made possible by Africans themselves.

It is important to note that African Christianity has experienced remarkable growth over the past century, representing an often-overlooked triumph in global religious history. In 1900, West Africa had fewer than 10 million Christians, including non-native missionaries. However, by 2000, the number of African Christians surged to 350 million. This impressive trend is projected to continue, with expectations of nearly doubling the Christian population to approximately 630 to 700 million believers by 2025.[147]

DEEP DIVE

Assignment 1

Objective

The objective of this assignment is to ensure that students complete the reading of Chapter 11 and to get them to consider the elements that encouraged and discouraged the spread of Christianity. Students will be expected to provide specific examples of obstacles or opportunities that impacted European success in converting Africans to Christianity.

Method

Students will be expected to write a short note in response to the question.

Reading Comprehension

What inhibited and contributed to the spread of Christianity in West Africa?

Assignment 2

Discussion

How did Africans redefine Christianity?

Objective

The objective of this assignment is to get students to consider how Africans indigenized Christianity.

Method

Students will be expected to have a group discussion (either in person or on the online discussion forum) to talk to their peers about the question. Each student would be expected to create a post and respond to at least one other student. If this were to take place in person, then it would simply be a class-wide discussion

Notes

1 Kenneth Onwuka Dike, *Origins of the Niger Mission 1841–1891* (Ibadan: Ibadan University Press, 1962).
2 Adrian Hastings, *The Church in Africa: 1450–1950* (Oxford: Oxford University Press, 1994).
3 David W. Kling, *The Bible in History: How the Texts Have Shaped the Times* (Oxford: Oxford University Press, 2004), 25.
4 Lois M. Farag, ed., *The Coptic Christian Heritage: History, Faith and Culture* (London: Routledge, 2014).
5 Farag, *The Coptic Christian Heritage.*
6 H. V. Canter, "Roman Civilization in North Africa," *The Classical Journal* 35, no. 4 (1940): 197–208.

7 Archibald Cary Coolidge, "The European Reconquest of North Africa," *The American Historical Review* 17, no. 4 (1912): 723–734.

8 François Decret, *Early Christianity in North Africa* (Cambridge: James Clarke & Co, 2014).

9 J. Okoro Ijoma, "Portuguese Activities in West Africa before 1600: The Consequences," *Transafrican Journal of History* 11 (1982): 136–146.

10 Alan F. C. Ryder, "Portuguese Missions in Western Africa," *Tarikh* 2, no. 1 (1969): 1–13.

11 Christopher R. DeCorse, "Contact, Colonialism, and the Fragments of Empire: Portugal, Spain, and the Iberian Moment in West Africa," in *The Global Spanish Empire: Five Hundred Years of Place Making and Pluralism*, eds. Christine Beaule and John G. Douglass (Arizona: The University of Arizona Press, 2020).

12 Ruth Danenhower Wilson, "Justifications of Slavery, Past and Present," *The Phylon Quarterly* 18, no. 4 (1957): 407–412.

13 Hastings, *The Church in Africa*.

14 Hastings, *The Church in Africa*.

15 Isaac Boaheng, "Early Christian Missions in West Africa: Implications of Rethinking the Great Commission" in *Rethinking the Great Commission: Emerging African Perspectives*, eds. Emmanuel Asante and D. N. A. Kpobi (Accra: Type Company Limited, 2018), 1.

16 J. Kofi Agbeti, *West African Church History: Christian Missions and Church Foundations 1482-1919* (Leiden: E.J. Brill, 1986), 3.

17 Agbeti, *West African Church History*, 4.

18 Honor Sewapo, "Christianity in Africa," in *African Culture and Civilization: A Textbook for GES 102*, eds. M.O. Muritala and O.C. Adesina (Ibadan: Ibadan University Press, 2019), 6.

19 Ogbu Kalu, *The History of Christianity in West Africa* (London: Longman,1980), 3.

20 G. A. Oshitelu, *Expansion of Christianity in West Africa* (Ibadan, Oputoru Books, 2002).

21 Agbeti, *West African Church History*, 4.

22 Agbeti, *West African Church History*, 5.

23 Boaheng, "Early Christian Missions in West Africa," 1.

24 Philip Tachin, "Unit 4: Historicity of the Missionary Activities in West-Africa (Nigeria)," in *CRS832: The Growth of Western Christianity in Africa*, ed. Michael Enyinwa Okoronkwo Department of Religious Studies (Abuja: National Open University of Nigeria, 2021), 30-32.

25 Jacob F. Ade-Ajayi, *Christian Missions in Nigeria, 1814-1891: The Making of a New Elite* (London: Longman, 1964).

26 Ajayi, *Christian Missions in Nigeria, 1814-1891*.

27 Boaheng, "Early Christian Missions in West Africa," 4.

28 Boaheng, "Early Christian Missions in West Africa," 4.

29 Richard Gray, "Origins and Organization of the Nineteenth-Century Missionary Movement," *Tarikh* 3, no. 1 (1969): 18-19.

30 Boaheng, "Early Christian Missions in West Africa," 5.

31 Sewapo, "Christianity in Africa," 6.

32 Sewapo, "Christianity in Africa," 6.

33 Onyeka Egwuonwu, "An Appraisal of the Ex-Slaves Factor in the Spread of Christianity in Nigeria, 1841-1900," *Nigerian Journal of African Studies* 3, no. 2 (2021): 185-186.

34 Sewapo, "Christianity in Africa," 6.

35 Ajayi, *Christian Missions in Nigeria 1814-1891*

36 Paul Kollman, *The Evangelization of Slaves and Catholic Origins in East Africa* (New York: Orbis Maryknoll, 2005); Terence Ranger, "Missionary Adaptation of African Religious Institutions: The Masasi Case," in *The Historical Study of African Religion*, eds. Terence Ranger and I. N. Kimambo (London: Heinemann, 1972), 221–251.

37 David Maxwell, "Freed Slaves, Missionaries and Respectability: The Expansion of the Christian Frontier from Angola to Belgian Congo," *The Journal of African History* 54, no. 1 (2013): 79-102.

38 Egwuonwu, "An Appraisal of the Ex-Slaves Factor," 186-187.

39 Egwuonwu, "An Appraisal of the Ex-Slaves Factor," 185-186.

40 Egwuonwu, "An Appraisal of the Ex-Slaves Factor," 185-187.

41 Boaheng, "Early Christian Missions in West Africa," 18-19.

42 Tiwalola A. Falaye, "A Review of African Initiated Churches and Their Contributions to Development of Education in Nigeria," *International Journal of African and Asian Studies*, no. 15. (2015): 88-92.

43 Ogbu U. Kalu, "African Christianity, African Initiated Churches, and Theological Education in Africa," *International Bulletin of Mission Research* 25, no. 3 (2001): 104-111.

44 Chris Obiukwu, and Nwaocha Ogechukwu, "Major Challenges Encountered by Christian Missionaries in Africa: Encounters with Nigerian Communities in 19th Century," *West African Journal of Industrial & Academic Research* 18, no. 1 (2017): 106-117.

45 Obiukwu and Ogechukwu, "Major Challenges."

46 Onyeka Egwuonwu, "An Appraisal of the Ex-Slaves Factor," 185.

47 Paul Gifford, *African Christianity: Its Public Role* (Bloomington: Indiana University Press, 1998).

48 B. K. Ampadu, *Notes on History of Ghana for Senior High Schools* (Kumasi, Ghana: NUUT Co. Ltd., 2011).

49 Tachin, *CRS832: The Growth of Western Christianity in Africa*, 9.

50 Okechukwu E. Okeke, "Prophetism, Pentecostalism and Conflict in Ikenanzizi (1945 and 1972)," *Journal of Religion in Africa* 19, no. 3 (1989): 228–243.

51 Cephas N. Omenyo, "African Pentecostalism," in *The Cambridge Companion to Pentecostalism*, eds. Cecil M. Robeck, Jr and Amos Yong (Cambridge: Cambridge University Press, 2014), 132–151.

52 Allan Heaton Anderson, *An Introduction to Pentecostalism: Global Charismatic Christianity* (Cambridge: Cambridge University Press, 2014).

53 Ogbu Kalu, *African Pentecostalism: An Introduction* (Oxford: Oxford University Press, 2008).

54 Richard Burgess, *Nigerian Pentecostalism and Development: Spirit, Power, and Transformation* (New York: Routledge, 2020).

55 Burgess, *Nigerian Pentecostalism and Development*.

56 Asonzeh Ukah, "Piety and Profit: Accounting for Money in West African Pentecostalism (Part 1)," *Dutch Reformed Theological Journal* 48, no. 3–4 (2007): 621–632.

57 Alex R. Mayfield, "The Question of Power in African Pentecostalism," *Spiritus: ORU Journal of Theology* 3, no. 1 (2018): 87–107.

58 Joel Foster, "African Pentecostalism Has Grown Large Enough to Begin to Influence World Christianity," *Evangelical Focus Europe*, last modified December 20, 2021, https://evangelicalfocus.com/world/14667/african-pentecostalism-has-grown-large-enough-to-begin-to-influence-world-christianity.

59 Foster, "African Pentecostalism."

60 "How Adeboye Became RCCG's General Overseer," *Premium Times*, last modified February 14, 2021, https://www.premiumtimesng.com/news/top-news/442851-how-adeboye-became-rccgs-general-overseer.html?tztc=1.

61 "Winners Chapel Has Six Million Members Spread across 147 Countries — Oyedepo," *Vanguard*, last modified, December 27, 2014, https://www.vanguardngr.com/2014/12/winners-chapel-has-six-million-members-spread-across-147-countries-oyedepo/.

62 Saifaddin Galal, "Share of Christian Population in Africa 2023, by Country," *Statista*, last modified, April 28, 2023, https://www.statista.com/statistics/1239389/share-of-christian-population-in-africa-by-country/.

63 Birgit Meyer, "Christianity in Africa: From African Independent to Pentecostal-Charismatic Churches," *Annual Review of Anthropology* 33 (2004): 447-474.

64 Johnson Asamoah-Gyadu, *African Charismatics: Current Developments within Independent Indigenous Pentecostalism in Ghana*, vol. 27, *Studies of Religion in Africa* (Leiden, The Netherlands: Brill, 2004).

65 Molly Manyonganise, "African Independent Churches," in *Multiplying in the Spirit*, vol. 15, *Bible Studies in Africa*, ed. Ezra Chitando, Masiiwa Ragies Gunda, and Joachim Kügler (Bamberg: University of Bamberg Press, 2014): 161.

66 Manyonganise, "African Independent Churches."

67 Allen Olatunde, "The Effects of Adversity in African Indigenous Churches and its Consequence on 21st Century Churches," *African Theology*, last modified February 13,

2016. https://africantheology.wordpress.com/2016/02/13/the-effects-of-adversity-in-african
-indigenous-churches-and-its-consequence-on-21st-century-churches/.

68 Olatunde, "The Effects of Adversity."

69 Ibrahim B. Anoba, "Africa Shall Stretch Her Hands unto God: Ethiopianism as a Pan-African Religious Freedom Movement (1880–1940)," *Journal of Church and State* 64, no. 1 (2022): 42-67.

70 Olatunde, "The Effects of Adversity."

71 Samuel Crowther, and Jacob Friedrich Schoen. *Journals of the Rev. James Frederick Schön and Mr. Samuel Crowther, who, with the sanction of Her Majesty's Government, accompanied the expedition up the Niger in 1841, on behalf of the Church Missionary Society. With appendices and a map.* Hatchard & Son, 1842.

72 Kanayo Louis Nwadialor, "Christian Missionaries and Civilization in Southern Nigeria, 1841-1960: Implications for Contemporary Christians," *UJAH: Unizik Journal of Arts and Humanities* 14, no. 2 (2013): 173-193. See also, Richard Anderson, "Uncovering Testimonies of Slavery and the Slave Trade in Missionary Sources: The SHADD Biographies Project and the CMS and MMS Archives for Sierra Leone, Nigeria, and the Gambia," *Slavery & Abolition* 38, no. 3 (2017): 620-644.

73 Ezekiel Oladele Adeoti, "Evolution, Development and Impact of Western Education in Lagos: 1852-1978," *American Journal of Social Issues and Humanities* 4 (2014): 93-98.

74 M. Louise Pirouet, "East African Christians and World War I," *The Journal of African History* 19, no. 1 (1978): 117-130.

75 John Zarwan, "William Wade Harris: The Genesis of an African Religious Movement," *Missiology* 3, no. 4 (1975): 431-450.

76 Cornelius A. Olowola, "An Introduction to Independent African Churches," *East African Journal of Evangelical Theology* 3, no. 2 (1984): 21-49.

77 Olowola, "An Introduction to Independent African Churches,"

78 P. E. Nmah, "The Rise of Independent African Churches, 1890-1930: An Ethical-Genesis of Nigerian Nationalism," *African Research Review: An International Multi-Disciplinary Journal, Ethiopia* 4, no. 4 (2010): 482-493.

79 Philomena Njeri, "The Akurinu Churches: A Study of the History and Some of the Basic Beliefs of the Holy Ghost Church of East Africa 1926-1980" (PhD diss., University of Nairobi, 1984).

80 Akurinu Community, "A Story on Akurinu Church Community," *General Conference of Akurinu Churches Assembly*, accessed September 5, 2023. https://www.akurinucommunity .org/akurinu-history.html

81 Akurinu Community, "A Story on Akurinu Church Community."

82 Graham A. Duncan, "Ethiopianism in Pan-African Perspective, 1880-1920," *Studia Historiae Ecclesiasticae* 41, no. 2 (2015): 198-218.

83 Christopher C. Saunders, "Tile and the Thembu Church: Politics and Independency on the Cape Eastern Frontier in the Late Nineteenth Century," *The Journal of African History* 11, no. 4 (1970): 553-570.

84 Gerhardus Cornelis Oosthuizen, "The African Independent Churches in South Africa: A History of Persecution," *Emory International Literature Review* 14 (2000): 1089.

85 Allan H. Anderson, "Types and Butterflies: African Initiated Churches and European Typologies," *International Bulletin of Missionary Research* 25, no. 3 (2001): 107-113.

86 Taiye Adamolekun, "Main Trends in the Church Growth in Nigeria," *European Scientific Journal* 8, no. 23 (2012).

87 Adamolekun, "Main Trends in the Church Growth in Nigeria."

88 Adamolekun, "Main Trends in the Church Growth in Nigeria."

89 Adamolekun, "Main Trends in the Church Growth in Nigeria."

90 Gloria Lotha, "Aladura: Nigerian Religion," *Britannica: History & Society*, last modified November 7, 2021, https://www.britannica.com/topic/Aladura

91 Lotha, "Aladura: Nigerian Religion."

92 Peter Clarke, ed. *Encyclopedia of New Religious Movements*, (London: Routledge, 2004)

93 Robert W. Wyllie, "Pioneers of Ghanaian Pentecostalism: Peter Anim and James McKeown," *Journal of Religion in Africa* 6, no. 2 (1974): 109-122.

94 Michèle Miller Sigg, Eva M. Pascal, and Gina A. Zurlo, "Indigenous and Vernacular Christianity," in *The Wiley Blackwell Companion to World Christianity*, eds. Lamin Sanneh, Michael J. McClymond (Hoboken: Wiley Blackwell, 2016), 664-681.

95 The Editors of Encyclopaedia Britannica, "Kimbaguist Church: African Religion," *Britannica*, last modified July 20, 1998, https://www.britannica.com/topic/Kimbanguist -Church.

96 Gary W. Trompf, "Christianity in Melanesia," in *Introducing World Christianity*, ed. C. Farhadian (Oxford: Blackwell, 2012), 244.

97 Yolanda Covington-Ward, "'Your Name Is Written in the Sky' Unearthing the Stories of Kongo Female Prophets in Colonial Belgian Congo, 1921–1960," *Journal of Africana Religions* 2, no. 3 (2014): 317-346.

98 Allan Anderson, *African Reformation: African Initiated Christianity in the 20th Century* (Trenton: Africa World Press, 2001).

99 Lovemore Togarasei, "Modern Pentecostalism as an Urban Phenomenon: The Case of the Family of God Church in Zimbabwe," *Exchange* 34, no. 4 (2005): 349-375.

100 James Owino Kombo, "The Story of the African Independent Churches and its Implications for Theology," *African Journal of Evangelical Theology* 20, no. 2 (2001): 157-175.

101 Kombo, "The Story of the African Independent Churches."

102 Bengt G. M. Sundkler, "The Concept of Christianity in the African Independent Churches," *African Studies* 20, no. 4 (1961): 203-213.

103 Omololu Fagunwa, "African Pentecostalism and the 1918 Influenza Pandemic: The Supernatural Amid the Fearful and Implications for the COVID-19 Pandemic," *Christian Journal for Global Health* 7, no. 5 (2020): 52-64.

104 Karen Hull Brown, *The Function of Dress and Ritual in the Nazareth Baptist Church of Isaiah Shembe (South Africa)* (Indiana: Indiana University, 1995).

105 Patrick Enoch Nmah, "What is New in "New" Religious Movements in Africa? An Analytical Approach," *IGWEBUIKE: African Journal of Arts and Humanities* 3, no. 2 (2017): 46-62.

106 Kombo, "The Story of the African Independent Churches."

107 Anderson, "Types and butterflies," 107-113.

108 Kombo, "The Story of the African Independent Churches."

109 Kombo, "The Story of the African Independent Churches."

110 Getnet Tamene, "Features of the Ethiopian Orthodox Church and the Clergy," *Asian and African Studies* 7, no. 1 (1998): 87-104.

111 Philomena Njeri Mwaura, "African Instituted Churches in East Africa," *Studies in World Christianity* 10, no. 2 (2004): 160-184.

112 Kombo, "The Story of the African Independent Churches."

113 Mwaura, "African Instituted Churches in East Africa."

114 Walle Engedayehu, "The Ethiopian Orthodox Tewahedo Church in the Diaspora: Expansion in the Midst of Division," *African Social Science Review* 6, no. 1 (2013): 8.

115 Kombo, "The Story of the African Independent Churches."

116 Kombo, "The Story of the African Independent Churches."

117 Jacqueline Martha Francisca Wouters, "An Anthropological Study of Healing Practices in African Initiated Churches with Specific Reference to a Zionist Christian Church in Marabastad," PhD diss., University of South Africa, 2014.

118 James N. Amanze, "Christianity and Ancestor Veneration in Botswana," *Studies in World Christianity* 9, no. 1 (2003): 43-59.

119 Linda E. Thomas, "South African Independent Churches, Syncretism, and Black Theology," *Journal of Religious Thought* 53, no. 1/2 (1997): 39.

120 Allan Anderson, *Moya: The Holy Spirit in an African Context* (Pretoria: University of South Africa, 1991).

121 George C. Oosthuizen, "Interpretation of Demonic Powers in Southern African Independent Churches," *Missiology* 16, no. 1 (1988): 3-22.

122 Dean S. Gilliland, "How "Christian" are African Independent Churches?" *Missiology* 14, no. 3 (1986): 259-272.

123 James Pfeiffer, "Commodity Fetichismo the Holy Spirit, and the Turn to Pentecostal and African Independent Churches in Central Mozambique," *Culture, Medicine and Psychiatry* 29 (2005): 255-283.

124 Taiye Aluko, "Naming Ceremony in African Independent Churches—A Cultural Revolution," *Indian Journal of Theology* 35, no. 2 (1993): 20-32.

125 J. D. Y. Peel, "Syncretism and Religious Change," *Comparative Studies in Society and History* 10, no. 2 (1968): 121–41.

126 Peel, "Syncretism and Religious Change."

127 Cas Wepener and Bethel Muller, "Water Rituals as a Source of (Christian) Life in an African Independent Church: To be Healed and (Re) Connected," *Dutch Reformed Theological Journal (Nederduitse Gereformeerde Teologiese Tydskrif)* 54, no. 1/2 (2013): 254-266.

128 Dionne Crafford, "The Church in Africa and the Struggle for an African Identity," *Verbum et Ecclesia* 14, no. 2 (1993): 163-175.

129 Crafford, "The Church in Africa,"

130 Crafford, "The Church in Africa,"

131 Crafford, "The Church in Africa,"

132 Matsobane J. Anala, "The Impact of Christianity on sub-Saharan Africa," *Studia Historiae Ecclesiasticae* 39, no. 2 (2013): 285–302.

133 Francisco A. Gallego and Robert Woodberry, "Christian Missionaries and Education in Former African Colonies: How Competition Mattered," *Journal of African Economies* 19, no. 3 (2010): 294–329.

134 Jacob F. Ade Ajayi, *Christian Missions in Nigeria, 1841–1891: The Making of a New Elite* (Evanston: Northwestern University Press, 1965).

135 Philip B. Wood, "Church/Mission Hospitals in Africa," *Evangelical Missions Quarterly* 37, no. 2 (2001): 174–177.

136 Wood, "Church/Mission Hospitals in Africa."

137 Robin Law, "Slave-Raiders and Middlemen, Monopolists and Free-Traders: The Supply of Slaves for the Atlantic Trade in Dahomey c. 1750-1850," *The Journal of African History* 30, no. 1 (1989): 45–68.

138 Joseph E. Inikori and Stanley Engerman, "Introduction: Gainers and Loosers," in *The Atlantic Slave Trade: Effects on Economies, Societies, and Peoples in Africa, the Americas, and Europe*, eds. Joseph E. Inikori and Stanley Engerman (North Carolina: Duke University Press, 1992).

139 Metala, "Christianity and African Culture in Nigeria," 26-33.

140 Ajana Clinton Metala, "Christianity and African Culture in Nigeria," *Journal of Religion and Theology* 3, no. 2 (2019): 26-33.

141 Metala, "Christianity and African Culture in Nigeria," 26-33.

142 Peter Iwunna, "The Impact of Christian Missionary Education on the Educational Development of Nigeria: A Case Study of the Educational Activities of the Catholic Mission in Igboland-Nigeria (1925-1970)," (PhD diss., Katholieke Universiteit Leuven Faculteit Psychologie en Pedagogische Wetenschappen, 2006).

143 Iwunna, "The Impact of Christian Missionary Education."

144 Tachin, *CRS832: The Growth of Western Christianity in Africa* 42-45

145 Tachin, *CRS832: The Growth of Western Christianity in Africa*, 42-45

146 Samson A. Fatokun, "Christianity in Africa: A Historical Appraisal," *Verbum et Ecclesia* 26, no. 2 (2005): 357-358.

147 Michael M. Canaris, "The Rapid Growth of Christianity in Africa," *Catholic Star Herald*, December 13, 2018, https://catholicstarherald.org/the-rapid-growth-of-christianity-in-africa/.

12

THE TRANSATLANTIC SLAVE TRADE

Introduction

Many historical accounts established that the infamous slave trade began in the six-teenth century.[1] Other reasonable sources dated the timeline of the transatlantic slave trade from the fourteenth century onward,[2] but revisionist historians are unconcerned about the differences in dates. The argument is clear that the fixation on the sixteenth-century timeline tends to support the view that only around ten million Africans were funnelled into the Atlantic world. Meanwhile, the number of enslaved Africans is esti-mated to exceed this projected number. Some accounts put the number around 12 to 15 million.[3] Perhaps the slave trade started in the fifteenth century (Figure 12.1).

The slave trade was a cruel enterprise that dealt in the exchange of humans for mon-etary or material values.[4] The trade came into existence through the Euro-American intention to increase economic opportunities by creating extensive agricultural plan-tations in satellite areas, which required the use of an able-bodied workforce. This definition by no means suggests that the experience of enslavement emerged with the introduction of European merchants to the global market in Africa. It only emboldens the claim that the institutionalization of enslavement as a global business was estab-lished by the Europeans.[5] The conditions of enslavement were not new to human his-tory.[6] As far back as the first century, there had been the commodification of humans for monetary value. In addition, stating that Europeans instigated the beginning of the slave trade is not meant to create the impression that slavery or enslavement generally was alien to the African people, as this would not be correct.

Different historical accounts affirm that there had been internal slavery among African groups even before their contact with European and American traders.[7] African slavery was a product of different factors mostly connected to the reality of the quest for dominance—people engaged in wars over land, misunderstandings, labor needs, and deliberate intentions to show supremacy, which often led to situations that warranted the enslavement of others.[8] In other words, enslaving conquered people was evidence

DOI: 10.4324/9781003198260-15

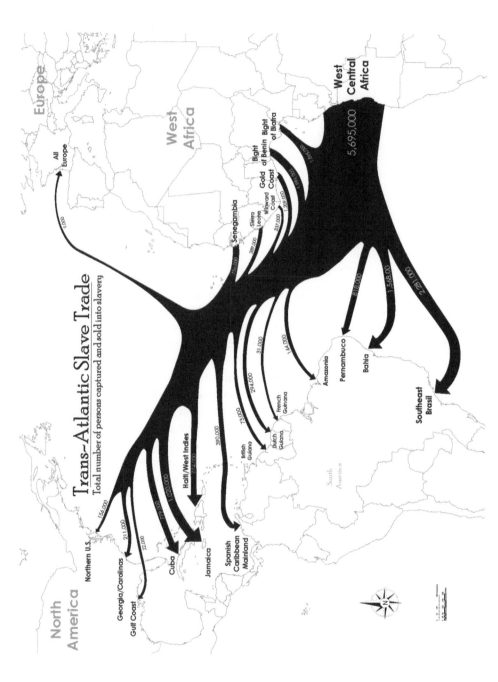

Trans-Atlantic Slave Trade

Total number of persons captured and sold into slavery

North America

Northern U.S. 156,000
Georgia/Carolinas 211,000
Gulf Coast 22,000
Cuba 779,000
Jamaica 1,020,000
Haiti/West Indies 774,000
Spanish Caribbean Mainland 390,000
British Guiana 73,000
Dutch Guiana 294,000
French Guiana 31,000
Amazonia 144,000
Pernambuco 818,000
Bahia 1,568,000
Southeast Brasil 2,218,000

Europe — All Europe 9,000

West Africa

Senegambia 756,000
Sierra Leone 389,000
Windward Coast 337,000
Gold Coast 1,209,000
Bight of Benin 1,999,000
Bight of Biafra 1,595,000

West Central Africa 5,695,000

South America

FIGURE 12.1 Map of the transatlantic slave trade. Author's collection.

of superiority over others and the demonstration of military power. Captives were conferred some respectable status on the occasion that they satisfied laid-down regulations around their freedom.

Another incidence leading to enslavement in the pre-Atlantic trade in Africa was debt payments, where defaulting on a financial agreement could lead to the seizure of freedom. People in this category were mandated to serve their usurers for a stipulated time, after which they could attain their freedom.[9] Thus, slaves and pawns enjoyed a considerable degree of freedom and honor, as many had the opportunity to advance in society.

However, the situation was different from the transatlantic slave trade because human dignity was terminated when they were captured from their African abodes and taken to Europe and the Americas. No fewer than 12.5 million people were carted away from Africa to the Americas in the era of the transatlantic slave trade.[10] Since the enslavement of the African people spanned at least 400 years, specifically between the fifteenth and the nineteenth centuries, Africa encountered the presence of a multitude of slave dealers from different European and American countries.[11] The varied methods and styles of enslavement substantially affected African political, social, and economic institutions.

Active Players in the Transatlantic Slave Trade

The Portuguese

There is a hasty conclusion that there truly was a high probability of African complicity in the booming of the slave trade because of the understanding that a few of the African nobles in positions of power sold "their people" into slavery.[12] However, no historical evidence reports that these complicit Africans represented a significantly higher percentage than the Europeans and Americans who systematically engaged in the commodification of human beings. In the calculation of the early players in the business of enslavement was the understanding that the African people were inferior to the Europeans and, therefore, were suited for slave labor.[13] As disingenuous as the accusation that Africans sold themselves into slavery may be,[14] as noted by Cameroonian sociologist Axelle Kabou, it is more unsettling that a people from a distant geographical territory would instigate and enforce it systematically. It was a decision set in motion to reflect the perception and position that Africans as a people could be exploited.

European slave dealers were so confident about the African "subhuman conditions" that they believed that the trade was not immoral. Some even saw it as justified. In fact, consistent with some "(un)scientific" claims, even among the intellectuals of the post-slavery era, Africans were considered to be at the level of animals. The slave trade received justification in prominent European and American circles. This explains the justification for slavery, as presented by a 1696 French King, Louis XIV.[15]

In 1471, the Portuguese entered into the business of slave trading in Africa to augment their not-too-strong economic system.[16] Unlike the British who appeared on the radar much later, the Portuguese had a comparatively weaker manufacturing industry that could have enhanced a mutual exchange of goods and services between them and Africans.[17] Trade with Africa was intended to boost their economy. The relative underdevelopment that characterized the industrial and economic platforms in Portugal made it difficult to consider a fair-trade relationship with Africans (Figure 12.2).

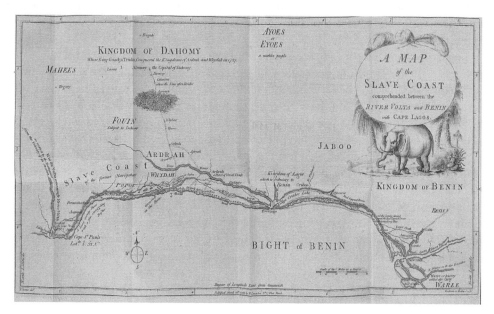

FIGURE 12.2   Map of the Slave Coast https://commons.wikimedia.org/wiki/File:Map_of_Slave
_Coast-1789.jpg.

The Portuguese lobbied for the occupation of some of the African territories along the coast to serve as trading colonies.[18] Of course, this was to establish an African trade in which they would serve as middlemen to a much more industrial Europe that would eventually be connected to the Americas. This led to the capitulation of the "Slave Coast" and the penetration of places such as Guinea and Benin, from where they encouraged the raiding of men and women for enslavement.[19] The Portuguese carted the people to Europe and later to the Atlantic world.

After a decade of involvement in the slave trade, the Portuguese succeeded in capturing the Gold Coast (the place, not the people) and developed a trading post named Elmina in 1482, with strategic positional advantage to enhance smooth business operations.[20] From the Portuguese occupation of the Elmina (or *Costa da Mina*) in the fifteenth century to around the 1630s, the number of enslaved Africans uprooted from their native land remains largely unknown.[21] The Portuguese maintained a monopolistic market, which provided, or perhaps enhanced, their opportunity to lift fewer than a thousand people from Africa who were then transported to the Atlantic environment to serve the purpose of enslavement (Figure 12.3).

The experience continued unabated because the beneficiaries of the slave trade had perfected the art of instigating violence among different African groups, which, in the long run, enabled them to derive maximum benefits from the trade. The search for slaves instigated widespread violence.

The continuous forceful capture of Africans as slaves was a potential threat to African societies: slavery brought about depopulation, which invariably led to the internal degradation of the economic systems.[22] Internal frictions that contributed to the enslavement of Africans were promoted because of the economic incentives offered to those in

FIGURE 12.3   São Jorge da Mina https://commons.wikimedia.org/wiki/File:5540_Elmina_Sao
_Jorge.jpg.

political positions to instigate violence. In other words, breaking the social order and
regulations depended on financial gains. As the assurance of getting more economic
opportunities increased, so did the internal unrest that consolidated enslavement.[23]

Meanwhile, the combination of lawlessness encouraged by the Portuguese slave
traders and their African collaborators, and the depopulation from their respective
enslavement were unsuitable for economic prosperity, especially for the poor in affected
societies. Agriculture, their predominant mainstay, was thus challenged, as there was a
reduction in the amount of labor available to engage in farm work. Through all of this,
the Portuguese continued with the impression that their prey were subhumans.[24]

The Dutch

Toward the end of the sixteenth century, another player—the Dutch—surfaced in the
unethical slavery business on the Coast of Guinea.[25] Coming with the intention to
compete and overtake, the Dutch were committed to challenging the monopolies the
Portuguese had enjoyed for a considerable number of years.[26] The establishment of the
Elmina by the Portuguese signaled their conquest of the area for the foundation of their
business empire. This was the same way the Dutch overtook the *Costa da Mina* in
1637,[27] which can be interpreted as the decline of the Portuguese's influence.

Some circumstances led to the uncompromising commitment of the Dutch to overtake the Portuguese from the base they established along some African coasts.[28] First,
they had already established a sugar plantation in Brazil after conquering its northeastern part in the 1630s. Second, it appeared that the only way they could consolidate their

economic gains in these places was to create an unimpeded trade system, regardless of the fact that the object of trade would be Africans themselves in (or with) Africa. Sequel to this ambition, they had to defeat opponents with the capacity to stand in their way, either real or imagined. As such, they consciously remained committed to their ambition.

Just before the ascension of the Dutch, Africans had engaged in struggles against the Portuguese traders.[29] However, the Portuguese would not relent, nor would they cede their place in Guinea and the Gold Coast to the ambitious Dutch without a fight. Luanda and Angola were prominent suppliers of enslaved Africans, which became a conquered territory by the Dutch after several attempts.

In 1641, even though they experienced some critical challenges, the two places or trade zones came under the influence of the Dutch. In their show of resistance and protest, these places were reclaimed by the Portuguese shortly after they came under the control of the Dutch, but it seemed that they had permanently lost the Gold Coast to the Dutch. After much non-compliance and a series of open confrontations between the two players, they came to a mutual understanding in 1662,[30] which was reflected in the de-monopolization of the market control previously enjoyed by the Portuguese.

Due to their comparatively lower levels of organized strategies, the Dutch collected a smaller number of enslaved Africans. Although different authors give contradictory accounts of slave estimates ascribed to them, they all agreed that they did not gather as many enslaved Africans as the Portuguese. For example, Phillip Curtin reports that the number of Africans enslaved and transported to the Atlantic world by the Dutch was 554,300,[31] though reaching the exact number remains a difficult task. Because of the nature of human business, mercantilism became the watchword for the Dutch, whose primary interest was the possible overtaking of the Portuguese, as losing a fort to other European countries meant a decline in business.

Indeed, the understanding that a once-defeated expansionist in these African territories potentially portends danger, given their capacity for regrouping and recovering lost grounds. Centuries later, it inspired an organized meeting among European powers in 1884/5 in Berlin that led to "The Scramble for Africa."[32] This meeting came into existence to guide them in occupying these territories to avoid the belligerence-leaning competitions they had previously while struggling to control the slave trade. What happened between the Dutch and the Portuguese was soon replicated extensively when other European powers entered the business. The intergroup contestations for territories were the only visa for access to African polities, and nothing would prevent the ambitious Europeans from achieving this.[33]

The English

The English participation in the slave trade was announced by their emergence between 1631 and 1632.[34] Although the British eventually became the second largest conveyors of enslaved Africans into the transatlantic world, their beginning was shrouded in uncertainties.

After a decade of their appearance in the slave trade, the English Civil War erupted in 1642 and lasted for almost a decade.[35] This created a series of internal contradictions and generated insurrections that provoked an acrimonious atmosphere. In 1600 AD, the East India Company surfaced to bring about an advantage in competition to the English.[36] The company attempted to enter the trade in a manner that revealed a calculated tactic to upstage the dominant forces in that market—the Dutch. Although this penetration would eventually remain superficial, it affected their trading system.[37]

Perhaps after the decisive dismemberment of the East India Company from the Guinea Coast, the English began a rejuvenation of their interest in September 1663 when two of their slave ships sailed safely to Allada.[38] Wealthy aristocrats in Great Britain were understandably the brains behind the funding of these ships, thus representing their interest in the expansion of their business empire by investing heavily in the slave trade, obviously after knowing about its immense profits. It must be noted that other European countries involved in the slave trade also had a heavy presence.[39] The emergence of the English not only centralized their economic stronghold on the people and places, but these countries had the potentiality of upstaging them completely for obvious reasons. The knowledge that Britain had sufficient materials and resources to trade with Africans inspired the Dutch and the Portuguese to rise up against their presence in Allada. The Dutch and the Portuguese had to live with the understanding that the British had come to stay.[40]

The presence of Great Britain meant that the slave trade had to be redefined, particularly if the preceding countries were to still hold on to their economic or financial advantages. One of the eventual responses to the competition was the dramatic rise in slave raiding and trading. The English were astute in being assertive. Perhaps in an unquenchable urge to rival their predecessors in the business, they increased the number of slaves by making the conditions more attractive to their corresponding African facilitators.[41] One of the most important ways to emphasize the participation of these English players in the business is to invoke the number of slaves they took within the period of their emergence and the time when slavery officially ended.[42] Except for the Portuguese who started long before them and for the singular fact that they did not initially have a receptive environment as the British had in the Americas, none of the preceding actors in the trade extracted as many people as the English. Curtin, for example, puts the number at around 3,259,400,[43] although it does not represent a final figure (Figure 12.4).

The French

Like the history of the other European players in the slave trade, the French also went into it with some measures of grandstanding.[44] It is common to come across contradicting positions about the actual year of emergence and the proportion of Africans they carted off as slaves to the Americas. However, the argument is aligned with Fuglestad's position that the French went into the business in approximately 1670,[45] when they came into Offra/Jakin with ships belonging to the French West India Company, regardless of the presence of the Dutch ships, signifying the already established influence of the Dutch in the first place.

Some other accounts assert that the French's involvement in the slave trade dates to the sixteenth century.[46] Even though they had a significant presence in present-day Senegal, in the seventeenth century,[47] the number of slaves captured by the French did not increase significantly until the nineteenth century. Throughout the sixteenth and seventeenth centuries, the total number of Africans enslaved and carted away to the Atlantic world by the French was below 50,000.[48] Conversely, this was the period when

FIGURE 12.4   Sierra Leone Bunce Island plaque https://commons.wikimedia.org/wiki/File
:Bunce_Island_Historical_Summary_panel.jpg.

Portugal traded more than one and a half million enslaved people, whereas their contending rival recorded more than half a million people. The reason for their low number, compared to Europeans such as the English or the Portuguese, was not because
their interest in enslaving people waned. Rather, it was connected to the fact that those
places from where slaves were mostly extracted had been dominated by other powerful European rivals. As a result, Portugal, Britain, and the Netherlands predominantly
occupied areas that would become known as future Ghana and Cameroon, leaving little
chance for competition (Figure 12.5).

   Alternatively, the French had to dabble in an economic practice that involved trading gums, groundnuts, cotton, and other items with African slave traders. Before their
involvement in this unfair trade between them and Africans, the French had already made
unsuccessful attempts to dislodge the Dutch from their strongholds.[49] The expectation
was that the displacement of these slave traders would earn them a chance at the coast,
from where they would penetrate the interior to replicate what others had been doing
centuries before. Ironically, the initial poor performance of France in enslaving Africans
and a commodification process in the Americas did not, by any means, indicate overall
failure. They were only outperformed in the business by the Portuguese and British.
Nantes, the major slaving port located on the west coast of France, recorded many
enslaved Africans.[50] Some single-family slave traders sent around 375 ships to dredge up
these African humans. La Rochelle, Le Havre, Nantes, and Bordeaux remained active

FIGURE 12.5   Bimbia Slave Port (Cameroon) https://commons.m.wikimedia.org/wiki/File
:Bimbia_Slave_Port.jpg.

during this period, and they continued to challenge the supremacy of one another in
their quest for the domination of the slave market.

Eventually, the French were consistent because they had ensured a virile atmosphere
for their trade in slaves. In most cases, they were assisted by merchants who willingly
continued to make the business possible and relatively easy. However, their consistency
also petered out because of factors connected to strife and struggles that characterized
the slave trade. The fact that nearly all of those slave traders were competing for dominance and relevance severely affected how far they went in the accumulation of more
and more enslaved persons.[51]

The Spanish

The Spanish incorporation into the list of European countries that ravaged the West African
region was connected with their foraging into the Caribbean world,[52] seeking slaves long
before others who looked for slaves in Africa. Thus, the emergence of the Spanish in West
African territories was connected to epochal events in the Americas. The Spanish found
about 1.1 million Taíno indigenous population on Hispaniola in the fifteenth century,[53] and
a substantial number of those people died by the time Spain established itself. Meanwhile,
the sudden decline of the labor population in this base pushed them into further extraction
of humans from nearby settlements to fill the island of Hispaniola.[54]

Although several accounts have hinted that this reduction in the number was associated with the immediate surge of diseases as well as acts of genocide,[55] the demand
for labor led the Spanish to Africa.[56] They turned to West Africa to meet their labor
demands through the enslaved.

It is not difficult not to see the connection between the genocide in the Caribbean and the slave trade in West Africa. According to Toby Green, it was Las Casas who persistently persuaded Charles V, pleading that he legally approve the transportation of slaves from Africa to the Caribbean in 1518.[57] After much consideration, Charles V granted the license to Laurent de Gouvenot, the governor of Bresse, who later contracted it to Genoese merchants.[58] Subsequent to these developments, the Spanish immediately launched themselves into the slave trade, making aggressive leaps in the carting away of West Africans to the Caribbean.[59]

Many enslaved Africans were transported to Hispaniola as early as 1502.[60] King Fernando had sanctioned the transportation of one hundred enslaved Africans to the Caribbean for his mining works circa 1505.[61] A few years later, he also purchased more enslaved Africans he sent to Hispaniola for similar assignments. From there, the number of enslaved Africans carted to the Caribbean was such that Black people could organize a revolt.[62] The occupation of the Spanish in parts of the West African coastal areas began around the 1510s and continued for succeeding years.[63] Countries such as Guinea, Senegal, and Cameroon supplied enslaved Africans to Cabo Verdean and Iberian[64] markets. The Spanish economy was supported by the provision of slaves from Africa to the Caribbean, which eventually contributed to the improvement of their agricultural production. In what would be estimated by Curtin, more than a million Africans were carted away to the Atlantic world by the Spanish by the end of the slave trade.[65]

The Triangular Trade and The Middle Passage

Understood as the voyage of human cargo from the West coast of Africa to the Americas, the Middle Passage was part of the historical triangular movement of goods and people from European countries down to the African polities, then to the Americas, and back to the European countries.[66] These trips were usually characterized by the movement of goods between places. To the Europeans, the Africans, and the Americans, the concept of goods had a different meaning; therefore, the trade and the Middle Passage evoked different emotional and psychological feelings.[67] To the Europeans, their relationship with Africa and the Americas was based on profit calculations.

To the Americans, the goods were humans to be exploited. However, for Africa, it was a relationship that created a sour experience of brutality and exploitation.[68] From the beginning, it was established that Europeans had a reasonable number of processed products and goods needed in Africa. As such, Europeans, on one of the legs of this triangular trade, brought manufactured goods to Africa. On the second leg of this business, African men and women would be exchanged for these manufactured goods before being carted off to the Americas for labor work on plantations. In the third part of the triangular movement, American finished products (sugar and cotton) would be taken to European countries (Figure 12.6).[69]

The triangular trade had different outcomes for these three continents. The Europeans who instigated the business gained disproportionately compared to the Africans. The gains of the Europeans cannot be measured only materially, as the relationship ultimately ended in colonization. Moreover, even though slavery ceased centuries ago, its consequences remain.

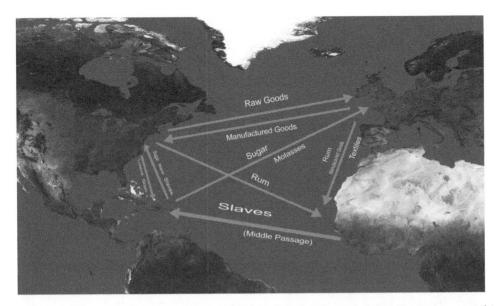

FIGURE 12.6   Map of the products being traded in the triangle trade https://commons.m.wiki-
media.org/wiki/File:Detailed_Triangle_Trade.jpg.

We should not underestimate the magnitude of the damage done to the African people. The slave trade came with violence and suffering. It was inhuman to exchange
goods for people. The Middle Passage brought horror stories and tragedies. The horrible
experience of the Middle Passage created a unifying identity of pain, anguish, sickness,
and death.

The Transatlantic Slave Trade: Implications for the West and West Africans

It is incontestable that such a large-scale extraction of human beings would come with
horrible consequences.[70] The action of forcefully taking people away from their cultural and religious homeland to a relatively strange environment would incapacitate and
unleash anguish on them. Detailed studies have shown how the Americas benefitted
in terms of contributing to the expansion of capitalism while Africa suffered a loss of
population and prestige. The racism that the slave trade created remains with us today.
The following sections are several dimensions of the implications of the transatlantic
slave trade (Figure 12.7).

Economic Impact

The economic consequences of the transatlantic slave trade for the West were immense,
with positive results, while the negative downsides for the West African region were
sadly various.[71] West Africans were agrarians, as their societies were predominantly
supported by developed agriculture. They required human resources to increase productivity and activity in agriculture.

FIGURE 12.7   The slave trade (slaves on the West Coast of Africa) https://commons.wikimedia
.org/wiki/File:The_Slave_Trade_by_Auguste_Francois_Biard.jpg.

However, the market culture of the slave trade era demanded strong men and women for the continuation of Euro-American economic and financial domination. By taking Africans in large numbers, it became challenging for the African people to sustain impressive economic growth. Apart from the emotional trauma of the loss of close relations, it ruptured the social fabric of society.[72] However, there was a boost in the economic activities of the slave receivers. For example, it led to an increment in the production of sugar and cotton, among others.[73] If the slave trade destroyed West African economies, slaves contributed to the development of American and European economies and capitalism.

Enslavement came with objections and resistance, both in the Americas and Africa. The enslaved sought their freedom and moral authorities in Africa objected to the trade.

Meanwhile, people were not constrained from demonstrating their resistance in violent ways. In some cases, compounds were burnt, farms were razed, and other destructive habits were normalized. Mutual suspicion and contempt increased exponentially, thereby causing serious damage to friendships and relationships. Wars were maintained because of the necessity to capture humans to meet financial commitments made to the Europeans. With instability, many of them could not confidently pursue agricultural interests.[74]

The success in enslaving people represented a defeat with emotional consequences.[75] By consistently creating the impression that Africans were inferior in every way conceivable, the business of enslavement went along with the ideology of racism. It is benumbing to exchange healthy people for items as ordinary as umbrellas, shoes, mirrors, and other items. Enslavement was traumatic, and minds were destroyed.

The political consequences were grave. When leaders consciously lose their (governed) members to outsiders, they run out of leadership relevance. The leaders were unable to protect their citizens in areas raided for slaves.[76] Slave raiders destroyed their societies by the use of violence to produce slaves.[77] The dwindling number of people in affected places, however, was catastrophic to the political stability of societies and the sustenance of political sovereignty. Having a fear of possible capture, people migrated and fled in search of permanent safety. The cost of instability was high.

Conclusion

Although the players in the business of slavery were more than those identified in this chapter, the roles played by the Spanish, the Portuguese, the Dutch, the English, and then the French in the sustenance of the slave trade have been pinpointed.

Available literature does not confirm the number of Africans who were victims of the transatlantic trade, but one point of agreement is that more than 12 million Africans were taken into slavery.[78] While most accounts are silent regarding the number of individuals who died in the wars waged to produce slaves, we cannot underestimate the undocumented number of people lost in the process. It is also believed that the brutal traffic of slaves had enduring negative economic, social, ecological, political, and psychological effects on West Africa.

DEEP DIVE

Assignment 1

Objective

The objective of this assignment is to ensure that students complete the reading of Chapter 12 and to get them to understand how much the slave trade impacted, disrupted, and transformed African life and society.

Method

Students will be expected to write a short essay in response to the question.

Reading Comprehension

Discuss the impact of the transatlantic slave trade on West African societies.

Assignment 2

Objective

The objective of this assignment is to make students understand that slavery existed in West Africa and also to consider how Europeans commercialized slavery on an international scale.

Additionally, students will be expected to explain why chattel slavery was permissible and beneficial.

Method

Students will be expected to have a group discussion (either in person or on the online discussion forum) to talk to their peers about the question. Each student will be expected to create a post and respond to at least one other student. If this were to take place in person, then it would simply be a class-wide discussion.

Discussion

How did indigenous slavery in Africa differ from the transatlantic slave trade? How did Europeans and Americans justify slavery?

Notes

1 Toney Allman, *The Transatlantic Slave Trade* (India: Lucent Books, 2009).
2 Toby Green, *The Rise of the Transatlantic Slave Trade in Western Africa, 1300–1589* (New York: Cambridge University Press, 2012).
3 James W. Blake, ed., *Europeans in West Africa: 1450–1560* (London: Hakluyt Society, 1942).
4 Herbert S. Klein and Jacob Klein, *The Atlantic Slave Trade* (Cambridge: Cambridge University Press, 1999).
5 Pieter C. Emmer, *The Dutch in the Atlantic Economy, 1580–1880: Trade, Slavery and Emancipation* (Aldershot: Ashgate, 1998).
6 Milton Meltzer, *Slavery: A World History* (New York: Da Capo Press, 1993).
7 Paul Lovejoy, "Indigenous African Slavery," *Historical Reflections* 6, no. 1 (1979): 19–83.
8 Walter Rodney, "African Slavery and other Forms of Social Oppression on the Upper Guinea Coast in the Context of the Atlantic Slave-Trade," *The Journal of African History* 7, no. 3 (1966): 431–443.
9 Paul E. Lovejoy and David Richardson, "The Business of Slaving: Pawnship in Western Africa, c. 1600–1810," *The Journal of African History* 42, no. 1 (2001): 67–89.
10 Finn Fuglestad, *Slave Traders by Invitation: West Africa's Slave Coast in the Precolonial Era* (New York: Oxford University Press, 2018).
11 Hilary Beckles and Verene Shepherd, *Trading Souls: Europe's Transatlantic Trade in Africans* (Kingston: Ian Randle Publishers, 2007).
12 Adaobi T. Nwaubani, "My Great-Grandfather, the Nigerian Slave-Trader," *The New Yorker*, July 15, 2018, https://www.newyorker.com/culture/personal-history/my-great-grandfather-the-nigerian-slave-trader.
13 Gabriel O. Apata, "A Response to Adaobi Tricia Nwabuani's 'My Nigerian Great Grandfather Sold Slaves," *The Cable*, August 10, 2020, https://www.thecable.ng/a-response-to-adaobi-tricia-nwabuanis-article-my-nigerian-great-grandfather-sold-slaves.
14 Axelle Kabou, *Et si l'Afrique Refusait le Développement?* (Paris: Le Harmattan, 1991).
15 Kabou, *Et si l'Afrique Refusait le Développement?*
16 Mohamed I. Nugud, "Pioneers of Enslavement and the Slave Trade in Africa," in *Slavery in the Sudan: History, Documents, and Commentary*, eds. Sharon B. Asma, Mohamed A. Halim and Mohamed I. Nugud (New York: Palgrave Macmillan, 2013), 27–35.
17 J. Okoro Ijoma, "Portuguese Activities in West Africa before 1600: The Consequences," *Transafrican Journal of History* 11 (1982): 136–146.
18 Ijoma, "Portuguese Activities in West Africa."

19 Anthony Luttrell, "Slavery and Slaving in the Portuguese Atlantic (to about 1500)," in *The Transatlantic Slave Trade from West Africa*, ed. Christopher Fyfe (Edinburgh: University of Edinburgh, 1965), 293–304.
20 Paul E. H. Hair, "Columbus from Guinea to America," *History in Africa* 17 (1990): 113–129.
21 Malyn Newitt, ed., *The Portuguese in West Africa, 1415–1670: A Documentary History* (Cambridge: Cambridge University Press, 2010), 90.
22 Cameron J. Monroe, "Demographic Change and the Transatlantic Slave Trade in West Africa: An Example from the Abomey Plateau, Bénin," Paper presented at the 84th Annual Meeting of the Society for American Archaeology, Albuquerque, NM. 2019.
23 Bruno da Ponte, *The Last to Leave: Portuguese Colonialism in Africa: An Introductory Outline* (London: International Defence and Aid Fund, 1974).
24 Alvin O. Thompson, "Race and Colour Prejudices and the Origin of the Transatlantic Slave Trade," *Caribbean Studies* 16, no. 3/4 (1976–1977): 29–59.
25 Rik Van Welie, "Slave Trading and Slavery in the Dutch Colonial Empire: A Global Comparison," *New West Indian Guide* 82, no. 1/2 (2008): 47–96.
26 Welie, "Slave Trading and Slavery."
27 Jean-Pierre Chauveau, "Une Histoire Maritime Africaine Est-elle Possible? Historiographie et Histoire de la Navigation et de la Pêche Africaine à la Côte Occidentale Depuis le XVe Siècle," *Cahiers d'Études Africaines* 26, no. 1–2 (1986): 173–235.
28 Filipa I. Ribeiro da Silva, "The Dutch and the Portuguese in West Africa: Empire Building and Atlantic System (1580–1674)" (Ph.D. diss., Leiden University, 2009).
29 Albert van Dantzig and Priddy Barbara, *A Short History of the Forts and Castles of Ghana* (Accra: Ghana Museums and Monuments Board, 1971).
30 Charles R. Boxer, *The Dutch Seaborne Empire 1600–1800* (London: Hutchinson, 1965).
31 Phillip Curtin, *The Atlantic Slave Trade: A Census* (Madison: University of Wisconsin Press, 1969).
32 Ewout Frankema, Jeffrey Williamson and Pieter Woltjer, "An Economic Rationale for the West African Scramble? The Commercial Transition and the Commodity Price Boom of 1835–1885," *Journal of Economic History* 78, no. 1 (2018): 231–267.
33 Stig Förster, Wolfgang J. Mommsen and Ronald E. Robinson, eds., *Bismarck, Europe and Africa: The Berlin Africa Conference 1884–1885 and the Onset of Partition* (Oxford: Oxford University Press, 1988).
34 Margaret Makepeace, "English Traders on the Guinea Coast, 1657–1668: An Analysis of the East India Company Archive," *History in Africa* 16 (1989): 237–284.
35 Makepeace, "English Traders on the Guinea Coast."
36 Huw V. Bowen, *The Business of Empire: The East India Company and Imperial Britain, 1756–1833* (Cambridge: Cambridge University Press, 2005).
37 Robert Garfield, *A History of São Tomé Island, 1470–1655, The Key to Guinea* (Lewiston: Mellen Research University Press, 1992).
38 Robin Law, "The Slave Trade in Seventeenth-Century Allada: A Revision," *African Economic History* 22 (1994): 71.
39 Beckles and Shepherd, *Trading Souls*.
40 David Ormrod, *The Rise of Commercial Empires: England and the Netherlands in the Age of Mercantilism, 1650–1770* (Cambridge: Cambridge University Press, 2003).
41 David Eltis and Stanley L. Engerman, "The Importance of Slavery and the Slave Trade to Industrializing Britain," *The Journal of Economic History* 60, no. 1 (2000): 123–144.
42 Katie Donington, Ryan Hanley and Jessica Moody, eds., *Britain's History and Memory of Transatlantic Slavery: Local Nuances of a National Sin* (Liverpool: Liverpool University Press, 2016).
43 Curtin, *The Atlantic Slave Trade*.
44 David Geggus, "The French Slave Trade: An Overview," *The William and Mary Quarterly* 58, no. 1 (2001): 119–138.
45 Fuglestad, *Slave Traders by Invitation*. See also Jutta Wimmler, *The Sun King's Atlantic: Drugs, Demons and Dyestuffs in the Atlantic World, 1640–1730* (Leiden: Brill, 2017), 11–38.
46 Douglas Harper, "French Slavery," *The Sciolist*, http://slavenorth.com/columns/frenchslavery.htm.

47 James F. Searing, *West African Slavery and Atlantic Commerce: The Senegal River Valley, 1700–1860* (Cambridge: Cambridge University Press, 1993).

48 Curtin, *The Atlantic Slave Trade*.

49 Pieter C. Emmer and Jos J. L. Gommans, *The Dutch Overseas Empire, 1600–1800* (Cambridge: Cambridge University Press, 2020), 125–244.

50 Robert Stein, "The Profitability of the Nantes Slave Trade, 1783–1792," *The Journal of Economic History* 35, no. 4 (1975): 779–793.

51 Christopher L. Miller, *The French Atlantic Triangle: Literature and Culture of the Slave Trade* (Durham: Duke University Press, 2008).

52 Ida Altman and David Wheat, eds., *The Spanish Caribbean and the Atlantic World in the Long Sixteenth Century* (Lincoln: University of Nebraska Press, 2019).

53 Bartolomé de Las Casas, "Brevíssima Relación de la Destruyción de las Indias," in *Colección de Documentos Inéditos para la Historia de España*, Vol. 1 (Vaduz: Kraus Reprint Ltd., 1996), 1–72.

54 Bartolome Las Casas, *A Short Account of the Destruction of the Indies* (London: Penguin Classics, 1992).

55 Noble D. Cook, "Sickness, Starvation, and Death in Early Hispaniola," *The Journal of Interdisciplinary History* 32, no. 3 (2002): 349–386.

56 Alejandro T. M. Okuno and Daniel Ventosa-Santaulària, "Fall in the Indian Population after the Arrival of the Spaniards: Diseases or Exploitation?" *Investigación económica* 69, no. 272 (2010): 87–104.

57 Green, *The Rise of the Transatlantic Slave Trade*, 187.

58 William D. Phillips, *Slavery from Roman Times to the Early Transatlantic Trade* (Manchester: Manchester University Press, 1985).

59 David Wheat, *Atlantic Africa and the Spanish Caribbean, 1570–1640* (North Carolina: University of North Carolina Press, 2016).

60 Green, *The Rise of the Transatlantic Slave Trade*.

61 Helen Nader, "Desperate Men, Questionable Acts: The Moral Dilemma of Italian Merchants in the Spanish Slave Trade," *The Sixteenth Century Journal* 33, no. 2 (2002): 401–422.

62 Erin W. Stone, *Captives of Conquest: Slavery in the Early Modern Spanish Caribbean* (Pennsylvania: University of Pennsylvania Press, 2021).

63 David Wheat, *Atlantic Africa and the Spanish Caribbean*.

64 David Davis, *Slavery and Human Progress* (Oxford: Oxford University Press, 1984).

65 Curtin, *The Atlantic Slave Trade*.

66 Ruth Mayer, "'Africa as an Alien Future': The Middle Passage, Afrofuturism, and Postcolonial Waterworlds," *American Studies* 45, no. 4 (2000): 555–566.

67 See, for instance, Rinaldo Walcott, "Middle Passage: In the Absence of Detail, Presenting and Representing a Historical Void," *Kronos* 44 no. 1 (2018): 59–68; and Shizen Ozawa, "On Naipaul's Cultural Positions in The Middle Passage," *CLCWeb: Comparative Literature and Culture* 14, no. 5 (2012): 1–9.

68 Cathy Caruth, *Unclaimed Experience: Trauma, Narrative, and History* (Maryland: Johns Hopkins University Press, 1996).

69 Stephanie E. Smallwood, *Saltwater Slavery: A Middle Passage from Africa to American Diaspora* (Cambridge: Havard University Press, 2007).

70 Joseph E. Inikori and Stanley L. Engerman, eds. *The Atlantic Slave Trade: Effects on Economies, Societies and Peoples in Africa, the Americas, and Europe* (Durham: Duke University Press, 1992).

71 Joseph E. Inikori and Stanley L. Engerman, "Introduction: Gainers and Losers in the Atlantic Slave Trade," in *The Atlantic Slave Trade: Effects on Economies, Societies and Peoples in Africa, the Americas, and Europe*, eds. Joseph E. Inikori and Stanley L. Engerman (Durham: Duke University Press, 1992), 1–24.

72 Barbara L. Solow, *The Economic Consequences of the Atlantic Slave Trade* (Maryland: Lexington Books, 2014).

73 Daron Acemoglu, Simon Johnson, and James A. Robinson, "The Rise of Europe: Atlantic Trade, Institutional Change and Economic Growth," *American Economic Review* 95, no. 3 (2005): 546–579.

74 Suzanne Miers and Igor Kopytoff, "African 'Slavery' as an Institution of Marginality," in *Slavery in Africa: Historical and Anthropological Perspectives*, eds. Suzanne Miers and Igor Kopytoff (Wisconsin: University of Wisconsin Press, 1977), 3–81.

75 Joy DeGruy Leary, *Post Traumatic Slave Syndrome: America's Legacy of Enduring Injury and Healing* (Oregon: Joy DeGruy Publications, 2005).

76 Martin A. Klein, *Slavery and Colonial Rule in French West Africa* (New York: Cambridge University Press, 1998).

77 John Thornton, *Africa and Africans in the Making of the Atlantic World, 1400–1800* (Cambridge: Cambridge University Press, 1998).

78 Nathan Nunn, "Shackled to the Past: The Causes and Consequences of Africa's Slave Trades," in *Natural Experiments of History*, eds. Jared Diamond and James A. Robinson (Cambridge: Harvard University Press, 2010), 142–184.

13

ECONOMY AND SOCIETY

External Commerce

Introduction

Following Christopher Columbus' "rediscovery" of the peoples of the New World[1] and the available economic bounties like land and minerals on the continents, Europe's attention switched to the Americas. Not only were the American continents exploited with massive exportation of raw materials, but agrarian plantations also rose in their numbers. The economic labor demands proved fatal for the indigenous population,[2] turning Europeans' attention to Africa. This marked the commencement of the transatlantic or triangular trade, as it was also known.[3] The trade in humans became dominant until the early nineteenth century when concerted activities yielded positive results to end the slave trade. Looking away from the humanitarian perspective, the abolitionists were backed by former large importers of slaves. Before the British abolition of slavery in 1807, Denmark had abolished the trade in humans in 1803.[4] Other Western powers followed suit, starting with the United States in 1808, Holland in 1814, and France in 1817. However, this widespread abolition only triggered a renewed concentration on "legitimate commerce,"[5] the collapse of which economists and historians like Hopkins believe was responsible for European incursion into West Africa as well as the rest of Africa.

By the seventeenth century, trade in humans had replaced virtually every other form of trade and commerce in West Africa. Thus, when this trade collapsed in the aftermath of abolition, its replacement—the "legitimate" trade/commerce—became the major force in West Africa's economy and dictated the pace of development in society. It is important to note that the 1807 abolition of the slave trade and the 1833 abolition of slavery did not immediately end either of these phenomena as they thrived until the late nineteenth century (Figure 13.1).[6]

According to Manning and Akyeampong, West African slaves at the end of the century dwarfed the numbers at the beginning of the century.[7] In Nigeria, for instance, between 1780 and 1850, there was further slavery expansion consequent of wars involving Hausaland, the Fulani, and especially Yorubaland in the aftermath of the fall of Old

DOI: 10.4324/9781003198260-16

FIGURE 13.1   The official medallion of the British Anti-Slavery Society https://commons.wiki-media.org/wiki/File:Official_medallion_of_the_British_Anti-Slavery_Society_(1795).jpg.

Oyo.[8] While the slave trade across the Atlantic dropped massively around this period, it continued across the Sahara till the late nineteenth century, averaging 10,000 people per year.[9] For Eric Green, "at first the gold trade dominated, but later the trades in copper and salt became more important. These valuable goods were used for long-distance trades across the Sahara Desert."[10] Green further highlights the relationship of the slave trade with other major economic activities in West Africa thus:

> Another kind of specialization in West Africa was the development of commercial centers. New centers became important and older ones lost their importance as the types of trade and the goods traded changed over time. Hausaland, for example, was a leading regional center in the 16th century. It grew in strength because of its successful engagement in the gold trade. But as the gold trade became less important in the 17th century, Hausaland was replaced as a major commercial center by the Dahomey kingdom, in the area known today as Benin. This kingdom had become a key player in the growing trade in people as goods – in other words the slave trade. It grew richer and richer as it profited from the 17th century trans-Atlantic slave trade.[11]

Indeed, the West African precolonial economy and society depended heavily on the use of labor during this period. During this period, wealth was determined by the vastness of a person's farmland, businesses owned, and the number of people in the person's employ. Rich plantation owners used slaves as cheap labor to expand their farmlands, a practice similar to the European slave trade and slavery in the Americas. Manning and Akyeampong support this assertion with the following:

> As the nineteenth century continued, a thriving system of slavery and slave trade developed in the West African savanna, especially in the Sokoto Caliphate, but also in the middle Niger and in Borno. Now the system came to depend as much on local demand as on external demand. Slave labor was used for grain production, for textiles, and for leather work. Control of slave women and children became the prerogative of wealthy men throughout the region. Thus a new social system developed, as substantial numbers of males were held in slavery.[12]

The transatlantic slave trade lasted till around the mid-nineteenth century and had both negative and positive effects on the economy of West Africa.[13] The negatives undoubtedly outweighed the positives, and the fact remains that trade in humans was completely evil and unforgivable.

In facilitating trade in nineteenth-century West Africa, cowry shells were the common currency. This made long- and short-distance trading possible throughout the century. Boge emphasizes the existence of trade associations, such as guilds, as they sought to protect their "socio-economic interests."[14] Some of their activities included pooling financial resources together, a practice known as *esusu,* whereby each member would get the total amount contributed rotationally at the end of a given period.[15] This practice still thrives in present-day West Africa, albeit in modern form, with little to no changes. They also assisted each other on their farmlands rotationally. They would work together on a member's farmland without direct remuneration, and in most cases, the person on whose farmland they worked would provide food and water or palm wine during the period. Afterward, the group would go on to another member's farmland until all of the farms had been covered. This communal system ensured they saved money, and at the same time, worked at a faster pace.

The transatlantic slave trade undermined the continual development of local industries.[16] This is because humans began to fetch more money than the industries could afford. The wealthiest were those who had slaves to sell; therefore, many left their legitimate businesses for the lucrative slave trade. On the one hand, it ruined the development of these local industries, and on the other hand, it exposed West Africans, like their counterparts, to the merchant/middleman business. It is close to what is known as affiliate marketing in modern times, where a middleman connects a seller to potential buyers and gets a share of the proceeds. Although they had suffered a huge blow, it is safe to say the industries continued well into the nineteenth and twentieth centuries, albeit with fewer hands in the business.

According to Boge, the transatlantic slave trade also significantly influenced the establishment of new commercial centers/ports such as Lagos, which gained popularity by 1810, when slaves, agricultural products, and other economic resources were exported from the Yoruba heartland.[17] While this did occur, it had repercussions. Although the dominant aspect of economy and society in the nineteenth century was "legitimate commerce," the above demonstrates that slavery, slave trade, agrarian plantations, and even produce trade within and beyond the shores of the region were all active as part of West African economic and societal life.

Pre-"legitimate" Commerce

Despite commercial diversification in other parts of the world, agriculture remained the most prominent economic activity in West Africa, even until the twentieth century, with the primary focus on food and cash crop production, pastoral farming, hunting, and fishing, depending on the environment.[18] This is corroborated by Hopkins as he regards agriculture as the "matrix" upon which all other local economic activities in the region rested.[19] Crucial to economic activities is its facilitation from one place to another, from the point of production to the point of consumption or trade.

Before the advent of colonialism and the subsequent motorized means of transportation, West Africans had their means of transportation for commercial activities. There was human porterage, which is still very much alive in some parts of West Africa today.[20] For instance, some porters could be seen, especially in marketplaces such as Bodija, Oja Oba, and Ogunpa in the western part of Nigeria, lifting heavy, purchased goods from the inner market to the roadside where a vehicle was waiting to ferry them to their destination. In the nineteenth century, however, before the advent of these vehicles, porters—mainly slaves—were required to carry goods to their expected destinations—another notable factor that sustained slavery in West Africa as part of its economic society.[21] The use of animal transport was also popular in West African history, especially to facilitate the trans-Saharan trade.[22] This mode of transportation to carry goods across the region and from the hinterland to the coast for trade with the Western powers continued in West Africa. Besides these two, with fishing a common practice, using boats and canoes, water transportation also aided the conduct of trade during the period under examination.[23]

"Legitimate" Commerce

Before the intense scramble for colonies in Africa, the United States was as big an influence on West African commerce, as was Britain and France, the leading commercial powers in the region. In the early part of the century, the United States, Britain, and France were the biggest "trading partners" with West African societies, especially in Senegal, Sierra Leone, Ghana, and Nigeria. Given how trade in humans became branded as illegal and improper, trade in agricultural products such as groundnut and palm oil was branded as "legitimate trade". In fact, this trade did not start in the nineteenth century, nor was it a consequence of the decline in the slave trade. As far back as 1588, Britain had been exporting palm oil from West Africa.[24] The only difference was that the quantity was low, which remained that way until the eighteenth century.

However, the nineteenth century witnessed a major upsurge in the demand for agricultural products (especially palm oil) from West Africa. This high demand for palm oil is not unconnected to the industrial revolution in Europe and the United States and the need for oil for their machines. According to Martin Lynn, data shows that palm oil exported to the United Kingdom increased by about 500 percent between 1800 and 1810, and between 1810 and 1850, the demand had risen by over 1,600 percent.[25] Lynn expounds his assessment of the volcanic growth further:

During the nineteenth century, the volume of palm oil imports into Britain from West Africa grew from 2,233 *cwt* in 1807 to reach a peak of 1,058,989 *cwt* in 1895 ... In terms of the trade's value, however, sharp increases in the early part of the century, with the £1 million figure being first reached in 1853, were followed by a plateau between the 1850s and early 1870s, which can be seen as the trade's heyday, before decline set in. In this period, Britain was importing some £1.5m p.a. from West Africa, with the trade's apogee being reached in 1868 when Britain imported £1,873,147 of palm oil from the region.[26]

As earlier pointed out, palm oil was not the only object of trade in West Africa. By the mid-nineteenth century, the United Kingdom was importing a vast amount of palm kernel from West Africa, with the first major export from Sierra Leone in 1846. The trade in palm kernels peaked with Britain from 592 tons of kernels and nuts in 1855 to about 43,372 tons in 1884,[27] before the Berlin Conference, after which they no longer needed to trade when they could easily expropriate these resources and more to the metropolis. Britain was not alone in this trade; in fact, by the 1870s, following its unification, Germany rivaled Britain as West Africa's biggest customer, especially for palm kernels. Other than the Gold Coast, where other Western powers could import as much as Britain, the latter controlled the trade in palm oil and kernels from the Bight of Benin and Biafra.[28]

According to Lynn, by the mid-nineteenth century, while the Gold Coast accounted for 10 percent of British imports in the oil trade, the Bight of Benin emerged as the largest contributor to British imports, peaking at over 30 percent.[29] Some of the other major exporting markets in West Africa included Old Calabar, Kalabari, Nembe, Lagos, Ikorodu, Egba (which peaked at the export of 15k tons of oil per year from 1856), Ibadan, Isoko, Itsekiri, Warri, Opobo, Bonny, and Ijebu Ode (in Nigeria); Egbado, Port Novo, Abomey, and Whydah (in the Republic of Benin); Krobo, Apollonia, Anomabu, Sekondi, Komenda, Dixcove, and Tantumquery (in Gold Coast); Sierra Leone, and the Dukwia River in Liberia, among others. In Sierra Leone, the value of palm oil exports grew from £182 in 1825 to £43,276 in 1849,[30] before it started declining until it peaked again before the Berlin Conference. Yorubaland's active participation in the palm oil business is largely connected to its fratricidal wars from the mid to late nineteenth century. Ibadan, which emerged as the strongest power in Yorubaland,[31] exported palm oil in large quantities, as much as slaves, for tributes upon conquests from their vassal states and those who looked up to them for protection.[32] With palm oil, they could participate in trade with foreign powers. The Ijebu, in particular, traded this for firearms to strengthen their military and aid their wars against Ibadan and Egba.

By 1892, there were about 15 million palm trees in Yorubaland purposely for export in response to the high demands from the West.[33] The above highlights that West Africa, in various ways, responded to the high demand for palm oil by the Europeans who needed it to oil their machines and for the production of candles and soaps. The ability of West Africa to respond in kind to the high demand for palm oil is an important subject not discussed enough in literature. As I mentioned earlier, palm oil production existed long before the nineteenth century. It was used mainly for cooking and other traditional or domestic needs. However, when the Industrial Revolution dawned on the world and the West responded with massive production, West Africa also actively participated in the process. With a tremendous rise in palm oil and palm kernel plantations came an increase in processing and shipping, which heavily contributed to the development of industries in Europe. The prospect of more profit contributed to the European penetration into the hinterland. Edmund Morel describes the importance of palm oil to West Africans and the process of export thus:

> There is not another tree in the whole world which produces money with so little expense as this particular crop. In Nigeria, the oil is prepared usually in small quantities, in the small villages scattered over the country. After being prepared, it is in many instances carried by women and children to some central native market, situated as a rule on the edge of a waterway. There it is bought by the middlemen so called, who are really the carriers of the country, and put by them into the casks previously supplied by the European merchants. The casks are packed away in canoes, and the middlemen paddle down through the creeks for distances varying with the length and character of the waterways, to the merchant's factory at the mouth. The merchant then pays for the oil, gives the middleman an empty cask in exchange for the full one, and ships the latter by the first steamer that comes along.[34]

The palm oil trade did not come without its challenges, as shipping of these palm oil and kernels was mainly carried out via waterways without road networks or vehicles for transportation. For example, this proved particularly arduous for Ibadan, which could not be active until the emergence of reliable trade routes to Lagos in the 1850s and through Egbaland, which caused another major source of conflict involving the Ijebu. In the case of this limitation, parts of Yorubaland that wanted to do business with European traders but lacked access to the coast had to either fight their way through or establish trading arrangements with those guarding the coast. Therein lies some of West African societies' economic and social networks.

The decline of the oligarchic elite, which had developed as a result of the transatlantic slave trade, was one significant aspect, or, possibly, advantage, of the rise of legal commerce. The rulers and chiefs who had monopolized the slave trade due to its reliance on sheer force and power lost their influence on commerce in West Africa to two main sets of people. First were the rising small-scale farmers. The Europeans became interested in dealing with anyone with agricultural products, which meant they eclipsed those dealing in the sale of slaves.[35] The Europeans' high demand for these raw materials meant that the monopoly by a few hands did not exactly work in their favor as it used to be. The second factor was the return of former slaves to parts of West Africa, especially Lagos, Abeokuta, and Sierra Leone.[36] These returnees had the advantage of language and, thus, began to act as middlemen. As they were new, they needed clients to promote their products to Europeans, which led them to assist farmers who were just starting out in the industry at the expense of the existing oligarchs. Some of these new merchants included "Shitta Bey, Taiwo Olowu, Seidu Olowu, Madam Tinubu, Da Rocha, J. H. Doherty, Sedu Williams, the Crowther family,"[37] as well as the famous Omu Okwei of Osomari,[38] who began to dominate foreign trade with the Europeans.

However, the legitimate trade was not entirely without problems. This is especially a given fact, as the palm oil business did not always boom throughout the entire nineteenth century. The depression that hit the global economy between 1873 and 1895 affected the economy of West Africa, too.[39] As a result, the price of palm oil—like other agricultural products—plummeted, which Hopkins believes was one of the major factors that "provoked intra-African conflicts over shrinking export revenues, which provoked African elites to secure rents by raising tolls and tariffs, and that this undermining of free trade by Africans motivated European intervention."[40]

In 1890, cocoa was imported into Yorubaland for the first time,[41] becoming a major source of wealth and mainstay of the Nigerian economy until the discovery of crude oil in the mid-twentieth century. While cocoa was introduced into the region, the lack of processing mechanisms meant West Africa was only used as a source farm where cocoa was planted, harvested, and exported to Europe that had the wherewithal to convert the produce into finished goods such as beverages. This has remained a common practice today. Besides cocoa, planting, harvesting, and exporting rubber was another big commercial breakthrough of the nineteenth century. Boge identifies and further discusses it thus:

> During the 1890s the international price of rubber rose and this fired the interest of the local farmers in its production even though the necessary skills to handle its tapping were lacking. As a result of the poor tapping methods by the local farmers, the Agricultural and Forestry Department introduced new types of the rubber plants in order to increase the yields. Later on, the department embarked on the program of demonstrating to the local farmers the techniques of efficient planting and production of the newly introduced species.[42]

The above further shows that another benefit of legitimate commerce in the nineteenth century was not limited to introducing new crops as the European powers began to train local farmers on more efficient ways to farm, especially the newly introduced crops. In truth, while this training aimed at efficiency and higher productivity, it was a selfcentered design by the Europeans to improve the quantity and quality of their imports. West African farmers were taught advanced means of cultivation, harvesting, and processing. New methods of agricultural activities, such as plowing, were also introduced, which revolutionized agriculture in West Africa, particularly Yorubaland. Again, the size of the farmland and the quantity of cash crops grown were more important indicators of wealth than the ownership of slaves, which by that time had significantly decreased.

Another major feature of legitimate commerce in the economy of West African societies was the gradual introduction and circulation of foreign legal tenders. Although, in Hopkins' view, a formal monetary system for commercial transactions was not inaugurated until the establishment of the West African Currency Board in 1912,[43] the British currency had begun to flood West Africa from the 1870s and 1880s.[44] The use of copper rod standard as currency in Cameroon and parts of Nigeria, such as the Cross River basin, and cloth-made money in Senegambia, was already common before the turn of the twentieth century.[45]

In 1880, Britain passed an ordinance that sought to domesticate metallic coins and make the Sterling the legal tender in the region, especially in its areas of trade influence.[46] As a result, according to Lovejoy, the cowrie, which was already gradually declining, fluctuated heavily, and its value depreciated completely between 1880 and circa 1895.[47] The massive importation of the British silver coin and other currencies not only depreciated the cowrie system but also further destroyed and ended the trade-by-barter system that had served the region for several centuries. Ironically, perhaps, the century is regarded as the time of currency revolution for West Africa and the continent at large. Leigh Gardner emphasizes the conscious effort by the British, in particular, to eliminate the use of cowries as legal tender thus:

> By the late nineteenth century, therefore, colonial governments began enacting legislation banning the importation of cowries and manilas and declaring that they were no longer legal tender within colonial boundaries. They then began to issue new currencies which were intended to replace the old commodity currencies. These included the West African pound, the East African rupee, the East African shilling, and the Congolese franc, among others.[48]

However, despite the above effort, the use of cowries and manilas continued in parts of West Africa. In other words, the entirety of West Africa did not embrace the use of the foreign-introduced legal tender. It did not become a universal practice until decades into the twentieth century. In Yorubaland, for instance, the use of cowries continued as the recognized means of transaction (contrary to the use of metallic currencies such as gold, copper, and silver), especially in the hinterland, until well into the colonial era.[49] This means the British imposition of metallic coins was only effective on the coast and in trade relationships between West Africans and European powers. In trade relations involving West Africans, or other regions in Africa, the use of cowries and manilas continued as legal tender for a long time until they gradually became scarce before the 1930s.

With the growth of commerce and the gradual introduction of currency, an institution for their regulation became a necessity. The British needed this institution particularly to regulate its newly introduced currency, sanction exchanges, as well as circulate metallic currencies. The banking institution can be traced to the establishment of the African Banking Corporation (ABC) in Lagos, Nigeria, by the British in 1892.[50] It had its roots in South Africa. Barely a year later, another one was established, known as the British Bank of West Africa (BBWA), which originally commenced as a trust fund under Sir Alfred Jones.[51] It was not until a year after that it fully commenced banking activities with its headquarters in Lagos and first branch in Calabar. That same year, 1894, the BBWA merged with the ABC and went on to evolve, assuming several names such as Bank of West Africa in 1957, Standard Bank of West Africa, Standard Bank of Nigeria later in 1965, and finally settling for First Bank of Nigeria in 1979.[52]

Similarly, society invented the practice of the credit or trust system. While it had been in practice since the establishment of coastal relationships between West Africa and Europe, it grew in practice in the nineteenth century, chiefly owing to increased trade relations between both parties. Giving of trust, which peaked in the nineteenth century, according to Njoku, was a credit system where European merchants "advanced on trust considerable amount of goods to African middlemen for a specified period during which the middlemen were expected to repay to their European creditors the equivalent in such goods as slaves, palm oil, cloths and ivory."[53] Simply put, it was a system in which goods were given "on credit" based on trust in exchange for subsequent payment in kind using commodities such as palm oil and kernels. However, the "trust" was not one-way or monopolized by the Europeans with West Africans merely receiving, which would have represented a false narrative of the system. Njoku documents that in many places in West Africa, the local people served as middlemen who initiated the "trust" system by issuing it to European merchants, going as far as to suggest that the system predates the encounter with the Europeans. He cites examples thus:

> It may be appropriate to preface comments on the above impression by pointing out that the giving of credits in West Africa ante-dated the coming of the Europeans. As A. G. Hopkins has indicated, credits were usually provided by established indigenous lenders in the long-distance domestic trade ... The Portuguese, who first visited Benin adapted the existing indigenous system by adding their own system of fixed prices in place of indigenous bargaining method. They then probably exported this new method to other areas on the West African coast ... In the Benin area, as Ryder has noted, credit was extended by the Edo to Europeans, not vice-versa, as happened in the later phase. In 1783, J. F. Landolphe, a French sea captain and merchant, requested the Oba of Benin to supply him, on credit, yams and other items with which he would feed his slaves *en route* to America. In the late 19th century, Charles Patridge, a British official was impressed by the fact that the Cross River indigenous traders were extraordinarily credulous in giving credits.[54]

Besides the trust and credit system, there was also the insurance system in precolonial West Africa. Using Nigeria as a case study, there is material evidence that the country boasted of a traditional system where misfortunes, like the death of any member of a community, did not result in the end of their business. As Ogbeidi further corroborates, southern communities in Nigeria, in particular, were not only communal, but they also functioned with high value for the kinship system, "which provided the basis for protection against loses, but the mode of practice differed from one community to another."[55] Examples include the *otu* organization among the Apoi-Ijo people in the Eseodo Local Government found in today's Ondo State in Southwest Nigeria. According to Ogbeidi, the *otu* was often established by mutual consent of youths who, for instance, worked together to render financial assistance to members for house-warming, titling, funeral, marriage, and naming ceremonies, to which they would have contributed in advance.[56] In their world, the problem of one was a problem for others. Other examples abound in precolonial Yorubaland in the form of *esusu, aro, ogbo, isusu, mitiri,* and *Egbe Ode,* some of which were guilds formed to help colleagues of a similar profession.[57]

Apart from the economy and geography, the transportation system is also one of the most crucial infrastructures of any society because it determines the growth and development of the economy and society at large. The use of animal transportation, slaves, *iwofa*, and human porterage gradually gave way to modernized transportation systems from the last two decades of the nineteenth century. This was necessary for ease of commercial activities, and as colonialism began to gain momentum, the regular movement of colonial administrative personnel also became a priority. This necessity engendered the introduction of wheeled transport into West Africa.

Notably, the first form of wheeled transport did not appear in the nineteenth century. The earliest sighting of a wheeled vehicle in West Africa was in 1670, which was a ceremonial carriage presented to the royal king of Allada in the present-day Republic of Benin by the French *Compagnie des Indes Occidentales*.[58] While there are disputed sources on when the actual first wheeled vehicle was used in West Africa, dating to earlier Portuguese encounters in West Africa, none could be proven or solidified with any material evidence—hence the general acceptability of the 1670 narrative. According to Law, the next wheeled carriage was not seen in West Africa until a European on a visit to Dahomey, in modern-day Benin Republic, used two coaches in a ceremonial procession at Abomey in 1772.[59]

While humans were used in the earliest introductions and subsequently after until the eighteenth and nineteenth centuries, when the use of horses in pulling these carriages became prominent, the carriages were used by the political and the wealthy classes for recreational purposes and the occasional grand visits as they spread to several parts of West Africa. However, it is very important to note that the carriages were not used to transport goods due to their heavy nature, even though the nineteenth century had ushered in increased agricultural exports.[60] Until the introduction of vehicular transport, the movement of goods remained through human porterage (using slaves and servants), water, and animal transportation.

A major breakthrough occurred in 1885 when the British embarked on road construction in Lagos following the legislative issuance of the road construction ordinance.[61] In 1889, the passing of this ordinance led to the construction of over 250 miles in the Lagos Colony.[62] However, a shortage of manual laborers created challenges for the rehabilitation and reconstruction of roads. Many laborers left the construction site for farms, which promised them more wealth due to the introduction of cash crops like rubber and cocoa, as discussed above. With this "labor migration," progress on road construction was further halted until the twentieth century.

The attempt at modernizing transportation in West Africa did not end there. The use of railway transportation was introduced into Nigeria in the last decade of the nineteenth century.[63] While Gilbert Carter, the then-Governor of Lagos Colony, is credited with being the first to conceive the idea of a railway in Nigeria in 1893 to connect the coastline to the hinterland, the actualization of railway lines in Nigeria, and West Africa at large, was implemented in 1895 by Joseph Chamberlain, the then-Secretary of State.[64] The railway project faced the same problem as the road construction project due to a labor shortage.

Beyond the economic benefits of farming during the period of study, Nigerians, like other Africans, were more comfortable being their own boss rather than taking orders from persons who would otherwise and especially determine their pay. Oyemakinde identifies other problems, including "the difficulty of cutting through thick tropical forest from the coast inwards" and irregular supply of construction materials "owing to shipping and landing difficulties in the Lagos harbor."[65] Although these factors stifled the progress of railway construction in Nigeria, the first transportation by rail took place in 1901. The introduction of the railway would prove even more vital in expropriating raw materials from West Africa to the metropolis, where they were often processed and sold back to the continent as finished goods. Several feeder roads were constructed by early colonial administrations to further facilitate movement by rail.

FIGURE 13.2   Proclamation of the Abolition of Slavery in the French Colonies, 27 April 1848
https://commons.wikimedia.org/wiki/File:Biard_Abolition_de_l%27esclavage
_1849.jpg.

While the infrastructural development purposefully and deliberately served the colonial government to the detriment of the growth and development of the African economy, some positives can be identified from the economic relations between the West and West Africa.[66] Most notably, the abolition of the slave trade and the increase in the conduct of legitimate trade in West Africa revolutionized the socioeconomic pattern of living in West Africa. In the labor force, a new class of individuals emerged—professionals such as bricklayers, carpenters, traders, merchants, artisans, marketers, bankers, and horticulturists.[67] While many of them were slave returnees who now had the advantage of exposure to the Western professional class and replicated the knowledge upon return, some locals began to acquire skills in some of these professions. It should come as no surprise that these slave returnees, in most cases, were responsible for training the locals who spread the vocations around the region (Figure 13.2).

Conclusion

The economic situation of West Africa, like the rest of Africa, was revolutionary in its circumstances and aftermath. While the transatlantic slave trade—the bane of West Africa's economy for almost three centuries—gradually faded, slavery lingered, especially owing to increased war situations in the region. These wars were further exacerbated by the availability of firearms,[68] which were in high supply as the Europeans traded them in large quantities for palm oil, palm kernel, and other agricultural products. While that was the case, there was also the ascendance of legitimate trade. Its expansion led to several innovations and new ways of doing things, as well as an increase in production out of West Africa. As a result, West Africa, like the rest of Africa, reverted to the post-European encounter when agriculture was the order of the day.

However, the boom in agricultural products and trade with West Africa could not last the century. The global depression of the 1870s and 1880s affected legitimate trade, inviting the Europeans into the continent as they sought economic relief.[69] Invariably, the demands for palm oil and kernels from the Western world, particularly Britain, France, and the United States, increased throughout the nineteenth century and progressed until interest shifted to colonization. This was due to certain circumstances, some of which are linked to commercial fallouts between Western powers and Africa. Several features of the economy of West Africa around this period were also discussed in the chapter, ranging from the "trust and credit" system, the introduction of metallic legal tender, infrastructural developments such as banking, road, and rail transportation, and the emergence of the professional class in West Africa.

DEEP DIVE

Assignment 1

Objective

The objective of this assignment is to ensure that students complete the reading of Chapter 13 and to get them to understand how legitimate trade was expanded by the need for manufactured goods and to ensure the continuation of manufacturing industries in Europe. Additionally, students will be expected to address how crucial palm oil was to the legitimate trade industry and Western societies.

Method

Students will be expected to write a short note in response to the question.

Reading Comprehension

How was legitimate trade connected with the European economy? What role did palm oil play in the legitimate trade?

Assignment 2

Objective

The objective of this assignment is to ensure that students complete the reading of Chapter 13 and to get them to think about how legitimate trade and the implementation of foreign currency depreciated the value of African currencies and affected African trade.

Method

Students will be expected to write a short note in response to the question.

Reading Comprehension

How did "legitimate trade" affect social and economic institutions in West Africa?

Notes

1 Wendy R. Childs, "1492–1494: Columbus and the Discovery of America," *The Economic History Review* 48, no. 4 (1995): 754–768.
2 Tony Horwitz, *A Voyage Long and Strange: Rediscovering the New World* (New York: Henry Holt and Co., 2008).
3 Herbert S. Klein, *The Atlantic Slave Trade* (Cambridge: The University of Cambridge, 1999).
4 Joel Quirk and David Richardson, "Anti-slavery, European Identity and International Society," *Journal of Modern European History* 7, no. 1 (2009): 68–92.
5 Robin Law, "The Transition from the Slave Trade to Legitimate Commerce," *Studies in the World History of Slavery Abolition and Emancipation* 1, no. 1 (1996): 1–13.
6 David Eltis and James Walvin, eds., *The Abolition of the Atlantic Slave Trade: Origins and Effects in Europe, Africa, and the Americas* (Wisconsin: University of Wisconsin Press, 1981), 6.
7 Patrick Manning and Emmanuel Akyeampong, "Slavery and Slave Trade in West Africa, 1450–1930," in *Themes in West Africa's History*, ed. Emmanuel Akyeampong (Oxford: James Currey, 2006), 99–117.
8 Olatunji Ojo, "The Atlantic Slave Trade and Local Ethics of Slavery in Yorubaland," *African Economic History* 41 (2013): 73–100.
9 David Eltis, *Economic Growth and the Ending of the Transatlantic Slave Trade* (New York: Oxford University Press, 1987).
10 Erik Green, "Production Systems in Pre-Colonial Africa," in *The History of African Development*, eds. Ewout Frankema and Ellen Hillbom (African Economic History Network, 2015), 13.
11 Green, "Production Systems in Pre-Colonial Africa."
12 Manning and Akyeampong, "Slavery and Slave Trade in West Africa."
13 Albert Van Dantzig, "Effects of the Atlantic Slave Trade on Some West African Societies," *Revue française d'histoire d'outremer* 62, no. 226–227 (1975): 252–269.
14 Faruq Idowu Boge, "The Dynamics of the Abolition of Slave Trade and the Changing Nature of Yoruba Economy in the Nineteenth Century," *RIMA International Journal of Historical Studies (RIJHIS)* 1, no. 1 (2018): 129.
15 Ayodele Thomas, "Revolving Loan Scheme (Esusu): A Substitute to the Nigerian Commercial Banking?" *IOSR Journal of Business and Management* 17, no. 6 (2015): 62–67.
16 Walter Rodney, *How Europe Underdeveloped Africa* (London: Bogle-L'Ouverture Publications, 1972).
17 Boge, "The Dynamics of the Abolition of Slave Trade," 133.
18 Santosh C. Saha, *A History of Agriculture in West Africa: A Guide to Information Sources* (New York: E. Mellen Press, 1990).
19 Anthony Hopkins, *An Economic History of West Africa* (New York: Routledge, 2014).
20 Robin Law, "Wheeled Transport in Pre-colonial West Africa," *Africa* 50, no. 3 (1980): 249–262.
21 Deji Ogunremi, "Human Porterage in Nigeria in the Nineteenth Century," *Journal of the Historical Society of Nigeria* 8, no. 1 (1975): 37–59.
22 Gabriel O. Ogunremi, *Counting the Camels: Economics of Transportation in Preindustrial Nigeria* (New York: NOK Publishers International, 1982).
23 Robert Smith, "The Canoe in West African History," *The Journal of African History* 11, no. 4 (1970): 515–533.
24 Martin Lynn, *Commerce and Economic Change in West Africa: The Palm Oil Trade in the Nineteenth Century* (Cambridge: Cambridge University Press, 2002).
25 Lynn, *Commerce and Economic Change in West Africa*.
26 Lynn, *Commerce and Economic Change in West Africa*.
27 Lynn, *Commerce and Economic Change in West Africa*.
28 Lynn, *Commerce and Economic Change in West Africa*.
29 Lynn, *Commerce and Economic Change in West Africa*.
30 Lynn, *Commerce and Economic Change in West Africa*.
31 Bolanle Awe, *The Rise of Ibadan as a Yoruba Power in the Nineteenth Century* (Oxford: University of Oxford, 1964).

32 Olawale B. Salami, "Ibadan Slaves and Ibadan Wars in Pre-Colonial South Western Nigeria, 1835–1893," *IOSR Journal of Humanities and Social Science* 7, no. 3 (2013): 33.
33 Boge, "The Dynamics of the Abolition of Slave Trade," 136.
34 Edmund Dene Morel, "Affairs of West Africa," *Psychology Press* 62 (1968): 73.
35 Boge, "The Dynamics of the Abolition of Slave Trade," 136.
36 Kwesi Kwaa Prah, *Afro-Brazilian Returnees and Their Communities* (Rondebosch: CASAS, 2009).
37 Boge, "The Dynamics of the Abolition of Slave Trade," 136.
38 Felicia Ekejiuba, "Omu Okwei of Osomari," in *Nigerian Women in Historical Perspective*, ed. Bolanle Awe (Lagos: Sankore Publishers, 1992), 89–104.
39 Ian Brown, *The Economies of Africa and Asia in the Inter-war Depression* (New York: Routledge, 1989).
40 Ewout Frankema, Jeffrey Williamson and Pieter Woltjer, *An Economic Rationale for the African Scramble: The Commercial Transition and the Commodity Price Boom of 1845–1885* (Cambridge: National Bureau of Economic Research, 2015).
41 Boge, "The Dynamics of the Abolition of Slave Trade," 136.
42 Boge, "The Dynamics of the Abolition of Slave Trade," 136–137.
43 Hopkins, "The Creation of a Colonial Monetary System."
44 Boge, "The Dynamics of the Abolition of Slave Trade," 137.
45 Paul Lovejoy, "Interregional Monetary Flows in the Precolonial Trade of Nigeria," *The Journal of African History* 15, no. 4 (1974): 563–585.
46 Boge, "The Dynamics of the Abolition of Slave Trade," 137.
47 Lovejoy, "Interregional Monetary Flows."
48 Leigh Gardner, "From Cowries to Mobile Phones: African Monetary Systems Since 1800," in *The History of African Development: An Online Textbook for a New Generation of African Students and Teachers*, eds. Frankema Ewout, Ellen Hillbom, Ushehweu Kufakurinani and Felix Meier zu Selhausen (African Economic History Network, 2020).
49 Akanmu G. Adebayo, "Money, Credit, and Banking in Precolonial Africa: The Yoruba Experience," *Anthropos* 89, no. 4/6 (1994): 379–400.
50 Olubisi Friday Oluduro, "History and Evolution of Banking in Nigeria," *Academia Arena* 7, no. 1 (2015): 9–14.
51 Oluduro, "History and Evolution of Banking in Nigeria," 10.
52 Oluduro, "History and Evolution of Banking in Nigeria," 10.
53 Onwuka N. Njoku, "Some Thought on the 'Trust' System in Eastern Nigeria," *Africa Development/Afrique Et Développement* 5, no. 2 (1980): 37–49.
54 Njoku, "Some Thought on the 'Trust' System in Eastern Nigeria," 38.
55 Michael M. Ogbeidi, "Insurance Institutions in Pre-Colonial Nigeria," *Lagos Notes and Records* 9, no. 1 (2003): 115–133.
56 Ogbeidi, "Insurance Institutions in Pre-Colonial Nigeria," 120.
57 William Bascom, "The Esusu: The Credit System of the Yoruba," *Journal of the Royal Anthropological Institute* 92, no. 1 (1952): 63–69.
58 Robin Law, "Wheeled Transport in Pre-Colonial West Africa," *Africa: Journal of the International African Institute* 50, no. 3 (1980): 249–62.
59 Law, "Wheeled Transport in Pre-Colonial West Africa," 253.
60 Law, "Wheeled Transport in Pre-Colonial West Africa," 255.
61 Boge, "The Dynamics of the Abolition of Slave Trade," 138.
62 Boge, "The Dynamics of the Abolition of Slave Trade," 138.
63 Wale Oyemakinde, "Railway Construction and Operation in Nigeria, 1895–1911: Labor Problems and Socio-Economic Impact," *Journal of the Historical Society of Nigeria* 7, no. 2 (1974): 303–324.
64 Oyemakinde, "Railway Construction."
65 Oyemakinde, "Railway Construction," 304.
66 S. R. Tolofari and E. J. Gubbins, "Nigerian Railways: Problems and Prospects," *Transportation Planning and Technology* 8, no. 4 (1984): 225–235.
67 Boge, "The Dynamics of the Abolition of Slave Trade," 138.
68 W. A. Richards, "The Import of Firearms into West Africa in the Eighteenth Century," *The Journal of African History* 21, no. 1 (1980): 43–59.

69 Patrick Manning, "Slave Trade, 'Legitimate Trade', and Imperialism Revisited: The Control of Wealth in the Bights of Benin and Biafra," in *Africans in Bondage: Studies in Slavery and the Slave Trade: Essays in Honor of Philip D. Curtin*, ed. Paul E. Lovejoy (Wisconsin: University of Wisconsin Press, 1986), 203–233.

14

TRANSFORMATIONS AND REVOLUTIONS

Introduction

Following the colonialists' subjugation of West Africa at the end of the nineteenth century, control of the region's narratives was planted within their grasp. West Africa was painted as a region in a state of sociopolitical decline, a condition that justified intervention. These stories were part of the fabrication of a "Dark Continent." Many West African states at that point were reeling from the abolition of the slave trade on which they had so heavily depended. However, even as there were problems, certain provinces in this region were still remarkable in their survival. For example, Dahomey's military, economic, and political competence saw it through the abolition and the attacks of the French for a few years.[1] However, this chapter is not solely concerned with counteracting imperial narratives. It aims, among other things, to interrogate changes in the West African landscape in the context of the collapse of once-powerful states, the abolition of the slave trade, the new trade in raw materials, and the advent of jihadism.

Trade, Politics, and Imperialism

Trade and politics constituted the twin paradigm of interrelated activities in nineteenth-century West Africa.[2] Essentially, both were at the core of intergroup and other forms of contact and interactions among different communities. The economy of West Africa adjusted to the Atlantic economies,[3] and many of the long-established trade routes remained.[4] Internal trade connected the hinterland with the coastal areas.[5] The course of African trade shifted toward the Atlantic route with interest in palm products, ivory, pepper and others.[6] The Industrial Revolution, coupled with a series of social disruptions heralded by the revolutionary tide of the eighteenth century that lasted till the nineteenth century and beyond, dramatically changed the mechanism of relations between West Africa and Europe[7] in what scholars collectively defined as the Atlantic Age. In addition, this period further integrated West Africa into the world market with a palpable impact

DOI: 10.4324/9781003198260-17

on the social relations among the people of the region.[8] As the European economy was expanding and transforming from agriculture and manufacturing into services, West African states were in no small measure impacted.

In the same way that the nineteenth century marked a turning point in the evolution of West African states, the eighteenth century was conspicuous for its massive disruptions and transformations in Europe since the region's maritime breakthrough/advancement from the fifteenth century. These changes covered the political and economic scenes and went far into the social fabric of society, including religion, technology, science, and investment.[9] Following the French Revolution, whose ideals steadily spread to other parts of Europe, a new standard of social conduct, norms, and philosophy emerged, revolving around the ideals of humanitarianism and liberalism, considered to be universal and innate to every human on earth.[10] With the Industrial Revolution, which began to mechanize production, these ideals became popular in Europe and were put into practice by the European elite. Merchants, missionaries, humanitarian bodies, and governments spearheaded this campaign to transform other civilizations.[11]

One of the immediate implications was the abolition of the trade in human commodities, first by the French government, which was later enacted, and then by the British Act of 1807.[12] Notably, the abolitionist movement and the elite consensus galvanized into action were immensely impacted by the series of revolutions and actions staged by Europeans against the establishment and the rebellions raging among the Black communities in Europe and the Americas. Rebellions intensified as slave practices continued on both sides of the Atlantic.[13] This development alone had immeasurable consequences on the dynamics of the evolution of West African states during the nineteenth century as it spurred on and shaped every other contour that characterized centrifugal inputs into this process.

Following abolition, there was an intense pursuit to organize and promote the so-called legitimate trade meant to feed the emerging mechanized industries in Europe.[14] However, it was believed that the sociopolitical landscape of the people must be altered to accommodate more involvement in carrying out this economic transformation. In other words, it replaced the people's crony capitalist practices with liberal ones, resulting in a laissez-faire economy.[15] To achieve this, a new class of economic actors needed to be created as agents of sociopolitical transformation in society. This would be the middle-class, which only began to emerge in Europe following the deconstruction of the feudal ownership of property and wealth at the turn of the modern era. The middle class also directly impacted the pattern of trade and agricultural and industrial production in the region.[16]

Evidently, various Western imperial agents conceived traditional authorities in West African societies in light of the feudal lords in the pre-modern European era who stood between trade and commerce and society's interests to promote legitimate trade and the reconstruction of the social stratification dynamics of nineteenth-century Africa. Instructively, this transition implied that the pigmy property of the many was replaced with the huge property of the few. This was to the extent that the creation of a new elite class and the emergence of the middle-class population evaporated the basis of the communal structure of wealth, economic production and distribution, and social relations. It should be noted that in the previous practice, individuals earned their living through a collective source of communal wealth that provided shelter, food, land, and means of production, and this did not imply that an element of the latter was absent in society.[17]

What had previously been limited by the people's crony capitalist practices, which favored the few, exploded with the emergence of its liberal form. If there were any barriers to trade with the people of the region in the past—and there were many—the nineteenth century offered a great remedy through science, technology, and growing investment in these two areas, as well as trade. Diop observes that "it would seem to be more judicious to explain the development of mechanization by the needs of capitalist production, rather than to justify the system as being a consequence of the use of machinery."[18] As the revolutionary tide was recalibrating European societies in the late eighteenth century, organizations like the Association for the Promotion of Scientific Knowledge about Africa were already debating the possibility of exploring Africa's interior.

Following the engagements of these bodies, the exploratory missions became a compartment of selected professionals from different fields of scientific research—medicine, anthropology, geography, botany, and even administration.[19] Added to this were Christian missionaries and representatives of the merchant companies. Until the formal annexation of these polities into various European empires, these missions were propelled and financed, particularly for in-depth exploration and collection of data on flora and fauna and all that made up the wealth of the region. It also opened a safe passage for European ships, missionaries, merchants, and others into the interior (Figure 14.1).[20]

From the twilight of the eighteenth century were simultaneous massive investments by European governments, merchants, and other elite classes in transportation, telecommunication, and weapons of war. Innovations from these endeavors became the tangible vehicle in the Western imperial project in West Africa and elsewhere. The development of railway-line technology and the steam-engine ship later in the mid-nineteenth century accelerated the exploration of West African resources and the distribution of trading commodities. This aided in reducing the time and duration of navigation and increasing the exploitative capacity of the economic actors.[21] The railway, which began to emerge in European capitals in the late eighteenth to the early nineteenth centuries,[22] became even more important to the imperial project for the same reason it was developed in the first place. As the development was ongoing in Europe, the abolitionists desired and debated that this was developed in Africa to expedite trade in the region's resources. The project began earnestly in the late nineteenth century and, before the First World War, it had become an integrating factor in the West African economy, connecting producing areas in the interior to the coast and distribution centers.

Similarly, by 1865, when the British government needed to consolidate its West African settlements into a single administrative unit comprising Lagos, Gold Coast, Sierra Leone, and The Gambia, with the administrative headquarters in Sierra Leone, the steamship came in handy.[23] Advancements in telegraphs also facilitated the coordination of the imperial project, leading to the region's colonial experience by the turn of the twentieth century. Although there was intense lobbying for European weapons by different political actors that emerged from the nineteenth-century crisis in the region, innovations in weaponry did little to contribute to successful military campaigns by these actors. They lobbied more for the Dane and the Gatling guns than they did in preparing their men to deploy them efficiently for the prosecution of wars.[24] Hence, even with the guns at the disposal of the Dahomeans at the time the Old Oyo was at its lowest ebb of military might, the latter had its archers defeating the former decisively. Likewise,

Scale 1 : 41,000,000.

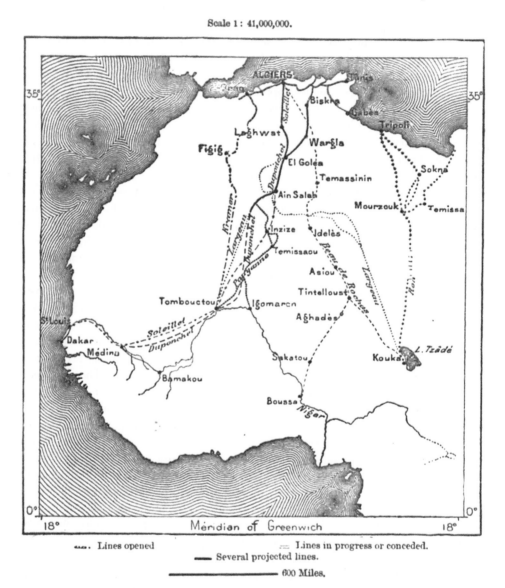

FIGURE 14.1   Projected railways across West Africa https://commons.wikimedia.org/wiki/File
:AFR_V2_D053_Projected_railways_across_West_Africa.jpg.

despite the massive stockpile of ammunition in the arsenal of the Sultan of Sokoto and
other authorities in the caliphate from Bida to Kano, they could only engage with the
"square" formation of the British invading forces with a few of these weapons that were
haphazardly handled by their forces.[25]

Essentially, the accumulation of modern European arms and ammunition only served
as a deterrent among West African political actors rather than deciding the result of
the nineteenth-century wars. Therefore, javelins, machetes, bows and arrows, and other

locally produced weapons decided the tide of war during this period. However, alongside the steamship and other innovations, modern munitions and arms were used as a medium of diplomacy and military force to subdue West African polities under the expanding Western imperial empire of the time. In places like Opobo, it was used to force the authorities to renounce their rights and the sovereignty of their kingdoms; however, colonial forces engaged in all-out wars in Asante, Lagos, the Sokoto caliphate, and other places.[26]

It was not only the acquisition of these weapons that triggered the scramble for European support/alliance among the emerging political actors in the region; the presence of Europeans, usually missionaries and merchants, in any of these polities from the mid-nineteenth century also provided a formidable shield for the people.[27] To understand why this became integral to the evolution of society during this period, it is important to recall that this epoch marked the devastation and reconstitution of communities and kingdoms in the region. As such, one of the criteria for the resettlement of the people, formation of new polities, and the expansion of the surviving ones was the provision of basic and social security as it was when these polities first emerged centuries back. This was facilitated by the presence and activities of European merchants and missionaries.

In addition to their role as agents of Western civilization and as acculturated individuals to Western culture, the returnees from the Americas and Sierra Leone also propelled the same aura among the people. By the mid-nineteenth century, they had become a formidable bloc in the political, economic, and sociocultural evolution of society.[28] For instance, in Yorubaland, from Abeokuta to Lagos, they dominated the political waves in the cities through their engagement with the nascent British authorities in these areas, steadily displacing the local authorities.[29] This was not so much the case in Calabar and Bonny, where English culture and civilization had influenced their sociopolitical landscape since around the seventeenth century.[30] However, the place of the returnees in other parts was necessitated by the role of literacy and Western education in society's evolution, a process that had dominated palace businesses and administration in parts of the delta states.[31] In the whole of the Yoruba region, alongside the missionaries, they became intermediaries between the traditional political authorities and the Lagos government during war and peace times.[32] Their presence propelled Christian missions in the region and beyond and was cardinal to the development and spread of other forms of Western taxonomic modernity, including education and social relations and the creation of the proposed middle class.

Leaning toward what they characterized as benign colonization, this new community promoted the idea of Western imperialism and began to articulate their views on the colonial project vis-à-vis what they thought to be their undeniable right in the political power-sharing of the emergent state.[33] This was made possible by the development of the printing press in the mid-nineteenth century, which triggered the production of newspapers, pamphlets, and other literature contributing to the changing face of society.[34] Some were instructional books designed to encourage the development and spread of Christianity, while others were referred to as improvement pamphlets, teaching the people about Western manners and etiquette. During this period, the preliterate traditional West African cultures were transformed into literate societies.

Christian missionaries taught the people the art of reading, writing, and basic arithmetic.[35] These skills were deployed in the service of missionary activities and the emerging merchant companies, relatively bringing society's economy in line with what evolved in the modern transition in Europe. This was particularly so in the service and labor sector, which propelled the cash economy and deconstruction of the communal morphology of society.[36] New crops were also introduced, and some existing ones were enhanced through the missionaries' efforts.

As railway construction began in the twilight of the nineteenth century, together with the clearing of the waterways and general improvement on the transportation network in the region, botanical farms were established for the experimentation of crops, mainly cash crops like cocoa, cotton, and palm oil seed, for the expansion of trade. Hence, the evolution in agricultural production in the region coincided with development in the medium of exchange. Centuries of trade and commercial activities in the region have evolved from the barter system to the adoption of cowries and coins of different values. At different times of their adoption, all these systems and media of exchange existed side by side.[37]

Under Herbert Taylor Ussher, the Governor-in-Chief of the Gold Coast colony, and the public seal of the colony, at the Government House, Christiansburg, on April 13, 1880, and on the forty-third reign of Her Majesty, the British coin replaced all other forms and means of exchange on the Gold Coast. This consisted of several notable African kingdoms and civilizations.[38] Reforms in the newly created financial sector of the West African economy continued with the development of banks such as the African Banking Corporation, which evolved into the Bank of British West Africa in 1894 out of the crisis created by the former.[39] This helped to increase West African economies' link to the British economy through the Chambers of Commerce in British financial and trading capitals in London, Manchester, Liverpool, and elsewhere. Likewise, since the establishment of the first Court of Equity in Bonny in the mid-nineteenth century, English law increasingly became an integral part of the administration of criminal justice in the region at various times.[40]

Through the same official communication that proclaimed the British coins as the only valid medium of exchange (with other gold coins) and the debate in the Legislative House that brought this to light, the Supreme Court's legal authority was reinforced through Ordinance No. 3 of 1880. This, thereby, reinforced English laws over and above customs and norms that had governed the trade and social coordination of the people for centuries. These developments imply that traditional authority had collapsed in the region. The British and French governments did not always deploy military force or diplomatic entreaties to initiate the takeover of these territories. Some of the traditional authorities had called for the intervention, or rather protection, of the British government, to enhance or sustain their geopolitical power. So, while all these reforms were ongoing with clear implications for their authority, they were in no way powerful enough to resist them.

The Slave Trade and the Rise of "Legitimate Commerce"

As pointed out in a previous chapter, the conquest of the Americas was a major incentive for the expansion of the slave trade. African states, which had found little use for slaves beyond routine farming and domestic interests, embarked on expeditions to export human capital. The transatlantic exodus of slaves from West Africa grew from an annual estimate of 600 persons between 1450 and 1500 to around 50,000 by 1780.[41] Alongside this was the trans-Saharan slave trade, which was rising steadily within the same period.[42] Although there were adverse consequences in terms of population shrinkages on the West African coast, the trade was beneficial to both sides. The Americas accessed the labor it needed for economic exploitation while West African states, at least the ones with enough military resources for enslavement, reaped gains in terms of European goods and revenue. Therefore, it was a considerable oddity when Britain, having exploited slaves for so long, suddenly deemed it immoral to sustain it. The British antagonism to the transatlantic slave trade was an outgrowth of slave resistance and the activities of the abolitionist movement. Led by activists Granville Sharp, Thomas Clarkson, the parliamentarian William Wilberforce, Olaudah Equiano, and several others of less renown, the anti-slave movement was an organization that cut across England's social classes.[43] The expansion of the country's reading population and the backing of interest groups such as the Religious Society of Friends (Quakers) and the Methodists were significant factors that influenced the ban in 1807 (Figure 14.2).[44]

Although scholars have debated the extent to which humanitarianism rather than practical economic calculation necessitated Britain's move, there is consensus that activists had a genuine interest in seeing the end of slavery.[45] This is evidenced by late eighteenth-century campaigns at the grassroots of English society wherein petitions to legislators were signed by hundreds of thousands of citizens.[46] Nevertheless, even as that was the case, the doubt in academic circles was probably influenced by the fact that the institution of religion, which occupied the frontlines in the abolition movement, also supplied justifications for the subjugation of Black people when slavery was at its

FIGURE 14.2   Quakers meeting in the eighteenth century https://www.shutterstock.com/image -photo/quakers-meeting-18th-century-after-old-86630713.

peak.[47] The turn to morality has equally been attributed to the rise of industrialization in Britain. Under this line of reasoning, the need for fresh sources of raw materials, new export destinations, and evolving socioeconomic dynamics in England due to industrialization coincided with the upsurge of anti-slavery sentiments. In other words, the bill was passed when it had become convenient for the British to call a halt to slave exports.

In Europe, Britain was initially the only nation particular about ending the transatlantic slave trade. Discussing Britain's military and diplomatic efforts is important because it provides an opportunity to understand the constraints to discontinue human exports from West African coasts. Indeed, had the English not added bite to their eager anti-slave declarations, the trade would have persisted unhindered. Yet, even as that is asserted, scholars dispute the actual effectiveness of Britain's efforts on the high seas. A consensus exists that while the British successfully prevented transatlantic exports, the same could not be said for the perpetuation of slavery on West African territory. Thus, when the potential of a foreign market began to diminish, slavers found an alternative on domestic soil. These factors combined to justify colonization.

On the diplomatic front, Britain relied on a system of treaties and negotiations with its European counterparts. These treaties were, however, not fully effective in stopping the slave transits across the Atlantic. The international political climate was delicate in the early post-abolition years as France, a major participant, had just emerged from the Napoleonic wars. The United States was equally uninterested in fully committing to Britain's fervor. In addition, there was the need to respect sovereign waters by staying a cannon shot's distance (three miles) away from a country's ports. As a result, the Royal Navy could not board and seize vessels of other nations as that would provide sufficient justification for war. Consent was integral.

To navigate this, the British embarked on a series of negotiations with participating countries to secure permission to board ships suspected of carrying slaves. As highlighted by Bethell, these manifested as conventions under which special warrants were granted to the signatories to search each other's ships for human cargo. But while the agreements had a surface appearance of reciprocity, in practice, Britain was the sole enforcer. Its merchant vessels had ceased to engage in the trade, and it was the only navy capable of the kind of patrols needed to halt it.[48] Although the British experienced resistance from its European partners, it got more nations to agree to the right of search. Under the conventions, seized ships were prosecuted by Britain and the country to which the vessel belonged. They effected this by establishing courts of mixed commissions at various slave trading hotspots across the Atlantic. These commissions were essentially tribunals with adjudicators from either country. Thus, an Anglo-Brazilian commission had officials from England and Brazil on its prosecutorial panel. In West Africa, Sierra Leone was the seat of the commissions.[49]

When countries, for separate interests of their own, decided to resist Britain's diplomatic advances, the latter took it upon itself to board their vessels without consent. This was demonstrated by Britain's willingness to board Brazilian vessels under the backing of the Equipment Act. The Act, with the agreement of other signatories, allowed the Royal Navy to detain ships whose equipment indicated that slaves had been embarked at some point. These included shackles, an unusual supply of fresh water and other provisions, extra planks, etc.[50] Brazil eventually agreed to an equipment clause in 1842.[51] The

Act was designed to expand the remit of naval officials who could only detain vessels with slaves on board.

On West African shores, similar regard for international edicts was initially applied. The British had little interest in establishing overseas territory beyond their trading posts and were restrained from interfering explicitly with internal affairs. However, as emphasis shifted to legitimate commerce, the region lost respect for its territorial waters. An instance of violation is the bombardment of the Dahomean port of Whydah in 1841 and Lagos in 1851.[52] A series of tactics was equally deployed to pressure African rulers to indulge in legitimate trade. Some of these were treaties of cession, mediation, and military protection. The application of treaties rather than outright occupation was an outgrowth of British reluctance to occupy West African territory. Britain's administrators were unwilling to undertake the resource burden that administrative commitments would impose and, as such, preferred minimal involvement in local affairs.

However, it was not always the case that British agents on the ground agreed with their faraway superiors. Officials sometimes deemed it necessary to negotiate treaties of cession with African rulers to ensure the continuous flow of legitimate trade in commercially viable areas.[53] These treaties enabled officials to deploy troops to interfere with the slave business. But even as they did this, requests for ratification, which were sent back home, were frequently rejected. These provided an unintended benefit: the British avoided investing resources in ceded areas, saving costs, but could also respond to economic threats in local areas of responsibility. In other words, without the support of superiors, British agents established a semblance of authority in strategic sectors. The unratified treaties would later prove instrumental in advancing British interests in the late nineteenth century. The same people who had refused to grant approval for treaties later accepted.[54]

Treaties of military protection were equally utilized to create relationships with African rulers and prevent trade disruptions. Often, the communities, for economic or other reasons, were prone to war with one another. These conflicts interfered with the British merchants' security and their trade routes. With British support, protected territories could fend off competitors. However, these agreements to protect were not without costs. They enabled foreign agents to meddle in internal politics, even appointing favorites to local positions. They could also determine which enemy communities could wage wars against others and which were to be avoided.[55]

Added to this was the use of mediation. It was not unusual for the British to be invited to mediate between conflicting parties, reducing the possibility of an outbreak.[56] Mediation can be said to have increased British influence in a way that was unconnected to its ability to deploy force. Imperial agents were tagged "unbiased" parties, suggesting either some measure of trust or a simple acknowledgment of the enforcing powers they could bring to the table.

It is inadequate to consider West Africa's interaction with "legitimate commerce" as a blanket case. There were separate narratives across the region, each describing the nature of reactions to the European endeavor. As such, to account for individual territories, we shall be taking a specific approach.

The Bight of Benin

Dahomey was one of the most prominent kingdoms in the Bight of Benin and a West African territory that has received immense scholarly attention in terms of its military, political, and economic systems. A brief outline of its historical progression is important to understanding its adaptation to "legitimate commerce." Dahomey grew out of a dispute between members of the Allada royal household. At the time, Allada was the dominant kingdom, and it demanded tributes from neighboring subordinates. Dakodonu, one of its princes, departed the kingdom to establish a new home on the Abomey plateau. According to historical sources, he was allowed to settle by local ruling elites whose territories were later usurped by his son, Wegbaja.[57]

Later, the kingdom evolved into a regional hegemon, subjugating its neighbors, Hueda and Allada. Dahomey's military culture was deeply connected to holdovers from these two kingdoms. Both were keen on conflict and were known to attack each other for control of trade. Hueda was home to the famous port of Whydah, through which slaves were exported from the coast. The port was also the subject of diplomatic controversies during the post-abolition era. Before Hueda and Allada were eventually defeated by the Dahomean King, Agaja, in the 1720s, Dahomey supplied slaves from the interior.[58]

Dahomey's expansion has been identified as likely growing out of a defensive strategy to protect itself from being raided for slaves by these kingdoms and a desire for direct control over trade with the Europeans. Dahomey's conquest of rival territories also came at an opportune time when the other states had warred against each other and weakened themselves in the process. Its military was highly organized, relying on firearms for superiority. However, this did not discourage the cavalry-based Oyo military from harassing it until the early nineteenth century; therefore, it had to maintain a professional army for two reasons: to protect its borders against incursions and to secure its economic interests, which largely depended on its ability to capture slaves for sale.

Also, to administer subservient territories, it developed a system of tributes similar to what existed in those areas. Its leaders relied on a redistributive mechanism necessary to maintain the loyalties of its chiefs and control them. There were ceremonies wherein the public would feast and local officials would be indebted to their monarchical overlords for these benefits. Thus, once the material needs of regional administrators were served, they willingly submitted tributes, but as the decades wore on, the ruling elites at Abomey, the Dahomean seat of power, began to develop an interest in creating architectural symbols of authority. This was not solely an experiment in political theory; it was born out of a need to control trade routes.

Significantly, this interest manifested as country palaces were built across the Dahomean state.[59] The palaces, which housed everything from state officials to slaves and revenue, were designed to reflect the extent of the monarchy's reach. While royalty and top ministers mainly sequestered themselves in Abomey, the regional palaces handled the dispersed nuances of state administration. Before the nineteenth century, they had two central roles: providing vital links between Abomey and trade routes to the coast, and executing ritual ceremonies that displayed monarchical power. The latter involved annual ceremonies in which wealth and the state's capacity for violence were displayed. Palace walls were usually decorated with the heads of slain enemies,[60] ostensibly demonstrating the severe tendencies of those within. Besides their physical benefits, slaves played a spiritual role in the preservation of the Dahomean monarchy. They were offered as human sacrifices at rituals, and while this may be dismissed as an extreme demonstration of barbarity, it was critical to maintaining the seat of any monarch.

The kings were customarily viewed as symbols of strength, an attribute they displayed through brute force and military expertise. They were also beholden to the tradition of flagrantly exhibiting wealth. Adandozan, whose reign was usurped by Gezo in the early nineteenth century, is cited in some quarters as possessing an imagination far ahead of his time. He was said to have neglected customs such as rituals involving human sacrifices and was ineffective in his management of military onslaughts. While these may have contributed to his downfall, the narratives surrounding his reign are equally interesting. Adandozan was widely regarded as an evil monarch committed to sadism, and his name was expunged from the official list of Dahomean monarchs. In Elisee Soumonni's opinion, the propagation of these views may be partly due to his policies toward the Portuguese. Adandozan had expelled and detained foreign traders as he deemed fit, and his deposition, in Soumonni's analysis, may be related to this.[61]

The Dahomean dedication to militarism and its consequent fear of being perceived as weak by its constituents made its rulers reluctant to encourage agriculture, and though its ecology was suited for palm oil production, its perpetual war footing demanded a commitment to promoting martial strength. The advent of legitimate trade and pressures from Britain forced an acknowledgment of the agricultural sector. However, even that did not compel Dahomey to completely shed its captive tendencies. The slave economy existed alongside the agrarian one and is cited as an exception to the British claim that the slave trade could not exist alongside legitimate commerce.

As trade dynamics evolved in the early nineteenth century, so did architectural projects in Dahomey. With the collapse of the slave trade, the manner of administration took on a more centralized nature. Earlier, the focus was on routes linking the coast and important cities, but the potential of rural areas eventually came to be acknowledged. The closure of the business of dealing in humans forced the unsettled elite, who had been deprived of a crucial source of income, to emphasize agriculture. Palm oil was a highly valued crop, and the state deployed human and material resources to ensure its exploitation. Slave labor was also deployed to ensure production at the scale required for meaningful export.

The bureaucracy of the eighteenth century developed into one that penetrated the interior. Land use for agriculture was state-regulated, with established structures comparable to modern-day offices of local administrators. Unlike slavery, however, the tools of resource exploitation were not limited to the hands of the elite. Palm oil could be farmed on a small scale by individuals, although under taxation and the state's watchful eyes. Taxes were imposed on virtually every commodity traded in Dahomey, with collection centers at city entrances and major routes to ensure a constant flow of dividends to the monarchy.

While the shift to agriculture resulted in the creation of household wealth, scholars have argued that the international aspect of the trade was dependent on the elite. Individuals might have been capable of farming the produce, but they still required the advanced networks of the highly placed elites to export it. In this era, Dahomey recorded a boom in its population and an expansion in its economic activities. The importance of agriculture to its post-slave trade survival also meant region-wide connectivity. For remuneration, tax collectors were allowed to take fractions of the monies they collected for themselves.

The Gold Coast

Similar to the Bight of Benin, the Gold Coast conducted its trade through a few ports—Elmina, Cape Coast, and Anomabo—which were among the Fante, the territory of the coastal state. The ports were the contact points with European ships that imported slaves into the region before the nineteenth century and left with gold and ivory. The former's reliance on slave exports was a major area of divergence between the Bight of Benin and the prominent state of Asante on the Gold Coast. Dahomey's real foray into its agricultural sector began after the British grip on its slave export channels suffocated it. According to Dalrymple-Smith, the Asante kingdom, whose dominance among the multiple ethnicities of that region makes it our focus here, had been involved in the commodity trade for centuries.[62] Before it became a central hub for slave exports, it indirectly supplied Europe with gold exports pre-nineteenth century and was a recipient of slaves from the Portuguese before American territories were acquired.[63] The kingdom had relied extensively on slave labor to shore up its agricultural outputs (Figure 14.3).

The Asante story is one of opportunity and an abundance of resources. In Austin's study, the British withdrawal from the slave trade coincided with jihadist conquests in the savannah. The emergence of the Sokoto Caliphate in Hausaland enabled the Asante to open a new export channel, simultaneously allowing them to import materials they did not produce.[64] There was also a system that favored material acquisition by households, contrary to the Dahomean mindset of concentrated wealth. While there is some debate about the level of state control of its economy, it is contestable whether the Asante

FIGURE 14.3   Gold in the nineteenth century, Gold Coast https://commons.wikimedia.org
/wiki/File:Guinea_Coast,_Ghana,_Asante,_19th_century_-_Gold_Weight-_
Geometric_-_1969.265_-_Cleveland_Museum_of_Art.tif.

would have achieved as much upshoot in productivity as they did had all the production avenues focused on the elite alone.

In terms of coastal trade, the Asante were too distant from the ports to interact directly with the Europeans. They exported slaves and other products through the Fante, who served as middlemen. The Fante's proximity to the coast also meant they could evolve into a palm oil-based economy. Attempts by the Asante to control the coast through military action resulted in a defeat in 1824 and another at the famous battle of Katamanso in 1826. Its opponents were supported by British forces. Asante's relationship with the territories in the Savannah preceded Britain's withdrawal from the slave trade. Historical evidence suggests that there were Hausa traders in Kumasi whose activities were protected by the state.

In the early nineteenth century, the kingdom had also focused its trading activities on the Salaga region, enabling easier connection to foreign contacts. Wilks and Lovejoy suggest that this move might have resulted from the need to minimize reliance on coastal trade.[65] Usman dan Fodio's jihad in much of what is now the modern-day northern region of Nigeria expanded Asante's choices. The Muslim areas were immense consumers of kola nuts, particularly the "cola nitidia."[66] Its reception among the people of the savannah was fostered by its non-prohibition as haram in the Qur'an. Asante lands were well attuned to the growth of kola nuts, with surpluses existing across its forest domain. Thus, it was a matter of transporting this produce to the Hausa interior in exchange for textiles, which had started improving in quality.

There was lower demand for Asante gold in the savannah, which meant that the mineral was readily available for sale to its Atlantic contacts. For textiles and other products, the Hausa demanded kola nuts, which required minimal labor and were quite accessible compared to gold. This enabled the Asante to focus human resources on its labor-intensive mining sector without impacting supplies to its other market. Ultimately, this implied that the Asante had well-established alternatives for trade before abolition. The availability of produce other than humans created economic flexibility.

In addition to the above, the British withdrawal from the purchase of slaves led to the existence of a surplus. Not only was Asante receiving tributes in the form of slaves from subordinate communities, but it also exchanged its produce for slaves in the savannah. Without European ships to convey them abroad, they were essentially stuck in the local economy. The Asante responded to this challenge in the early nineteenth century by integrating slaves into the households of its political elites, who then utilized them in productive enterprises. Austin's work on this particular dynamic in Asante's history highlights a decline in the market price of slaves. He submits that slaves were committed to improving economic outputs and assisting ancestors in their sojourn in the afterlife.[67]

Slaves were sacrificed for funeral and ceremonial purposes, but they were also retained for labor. In the mid-nineteenth century, as prices for slaves increased, a corresponding drop in sacrificial executions was recorded. As enunciated by Austin, the reason for this was the demand for slaves by palm oil exporters on the coast and within Asante itself.[68] Popular participation in the kola nut and gold production sectors necessitated the use of slaves by households other than those belonging to chiefs and other elites. There was more profit in exploiting slaves than in employing wage labor. Yet, as adapted as the Asante economy may have been, its dominance seemed to run contrary to Britain's economic interests. As shown in the early nineteenth-century battles of 1824 and 1826, clashes between the British and the Asante militaries for economic reasons were not unusual. Moreover, while there was a cession of southern tributaries controlled by the Asante in the latter, there were minimal efforts to determine its course of trade.

However, by the late nineteenth century, the middleman position occupied by the Asante in terms of trade contacts with the Hausa-Fulani in the northern savannah was becoming unacceptable. Still, Britain's reluctance to assume the administration cost prevented any significant attempt to intervene, a stance that continued until the 1873 conflict. The battles culminated in the burning of Kumasi, Asante's capital. Unfortunately, the defeat was one from which the state could not recover. After the withdrawal of the British forces from its nerve center, Asante's authority over its tributaries weakened considerably, resulting in a series of internal conflicts that affected its trade with the coast. At home, the British government was under pressure from its business entities to establish some form of colonial control over the area, and this option was made more practicable by advancements in medical, military, and communications technology. Eventually, in 1896, the British assumed administrative authority over Asante, starting a decades-long history of foreign occupation in that region.

The Bight of Biafra

Compared to the case study region examined above, the Bight of Biafra is unique in its interaction with the slave trade and institutional response to legitimate commerce. In this section, we shall consider the structure of Biafran society, its relationship with the slave trade, and the impacts of legitimate commerce on established sociocultural norms. In terms of ecology, the Bight of Biafra was divided into three areas, each with varying levels of productive abilities. There was a coastal area unsuitable for agriculture, and inhabitants of this area relied on trading fish and salt in exchange for produce from the interior. Further inland were dense rainforests that sustained equally large populations. The locals could farm at scales required for subsistence and exports, churning out yams, palm oil, and the importation of new crops, cocoyam, maize, and tomatoes. Following this area were lands that were similar to savannah regions and could not support sizable numbers of people.[69] This distribution was a great determiner of trade patterns and social structures within Biafran communities.

As with the Asante–Fante relationship, and to a lesser extent, Dahomey and its coastal regions, inland communities depended on the coastal regions to access foreign goods. However, the difference was that this economic contract system was relatively settled. Rather than organized militaries, business elites oversaw the connections between both peoples for nearly two centuries. The Aro Network, a group of business-minded individuals, was depicted as a secret society open only to men. Their network extended across multiple small communities in Biafra in liaison with the local heads of these locations. They evolved into indigenous groups in some areas, like the *Okonko* secret society of the Ngwa people, the *Ekpe* of the Ibibio, and the *Ekong* at Old Calabar.[70]

At a less intercommunal level, Biafra contained multiple settlements, which, despite their distributed nature, were bound by a shared history and language. Evidence of this unity lies in the popular regard of Arochukwu as a spiritual center. The area was home to the *Inbiniukpabi*, deemed the highest court of appeal.[71] In her study of the Ngwa, Martin describes a familial structure that revolved around households. A family consisting of a male head and other members (children, wives, and slaves) cohabitated in a compound called the *Onu Ovu*. This household formed the basic unit of production.[72] Oriji argues that members of the *Okonko* society rivaled community leaders in terms of how much influence the latter could wield beyond the allocation of land and collection of a share of produce.[73]

Like its umbrella institution, the Aro, the society recruited people with strong entrepreneurial mindsets. It did this due to the Biafran focus on an individual's potential to generate wealth rather than a limited number of elites. Thus, Aro traders as a whole were not necessarily in the privileged class of title holders. They could project their authority through ties to the Arochukwu deity mentioned earlier. This spiritual symbolism also played a role in how the Aro acquired slaves on a large scale. Since the oracle was the ultimate adjudicator, those condemned were sent into slavery.

Notably, spiritual, rather than martial dictates, were the primary source of slaves exported from the Biafran region. Although kidnapping and small-scale intercommunal invasions played a role in the acquisition of slaves, these had less influence on the number of embarkations. Biafra differed from the Gold Coast and Benin in this aspect. There was little need for heavy militarization for self-defense because slaves were mostly condemned through judicial authority. Kidnappers faced severe consequences, and dispute-resolution mechanisms were available in potentially explosive situations.

Interestingly, Biafra's population density suffered the demographic consequences of the slave trade even without intensive military operations. The region, which had previously been of scant repute in the eyes of European slave traders, transformed around the mid-eighteenth century into one of the important sources of trade in West Africa. According to Dalrymple-Smith, the reasons for the initial lukewarm patronage were the region's lack of gold, the existence of embarkations from West Africa, and the view of Biafran slaves as weaker than those from other areas.[74] Therefore, it was not until the 1730s that Biafra became a popular hub for the supply of slaves. Before this, it was known for its participation in provisioning merchant vessels. Hinterland goods sold on the coast centered majorly on livestock, yams, and slaves. These were offered in exchange for salt and protein sources, which were scarce in the interior. These production, transportation, and trade systems were instrumental in the Biafrans' ability to meet Europe's demands.

The rise of slave exports in Biafra coincided with the expansion of the Aro into areas outside Arochukwu in the early eighteenth century. Aside from their spiritual significance, they acquired prominence through the formation of ties with elites at local community levels. Martin estimates the number of slaves derived from this region in the 1750s at 10,600 per annum, an extensive upshoot from 2,300 in the opening decade of the eighteenth century.[75] By the end of that period, Biafra had overtaken Benin as a prolific source of slaves in West Africa and continued to ship thousands even after abolition.

Biafra relied on several ports to export slaves: Old Calabar, Elem Kalabari, and Bonny. Being coastal areas, the ports possessed land unsuitable to agriculture, and its inhabitants positioned themselves as conduits between the interior and European ships. Due to Bonny's geographical linkages with some of the most densely populated areas, it enjoyed prominence above the other ports. Sources also indicate that its centrality may have been due to the ease of embarkation and its efficiency at sorting credit with Europeans.[76] Besides the ports, Biafra had a series of waterways through which commodities and slaves could be transported to the exportation centers. The boatbuilding capabilities of the people of this area probably played a role in their recognition by foreign partners. Trade at the ports typically involved large canoes capable of carrying close to a hundred men. If this was the case, the same could be said for the haulage of commodities, particularly palm produce.

Commodity exports began to grow at the ports in the late eighteenth century in response to the increase in demand. Initially, Old Calabar was the center of attention, while Bonny held sway as the dominant outlet for human trade. This changed in the years following the abolition of the slave trade as Bonny once again overtook its rival. As described earlier, abolition did not translate into an immediate halt in the slave trade. There were other channels, even with Royal Navy intervention, through which slaves could be sold to French, Portuguese, or Spanish buyers. Regardless, exports slowed, and commodity exports took over. The question now is whether Biafra, like the Bight of Benin and the Gold Coast, faltered substantially or even at all as a result of the shift to commodity trade. If it did suffer, then its method of recovery also demands interrogation.

Biafra is a notable exception to the British narrative that legitimate commerce could not survive in tandem with the slave trade. In expanding its commodity outputs, the region utilized slaves in food production. This dynamic was especially important due to the labor-intensive nature of palm oil. Susan Martin's analysis of household hierarchies and ownership rights describes the operation of labor on farmlands. In addition to their traditional duties of childcare and home maintenance, women were tasked with the collection and processing of palm oil. Before it rose to commercial prominence, palm oil processing for cooking was a female chore. As demand rose, men who engaged in clearing forests for agricultural purposes became more mindful of palm trees. They dealt with the initial phases of vigorous pounding before ceding the produce to women for onward distillation.[77] Its exerting nature is reflected in Lynn, Maier, and Northrup's analyses of the time required to produce hard and soft oil. The density or otherwise of palm oil in terms of fatty acid determined its application in the British production chain.[78] Therefore, to greatly increase output, households needed to use slaves in laboring for oil palm and other agricultural products.

Where communities had shifted to producing palm oil, they created slave villages which compensated by producing yams and other foods. Even with that, the size of individual families played a role in how much they could generate. Marriage to multiple wives translated to increased labor strength, which was a prerequisite for higher productivity. This takes us to the conclusion that the abolition of slaves did not unhinge a shortfall in demand. For the Aro traders who interacted with Europeans, Dalrymple-Smith's inquiry into customs duties at Biafran ports indicates some loss for the merchants. Traders at Elem Kalabari, which did not enter the palm oil trade until the mid-nineteenth century, may have suffered worse returns than their mixed counterparts.[79] However, the general submission in the literature is that the Aro's strategic position as handlers of trade routes and the internal demand for slave labor softened the blow that would otherwise have been occasioned by abolition. There was also the stability of the palm oil trade and the boom in early nineteenth-century prices to motivate the Aro's transition.

Aside from these, it is possible that Britain's efforts to foster legitimate commerce through the reduction of import duties were influential in the ease of adaptation.[80] But the Aro were not to stay immune forever. The eruption of conflict in coastal areas meant that producers began to seek new routes outside the Aro's domain to market their goods. Advancements in ship-building technology, particularly the emergence of steamships, also meant that British merchants could connect directly with hinterland agricultural sources. Thus, in the long run, the Aro network was impacted.

Warfare and State Formations

Oyo Empire: Wars, Military, and Political Collapse

Accounting for the evolution of societies in West Africa encompasses other elements and mechanisms of change during the nineteenth century, as it embodies the impact of the slave trade, transition to legitimate trade, migration, state formation, missionary and European merchants' activities, spread and distribution of arms, and much more. It is also the fundamental basis upon which the nineteenth-century history of West African States can be understood. The military factor in the evolution of precolonial states in this region, like elsewhere, cannot be overemphasized. Kingdoms and polities emerged and grew in proportion to the military acumen of their progenitors and their descendants' abilities to sustain this tradition. The primacy of military power in the formation of states before the nineteenth century characterized the evolution of states in this region and the strategic roles played by hunters and warriors.[81]

Whereas military capacity had previously been built around society's royal tradition, ensuring that warriors and hunters deployed their skills in the service of the monarch, this tradition began by the turn of the nineteenth century and with the rise of independent military chiefs and warlords.[82] At this time, political power and hegemony had declined to the point that everything that occurred in the sociopolitical and economic space of the region was defined by military adventurism.[83] As against the previous practice, military lords in some areas, such as among the Yoruba, began to exert political power and authority without the sanction of a monarch. Warriors organized their men against existing political authorities instead of waiting to get orders from them. The military became the most important class in every aspect of society through civil wars, raids, kidnapping, invasions, collecting tributes (a privilege traditionally enjoyed by the monarchs), and control of the largest share of the trade.[84] Until colonial incursion, the successful warriors in a place like Ibadan owned the largest wealth, controlled political power, and dictated the terms of politics.

Before its decline in the late eighteenth century and eventual collapse around 1830, European traders, travelers, and others within and without the region navigating this area often referred to the Old Oyo Empire as one of the largest and most powerful of all the polities in the region.[85] The Empire's growth and expansion leaned primarily on its military capabilities.[86] With this, Oyo expanded to reach places in parts of Ghana, Togo, and the present-day Republic of Benin. However, this expansion did not guarantee the Alaafin's total subjugation of polities around this area. In a complex web of relations between the Alaafin and these polities, namely Nupe, Borgu, and Dahomey, the former paid tributes to these polities and collected the same from them (Figure 14.4).[87]

Until the involvement of the Alaafin in the West African slave trade in the first half of the seventeenth century, the trade remained at its lowest point. Bringing its military prowess and political hegemony to bear, the Oyo Empire became one of the main

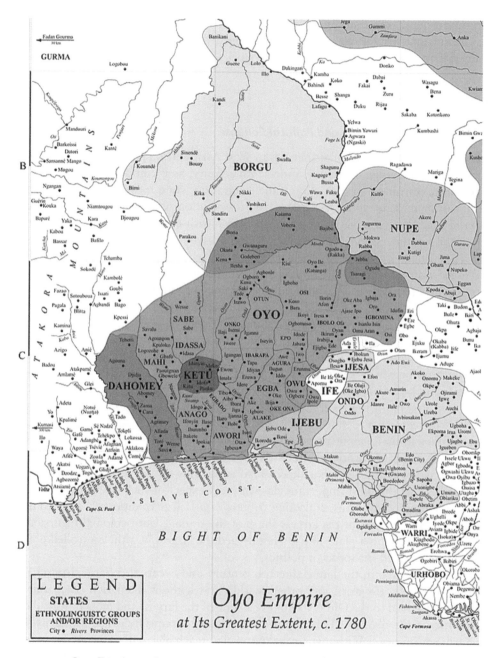

FIGURE 14.4 Oyo Empire at its greatest extent, circa 1780 https://commons.wikimedia.org/wiki/File:Oyo_Empire_at_Its_Greatest_Extent,_c._1780_(5).jpg.

sources of human commodities for the European slave market.[88] The role of the Empire during this era of slave dealing positioned it as a central stabilizing force. As a result, its disintegration would result not only in the independence of several other polities but also in the formation and expansion of some others.[89] This was the situation until the rise of the political intrigues ignited by Basorun Gaa, which was further propelled by factors that have been extrapolated by scholars from events of the time.[90] Between the late eighteenth and the nineteenth centuries, the empire, like others in the region, was affected by the changing sociopolitical and economic landscape of the time, despite the varying degrees of opinion on the events that led to the absolute collapse of the Alaafin's political authority over the Oyo Empire. This takes us expressly to the developments in some other parts of West Africa.

Apart from the massive and widespread impact of the Old Oyo Empire's expansion on the region, the areas north of Oyo populated by Hausa states may have had more intense implications for the Empire. Since the transformation of the political morphology of West African cultures from around the eighteenth and nineteenth centuries, events were geared toward the political consolidation of these established traditions with different groups guarding their geopolitical interests jealously. However, the nineteenth-century disrupted this process and formation.[91] Going by this trajectory, the late eighteenth century brought about different elements of strife and contention in the region, which spilled over to the better part of the nineteenth century. By this time, the spread and influence of Islam into the region had been well reinforced with the torrential and massive migration of *ulama* and other Muslim populace from places like Mali, driven by the political unrest that followed the tide of migration from the Maghreb region.

With this continuous migration, what have been described as Islamic revivalists emerged across the region.[92] Led mainly by the Tuaregs and the Fulani, these new elements in society preached what they considered pure Islam to the people across the region, from Senegal to the Hausa states and the Kanem-Borno in the Lake Chad region and beyond. They mobilized the people around Islamic doctrine to arm the population with Islamic knowledge and military might against the extant political authorities in this area.[93] It should be recalled that Islam had been a major factor in the organization and evolution of states in West Africa since around the eleventh century, especially in the Sahel region.[94] Its role as the harbinger of a new and advanced civilization that cared for the converts within the social stratification of the society and establishment of true justice was reinforced and retooled by the emerging *ulama* preaching "pure Islam."[95]

As with the rise of Gaa in the Old Oyo, Islamic scholars found a common bond with the ordinary people within the realm of the oppressive and exploitative regimes of the Hausa states. Before the mobilization of the population for the usurpation of the political authority in the area, the reformists, as they were called, went around towns and cities preaching and admonishing the authorities and the people to accept Islam under its true tenets.[96] As Akinjogbin postulated, on one of these missions, Aole, an itinerant trader and the reigning and last Alaafin to be properly installed in the old capital, according to traditions, must have been converted to Islam or, at least, had huge sympathy for the religion.[97]

Going by the traditions that established the relationships between Yoruba kingdoms and monarchs, which prohibited any of the polities from invading Ife territory under any guise,[98] the Alaafin's general disposition during this period pointed to his leaning toward Islam even though none of the jihadists' demands from the established authorities in the region, which became the modus operandi of the movement, were conceived in Aole's action against Ife hegemony. Driven by the disposition to protect the religion, the Alaafin had no qualms about fighting the Basorun, one of his most powerful chiefs. In his illuminating reinterpretation of events during this period, Akinjogbin described the ensuing quarrel between the Alaafin and the said chief as a conflict between those who wanted to spread Islam, represented by Alaafin Aole, and those determined to curb it, represented by the Basorun.

Alaafin Aole's position should be understood from the Alaafin's diminishing authority and the thought of reinforcing this authority through new alliances and Islamic social strength. Owing to the devastating economy of the late eighteenth century that followed the demise of Alaafin Abiodun, which was animated in folksongs and tales, Islam was also gaining intensive roots among the Empire's population. Tellingly, the spread of Islam in the Empire altered the social value and conduct of some of the populace, including the Alaafin.[99] In addition to the pride in authority, this explains why the Alaafin could fight the Basorun for not returning the Quran of a Hausa trader who had come to him for justice and ordered the invasion of "sacred" Ife territory. The decisive role played by Islam in the occurrences of this period was more evident in the implosion of the empire and its counterparts in the Hausa states, the reformation of Nupe politics, and the reconstitution of political power in the region until the presence of Western imperial powers.

Following his encounter with his Basorun, the Alaafin, still in a bid to reinforce the authority of the Alaafinate, which made the Alaafin the most feared and respected figure in the Empire, also took on his Generalissimo (the Are Ona Kakanfo), Afonja, whom he considered a threat to this path. Indeed, every step taken by the Alaafin brought him into conflict with his most powerful chiefs and the traditions regulating the conduct of monarchs. Afonja deserted the Alaafinate to build an equally powerful state at the garrison town of Ilorin when he got wind of the Alaafin's plot to assassinate him. Hence, by the turn of the nineteenth century, the Alaafinate was left without its strong army and powerful allies. This was particularly so with the cavalry soldiers that formed the basis of the strength of its army from the sixteenth century.

Rather than looking after the Alaafin's interest, these elements began to advance their interests in different directions, converging at supplanting the authority of the Alaafinate and instituting a new order. Subsequently, the Alaafin was forced to take his own life, and the scramble to replace the old authority of the Alaafinate within and outside of the capital and, indeed, the Yoruba region began, followed by seismic turmoil.[100] Even though Alaafin Abiodun was reputed to have been the last Alaafin in the days of the Empire's prosperity, the crack in the authority of the Alaafinate was made evident during the later eighteenth century in the assertiveness of Borgu, Egba, and Nupe. However, not only did they successfully wrestle their independence from the Alaafin, they also raided Oyo protectorates and outlying areas. During this same period, Dahomey was constituting a massive nuisance to the hegemony of the Alaafin to the south of the Yoruba country. Although a nascent power in the West African geopolitical dynamics, Dahomey lords wrestled and exacted political authority to the detriment of the Old Oyo.[101]

The case of its activities in Ajase Ipo port, known as Porto Novo, the center of Oyo external commerce, was even more instructive. With the French government in pursuit of its anti-slavery law, Dahomey forces rendered trade in this area redundant to divert trade to its ports. Expectedly, this was not without a tremendous impact on Oyo trade, commerce, and wealth. As if all these were not enough, the British Abolition Act of 1807 spelled the final doom for the great Oyo Empire and the entire region. This was followed by the Anglo-Portuguese treaty of 1810, which legally closed Porto Novo and other major slave ports in West Africa.[102] Although trade, which constituted the major source of state revenue in many parts of the region, continued clandestinely until the second half of the nineteenth century, especially in the Lagos port and with the permission of the British government in designated ports, namely, Dahomey and Whydah, the Old Oyo Empire was unable to operate along these lines due to the lack of political organization and authority. Rather, the massive eruption of people and polities in the area that could have produced human commodities for Oyo commerce came under the organization of its chiefs, the military, and other regional powers in the country from Ijebu, Ife, Abeokuta, Ibadan, Ijaiye, Ilorin, and others.[103]

Regardless, until its final collapse in the 1830s, the Old Oyo Empire continued to wield some level of influence in the region, and as such, the scramble to replace its authority did not intensify and expand among several emerging and extant actors until after this period.[104] Before this time, practically all the dependents that constituted its political authority and hegemony had declared their independence from the empire or were displaced by the geopolitical developments over which the empire had little or no control in terms of protection.

Oyo and Islamic Reforms

Simultaneously, as the Old Oyo calamities were ongoing with reverberating effects across the Yoruba country, the Islamic reformists' activities in Western and Central Sudan culminated in the Uthman Dan Fodio Jihad that erupted in 1804. Between 1785, when the reformists sealed a bargain with Bawa, the then Sultan of Gobir and his successors on some of the demands of the movement, and 1804 when the war broke out, the acrimony between the Hausa establishments and the reformists had escalated from diplomatic maneuvering on both sides to outright confrontation. The final straw that broke the camel's back was the threat issued against Dan Fodio by the authorities in Gobir that year, necessitating his escape to Gudu.[105]

In no time, his followers, now in their hundreds and thousands, began to desert Gobir with the implication that the Sultan sought to coerce their return for socioeconomic purposes and the exertion of his political authority. Resisting all the Sultan's threats and coercion, within a few months of their flight from Gobir, they mobilized from Gudu and launched the Jihad campaign from Gobir.[106] Within four years (1804–1808), the first phase of the series of the campaign was concluded and had effectively swept through the major Hausa states of Katsina, Kebbi, Kano, and Gobir.[107] The campaign was taken across the Niger from here, through several routes coordinated by different independent but interdependent cells of the movement, only to be stopped in 1840 by Ibadan forces at the popular Jalumi war at Osogbo, where they were driven through Offa.[108] Faced with immense competition for the occupation of the vacuum left by the collapse of the Old Oyo, the successful campaign of the Ibadan forces in this war established Ibadan's primacy over and above all other Yoruba powers.[109] If this did not bring Ibadan to the pedigree of the Old Oyo as intended, it did serve as a yardstick to measure the military prowess of the competing emerging powers in the country as the scramble continued.

Against the clear personal interests that drove Afonja and other revolutionary actors in nineteenth-century Yoruba politics as a result of the vacuum created by the dwindling authority of the Alaafinate, jihadists from the Hausa states were driven by the demand for the reconstitution of Islam, which spoke to the sociopolitical practices of the states and their people. These included immodest dressing, bribe-taking, especially by the political elites, for political favors, Muslims' enslavement, taxation and loan advancement, deity worship, and other practices considered antithetical to Islamic tenets.[110] Following the reformists' campaign, all the Hausa states were reconfigured under the caliphate system headquartered in Sokoto and Gwandu.[111] However, this did not translate into the realization of the set objectives and goals of the movement. The old practice continued until the British government injected another series of reforms into the system at the turn of the twentieth century. As it did in Central and Eastern Sudan, except for the great Kanem-Borno Empire, it displaced the political authorities in Nupe and instituted a new order under the Gwandu central administrative headquarters of the new caliphate.[112]

The alliance between Afonja and Alimi, the itinerant Islamic Fulani scholar and warrior, had collapsed by the 1830s and was being prosecuted by several forces in Yorubaland,[113] resulting in the death of the former and the usurpation of political power in Ilorin by the Jihadists.[114] Due to the limitations of the chronology of events during this period, it remains unclear if Alimi ever took charge of Ilorin. However, the turn of events between Alimi and his host, who had requested his resources—military and magic in the main—in his political pursuit, had ensured the effective occupation of Ilorin by Fulani forces and the transformation of its political landscape.[115] From Ilorin, Shitta, Abdullahi, and their successors consistently launched fierce attacks and raids on other parts of Yorubaland,[116] even though owing to several factors, including the topography of the southeastern Yoruba states and the special arrangement between the Old Oyo Empire and Benin, the former had very limited influence in this area. The latter, with tremendous influence over various factions, was too weak to protect Oyo and Ilorin against the encroachment of the Fulani forces. Consequently, Ilorin came under the influence of the caliphate and became one of its important states.

The Rise of Ibadan

The area known today as the "brown roof city" has a colorful history behind it. Spanning 3,080 sq km, Ibadan is one of Africa's largest cities. It was founded around 1829 following the collapse of the Oyo Empire. Oral sources say Ibadan was established three times, only taking root at the third. The first time it was founded by Lagelu, a prince from Ife. This Ibadan was remarkable for its 16 gates and 70 blacksmith shops, not one of which exists any longer.[117] However, these sources tend toward the apocryphal, as Salami Olawale, in discussing nineteenth-century Ibadan's military architecture, mentioned that slaves were responsible for defending the city's 16 gates, raising the question of which Ibadan he was referring to.[118]

Notwithstanding, the first Ibadan drew the ire of the *Egungun* cult and was destroyed for it. The second similarly faded into oblivion, while the third, our concern here, evolved from being a war camp into one of West Africa's most remarkable governance systems.

This transformation was set off by the Fulani attacks on northern Oyo, which forced a southward migration by the Yoruba in those areas. After a spell in the Owu conflict of the early nineteenth century, refugees made their camp at Ibadan. It quickly developed its government with vast opportunities for commerce to flourish. Ibadan was peopled by members of diverse Yoruba communities such as the Ijebu and the Egba. The multiplicity of cultures meant it could tap into the specialties that came with it. There were traders, artisans, and farmers, all serving to position the city as important. Its geographical placement was also fortuitous because it was located between the grasslands and forests, making it a natural center of trade.

But underneath this glamor was the military exigency that founded it in the first place. Its legacy of warfare made its government almost inevitably martial. Political offices were occupied by commanders who had distinguished themselves in battle. Besides the fact that military leadership was certain, given the proportion of professional soldiers among the first settlers, it was also born out of necessity, as Yorubaland at the time was wracked by conflicts, making it important that states were always prepared. However, contrary to the monarchical system of government, Ibadan's military chiefs ruled collectively. Of this number, a few chiefs are worthy of mention: Aare Latosa, who was militarily ambitious and sought to expand Ibadan's authority to other parts of Yorubaland but was defeated; Basorun Ogunmola, who was reputed for his judicial competence and reformative ventures; and Basorun Oluyole, whose visionary leadership transformed Ibadan from a raw camp of refugees into a dominant city in Yoruba history.[119] Ibadan's military leaders later designed a framework to introduce civilians into government. This gave birth to the office of Baale, which became known as Olubadan in the twentieth century.

On its actual methods of administration, Ibadan relied on slaves to carry out most of its functions. Slaves were converted into soldiers and enforcers of order; they worked on farms, protected the elite, served as emissaries, and even became political managers. Olawale describes the role of slaves as guards and toll-collectors at the city gates. According to him, slaves were charged with taking tolls from farmers and traders as they entered and departed the city. He stated that their role was not born out of contempt but from a need to remunerate them for their work.[120] The slaves could take a cut of toll revenue and hand most of it over to their masters.

Also, there was a need for slave labor in the justice system. They formed part of market administrations and helped to maintain order. They could adjudicate minor cases while transferring severe ones to their superiors. These slaves also served as enforcers in dispensing justice by lineage courts. They could plunder the homes of the condemned when given the order to do so. Besides these, they played a critical role in securing Ibadan's commercial interests in times of strife. They would escort traders in return for the payment of a fee. The level of reliance on slave labor by Ibadan rulers becomes more astounding with the tendency to trust them with the delivery of diplomatic messages.[121] This was considered a security threat and has been cited as one of the causes of Ibadan's fall late in the nineteenth century.

In politics, the metropolis found a use for its slaves in the leadership of satellite towns. Ibadan had made conquests in surrounding areas and needed a way to oversee these territories without the consistent presence of a standing army. The answer to this was the *Ajele*. The *Ajele* was a subordinate of the *Ologun,* a senior military officer who had earned merit in battle. The *Ologun* possessed supervisory authority over one or several subjugated towns and appointed the *Ajele* to supervise the running of those places. These individuals were slaves of outstanding battlefield qualifications, loyal to their masters and Ibadan. They collected taxes, deliberated in the territories' councils, and saw to it that Ibadan's army was neither lacking in labor nor combatant personnel when conflicts emerged. They also had the responsibility of warding off invaders from their domains until Ibadan was able to send reinforcements. As for the *Ologun*, they maintained control of these administered territories by determining the direction of their diplomatic policy as well as paying occasional visits to the area, either personally or through representatives.

The decentralized approach to administration, while impressive in itself, later created problems for the state. The *Ajele* were at near liberty to do as they pleased and were highhanded in executing some of their duties. Slaves entrusted with day-to-day engagements with civilians, such as law enforcement and tax collection, also leaned toward abuses when they saw fit. Even among the free elites, there were cases of political opposition to one another. Each elite's control over large areas created fissures in the political system, making foreigners and internal enemies willing to exploit them. Military adventures in a city accustomed to war finally abated when the British assumed colonial authority in 1892.

Missionary Activities

It is utterly simplistic to consider missionary interventions in Africa as born out of purely religious motives. Certainly, religion was an influential factor, but it was not the exclusive rationale for penetration. One of the major reasons for the appearance of missionaries was the elimination of the slave trade. Earlier, we described the association of religious groups with the abolition movement. This drive was a result of a renaissance of the European conscience. But it was not sufficient for the church to merely advocate an end to embarkations on the high seas; it was also critical that slavery was abolished in African societies. Thus, the nineteenth century witnessed renewed efforts to preach Christianity to indigenous communities.

Traditions and customs in these communities were deemed barbaric and only redeemable by the European religion. In other words, proselytizers perceived themselves as having a duty to reform. An attestation to this is the effect of narratives of the African situation on Christian minds in Europe. The bleaker the continent was painted, the higher the likelihood of fervor among home-based evangelists. This is seen in Hastings's statement, cited in Boaheng:

> In fact, neither in the nineteenth nor in the early twentieth centuries did missionaries give much thought in advance to what they would find in west Africa. What struck them, undoubtedly, was the darkness of the continent, its lack of religion and sound morals, its general and pitiful condition made worse by the barbarity of the slave trade. Evangelization was seen as liberation from a state of absolute awfulness and the picture of unredeemed Africa was often painted in colors as gruesome as possible, the better to encourage missionary zeal at home.[122]

Missionaries quickly attacked Africa's sociocultural institutions, attempting to dismantle them as a prerequisite for conversion to Christianity. This may have contributed to the hostility with which the religion was received in many societies. Some of the strictures of European missionaries include the ban on converts from engaging in polygamy, participating in traditional rites, and isolation in townships when converts were excommunicated by their families.[123] In particular, banning polygamy was antithetical to the foundational beliefs of communities. Marriage to multiple wives ensured there was sufficient labor on farms and was also a status symbol in itself. There was also the concept of family, which missionaries were overturning by separating converts from their households. This was against the communality that characterized traditional societies.

Clashes between Christianity and African religions also emerged in the area of medicine. While the early nineteenth century was not so far advanced in discoveries in this sector, its knowledge was still ahead of its African traditional counterpart. Thus, Europeans were keen on emphasizing this aspect of their superiority. More expressive of this notion among missionaries entering West Africa is the conversation between Cecil Tyndale-Biscoe, an active missionary in the nineteenth and twentieth centuries, and Frederick Temple, then Bishop of London. Biscoe wrote in his autobiography:

On his desk were my examination papers, and as he turned over the sheets he exclaimed loudly: 'Shocking! Shocking! You don't know anything Biscoe'. 'I know I do not', I replied.
Bishop: Then how do you think you can teach anybody if you do not anything yourself?
Biscoe (scratching his head): Well, sir, perhaps there may be some people in the world almost as ignorant as I am.
Bishop: I doubt it! You are only fit to teach the blacks, there now!
Biscoe: Sir, if you can only persuade my parents to and the Church Missionary Society to send me to central Africa, I shall be most grateful.
Bishop: Ah, then you'll do! You'll do![124]

Chronologically, missionary contact with West Africa began in the fifteenth century. The Portuguese were on a mission of trade and scientific discovery when they arrived on its Atlantic coast. In 1482, they commenced missionary exploits in the subregion with the ceremonial hoisting of the Portuguese flag at Elmina, Gold Coast.[125] This was followed by subsequent interplays between missionaries and African rulers. Their engagements with indigenous rulers were sometimes colored by economic reasons on both sides, making it difficult to achieve true missionary objectives in certain areas. They began to receive popular support in their home countries, particularly Britain, when their evangelical missions intertwined with efforts to end the slave trade.

In Sierra Leone, missionaries under the Church Mission Society founded the Fourah Bay College to build an African clergy. This was succeeded by the establishment of the Anglican Diocese of Sierra Leone in 1852. Other West African territories, such as Liberia, the Gold Coast, and Nigeria, witnessed a similar expansion in missionary activities. Of particular importance to the Christian project were liberated slaves who penetrated the interior and spread the gospel. Africans were equally instrumental in ensuring that the message of proselytizers was well understood as they translated the Bible into local languages. The Europeans' realization that they could not be impactful without understanding the local languages was also helpful. The missionary movement in Africa provided a further rationale for imperialism. Indeed, missionaries and traders encouraged colonial intervention to assist their interests in the communities. This is

shown in the British officials' compulsion to react through military or diplomatic channels to internal problems that threatened the safety of their nationals.

Today, an interesting turn of events is Africa's stronger consciousness of religious values than some of the societies that introduced them. Forced by issues of security, poverty,
and political crises, its people have substituted the custom of seeking answers from traditional deities for communion with a monotheistic God. Conversely, the people across
the Atlantic lean further toward secularity, believing instead in human actions and their
natural consequences. Like nineteenth-century ideological imperialism, Africans may be
assimilating again, albeit within a subtler and less imposing structure. The implications
of this merit a separate study of its own.

DEEP DIVE

Assignment 1

Objective

The objective of this assignment is to ensure that students complete the reading of Chapter
14 and to get them to understand the various factors that created the transformations and
revolutions that emerged in the nineteenth century. Students are expected to explain the
implications of these changes on West Africa during and after the nineteenth century.

Method

Students will be expected to write a short note in response to the question.

Reading Comprehension

In what ways did the abolition of the slave trade and the enthronement of legitimate trade
reform the sociopolitical and economic fabric of West Africa in the nineteenth century?

Assignment 2

Objective

The objective of this assignment is to ensure that students complete the reading of Chapter
14 and to get them to think about how political power in West Africa shifted from filial privileges to those with military skills and individual capacity.

Method

Students will be expected to write a short note in response to the question.

Reading Comprehension

What were some of the underlying factors that led to the collapse of the Old Oyo Empire,
and how did this lead to the formation of new sets of equally powerful hegemons in West
Africa?

Notes

1 Cameron J. Monroe, *The Precolonial State in West Africa: Building Power in Dahomey* (Cambridge: Cambridge University Press, 2014).

2 Chima J. Korieh, "The Nineteenth Century Commercial Transition in West Africa: The Case of the Biafra Hinterland," *Canadian Journal of African Studies* 34, no. 3 (2000): 588–615.

3 Gabriel O. Ogunremi, *Counting the Camels: The Economics of Transportation in Pre-industrial Nigeria* (New York: Nok Publishers International, 1982).

4 Nöthling F. J., *Pre-colonial Africa: Her Civilisations and Foreign Contacts* (Johannesburg: Southern Book Publishers, 1989).

5 Ghislaine Lydon, *On Trans-Saharan Trails: Islamic Law, Trade Networks, and Cross-Cultural Exchange in Nineteenth-Century Western Africa* (Cambridge: Cambridge University Press, 2009).

6 Kristin Mann, *Slavery and the Birth of an African City Lagos 1760–1900* (Bloomington: Indiana University Press, 1997).

7 David Armitage and Michael J. Braddick, *The British Atlantic World 1500–1800* (New York: Palgrave Macmillan, 2002).

8 Nektarios Aslanidis, Oscar Martinez and Federico Tade, "The Integration of West Africa in the Global Economy, 1842–1938," Working Paper, ECO-SOS, Centre de Recerca en Economia i Sostenibilitat, 2020.

9 Bernard Semmel, *The Methodist Revolution* (London: Heinemann Educational Books, 1974).

10 Francis Fukuyama, "The End of History?" *The National Interest* 16 (1989): 3–18.

11 Robert A. Bickers and Rosemary Seton, eds., *Missionary Encounters: Sources and Issues* (London: Curzon Press, 1996); and Emmanuel A. Ayandele, *Missionary Impact in Modern Nigeria 1842–1914* (London: Longman Group, 1966).

12 Lawrence C. Jennings, "The Interaction of French and British Antislavery, 1789–1848," *Proceedings of the Meeting of the French Colonial Historical Society* 15 (1992): 81–91.

13 Manuel Barcia, *West African Warfare in Bahia and Cuba: Soldier Slaves in the Atlantic World 1807–1844* (London: Oxford University Press, 2016); and Henry Lovejoy, *Prieto: Yoruba Kingship in Colonial Cuba during the Age of Revolutions* (North Carolina: University of North Carolina Press, 2019).

14 Robin Law, ed., *From Slave Trade to 'Legitimate Commerce': The Commercial Transition in Nineteenth-Century West Africa* (Cambridge: Cambridge University Press, 1995).

15 This went through the letters of the treaties signed by the traditional authorities and proclamations and ordinances issued by the government afterwards. See, for instance, The Treaty of Epe, September 28, 1854. Agreement entered into this 28th day of September 1854 between Kosoko his Caboceers and Chiefs, and Benjamin Campbell Esquire Her Britannic Majesty's Consul for the Bight of Benin, and Thomas Miller Esquire Commander H.M. Sloop "Crane" Senior Officer in the Bights of Benin and Biafra.

16 Christof Dejung, David Motadel and Jürgen Osterhammel, eds., *The Global Bourgeoisie: The Rise of the Middle Classes in the Age of Empire* (Princeton: Princeton University Press, 2019).

17 Anthony G. Hopkins, *An Economic History of West Africa* (London: Longman, 1973).

18 Cheikh Anta Diop, *Precolonial Black Africa: A Comparative Study of the Political and Social Systems of Europe and Black Africa from Antiquity to the Formation of Modern States* (Connecticut: Lawrence Hill Books, 1987), 145.

19 Felix K. Ekechi, *Missionary Enterprise and Rivalry in Igboland 1857–1914* (London: Frank Cass, 1972).

20 In a somewhat different form, this practice continued well all through the colonial era as it constituted the core of the colonial project. Lord Lugard, *The Dual Mandate in British Tropical Africa* (New York: Routledge, 1965).

21 Olufemi Ekundare, *An Economic History of Nigeria 1860–1960* (London: Methuen, 19673), 140–158.

22 Paul Caruana-Galizia and Jordi Martí-Henneberg, "European Regional Railways and Real Income, 1870–1910: A Preliminary Report," *Scandinavian Economic History Review* 61, no. 2 (2013): 167–196.

23 John A. Payne, *Paynes Lagos and West African Almanack and Diary* (London: W.J. Johnson, 1882), 22.

24 Joseph Smaldone, *Warfare in the Sokoto Caliphate: Historical and Sociological Perspective* (London: Cambridge University Press, 1977).

25 Smaldone, *Warfare in the Sokoto Caliphate.*

26 M'baye Gueye and Adu Boahen, "African Initiatives and Resistance in West Africa, 1880–1914," in *General History of Africa: VII Africa Under Colonial Domination 1880–1935*, ed. Adu Boahen (Paris: UNESCO, 1990), 147.

27 Paul M. Mbaeyi, *British Military and Naval Forces in West African History 1807–1874* (New York: NOK Publishers, 1978).

28 Femi J. Kolapo, "The Saro of West Africa," in *Oxford Research Encyclopedia of African History*, https://oxfordre.com/africanhistory/view/10.1093/acrefore/9780190277734.001 .0001/acrefore-9780190277734-e-762.

29 Nicholas Omenka, "The African-Brazilian Repatriates and the Religious and Cultural Transformation of Colonial Lagos," *Abia Journal of the Humanities and the Social Sciences* 1, no. 1 (2004): 27–45.

30 Abiodun Adetugbo, "The Development of English in Nigeria up to 1914: A Socio-Historical Appraisal," *Journal of the Historical Society of Nigeria* 9, no. 2 (1978): 89–96.

31 Mac Dixon-Fyle, "The Saro in the Political Life of Early Port Harcourt, 1913–49," *The Journal of African History* 30, no. 1 (1989): 125–138.

32 Toyin Falola and Ann Genova, eds., *Yoruba Identity and Power Politics* (Rochester: Rochester University Press, 2006).

33 Valentin Y. Mudimbe, *The Invention of Africa: Gnosis, Philosophy, and the Order of Knowledge* (Indianapolis: Indiana University Press, 1988), 98–134.

34 Julia Cagé and Valeria Rueda, "The Long-Term Effects of the Printing Press in sub-Saharan Africa," *American Economic Journal: Applied Economics* 8, no. 3 (2016): 69–99.

35 Francisco A. Gallego and Robert Woodberry, "Christian Missionaries and Education in Former African Colonies: How Competition Mattered," *Journal of African Economies* 19, no. 3 (2010): 294–329.

36 Melville J. Herskovits and Mitchell Harwit, *Economic Transition in West Africa* (London: Routledge, 1964).

37 Anthony G. Hopkins, "The Currency Revolution in South-West Nigeria in the Late Nineteenth Century," *Journal of the Historical Society of Nigeria* 3, no. 3 (1966): 471–483.

38 Payne, *Payne's Lagos and West African Almanack*, 36.

39 Chibuike Ugochukwu Uche, "Foreign Banks, Africans, and Credit in Colonial Nigeria, c. 1890–1912," *The Economic History Review* 52, no. 4 (1999): 669–691.

40 Mieke van der Linden, *The Acquisition of Africa (1870–1914): The Nature of International Law* (Netherlands: Brill I Nijhoff, 2017), 95–138.

41 Patrick Manning, *Slavery and Slave Trade in West Africa 1450–1930* (Ohio: Ohio University Press, 2016), 111.

42 Michael Kehinde, "Trans-Saharan Slave Trade," in *Encyclopedia of Migration*, eds. Frank D. Bean and Susan K. Brown (Dordrecht: Springer, 2013), 1–14.

43 Jason Kelly, "Anti-slavery Movement, Britain," *The International Encyclopedia of Revolution and Protest*, 2009, 8, https://www.revolution.protestencyclopedia.com .proxy.ulib.uits.iu.edu/subscriber/tocnode.html?id=g9781405184649_yr2012-chunk _g9781405184649103>.

44 Kelly, "Anti-slavery Movement," 3–4.

45 Angus Dalrymple-Smith, "A Comparative History of Commercial Transition in Three West African Slave Trading Economies, 1630 to 1860," Ph.D. diss., Wageningen School of Social Sciences (2017): 18.

46 Kelly, "Anti-slavery Movement," 8.

47 Kelly, "Anti-slavery Movement," 2.

48 Leslie Bethell, "The Mixed Commissions for the Suppression of the Transatlantic Slave Trade in the Nineteenth Century," *The Journal of African History* 1 (1966): 80.

49 Bethell, "The Mixed Commissions," 81.

50 Bethell, "The Mixed Commissions," 86.

51 Dalrymple-Smith, "Comparative History," 29.

52 Dalrymple-Smith, "Comparative History," 29–30.
53 Inge Van Hulle, *Britain and International Law in West Africa* (Oxford: Oxford University Press, 2020), 56.
54 Hulle, *Britain and International Law*, 55.
55 Hulle, *Britain and International Law*, 61.
56 Hulle, *Britain and International Law*, 62.
57 Cameron Monroe, "Building the State in Dahomey: Power and Landscape on the Bight of Benin," in *Power and Landscape in Atlantic West Africa: Archaeological Perspectives*, eds. Cameron Monroe and Akinwumi Ogundiran (Cambridge: Cambridge University Press, 2012), 195.
58 Monroe, "Building the State in Dahomey," 201.
59 Monroe, "Building the State in Dahomey," 195–215.
60 Monroe, "Building the State in Dahomey," 195.
61 Elisee Soumonni, "Between Abolition and the Jihad: The Asante Response to the Ending of the Atlantic Slave Trade, 1807–1896," in *From Slave Trade to "Legitimate" Commerce: The Commercial Transition in Nineteenth-century West Africa*, ed. Robin Law (Cambridge: Cambridge University Press, 1995).
62 Dalrymple-Smith, "Comparative History," 112.
63 Dalrymple-Smith, "Comparative History," 116.
64 Gareth Austin, "Plantations and Labour in the South-east Gold Coast from the Late Eighteenth to the Mid-nineteenth Century," in *From Slave Trade to "Legitimate" Commerce: The Commercial Transition in Nineteenth-century West Africa*, ed. Robin Law (Cambridge: Cambridge University Press, 1995), 96.
65 Dalrymple-Smith, "Comparative History," 118.
66 Dalrymple-Smith, "Comparative History," 112.
67 Austin, "Plantations and Labour," 102–105.
68 Austin, "Plantations and Labour," 102–105.
69 Dalrymple-Smith, "Comparative History," 145.
70 Dalrymple-Smith, "Comparative History," 162.
71 Dalrymple-Smith, "Comparative History," 160.
72 Susan Martin, "Slaves, Igbo Women and Palm Oil in the Nineteenth Century," in *From Slave Trade to "Legitimate" Commerce: The Commercial Transition in Nineteenth-century West Africa*, ed. Robin Law (Cambridge: Cambridge University Press, 1995), 176.
73 Martin, "Slaves, Igbo Women and Palm Oil in the Nineteenth Century," 177.
74 Dalrymple-Smith, "Comparative History," 160.
75 Martin, "Slaves, Igbo Women and Palm Oil in the Nineteenth Century," 176.
76 Dalrymple-Smith, "Comparative History," 146
77 Martin, "Slaves, Igbo Women and Palm Oil in the Nineteenth Century," 183.
78 Dalrymple-Smith, Comparative History, 164.
79 Dalrymple-Smith, Comparative History, 153.
80 Dalrymple-Smith, Comparative History, 158.
81 Jan Vansina, *Oral Tradition as History* (Madison: University of Wisconsin Press, 1985).
82 Godfrey N. Uzoigwe, "The Warrior and the State in Precolonial Africa," *Journal of Asian and African Studies* 11, nos. 1–4 (1977): 20–47.
83 Robin Law, "Horses, Firearms, and Political Power in Pre-Colonial West Africa," *Past and Present* 72, no. 1 (1976): 112–132.
84 Philip D. Curtin, ed., *Africa Remembered: Narratives from West Africans from the Era of the Slave Trade* (Madison: University of Wisconsin Press, 1967); and Toyin Falola and Dare Oguntomisin, *The Military in Nineteenth Century Yoruba Politics* (Ile-Ife: University of Ife Press, 1984).
85 Robin Law, *Contemporary Source Material for the History of the Old Oyo Empire, 1627–1824* (Toronto: York University, 2001).
86 Robin Law, "A West African Cavalry State: The Kingdom of Oyo," *The Journal of African History* 16, no. 1 (1975): 1–15.
87 Robin Law, *The Oyo Empire c.1600-c.1836: A West African Imperialism in the Era of the Atlantic Slave Trade* (London: Oxford University Press, 1977).

88 Robin Law, "Trade and Politics Behind the Slave Coast: The Lagoon Traffic and the Rise of Lagos, 1500–1800," *Journal of African History* 24, no. 3 (1983): 321–348; and Alan F. C. Ryder, *Benin and the Europeans 1485–1897* (New York: Humanities Press, 1970).

89 Stephen A. Akintoye, *Revolution and Power Politics in Yorubaland 1840–1983* (London: Longman, 1971).

90 Robin C. C. Law, "The Constitutional Troubles in Oyo in the Eighteenth Century," *The Journal of African History* 12, no. 1 (1971): 25–44.

91 Jacob F. A. Ajayi, *General History of Africa- VI: Africa in the Nineteenth Century until the 1880s* (Oxford: Heinemann Educational Publishers, 1995).

92 Hamza Muhammad Maishanu and Isa Muhammad Maishanu, "The Jihad and the Formation of the Sokoto Caliphate," *Islamic Studies* 38, no. 1 (1999): 119–131.

93 Maishanu and Maishanu, "The Jihad and the Formation of the Sokoto Caliphate."

94 Nehemia Levtzion, *Islam in West Africa: Religion, Society and Politics to 1800* (New York: Routledge, 1994).

95 Aziz A. Batran, "The Nineteenth Century Islamic Revolutions in West Africa," in *General History of Africa. Vol. VI: Africa in the Nineteenth Century until the 1880s*, ed. Jacob F. A. Ajayi (Paris: UNESCO, 1989), 537–554.

96 Murray Last, *The Sokoto Caliphate* (London: Longman, 1977).

97 Isaac A. Akinjogbin, "The Prelude to the Yoruba Civil Wars of the 19th Century," *Odù: Journal of Yoruba and Related Studies* 1, no. 2 (1965): 24–46.

98 Isaac A. Akinjogbin, ed., *The Cradle of a Race: Ife from the Beginning to 1980* (Port Harcourt: Sunray Publications Ltd., 1978).

99 Insa Nolte, "Imitation and Creativity in the Establishment of Islam in Oyo," in *Landscapes, Sources and Intellectual Projects of the West African Past: Essays in Honour of Paulo Fernando de Moraes Farias*, eds. Toby Green and Benedetta Rossi (Leiden: Brill, 2018), 91–115.

100 Adekunle Adekoya, "Afonja: The Kakanfo and Fall of Oyo Empire," *Vanguard*, January 9, 2018.

101 Robin Law, "A Lagoonside Port on the Eighteenth-Century Slave Coast: The Early History of Badagri," *Canadian Journal of African Studies* 28, no. 1 (1994): 32–59.

102 L. M. E. Shaw, *The Anglo-Portuguese Alliance and the English Merchants in Portugal 1654–1810* (London: Routledge, 1998).

103 Olatunji Ojo, "The Organization of the Atlantic Slave Trade in Yorubaland, Ca. 1777 to Ca. 1856," *The International Journal of African Historical Studies* 41, no. 1 (2008): 77–100.

104 Joseph A. Atanda, "The Fall of the Old Oyo Empire: A Re-consideration of its Cause," *Journal of the Historical Society of Nigeria* 5, no. 4 (1971): 477–490.

105 Kim Searcy, *The Formation of the Sudanese Mahdist State: Ceremony and Symbols of Authority: 1882–1898* (Leiden: Brill, 2011), 82.

106 Searcy, *The Formation of the Sudanese Mahdist State.*

107 Alkasum Abba, *History of Yola, 1809–1914: The Establishment and Evolution of a Metropolis* (Zaria: Ahmadu Bello University, 2003).

108 Hakeem O. Danmole and Toyin Falola, "Ibadan-Ilorin Relations in the Nineteenth Century: A Study in Imperial Struggles in Yorubaland," *Transafrican Journal of History* 14 (1985): 21–35.

109 Bolanle Awe, "The Ajele System: A Study of Ibadan Imperialism in the Nineteenth Century," *Journal of the Historical Society of Nigeria* 3, no. 1 (1964): 47–60.

110 Thomas Hodgkin, "Islam and National Movements in West Africa," *The Journal of African History* 3, no. 2 (1962): 323–327.

111 Rowland A. Adeleye, *Power and Diplomacy in Northern Nigeria, 1804–1906: The Sokoto Caliphate and its Enemies* (London: Longman, 1971).

112 Idris Sha'aba Jimada, *The Historical Background to the Establishment of Patigi Emirate: c1810–1898* (Zaria: Ahmadu Bello University, 2016).

113 Although a popular event in the evolution of Yorubaland in the nineteenth century, the exact date of the war and chronology of events around this time have remained one of the knotting aspects of the time. However, this has been put between circa 1817 and 1825.

114 Abdullahi Smith, "A Little New Light on the Collapse of the Alafinate of Yoruba," in *Studies in Yoruba History and Culture: Essays in Honour of Professor S. O. Biobaku*, ed. Gabriel O. Olusanya (Ibadan: Ibadan University Press, 1983), 42–71.

115 Samuel N. Nwabara, "The Fulani Conquest and Rule of the Hausa Kingdom of Northern Nigeria (1804–1900)," *Journal de la Société des Africanistes* 33, no. 2 (1963): 231–242.

116 Ade Obayemi, "The Sokoto Jihad and the 'O-Kun' Yoruba: A Review," *Journal of the Historical Society of Nigeria* 9, no. 2 (1978): 61–87.

117 Olufunke Adeboye, "The City of Ibadan," in *Yoruba Towns and Cities, Vol 1*, ed. Gabriel. O. Oguntomisin (Ibadan: Bookshelf Resources, 2003), 8.

118 Salami Olawale, "Slaves, Government and Politics in Ibadan, 1835–1893," *Journal of Humanities and Social Sciences* 6 (2012): 13.

119 Adeboye, "The City of Ibadan," 9.

120 Olawale, "Slaves, Government and Politics," 13.

121 Olawale, "Slaves, Government and Politics," 15.

122 Isaac Boaheng, "Early Christian Missions in West Africa: Implications for Rethinking the Great Commission," in *Rethinking the Great Commission: Emerging African Perspectives*, eds. Emmanuel Asante and David N. A. Kpobi (Accra: Type Company Limited, 2018), 6.

123 Boaheng, "Early Christian Missions in West Africa," 10.

124 David Maxwell, "The Missionary Movement in African and World History: Mission Sources and Religious Encounter," *The Historical Journal* 58, no. 4 (2015): 901–930.

125 Boaheng, "Early Christian Missions in West Africa," 2.

15

NINETEENTH-CENTURY JIHADS

Introduction

In the nineteenth century, West Africa (Bilad-al-Sudan) became the setting of the culmination of an Islamic religious fervor traced back to the seventeenth century (the 1670s).
Of the several earlier historical instances of Islamic revivalist/militant activity (prominent among which was the Almoravid invasion of Ghana in the eleventh century) aimed
at the overthrow of non-Islamic authorities, attempts at finding a common origin for
the jihad have presented (among others) the campaigns of Awbek Ashfaga, otherwise
known as Nasir al-Din (protector of the faith), against the nomadic clans of the western
Sahara as the first instance of jihad in West Africa.[1] By the eighth century, the region
was populated by a combination of settled agriculturalists and sedentary and pastoral
nomads who eked a living from its varied geographies (desert, savannah, and forest).
Also, the region accommodated foreign elements in the form of traders and trading communities from the trade across the Sahara Desert through northern Africa to the Middle
East.[2] The religion (Islam) introduced into the region by these foreign (Arab) elements
and their (Berber) converts produced an added dimension to the socioeconomic and
political intrigues formerly expressed through established social dichotomies. Between
these were farmers and herders, rural and urban dwellers, slaves and freeborn, and the
nobility and peasantry, to which the coming of Islam provided overarching divisions
between the adherents of traditional beliefs and Muslims on the one hand and between
Muslim (orthodoxy) agitators and pacifists on the other.

As the number of Muslim converts within West African populations—for instance,
both among the Fulani and non-Fulani in the central Sudan—grew, so did the awareness
that "the states in which they lived were by Islamic standards corrupt."[3] By 1804, the
extent of Islam's integration in the area had produced a level of awareness and solidarity
among Muslims strong enough to instigate a succession of Islamic reformist campaigns
(jihad) led by various charismatic Muslim scholars from groups of clerical Fulani. They
successfully rallied both (sedentary and nomadic) Fulani and non-Fulani peoples of the

DOI: 10.4324/9781003198260-18

"central Sudan" to their reformist cause against the nominally Muslim Hausa rulers and other "pagan" peoples in the region (Figure 15.1).

This Sokoto jihad (holy war) had, as its justification, a charge made by the reformers (the leading Fulani scholastic/clerical elements) of "religious laxity" against their mostly Hausa overlords, as well as the unbelief of other "pagan" peoples. However, the issue of the ethnic composition of a significant number of the jihadist leadership and beneficiaries, including the irrefutable role of Fulani nationalism, has been a source of controversy as to the underlying cause of the jihads. This is especially against the backdrop of an age-long tradition of skirmishes between settled agriculturalists and nomadic cattle herders in the region,[4] as well as the fact that most of the principalities affected were at least nominally Muslim. The role of Islam as the rallying ideology and guiding principle of these jihads was strong, even when doubts were expressed about the religious sincerity of the reformers. Islam, with its instrument of jihad, remained a major driving force behind the social, political, and economic transformations witnessed in West Africa in the nineteenth century.[5]

Islam in West Africa: The Call for Reformation

The exact date of the introduction of Islam into the West African region is not specific because many of the earlier instances of contact and conversion were not recorded by early Arab sources, except where they marked the conversion of a reputable figure (royalty) which was considered a victory for the faith. Nonetheless, what is cited is that Islam was introduced into the West African region by the Lumunta, a group of Berber traders belonging to the *Ibadi* (a Kharijite sect) who were converted via conquest and trading relations with Arabs by the second decade of the eighth century.[6] By this period, trade across the Sahara—led by the aforementioned Saharan groups—had begun to some

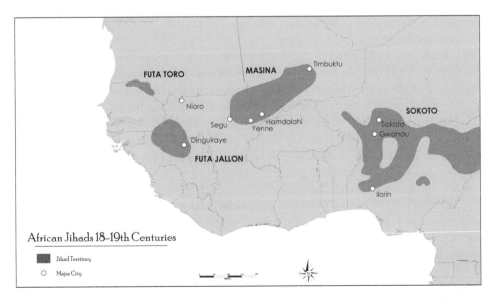

FIGURE 15.1 Map of African jihads, eighteenth to nineteenth centuries. Author's collection.

extent and was the main driver of contact and vehicle for disseminating the Islamic faith. The introduction of the Islamic faith into West Africa, thus, followed a pattern where Muslim traders of Berber and later Arab origins traded, settled, and established—with the approval of "pagan" sovereigns—their separate Muslim communes within the great centers of trade—Ghana, Gao, Awdaghust, Ghayaru, Tademekka, Kugha and Zajunu.[7]

Contrary to perceptions of the expansion of Islam as one great advancing frontier, gradually incorporating non-Islamic lands through successive successful religious campaigns, Hrbek clarifies that its development at the onset took the form of "a series of Urban enclaves at the centers of trade and political power, while peasants were little touched by Islam. These settlements along the trade routes and in major centers constituted the nursery for the eventual propagation of Islam."[8] Hence, widespread dissemination mostly depended on "the group most commercially active in later centuries, the Dyula, the Hausa and the Dyakhanke, [who] were among the first to be converted to Islam when their respective countries came into contact with Muslims."[9] In this role, the Soninke (Wangara/Dyula) merchants led the way, spreading Islam through their ever-expanding commercial networks that stretched from the Sahel to the fringes of the tropical forest.[10] After the Dyula (credited by some traditions as having brought Islam to Hausaland), the Hausa were the second most commercially active class of Muslims. They were also to play important roles in spreading the religion to forest regions, down to the coastal areas of modern Ghana.[11]

Another factor critical to the advancement of Islam in West Africa was the development of an indigenous clerical class.[12] Before the Sudan region developed its indigenous clerical class, it depended on "North African coreligionists" to meet its developing spiritual needs. Moreover, just as the value in trade commodities (particularly gold) from the region had attracted Muslim merchants to the area, so did the growing demand for Islamic teachers, scribes, diviners, and healers attract groups devoted to the provision of such spiritual needs, which quickly translated to political relevance for the *ulama*. These were soon scattered around the region, finding their way into the courts of important rulers, where their services as scribes, religious instructors, and administrative advisers were welcomed and rewarded. The expansion of Islam in the region, however, witnessed a remarkable leap in reaction to the development of indigenous clerical classes, not least because it toned down—in the eyes of the local people—the expatriate character of the religion and made it an African religion, which facilitated acceptance. More so, armed with a better grasp of local languages, traditions, and beliefs, this local clerical class was inclined to make a deeper impression on the locals. One of such (Fulani) clerical clans, the Torodbe, from Tarkrur, famed for being the "first West African Muslim country,"[13] would go on to play a most decisive role in the direction of the development of Islam in West Africa, especially from the sixteenth century.

Gradually, through extended periods of interaction (mainly trade and proselytization), Islam began to spread from the merchant class to record important gains in the royal courts and, even more slowly, extended to the general populace. This process, slow as it was, was encouraged by several factors. First, to encourage critical trading relations with North Africa, the rulers of West African states thought it wise to provide special housing privileges for Muslim merchants who preferred to keep some physical distance from the unbelieving (pagan) populace and maintain certain political and judicial autonomy in the process. It was also meant to present an Islamized front to inspire confidence in their clients and partners from the Islamic north. This meant formal royal conversions, adjustments to court organization, and an obligation of religious pilgrimages. Second, there were incentives for the adoption of Islam, which lay in its quality as an instrument for administration. Not only was the literacy it offered important for administering large empires, but also universalism in the common practice of Islam offered solutions to the problem of securing "the allegiance of other subjected pagan clans and peoples which possessed totally different ancestor and land cults from those of the ruling dynasty."[14] Thirdly, in the case of the masses, beyond the reason of avoiding taxes imposed on non-believers by certain "pious" rulers,[15] the attraction also lay in the protection provided against enslavement by fellow Muslims—which Islamic laws forbade.

The eleventh century is believed to be the period Islam made its first major gains in West Africa due to the conversion of many of the region's rulers to the religion. Describing the situation, Hrbek submits that:

> The eleventh century seems to represent the first real period of breakthrough for Islam in Western and Central Sudan: from the lower Senegal to the shores of the Lake Chad Islam was accepted by various rulers and chiefs thus gaining an official recognition in the framework of African societies. The same century brought about the conversion of the most famous and at the time the most powerful of the Sudanese states, that of Ghana.[16]

Nevertheless, even where the rulers of Borno (in the eleventh century), Mali (in the thirteenth century),[17] and the Hausa kingdoms (from the fourteenth century)[18] and their courts converted to Islam, it was, in most cases, more a strategic decision than it was a concern for religious piety. In some instances, conversion was limited to princes,[19] and even where the converts were actual sovereigns, the conversions were often superficial or personal for social, political, and economic reasons.

From the moment of its appearance on the West African scene, Islam had to contend with the preexisting norms and traditions established many centuries before its arrival. For a period, the liberal approach to proselytization of early Muslim leaders allowed for the conversion of many. However, the inevitability of conflict lay in the nature of the Islamic faith, being, as it were, more than a basic subscription to monotheism. In the words of Hesket, "Islam is a religion and a way of life."[20] As a worldview, complete with a belief system that covers an extensive spectrum of human activity, "the individual and social, material and moral, economic and political, legal and cultural, national and international,"[21] Islam reflected the social-cultural milieu (the Arab world) that produced it. Hence, when strict adherence to its precepts was to be later demanded, it naturally met with some stiff resistance from the people who were already set in their ways. Describing the intricacies involved in such sociocultural dissimilarity as a source of conflict, Dramani-Issifou explains thus:

> The black African societies which were penetrated by Islam were rural; they had functional links with the land and with all features of their immediate environment (mineral, vegetable, air and water). In these agrarian cultures, based on the oral tradition, it may be possible to see analogies with certain socio-cultural aspects of the

pre-Islamic Arab World. That does not mean that the social structures of the Islamic world resembled those of Africa ... The important thing is that these communities, whatever their size, considered that their bonds — even if they were fictive—were religious and were shared by the totality of their ancestors, the living and children as yet unborn, in an unbroken chain of generations, having a sacred bond with the soil, with the bush, and with the waters, which provided food and were objects of worship. These socio-religious structures could not be dissociated without destroying the entire balance of their life.[22]

Even among the more evolved societies, whose level of social sophistication had produced socioeconomic categorizations and specialization, "the African man retained his vision of the world as a vast confrontation of forces that were to be exorcised or exploited."[23] Resistance to Islam came in two major forms: active and passive/partial. Among "pagan" peoples were the Mossi,[24] Bambara,[25] and Bariba,[26] as well as other chieftaincies—among the Mande and Denianke Fulani—which had relatively little interaction with Islam or had had such interaction disrupted[27] before facing attempts at coercive conversion. To this group of people, resistance was very active as it was a matter of defending the threat to their independence and their (established) ways of life from a usurping alien culture. However, in the case of the Soninke/Malinke (of Ghana and Mali), Songhai, parts of Hausa and other such groups, which boasted of some history of cordial Islamic interaction—mostly through a long tradition of trans-Saharan trading—before attempts at wholesome enforcement of adherence to Islamic precepts, the resistance was rather relatively passive/partial (a combination of non-receptiveness, ambivalence, and partial acceptance).

Moreso, for these latter populations, the situation was more a matter of adjusting to the demands of a new religion—one which, although its tenets did not always agree with their traditional religious beliefs, posed no perceivable threat to their political and social-cultural establishments. As such, in places like Mali, Songhai, and Borno, which boasted of a longer Islamic tradition, Islam made quite the inroad, achieving varying levels of institutional integration before the nineteenth-century jihads.[28] This is, however, not suggesting that there was no sense of religious antagonism between adherents of both Islam and traditional African religions in these areas via passive/partial resistance, but that, for a time—in the heyday of pacifist Islam—they had coexisted peacefully until the spark which ignited reformist ideas.

Even in the face of subsequent inroads Islam made into West Africa by the fifteenth century through "the constant flow of ideological communication, of books and scholarship, of pilgrims and marabouts along the trade routes,"[29] the majority of Sudanic peoples still maintained this system of passive/partial resistance. This provided some basis for both the early and latter nineteenth-century jihad movements. At this point, this system of passive/partial resistance had evolved into a tradition of "mixed Islam"—a compromise between Islam and traditional practices, existing "eclectically," either in parallel or as a combination of Islam and traditional African religion.[30] This religious compromise (mixed Islam) was sustained by two types of factors: political and economic.

Politically, as Muslim converts, the rulers of most West African territories could not abandon the traditional beliefs from whence they drew their legitimacy. As such, they were powerless to demand a blanket conversion of their subjects, as this would compromise the loyalty of the non-Muslim population.[31] Moreso, notwithstanding the various administrative and trade opportunities a relationship with Islam offered, African rulers were wary of its

> concept of a loyalty overriding the ordinary duties of a citizen towards his state. The Fulani jihad was to prove the outstanding instance of the way in which the sword of faith might turn in the hands of those traditional rulers who had sought to brandish it to their own advantage.[32]

Economically, just as conversion improved external trading prospects with the Islamic world, internally, it threatened some aspects of economic activity that derived their vitality from established indigenous cultural norms. Daramani-Issifou presents such a scenario where:

> In the eighth/fourteenth century ... al-'Umarï explains that the Mansa of Mali tolerated in his empire 'the existence' of populations still practising traditional religions which he exempted from the tax that was imposed on unbelievers but which he employed in gold-mining. The situation appears to have remained much the same until quite recent times. The fundamental reason really is that gold prospecting and production were accompanied by a number of magical operations and were bound up with a system of beliefs of which we can still discern trace. The same applied to iron which provides perhaps an even clearer example than gold. In many areas, accounts describing power relations indicate the close association between royal authority and the master smelters and smiths. The figure of the 'blacksmith' is also associated with magic, with the dangerous power of the ironmasters.[33]

By the eighteenth century— four centuries after the introduction of Islam to Hausaland and two centuries before the onset of the reform movements—however, Islam had achieved some integration into the social and political systems of the Savannah states,[34] that is, "Islamic mores and attitudes, if not full Islamic confession, became more pervasive."[35] This was such that, by the end of that (eighteenth) century, Islam in Hausaland—the locus of the origins of the nineteenth-century Islamic reform movements—had developed enough to entertain an active controversy. Hiskett corroborates this when he avers that "various groups of Muslims took up positions from extreme rigorism to total quietism, towards the mixed Islam by which they were surrounded."[36] Commenting on the prevailing sentiment among the would-be nineteenth-century reformers, Bartan points out that:

> Islam in the nineteenth-century Western Sudan undoubtedly fell far short of the ideals of the reformers and their committed followers. The reformers complained of the pervasiveness of non-Islamic practices among rulers and subjects alike. They condemned the injustices and oppression perpetrated by the ruling dynasties and accused them of mixing Islam with traditional religious customs (takhlit), and even outright unbelief. They assailed the *'ulama'* for tolerating, indeed endorsing the debased state into which Islam had sunk.[37]

Furthermore, leading the call for a return to strict adherence to Islamic orthodoxy were the duo of the early eighteenth century—Muhammed al-Barnawi, who condemned all forms of deviation from strict orthodoxy and Shayk Jibril B. Umar, who postulated that any sin, including all non-Islamic practices, amounts to apostasy. The Maghribian scholar, Muhammad ibn Abd al-Karïm al-Maghïlï, represented another prominent voice against syncretism and the issue of *ulama al su*, which he condemned as unbelief necessitating jihad.[38] At the other end of the argument were the pacific Muslims, made up of literates who enjoyed the patronage of Hausa courts, in the employ of which they served as counselors, scribes, rain-makers, and diviners. They were disposed to a wide range of compromises with African religion at the cost of their privileged standing. Hiskett presents a description of their conduct, as captured in the "Hausa Chronicles," which explains that, "At this time all the Hausa kings gave judgement arbitrarily, without laws; learned Mallams [Hausa Malam, the equivalent of Arabic' *alim* learned man] were attached to them, but they did what the kings ordered them."[39] This points to another critical aspect of the ongoing controversy in Hausaland in the eighteenth century, which is the objection of the pro-orthodoxy Muslim elite to the un-Islamic policies of the Hausa rulers. They desired a political administration guided by Islamic (sharia) law, which, in their view, was the only way to ensure justice and equity.

Some quietists combined their literate functions with trading interests and were against changing the status quo. The clerical class, which comprised mainly of Hausa with some elements of clerical Fulani who had been enticed away from the customary strict independence of their ethnic kin, were qualified in Arabic as *ulama al su*. Another contributory element in this division between reformists and quietists was the role of the jurists concerned, the likes of Muhammad ibn Abd al-Karïm al-Maghili, Muhammed al-Barnawi, Shayk Jibril B. Umar, and Shaykh al-Mukhtâr al-Kunti. As Daramani-Issifou elucidates:

> The jurists from the north, armed with their learning and proud of the society they represented, tended to see in the 'non-conformist' actions of black societies the proof that they belonged to a world that was alien to Islam and must be opposed; the black Muslims who were born in these societies and who wished to live in them, sometimes as small and tolerated minorities, were much more inclined to regard the practices of African religions as not constituting a real obstacle to the acceptance of Islam; their tolerance might be very extensive and their coreligionists from the north readily accused them of permissiveness, of collusion or even of treason to Islam.[40]

However, this is not to say there were no genuine peace-loving Muslims who simply eschewed violence. The exchange between these two main categories of Muslims, and others in between, was carried out in classical Arabic or Ajami prose and verse that sometimes resulted in verbal confrontations. Available to maintain the vitality of these debates were the opinions and contributions of newly returned pilgrims from Mecca, Medina, Cairo, and Fez, who arbitrated on the authority of the famous *shaykhs* whom they had consulted while away in what were then the major centers of Islamic learning and the ferment of contemporary ideas. Keeping with this tradition of ideological wrangling, the atmosphere in Hausaland became pregnant with the possibilities that contributed to the birth of the reform movements in the nineteenth century.

The Ideological, Social, and Political Background of the Jihads

The ideological premise of the jihad can be traced back to the time of the Prophet Muhammad—the progenitor of the Islamic faith—and a campaign he prosecuted against an unbelieving Arab *Kabila* (group).[41] Regardless of the controversy surrounding its designation as "holy war" over the centuries, the jihad has, since its first application in said context, continued to qualify an idea of the overthrow of a "pagan" (un-Islamic) political leadership and its replacement with an Islamic one. This is especially so when the latter is perceived as detrimental to the practice and propagation of Islam, as signified by the absence of the Islamic penal code, *sharia*, and the institutionalization of un-Islamic practices.

To also inspire the tradition of jihad was the Prophet Muhammad's prophecy that "Allah will send to this *umma* (Muslim community) at the beginning of every hundred years he who will renew her religion for her."[42] This tradition of eschatology, promoted over the centuries, became a point of reference to many of the jihad leaders of the seventeenth, eighteenth, and nineteenth centuries. Bartan presents a comprehensive description of this eschatological tradition and the extent of its influence among West African Muslims in the nineteenth century thus:

> Nowhere in *dar al-Isläm* did the concept of *tadjdid* have a more profound effect than in nineteenth-century West Africa. In that century, the Muslims in West Africa anxiously awaited the advent of the *mudjaddid* (reformer/renewer). It is claimed that Muhammad had prophesied that twelve caliphs *(mudjaddidun)* would follow him. Thereafter, a period of anarchy heralding the end of the world would prevail. Local traditions proudly maintain that the Prophet had honoured Takrür (West Africa) with the last two *mudjaddidun*. It was generally believed in the Western Sudan that the first ten reformers had already appeared in the Muslim East (five in Medina, two in Egypt, one in Syria, and two in Iraq) and that Askia al-Muhammad, the great Songhay monarch (1493-1528), was designated the eleventh. The twelfth and last *mudjaddid*, so it was said, was to make his appearance in the Western Sudan during the thirteenth century of the *Hidjra*, i.e., between 1785 and 1881. This millennial climate was exploited by the nineteenth-century West African *djihad* leaders to their own advantage. That both Shaykh' Uthman dan Fodio and Seku Ahmadu claimed to be the *mudjaddid* of the fateful thirteenth century of the *Hidjra* had already been noted. Although al-'Hadjdj 'Umar never took the title of either *mudjaddid* or makdi, he nonetheless assumed a Tijäni-süfi variation, that of *Khalifat Khatim al-Awlyya'* (successor of the Seal of Saints, that is, Ahmad al-Tijani, founder of the Tijàniyya *tarika*).[43]

As established, Islamic fundamentalism was not new to Muslims of Western and Central Sudan. Beyond its premise in the *hadith*, the jihad found expression in West Africa in the seventeenth century (with Nasir al-Din) and eighteenth century (among the Torodbe in the regions of Futa Jallon and Futa Torro).[44] Another important expression of Islamic fundamentalism, which contributed to stirring the spirit of Islamic revivalism in West Africa, was the *Wahhabi* movement, which was "an angry surge of Islamic fundamentalism that swept the slothful Turk out of Arabia and established its first, puritanical regime there from circa 1747 to 1812."[45]

In maintaining a constant stream of interaction with the outside world—North Africa and the Middle East—through the trans-Saharan trade and acts of pilgrimage, Muslims in West Africa had kept abreast with developments in the wider Muslim world, which, in turn, maintained some influence on the area as part of *dar al-Islam*. Thus, the "Wahhabi's revolt against Islam's lethargy and its otiose way of life"[46] and, perhaps even more importantly, the *Sufi* reactions to the attack on mysticism, a central pillar of the *Sufi* tradition movement, contributed to enflaming an Islamic fervor which was already brewing underneath in Western Sudan.[47] The *Sufi* revival, "which reached a climax during the second half of the eighteenth century in the mosque of al-Azhar in Cairo,"[48] also led to the founding of the Tijaniyyah order.[49] Its influence on the nineteenth-century Islamic reform movements in West Africa is evident in the strategic role of the al-Azar mosque—as the locus of ideological affirmation and dissemination—in Cairo. Lastly is the impact of the Napoleonic conquest and occupation of Cairo on attitudes in the rest of the Islamic world (*dar al-Islam*).

As the main precursor of the nineteenth-century jihads in West Africa, *Shehu* Uthman dan Fodio, like his jihad successors, was a member of one of these Islamic orders (*Qadiriyya*) whose activities were centered at the al-Azar Mosque in Cairo in the eighteenth century. The *Shehu*, his family, and his followers "were deeply involved in a Sufi network extending from Hausaland into the Sahara, North Africa, Egypt and, ultimately, Mecca and Medina. Their involvement included not only membership of the Qadiriyya but also links with other powerful orders such as the *Shadhiliyya* and the *Khalwatiyya*."[50] However, unlike the *Shehu* and his immediate band of followers, the largely non-literate members of his extended followership, with the help of whom he conquered Hausaland, drew their inspiration from a slightly different kind of "Islamic excitement." Hiskey refers to it as the sense of divine reward and punishment gained through years of audience to "an oral Islamic verse literature" delivered in the vernacular (Fulfulde and Hausa).[51]

The social and political foundations of the nineteenth-century jihads in West Africa can be traced to several factors, some of which were briefly highlighted earlier.[52] An example was the long-standing tension between the sedentary (mainly agrarian) non-Fulani peasantry and the settled and nomadic Fulani groups, which comprised many populations in the area. In the areas that later became the Sokoto Empire, it was common for Hausa rulers to accommodate nomadic Fulani clans within their domains and to make grazing concessions available, for which the Fulani paid tax. However, over time, such Fulani clans developed some resentment towards their benefactors, either for the amount of *jangali* (cattle tax) or for the restrictions—like limitations on water usage and penalties for grazing over cultivated farms, the latter imposed to protect their indigenous subjects. Perhaps what heightened the resentment was that, even after long periods of settling among the Hausa, the *fulanin gida* (settled Fulani) were still not accorded the same privileges as their Hausa counterparts.[53] The resentment harbored by such Fulani groups created ready recruits for the jihad movements led by their fellow kinsmen. During the jihads, such clan leaders prosecuted their holy wars against the Hausa rulers, whom they promptly replaced as Emirs at the end of successful campaigns.

In Masina and Senegambia, where the *Fulbe* had to embark on seasonal searches for water and pasture that took them up north into Tuareg territory and down south into the farmlands of settled agriculturalists, they were subjected to taxation and restrictions on the use of water and movement of herds. Like their kinsmen in Hausaland, they were also compelled to pay for damages whenever their herds trampled on the farms of local peoples and had to contend with cattle raids from the Tuareg when they moved their cattle up north in the wet season.[54] In addition to all these challenges to their livelihood, the *Fulbe* of Masina was reduced to a humiliating tributary status by the Bambara of Segu, exacted by proxy through the *famas*, which is said to have consisted of "100 boys, 100 girls, 100 male horses, 100 female horses, a measure of gold', and a large number of cattle."[55] Their counterparts in Senegambia hardly fared any better as they also bore the ravages of living under the harsh dispensation of the Torodbe *alammis*. Hence, the Fulbe clan had ample reasons to unite in a jihad against the oppressive regimes and other unfavorable sociopolitical conditions in Masina and Senegambia.

Slavery was another factor that brewed resentment among the people, thus, amassing support for the Fulani revolutionary cause within the Hausa states and beyond. Although Islam banned the enslavement of Muslims of non-servile parentage by other Muslims, slavery was rife in Hausaland.[56] This was particularly common among the Hausa aristocracy, who, unlike the reformers who also participated in slave raiding, made no efforts to distinguish between Muslims and non-Muslims or even their Hausa kin. The place of slavery/slaves in the emergence and success of the reform movements is further reinforced by their role as instigators (from running away to join the ranks of reformers). They also emerged as foot soldiers whose interest was winning their freedom as Muslims in a reformed Islamic society where *sharia* prevailed.

Another important sociopolitical factor that contributed to the reform movements in Hausaland in the nineteenth century was the charge of tyranny and corruption leveled against the Hausa rulers by the reformers. In this case, the matters of the enslavement by the aristocracy, of peasants, pastoralists, as well as Muslims and non-Muslims alike, and others involving the exaction of extreme and abusive tributes on the conquered Fulani, cases of tax abuse and extortion, and the restrictions placed on rights and privileges of both peasants and nomadic Fulani, were enough to inspire such accusations. Undoubtedly, some of these acts labeled "tyrannical" were likely customary decisions imposed by rulers in the interests of their indigenous subjects, which might appear as "corruption" in the eyes of the *sharia* reformers. However, this does not negate the plausibility of the accusations of tyranny and corruption, as the fact that the jihad had advocates from within the indigenous populations supported the existence of royal excesses.

The decision by members of the clerical class to interfere in the political affairs of their respective localities disrupted the tacit understanding between them and the political class that they would stay out of such matters as a price for the relative autonomy they were afforded.[57] Such understanding also formed the basis of a successful cohabitation between Islam and traditional African culture in the region for centuries. However, as adherents of Sunni Islam, the decision to interfere was an obligation, not an option, according to the *Sunni* creed. Moreso, this was in tandem with a long Islamic tradition that "the best kind of political overlord was a caliph or successor of the prophet who could combine political and religious leadership in the tradition of the first Islamic empires."[58] The calls for reform were rooted in such a belief trajectory, setting the stage for an inevitable clash between reformers and established authorities.

The Jihad of Uthman dan Fodio (1804–1810)

Born on December 15, 1774, in Maratta (in the Hausa kingdom of Gobir), Uthman b. Muhammad b. Muhammad b. Salih, also known as *Shehu* Uthman dan Fodio, hailed from a clerical clan of Fulani known as the *Toronkawa*.[59] His father, an Imam, was the young *Shehu* in the family tradition of Islamic scholarship, which brought him under the influence of radical figures such as the Berber Shaykh Jibril b. Umar. Notwithstanding his origins from a family of distinguished quietist scholars and an early interaction with (Islamic) mystic neighbors devoted to the existence of recitation and seclusion, the *Shehu* chose a life of scholarship and teaching (proselytization).[60]

During his conventional Islamic education, when he showed himself as a devout and determined scholar, he came under reformist influences through the agency of two teachers who were already imbued with this spirit of reform. Young dan Fodio was particularly influenced by the latter of the duo, which included his uncle Uthman Binduri and Jibril b. Umar, the ideas of whom he would subsequently reject for their extremism at a period (before 1804) when he had a more moderate stance. Though he had always condemned the complete complacency of quietists, the *Shehu*, as shown "in an early work *Ibya al Sunna* (revivification of orthodoxy) ... stressed that the common people should not be subjected to excessive fault-finding, or be expected to conform to standards of Islamic observance beyond their capacity to attain."[61]

Despite his moderate views, the *Shehu*'s enthusiasm for reform remained unaffected. Around 1774, when he was about twenty years of age, the *Shehu* kicked off his career as a traveling Muslim missionary, preaching along the length and breadth of the Hausa kingdom of Gobir and the neighboring regions of Zamfara and Kebbi to reform "imperfect" Muslims.[62] His passion for teaching saw him providing instructions on the fundamentals of Islam to ill-informed Fulani pastoral groups whom he shared ties with as a Fulani scholar and the Hausa peasants. This passion for proselytization extended beyond the male folk to include women whom the *Shehu* was willing to accommodate in his gatherings, though confined to a secluded area. Soon enough, his popularity grew, aided by his ability to communicate Islamic instruction to his kinsmen through instructional poems in Fulfulde, preach to indigenous peasants in Hausa, and win over fellow students/intellectuals through his Arabic books/pamphlets rendered in classical Arabic.[63]

Giving urgency to the *Shehu*'s teachings and call for reform was millenarism—a belief in an imminent end of the world, widespread in the area on the eve of the nineteenth century. Driving the excitement among believers was the belief that dan Fodio was the expected Mahdi, a charge which he denied, though he conceded instead, like al-Maghili before him, to be the forerunner, the *mujaddid*—"the centurial 'Renewer of the Faith' whom God sends once every hundred years to reform Islam and prepare the way for the Mahdi."[64] Last explains the extent of the influence of this Islamic tradition on the jihad movement, stating that:

> The excitement such expectations aroused should not be underestimated: it gave martyrdom an extra value; it made risks seem less great with the end so near. Even the marginally Muslim must have been stirred to join in the final jihad; the Shaikh's preaching dwelt heavily on the joys of paradise and the terrors of hell. The call was urgent and unequivocal.[65]

Beyond the claims of messianic affiliations, the *Shehu* also drew his inspiration from divine revelations. Beginning in 1789, the *Shehu*, at 36 years of age, started to experience visions in which the nature and implications of his divine appointment were made known to him. In the series of visions he had, the *Shehu* received the power to perform miracles, the grace to intercede on behalf of his followers, and was confirmed and ordained the *"imam* of the *Walis"* (Muslim holy men) by a host of Islamic saints and the Prophet Muhammad himself before God and the host of heaven. In one of these visions, he was also handed "the Sword of Truth to unsheathe it against the enemies of God."[66]

Dan Fodio became a person of great interest to the Bawa Jagwarzo, the King of Gobir, after amassing a following in Gobir, Katsina, and Zamfara substantial enough to command the attention of the king. Some traditions claim that an outright demand from the *Shehu* for strict adherence to Islamic precepts drew the ire of the king and his successors,[67] while others claim that the reformer's rising popularity and followers disturbed the leadership and started them on a path of conflict with him and his followers.[68] Whatever the incentive, dan Fodio, after several instances of persecution against his followers by successive kings of Gobir, *Sarki* Bawa, Nafata, and Yunfa, was compelled to vacate the settlement in Dengel. He and his followers made their way to Gudu in the manner of the Prophet Muhammad during the *hijra*. It was in Gudu that the *Shehu* mobilized his followers, comprised of the Hausa, Fulani, and Tuareg people, in a jihad (holy war) against the syncretistical and "pagan" peoples of the kingdoms—Gobir, Daura, Kebbi, Kano, Zamfara, and Zaria—of Hausaland.

The Jihad of Ahmad b. Muhammad b. Abi Bakr b. Sa'id (Ahmad Lobbo) in Masina (1810–1818)

Born to a minor scholar family from a less important Fulani clan, Ahmad Lobbo was orphaned as a young child and was raised by his maternal family. His education, which he combined with paid cattle herding, was delivered to him and his cousins by his maternal relations and friends of his family. As a young lad, Ahmad Lobbo was a serious and solitary student, a trait perhaps developed from the constant teasing he endured at the hands of his contemporaries. He was also very critical of *"ardo'en,* the traditional and faintly Muslim chiefs in Masina, whom he accused of idolatry."[69] An acquaintance of the *Shehu* Uthman dan Fodio, Ahmad Lobbo was no stranger to the reformist ideas. He is claimed to have sought not only the Shaikh's blessing to embark on his campaign but also ideological materials (books) on which to base it.[70]

Similar to the situation in Hausaland on the eve of the jihad, the society in Masina was characterized by mixed Islam. The region (Niger Bend) had been settled by former nomadic Fulani groups, creating literate Muslim reserves in the midst of surrounding Bambara paganism. While the Fulani *ardo en* in Masina and the somewhat acquiescent *ulama* had come to terms with the paganism of the Bambara overlord, many within the literate Muslim Fulani class harbored an enthusiasm for Islamic reform and intolerance for the compromise that was the norm.[71] Capitalizing on the discontent created by the pervasiveness of syncretism, the tributary relations with the Bambara of Segu who had extended their suzerainty over Masina, and the vacuum created by the decline of the *arma*—descendants of Moroccan alcaides—Ahmad Lobbo rallied these interests and declared jihad against the Bozo, the Bambara, and other pagan and partly Islamized peoples in the region.

Murray Last presents a succinct description of Ahmad Lobbos' rise to relevance and how he managed to utilize the opportunities this afforded him in advancing his jihad cause, as follows:

> Apart from his preaching, Ahmad Lobbo achieved a certain fame by antagonising the Ardo'en and their followers. He accused them not merely of non-Muslim habits (like drinking alcohol) but also of being tools of their Bambara overlords. He had also openly insulted the group of notable foreign scholars in Jenne, and attacked them for their laxity in the Faith and for their fine living. He appealed strongly to the more austere and nationalistic among the Fulani who on either religious or political grounds resented alien domination. Finally, in a society where castes were entrenched, he seemed to oppose both tribal and academic aristocracies and their extortions. He offered, as the Shaikh 'Uthman had offered in Sokoto, hope for the oppressed in the form of a Muslim society based solely on the rule of Law.[72]

The Ahmad Lobbo jihad thus offered different opportunities for the various participants. For the Tukolor and Fulani, it was an opportunity to throw off the yoke of Bambara imperialism. It was also a refuge for escaped slaves of the Bambara and other inferior people in that society. The jihad movement of Ahmad Lobbo culminated in overthrowing the "pagan" Bambara supremacy and its replacement with an Islamic theocracy centered at Hamdallahi, where he founded the capital city of his large empire.

There were similarities between the *jihad* of Ahmad Lobbo in Masina and that of the *Shehu* in Hausaland. Like the *Shehu*'s jihad in Hausaland, much of the support for the Ahmad Lobbo *jihad* movement came from within the Fulani genealogical pool. Like in Hausaland, the Masina jihad also drew ideological inspiration from the *Sufi* revival movement at Al-Azar, Cairo. Like his predecessor, Ahmad Lobbo adopted the role of *mujaddid* or, more precisely, presented himself as a successor to the Prophet. Hence, like the *Shehu*, he took advantage of the messianic expectancy prevalent in the Islamic world at the time. Therefore, the jihad of Ahmad Lobbo proved to be a continuation of the reformist ideas that had taken root in Hausaland and were spreading across the region of West Africa owing to a similarity in the sociopolitical and cultural landscape that can be traced to the introduction of Islam.

The Jihad of Al-Hajj Umar b. Sa'id (1853–1864)

Born in Futa Toro in about 1789, Al-Hajj Umar b. Sa'id, also known as Al-Hajj Umar Tal, was the youngest son of a Fulani scholar. He is said to have distinguished himself early on as a student. Other remarkable achievements were recorded during his pilgrimage to Mecca and Medina, where he spent many years and is said to have impressed the authorities with his intellect so much that they appointed him the *Khalifa* (Vicar) of the *Tijaniyya* order in West Africa.[73] On a sojourn in Egypt, he is alleged to have had some contact with the *khalwati* shaykhs at Al-Azar Mosque in Cairo.[74] On his way back, Al-Hajj Umar antagonized the leaders of the states where he stopped by inducting men into the Tijaniyya order, especially where such converts were influential men; the brotherhood grew to pose a threat to the ruler's authority. In Borno, he fell out with Amin Al-Kenemi. In Sokoto, he had to leave after the death of Mohammed Bello, under whose protection he could stay and win converts. He also made some progress in Masina before moving on to Segu, where he was imprisoned for subversive activities against the non-Muslim leadership. Due to his growing reputation as a sophisticated and influential scholar, Al-Hajj Umar was not welcomed in many Islamic states, including his home, where it was feared he could disrupt the established order. Hence, he was forced to establish his community at Dinguiray, outside any of the Islamic states within the region,[75] from where he launched his jihad campaign and fulfilled the jihad tradition of *hijra* (Figure 15.2).

Celebrated as the most widely traveled of the three jihadists, Al-Hajj Umar's travels exposed him to all of the intellectual and ideological currents sweeping across the Islamic world. His experiences abroad impressed on him the strength of a united Muslim community and, at the same time, underlined the inadequacy of the mixed Islam practiced at home. Hence, reform was already on his mind upon returning from his travels abroad. In 1853, when he declared war on all the *infidels* (unbelievers) in Sudan, it was with a relatively small army of his students, some Fulani kinsmen, and runaway slaves. Al-Hajj Umar, with the deployment of firearms and a well-trained army, managed to win some important victories, which improved his image as a capable leader among like-minded interests and grew his following among various ethnicities. At some point, he could boast of as many as 15,000 to –30,000 men on the battlefield.[76]

As the last of three—interrelated—significant Islamic reform movements in nineteenth-century West Africa, the jihad of Al-Hajj Umar stands out as the exception to the rule in several ways. Most important is the fact that it took place at a period when the French colonial expansion into Africa was already in full swing. For this reason, it is often classified as part of the African resistance efforts against European colonialism,

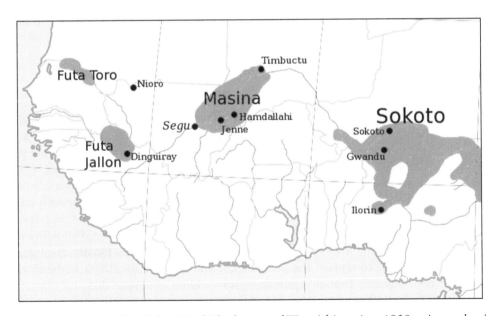

FIGURE 15.2 Major Fula / Fulani /Peul Jihad states of West Africa, circa 1830, prior to the rise of Umar Tall https://commons.wikimedia.org/wiki/File:Fula_jihad_states_map _general_c1830.png.

a view that Hiskett argues is too simplistic, even if it is not "entirely invalid."[77] It was also the first instance in the history of jihad in West Africa where a professional army equipped with guns would attack a state with no prior engagements. Unlike the other jihad movements, that of Al-Hajj Umar could hardly be called a revolution or an aspiration for independence. It was an attempt at Islamic imperialism in West Africa. Such ambitions soon pitched the jihad armies of Al-Hajj Umar with that of Ahmad Lobbo against each other over the Segu, which the latter had hastily declared a "pagan" protectorate to stave off the former's ambitions. In the ensuing battle, Al-Hajj Umar emerged victorious. Hiskett captures it thus:

> By 1862 he had destroyed the empire of Masina and occupied Hamdallahi. His conquests now formed a great wedge of territory, stretching from the lower Senegal in the west to Timbuktu in the east, from Guèmou in the north to Dinguiray in the south. But in 1863 a substantial body of his non-Tukulor subjects rose in revolt against him and besieged him in Hamdallahi. Early in 1884 he was killed while trying to break this siege.[78]

Notwithstanding these various dissimilarities between the jihad movements of Al-Hajj Umar with those of his predecessors, there were enough similarities in their procedures to suggest an ideological connection. Beyond the performance of the *hijra,* which became a standard procedure for all reformers, Al-Hajj Umar also demonstrated the divine element in his emergence as leader of the faithful. In his visionary visitations, where he encountered the Prophet Muhammad, he was bestowed with "the gift of *istikhara,* a special esoteric formula that assured him of direct divine guidance in time of difficulty."[79] He also exploited the messianic expectations prevalent in the era and took the trademark title of *mujaddid al-din al-tnubarnniadiyya,* "the renewer of the Muslim faith."[80]

Consequences of the Nineteenth-Century Jihads in West Africa

The jihad altered the social and political character of many affected societies.[81] In the attempt to implement reforms (*sharia*) that would ensure the survival of Islam (in its orthodox form), certain social structures were affected. The place and role of women as provided for in traditional African culture, where "women had been important participants not only in specific fertility cults but also generally in social gatherings,"[82] was taken up by restrictions placed on their movement and activities, as they were mostly confined to the home. Also affected were African traditional ceremonies, especially dancing and the use of musical instruments, which were banned and considered un-Islamic.

The jihad also resulted in a general transference of political and social standing to a new elite, mostly, but not always, from a different ethnic group than the one displaced.[83] Most also attempted to replace the old political and constitutional systems with new ones, and their success, though significant, was seldom complete. Masina offers the best example of a (relatively) successful political and institutional introduction in an attempt to initiate the necessary sociopolitical reforms. Moreover, this was largely possible owing to the absence of a centralized system of government among the pastoral Fulani. Hence, the entire framework of Islamic administration was introduced.[84] The jihads also produced the first, and perhaps the last, instance of large Islamic theocracies in *Bilad-al-Sudan.*

Another, and maybe the most important area of jihad influence, was in education:

> They greatly accelerated the dissemination of Islamic literacy, particularly in Hausa and Fulfulde-speaking areas, and they also led to the wider dispersal of Muslim literates and to the setting-up of additional centers of Islamic education, especially in the southern areas of the western Sudan. While this certainly strengthened orthodoxy where Islam was already well established, it also, paradoxically, extended the area of mixed Islam.[85]

In the long run, the existence of a tradition of Islamic education and literacy delayed the implementation of secular education in (mostly northern) Muslim-dominated areas of Nigeria. In these areas, the progress of Western education was slow, owing mainly to the active resistance put up by the resident *ulama*. As a result, the northern part of Nigeria's embryonic nation was educationally and technologically undeveloped on the brink of independence.[86] Additionally, the solidarity facilitated, based on common adherence to Islam between ethnic groups in the northern regions, tended to result in a pan-Islamic outlook as against the pan-African aspirations of the non-Muslim areas.

Conclusion

The nineteenth-century jihads in West Africa were undoubtedly one of the most important factors that contributed to social and political developments in the region in that period. They were responsible for radical changes in the political structure and socioeconomic organization of West African states. Politically, the impact of the jihads was felt in the proliferation of centralized systems of governance. The jihads also highlight the place of religion as an age-old outlet for the expression of socioeconomic grievances. Additionally, the jihads represent a coming of age for Islam, that is, the triumph of "African Islam," as a reinforcement of centuries-old transformative influences brought about by the introduction of Islam in the eighth century.

DEEP DIVE

Assignment 1

Objective

The objective of this assignment is to ensure that students complete the reading of Chapter 15 and to get them to understand how the culmination of an Islamic religious fervor dating back several centuries triggered the jihads (holy wars) of the nineteenth century in West Africa. Students are expected to explain the long-term impacts of these sudden religious interjections on West Africa in the nineteenth and twentieth centuries.

Method

Students will be expected to write a short note in response to the question.

Reading Comprehension

What different contexts triggered the nineteenth-century jihads and their impacts on West Africa?

Assignment 2

Objective

The objective of this assignment is to ensure that students complete the reading of Chapter 15 and to get them to think about the circumstances that fostered the need for a religious shift in West Africa based on doctrines central to orthodox Islam, whose ideas were drawn from north Africa and the Arabian Peninsula.

Method

Students will be expected to write a short note in response to the question.

Reading Comprehension

What are the points of convergence and divergence in the concerns of Uthman dan Fodio, Ahmad b. Muhammad b. Abi Bakr b. Sa'id, and Al-Hajj Umar b. Sa'id, which spurred the call for reformation and revolution in West Africa in the nineteenth century?

Notes

1 See Paul Lovejoy, *Jihad in West Africa During the Age of Revolutions* (Ohio: Ohio University Press, 2016), 51; Aziz Bartan, "The Nineteenth-Century Islamic Revolutions in West Africa," in *UNESCO General History of Africa, Vol. VI: Africa in the Nineteenth Century Until the 1880s*, ed. Jacob F. A. Ajayi (California: Heinemann, 1989), 540–541; Philip D. Curtin, "Jihad in West Africa: Early Phases and Inter-Relations in Mauritania and Senegal," *Journal of African History* 12, no. 1 (1971): 14–15; Nehemia Levtzion, "North-West Africa: From the Maghrib to the Fringes of the Forest," in *The Cambridge History of Africa Vol. 4: From 1600–1790*, ed. Richard Gray (New York: Cambridge University Press, 1975), 199–201; and M. Hiskett, "The Nineteenth-Century Jihads in West Africa," in *The Cambridge History of Africa, Vol. 5: From 1790–1870*, ed. John E. Flint (New York: Cambridge University Press, 1975), 128–130.
2 Basil Davidson, *A History of West Africa* (England: Longman, 1977), 36.
3 Murray Last, "Reform in West Africa: The Nineteenth Century Jihad Movements," in *History of West Africa Vol. II*, eds. Jacob F. A. Ajayi and Michael Crowder (New York: Columbia University Press, 1973), 3.
4 Bartan, "The Nineteenth-Century Islamic Revolutions," 547–549; and Stephanie Zhenle, *A Geography of Jihad: Sokoto Jihad and the Islamic Frontier in West Africa* (Berlin: De Gruyter, 2020), 411–412.
5 Murray Last, "The Sokoto Caliphate and Borno," in *UNESCO General History of Africa, Vol. VI*, ed. Jacob F. A. Ajayi (California: Heinemann, 1989), 557.
6 Mohammed El Fasi and Ivan Hrbek, "Stages in the Development of Islam and its Dissemination in Africa," in *UNESCO General History of Africa, Vol III: Africa from the*

Seventh to Eleventh Century, eds. Mohammed El Fasi and Ivan Hrbek (Paris: UNESCO, 1988), 68.

7 Fasi and Hrbek, "Stages in the Development of Islam," 69.

8 Fasi and Hrbek, "Stages in the Development of Islam," 72. See also Levtzion, "North-West Africa," 191.

9 Fasi and Hrbek, "Stages in the Development of Islam," 71.

10 Fasi and Hrbek, "Stages in the Development of Islam," 75.

11 Fasi and Hrbek, "Stages in the Development of Islam," 80; and Levtzion, "North-West Africa," 189.

12 Fasi and Hrbek, "Stages in the Development of Islam," 72 and 78.

13 Fasi and Hrbek, "Stages in the Development of Islam," 73.

14 Fasi and Hrbek, "Stages in the Development of Islam," 76. See also Jacob F. A. Ajayi and Benjamin O. Oloruntimehin, "West Africa in the Anti-Slave Trade Era," in *The Cambridge History of Africa, Vol. 5: From 1790–1870*, ed. John E. Flint (Cambridge: Cambridge University Press, 1977), 202.

15 The fourteenth-century Mansa of Mali is known to have imposed such tax on unbelievers in his domain. See Z. Daramani-Issifou, "Islam as a Social System in Africa Since the Seventh Century," in *UNESCO General History of Africa, Vol III*, eds. Mohammed El Fasi and Ivan Hrbek (Paris: UNESCO, 1988), 102.

16 Fasi and Hrbek, "Stages in the Development of Islam," 74.

17 Fasi and Hrbek, "Stages in the Development of Islam," 73, 76.

18 Hiskett, "The Nineteenth-Century Jihads in West Africa," 131; and M. El Fasi and I. Hrbek, "The Coming of Islam and the Expansion of the Muslim Empire," in *UNESCO General History of Africa, Vol III: Africa from the Seventh to Eleventh Century*, eds. M. El Fasi and I. Hrbek (Paris: UNESCO, 1988), 79.

19 Daramani-Issifou, "Islam as a Social System in Africa," 101.

20 Hiskett, "The Nineteenth-Century Jihads in West Africa," 125.

21 Fasi and Hrbek, "The Coming of Islam," 40.

22 Daramani-Issifou, "Islam as a Social System in Africa," 104.

23 Daramani-Issifou, "Islam as a Social System in Africa," 105.

24 Levtzion, "North-West Africa," 195; and Fasi and Hrbek, "Stages in the Development of Islam," 80.

25 Fasi and Hrbek, "Stages in the Development of Islam," 80.

26 Levtzion, "North-West Africa," 196.

27 Ajayi and Oloruntimehin, "West Africa in the Anti-Slave Trade Era," 202.

28 Humphrey J. Fisher, "The Central Sudan and Sahara," in *The Cambridge History of Africa Vol. 4*, ed. Richard Gray (New York: Cambridge University Press, 1975), 64; and Ajayi and Oloruntimehin, "West Africa in the Anti-Slave Trade Era," 202.

29 Levtzion, "North-West Africa," 191.

30 Hiskett, "The Nineteenth-Century Jihads in West Africa," 131; and Fasi and Hrbek, "Stages in the Development of Islam," 80.

31 Fasi and Hrbek, "Stages in the Development of Islam," 76.

32 Fisher, "The Central Sudan and Sahara," 65.

33 Daramani-Issifou, "Islam as a Social System in Africa," 102.

34 Levtzion, "North-West Africa," 197. See also Ajayi and Oloruntimehin, "West Africa in the Anti-Slave Trade Era," 202.

35 Hiskett, "The Nineteenth-Century Jihads in West Africa," 131.

36 Hiskett, "The Nineteenth-Century Jihads in West Africa," 131.

37 Bartan, "The Nineteen-Century Islamic Revolutions," 545.

38 Bartan, "The Nineteen-Century Islamic Revolutions," 543.

39 Hiskett, "The Nineteenth-Century Jihads in West Africa," 132.

40 Daramani-Issifou, "Islam as a Social System in Africa," 106.

41 Fasi and Hrbek, "Stages in the Development of Islam," 46.

42 Bartan, "The Nineteen-Century Islamic Revolutions," 538.

43 Bartan, "The Nineteen-Century Islamic Revolutions," 539.

44 Bartan, "The Nineteen-Century Islamic Revolutions," 540.

45 Hiskett, "The Nineteenth-Century Jihads in West Africa," 126.

46 Hiskett, "The Nineteenth-Century Jihads in West Africa," 126.
47 Bartan, "The Nineteen-Century Islamic Revolutions," 543.
48 Hiskett, "The Nineteenth-Century Jihads in West Africa," 126.
49 Bartan, "The Nineteen-Century Islamic Revolutions," 543; and Hiskett, "The Nineteenth-Century Jihads in West Africa," 126.
50 Hiskett, "The Nineteenth-Century Jihads in West Africa," 137.
51 Hiskett, "The Nineteenth-Century Jihads in West Africa," 137.
52 See also Lovejoy, *Jihad in West Africa*.
53 Zhenle, *A Geography of Jihad*, 411.
54 Bartan, "The Nineteen-Century Islamic Revolutions," 547–548.
55 Bartan, "The Nineteen-Century Islamic Revolutions," 548.
56 Mostly because of the demand for muskets, which is said to have been accessible in the period and, could be paid for mainly in slaves. See Hiskett, "The Nineteenth-Century Jihads in West Africa," 138.
57 See Curtin, "Jihad in West Africa," 14; and Bartan, "The Nineteen-Century Islamic Revolutions," 550.
58 Curtin, "Jihad in West Africa," 14.
59 Hiskett, "The Nineteenth-Century Jihads in West Africa," 131.
60 Last, "Reform in West Africa," 4.
61 Hiskett, "The Nineteenth-Century Jihads in West Africa," 133.
62 Hiskett, "The Nineteenth-Century Jihads in West Africa," 134.
63 Last, "Reform in West Africa," 5.
64 Hiskett, "The Nineteenth-Century Jihads in West Africa," 134.
65 Last, "Reform in West Africa," 6.
66 Hiskett, "The Nineteenth-Century Jihads in West Africa," 136; and Bartan, "The Nineteen-Century Islamic Revolutions in West Africa," 539.
67 Hiskett, "The Nineteenth-Century Jihads in West Africa," 134–135.
68 Last, "Reform in West Africa," 6–7.
69 Hiskett, "The Nineteenth-Century Jihads in West Africa," 152.
70 Last, "Reform in West Africa," 14.
71 Hiskett, "The Nineteenth-Century Jihads in West Africa," 152.
72 Last, "Reform in West Africa," 15.
73 Last, "Reform in West Africa," 18; and Hiskett, "The Nineteenth-Century Jihads in West Africa," 155.
74 Bartan, "The Nineteen-Century Islamic Revolutions," 543.
75 Last, "Reform in West Africa," 19.
76 Hiskett, "The Nineteenth-Century Jihads in West Africa," 158.
77 Hiskett, "The Nineteenth-Century Jihads in West Africa," 155.
78 Hiskett, "The Nineteenth-Century Jihads in West Africa," 158.
79 Hiskett, "The Nineteenth-Century Jihads in West Africa," 162.
80 Hiskett, "The Nineteenth-Century Jihads in West Africa," 162.
81 Yusufu B. Usman, "The Transformation of Political Communities: Some Notes on a Significant Dimension of the Sokoto Jihad," in *Studies in the History of Sokoto Caliphate*, ed. Yusufu B. Usman (Zaria: Ahmadu Bello University, 1979).
82 Last, "Reform in West Africa," 24.
83 Hiskett, "The Nineteenth-Century Jihads in West Africa," 167; and Bartan, "The Nineteen-Century Islamic Revolutions," 550.
84 Last, "Reform in West Africa," 26.
85 Hiskett, "The Nineteenth-Century Jihads in West Africa," 167.
86 Peter K. Tibenderana, "The Emirs and the Spread of Western Education in Northern Nigeria, 1910–1946," *The Journal of African History* 24, no. 4 (1983): 517–534.

PART IV

The Colonial Era

PART IV

The Colonial...

16

COLONIAL RULE AND ITS IMPACT

The Imposition of Colonial Authority

The imposition of colonial authority in West Africa commenced with the acquisition, conquest, and possession of the region by the colonialists. According to Michael Crowder, "during the nineteenth century, Europeans whether French or British had accepted Africans as men of equal capabilities once they had accepted the European way of life."[1] This partially accounted for why a new class of Africans sought to become like Europeans. With the imposition of colonial rule, West Africans were regarded as inferior citizens, and they could only be considered equivalent to Europeans when they embraced the colonialists' practices and culture. This belief among Europeans was responsible for the administrative policies they adopted in their colonies, such as the French policy of assimilation that sought to make French men out of Africans. One of the first measures they employed to implement their rule and authority was to gain adequate knowledge of the region and its people. Gann and Duignan state that:

> Colonial governments recognizing early in this century the need to know more about the people they governed, employed anthropologists or encouraged colonial officers to act as anthropologists ... [and] after 1920 British colonial governments increasingly used anthropologists to help them formulate and execute policy. There was a great need for information about traditional societies, and governments felt an increased sense of social responsibility to modernize traditional life. Thus they called on the anthropologist to sketch in the habits, thoughts and patterns of behaviours of the colonized people.[2]

Colonialists acquired strategic knowledge and information that aided the dispensation of their regional policies and administration, vital to consolidating their influence and entrenching their presence. In addition to the information gathered by missionaries and explorers, "colonial researchers" were also employed to supplement the

DOI: 10.4324/9781003198260-20

existing knowledge about West Africa.[3] With this information, colonialists established a policy, generally known as "native policy,"[4] because it involved using Africans as ancillary administrators. The decision to adopt this tactic was informed by several reasons. Having studied the people, the colonialists discovered many were obsequiously submissive to their kings and chiefs, so using them in governance was believed to be an efficacious way to manage colonial rule. Moreover, this strategy also proved to be cost-effective.

The method of imposing colonial rule varied from colony to colony, but common to all was the direct control of West Africans economically and politically. As with the rulers, existing political and economic structures and institutions in Africa were retooled in service of the new administration. Furthermore, the colonialists sought to eliminate the intermediaries with whom they traded on the shores to gain direct access into the hinterland and oversee activities there, especially the farm plantations and mines. Political control over West Africans was necessary to access cheap labor without resulting in

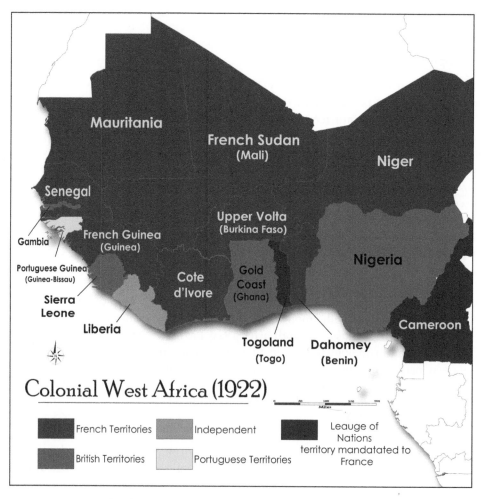

FIGURE 16.1   A map of Colonial West Africa (1922). Author's collection.

revolts or rebellions, which was made possible through proclamations from the local rulers doing the bidding of the colonialists (Figure 16.1).[5]

The West African economy became tethered to the imperial nations. Colonialists utilized peasant labor to grow cash crops for export.[6] Labor was also employed in the mines and factories, and the resulting resources were extracted and exported to Europe. The colonies were restricted to trading exclusively with their imperial nation,[7] while the only legal tender acceptable was that introduced by the colonialists tied to those of the colonizing power. The use of local currencies, which West Africans had previously relied on to exchange goods and trade, was consequently abolished.[8]

After gaining control of West African peoples politically and economically, the colonizers subjected them to taxes. One such onerous tax was the "hut tax" in Sierra Leone, which required affected Africans to labor for the colonialists.[9] This was the situation for many West Africans who had to labor in exchange for the colonial currency required for the payment of taxes. Taxation was very effective at making West Africans fund the cost of administration; since it was considered a civic and legal obligation, tax evasion was a serious offense as the people were extremely frightened of its consequences.[10] Another strategy devised to keep the people in the service of the colonizers was by paying them paltry wages. The amount earned was usually insufficient to sustain a family, especially in emerging cities.

Administration of Colonies

At the apex of the structure of colonial administration in British colonies was the Governor-General, who resided in the colony.[11] As a representative of the Crown, he possessed executive power and functioned as a supreme ruler, aided by a colonial council. Colonies had internal units that could be referred to as a precinct or a district, and at the center of the system was the warrant or colonial chief, who served as the bridge between the colonialists and the colonized.[12] These chiefs were obliquely used in an administrative process termed "indirect rule." Betts notes that:

> Although there was initially no universally accepted approach to colonial administration in Africa, most lines of thought converged on what might be called conjunctive administration (usually termed indirect rule); that which joined African authorities, in traditionally-held or European-imposed political role, to the colonial government, but in an obviously subordinate capacity.[13]

Indirect rule was primarily the system of administration employed by the British, while the French and Portuguese enlisted the services of African chiefs directly in their colonies. Whether directly or indirectly, the use of African chiefs in West Africa was a central theme in the system of administration of the colonialists.[14]

Indirect Rule

The new African elites were excluded from indirect rule's use of African chiefs, kings, and existing traditional institutions in the administrative process of the colonies. Colonial officials justified this exclusion by claiming they did not genuinely care for or understand the "real Africans" in the towns and villages.[15] The resulting grievances of the elites primarily accounted for the nationalist movements and campaigns for the end of colonial rule. The chiefs were incorporated and integrated into the administrative system for numerous reasons, including convenience, cost, size of the colonies, and the availability of personnel.[16] Moreover, since the colonial officers were few, expected high incomes, and were usually homesick, it was easier and cheaper to use existing rulers than to bring in more officials from the home country.

Also, the colonies were often too large for the limited number of European officials to cover effectively, which contributed to the decision to use indirect rule. Lack of knowledge of the local languages also made indirect rule preferable. Indirect rule ensured the continued preservation of indigenous institutions, as the positions of the preexisting rulers were not abolished; instead, they were employed and modernized by the new administration.[17] This system was used in British colonies, and it was most successful in Northern Nigeria under the leadership of Lord Frederick Lugard, who served as High Commissioner between 1900 and 1906 and as Governor-General between 1912 and 1919.[18] Lord Lugard and his successors held the Emirs of Northern Nigeria in high esteem as if they were fellow aristocrats;[19] unfortunately, this was not the case in other parts of Nigeria. The Emirs levied taxes and ran their courts of law and prisons.

In addition, the system of Native Treasuries metamorphosed out of the taxation system, where the Emirs paid a quarter of the taxes they levied to the central government, with the district and village heads subject to the Emirs' assistance in tax collection. The policy of indirect rule often made the British colonial officials ignore things they considered abuses; thus, despite the gradual reduction of the political, economic, and social inequalities in Britain during this period, they exacerbated those inequalities in West Africa.

Conversely, indirect rule succeeded only partially in Southern Nigeria.[20] It featured small societies that had complex governments, and the British colonialists did not fully understand their administrative system. They were a poor fit for bureaucratic administration due to their small size, complex decision-making processes, and excessive dependence on preternatural sanctions. The colonialists created native courts, and the chiefs who presided in the eastern region were referred to as warrant chiefs.[21] They tried cases and directed the implementation of forced labor, becoming exceedingly powerful, influential, and wealthy. Since their office was not a traditional one, they had no guiding cultural principles, were often corrupt, and used forced labor for their selfish needs. The warrant chiefs' highhandedness occasionally drove the people to rebel against colonial rule, including the Aba Women's War of 1929,[22] caused by the imposition of taxes and corrupt practices by the warrant chiefs.

Indirect rule was also extended to the other British colonies in West Africa. In Sierra Leone, the ruling governor resided in Freetown, where he had his headquarters and subordinates assisted him. In 1937, Lugard's native system of administration was introduced into the protectorate.[23] Traditional rulers who were members of a ruling house were made paramount chiefs and elected for life.[24] They were put in control of the local government, the collection of taxes, and the administration of justice, functioning in the same capacities as the other chiefs in the British colonies. There was a hierarchy of traditional leaders, with the paramount chiefs on top, then the village chiefs and section chiefs. The British indirect rule system was also extended to Togo and Cameroon, the newly acquired German territories administered similarly to the other British West African territories.[25]

The Policy of Assimilation and Association

Apart from the indirect rule system, there was also the policy of assimilation implemented in parts of areas controlled by the French. This policy was based on the notion of parity among men and women and, in the context of colonial rule, meant that West Africans should be treated with equality, allowed to live as Frenchmen and women, and allowed to become French citizens if they desired.[26] This belief was embodied in France's description of its colonial territories, "overseas France," and assimilation operated most successfully in the four communes of Senegal—Dakar, Goree, Rufisque, and Saint-Louis. The "natives" of these communes were called *originaires*, and they became French citizens once they were accustomed to French culture over time. The term *évolué* was given to those few Africans who had pursued higher education and had been granted the right to vote, including Blaise Diagne, who became the first African to be elected to the French Assembly (Figure 16.2).[27]

The colony of Senegal was the oldest, and Africans born there became citizens of France automatically, unlike the other colonies. The acceptance of the policy of assimilation was controversial, as some elites supported it while others rejected it. Also, the system was expensive to run since facilities such as schools, hospitals, and churches had to be provided; however, most of the infrastructure was limited to small areas in Senegal,

FIGURE 16.2   Diagne, Deputy of Senegal and High Commissioner of the Pan Noir Congress
https://commons.wikimedia.org/wiki/File:Blaise_Diagne-1921.jpg.

Côte d'Ivoire, and Guinea.[28] Each year, the French administrators had to determine the number of schools, teachers, hospitals, and doctors needed and how much should be allocated.

The structure of the French administration comprised the "governors-general, the lieutenant-governor, the *commandant du cercle,* and the African chiefs who headed the cantons."[29] The colonies were divided into *cercle*, the basic unit of French administration in West Africa, and each was controlled by a colonial officer.[30] A *cercle* was divided further into cantons and villages, headed by cantonal and village chiefs. The *commandants du cercle* wielded tremendous influence and power over the colonies. The French colonies in Senegal were clustered along the coast, making the policy of assimilation relatively easy to enforce, but when the French colonies began to expand, assimilation became more challenging to implement. Treating West Africans as Frenchmen seemed difficult for the French due to Africans' unfamiliarity with French culture, which partially accounted for the difficulty West Africans encountered in their attempt to become citizens of France (Figure 16.3).

While the right of citizenship by birth was maintained in Senegal's four communes, citizenship would only be granted if the applicant could speak, read, and write French fluently, had only one wife, had worked at least ten years for the French, and had completed military service, all of which were difficult to achieve. Besides the Senegalese French citizens, only about 500 people from the 15,000,000 West Africans living in the French territories had attained citizenship by 1939.[31] Christian missionaries were mostly absent in the region, unlike in British West Africa, probably because the French parliament in 1903 voted for the removal of subsidies granted to the missionaries.[32]

FIGURE 16.3   French settlements in Senegal https://commons.wikimedia.org/wiki/File:Histoire
_des_Colonies-Guillon-Bakel_(S%C3%A9n%C3%A9gal).jpg.

The difficulties in managing the assimilation policy led to the adoption of the policy of association.[33] Outside the Senegalese colonies, the French used West African chiefs like the British. However, the position and authority of the chiefs in French West Africa differed from those in British West Africa.[34] In French West Africa, the chiefs had no legal jurisdiction, nor did they control the prisons or the police. Although they collected taxes, they were remitted to the colonial government, from whom they received their salary. In contrast, the chiefs in British West Africa used the taxes they collected to directly finance their administration. The French colonial chiefs served as the pawns of the colonial masters, doing all their "dirty" jobs, such as collecting taxes and recruiting West Africans for forced labor on the plantations and in the army (Figure 16.4).[35]

Like their British counterparts, the French colonial chiefs became corrupt and were usually treated dismissively by the colonial masters. In many cases, they were ordinary people rather than members of traditional ruling houses,[36] while the African rulers were mostly reduced to lesser chiefdoms and made ceremonial functionaries. In both British and French West Africa, the chiefs often became authoritarian, and their excesses could only be checked by the educated elites. One such instance was the case of the Awujale of Ijebuland, who arbitrarily increased his authority under the indirect rule system.[37] A significant difference between the British and French colonial chiefs was that the former exercised more power and control over their subjects than the latter, although both were under the control of the colonial masters.

The assimilation policy in Portuguese colonies was much like the French colonies, with the Portuguese also seeking to integrate the West Africans into their culture. Together with the emphasis on assimilation, the Portuguese administered their West African territory with a policy of paternalism.[38] The Portuguese were the most brutal of all the colonial masters in West Africa, as their decline as a global power pushed them to brutally exploit their colonies.[39] The term *assimilado* was given to those West Africans who had attained a certain level of "civilization," as defined by Portuguese

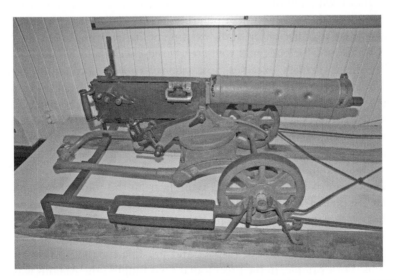

FIGURE 16.4   Maxim gun https://commons.wikimedia.org/wiki/File:Maxim_m_1905_Mikkeli _2.JPG.

standards, and were qualified to become Portuguese citizens.[40] In Guinea, for example, applicants for Portuguese citizenship had to demonstrate genuine dedication to Portugal. Like the French, the Portuguese administration did not have an indigenous court system.

The Impacts of Colonial Rule

Colonial rule was a double-edged sword that produced some positive impacts in West Africa, but the adverse effects outweighed them.[41] Moreover, the subjugation of a people hitherto independent and autonomous could not have happened without dire consequences. Although colonial rule ended over 50 years ago, its legacy can still be felt. The most profound and immediate result of colonial rule was the emergence of new political entities that evolved into modern-day West African nation-states.[42] While existing West African states and societies had lost their sovereignty, new sovereign states emerged following the region's decolonization. The borders of the post-independent West African states were patterned after those of the imperial nations from whom they inherited their systems of government. This was achieved by "sharing the imposition of artificially created nation-states and state structures developed through coercive mechanisms."[43]

The colonialists merged different societies with varying cultural backgrounds and religions, resulting in a lopsided arrangement attributed to the ethnic conflicts in modern nation-states.[44] For example, Nigeria's structural unevenness can be traced to the amalgamation of the northern and southern protectorates, as the former was twice the size of the latter.[45] The amalgamation was to enable effective administration in both protectorates, but the British amalgamated only the formal political structures and not the people, laying the foundation for future intergroup conflicts in Nigeria.[46] The situation was similar in other West African nation-states, especially the former British colonies. The colonial policies of the British did not advance Pan-Africanism within their colonies; rather, they brought ethnic division to the surface[47] because, as much as the populations had been brought together under one rule, no effort was made to integrate them.

Colonial rule led to a disruption of the existing political arrangements in West Africa. Precolonial states and societies had well-structured checks and balances systems, curtailing the traditional rulers' excesses. Since the rulers were accountable to the people, they could be deposed if they became unpopular. With the advent and imposition of colonial rule, they became more interested in serving the colonial masters rather than their constituents and enforced colonial policies that put them at a disadvantage. The presence of colonial authorities also encouraged traditional rulers to practice injustice and corruption.

Furthermore, colonial rule created a new category of native chiefs, sometimes ordinary people, who derived their authority entirely from the colonial masters, and other policies that weakened existing indigenous systems of government. Some states and societies that were acquired by force had their leaders deposed, and their successors were installed by the colonialists to carry out their bidding. This disruption in political arrangements engendered a loss of respect and prestige for the traditional rulers and their positions. For example, in the precolonial Oyo Empire, the Alaafin was referred to as *alase ikeji orisa* (second to the gods), but their near divinity status became inalterably degraded once they began to dance to the tune of the colonialists.[48]

Colonial rule also distorted the pattern of urbanization. The social amenities put in place by the colonialists were concentrated in particular central locations, forcing many people from the hinterlands to migrate into the urban centers where these amenities were established. This widened the gap in the standard of living between the urban and rural areas and caused overuse and overcrowding of the urban centers.[49] Additionally, it led to the rapid spread of infectious diseases, poor hygiene conditions, rising social offenses, and other ills. Poor management of these issues still constitutes a major problem in West Africa.

Virtually all aspects of people's lives were affected by colonial rule. Medically, colonial rule influenced native healing practices. Among the Asante in the Gold Coast, the indigenous medical practitioners attempted to modernize their medical practices as required by the colonialists, spurring the formation of indigenous healers' societies.[50] One such group was the Society of African Herbalists, formed on December 12, 1931, at Sekondi.[51] The colonial administration had dismissed the indigenous medical practitioners as unprofessional charlatans because they used religious and magical practices in their healing, which the colonialists discounted. Meanwhile, societies were formed to help improve their medical practices and reputations.

Infrastructure development was also affected, with the colonial era witnessing the construction of infrastructure aimed at aiding colonial administration. Specifically, fostering trade was the utmost priority, so they built internal infrastructure that facilitated the transportation and export of raw materials to Europe and the importation of produced goods into the colonies from the coast. These construction projects, such as railways and roads, were strategically built to connect the hinterlands and coastal markets, but not between inland communities within the colonies,[52] leading to a distortion of transportation in West Africa. The developed transport system network consisted primarily of seaports and railways, whereas inland road networks were left undeveloped. Not only did this hinder intergroup relations between West African societies, but it also reduced the overall quality of life and prevented agricultural integration within the colonies.

Western education and civilization have been argued to be positive aspects of colonial rule, and, on a superficial level, this would appear to be true. When examined critically, colonial education was a limited formal model designed to produce technocrats, interpreters, and administrative staff but not directed toward industrialization or to promote technological advancements. Colonial education had no roots in West African cultures, leading to a deviation from the native system of indigenous education. Some people who were skilled craftsmen, weavers, carvers, sculptors, or other tradesmen abandoned—though not willingly—their indigenous crafts and skills in favor of education focused on reading, writing, and arithmetic.[53]

Also, colonial rule undermined traditional religions. Missionary activities increased with the establishment of colonial rule and converts gave up their traditional religions and converted to Christianity.[54] Devotion to the local deities was minimized, while Christian gatherings were fostered. Although the missionaries were discouraged from proselytizing in some areas, they still succeeded in spreading Christianity to many parts of the region, reshaping its culture up to the present.

Additionally, not only did colonial rule and the colonial era distort the nature of the precolonial economy, but it also halted its growth. The economy was restructured to benefit the colonialists, and emphasis was laid on the extraction of raw materials in high demand in Europe.[55] The colonialists also ensured the production of certain foods and spices that could produce lucrative profits through exportation. The production of these goods for external markets made it difficult for rural areas to produce enough food to match the needs of the urban centers. A direct result of this was an increase in crop production in the colonies for export into the imperial country.[56] The imposition of colonial rule drastically changed the role of West Africans in the international economy. It made them primary producers of raw materials for industrialized nations, also becoming consumers of manufactured goods in Europe.

This was the situation up till the end of colonial rule, and it continued after decolonization, with West African nation-states still relying on the importation of industrial goods from Europe, and now from Asia in the present day. The colonialists made little to no attempts to industrialize West Africa, thereby hampering its development and perpetually making it a dependent economy.[57] If they had been left to industrialize and produce finished goods rather than only extract raw materials, there would have been a much more limited market for European goods. The agricultural economy was also controlled. The colonialists deliberately chose what cash crops the farmers should cultivate based on their goals. In Nigeria, it was essentially palm oil;[58] in The Gambia and Senegal, groundnuts; cocoa in the Gold Coast; and rubber in Guinea. After independence, West Africans continued to produce these crops even without the dictates of the colonial masters, and this heavy dependence on cash crops hindered and prevented a diversification of their internal economies.[59] As the production of food crops diminished in later years, food had to be imported from abroad (Figure 16.5).

Colonial rule established a monetized economy. By the 1930s, a new measure of wealth was introduced, based on physical cash rather than the quantity of produce or animals owned.[60] The introduction of this type of economy led to the emergence of banking activities and tremendously expanded trade between colonial West Africa and

FIGURE 16.5   Cocoa beans https://commons.wikimedia.org/wiki/File:Cocoa-1580724.jpg.

European countries. Hopkins described this as, "The completion of the integration of West Africa into the economy of the industrial world through the creation of conditions which gave Europeans and Africans both the means and the incentive to expand and diversify legitimate commerce."[61] Unfortunately, the West African economy benefited less from this change. The trading companies who regulated the prices of exported and imported goods accrued to themselves profits that came with the enormous trade. West African economy became increasingly tied to that of Europe in a disadvantageous and exploitative manner.

Notably, colonial rule did not always encourage intra-African trade. Precolonial West Africans traveled short and long distances to trade among themselves, fostering inter-group relations. With the advent of colonial rule, such business exchanges were reduced in some areas.[62] According to Rodney, "the arbitrary political boundaries of each colony were generally taken to mean the limit of the economies."[63] West Africans did not trade directly with China and India, preventing them from creating new links.

New socioeconomic and political classes emerged under colonial rule, "include[ing] European comprador bourgeoisie, African petty bourgeoisie, proletariat and the peasant."[64] The comprador bourgeoisie was a category of middle-class Africans affiliated with Europeans, while the petty bourgeoisie was made up of the semi-independent peasantry and mini-scale traders. The proletariat included the new urban workers, just as peasants stood at the bottom of the new hierarchy. The petty African bourgeoisie bridged the colonialists and the indigenous people.[65] They had an inextricable link with the European comprador bourgeoisie and also took over power from the colonialists at independence and maintained the status quo of the exploitation of the working class. The severe oppression, marginalization, and impoverishment of West Africans by the petty bourgeoisie are offshoots of colonial rule and persist in present-day West African nation-states.

Conclusion

Exploitation was the basis of colonial rule, and this caused more harm than good. Things termed the gains of colonial rule, such as education, infrastructure, and other forms of development, were by-products of colonial rule that came about not because the colonialists had the best interests of West Africans at heart but because they were necessary for the smooth administration of their colonies. Moreover, Western education was not introduced into all parts and regions of West Africa. In colonial Nigeria, for example, the British colonialists restricted the missionaries' activities and fostered Arabic education in Northern Nigeria. This effort to preserve the north from extraneous influences led to a disparity in the educational level between Northern and Southern Nigeria and has continued to be a major factor in the lingering north-south divisions in Nigeria.[66] Colonial rule was dictatorial and was implemented through force and tactics passed down to postcolonial West African leaders. The legacies of colonial rule live on in post-independent West African nation-states, leaving them to inherit its evils. Colonial rule "greatly impacted their way of administration which is highly autocratic."[67]

It is imperative to note that some Europeans were not favorably disposed to colonial rule. In J. A. Hobson's work, he criticizes imperialism as a social injustice.[68] According to him, if income distribution in the colonies were equal, it would increase the standard of living and create more markets for surplus capital in the home country. A French account, *Colonial Crimes* in 1911, describes a common opposition:

> I had a dream: at last there existed on this earth justice for all subject races and conquered peoples. Tired of being despoiled, pillaged, suppressed and massacred ... [they] drove their oppressors ... And forgetting that I was French—which is nothing—I remembered only one thing: that I was a man—which is everything—and I felt an indescribable joy in the depth of my being.[69]

Eventually, this dream was realized as West Africans fought to end colonial rule and gain their independence and freedom from the colonialists. The transition period from colonial rule to independence was not easy, but ultimately, they had victory. The decolonization period began after the end of the Second World War,[70] and beginning from colonial rule, began to be terminated, although not successfully, by way of dismantling the colonial institutions.

DEEP DIVE

Assignment 1

Objective

The objective of this assignment is to ensure that students complete the reading of Chapter 16 and make them understand how European colonizers promoted changes.

Method

Students will be expected to write a short note in response to the question.

Reading Comprehension

Describe the meaning of "making Frenchmen out of Africans." Was this ideology successful in granting Africans economic opportunity and equality? Compare this concept to the definition of "*évolué*." How are they similar?

Assignment 2

Objective

The objective of this assignment is to ensure that students complete the reading of Chapter 16 and to encourage them to pursue outside research to understand the impact of colonial rule.

Method

Students will be expected to conduct research and write a short note in response to the question.

Reading Comprehension and Research

What are some of the lingering effects of colonial politics and economy? How have they influenced identity politics and conflicts within the continent?

Notes

1 Michael Crowder, *Colonial West Africa: Collected Chapters* (Hove: Psychology Press, 1978), 11.
2 Lewis Gann and Peter Duignan, *Colonialism in Africa, 1870–1960*, vol. 5, *A Bibliographical Guide to Colonialism in Sub-Saharan Africa* (London: Cambridge University Press, 1969), 19.
3 Helen Tilley, *Africa as a Living Laboratory: Empire, Development and the Problem of Scientific Knowledge, 1870–1950* (Chicago: The University of Chicago Press, 2011).
4 Adu Boahen, ed. *General History of Africa*, vol. 7, *Africa Under Colonial Domination 1880–1935* (Berkeley: University of California Press, 1990), 312.
5 Stephen Ocheni and Basil C. Nwankwo, "Analysis of Colonialism and Its Impact in Africa," *Cross-Cultural Communication* 8, no. 3 (2012): 46–54.
6 Roger G. Thomas, "Forced Labour in British West Africa: The Case of the Northern Territories of the Gold Coast 1906–1927," *The Journal of African History* 14, no. 1 (1973): 79–103.
7 John W. Cell, *Hailey: A Study in British Imperialism, 1872–1969* (Cambridge: Cambridge University Press, 1992).
8 Walter I. Ofonagoro, *The Currency Revolution in Southern Nigeria 1880–1948* (Los Angeles: African Studies Center, 1976).
9 Michelle Gordon, *Extreme Violence and the 'British Way': Colonial Warfare in Perak, Sierra Leone and Sudan* (London: Bloomsbury Academic, 2020).
10 Barbara Busha and Josephine Maltby, "Taxation in West Africa: Transforming the Colonial Subject into the 'Governable Person,'" *Critical Perspectives on Accounting* 15, no. 1 (2004): 5–34.
11 Lewis H. Gann and Peter Duignan, *The Rulers of British Africa, 1870–1914* (London: Croom Helm, 1978).
12 Anthony Kirk-Greene, *Britain's Imperial Administrators, 1858–1966* (London: Palgrave Macmillan, 2000), 125–163.
13 Ocheni and Nwankwo, "Analysis of Colonialism," 315.
14 Liya Palagashvili, "African Chiefs: Comparative Governance under Colonial Rule," *Public Choice* 174 (2018): 277–300.
15 Elizabeth Isichei, *History of West Africa Since 1800* (Teaneck: Holmes & Meier Publishers, 1977), 201.
16 Michael Crowder and Obaro Ikime, eds. *West African Chiefs: Their Changing Status under Colonial Rule and Independence* (New York: African Publishing Corporation), 255–270.
17 Frederick J. D. Lugard, *The Dual Mandate in British Tropical Africa* (London: Routledge, 1965).
18 Isichei, *History of West Africa*, 204.
19 Robert Heussler, *The British in Northern Nigeria* (Oxford: Oxford University Press, 1968).
20 Adiele E. Afigbo, *The Warrant Chiefs: Indirect Rule in Southeastern Nigeria, 1891–1929* (London: Longman, 1972).
21 Isichei, *History of West Africa*, 206.
22 Felicia I. Abaraonye, "The Women's War of 1929 in South-Eastern Nigeria," in *Women and Revolution: Global Expressions*, ed. Marie J. Diamond (Netherlands: Kluwer Academic Publishers, 1998), 109–132.
23 Magbaily C. Fyle, *Historical Dictionary of Sierra Leone* (Lanham: Scarecrow Press, 2006), xxi.

24 Daron Acemoglu, Isaías Chaves, Philip Osafo-Kwaako and James Robinson, "Indirect Rule and State Weakness in Africa: Sierra Leone in Comparative Perspective," in *African Successes, Vol. 4: Sustainable Growth*, eds. Sebastian Edwards, Simon Johnson and David N. Weil (Chicago: University of Chicago Press, 2016), 343–370.

25 Jonathan Derrick, "The 'Native Clerk' in Colonial West Africa," *African Affairs* 82, no. 326 (1983): 61–74.

26 Martin D. Lewis, "One Hundred Million Frenchmen: The 'Assimilation' Theory in French Colonial Policy," *Comparative Studies in Society and History* 4, no. 2 (1962): 129–153.

27 Tony Chafer, "Teaching Africans to be French?: France's 'Civilising Mission' and the Establishment of a Public Education System in French West Africa, 1903–30," *Africa: Rivista trimestrale di studi e documentazione dell'Istituto italiano per l'Africa e l'Oriente* 56, no. 2 (2001): 190–209.

28 Elise Huillery, "History Matters: The Long Term Impact of Colonial Public Investments in French West Africa," *American Economic Journal: Applied Economics* 1, no. 2 (2009): 176–215.

29 Huillery, "History Matters: The Long Term Impact of Colonial Public Investments in French West Africa."

30 William B. Cohen, *Rulers of Empire: The French Colonial Service in Africa, 1880–1960* (California: Hoover Institution Press, 1971).

31 Isichei, *History of West Africa*, 203.

32 Isichei, *History of West Africa*.

33 Raymond F. Betts, *Assimilation and Association in French Colonial Theory, 1890–1914* (New York: Columbia University Press, 1961).

34 Michael Crowder, "Indirect Rule: French and British Style," *Africa: Journal of the International African Institute* 34, no. 3 (1964): 197–205.

35 Crowder, "Indirect Rule: French and British Style," 197–205.

36 Crowder and Ikime, *West African Chiefs*, xviii.

37 Michael Crowder, *Colonial West Africa*.

38 Allen Isaacman, "Coercion, Paternalism and the Labour Process: The Mozambican Cotton Regime 1938–1961," *Journal of Southern African Studies* 18, no. 3 (1992): 488.

39 Ngozi Kamalu, "British, French, Belgian and Portuguese Models of Colonial Rule and Economic Developments in Africa," *Annals of Global History* 1, no. 1 (2019): 37–47.

40 William Minter, *Portuguese Africa and the West* (New York: Monthly Review Press, 1973), 20.

41 Jean Suret-Canale, *The Effects of Colonialism on African Society* (South Africa: South African Communist Party, 1962), 52–60.

42 Nathan Nunn, "The Legacy of Colonialism: A Model of Africa's Underdevelopment," *Occasional Paper Series* 2, no. 1 (2003).

43 Jo-Ansie van Wyk, "Political Leaders in Africa: Presidents, Patrons or Profiteers?" *Occasional Chapter Series* 2, no. 1 (2007): 7.

44 Emmanuel M. Gbenenye, "African Colonial Boundaries and Nation-building," *Inkanyiso: Journal of Humanities and Social Sciences* 8, no. 2 (2016): 117–124.

45 Jacob F. Ade Ajayi, *Milestones in Nigerian History* (London: Longman, 1962), 36.

46 Ngozika A. Obi-Ani, Paul Obi-Ani, and Mathias C. Isiani, "The Mistake of 1914: 100 Years After?" *Nsukka Journal of the Humanities* 24, no. 2 (2016): 27–35.

47 Michael Crowder, "Colonial Rule in West Africa: Factor for Division or Unity," *Civilisations* 14, no. 3 (1964): 167–182.

48 Joseph A. Atanda, "The Changing Status of the Alaafin of Oyo under Colonial Rule and Independence," in *West African Chiefs: Their Changing Status under Colonial Rule and Independence*, eds. Michael Crowder and Obaro Ikime (New York: Africana Publishing Corporation, 1970), 212–230.

49 Muritala M. Olalekan, "Urban Livelihood in Lagos 1861–1960," *Journal of the Historical Society of Nigeria* 20 (2011): 193–200.

50 Samuel Adu-Gyamfi, "A Historical Study of the Impact of Colonial Rule on Indigenous Medical Practices in Asante: A Focus on Colonial and Indigenous Disease Combat and Prevention Strategies in Kumase, 1902–1957" (Ph.D. diss., Kwame Nkrumah University of Science and Technology, 2010), 102.

51 Adu-Gyamfi, "A Historical Study."
52 Joshua Dwayne Settles, "The Impact of Colonialism on African Economic Development" (Thesis Projects, University of Tennessee Honours, 1996).
53 Ocheni and Nwankwo, "Analysis of Colonialism."
54 Tugume Lubowa, "Attitudes of Christian Missionaries Towards African Traditional," *African Journal of History and Culture* 7, no. 10 (2015): 193–199.
55 Eno J. Usoro, "Colonial Economic Development Planning in Nigeria, 1919–1939: An Appraisal," *Nigerian Journal of Economic and Social Studies* 19, no. 1 (1977): 121–141.
56 Usoro, "Colonial Economic Development."
57 Ocheni and Nwankwo, "Analysis of Colonialism," 56.
58 Noah Echa Attah, "Nigerian Oil Palm Industry, 1920–1950: A Study in Imperialism," *African Historical Review* 46, no. 1 (2014): 1–21.
59 Boahen, *General History of Africa*, 793.
60 Boahen, *General History of Africa*, 791.
61 Anthony Hopkins, *An Economic History of West Africa*, 2nd ed. (London: Routledge, 2020).
62 Anthony I. Nwabughuogu, "From Wealthy Entrepreneurs to Petty Traders: The Decline of African Middlemen in Eastern Nigeria, 1900–1950," *Journal of African History* 23, no. 3 (1982): 365–379.
63 Walter Rodney, *How Europe Underdeveloped Africa* (London: Bogle-L'Ouverture Publications, 1972), 795.
64 Ocheni and Nwankwo, "Analysis of Colonialism."
65 Stephen Thornton, "The Struggle for Profit and Participation by an Emerging African Petty-bourgeoisie in Bulawayo, 1893–1933," *Societies of Southern Africa* 9 (1980): 70.
66 Eyiuche I. Olibie, Gloria O. Eziuzo, and Chika P. Enueme, "Inequalities in Nigerian Education Sector: Some Perspectives for Improvement," *IOSR Journal of Research & Method in Education* 3, no. 6 (2013): 7–14.
67 Endalcachew Bayeh, "The Political and Economic Legacy of Colonialism in the Post-Independence African States," *International Journal in Commerce, IT & Social Sciences* 2, no. 2 (2015).
68 John A. Hobson, *Imperialism: A Study* (London: Allen & Unwin, 1938).
69 Isichei, *History of West Africa*, 200.
70 David Birmingham, *The Decolonization of Africa* (London: University College London, 1995).

17

WORLD WARS

West Africa in World War I (1914–1919)

Given that the First World War did not end all wars and enmity in Europe, a second war was imminent and inevitable. The British recruited over 80,000 West African men during the second war, while the French recruited over 100,000.[1] The outcome of the Second World War was more intense than the first and had more effects on West Africans, though both wars shattered the myths of European supremacy. At the end of the First World War, West Africa was re-partitioned, and the colonies of Germany, the aggressor, were given to the victors of the war.[2] Meanwhile, the end of the Second World War paved the way for nationalist movements and increased the political consciousness of West Africans.[3]

The assassination of Archduke Franz Ferdinand, the Austrian Crown Prince, and his wife, Sophie, by a Bosnian Serb student, Gavrilo Princip, on June 28, 1914, was the spark that ignited the flames of war in Europe in the early twentieth century.[4] A direct result of this was the declaration of war on Serbia on July 28 by Austria-Hungary, who had the support of Germany. Britain and France were then dragged into the war when they pledged support for Serbia; likewise, other European powers were brought into the conflict upon supporting Serbia or Austria-Hungary. At the outbreak of the war in Europe, Britain and France had to determine a plan of action concerning the strategic German colonies of Togo and Cameroon. Togo possessed the Kamina wireless transmitter, which was crucial for communication, while Cameroon possessed a deep-water port.

Germany's attempts to prevent military confrontations in these regions were unsuccessful as Britain and France were convinced that targeting these areas to seize control was vital to defeating Germany. As a result, Togoland and Cameroon became battlegrounds during World War I.[5] The colonial powers in West Africa mobilized and recruited West Africans to fight on behalf of European interests. Germany militarized its colonies, while France also made strategic calculations to depend on its holdings.[6] In

DOI: 10.4324/9781003198260-21

the British colonies, West Africans were drafted into two military divisions—the West African Frontier Force and the West African Regiment.[7] The West African Frontier Force comprised mostly Hausa groups from Northern Nigeria, while the West African regiment was stationed in Sierra Leone and was part of an official army. The Frontier Force comprised over 7,500 soldiers, with Nigerians numbering over 5,000.[8] West Africans numbering 17,000 from Nigeria were recruited to fight in Cameroon and East Africa by September 1918, and 4,000 to fight along the Nigerian-Cameroonian border and within Nigeria.[9] Recruitment methods varied from colony to colony, but in most cases usually involved force. For example, some West Africans willingly volunteered in the central and western parts of the Gold Coast, although most of the soldiers from the area were conscripted.[10]

Non-native visitors and native residents of the region were at risk of being captured and recruited forcefully. Also, colonial officers often forced and threatened traditional chiefs to provide soldiers for the army. Some chiefs were, however, uncooperative, like the rulers in Zungeru and Yorubaland, who blatantly refused to comply with the British directives.[11] Marriages were fast-tracked to secure the enlistment of young men into the army, and intending grooms were additionally offered incentives. For example, "every man, who wanted an unmarried girl who wanted him, was assured of a favourable decision before the Commissioner even if the girl's father was reluctant to part with her."[12]

Despite all these attempts, some prospective soldiers were still not persuaded to fight. In fact, in reaction to the recruitment and conscription efforts, many West Africans committed to some measures of revolting and rebelling. To these individuals, the option of being cocoa farmers was preferable to fighting in an army, while others who did not revolt fled into the forests to prevent being conscripted. In Nigeria, some traditional leaders sought to use the recruitment of soldiers to their advantage. For example, the Emir of Yola, who wanted to control the northern part of Cameroon, supplied soldiers to participate in the British onslaught in Garoua.[13] Other chiefs who provided soldiers for the army did so forcefully and intentionally.

Unlike the British, the French adopted a fiercer and more formal policy of recruitment.[14] They coerced West Africans into the military, and in response, many people revolted and fled into neighboring colonies. One such revolt nearly cost France its colonies in West Africa.[15] Colonial officials and traditional chiefs worked tirelessly together to recruit soldiers into the army, targeting all aspects of their intended soldiers' lives if they resisted. Family members of uncooperative potential recruits were imprisoned while the livestock and crop produce were destroyed. Colonial officials strategically identified areas that had men eligible for military service, usually focusing on the interior, where the majority of the recruits came from.

Between August 1914 and October 1915, France recruited over 32,000 West Africans, and in October of the same year, the French government declared that an additional 50,000 soldiers would be recruited.[16] The French recruits were not given adequate training, leading to high death rates among them. In 1918, under Blaise Diagne, the first black African elected to the French Chamber of Deputies, France launched a successful recruitment drive using persuasive methods, resulting in 63,000 West Africans being recruited in August and mobilized to Togo and Cameroon for war with the Germans.[17] The Germans also recruited West Africans as soldiers to defend their colonies from the British and the French.[18] Karl Ebermaier, the governor of Cameroon, who sought to make amends for the colonial brutality in the region, issued a decree that was regarded as a "liberal piece of policy."[19] With this decree, recruitment began from the Beti area, especially in Yaounde. In letters circulated to the northern chiefs, colonial officials in Germany appealed to the sentiments of Muslims by declaring that the war was a religious one and that the Germans were fighting for the cause of Islam. With this, the Germans recruited thousands of Muslims into the army.

In other areas, the potential recruits were bribed, old recruits were rewarded with slaves, pillaging rights, and captured women, and some traditional rulers even used conscription as a means of punishment. When the Allies (Britain, France, and Belgium) invaded Cameroon, the climate and their unfamiliarity with the region's terrain worked against them. The campaign against the Germans lasted 18 months, and their major target areas were Douala, which was conquered on September 27, the capital of the port of Victoria, Buea, captured on November 15, 1914, and Garua, which was captured in June 1915.[20] Yaounde was captured next in 1916, after which the Germans retreated to Ntem, their base.

In Togoland, German forces could not defend themselves because their size was comparably smaller than that of their adversaries. The British and French troops numbered about 1,738 against the German force of about 1,500.[21] In addition to numerical superiority, the Allies, of which Portugal later became a member, had more advanced weapons. The governor of Togoland suggested to the Allies that the Africans be left out of the war and be prevented from seeing the Europeans fight themselves, as this would damage their prestige. However, this suggestion fell on deaf ears, and Togoland was invaded. Major Hans-Georg Von Doring, the governor, realizing his small force could not defend the whole of Togo, decided to concentrate his defense on the Kamina communication station. This effort was ultimately unsuccessful, and Togoland fell to the Allied forces.[22]

The impact of recruitment and war on West Africans cannot be overemphasized. A major impact of the recruitment efforts on West Africans was demographic imbalance.[23] In an attempt to evade capture, many West Africans crossed borders. For example, those in British West Africa crossed to French and Portuguese territories and vice-versa. The trend became popular to the extent that "[i]n February 1916, the Governor of Gambia reported to the Secretary of State that a large number of Senegalese, in particular, Diola from Casamance, had crossed into his territory."[24] Escapees from Upper Volta and Ivory Coast took refuge in the Gold Coast, while those from Niger and Dahomey took refuge in Nigeria. The nomadic people of Niger were relatively easily able to cross the border into Nigeria to avoid recruitment, while the district officers in Nigerian Borgu recorded large amounts of Dahomeyan Borgu in the region.

These demographic changes caused by an "exodus of population" affected the recruitment efforts and the colonial economy as farmers migrated and stopped working on the plantations in the colonies. The French appealed to the other colonial governments to send the escapees and deserters back,[25] an appeal that the British granted, though not wholeheartedly. The deserters in some areas, such as The Gambia, were arrested and sent back to the French territory, and in Asante, a proclamation permitting the deportation of the deserters was passed. However, in other instances, the British re-recruited these deserters, especially the Cameroonian escapees who fled from the Germans.

These escapees were recruited for logistic purposes, such as navigating the unknown Cameroonian terrain in the war against the Germans.

Recruiting the displaced Cameroonian refugees was a determining factor in the victory of the Allied forces. By 1918, in the Gold Coast, there were about 17,000 immigrants from neighboring French colonies,[26] and the British employed them in the local farming and mining industries while others were drafted by the army. This emigration and immigration created a mass refugee problem in West Africa during the war, resulting in most of the escapees ending up homeless in bushes and forests.[27]

Resistance to military recruitment by subjects of the colonial government led to the execution of raids among the citizens. The raids, carried out by recruiting agents, stirred up organized opposition against the colonial governments and attempts to repress the resistance often resulted in the deaths of activists. In Southern Nigeria, for example, about 200 Igbo died in the brutally suppressed rebellion in 1915,[28] of which colonial officials maintained records. There were more revolts, political disruptions, and economic disturbances in the French colonies than in the British.[29] The Governor-General of French West Africa stated that:

> Out of the recruitment has resulted [in] ... unpopularity that has become universal from the very day when recruits were asked to serve in Europe and grim, determined, terrible revolts started against the white man, who had hitherto been tolerated, sometimes even loved, but who, transformed into a recruiting agent, had become a detested enemy.[30]

Revolts against French recruitment efforts and policies took place across the French colonies, "in Beledougou in 1915, in Western Volta in 1915/16, and in Northern Dahomey in 1915 and 1917."[31]

Military recruitment interfered in the economic transactions of the colonies and intensified the demand for labor and supply in West Africa. The laborers who worked in the mines, railways, roads, etc., and the farmers who worked on plantations and farms fled to avoid conscription, which disrupted agricultural production and adversely affected the colonial economy. Laborers were drafted into war out of necessity, and those targeted for substituting these new soldiers were all too often drafted themselves, leading to an imbalance in the supply and demand of necessities. The colonies and their European authorities experienced a reduction in the number of raw materials, cash, and food crops as the availability of workers in Europe and West Africa decreased. For instance, in the Gold Coast, the labor force from the mining sector fell from 17,400 to 10,800 from the beginning to the end of the First World War.[32] As a result of poor labor and low production, nearly all sectors of the colonial economy suffered throughout West Africa.

The war severely impacted the residents of the West African region.[33] It led to the destruction of land and property in some places, the spread of disease, as well as death, and economic hardship.[34] West African producers and merchants were confronted with the problem of searching for new markets. For example, prewar Germany imported large amounts of palm kernel from Sierra Leone and Nigeria, and cocoa from the Gold Coast. However, due to financial restrictions imposed by the war and the postwar reallocation of land and bans placed on trading, these colonies had to find new markets for their exports. The search for new markets was made even more difficult by the reduction in the price of raw materials. The war wrought tremendous changes in the region, "whether in the form of price control, requisition of food crops, compulsory cultivation of crops, recruitment of labour for essential projects or allocation of shipping space."[35] The colonies confronted issues brought on by the imposition of European interests in their territories.

West Africa in the Interwar Years (1919–1939)

The period between 1919 and 1939 in West Africa were years of replenishment for European colonial governments. Joost van Vollenhoven, the Governor-General of French West Africa, stated in 1917 that "the African empire is poor in men but rich in products, so let us use its miserable population for food supply during the war and for postwar times."[36] Colonial governments in West Africa anticipated an era of peaceful administration in which they could continue the economic exploitation of the region. These years were the most distinctive of colonial rule in West Africa; new policies of administration were formed and implemented with the end of the war.

The indirect rule system, which was perfected in Nigeria, was introduced into the other three British colonies. During this period, France abandoned the policy of assimilation, which was very difficult to practice and resulted in only a handful of West Africans being able to attain French citizenship, and adopted the policy of association. However, the policy of association was never put into practice in West Africa due to the economic depression that came in the 1920s and 1930s.[37] Therefore, in the interwar years, the French colonies in West Africa did not have a universal policy of administration, though officials followed similar guidelines that characterized their administrative policies.

Britain and France consolidated themselves in West Africa by taking control of Togoland and Cameroon, the former German colonies.[38] Togo was partly administered with French West Africa under the mandate of the League of Nations, which was established in Europe after the war, to maintain a balance of power in Europe and prevent the outbreak of another war. From 1934 to 1936, however, Togo, which was previously governed as an independent entity, was administered conjointly with Dahomey, and from 1939 to 1945, it was under the control of the Governor-General of Dakar in Senegal.[39] On March 31, 1916, Cameroon was officially split between France and Britain, with France getting four-fifths of the region.[40] During the interwar years in Portuguese West Africa, the colonial policy was similar to the French administration though it was more centralized. However, Portugal's internal economic and political problems prevented the effective administering of the colonies (Figure 17.1).

In the West African colonies, the policy of the colonial economy was primarily laissez-faire during this interwar period.[41] The colonial governments encouraged but did not directly interfere with trade. Their central principle was to promote the cultivation and export of cash crops, increase the importation and consumption of manufactured goods from Europe, and, most importantly, conduct trade only with the metropolitan nations in Europe. To ensure these objectives were met, the governments introduced certain measures to ensure the perpetual domination of a handful of foreign companies. Alongside the export–import trade between the governing nation and the colony, the administration also fostered internal trade. Locally manufactured goods, such as woven clothes, household equipment, and subsistence crops, were bought and sold internally.

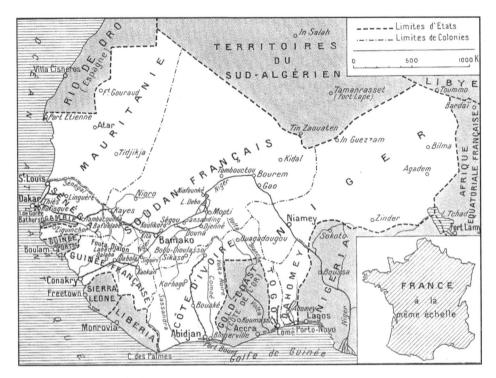

FIGURE 17.1   Map of French West Africa on the eve of war (1936) https://commons.wikimedia
.org/wiki/File:AOFMap1936.jpg.

While the colonial governments were affected by the war, the people also had their fair share of economic and social problems. The reintegration and incorporation of ex-soldiers into non-military life and affairs were difficult, especially for those not literate.[42] Those who were literate or who had gained some technical skills were employed by the government or commercial institutions. The colonial government in Nigeria tried to ameliorate the situation by introducing a land settlement plan, but this plan was unsuccessful as ex-soldiers who had explored the world and participated in wars had little to no interest in land and farming activities. Sierra Leone's situation was not different. The 1921 census reported that the former soldiers who had seen the attractions of the "civilized world" refused to return to their unexciting and boring lives and preferred to remain in the colony's capital.[43]

Lord Lugard, the Governor-General, expressed his concerns that these former soldiers might pose a threat to the colonial authorities since they had learned to handle rifles and other weapons. However, this social problem of reintegration did not constitute any large-scale social disturbance, as the issues primarily resolved themselves without any upheaval. In French West Africa, the reintegration of the former soldiers was less problematic than in the British colonies.[44] Compulsory tax payments made former soldiers seek any form of employment, especially land work. Moreover, fewer jobs for the literate increased competition among the soldiers for employment.

Furthermore, West Africans were confronted with problems as a result of the global depression that hit Europe in the 1930s.[45] International trade plummeted, which meant a reduction in the number of exported products bought in the international market for West Africa. Davidson states that:

> In 1929 the total value of the export-import trade of the four British West African colonies was £56 million; by 1931 it had collapsed almost by half to £29 million ... The fourteen French West and Equatorial colonies (including the two 'mandated territories' of Cameroon and Togo) met the same hard fate. Their total export-import trade fell from £30 million in 1929 to less than £18 million in 1931.[46]

The reduction in the number of goods, products, and raw materials sold led to a fall in prices, which resulted in a reduction in the wages of the workers and producers in West Africa. In some cases, workers could not even be paid, resulting in high unemployment rates. The great depression was severe, laying the foundation for the Second World War, and did not end until the 1940s in some colonies.[47] As a result of the economic hardships, European nations resumed expansionist policies and imperialistic agendas, resulting in another World War in Europe.

West Africa in World War II (1939–1945)

On September 1, 1939, Germany invaded Poland, marking the start of the Second World War in Europe.[48] Germany then invaded Belgium, Holland, and France and unsuccessfully attempted to invade the USSR and Britain. It then partnered with Italy and Japan to form the Axis powers.[49] West Africans were again dragged into the war when their colonial rulers were attacked. However, unlike the First World War, West Africa only served as a channel for conveying troops (and others arriving from Europe), provisions, and other supplies to other African regions while battles were carried out in Ethiopia and parts of North Africa.[50]

With the experience of recruiting colonial subjects from the First World War, recruitment strategies were organized into three forms, with West Africans serving as combatants or non-combatants. They were "coercive recruitment, conscription and compulsory secondment and voluntary enlistment."[51] Coercive methods took the form of raids and kidnappings organized with the help of traditional chiefs, who had recruitment targets to meet, with captives being forced to the European fronts. Once soldiers were recruited, they served as either non-combatants, clerks, officials, or combatants and soldiers sent to the battlegrounds.

In British West Africa, 167,000 men were recruited and grouped into seven military units or brigades.[52] One group was sent to Sierra Leone; one was deployed to the Gambia; two were sent to the Gold Coast; three were placed in Nigeria and further classified as 81st and 82nd divisions.[53] These soldiers fought and repelled the Italians who attacked Somaliland and drove out the final fascist Italian army from East Africa. In 1939, the British colonial office opposed the recruitment of soldiers forcefully because it was an ineffective means of obtaining reliable soldiers for war.[54] As a result, conscription was done to fill non-combatant roles and services that required educated men who would not voluntarily give themselves up for military service.

Additionally, convicts and vagrants were conscripted into the army to punish those arrested for illegal mining in Sierra Leone. Likewise, in the Gold Coast in 1943, about 400 Bathurst "corner boys" were captured and taken to an army camp, while in March 1944, some eight boys, believed to be the ringleaders of the King's College strike, were conscripted.[55] In the northern parts of the Gold Coast, incentives in the form of regular salaries were given to the traditional chiefs to facilitate the recruitment of West Africans. Recruitment into the army in the Gold Coast was not limited to the common people, but the sons of chiefs and rulers were also pushed into military service to supplement the authority of their fathers. The compulsory secondment was integrated into laws passed in wartime, like the Defense Regulation of the Colonies and the Compulsory Service Bill in the Gold Coast.[56] Recruited soldiers were trained, both fighters and non-combatants, although training was often unsuccessful owing to language problems and insufficient supplies.

British officials frequently raided the Gold Coast, arresting young and agile men and transporting them to military camps while also trying to convince young men to enlist voluntarily and fight for their colonizers.[57] Officials visited their communities and organized drills, parades, sporting events, and other activities to serve as incentives and recruitment opportunities. In 1941, recruitment spilled into the everyday social activities of the colonial residents, and mobile cinema centers urged the people to join the military. Newspaper adverts encouraged literate men to sign up, and radio programs recounted the courageous deeds of West African soldiers to motivate potential recruits.[58] Prominent journalists hosted talk shows, musicians composed and sang songs to motivate people to sign up, and soldiers, for example, in Abeokuta, even toured the area performing drills, hoping to attract recruits (Figure 17.2).

Through the chiefs, Northern Nigeria had the highest number of recruits in Nigeria. For instance, the Emir of Kano actively assisted in the recruitment efforts. Also, soldiers' salaries and allowances prompted young men to enlist. A private in the West African army received one shilling per day, while a British private received two shillings. Educated combatants also received higher pay, and non-educated combatants received the lowest.[59] Separation allowances or allotments were also paid to the wives of West African recruits who became soldiers. The West African soldiers eventually discovered this disparity in payment, resulting in anger and a policy change.

From 1942 onwards, technical recruits began to receive higher payments to draw more West Africans into military service.[60] Volunteers in the early years of the war signed up willingly because of their awareness of the evils of Nazism and fascism they had been exposed to. This was especially true of Nigerians who were enthusiastic about fighting for their colonial country. Donations were also made under different names to support the war effort. "Kano raised £10,270 in 1942, of which £5,000 was used to buy a Spitfire bearing the municipal name, while in August 1943, a Mosquito Bomber named *Nigeria* was purchased with £20,000 from the Win the War fund."[61]

In French West Africa, about 118,000 troops opted for military service during the 1939 and 1940 recruitment efforts, and only 20,000 were adequately trained and deemed fit for battle.[62] France's African army was disbanded under the armistice, and French West Africa did not have any military role in the war except for self-defense, as was the case with Vichy France. France's defeat and the establishment of the Vichy government alarmed the French administrators. Also, Britain was threatened by the neutrality of

FIGURE 17.2   John Henry, servant, at headquarters, 3rd Army Corps, Army of the Potomac
https://www.loc.gov/item/2018672351/.

the new French government and could not withstand the pressures from Germany to militarize Dakar and make it a base for an onslaught on Freetown. Therefore, the nation hastily increased its West African forces and began to prepare for a possible attack by fortifying its ports and airfields.

Undoubtedly, the war impacted West Africans from start to end, with its greatest impacts being the death of a large number of West Africans and the exposure of the weakness of colonial rule.[63] By the end of the war, colonial governments began to collapse with the rise of nationalist movements.[64] Many West African soldiers expected that the end of Nazi Germany would mean an end to colonial rule. West Africans experienced fighting alongside Europeans for two world wars. They had witnessed their faults and shortcomings, and this opened their eyes to the fact that Europeans were not superior to them.[65] In reality, not only had West Africans succeeded in some combats where Europeans failed, but there was an understanding that without the efforts and numbers supplied by the West African army, the Europeans would not have been as successful, if at all, against the Axis Powers.[66]

Evidently, the Second World War also affected West Africans psychologically. At the end of the war, the efforts of the African soldiers received little or no recognition and gratitude, stirring anger among a large number of soldiers who were forced into service and those who felt committed to their colonial overlords.[67] While European soldiers received awards for their bravery at the battlefront, African soldiers got tickets back home.[68] This contributed to their resolution and determination to fight for their freedom. After all, if they fought successfully against advanced European forces in the name of their colonial masters, they were invariably capable of fighting for their own countries' independence. Most of the soldiers increased their educational, technical, and military skills and began to embrace the idea of independence. They mastered the art of coordination and communication, which they employed in the colonies, and some of them who sent letters home expressed their desire for freedom.

In 1945, a Nigerian soldier who fought in India sent a letter to Herbert Macaulay, a preeminent nationalist: "We all overseas soldiers are coming back home with new ideas. We have been told what we fought for. That is 'freedom'. We want freedom, nothing but freedom."[69] Numerous letters were sent to various parts of West Africa from soldiers who had been exposed to a different kind of lifestyle that changed their lives for the better. They were determined to act on the exposure and experience they had acquired, unlike those who came back after the First World War. This war especially revealed the evils and injustices of colonial rule, which the now-returned soldiers sought to end.

Also, the war dealt a huge blow to the colonial powers economically and politically. France, a major colonial power, was defeated by the Germans in 1940, creating a division in the governing of France and its colonies.[70] The northern region of France was subsequently occupied and ruled by Nazi Germany, while the Vichy government was created in the southern region of France.[71] This government in France was neutral, and the French colonies ruled by the administration became uninvolved and neutral. Those who opposed the Vichy government established the "Free French Government"; not only did this defeat damage the prestige of France in Europe, but it also affected the administration of its colonies, as well as its relationship with other colonial governments in West Africa.[72] Some colonies supported the Vichy, some the Free French Government, and others were pro-Nazi.

The disruption in the relations between colonies created roadblocks to the development of the colonies and interrupted the lives of the residents. For example, plans to construct railways and roads to link the colonies and other parts of West Africa were interrupted by the armistice with Nazi Germany in June 1940.[73] Colonial governments also experienced difficulty regulating their economies and supplying resources to their own citizens. The administration of French West Africa, for instance, was disorganized, and the exportation and importation of food crops were reduced considerably. This forced the population to produce goods in large quantities, not only for export but also for internal trade, since they were prevented by British blockades from importing food because of differences in ideological support among colonial administrators. Small-scale companies and industries were, in turn, created to increase the production of these goods and were referred to as "import-substituting companies." As a result, the peasants who relied on the income from the export crops suffered the most. In Senegal, for example, the peasants suffered from income deprivation and lack of food, especially when the importation of rice, a staple food crop, was halted.

In contrast, weavers and ironworkers benefitted from the blockade of exports and imports. The difficulty faced by the people in the rural areas further intensified rural impoverishment, disrupted farming activities and family life, and pushed the people into the towns to seek better living opportunities. Beginning in 1940, the number of people living in towns increased rapidly.[74] This rural-to-urban migration was one of the demographic changes the war caused, in addition to the displacements and migration fostered by colonial and native recruitment efforts.[75] Though the Allies eventually won the war,

Britain incurred a heavy cost. It committed its support and resources to the war effort resulting in a less-than-optimal economic position and the displacement and deaths of many West African soldiers.

After the war, the two major colonial powers in West Africa (the British and the French) became weak, and two new world powers emerged—the USA and the USSR.[76] They were more interested in maintaining their new positions as world powers rather than procuring a position within the colonial systems. Eventually, this led to the clamor for the independence of Asian nation-states, which fueled the flames of nationalism in West Africa. The war also gave rise to President Franklin Delano Roosevelt and Winston Churchill's Atlantic Charter, which supported the independence cause of all peoples after the war.[77]

At the end of the Second World War, the ex-soldiers faced similar problems as the soldiers who returned from the First World War. For Coates, "While recruitment had occurred in several waves from the late 1930s onward, demobilization was concentrated into 18 months starting in August 1945; the vast majority of enlisted servicemen left the army at the war's end."[78] The prolonged mission of demobilization was due to various reasons, including the preferential treatment of British soldiers. British soldiers were transported from the battlefronts and war camps before the West Africans, while the latter were stranded in India. The reintegration of former soldiers back into society did not pose as much of a problem as it had after the First World War: "The Resettlement Act of 1945, and the Employment of Ex-Servicemen's Ordinance formed an ambitious blueprint for government intervention in the local economies to secure employment for returning soldiers by means of loans, quotas, and training."[79] Registration platforms were set up in Enugu, Kaduna, Ibadan, and other provincial centers.

Naturally, educated and skilled ex-soldiers got employed quicker and easier than uneducated combatants. These ex-soldiers settled into society and participated in societal activities, especially revolts, like the one organized in 1947 against a Yoruba chief. Ex-soldiers in the Gold Coast formed an "ex-servicemen association"—a Gold Coast Legion modeled after the Legion in Britain was formed in February 1945—called the Nigerian Ex-Servicemen's Welfare Association (NEWA).[80] These associations provided medical assistance to former soldiers, especially the disabled, and gave loans to start or fund businesses.[81] For example, NEWA gave loans to two former soldiers in Awka to acquire sewing machines to set up a sewing school. Although not all ex-soldiers benefitted from the programs of the associations, a good number of them leveraged the provided opportunities and established themselves. These former soldiers also played active roles in West Africans' independence struggles.[82]

Conclusion

West Africans made significant contributions to the First and Second World Wars. Despite their lack of formal or adequate training, the soldiers recruited turned out to be good. Several reports from European officers attested to the proficiency of the West African soldiers in the First World War. For instance, Brigadier General Crozier recorded the meeting he had with an officer from West Africa who informed him about the exceptional way the West African Frontier Front fought in Cameroon.[83] The Cameroon West African soldiers were exceptional, as they were recruited during the war and received little or no military training, yet they demonstrated military adeptness. The training centers that were set up provided insufficient and limited training. Despite losing the Cameroon campaign, they gave the Allied forces a good fight. According to Njung, "That Cameroon soldiers brought their personal experiences to bear on the war is one powerful piece of evidence for the importance of Africa to the history of the first world war and for the importance of the war to the history of Africa."[84]

The First World War changed West Africa and partly laid the foundation for the independence struggles that came after the Second World War. Isichei observes that the First World War "solved nothing, but directly paved the way to the Second World War."[85] Indeed, the harsh treatment given to Germany by the victors after the First World War, set the stage for the Second World War. However, the First World War did bear some significance; it arose from the expectations of freedom in West Africa, which were based on Woodrow Wilson's Fourteen Points speech. However, these expectations were not acted upon until the end of the Second World War.

At the end of the Second World War, West Africans realized that Europeans were not "higher races" as they had been made to believe. This was a major catalyst for the agitations to end colonial rule in West Africa. The Second World War further intensified West Africa's ties with the outside world. Although it started as a European war, it evolved into a war against racism and colonial rule. West Africans desired the same level of freedom and independence as European countries and were determined to fight for and gain this freedom, whatever the cost.[86]

DEEP DIVE

Assignment 1

Objective

The objective of this assignment is to ensure that students complete the reading of Chapter 17 and to get them to explain why the World Wars I and II had consequences for Africa.

Method

Students will be expected to write a short response to the question.

Reading Comprehension

How and why was World War II the catalyst for nationalist movements in Africa? How did it awaken a sense of entitlement to freedom and equality among many Africans?

Assignment 2

Discussion

How did African military involvement in European wars create and contribute to a greater sense of equality among Black and white people? Did it successfully combat the idea of European supremacy?

Objective

The objective of this assignment is to encourage students to think about the contradictory nature of Europeans seeing Africans as inferior and then recruiting them to fight alongside white soldiers.

Method

Students will be expected to have a group discussion (either in person or on the online discussion forum) to talk to their peers about the question. Each student would be expected to create a post and respond to at least one other student. If this were to take place in person, then it would simply be a class-wide discussion.

Notes

1 Judith Byfield, Carolyn Brown, Timothy Parsons and Ahmad Sikainga, eds. *Africa and World War II* (Cambridge: Cambridge University Press, 2015), xix.
2 Lawrence Sondhaus, *World War One: The Global Revolution* (Cambridge: Cambridge University Press, 2011), 457.
3 W. F. Gutteridge, "The Nature of Nationalism in British West Africa," *The Western Political Quarterly* 11, no. 3 (1958): 574–582.
4 Hew Strachan, *World War I: A History* (New York: Oxford University Press, 1998), 9.
5 F. J. Moberly, *Military Operations, Togoland and the Cameroons, 1914–1916* (London: H.M. Stationery Office, 1931).
6 J. F. Ade Ajayi and Michael Crowder, eds. *History of West Africa, Vol. 2* (London: Longman, 1971), 484.
7 Oluwafunminiyi Raheem and Oluyemisi A. Disu, "Fighting for Britain: Examining British Recruitment Strategies in Nigeria," in *Unknown Conflicts of the Second World War: Forgotten Fronts*, ed. Christopher Murray (London: Routledge, 2019).
8 George N. Njung, "West Africa," in *1914–1918-Online; International Encyclopedia of the First World War*, eds. Ute Daniel, Peter Gatrell, Oliver Janz, Heather Jones, Jennifer Keene, Alan Kramer, and Bill Nasson (Berlin: Freie Universität Berlin, 2014), 3.
9 Njung, "West Africa," 3.
10 Raheem and Disu, "Fighting for Britain."
11 Njung, "West Africa," 3.
12 Melvin Page and Andy Mckinlay, *Africa and the First World War* (New York: Springer, 1987), 161.
13 George N. Njung, "Soldiers of their Own: Honor, Violence, Resistance and Conscription in Colonial Cameroon during the First World War" (Ph.D. Dissertation University of Michigan, 2016), 26.
14 Myron Echenberg, "'Morts Pour La France'; The African Soldier in France during the Second World War," *The Journal of African History* 26, no. 4 (1985): 363–380.
15 Ajayi and Crowder, *History of West Africa*, 484.
16 Njung, "West Africa," 3.
17 Njung, "West Africa," 3.
18 Bill Humphrey, "Remembering East Africa's WWI Fallen," *Arsenal for Democracy*, July 5, 2015, https://arsenalfordemocracy.com/2015/07/05/remembering-east-africas-wwi-fallen/.
19 Mahon Murphy, *Colonial Captivity during the First World War: Internment and the Fall of the German Empire, 1914–1919* (Cambridge: Cambridge University Press, 2017), 124–148.
20 Ajayi and Crowder, *History of West Africa*, 491.

21 Ajayi and Crowder, *History of West Africa*, 486.
22 Tony Jaques, *Dictionary of Battles and Sieges: F-O* (Connecticut: Greenwood Press, 2007).
23 Chima J. Korieh, *Nigeria and World War II: Colonialism, Empire, and Global Conflict* (Cambridge: Cambridge University Press, 2020).
24 Ajayi and Crowder, *History of West Africa*, 498.
25 Ajayi and Crowder, *History of West Africa*, 499.
26 Njung, "West Africa," 9.
27 Byfield, Brown, Timothy and Sikainga, *Africa and World War II.*
28 Njung, "West Africa," 3.
29 Page and Mckinlay, *Africa and the First World War*, 163.
30 Christian Koller, "The Recruitment of Colonial Troops in Africa and Asia and Their Deployment in Europe During the First World War," *Immigrants & Minorities* 26, no. 1–2 (2008): 111–133.
31 Koller, "The Recruitment," 9.
32 Njung, "West Africa," 9.
33 De-Valera NYM Botchway and Kwame Osei Kwarteng, eds. *Africa and the First World War: Remembrance, Memories and Representations after 100 Years* (Newcastle upon Tyne: Cambridge Scholars Publishing, 2018).
34 Richard Rathbone, "World War I and Africa: Introduction," *The Journal of African History* 19, no. 1 (1978): 1–9.
35 Adu Boahen, ed. *General History of Africa*, vol 7, *Africa Under Colonial Domination 1880–1935* (Berkeley: University of California Press, 1990), 302.
36 Koller, "The Recruitment," 9.
37 Ajayi and Crowder, *History of West Africa*, 518.
38 Stuart W. Allan, "Anglo-French Co-operation in Togoland, 1914 Lieutenant G. M. Thompson and General Order No. 9 of the French West African Command," *Journal of the Society for Army Historical Research* 74, no. 298 (1996): 96–101.
39 Ajayi and Crowder, *History of West Africa*, 519.
40 Willibroad Dze-Ngwa, "The First World War and Its Aftermath in Cameroon: A Historical Evaluation of a Centenary, 1914–2014," *International Journal of Liberal Arts and Social Science* 3, no. 2 (2015): 83.
41 Michael Crowder, *Colonial West Africa* (Hove: Psychology Press, 1978), 244.
42 Emmanuel E. Mordi, "'We Cannot Suffer in Burma and Return to Face Trials in our Own Country': Demobilization of Nigerian Soldiers, 1943–1953," *Journal of African Military History* 4, no. 1–2 (2020): 97–132.
43 Ajayi and Crowder, *History of West Africa*, 512.
44 Sarah J. Zimmerman, "Living Beyond Boundaries: West African Servicemen in French Colonial Conflicts, 1908–1962" (Ph.D. diss., University of California, Berkeley, 2011).
45 Ian Brown, *The Economies of Africa and Asia in the Inter-war Depression* (London: Routledge, 1989).
46 Basil Davidson, *Modern Africa: A Social and Political History*, 3rd ed. (New York: Longman, 1994), 51.
47 John E. Moser, *Global Great Depression and the Coming of World War II* (New York: Routledge, 2015).
48 John Skates and Wayne Dzwonchyk, *A Brief History of the US Army in World War II* (Washington, DC: Centre of Military History, 2011), 5.
49 Antony Beevor, *The Second World War* (New York: Little, Brown and Co., 2012).
50 Botchway and Kwarteng, *Africa and the First World War.*
51 Chris Murray, ed. *Unknown Conflicts of the Second World War: Forgotten Fronts* (Abingdon: Routledge, 2019), 15.
52 Toyin Falola, *Key Events in African History: A Reference Guide* (Westport: Greenwood Press, 2002), 206.
53 Davidson, *Modern Africa*, 62.
54 Oliver Coates, "New Perspectives on West Africa and the World War Two," *Journal of African Military History* 4 (2020): 5–39.
55 Coates, "New Perspectives," 15.
56 David Killingray, "Military and Labour Recruitment in the Gold Coast During the Second World War," *The Journal of African History* 23, no. 1 (1982): 83–95.

57 Edho Ekoko, "The West African Frontier Force Revisited," *Journal of the Historical Society of Nigeria* 10, no. 1 (1979): 47–63.
58 Coates, "New Perspectives," 16.
59 Michael Crowder, "The 1939–45 War and West Africa," in *History of West Africa, Vol. 2,* eds. J. F. A. Ajayi and Michael Crowder (London: Longman, 1974).
60 Coates, "New Perspectives," 17.
61 Coates, "New Perspectives," 18.
62 Ajayi and Crowder, *History of West Africa,* 598.
63 Wendell P. Holbrook, "The Impact of the Second World War on the Gold Coast 1939–45" (Ph.D. diss., Princeton University, 1978).
64 James Coleman, *Nigeria: Background to Nationalism* (Los Angeles: University of California Press, 1958).
65 Gabriel O. Olusanya, "The Role of Ex-servicemen in Nigerian Politics," *Journal of Modern African Studies* 6, no. 2 (1968): 221–232.
66 Olusanya, "The Role of Ex-servicemen."
67 David Killingray, *Fighting for Britain: African Soldiers in the Second World* (Suffolk: James Currey Publishing, 2012).
68 Killingray, *Fighting for Britain.*
69 Davidson, *Modern Africa,* 65.
70 Richard Carswell, *The Fall of France in the Second World War: History and Memory* (London: Palgrave MacMillan, 2019).
71 Elizabeth Isichei, *History of West Africa since 1800* (Teaneck: Holmes & Meier Publishers, 1977), 260.
72 Carswell, *The Fall of France.*
73 Ajayi and Crowder, *History of West Africa,* 606.
74 Davidson, *Modern Africa,* 63.
75 Holbrook, *The Impact of the Second World War.*
76 David Mayers, *America and the Postwar World: Remaking International Society, 1945–1956* (London: Routledge, 2018).
77 Warren Kimball, *Forged in War: Churchill, Roosevelt and the Second World War* (New York: HarperCollins, 1997).
78 Coates, "New Perspectives," 26.
79 Coates, "New Perspectives," 25.
80 Coates, "New Perspectives," 26.
81 Olusanya, "The Role of Ex-Servicemen."
82 Olusanya, "The Role of Ex-Servicemen."
83 Ajayi and Crowder, *History of West Africa,* 491.
84 Njung, "West Africa," 10.
85 Isichei, *History of West Africa,* 260.
86 Gabriel O. Olusanya, "The Zikist Movement – A Study in Political Radicalism, 1946–50," *The Journal of Modern African Studies* 4, no. 3 (1966): 323–333.

18

CONTINENTALISM, NATIONALISM AND INDEPENDENCE

Introduction

The racial denigration of Africans, which became commonplace in white sociopolitical trajectories from the inception of slavery, crept into American political culture as far back as the time of Americans' struggles for freedom.[1] The construction of racial identity had its foundation laid in the Declaration of American Independence in 1776 by the events that followed the epochal moment. The Statue of Liberty, which emphasized the equality of men and women at the pronouncement of American independence, had a different semantic concentration; people were only defined by color or gender in terms of the social, economic, political, and cultural definition of these groups of Americans. This definition of a "man" in a racialized category was not inscribed in the iconic symbol of the Statue of Liberty. Characteristically, they allowed their social and political treatment of Africans in the Americas to make the announcement. In other words, people who shared the black color could not be considered human, as they were reduced to an inferior status where they were forced to accept subaltern and debased treatment.

According to G. W. F. Hegel, a Western scholar, African history was non-existent.[2] With his intellectual stature in the global academic circle, it is incontestable that his conclusion about Africans pronounced European bias, as those who heard it in the academic circle accepted his idea, even if it consolidated the already established racial prejudices. This unsubstantiated claim survived until African nationalist scholars challenged the veracity of the racialized claim, staging their intellectual protest from the staple of both organic and academic history.[3] Many Afrocentric scholars, including the energetic titan Cheikh Anta Diop, destroyed the foundation of Eurocentric revisionist conclusions about Africa, birthing the assertive literature on cultural nationalism.[4]

DOI: 10.4324/9781003198260-22

Triggers of Resistance and Nationalism

Anti-colonial resistance occupied the central position of nationalist African struggle because they perceived colonial structures and institutions as instruments of racial reconstruction, where a subhuman identity was carved out and reserved for Africans.[5] At the end of the slave trade in the nineteenth century, colonial idealists installed themselves as agents of a revolution aimed to transform African polities into modern and civilized people.[6] Meanwhile, slavery was founded on the assumption that Africans were inferior and that their supposed status as debased humans justified their commodification and continued subjection to painful experiences. They believed that Africans, based on the theories developed about them, had a strong biological composition to withstand difficult challenges, knowing that their survival capacity was different.[7] Superficially covering this conclusion was the notion that Africans were given to promiscuity and appeared primitive, unclean, and dangerous to themselves and, therefore, required intervention from colonizers for the redemption of their identity.

Based on this jaundiced evaluation of Africans, some Europeans, including missionaries, argued that slavery was the price Africans had to pay for their souls to receive redemption.[8] Therefore, it is a paradox of a strange magnitude that Europeans who created the impression that Africans were in danger in the absence of interventionist efforts from civilizations like that of Europe became the source of Africans' challenges. In the diaspora and African homeland, the West created a Manichean binary that manifested in all aspects of human experience—economic, political, social, and spiritual. Colonial altruism was, thus, contradicted because the imperialists did not see anything in Black history that made Africans worthy of having equal rights and privileges with them.[9] As such, their relationship with Africans manifested in the apartheid policy in South Africa, created the elite-proletariat dichotomy in Sierra Leone (Freetown), enthroned the master-subordinate culture in Liberia, indirect rule in some British colonies, and the policies of assimilation in French West African countries.[10] These contradictions continued to signal to Africans that their fate under the West, the colonial imperialists, would continue to be clouded by several cases of racial injustices if preventive measures and actions were not put in place. To justify their nefarious policies and behaviors, Europeans had to create negative impressions about Africans, and we can see this in their assertion that the existing political structures were bad and thus must be changed.[11]

Also, the Europeans ruled that African educational systems were impractical for modern development. They introduced Western-oriented models of academic programs, which were used to undermine African systems.[12] After the 15th century, some parts of Africa entered a moment of stagnation as a consequence of the slave trade and racial prejudices. Black thinkers and revolutionaries began to think in terms of Black solidarity as a way of overcoming racial prejudices in the Americas and fighting European colonization in Africa.

African peoples were divided by colonial boundaries. Many probably did not have a clue that the balkanization of their various polities into different countries was a deliberate act of colonization.[13] However, their ignorance became history the moment they understood the importance of their oneness. Pan-Africanism became the vehicle they used to promote Black togetherness. In what other way can the contradictions of colonialism be more apparent than the decision of the conquerors to settle in urban communities while they asserted that they wanted to bring salvation to rural Africans? Could it be more obvious that they were so antithetical to their commitment to the discovery that they did not allow many Africans access to the social institutions they built? African identity and cultural traditions were redefined by the politics of difference and segregation, although negatively. There was an understanding that without appropriate resistance, even if it required violence, the demand for anti-colonial struggles that manifested in the nationalist agenda and continent-wide aspirations for Black freedom would be impossible.

Knowing the intricacies of freedom and the power of politics, Frantz Fanon argued for organized violence since colonialism or power control does not demand peaceful resolution because those who are benefiting from the existing practice would not willingly give up the privilege.[14] As such, it was apparent that the more they appealed to the moral sense of their oppressors, the more they suffered attacks from them. Their political freedom was tightened, such as in the case of the South African freedom fighter, Nelson Mandela. The same goes for their economic and financial resources that were pillaged, as in the case of French West African countries, and their cultures suffered devastating defeats as a result. To prevent all this, Africans had to embark on organized resistance and possibly violence. The demand for the ownership of African land was a demand for freedom, and since the enhancement of a nationalist economy was legal, it was within the natural rights of oppressed Africans. Moreover, the sociopolitical victimization of their race in America was unacceptable and, therefore, required a fundamental change.

All these political and social experiences created a national consciousness in the hearts of Africans who sought to escape the pangs of colonialism through the unification of their ideas and philosophies. This was inspired by the understanding that with the debasement of African values and identity in general, and because of its generality across the continent, it was necessary that the people also developed a radical mindset that would amplify the aspirations of Black people.[15] However, nationalism was not to be construed as a weapon needed to displace European domination or the despoliation of African culture alone; it was conceived within the context of all-round freedom from the entrapment of colonial institutions. Considering, for example, that Africans embarked on the reconstruction of the academic programs available in African schools immediately after independence, such efforts indicated a nationalist conviction necessary as a counter-reaction to the Europeans' position on African education. Significantly, the African universities created in the late 1940s embarked on finding out about the African past, and noted that some of Africa's histories had been deliberately masked by the Europeans to ensure that their disregard for Africans was promoted and supported.[16]

Pan-Africanism

As indicated in the above introduction, the racial prejudices experienced by African-Americans triggered a cyclone of reactions because the racially oppressed people could not bear the experience of an inferiority complex induced by their racial abuse from white Americans. Scholars have defined the idea differently based on their various evaluations of the movement's behavior. While some considered Pan-Africanism as a racial unification aimed at attaining freedom, others perceived it as the construction of a racial identity seeking to resist abuses, reject an inferior status, and demand recognition as humans, not pseudo-humans.[17] Africans in the Americas understood the deliberateness of the racial prejudices they were subjected to.

They became aware that a political structure that legitimized Europeans in America as free and gave them legal access to social and economic opportunities while restricting Blacks from doing so was deliberately practicing an ideology of racial superiority. Understanding that this system was detrimental to their collective development and racial success prompted a number of African-Americans to consider journeying back to Africa, which is their ancestral beginning and was believed to reserve some fair play for them.[18] Racial discrimination was behind the planned exodus of Africans from the Americas in the late nineteenth century. By 1870, for example, attempts to physically move away from the Americas were already in place.[19] Various organizations and companies contributed to the return of Blacks during the period.[20] The goal was to establish a satellite settlement in Africa where they could connect the diaspora people to their ancestral lineages, thus avoiding the unending human denigration they experienced in the Americas.

Therefore, Pan-Africanism considered Africa as the homeland of Black people and conceived of the forging of unity as the foundation for the redefinition of the continent. This would allow for the creation of appropriate institutions for its immediate transformation, the redemption of the Blacks and the negotiation of the African personality that would solely reflect African values and virtues, the remodeling of the African past for a beautiful future, and the evolution of African culture.[21] These were ways through which African identities would be appropriately reconstructed. All the political problems they had been exposed to continued to traumatize them, and the understanding that the white Americans' rise to economic and political stardom meant the relegation of others, especially Blacks, informed their decision to migrate.[22]

Perhaps developed as a "war" strategy, the concept of Blacks as a racial unit was a response to the challenges they faced. Once the construction of the Pan-African identity generated the needed energy to spark the determination for solidarity, the proponents of the concept became committed and steadfast. It is, therefore, no coincidence that scholars have considered Pan-Africanism as the collective efforts by Africans and their diaspora counterparts to promote issues that would locate the place of the people in global development.[23] Africans facilitated the growth of the Americas in unimaginable ways, and the experience of slavery drastically changed their destinies.

Without appropriately responding to the blatant oppression that the Europeans had subjected them to in collaboration with the Americans, Africans were submerged in the pool of political and economic marginalization, which invariably exposed them to all forms of oppression and prejudices. The consequences were devastating, and it was apparent that the unification of the people might unsettle white Americans who thought that Blacks were naturally inferior. With the systemic maltreatment of Blacks in the Americas, added to the previous history of slavery and the economic exploitation of Africans in their homeland, it was clear that without an organized platform enhanced by the Pan-African movement, Africans were in for a bumpy ride.[24]

The historical trajectory of Pan-Africanism was traced to the beginning of the slave trade and racial experiences in the New World.[25] They identified that people of color were subjected to a common treatment indicative of racial indictment and the impression that Africans were culturally and politically irredeemable because of the seeming inferiority of their continent. Creating the platform was necessary, as it was apparent that doing otherwise would only weaken their resolve for freedom. Black culture had to be harnessed as an instrument of freedom, and their engagements as the denigrated people in the Americas needed to indicate a common foundation.[26] Otherwise, they stood no chance of challenging the hegemonic foundation or, more particularly, confronting the racial expression that has institutionalized prejudice against them since the beginning of time. The Blacks were repressed at every opportunity because of their identity and tormented by several forms of abuse that got swept under the carpet. They were not protected by the systems of the country in which they had historically been a forceful part. As a result, they needed to create common economic, political, and social structures, even if conceived only in their minds at the beginning, as these were necessary platforms for achieving equality.[27] Equality was practically impossible in the white-dominated environment, but it could be achieved if they formed a powerful force through their unity and then left the societies that tormented them.

The train of Pan-Africanism started obviously from the African-Americans and various agonies from the slave trade era to the end of World War II, after which the continental Africans jumped on the train and used their intellectual and political power to chart a course for African freedom.[28] However, the debate about the actual time of the start of Pan-Africanism is yet to be resolved owing to the understanding that slaves, in a practical sense, began the quest for the struggles. Sojourner Truth's famous speech in 1851 titled, "Ain't I a Woman?" emphasized the struggles and strife that African women faced in the Americas.[29] Women of African ancestry in the New World suffered the double jeopardy of being Black and being female. The speech was a declaration of the rejection of the treatment and anguish that Blacks, especially Black women, were subjected to at the time.

Although there was no official designation of identity for the movement in the era of slavery, it cannot be contended that they laid down the foundation for the development of the Pan-Africanist agenda. On August 14, 1893, precisely four decades after Truth's popular speech, the Chicago Conference was held. This event lasted for a week, registering the attendance of some important Blacks, notably the Liberian Massaquo, Bishop Alexander Frederick Perry Noble; the secretary to the conference, Bishop Henry M. Turner (founder of the African Methodist Episcopal Churches in Sierra Leone and Liberia); and Alexander Crummell, among others.[30] The conference was thematically connected to the World Columbian Exhibition; however, the Blacks that presented chapters there highlighted the segregation and denigration experiences of the Blacks in the New World. Identifying their challenges underscored the intention to create a powerful structure or platform which would launch their resistance to the racial prejudices to which they had been abysmally subjected. These chapters examined the social and political marginalization of Black people and established that African freedom and access to quality of life could only be facilitated by Africans and their descendants, whether in the diaspora or continental Africa, making conscious decisions to contribute to its regeneration and rejuvenation. Perhaps, the foundation laid at this conference became the rallying point for similar protests.

Several other conferences came up in different states in the United States that focused plainly on the issues that affected Africans. To demonstrate their determination for an identity that represented the African people, several Africans and people of African descent dropped their European names in favor of their African names. For instance, a Nigerian, Mojola Agbebi, was formerly known as D. B. Vincent, while a Ghanaian, S. R. B. Attoh Ahuma, was formerly S. R. B. Solomon. It became a tradition to expunge some elements of foreign identity in their embracement, signaling the cultural reactions of frustrated Africans who responded this way. However, the potency of protest was usually underpinned by a suitable geographical location because it always served as the agency for harmonizing people's ideas and amplifying their sentiments. The anti-colonial and anti-European sentiments were growing, and the limitation of their coverage of the American space would achieve unintended results. The awareness of this inspired the redefinition of their tactics. Blacks in the diaspora extended their protest to England in 1897,[31] aware of the formation of the African Association, understanding that the English promoted slavery and enjoyed the benefits of religious expansionism. Therefore, registering a platform that had an African identity was calculated to have more sociopolitical weight.

Strengthened by the success recorded in the Americas, Africans were irrevocably committed to their struggle for freedom, not only physically but also in a political, cultural, religious, and economic sense. The primary political assignment of the group was to create the impression that Africans could now project their grievances because of the power in their unity. Of course, individuals in their separate existence were free to enunciate their various experiences of political victimization, which were blamed on racism. However, such would only provide mental gratification, not sociopolitical outcomes. Projecting the sufferings of Blacks required organized pressure groups, even against the background to know more about their history, as in the emergence of the Association for Promoting the Discovery of the Interior Parts of Africa, popularly known as the African Association, in London.[32]

Pan-Africanism was formally institutionalized in 1901, but the association crumbled in no time due to inhibitive challenges.[33] From insufficient funds to growing apathy by members, Africans' dream of reconnecting with their homeland was shattered at the maiden launch. However, ideas that would survive would always gather energy at a time when it seemed like there was no hope of continuing with the association.[34] The intensity of the commitment of the pioneer members of the movement sustained the initiative. More importantly, it revolutionized the ways Africans viewed themselves. The rise of these committed Pan-African groups changed the orientation and made the world have an urgent rethink of the heinous assumptions that Africans were inferior or too intellectually weak to have a respected identity. Africans' dedication to the course of their struggles from different geographical spheres represented by their unity tells a different story about their intellectuality and organizational capacity.

Those who attended the conferences in the United States and England in the 1940s made great efforts to replicate the content of the discussions in their various African countries to establish a point. African unity came at a cost, and they showed their presence in finance and other sectors, proving that they were convinced of their African identity, which was the foundation of Pan-Africanism. The desire of Blacks in the diaspora to return to their ancestral sources was simultaneous in the Americas and regions where slavery was commonplace. For example, in locations where some slaves were treated relatively better than others, many wanted to relocate.[35] Many of them made strenuous efforts to embark on the journey, and they eventually found themselves in Liberia, Sierra

Leone, Dahomey (present-day Benin Republic), Ghana, and Nigeria. Their decision to leave was informed by identity protection because they realized that reconnecting with their people would restore their human dignity. Meanwhile, many of them were displeased with the status of being slaves or ex-slaves because their experiences differed according to the general philosophy and disposition of the diaspora environment.

Being labeled an inferior race, which was how the Europeans perceived enslaved Africans, was repugnant and diminished the Africans' human dignity. The only effective support system was for the people to remove themselves from that environment and return to their ancestral places in Africa.[36] Therefore, the eighteenth and nineteenth centuries recorded a reasonable number of freed Africans in Freetown (present-day Sierra Leone), Ghana, Cameroon, and Nigeria. These returnees brought some astounding expertise in the different fields they had been introduced to in their former locations. Their reconnection with Africans came along with the dissemination of the knowledge they had gathered while in the diaspora, and this knowledge and experience were used to facilitate instant development in different areas.[37] For example, those who worked on sugarcane plantations in the Americas used their knowledge to improve the agricultural sectors in many African polities. They embarked on the production of international goods on large scales because they had mastered the basics of the business. Some of them were carpenters, while others were shoemakers, seamstresses, and traders, among others. Typically, they revolutionized each sector in which they found themselves, and with their records of success, evidenced by their productivity, more Africans in the diaspora nursed the ambition to migrate back to Africa.[38]

It is important to reiterate that Pan-Africanism was beyond mere reconnection with the motherland. Rather, it was a clear attempt to resist the unending extraction of people and resources, as well as the humiliation of unimaginable proportions that was the fate of Blacks in the Americas and other places where they were kept as marginals. Since the attainment of independence and despite co-struggling for it with African-Americans, the United States did not abate the economic, sociopolitical, and cultural strangulations of Black people. One way they could be free was to embrace the idea of an exodus to their motherland. Notably, the struggle to go back involved an arduous process because apart from the economic and financial responsibility they experienced, they also had to contend with the psychological problems that arose from their reconnection with a place they had been detached from. But the horror of living a lowly life in the diaspora appeared more gruesome and appalling, with significant political and economic damage to their existence. To these Pan-Africanists, it was more appealing to be exposed to harsh challenges in their various African roots than to eternally face the racial prejudices that characterized the American, European, and Latin American polities.[39] With their astounding zeal, the slave returnees laid the groundwork for African unity.

Expressions of Nationalism

Movements

Before independence, intellectually informed Africans were concerned about freedom from European imperialism. They had to respond to aspects of their identity that had faced political and economic devastation. Achieving this required different strategies, all of which were tailored toward the same goal. Since the Europeans were well-organized in their purported subordination and exploitation of Africa's human and natural resources, a counter-reaction required that Africans must be equally organized. The only reasonable solution was to create movements across all strata and systems so that they could gather sufficient momentum to challenge the existential crisis. From the establishment of a political movement to the emergence of labor groups, African methods of nationalism were carefully organized and well-structured.[40]

Radical movements such as Pan-Negroism, established in the West Indies by the 1920s, and Pan-Africanism, which started in North America,[41] were created differently but jointly contributed to the advancement of the African cause. They each contributed to the environment that allowed the institutionalization of African grievances and their collective demands for justice. Based on their general experience in these different societies, the most effective solution to the perpetual challenges confronting them racially was the reconstruction of African identity through reconnection to the homeland and struggles for liberation. Pan-Negroism was specifically concerned with the redemption of African dignity.[42] In other words, achieving a better image for Africans was predicated on the resolution to show reverence to the native and indigenous customs branded as uncivilized by the Europeans.

Alternatively, Pan-Africanism combined cultural and political struggles to construct an identity for the Africans who were traumatized by the callous political attitudes of white Americans against the Blacks.[43] Therefore, the movement created an avenue for Blacks to come together to project their grievances and seek lasting solutions to the perpetual challenges confronting them. Importantly, those who brought Blacks together under a common platform aimed to unify the people in their thoughts and political orientation; that is, to use their common experience of debasement to challenge the oppressors and the oppressions that had kept them below the system. Africans would not have succeeded in their ambitions for freedom if they had not galvanized their intellectual, political, and economic strengths. This formed the foundation for their unity and propelled them to their aimed positions in society. Pan-Africanism was unique because it not only sought the freedom of Blacks in the Americas but was also intended to establish a foundation of mutual understanding between the diaspora community and continental Africans.[44]

Continentalism

In 1961, under the leadership of Kwame Nkrumah, a Pan-Africanist political movement, later named the "Casablanca Bloc," was created, with its membership including Libya, Mali, Egypt, Ghana, Guinea, Morocco, and Algeria.[45] This political group wanted to unite Africans to achieve liberation and independence. Initially, it was apparent that the construction of this group was going to bring about the intended change to the ways Africans had been conducting themselves politically. Nkrumah remained committed to his ambition and the collective interest of the Casablanca Bloc, and in 1963, there was another significant move from the group to consolidate its identity regeneration focus.[46] He wrote to other African countries, proposing a union of African countries, which was predicated on the understanding that the unification of Africans on the political front would birth an economic system that would salvage Africans from their existential challenges.[47] This brought about ideas for a common policy on the international front, a unified currency, and a central African Bank, all of which primarily addressed the problems that confronted the African peoples.

Meanwhile, there was another movement of similar orientation but with a different approach to African regeneration. The "Monrovian Bloc" was led by Léopold Sédar Senghor, an intellectually radical Senegalese.[48] The group was composed of African countries like Nigeria, Liberia, Ethiopia, and many French West African countries still economically tied to France's apron strings.[49] Perhaps for individual political conditions and, more importantly, the understanding that the attraction of French ex-colonies would be difficult given their tied loyalty to France, the opposition to the Casablanca Pan-Africanist movement was fierce and unwavering.[50]

Realizing its potential damage to the collective course of African struggles, the Ethiopian emperor, Emperor Haile Selassie, intervened and brought the warring groups to a common ground.[51] He organized a reconciliation meeting to register the attendance of leaders from the different factions, whose goal was the emancipation of the African countries from the numerous identity degenerations that Europeans had masterminded against them. While the Nkrumah group believed that it was expedient that unity was achieved immediately and not delayed further, Senghor's faction thought it should be achieved gradually, although consistently. The firebrand approach of the Casablanca Bloc was considered ineffective for such an important agenda. What emerged was the Organisation of African Unity.

Prominent Leaders and Nationalists

Nnamdi Azikiwe

Nnamdi Azikiwe was a nationalist figure in Nigeria and a major proponent of Pan-Africanism in the twentieth century.[52] He devoted his life to the liberation struggle of the African people. While in the Gold Coast as an editor of the *African Morning Post* newspaper, Azikiwe used the medium to expose the ills of the colonial administration and was charged with sedition.[53] Consequently, he returned to Nigeria and established the *West African Pilot*, serving as its editor.[54] Azikiwe has been referred to as a preeminent Nigerian journalist who used his newspapers to influence the independence movement in Africa and emboldened Africans to demand self-government.[55] He was an ardent supporter and advocate of Pan-Africanism, which manifested in 1934 when he adopted an Igbo name, "Nnamdi," as his official name and discontinued the use of "Benjamin," his Christian name.[56] Azikiwe became a major source of motivation for other Pan-Africanists in West Africa, such as Kwame Nkrumah, who based his nationalist ideals partly on Azikiwe's philosophy.

Azikiwe was an active member of the Nigerian Youth Movement, and upon his resignation from this organization due to ethnic conflicts, he co-founded the first nationalist party, the National Council for Nigeria and the Cameroons (NCNC), in August 1944, and became its secretary while Herbert Macaulay was the party's president.[57] Azikiwe vehemently opposed the Richards Constitution, which included only four Africans in the Legislative Council. He gained more popularity following the strike organized by the working class and the publications of the *West African Pilot* exposing the assassination plots of the colonial government. Among the youth, Azikiwe became a unifying figure, and four prominent young men—Abiodun Aloba, M. C. K.

Ajuluchukwu, Nduka Eze, and Kolawole Balogun—formed the Zikist Movement.[58] Azikiwe was elected to the Legislative Council in Lagos in 1947. According to Olusanya, Azikiwe and his political party monopolized political affairs between 1944 and 1951.[59]

After Herbert Macaulay's death, Nnamdi Azikiwe became the President of the NCNC, and under him, a deputation was sent to London to request that changes be made to the constitution. He became the Premier of the Eastern Region when Nigeria became a federal entity.[60] Thereafter, he became the Governor-General of the newly independent state in November 1960, thus becoming the first Nigerian member of the Privy Council of the United Kingdom.[61] Nnamdi Azikiwe was elected the ceremonial president when Nigeria became a republic in 1963. The government was, however, toppled by the military coup of 1966. Nevertheless, he continued to advocate for the unity of Nigeria and served as a mediator and representative of the Biafran state to the Nigerian state.

Obafemi Awolowo

Obafemi Jeremiah Awolowo was a powerhouse in the struggle for Nigeria's independence.[62] He is regarded in some quarters as one of the forefathers of the nationalist movement. He received his formal education in the United Kingdom, where he studied law. Upon the completion of his degree, he became an active participant in Nigeria's fledgling politics. He was a strong advocate of self-determination for the various ethnic groups in Nigeria. He formed the Egbe Omo Oduduwa, an organization that became a rallying point for the Western people of Nigeria and gave them a cultural and political identity.[63] In 1951, he founded the Action Group (AG), which became the dominant party in Western Nigeria, based on the objectives of this organization.[64]

As a nationalist leader, Awolowo fought for Nigeria's political independence and the region's economic autonomy and social development.[65] He served as the Premier of the Western Region from 1954 till the country gained its independence in 1960. He also played active roles in constitutional parleys that resulted in subsequent adaptations. Awolowo espoused the political philosophy of federalism, which would ensure autonomy for the various ethnic groups and a more unified Nigeria. As the leader of the Action Group and Premier of the Western Region, he promulgated several progressive economic and social measures to develop the people of his region. Some of these measures included free and compulsory universal education in 1955, free health care, and a rise in the minimum wage.[66]

In 1959, he resigned as the Premier in preparation for the general elections into the Federal House of Representatives. He did not win the post of Prime Minister and opted to remain as the Opposition Leader in the Tafawa Balewa–led cabinet.[67] In 1963, Awolowo was detained and arraigned on charges of treasonable felony and was sentenced to ten years imprisonment. After a short stint in prison, he was released in 1966, before the 1967 civil war.[68] In 1967, Awolowo was named Chairman of the Federal Executive Council and represented Nigeria at the Commonwealth Prime Ministers' Conference in London.[69] He also served as the Finance Minister and Gowon's top advisor during the war and developed economic blockade policies to bring the seceding eastern region to its knees.[70]

Kwame Nkrumah

Kwame Nkrumah was at the forefront of Pan-Africanism and the nationalist movement in West Africa.[71] He was appointed secretary of the United Gold Coast Convention (UGCC), a position he effectively held. The UGCC organized protests, and during one of these protests, Nkrumah was arrested along with other notable party leaders. He broke away from the party and formed the Convention People's Party (CPP), whose aphorism was "self-government now," to distinguish it from the UGCC.[72] Under the new party, Nkrumah continued to stage protests and other forms of agitation. While behind bars, Nkrumah and his CPP won the 1951 general elections, resulting in his release from jail.[73] From this point, Nkrumah was referred to as *Osagyefo*—the redeemer—and he began to work toward the independence of Ghana.

Following Ghana's independence, Nkrumah stated that the emancipation of the African continent was his primary objective. Ghana's constitution contained a provision that the nation's sovereignty would be given up for the emergence of the United States of Africa.[74] Nkrumah referred to himself as a socialist, and most of his political ideologies emanated from socialism. He stated that once Ghana gained independence, a Pan-African policy must be executed to advance a political revolution in Africa.[75] Being a proponent of "socialism in Africa" instead of "African socialism," he advocated for the creation of "socialism in Ghana." Nkrumah was a Pan-Africanist to the core.

Amílcar Cabral

In Portuguese-Guinea, Amílcar Cabral was the leading nationalist figure. He was educated in Portugal, where he established relations with other colonized people from Africa who shared the same aversion to Portuguese colonial domination. Upon his return to Guinea-Bissau, he was appointed a field officer in the Ministry of Agriculture, which allowed him to acquire first-hand information about the people and the land, thus building a solid relationship with the people in the rural areas who were mostly peasant farmers. While in Europe, Cabral developed a keen interest in a radical Marxist group and was determined to establish such a radical group in his country.[76] With some other educated Africans, Cabral formed the Movimento de Independencia Nacional da Guinea Portuguesa (MING) under his leadership.[77] He committed himself to the recruitment of radical elements like himself who would join the political party. The members of this party were referred to as revolutionaries, and their revolutionary ideals were based on Marxism. This movement metamorphosed into a radical political party, the Partido Africano da Independence of Guinea and Cape Verde (PAIGC) African Party for the Independence of Guinea and Cape Verde, whose sole aim was to achieve independence at all costs. The Portuguese responded to the activities of Cabral and his fellow party members with force, but this did not prevent them from fighting for their independence.[78] Under Cabral's leadership, the PAIGC executed well-organized guerilla warfare, which was the major weapon employed in the fight against the Portuguese (Figure 18.1).

Furthermore, Cabral established contact with Guinea's (French) prominent nationalist figure, Sékou Touré, which significantly accounted for the success of the PAIGC.[79] Guinea became a primary command post and a training center and was also used as a landing base for the ammunition Cabral and his party received from other foreign nationals like China and the USSR. Cabral and his party rooted themselves firmly in

FIGURE 18.1   Monument to Amílcar Cabral, in Praia https://commons.wikimedia.org/wiki/File
:Monumento_a_Am%C3%ADlcar_Cabral,_Praia,_Cape_Verde.jpg.

Guinea-Bissau and became popular internationally. He wrote numerous articles that
exposed the flagitious nature of Portugal's colonialism and advertised the many achievements of his political party. He was an advocate of Pan-Africanism, and he exhibited
this in his writings.[80] The crux of his message was centered on African liberation and
unity. He desired a unified Guinea-Cape Verde entity and pledged himself to this cause.
In 1973, Guinea-Bissau received international recognition as an independent state
when Cabral announced its independence.[81] Regrettably, Cabral was assassinated on
20 January 1973, and did not witness the withdrawal of the Portuguese troops from
Guinea-Bissau.

Sékou Touré

Sékou Touré's political career began in Guinea as a trade unionist. During his tenure
as the General Secretary of the French Confédération Générale du Travail (CGT), he
used African trade unions as platforms to create political awareness. He was a trade
unionist and a political leader in the RDA in Guinea. During the 1953 general strike, he

FIGURE 18.2   Sékou Touré https://commons.wikimedia.org/wiki/File:Ahmed_S%C3%A9kou
_Tour%C3%A9_1962.jpg.

emphasized that workers' unity was necessary for the success of the trade unions.[82] He led
the Parti Démocratique de Guinee (PDG), a branch of the Rassemblement Démocratique
Africaine (RDA) in Guinea, against the chieftaincy institution. Touré rose to eminence
in the PDG due to his capability to restrain dissenting voices within the party. He won
the election to be Beyla's representative in the Territorial Assembly in 1953, and three
years later, he became a Guinean *deputé,* elected to the French National Assembly.[83] He
spearheaded the formation of the Confédération générale du travail African (General
Confederation of African Labor) (Figure 18.2).

   Sékou Touré was also instrumental to the formation of the Union Générale des
Travailleurs d'Afrique Noire (UGTAN) and articulated the union's ideologies—African
emancipation and unity. Like Kwame Nkrumah, Touré was willing to give up Guinea's
independence for the creation of the United States of Africa. He became the vice president
of the council of ministers when his party, the PDG, won the majority of the seats in the
elections for the Territorial Assembly. Consequently, he abolished the chieftaincy institution he had earlier fought against in Guinea, leading to grave changes and disturbances
in Guinea. Touré opposed the new constitution introduced under the French free government, and his territory, Guinea, voted against it, bringing about Guinea's independence.[84]

Radicalism and Trade Unionism

Trade unionism sprang from the political and economic conditions of colonies, and its
importance in the West African independence movement cannot be overstated. Trade

unions were one of the most vivid forms of radicalism in the independence struggles and nationalist movements in West Africa,[85] and the primary aim was to facilitate economic activities and improve the working conditions. With the emergence of nationalist movements, trade unions became political agencies that joined their voices to nationalist movements to fight colonial governments.[86] Some of the tools of action used by trade unions were strikes, protests, demonstrations, and negotiations.

In Nigeria, in its inceptive years, the Nigerian Trade Union Congress (NTUC) alienated itself from political activities.[87] Although it was not part of the nationalist movement, it worked with nationalists such as Nnamdi Azikiwe and Obafemi Awolowo. The African Civil Service Technical Workers' Union challenged the colonial government and requested that Nigerian Civil Servants be paid more and given the same benefits as the British expatriates. As a result, 17 unions that jointly had 30,000 members embarked on a general strike that lasted 37 days and affected essential public services.[88] The UAC Worker's Union, founded by Nduka Eze, organized the workers in the commercial sector to demand an increase in their living allowance.[89] This strike allowed the unionists to give their unwavering support to the nationalist movements.

The Trade Union Congress (TUC) in the Gold Coast was an outstanding trade union in West Africa in the pre-independence era.[90] There was a wide gap in the cost of living and the wages earned, which led to the call for industrial action by the TUC. Nkrumah's CPP and the TUC worked together to pressure the colonial government. Members of the CPP doubled as members of the political party as well as union members. However, the British suppressed the strike forcefully, and many of the nationalists were arrested and imprisoned, leading to the TUC's premature disintegration.[91] Although the TUC was re-established, it became a neutral union in political affairs.

In French West Africa, the trade unions were connected to the French Confédération générale du travail (CGT) and impeded nationalist development. A major aim of the Dakar trade union conference was to align trade unionism with the General Confederation of Labor (CGT) and the World Federation of Trade Union (WFTU), which did not refer to any political activity; rather, its focus was on economic and social issues. Nationalist ideas began to gain prominence in trade union conferences, starting from the trade union conference held at Bamako. The General Confederation of African Labor was formed and was remotely under the control of Rassemblement Démocratique Africain, the dominant party in French West Africa. The French colonial administration tried unsuccessfully to exclude the trade union from the political party and get it to work with the colonial administration. As a result, in a meeting in Conakry, a proposition for the creation of an autonomous African trade union movement was accepted to create a confederation of African Workers. The Union Générale des Travailleurs d'Afrique Noire (UGTAN) was another union formed in present-day Benin Republic, Dahomey. It was independent of the control of the colonial country and sought to unify all French workers in French West Africa.[92]

The Contributions of Women to Independence Struggles and Nationalist Movements

West African women were not mere bystanders in the independence struggle. Although their immense contributions to the Pan-Africanist movement have been mostly ignored, it is becoming clearer that women were active participants in the nationalist struggle in West Africa.[93] Since the fight for independence among African countries began, female liberation fighters have not received the accolades granted to their male counterparts, and their roles have been relegated to the background. History regales us with accounts of the acts of Kwame Nkrumah, Thomas Sankara, Nnamdi Azikiwe, and other nationalist heroes, but less is known about Funmilayo Ransome-Kuti, Constance Cummings-John, Yaa Asantewaa, Theodosia Salome Okoh, Charwe Nyakasikana, among others, who contributed to the development of their nations. Beside the Aba Women's War, academic literature has failed to document many other female uprisings and female leaders who resisted colonial rule that was detrimental to the women. Examples of such protests include the 1932/1933 Ewe market women of Lome protest against unreasonable taxes[94] and the 1958–1961 Kom women's Anlu rebellion against farming practices reforms in Cameroon.[95]

It should be noted that women's role in the anti-colonial and independence movements began with the imposition of colonial rule.[96] Yaa Asantewaa's contention against British rule is a prime indicator of this. She led the final battle mounted by the Asante of the former Gold Coast region against their British rulers at the time, being a member of a high-born family—the Asona royal family of the Besease lineage of Edweso Stool.[97] Although she had not undergone any formal Western education, she was held in high esteem for her intelligence and nationalist sentiments. She was also known for her abhorrence of imperialism and colonialism. This intense emotion led to one of the most famous wars in Asanteland, which was triggered by the demand of the British Governor to sit on the "Golden Stool," a sacred artifact of the Asante people. It became known as "the Yaa Asantewaa War" and resulted in defeat and the colonization of the kingdom.[98] Asantewaa proved to be a formidable foe and a proficient military strategist who fought against the British governor, trapping him and his people in a siege at the Fort of Kumasi.

Constance Agatha Cummings-John and Funmilayo Ransome-Kuti were organizers of the anti-colonial nationalist movements of the 1940s and 1950s. Cummings-John was the first female mayor in Sierra Leone, serving as the Mayor of Freetown in 1966.[99] An educationist and a politician, she participated in Pan-African organizations such as the League of Coloured Peoples and the West African Students' Union (WASU). She campaigned for Freetown's market women as a member of the city council. She also founded the Sierra Leone Women's Movement in 1952, established branches nationwide, created a women's trading cooperative, undertook educational and welfare projects, and floated its newspaper.[100]

Funmilayo Ransome-Kuti was one of the first Nigerian women to receive a post-primary school education in the 1920s. She actively participated in the political resistance against the British colonialists and was against the traditional local figureheads used to enforce their rules. Also, she established the Abeokuta Women's Union, which led demonstrations against unfair taxation, corruption, and the underrepresentation of women in decision-making.[101] In 1949, because of the unreasonable taxes imposed on the *Egba* women, Ransome-Kuti mobilized them in a revolt against Oba Ladapo Ademola II, the *Alake* (King) of Abeokuta at the time.[102] Oba Ademola was forced to suspend the taxation of women and went into exile in Osogbo. In a different instance, the British colonial authorities banned protests, but Ransome-Kuti mobilized the local market women for what she referred to as "picnics and celebrations."[103]

Another formidable yet relatively unknown female liberation fighter is Madame Ouezzin Coulibaly, a politician in former Upper Volta, present-day Burkina Faso.[104] She was a member of the political party Rassemblement Démocratique Africaine (RDA), where she served as the General Secretary of the Women's section and worked to organize women for political action.[105] She was described as "une femme formidable dans la politique," and her undertakings before the independence of her country attest to the moniker. In one case, when a female member of the RDA was arrested and jailed, she rallied together an army of female party members and staged a sit-in outside the jail. Their number was enough to achieve the release of the jailed member. In another instance, male leaders of the RDA were arrested, and Coulibaly organized a raid of the prisons by Abidjan women to free them. Where necessary, she stood in as a capable leader and inspiration to the chapters of the RDA in Ivory Coast and throughout Francophone Africa.[106]

To a great extent, the muted legacy of these women has spread across Africa. Women, educated or otherwise, played critical roles in the liberation and independence struggles of African countries, despite being relegated to the less relevant female wings of political organizations.[107] Although they had little to no opportunity to be part of the main political structure of these parties, African women were often able to show intuitive and proficient management ability.

Hopes and Expectations of Independence

When the actions of pioneer Pan-Africanists such as Leopold Sédar Sénghor, George Padmore, W. E. B. Du Bois, John Payne, Kwame Nkrumah, and Casely Hayford are evaluated, it is clear that they planned to have a politically and economically integrated Africa. This was a plan where members' interests were ascertained through institutionalizing a body of beliefs that can be realized in creating mutually inclusive platforms. It began with the rejuvenation of the African pride that had been wounded by centuries of humiliation and racial prejudices to the installation of policies that could facilitate instantaneous economic growth. Additionally, their proposed Africa would automatically have a definition of identity guided by available principles and philosophically in connection with African ideas.[108] Therefore, African politics expounded African political beliefs and desire for independence and development.

Essentially, the post-independence period was projected as a time in which Africans would carefully and effectively shed the burden of inferiority placed on them since the Atlantic slave trade. Africa would present a united front, with a common currency, implying that they would face the future together from a common perspective. In the proposed United States of Africa, all countries will be accorded their deserved status, and none will carry the burden of cultural despoliation and political servitude.[109] The recognition of these individual polities underscores the awareness of their cultural traditions and the desire to make them flourish in the current political design. Each country's linguistic property would be respected and kept in their engagement, even though the resistance to all forces of domination coming from the European imperialists or emerging predators would be entrenched at the heart of their unity.[110] This unity would give them the platform to resist external pressure and challenge all colonial structures that remained even after independence.[111] The foundation laid during this time would serve as the springboard for the contemporary African resuscitation of Pan-Africanist interests. Even though they were aware of their sociocultural and sociolinguistic differences, the experience that inspired their collective resistance to revolution was imposed on them by colonial rule.

Conclusion

The Pan-Africanism agenda embodied by the nationalists in West Africa enhanced the quality of African nationalism. In their search for an identity, the activists developed the concept of a Unified Africa, personified by Kwame Nkrumah, who was committed to African unity. He held strongly to the belief that the formation of the United States of Africa was the ultimate weapon against neocolonialism. However, the end of Nkrumah's government signaled the decline of Pan-Africanist ideas in Africa.[112] Whatever the shortcomings, the nationalists and Pan-Africanists devoted themselves to the emancipation of West Africa from the shackles of European colonialism and the attainment of African independence, identity, and unity.[113]

DEEP DIVE

Assignment 1

Objective

The objective of this assignment is to ensure that students complete the reading of Chapter 18 and to encourage them to explore the benefits of Pan-Africanism and how it was used to unite Black people across the globe.

Method

Students will be expected to write a short note in response to the question.

Reading Comprehension

How did Pan-Africanism contribute to the collective "Black" identity? How did Africans use this new-found identity to reclaim power and resist European dominance?

Assignment 2

Objective

The objective of this assignment is to ensure that students complete the reading of Chapter 18 and to encourage them to consider how African nationalist leaders carried out their political interpretations of Pan-Africanist ideas.

Method

Students will be expected to write a short note in response to the question.

Reading Comprehension

Compare and contrast the political ideologies, strategies, and beliefs of two African nationalist leaders.

Notes

1 Mathurin Owen, *Henry Sylvester Williams and the Origins of the Pan African Movement* (New York: New York University Press, 1975).
2 Rita Edozie, *"Pan" African Rising: The Cultural Political Economy of Nigeria's Afri-Capitalism and South Africa's Ubuntu Business* (Boston: Springer Nature, 2017).
3 John D. Omer-Cooper, "The Contribution of the University of Ibadan to the Spread of the Study and Teaching of African History within Africa," *Journal of the Historical Society of Nigeria* 10, no. 3 (1980): 23–31.
4 Ebere Nwaubani, "Kenneth Onwuka Dike, 'Trade And Politics,' and the Restoration of the African in History," *History in Africa: A Journal of Method* 27 (2000): 229–248.
5 Gregory Maddox, ed., *Conquest and Resistance to Colonialism in Africa* (London: Routledge, 1993).
6 Timothy C. Anyanwu and Kelechi J. Ani, "Slavery and Colonialism: The Roots of Postcolonial Conflicts in Africa," *World Affairs: The Journal of International Issues* 24, no. 1 (2020): 132–141.
7 Hugh Thomas, *The Slave Trade. The Story of the Atlantic Slave Trade: 1440–1870* (New York: Simon & Schuster, 1997).
8 Eric Williams, *Capitalism and Slavery* (North Carolina: University of North Carolina Press, 1944).
9 Luis Angeles, "Income Inequality and Colonialism," *European Economic Review* 51, no. 5 (2007): 1155–1176.
10 Gregory Maddox, *The Colonial Epoch in Africa* (New York: Garland, 1993).
11 Frederick Lugard, *The Dual Mandate in British Tropical Africa* (London: Frank Cass, 1965).
12 Michael Omolewa, "Educating the 'Native': A Study of the Education Adaptation Strategy in British Colonial Africa, 1910–1936," *Journal of African American History* 91, no. 3 (2006): 267–287.
13 Anthony I. Asiwaju, *Partitioned Africans: Ethnic Nations across Africa's International Boundaries 1884–1984* (Lagos: University of Lagos Press, 1984).
14 Frantz Fanon, *The Wretched of the Earth* (New York: Grove Press, 1963).
15 Olusola Olasupo, Isaac O. Oladeji, and Edwin O. C. Ijeoma, "Nationalism and Nationalist Agitation in Africa: The Nigerian Trajectory," *The Review of Black Political Economy* 44 (2017): 261–283.
16 Omer-Cooper, "The Contribution of the University of Ibadan."
17 Peter O. Esedebe, "Origins and Meaning of Pan-Africanism," *Présence Africaine* 73 (1970): 109–127.
18 David Jenkins, *Black Zion: The Return of Afro-Americans and West Indians to Africa* (London: Wildwood House, 1975).
19 Kenneth C. Barnes, *Journey of Hope: The Back-to-Africa Movement in Arkansas in the Late 1800s* (North Carolina: University of North Carolina Press, 2004).
20 Edozie, *"Pan" African Rising.*
21 Emma J. Lapsansky-Wener and Margaret H. Bacon, eds., *Back to Africa: Benjamin Coates and the Colonization Movement in America, 1848–1800* (Pennsylvania: Pennsylvania State University Press, 2005).
22 Ella Forbes, "African-American Resistance to Colonization," *Journal of Black Studies* 21, no. 2 (1990): 210–223.
23 Imanuel Geiss, *The Pan-African Movement: A History of Pan-Africanism in America, Europe, and Africa* (New York: Africana Publishing Co., 1974).
24 Charles F. Andrain, "The Pan-African Movement: The Search for Organization and Community in Twentieth-century Africa," *Phylon* 23 (1962): 5–17.
25 Imanuel Geiss, "Notes on the Development of Pan-Africanism," *Journal of the Historical Society of Nigeria* 3 (1967): 719–740.
26 Colin Legum, *Pan-Africanism: A Short Political Guide* (New York: F. A. Praeger, 1965).
27 Okechukwu S. Mezu, ed., *The Philosophy of Pan-Africanism: A Collection of Papers on the Theory and Practice of the African Unity Movement* (Washington: Georgetown University Press, 1965).

28 Tony Martin, *Pan-African Connection: From Slavery to Garvey and Beyond* (Dover: The Majority Press, 1985).
29 Sojourner Truth, *Ain't I a Woman?* (New York: Scholastic, 1992).
30 Peter O. Esedebe, *Pan Africanism: The Idea and the Movement, 1776–1963* (Washington D. C.: Howard University Press, 1982).
31 Esedebe, *Pan Africanism*.
32 William Sinclair, "The African Association of 1788," *Journal of the Royal African Society* 1, no. 1 (1901): 145–149.
33 John H. Clarke, "Pan-Africanism: A Brief History of an Idea in the African World," *Présence Africaine* 145, no. 145 (1988): 26–56.
34 James T. Campbell, "'A Last Great Crusade for Humanity': W. E. B. Du Bois and the Pan-African Congress," in *Making the American Century: Essays on the Political Culture of Twentieth Century America*, ed. Bruce J. Schulman (New York: Oxford University Press, 2014).
35 Mac Dixon-Fyle, "The Saro in the Political Life of Early Port Harcourt, 1913–49," *The Journal of African History* 30, no. 1 (1989): 125–138.
36 Kwesi K. Prah, *Back to Africa: Afro-Brazilian Returnees and their Communities, Volume 1* (South Africa: CASAS, 2009).
37 John M. Vlach, "The Brazilian House in Nigeria: The Emergence of a 20th-Century Vernacular House Type," *The Journal of American Folklore* 97, no. 383 (1984): 3–25.
38 Samuel Y. Boadi-Siaw, "Brazilian Returnees of West Africa," in *Global Dimensions of the African Diaspora*, ed. Joseph E. Harris (Washington: Howard University Press, 1982).
39 Sidney J. Lemelle and Robin D. G. Kelley, eds., *Imagining Home: Class, Culture and Nationalism in the African Diaspora* (London: Verso, 1994).
40 Barbara Bair, "Pan- Africanism as Process: Adelaide Casley Hayford, Garveyism, and the Cultural Roots of Nationalism," in *Imagining Home: Class, Culture and Nationalism in the African Diaspora*, eds. Sidney J. Lemelle and Robin D. G. Kelley (London: Verso, 1994), 121–144.
41 Ojo Olatunde, D. K. Orwa, and C. M. B. Utete, *African International Relations* (London: Longman, 1985).
42 Kiven Tunteng, *From Pan Negroism to African Paramountry: The Role of Kwame Nkrumah* (Montreal: Vanier College Press, 1977).
43 Geiss, "Notes on the Development of Pan-Africanism."
44 Fongot Kini-Yen Kinni, *Pan-Africanism: Political Philosophy and Socio-Economic Anthropology for or African Liberation and Governance, Volume 3* (Cameroon: Langaa RPCID, 2015).
45 Vincent Dodoo and Wilhelmina Donkoh, "Nationalism and the Pan-African State," in *Pan-Africanism, and the Politics of African Citizenship and Identity*, eds. Toyin Falola and Kwame Essien (London: Routledge, 2014).
46 Henry Kah, "Kwame Nkrumah and the Panafrican Vision: Between Acceptance and Rebuttal," *Austral Brazilian Journal of Strategy & International Relations* 5, no. 9 (2016): 141–164.
47 Kwame Botwe-Asamoah, *Kwame Nkrumah's Politico-Cultural Thought and Politics: An African-Centered Paradigm for the Second Phase of the African Revolution* (New York: Routledge, 2005).
48 Robert A. Mortimer, "From Federalism to Francophonia: Senghor's African Policy," *African Studies Review* 15, no. 2 (1972): 283–306.
49 Dodoo and Donkoh, "Nationalism and the Pan-African State."
50 Kwame Nkrumah, *Africa Must Unite* (London: Heinemann, 1963).
51 Getachew Metaferia, "The Ethiopian Connection to the Pan-African Movement," *Journal of Third World Studies* 12, no. 2 (1995): 300–325.
52 Mark Reeves, "A Gilded Cage? Nnamdi Azikiwe's Pan-Africanism as Governor-General of Nigeria, 1960–63," *Journal of West African History* 7, no. 1 (2021): 1–26.
53 Stanley Shaloff, "Press Controls and Sedition Proceedings in the Gold Coast, 1933–39," *African Affairs* 71, no. 284 (1972): 241–263.
54 Wale Adebanwi, *Nation as Grand Narrative: The Nigerian Press and the Politics of Meaning* (Rochester: University of Rochester Press, 2016).

55 Luke U. Uche, *Mass Media, People, and Politics in Nigeria* (New Delhi: Concept Publishing Company, 1989), 95.

56 Austine U. Igwe, "'Zik of Africa'–An Appraisal of the Contributions of Dr. Nnamdi Azikiwe to African Socio-Political and Economic Growth in the Twentieth Century," *Global Journal of Arts and Humanities and Social Sciences* 3, no. 4 (2015): 14–27.

57 Richard L. Sklar, *Nigerian Political Parties: Power in an Emergent African Nation* (New Jersey: Africa World Press, 2004).

58 Ngozika Obi-Ani and Paul Obi-Ani, "Zikist Movement 1946–1950: A Reappraisal," *Nsukka Journal of Humanities* 23, no. 2 (2015).

59 Obaro Ikime, ed., *Groundwork of Nigerian History* (Ibadan: Heinemann, 1980), 566.

60 Wilson Uwujaren, "Zik: The Exit of a Pioneer," *The News*, May 27, 1996.

61 Igwe, "'Zik of Africa.'"

62 Obafemi Awolowo, *Awo: The Autobiography of Chief Obafemi Awolowo* (Cambridge: Cambridge University Press, 1960).

63 John A. A. Ayoade, "Party and Ideology in Nigeria: A Case Study of the Action Group," *Journal of Black Studies* 16, no. 2 (1985): 169–188.

64 Lateef O. Buhari, "The Contributions of Chief Obafemi Awolowo to the Growth and the Development of Nigeria During First Republic," *Annals of Reviews and Research* 4, no. 4 (2019): 00115–00120.

65 Stephen N. Macauley, "Obafemi Awolowo (1909–1985)," *Black Past*, October 25, 2010, https://www.blackpast.org/global-african-history/awolowo-obafemi-1909-1985/.

66 Encyclopaedia Britannica, "Obafemi Awolowo, Nigerian Statesman," *Encyclopaedia Britannica*, November 13, 2021, https://www.britannica.com/biography/Obafemi-Awolowo.

67 Chukwudi Ukonne, "An Irony of History: The Complicated Legacy of Chief Obafemi Awolowo," *The Republic*, August 31, 2020, https://republic.com.ng/august-september-2020/an-irony-of-history/.

68 Daniel H. Ocheja, *The Rise and Fall of the Nigerian First Republic: History of Nigeria from Lord Lugard to Gen. Aguyi-Ironsi (1900–1966)* (Lokoja: Ogun De-Reuben, 2001).

69 Buhari, "The Contributions of Chief Obafemi Awolowo."

70 Buhari, "The Contributions of Chief Obafemi Awolowo."

71 David Birmingham, *Kwame Nkrumah: The Father of African Nationalism* (Ohio: Ohio University Press, 1998).

72 F. M. Bourret, *Ghana—The Road to Independence (Revised Edition)* (Stanford: Stanford University Press, 1960).

73 Phyllis Martin and Patrick O'Meara, eds., *Africa* (Bloomington: Indiana Press, 1977), 157.

74 Scott W. Thompson, *Ghana's Foreign Policy 1957–1966* (Princeton: Princeton University Press, 1969).

75 Frank Gerits, "'When the Bull Elephants Fight': Kwame Nkrumah, Non-Alignment, and Pan-Africanism as an Interventionist Ideology in the Global Cold War (1957–66)," *International History Review* 37, no. 5 (2015): 951–969.

76 Rui Lopes and Víctor Barros, "Amílcar Cabral and the Liberation of Guinea-Bissau and Cape Verde: International, Transnational, and Global Dimensions," *The International History Review* 42, no. 6 (2020): 1230–1237.

77 Peter K. Mendy, *Amílcar Cabral: A Nationalist and Pan-Africanist Revolutionary* (Ohio: Ohio University Press, 2019).

78 Mendy, *Amílcar Cabral*.

79 Ahmed Sékou Touré, *Afrika and Imperialism* (Newark: Jihad Publishing Co., 1973).

80 Carlos E. Sangreman and Rui J. Semedo, "The Struggle for Independence in Guinea-Bissau: Contribution to Understanding the Contradictions of the Process of State Building," *Journal of Contemporary Sociological Issues* 2, no. 1 (2022): 59–75.

81 Adiele Afigbo, Emmanuel A. Ayandele, R. J. Gavin, J. D. Omer-Cooper, and Robin Palmer, eds., *The Making of Modern Africa, Vol. 2 (Growth of African Civilization)* (Burnt Mill: Longman, 1986), 54.

82 Vincent Khapoya, "African Nationalism and the Struggle for Freedom," in *The African Experience*, 4th ed., ed. Vincent Khapoya (London: Routledge, 2012), 139–168.

83 Mairi S. MacDonald, "The Challenge of Guinea Independence, 1958–1971," Ph.D. diss., University of Toronto, 2009, 25.

84 Mohamed S. Camara, *Political History of Guinea since World War Two* (New York: Peter Lang, 2014).
85 Tiyambe Zeleza, "Pan-African Trade Unionism: Unity and Discord," *Transafrican Journal of History* 15 (1986): 164–190.
86 Zeleza, "Pan-African Trade Unionism."
87 Edmund O. Egboh, "The Nigerian Trade-Union Movement and its Relations with World Trade-Union Internationals," *Présence Africaine* 75 (1970): 76–88.
88 Jean Meynaud, *Trade Unionism in Africa: A Study of Its Growth and Orientation* (London: Methuen, 1967), 53.
89 Charles A. Orr, "Trade Unionism in Colonial Africa," *The Journal of Modern African Studies* 4, no. 1 (1966): 65–81.
90 Asuquo Cowan, *Evolution of Trade Unionism in Ghana* (Accra: Trades Union Congress (Ghana), 1969).
91 Adhemar Byl, "What Role for Unions?" *Africa Today* 9, no. 10 (1962): 7–9.
92 Jean Meynaud and Anisse S. Bey, *Trade Unionism in Africa* (London: Methuen, 1967), 60–61.
93 Susan Geiger, "Women and African Nationalism," *Journal of Women's History* 2, no. 1 (1990): 227–244.
94 Benjamin N. Lawrance, "La Révolte des Femmes: Economic Upheaval and the Gender of Political Authority in Lomé, Togo, 1931–33," *African Studies Review* 46, no. 1 (2003): 43–67.
95 Eugenia Shanklin, "Anlu Remembered: The Kom Women's Rebellion of 1958–61," *Dialectical Anthropology* 15, no. 2/3 (1990): 159–181.
96 Susan Geiger, Jean M. Allman, and Nakanyike Musisi, eds., *Women in African Colonial Histories* (Bloomington: Indiana University Press, 2002).
97 Abdul Kuba, "Women Nationalists in Nineteenth and Twentieth Century Ghana and Zimbabwe: Case Studies of Charwe Nehanda Nyakasikana and Yaa Asentewaa," *Journal of International Women's Studies* 19, no. 2 (2018): 159–171.
98 Kuba, "Women Nationalists."
99 Constance A. Cummings-John and LaRay Denzer, *Constance Agatha Cummings-John: Memoirs of a Krio Leader* (Ibadan: Sam Bookman for Humanities Research Centre, 1995).
100 Filomena Steady, *Women and Collective Action in Africa: Development, Democratization, and Empowerment, with Special Focus on Sierra Leone* (New York: Palgrave Macmillan, 2006), 62–65.
101 Judith A. Byfield, "Taxation, Women, and the Colonial State: Egba Women's Tax Revolt," *Meridians* 3, no. 2 (2003): 250–277.
102 Cheryl Johnson-Odim and Nina E. Mba, *For Women and the Nation: Funmilayo Ransome-Kuti of Nigeria* (Urbana: University of Illinois Press, 1997).
103 Byfield, "Taxation, Women, and the Colonial State."
104 Kenneth Little, *African Women in Towns: An Aspect of Africa's Social Revolution* (Cambridge: Cambridge University Press, 1973), 206–208.
105 Little, *African Women in Towns*, 206.
106 Little, *African Women in Towns*.
107 Jacqueline-Bethel Tchouta Mougoué, *Gender, Separatist Politics, and Embodied Nationalism in Cameroon* (Michigan: University of Michigan Press, 2019).
108 Nnamdi Azikiwe, *Renascent Africa* (London: Frank Cass & Company Limited, 1968).
109 Nkrumah, *Africa Must Unite*.
110 Kwame Nkrumah, *Towards Colonial Freedom: Africa in the Struggle against World Imperialism* (London: Heinemann, 1962).
111 Kwame Nkrumah, *Consciencism: Philosophy and Ideology for De-Colonisation* (New York: Monthly Review Press, 1970).
112 Adewumi, *West African Nationalism Rediscovered*.
113 Francis A. Kornegay, "The Pan-African Legacy: Some Historical and Contemporary Perspectives," *A Current Bibliography of African Affairs* 4, no. 1 (1971): 24–31.

19

THE ROAD TO INDEPENDENCE

Protests and Demands Before the Second World War

At the onset of colonial intrusion into West Africa, European colonists were met with stiff opposition from the indigenous people.[1] West Africans employed different strategies to guarantee their survival from the authoritarian colonial rule by the Europeans.[2] The Yaa Asantewaa War, fought by the British and the Asante, was a classic expression of the kind of resistance West Africans mounted against Europeans during the colonization period.[3] Some of the key protagonists in the journey to independence were the educated African elites, who were young Africans who had acquired Western-styled education, had imbibed some measure of Western acculturation and had suitable professions or trades.[4] Most of these educated elites would later become political leaders, trade unionists, and journalists who would spearhead nationalist ideas and efforts.[5]

From precolonial times in West Africa to the first half of the colonial period, power rested in the hands of traditional rulers such as kings, chiefs, emirs, and priests.[6] British and French colonists employed these rulers under the indirect rule system to govern people at the grassroots level. However, as Western-styled education aided the implementation of their policy of assimilation, leading to the production of a new social class order known as the educated elites, Europeans gradually shifted political power from traditional rulers to the educated elites.[7] It is perhaps only in Northern Nigeria that traditional rulers continued to have a certain level of political authority.

The rise of educated African elites could be ascribed partially to Western education and higher education.[8] Notably, the promotion of Western education was taken up by Christian missions as one of their principal responsibilities. As Ekechi notes, "formal education became the bait with which the young generation of Africans was enticed to Christianity."[9] Bassey also observes that higher education was seen as an opportunity for Africans to be European-trained and access untapped work opportunities and a medium for effective political and technological developments. For instance, in the mission churches, the civil service, colonial government, and European-owned enterprises,

DOI: 10.4324/9781003198260-23

job opportunities to serve as catechists, clerks, teachers, accountants, and sales representatives opened up to be filled by the educated African elites.[10] Undoubtedly, formal education became the most effective weapon in Africans' struggle against European colonists for self-rule.[11] Fairly quickly, the masses also began to look up to the educated elites as nationalist leaders and higher education as the medium for the transformation of Africa.

Aside from the "Scramble for Africa" and the period before the outbreak of the Second World War, the First World War was the singular event with the greatest influence on the trajectories of development in colonial West Africa.[12] The First World War broke out in 1914, hurling Europe into one of the greatest wars in its history, with much carnage and many casualties. Ironically, what European superpowers had aimed to prevent during the scramble for Africa—intense rivalry leading to war—surfaced and significantly impacted them and their territories in Africa. For instance, due to the defeat of Germany and its Central Powers allies (Austria-Hungary, Bulgaria, and the Ottoman Empire), German territories in West Africa—Togo and Cameroon—were taken up as trusteeship territories by France and Britain, respectively.[13] During the First World War, Africans were drafted into European armies to fight alongside their colonial masters.[14] The policy of assimilation, which European colonists implemented in their colonies and protectorates in Africa, projected to Africans the view that they were expected to be loyal subjects to the motherland in Europe. By the start of the war, some Africans hoped to benefit from this new perspective, but by the end of the war, Africans, especially those from West Africa, began to question their allegiance to European superpowers.

In the few decades that followed the scramble for Africa and before the outbreak of the First World War, European colonists were working toward consolidating their hold on colonies and protectorates in Africa. During this period, they also established social and economic policies to guide the administration of their territories in Africa. In West Africa, the cardinal principles that guided such social and economic policies were stimulating the production of cash crops and other agricultural produce from West Africa. The idea was to affect the export and processing of such products to the imperial country in Europe and their importation back to West Africa, where they were expected to be purchased by Africans at prices predetermined by European colonists. It is noteworthy that Europeans introduced a monetized market economy into Nigeria by using their currencies in trade as a medium of exchange.[15] To promote their economies in West Africa, they built railroads connecting West Africa to international trade and marketplaces.[16] Though it may be said that the development of railroads by Europeans contributed to infrastructural development, the inequality in the dividends generated from the construction of such railroads underlines the great extent to which Europeans exploited West Africa.

As suggested earlier, Christian missions bore the cost of providing education. Some West Africans embraced Western education provided by these Christian missions and converted to Christianity while holding on to their social and cultural identities. Some of the educated elites from this class spearheaded nationalist movements that later forced European colonists into drawing up policies that benefitted West Africans while guiding the region gradually toward self-rule.[17] The outbreak of the First World War added fuel to the raging flames of early nationalism in West Africa, for they became louder in decrying unfair, racist, and autocratic policies.

One of the significant movements that emerged before the outbreak of the Second World War was the National Congress of British West Africa (NCBWA). The NCBWA was formed in Accra, Ghana, in 1920 under the leadership of Joseph Cassely Hayford.[18] The organization brought together African intellectuals from different British West African countries such as Nigeria, The Gambia, and Sierra Leone. Branches were later established in each of these colonies.[19] According to Eluwa, the NCBWA differed from the previous nationalist organizations because while the previous protest organizations sought the emancipation of specific parts, states, or nations in West Africa, NCBWA was targeted at the emancipation of the entire British West African colonies.[20] Eluwa adds that: "The incipient nationalism which the movement embodied reflects a line in a chain of reactions to the British advent into and 'colonization' of West Africa."[21] Notably, the emergence of the National Congress of British West Africa spurred the rise of nationalism, among other activist responses that West Africans would give to Europeans to guide their indigenous nations to self-rule.[22]

In British West Africa, the rise of nationalism in the decade after the First World War was marked by the publishing of newspapers and magazines with incisive content that criticized colonial policies and advocated for the inclusion of West Africans in government.[23] For instance, the crude nature of the taxation system introduced by the British in the Colony and Protectorate of Nigeria and their attempts to extend such a tax system to women in the protectorate led to the Aba Women's War of 1929.[24] It should be noted, however, that West Africans' responses against unfair policies by European colonists led to major reforms of economic and political systems in the colonies and protectorates.[25]

For example, in the case of British West Africa, the Colonial Development Act was promulgated in 1929 to extend social, financial, and political developments to their colonies and protectorates in Africa. According to Shriwise, the Act was passed to serve two objectives: to develop agriculture and industry in Britain's colonies and to promote commerce or industry in the United Kingdom.[26] The Colonial Development Act opened a leeway for the development of British colonies in Africa. A large sum was set aside by Britain to fund education, health, and infrastructural developments in its four colonies. Britain extended the implementation of the funding policy initiated in 1929 to the 1940s, and it later encompassed social, economic, and political reforms. For instance, at the onset of colonial rule, the indirect rule system that Lord Lugard proposed for the colonial administration of British colonial territories in Africa allowed for the domination of government machinery by Europeans, with little to no representation of West Africans.[27] However, by the 1920s, and especially into the 1930s, the elective principle and party politics were introduced in different parts of British West Africa, allowing people to participate actively in political affairs.[28] This change in the political development of British West Africa underlay the emergence of a new era in the colonial history of most British colonies, especially in their journey to self-rule.[29]

Another significant landmark achieved in the 1920s was the formation of student bodies and political movements among West African educated elites. According to Adi, West African students and activists started organizing themselves into separate organizations partly due to concerns that the Pan-African movements that would emerge in Britain and the Americas during the time did not fully represent their identities, viewpoints, and interests.[30] One of the most influential student movements established during this period of rising nationalism was the West African Students' Union (WASU).[31] The movement was founded in 1925 when one of the leading members of NCBWA visited West African students in Britain and proposed the idea of forming an organization that would foster West African unity among them. In the history of colonialism and political developments, the 1920s were remarked upon as being when Africans began to stream-line liberationist ideas toward their specific nations and national interests. In that year, West Africans established political movements that served specific national interests. For instance, the Gold Coast Students' Association and the Nigerian Progress Union emerged during the decade and contributed significantly to nationalist struggles.[32]

Though the emergence of various student associations and political movements in West Africa in the 1920s later played a major role in the region's nationalist efforts, the most significant contributions to nationalism during that decade were made by the NCBWA. In 1920, the newly formed NCBWA sent delegates from among its members to the Secretary of State for Colonies in the United Kingdom, seeking, among other things, the following: the establishment of a legislative council in each British colony in West Africa and that half the membership of such legislative councils be elected Africans; the introduction of the elective principle and that the appointment and deposition of tradi-tional chiefs should be handled by African kingmakers and not by Europeans; and the creation of a judicial body independent of political or administrative control by other arms of the colonial government.[33] Though most of these demands were later adhered to, perhaps only the introduction of the elective principle by Sir High Clifford in 1922 has been identified as one of the results of the protests and demands made by West Africans through the National Congress of British West Africa.[34] It was not until the end of the Second World War that West Africans embraced political radicalism in their anti-colonial nationalist agitations.

The Second World War and Political Radicalism

The outbreak of the Second World War had a paradoxical impact on West Africans.[35] At the onset of the war, the Allied Powers—Britain, the United States of America, and France—peddled war propaganda that spurred their citizens to join the military and extended to their subjects in the colonies in Africa. According to Bonny Ibhawoh, the underlying premise of the war propaganda disseminated by Britain was that the war against Germany was not just one against an enemy nation of the imperial state but was to protect the world against the terrors of Nazism.[36] In one of the common declarations of purpose made by the United States of America and Britain, the political leaders of the respective states, President Theodore Roosevelt and Prime Minister Winston Churchill, mentioned that their countries recognized the rights of all peoples to determine the kind of government under which they would be governed.[37] These declarations were later documented in the Atlantic Charter of 1941, which promised Africans the right to determine the form of government under which they would be governed by the imperial powers.[38] Relying on the promise and premise of the Atlantic Charter, Africans began to demand that "the right to self-determination" be extended to themselves.[39]

Notably, historians have attempted to link the signing of the Atlantic Charter and the end of the Second World War to the emergence of radical nationalism in West Africa.[40] However, it is noteworthy that elsewhere in their African colonies, British colonists quickly denied the extension of the principles of the Atlantic Charter to their colonies.

In a speech he gave before the House of Commons, British Prime Minister Churchill asserted that the Atlantic Charter applied only to Europe. He observed that "At the Atlantic meeting, we had in mind, primarily the restoration of sovereignty, self-government and national life of the states and nations of Europe now under the Nazi yoke."[41] According to Ibhawoh, the matter of the interpretation of the Atlantic Charter was further complicated by the liberal interpretation that United States President Roosevelt would give. Expectedly, West Africans were outraged by the limited scope of interpretation that the British had applied to the Atlantic Charter. In its editorial on November 18, 1941, the *West African Pilot* expressed disappointment about the Prime Minister's statement, especially since the war had cost colonial peoples a lot of material and human resources. However, Churchill later expressed that the Atlantic Charter was not incompatible with the political evolution that was already taking place in West Africa, as the outburst of West African educated elites was not easily moderated.[42]

As ideas of self-determination began to take root in West Africa, militant nationalist organizations, such as the Zikist Movement that emerged in Nigeria, erupted. According to Olusanya, in his attempt to understand the factors responsible for the formation of the Zikist Movement, "the political situation in Nigeria after the Second World War had stimulated national awakening to an unprecedented degree."[43] In the aftermath of the Second World War, trade unions, ex-servicemen unions, political parties, and women's associations emerged.[44] While the Zikist Movement was the most militant of these groups in Nigeria, the United Gold Coast Convention was established in Ghana.[45] According to Dennis Austin, the post–Second World War account of nationalism in Ghana began with the establishment of the United Gold Coast Convention, an association of a small number of educated elites aimed at gradually leading Ghana to independence through the enactment and implementation of modern reforms.[46] Nationalist organizations of this type not only provided a training ground for the development of nationalists who would later commandeer the political sphere of newly independent states in West Africa, but they were also responsible for the speedy decolonization of West Africa in the aftermath of the Second World War.

While history books often showcase nationalist ideas and efforts masterminded by male-educated elites from colonial West Africa, only a few pay attention to women's ideas, efforts, and activities toward decolonization. It is pertinent to add that this prejudiced manner of writing historiographies is not limited to West Africa, as historians like Chadya have found traces of prejudice in the history of nationalism in Africa at large.[47] Meanwhile, revisiting the history of nationalism in West Africa has led to the knowledge of the participation of women. Social movements like the Lagos Market Women Association and the Abeokuta Women Association in Nigeria, as well as the Sierra Leone Women's Movement, were instrumental to the attainment of independence in the British West African colonies of Nigeria and Sierra Leone. These social movements were concerned about implementing wartime controls after the war, which militated against their income-generating endeavors. For instance, the Lagos Market Women Association, under the leadership of Madam Alimotu Pelewura, appealed to the Commissioner of the Colony of Lagos against the continuation of wartime economic restrictions.[48]

While the Second World War expedited the growth of radical anti-nationalism in British West Africa, nationalist struggles were rather sluggish in French West Africa.[49]

Though West Africans in British colonies were already proposing ideas for the expulsion of the British from their lands and the termination of imperial rule, West Africans in French colonies were dealing with the question of local involvement in the colonies' political machinery. The late onset of party politics is partly responsible for the differences in the level of national agitation between French and British West African colonies. For instance, before the outbreak of the Second World War, especially in the 1930s, political parties had already emerged in Nigeria, with the country's Nigerian Youth Movement, founded in 1933, serving as the most formidable political party in the Colony and Protectorate of Nigeria.[50] In British West Africa, Ghana and The Gambia followed suit with the establishment of the United Gold Coast Convention in 1947 and the Democratic Party, respectively.

The objectives and activities of the first generation of political parties in West Africa's political history were based on radical nationalism.[51] Political parties, especially after the end of the Second World War, became critics of the colonial government. For instance, the Nigerian Youth Movement was Nigeria's political organization with possibly the strongest stance against imperialism. According to Coleman, the party was "the nucleus of Nigeria's first genuine nationalist organization."[52] The National Youth Movement spearheaded protests, rallies, boycotts, and demonstrations in opposition to certain policies and actions by the British colonial government in colonial Nigeria. Like most other political parties or movements in colonial West Africa, the organization employed the medium of the mass media to attract support from the general public. The official newspaper of the National Youth Movement was the *Lagos Daily Service*. Through the newspaper, the National Youth Movement advocated for free education, universal adult suffrage, the independence of the judiciary, and better work conditions in the civil service, among others.[53] In one of the most incisive editorials ever published by the organization, the following was written of the British Prime Minister who sought to evade the obligations of imperial Britain under the Atlantic Charter:

> Winston Churchill is a bundle of contradictions. He believes in 'liberty and freedom for all men.' He is at the same time a die-hard imperialist. Imperialism and liberty are by no means coterminous. Churchill believes in ruling irrespective of the will of those who are ruled and yet he decries dictatorship of the world by Great Powers.[54]

In Nigeria, popular political parties that emerged after the Second World War were the Action Group, the Northern People's Congress, and the National Council of Nigerian Citizens. Of these three leading political parties, only the Northern People's Congress was conservative in articulating and pursuing nationalist objectives.[55] In Ghana, after the emergence of the United Gold Coast Convention, other formidable parties that would arise were the Convention People's Party and the National Liberation Movement.[56] According to Emmanuel, these political organizations erupted as a result of the merger of Ghanaian intellectuals and their preexisting organizations, such as the Aborigines' Right Protection Society, which was the precursor to the establishment of the United Gold Coast Convention.[57]

In Sierra Leone, in 1951, different social and political movements collaborated to form the Sierra Leone People's Party (SSLP).[58] The leadership of this political party would spearhead negotiations with the British colonial government to secure independence for the protectorate by the year 1961. As a precursor to the grant of independence in the 1950s and the 1960s, political parties, trade unions, and other remarkable associations in different British West African colonies would send delegates to London to attend certain constitutional conferences that would lay the framework for the decolonization of West Africa.

Constitutional Reforms in British West Africa

The decolonization of British West Africa was ushered in through constitution-making. Between the end of the Second World War and the grant of independence in the 1950s and the 1960s, a series of constitutional conferences were undertaken that required the presence and contributions of West African political elites.[59] According to Lodge, the first generation of constitutions drafted for West African colonial states were not particularly the result of extensive deliberation.[60] The author reckons that in British West Africa, constitution-making was conducted through a drafting process undertaken by colonial civil servants. It was only on certain minor issues that suggestions were encouraged by national political elites of respective colonies, and in that regard, there were usually divided opinions among the political elites on which constitutional concepts or principles to adopt. For instance, in situations where political parties were formed around ethnic groups, leaders of minority groups tended to support the devolution of powers, while those of dominant groups favored unitary constitutional arrangements. Thus, the decision on what constitutional systems would be established for colonies rested with European colonists.[61]

Nigeria has often been cited as one of the few African countries that held onto most of the constitutional principles handed down by the colonial government. As a heterogeneous nation, it is believed that a federal system was the best option for the country.[62] Meanwhile, efforts made by the colonial government to satisfy all interest groups proved abortive. Since the introduction of federalism into Nigeria with the enactment of the Richards' Constitution in 1946, concerns have been raised about the polarization of views on the kind of federalism to be adopted for the country. As suggested in the preceding paragraph, though political leaders of the major ethnic groups or regions in the colony favored unitary or regional constitutional arrangements, those in minor ethnic groups clamored for a system where all ethnic groups would be well-represented. This would continue to be a major constitutional issue for the country even after independence.[63]

Constitutional reforms began in Nigeria with the enactment of Clifford's Constitution of 1922.[64] Before then, governmental control of the colony and protectorate of Nigeria rested with the Governor-General, who had both an executive and a legislative council that advised him on policy-making and whose advice he had the power to veto. The major landmark in the enactment of Clifford's Constitution was the introduction of the elective principle, which, for the first time in colonial history, granted adult suffrage and the creation of political offices into which Africans were elected.[65] Also, the 1922 Constitution propelled the emergence of party politics in the country. Following Clifford's Constitution was Richard's Constitution, which introduced regionalism to Nigeria's political sphere. Richard's Constitution of 1946 saw the conversion of erstwhile provinces into regions as administrative units with some degree of governmental authority devolved to them from the central government.[66] However, ample historical records revealed that it was instead the Macpherson and Lyttleton Constitutions of 1951 and 1954. According to Ezera, these constitutions resulted from lengthy discussions at constitutional conferences.[67] This attribute distinguished the later constitutions from the previously enacted ones—the Cliffords' and Richard's constitutions—which were imposed on Nigerians without due consultation. Chief Obafemi Awolowo was a major critic of these constitutions (Figure 19.1).

As previously stated, the federal dimensions of the constitutions fashioned out during the decolonization era of the 1950s and the 1960s were retained only in Nigeria. In Ghana, another British West African colony, interest groups presented constitutional principles so varied that the constitution that was eventually drafted for the country was stiffly opposed.[68] For instance, the National Liberation Movement that emerged in opposition to the Convention People's Party led by Nkrumah preferred to have an indissoluble federation with elected regional parliaments and the revenue distribution between the central government and the federating units. The later Constitutional Assembly considered these suggestions, among other constitutional issues in colonial Ghana, and endorsed a British constitutional advisor's recommendation that regional assemblies with delegated powers should be established instead. Irritated at this incident, the National Liberation Movement boycotted the proceedings of the Constitutional Assembly. The independence constitution to be handed down to Ghanaians included the establishment of regional assemblies (whose powers were to be determined by the Parliament), a Prime Minister, a cabinet responsible to the Parliament, and the retention of the British monarch as head of state.[69]

The history of parliament and constitutional developments in Sierra Leone can be traced as far back as 1863 when the colonial government in Sierra Leone, at the time, established executive and legislative councils for the proper and effective administration of the colony.[70] Different political and economic reforms were introduced between 1863 and 1961 when Sierra Leone gained independence. However, the Slater Constitution of 1924 and the 1950 Stevenson Constitution had the most massive impact on the trajectories of development in the country.[71] Like Nigeria's 1922 Constitution, the 1924 Slater Constitution introduced the elective principle and granted minimal representation to Sierra Leoneans through the membership of certain traditional chiefs in the legislative council. The 1947 Constitution provided for increased membership of Africans in both executive and legislative councils. During the run-up to the grant of independence, delegates from ruling political parties and other interest groups in Sierra Leone joined those in other British West African colonies to participate in constitutional conferences, the outcomes of which included redesigning political and constitutional frameworks for the soon-to-be-independent nations.[72]

In The Gambia, the last British West African colony to gain independence, post–Second World War constitutional reforms were more radical than those previously made. In their review of the country's political history, Arnold Hughes and David Perfect observed that questions about the constitutional framework within which the territory would be governed were raised as early as the late nineteenth century when Europeans first settled in the territory.[73] It had also been suggested at different times that the territory be merged with Senegal or Sierra Leone and governed by either of those countries. However, by the 1950s, the status of The Gambia as a separate unit was inevitable. By 1960, which some have described as the year of the decolonization of Africa, unresolved

FIGURE 19.1 Portrait of Chief Obafemi Awolowo by Michael Efionayi. Author's collection.

constitutional issues delayed the decolonization of The Gambia. According to Hughes and Perfect, by this year, a new House of Representatives was established to replace the former Legislative Council as a parliament for the country.[74] At the constitutional conference in London in July 1961, alterations were made to the established constitutional framework. The 1962 elections that followed these reforms helped position The Gambia on the fast track to independence, a landmark that was achieved in 1965.[75]

The Independence of French Colonies

While 1960 is often called the "Year of Africa" in recognition of the grant of independence to many African nations that year, it is, perhaps, more befitting that it be nicknamed the "Year of French West Africa." Of the 17 African countries that gained independence that year, 11 were French colonies, and seven out of these were West African colonies. Seven of the eight French colonies in West Africa would gain their independence in the same year. The only colony not included in this decolonization process was Guinea, which had already chosen to opt out of continued colonization in a referendum that took place in 1958.[76] Historians and other scholars have taken a peculiar interest in the road to independence in French West Africa and how it differed from British West Africa.[77] As shown in the preceding section, constitutional reforms in British West Africa began in the early nineteenth century, though Britain would begin to implement radical constitutional reforms in its four colonies in West Africa soon after the Second World War. In this section, we attempt to narrate the trajectory of French West African countries on their journey toward independence.

A proper narration of the history of decolonization in French West Africa requires a distinction between Guinea and the other seven French colonies. In an empire-wide referendum in 1958, France proposed a continuation of colonialism pending the time when the colonists had helped fashion out a constitutional framework that would include each of them in a commonwealth of nations. According to Schmidt, historians and other scholars have not taken a serious interest in the factors that led to Guinea's rejection of the proposal.[78] The author, however, notes that the difference in the outcome of the referendum for Guinea might have resulted from the distinctive nature of the leading political movements in Guinea and the power of colonial chieftaincy in those other territories.[79] Schmidt observes that contrary to what was obtained in the other French colonies in Africa, the Guinea branch of the Rassemblement Démocratique Africain was effective in grassroots, class, gender, ethnic, and regional alliances, strong at the local level and operated on a principle of popular representation. She avers that "while parties in other territories generally were dominated by political, economic, and religious elites who had a stake in the colonial system, the Guinean RDA was led by low-level civil servants and trade unionists who were frustrated by the strictures of colonial rule."[80]

Although the 1958 referendum was often praised as responsible for the unexpected grant of independence to Guinea, the fight for the decolonization of Guinea started a few decades earlier.[81] As in most other West African colonies, the emergence of party politics in Guinea in the decade after the Second World War promoted radical nationalism to a greater degree than in other French West African colonies. As Schmidt argues, unlike what was obtained in other French colonies where professionals such as lawyers, accountants, and engineers formed and led political movements, anti-colonial nationalism was spearheaded by people on the lower rungs of the economic ladder.[82] This attribute helped articulate the demands of the masses, who had become disinterested in the continuity of colonial administration after the Second World War. Through movements such as the Rassemblement Démocratique Africain, the people of colonial Guinea expressed their dissatisfaction with colonial policies.[83] Opposition to the proposed 1958 constitution was voiced as soon as the referendum was called. After the referendum, it took two more years before independence would eventually be granted in other parts of French West Africa.[84]

In the case of other French West Africa colonies, the decade after the Second World War ushered in massive constitutional reforms that helped lay the foundation of later independent states with effective subordinate relationships with the French Empire. Unlike Britain, which allowed few contributions from African political leaders, France engaged representatives from its colonies during the constitution-making process. According to Lodge, changes were made to existing constitutional frameworks by introducing universal suffrage for advisory councils and the representation of West Africans in the French National Assembly in Paris in 1956.[85] By 1958, functional national assemblies had been established for each country. The author uses the case of Côte d'Ivoire to illustrate the extent to which France and African political leaders collaborated in the constitution-making process in French West African countries:

> After a nearly unanimous referendum in 1958 calling for the territory to become a republic within a francophone African community a Constitution was drafted by Ivorian officials, amended by a committee within the Ivorian National Assembly, approved by the leader of the main political party, then a parliamentarian in Paris, and subsequently adopted by the Ivorian Assembly.

In sum, earlier studies on the decolonization process in French West Africa portrayed it as a smooth process.[86] Contrary to other French colonies such as Indochina and Algeria, whose decolonization processes were marked by prolonged wars, French West African colonies successfully transitioned to independence. The key protagonists in the region's decolonization were the French colonial administration and African political elites who collaborated to drive different African countries toward independence. While the decolonization process in French West Africa did not crystallize into carnage, it is unbefitting to suggest that the process was not contingent. According to Chafer, decolonization in French West Africa was propelled by several factors, including the nature of colonial rule in the region, the rise of nationalism after the Second World War and the French responses. He also notes that "the perceived need to maintain empire at all costs to restore French grandeur after the humiliation of defeat and occupation in the Second World War" was another huge factor. As the author also rightly observes, when France eventually decided to grant independence to its colonies in West Africa in 1959, it took less than a year before they all gained independence. However, French dominance persisted several decades after, despite the acclaimed political independence granted to these countries.[87]

Conclusion

From the onset of colonial rule in the late nineteenth century, West Africans fought wars of resistance to oppose its imposition. Even though Europeans' superior military technology and tactics caused West Africans to lose the conquering wars, they refused to let Europe rule their political, economic, and sociocultural affairs. No sooner had Europeans finally established their base than the journey to independence began. In the early years of the history of nationalism, protests and demands were made to guarantee the inclusion of West Africans in the political machinery of government. Meanwhile, due to the changing world order after the Second World War, anti-colonial nationalism erupted across West African colonies. In British West Africa, constitutional reforms were made, and radical nationalist struggles blossomed. As this chapter shows, decolonization took a slightly different turn in French West Africa, where African political leaders engaged in the decolonization process. In South Africa, for example, Black Africans had to fight apartheid after the country gained independence to achieve political, economic, and social freedom. In British and French territories, it took several decades following independence for West Africa to be free of European colonial domination.[88]

DEEP DIVE

Assignment 1

Objective

The objective of this assignment is to ensure that students complete the reading of Chapter 19 and to get them to explain the factors that contributed to the rise of nationalism and independence of West Africa in the 1950s and 1960s.

Method

Students will be expected to write a short response to the question.

Reading Comprehension

How did political parties emerge in West Africa, and why did they become more radical after the Second World War?

Assignment 2

Discussion

What were some of the underlying protests and demands made by West African peoples before the commencement of the Second World War?

Objective

The objective of this assignment is to ensure that students have a deeper knowledge of the historical trajectory of how the people of West Africa struggled with colonial imposition and eventually fought their way through various methods to achieve independence.

Method

Students will be expected to have a group discussion (either in person or on the online discussion forum) to talk to their peers about the question. Each student would be expected to create a post and respond to at least one other student. If this were to take place in person, then it would simply be a class-wide discussion.

Notes

1 Mathew B. Gwanfogbe, "Resistance to European Penetration into Africa: The Case of the North West Region of Cameroon," *Journal of the Cameroon Academy of Sciences* 13, no. 3 (2016): 119–130.
2 Nigel Tussing, "African Resistance to European Colonial Aggression: An Assessment," *Africana Studies Student Research Conference* 2 (2017): 3–8.
3 Albert Adu Boahen, Yaa *Asantewaa and the Asante-British War of 1900–1* (Oxford: James Currey, 2003).
4 Magnus O. Bassey, "Higher Education and the Rise of Early Political Elites in Africa," *Review of Higher Education in Africa* 1, no. 1 (2009): 30–38.
5 Peter C. Lloyd, ed., *The New Elites of Tropical Africa* (London: Oxford University Press, 1966), 1–65.
6 Bassey, "Higher Education."
7 Michael Crowder and Obaro Ikime, eds., *West African Chiefs: Their Changing Status under Colonial Rule and Independence* (New York: Africana Publishing Corporation, 1970).
8 Emmanuel E. Ayandele, *The Missionary Impact on Modern Nigeria 1842–1914: A Political and Social Analysis* (New York: Humanities Press, 1967).

9 Felix K. Ekechi, *Missionary Enterprise and Rivalry in Igboland, 1857–1914* (London: Frank Cass, 1972).

10 Bassey, "Higher Education."

11 Eric R. J. Hussey, "Educational Policy and Political Development in Africa," *African Affairs* 45, no. 179 (1946): 72–80.

12 De-Valera NYM Botchway and Kwame Osei Kwarteng, *Africa and the First World War: Remembrance, Memories and Representations after 100 Years* (Newcastle upon Tyne: Cambridge Scholars Publishing, 2018).

13 Ieuan Griffiths, "The Scramble for Africa: Inherited Political Boundaries," *The Geographical Journal* 152, no. 2 (1986): 204–216.

14 David Killingray and James Matthews, "Beasts of Burden: British West African Carriers in the First World War," *Canadian Journal of African Studies* 13, no. 1/2 (1979): 7–23.

15 Harcourt Fuller, "From Cowries to Coins: Money and Colonialism in the Gold Coast and British West Africa in the Early 20th Century," in *Money in Africa*, eds. Catherine Eagleton, Harcourt Fuller and John Perkins (London: British Museum Research Publications, 2009), 54–61.

16 Remi Jedwab and Alexander Moradi, "Transportation Technology and Economic Change: Evidence from Colonial Railroads and City Growth in Africa," Unpublished Manuscript, Department of Economics, George Washington University, 2013.

17 Arif Hussain, "The Educated Elite: Collaborators, Assailants, Nationalists: A Note on African Nationalists and Nationalism," *Journal of the Historical Society of Nigeria* 7, no. 3 (1974): 485–497.

18 Gabriel I. C. Eluwa, "The National Congress of British West Africa: A Study in African Nationalism," *Présence Africaine* 77 (1971): 131–149.

19 Gabriel O. Olusanya, "The Lagos Branch of The National Congress of British West Africa," *Journal of the Historical Society of Nigeria* 4, no. 2 (1968): 321–333; Ayodele J. Langley, "The Gambia Section of the National Congress of British West Africa," *Africa* 39, no. 4 (1969): 382–395; and Akintola Wyse, "The Sierra Leone Branch of the National Congress of British West Africa, 1918–1946," *International Journal of African Historical Studies* 18, no. 4 (1985): 675–698.

20 Eluwa, "The National Congress of British West Africa."

21 Eluwa, "The National Congress of British West Africa."

22 Gabriel Eluwa, "Background to the Emergence of the National Congress of British West Africa," *African Studies Review* 14, no. 2 (1971): 205–218.

23 Fred I. A. Omu, "The Dilemma of Press Freedom in Colonial Africa: The West African Example," *The Journal of African History* 9, no. 2 (1968): 279–298.

24 Egodi Uchendu and Uche Okonkwo, "The Aba Women's War of 1929 in Eastern Nigeria as anti-colonial Protest," in *The Routledge Companion to Black Women's Cultural Histories*, ed. Janell Hobson (London: Routledge, 2021), 245–254.

25 Olakunle A. Lawal, "From Colonial Reforms to Decolonization: Britain and the Transfer of Power in Nigeria, 1947–1960," *Journal of the Historical Society of Nigeria* 19 (2010): 39–62.

26 Amanda Shriwise, "Social Policy and Britain's 1929 Colonial Development Act," in *International Impacts on Social Policy: Short Histories in Global Perspective*, eds. Frank Nullmeier, Delia González de Reufels and Herbert Obinger (Cham: Palgrave Macmillan, 2022), 73–87.

27 Frederick Lugard, *The Dual Mandate in British Tropical Africa*, 5th ed. (London: Frank Cass Publishers, 1965).

28 James Coleman, "The Emergence of African Political Parties," in *Africa Today*, ed. C. Grove Haines (Maryland: Johns Hopkins University Press, 1955), 225–256.

29 Britannica, "Western Africa – Decolonization and the Regaining of Independence," August 11, 2021, https://www.britannica.com/place/western-Africa/Decolonization-and-the-regaining-of-independence.

30 Hakim Adi, "Pan-Africanism and West African Nationalism in Britain," *African Studies Review* 43, no. 1 (2000): 69–82.

31 Ahmad A. Yusuf, "The West African Students Union and its Contribution to the Anti-Colonial Struggle," *Africa Quarterly* 38, no. 4 (1998): 101–124.

32 Adi, "Pan-Africanism."

33 Eluwa, "The National Congress of British West Africa."
34 Vincent B. Thompson, "Sir Hugh Clifford and the National Congress of British West Africa: A Reconsideration," *Kenya Historical Review* 3, no. 1 (1975): 109–125.
35 Oliver Coates, "New Perspectives on West Africa and World War Two," *Journal of African Military History* 4 (2020): 5–39.
36 Bonny Ibhawoh, "Second World War Propaganda, Imperial Idealism and Anti-colonial Nationalism in British West Africa," *Nordic Journal of African Studies* 16, no. 2 (2007): 221–243.
37 Andreas Eckert, "African Nationalists and Human Rights 1940s–1970s," in *Human Rights in the Twentieth Century*, ed. Stefan-Ludwig Hoffmann (Cambridge: Cambridge University Press, 2011), 292.
38 Douglas Brinkley and David R. Facey-Crowther, *The Atlantic Charter* (Basingstoke: MacMillan, 1994).
39 Ibhawoh, "Second World War Propaganda."
40 Anietie Inyang and Blessing J. Edet, "The Atlantic Charter and Decolonization Movements in Africa, 1941–1960," *African Journal of History and Archaeology* 4, no. 1 (2019): 1–13.
41 National Archives of the United Kingdom, CO 323/1848/7322/1942, extract from speech by Prime Minister Churchill to the House of Commons.
42 Ibhawoh, "Second World War Propaganda," 240–241.
43 Gabriel O. Olusanya, "The Zikist Movement – A Study in Political Radicalism, 1946–50," *The Journal of Modern African Studies* 4, no. 3 (1966): 323–333.
44 Olusanya, "The Zikist Movement."
45 Richard E. Nzeadighibe, *The United Gold Coast Convention and the National Liberation Movement as Opposition Parties in Ghana, 1947–1957* (Washington, DC: Howard University, 1969).
46 Dennis Austin, *Politics in Ghana, 1946–1960* (London: Oxford University Press, 1964).
47 Joyce M. Chadya, "Mother Politics: Anti-colonial Nationalism and the Woman Question in Africa," *Journal of Women's History* 15, no. 3 (2003): 153–157.
48 Cheryl Johnson-Odim, "Madam Alimotu Pelewura and the Lagos Marketwomen," *Tarikh* 7, no. 1 (1981): 1–10.
49 Frederick Cooper, "Alternatives to Empire: France and Africa after World War II," in *The State of Sovereignty: Territories, Laws, Populations*, eds. Douglas Howland and Luise White (Bloomington: Indiana University Press, 2009), 94–123.
50 Richard L. Sklar, *Nigerian Political Parties: Power in an Emergent African Nation* (New Jersey: Africa World Press, 2004).
51 Ndabaningi Sithole, *African Nationalism*, 2nd ed. (New York: Oxford University Press, 1968).
52 James S. Coleman, *Nigeria: Background to Nationalism* (Berkeley and Los Angeles: University of California Press, 1958).
53 Gabriel O. Olusanya, "The Nationalist Movement in Nigeria," in *Groundwork of Nigerian History*, ed. Obaro Ikime (Ibadan: Heinemann Educational Books, 1980), 545–569.
54 Daily Service, March 3, 1945, 2.
55 Sklar, *Nigerian Political Parties*.
56 David Rooney, *Kwame Nkrumah: Vision and Tragedy* (Accra: Sub-Saharan Publishers, 2007), 74–90; and Jean M. Allman, "The National Liberation Movement and the Asante Struggle for Self-determination, 1954–1957" (PhD diss., Northwestern University, 1987).
57 Paddy Emmanuel, "Nationalism in Ghana after 1945: Causes, Actors and Its Impact on Ghana Decolonization Drive" (Master's Thesis, University of Waterloo, 2021).
58 Peter L. Tucker, *Origin and Philosophy of the Sierra Leone People's Party* (Freetown: Mount Everest Publishers, 2001).
59 Victor T. Le Vine, "The Fall and Rise of Constitutionalism in West Africa," *The Journal of Modern African Studies* 35, no. 2 (1997): 181–206.
60 Tom Lodge, "First-Generation Constitutions in Africa," in *Checks and Balances: African Constitutions and Democracy in the 21st Century*, eds. Grant Masterson and Melanie Meirotti (Johannesburg: EIAA, 2017), 15–26.
61 Lodge, "First-Generation Constitutions in Africa."

62 Adiele E. Afigbo, "Background to Nigerian Federalism: Federal Features in the Colonial State," *Publius* 21, no. 4 (1991): 13–29.

63 Manko Rose Rindap and I. M. A. Mari, "Ethnic Minorities and the Nigerian State," *AFRREV IJAH: An International Journal of Arts and Humanities* 3, no. 3 (2014): 89–101.

64 Oluwole I. Odumosu, *The Nigerian Constitution: History and Development* (Lagos: African Universities Press, 1963).

65 Tekena N. Tamuno, "Governor Clifford and Representative Government," *Journal of the Historical Society of Nigeria* 4, no. 1 (1967): 117–124.

66 Kalu Ezera, *Constitutional Development in Nigeria: An Analytical Study of Nigeria's Constitution-Making Developments and the Historical and Political Factors that Affected Constitutional Change* (Cambridge: Cambridge University Press, 1960).

67 Kalu Ezera, "Nigeria's Constitutional Road to Independence," *The Political Quarterly* 30, no. 2 (1959): 131–140.

68 Tapan P. Biswal, *Ghana: Political and Constitutional Developments* (New Delhi: Northern Book Centre, 1992).

69 Lodge, "First-Generation Constitutions in Africa," 16.

70 Martin Kilson, *Political Change in a West African State: A Study of the Modernization Process in Sierra Leone* (London: Harvard University Press, 2013), 97–123.

71 Kilson, *Political Change in a West African State.*

72 Torrent Mélanie, "Crowning the Work of Wilberforce? The Settlers Descendants' Union and the Challenges of Sierra Leone's Independence," *Cahiers Charles V*, no. 46 (2009): 241–292.

73 Arnold Hughes and David Perfect, *A Political History of the Gambia, 1816–1994* (Woodbridge: Boydell & Brewer, 2006), 41–54.

74 Hughes and Perfect, *A Political History of the Gambia.*

75 Hughes and Perfect, *A Political History of The Gambia.*

76 Elizabeth Schmidt, "Anticolonial Nationalism in French West Africa: What Made Guinea Unique?" *African Studies Review* 52, no. 2 (2009): 1–34.

77 Tony Chafer, *The End of Empire in French West Africa: France's Successful Decolonization* (New York: Berg Publishers, 2002).

78 Schmidt, "Anticolonial Nationalism in French West Africa."

79 Schmidt, "Anticolonial Nationalism in French West Africa."

80 Schmidt, "Anticolonial Nationalism in French West Africa."

81 Elizabeth Schmidt, *Mobilizing the Masses: Gender, Ethnicity, and Class in the Nationalist Movement in Guinea, 1939–1958* (New Hampshire: Heinemann, 2005).

82 Schmidt, *Mobilizing the Masses.*

83 Michael Crowder and Donal Cruise O'Brien, "French West Africa, 1945–1960," in *History of West Africa*, Vol. 2, eds. Jacob F. A. Ajayi and Michael Crowder (New York: Columbia University Press, 1973), 664–699.

84 Schmidt, "Anticolonial Nationalism in French West Africa."

85 Lodge, "First-Generation Constitutions in Africa."

86 Chafer, *The End of Empire in French West Africa.*

87 Tony Chafer, "Decolonization in French West Africa," in *Oxford Research Encyclopedia of African History* (Oxford: Oxford University Press, 2022).

88 John D. Hargreaves, *The End of Colonial Rule in West Africa: Essays in Contemporary History* (London: Macmillan, 1979).

PART V
The Postcolonial Era

20

POSTCOLONIAL POLITICS

Introduction

All the political events of the ex-colonies in Africa, like Ghana after 1957, Nigeria after 1960, and South Africa after 1961 (and 1994), qualify as postcolonial politics, but, in line with Nasrullah Mambrol, the geographical coverage of postcolonial politics extends more broadly to ex-colonies such as in the "Caribbean, Central and South America, Africa, the South Pacific islands, and Malaysia."[1] It stretches even further into other former colonies like Canada, India, Philippines, New Zealand, and Australia, but our scope here is specifically limited to Africa, though we will make passive remarks about those experiences from other regions that reinforce our argument about postcolonial politics. Because it is nearly impossible to identify any postcolonial inadequacies and inconsistencies whose root is not deeply ingrained in colonial misadventures, postcolonial politics must address all the conditions of politics in the post-independence era, which have escalated the underdevelopment of the ex-colonies or threatened their chances of engendering advancement.

Different challenges are always emerging and combining on the continent to ridicule every effort toward development for reasons connected to slavery, economic sabotage, and the political desertification of African countries. Their postcolonial politics involve the discussion of these difficult experiences ranging from racism to apartheid, suppression, enslavement, economic strangulation, disenfranchisement, and the eventual responses to all the expressions of European superimposition on Africa. As opined by Ato Quayson, "post colonialism ... involves a studied engagement with the experience of colonialism with past and present effects."[2] The virulent consequences of colonialism outlived its existence and so must be accounted for.

Drawing on the insights of previous postcolonial scholars who have done extensive research on colonialism and its destructive consequences, our arguments unfold in three ways. Firstly, we argue that the political challenges confronting Africa in the present are the byproducts of all the painful experiences inherited or carried over from colonialism.

DOI: 10.4324/9781003198260-25

The current political misfortune of these African countries cannot be divorced from the abusive relationship between them and their erstwhile imperialists, an argument similar to Edward Said's conclusion about the disconnection of the past from the present.[3] In essence, the previous brutality experienced by Africans forms the basis for their ideological entrapment into an abyss of stagnation where it is difficult to register notable advancements or to return to their uncontaminated precolonial identities.

Secondly, the impression that the predatory reign of imperialists has ceased with their formal ends ignores that they largely continue to dictate Africa's future because of the instrumentality of colonization, deep-rooted in shared history. This may appear ambiguous on the surface, but the current struggles of Africans to sever every tie with the history of colonialism are undermined by the conscious and regular encroachment on their economies and politics by the former colonial powers, making it exceptionally challenging to improve their sociopolitical conditions.

Thirdly, Africa is trapped in the frenzy of globalization, pressured to preserve its identities and simultaneously prove the legitimacy of its claims of possessing a redoubtable history of civilization, all while trying to heal itself from the pains and scars of colonization.

Instability in Postcolonial Africa

Perhaps the best way to explain instability in postcolonial Africa is to invoke a vivid experience that illustrates it. For example, Donald Molosi, in his essay "On Decolonizing the Postcolonial African Classroom,"[4] presents his childhood experience while growing up in postcolonial Africa, describing the deep-seated immersion of Africans in colonial sentiments and temperament. As a pupil in Botswana, his teacher once told him that it was improper for males to keep hair on their heads in the name of proper hygiene. Surprisingly, however, there was an exemption to this rule: the male Indian students who shared the same classroom were not expected to observe this injunction. This creates an impression that African schools in the postcolonial environment are a battlefield for identity struggles, where the colonized Africans themselves become willing volunteers for the despoliation of African identity, perhaps unconsciously. The reason for his teacher's decision was the successful implantation of the orientation that anything African is probably inferior and, as such, naturally must undergo radical change through substitution or outright eradication. The magnitude of the mental colonization was demonstrated by how the teacher unconsciously accepted that Indians were model individuals, unlike the African students.

This anecdote pushes us to imagine the level of psychological trauma that Africans must contend with in their own political evolution and their perception of their African identity, as well as demonstrates the degree to which Africans have had to conform to their postcolonial environment just so they could be referred to as human. The postcolonial politics of the African people have never been peaceful for various reasons. It is difficult to find any African country immune to the devastating conditions that are the result of their abusive relationships with their erstwhile colonizers. Virtually all African ex-colonies suffer massive damage from the unceasing dredging of their economic resources that occurred for centuries by Western imperialists. They were victims of human exploitation that manifested most abjectly in their subjection to slavery, as well as many other brutish experiences. These have continued to challenge their attempts at development.

Inevitably, the wave of independence has caused the suppressed ex-colonized people to degenerate into the abyss of misrule and tensions. Approximately five years after many African countries had attained their independence in the 1960s, there was a contagious eruption of anger and grievance that appeared apocalyptic in its expression. Many were overtaken by military forces, promising the reclamation of peace and restoration of African identity, but the ensuing situations exposed stark contradictions between what the military proposed and the actions that defined their leadership. There was a strangulation of the economies that, in response to these contradictions, led to suppressed agitations.

Instability in postcolonial Africa has been characterized by different factors, including secessionist agitations, such as those that led to the Nigerian Civil War between 1966 and 1970, the violence in the Central African Republic in 1966, and Upper Volta—known today as Burkina Faso—in the same year.[5] The escalation of these tensions was engineered by the impracticality of the new identities bestowed on these different countries through colonization, creating conflicts that dictated their political and economic trajectories for decades.

Among the bloated, egotistical charade of Eurocentric scholars, whose evaluations of African challenges are clear attempts to downplay the contributions of the colonizers to the ensuing problems, is Samuel Huntington, who argues in his *Political Order in Changing Societies* that the situations in the ex-colonies are instead demonstrations of dissatisfaction from some groups to the social forces, acting according to their capabilities as, "the wealthy bribe, students riot, workers strike, mobs demonstrate, and the military coup."[6] A closer interrogation of the situation reveals that these explanations for the outbursts of social force are instead a demonstration of the inherent limitations of their philosophical or ideological convictions. The turmoil in the postcolonial environment does not actually represent any of these conjectures, rather revealing something more benumbing about the deep-rooted highhandedness of the colonial structures and their facilitators (Figure 20.1).

While the colonial governments ran their political systems by not anticipating the immediate termination of their stay in Africa, they allowed different groups to gather more strength in establishing a foundation to answer their groups' identities. They imagined they were strengthening these identities through their contributions or accomplishments while colonization lasted. However, this would not continue, especially with the sudden end of colonial rule. Groups were forced to emerge and mobilize swiftly in the post-independence era, inevitably necessitating clashing interests. Students wanted their agitations met, convinced that a desirable African future lay in heavy investment in education; the wealthy considered it necessary to form a bureaucratic political identity where they could usurp power to their advantage; and workers suddenly found their voices to demand a beautiful and better life.

These sectarian yearnings worked against the common course, instigated internal contradiction, and unavoidably led to a proliferation of tensions. Léopold Sédar Senghor of Senegal, for example, was a very committed "nationalist" who challenged European misrule in his country, but he made next to no changes to the existing social order after obtaining the mandate to serve his people and leading them away from the unjust

FIGURE 20.1 The Congolese leader, Patrice Loemoemba in Brussels https://commons. wiki-media.org /wiki /File :De _Congolese _leider _Patrice _Loemoemba _in _Brussel, _ Bestanddeelnr_910-9741.jpg.

strangulations they had been subjected to. Muammar Qaddafi of Libya was a liberal political leader who sought to oust the monarchy in Libya that he considered anti-democratic, but after coming to power, he abandoned these lofty ambitions.

One of the notable reasons for the explosion of conflicts was the colonial boundaries; the border lines were drawn by outmoded decisions hurriedly arrived at to enable European control over Africa. They demonstrated an outright disregard for the cultural makeup of the people whose lives were being affected, and the political structures available during the conquest. The problem was compounded because each of the different identities merged within these boundaries considered themselves qualified for the running of the political and economic systems of the countries bequeathed by the Europeans, with those groups able to use their numerical and social power to impose themselves on others and assume political office, resulting in a new type of internal colonization. The culmination of these parochial ambitions was impossible without occasional struggle and strife among those who contested for power. Mutual suspicion remains rife, breeding internal contradictions that reduce the possibility of achieving national objectives.

Another reason for the sudden political instability that engulfed African countries post-independence is a corollary of the colonial boundaries—the absence of clear negotiations of what the countries after independence would actually look like in practice. Africans suffering from the vestiges of colonization were principally interested in unseating their brutal conquerors, blinding their resolve for, and focusing on, a future beyond independence. As such, the social forces identified by Huntington could not be harnessed to build common bonds and institutions. This did not mean that they did not form unified ideological strata that pushed their shared agenda toward independence; rather, their agitations ended at the demand and they were not able to maintain the freedom that would follow. This is why, barely seven years after independence,

FIGURE 20.2 Map of West Africa today. Author's collection.

Nigeria slid into civil war, and the challenges that consumed Burkina Faso inflicted heavy damage on the country. These occasions of instability caused the manifestation of military interventions, with all the negative effects they brought, as shown in African history (Figure 20.2).

Military Intervention as Postcolonial Politics

Many political scientists conforming to the intellectual perspectives of the Global North perceive the implosion of African countries into wars and hostility as evidence of their incapacity for self-rule or political adroitness. Regrettably, these scholars do not factor in the circumstances and conditions introduced and institutionalized by the Europeans during their colonial expeditions and how they made war inevitable, peace an elusive commodity, and internal politics difficult. Gabriel Almond, for example, understood African dysfunctional postcolonial politics as a weakness of political structures that were incompatible with a modernization agenda.[7] To those whose evaluations aligned with Almond, the fault of underdevelopment rests exclusively on the African people. In their postcolonial conditions, most African countries were a hotbed of crisis, fractions, and internal infractions, all of which ordinarily justified the appropriation of political control by those who could seize it. During these periods, power was not defined by social or political affiliations but rather attached to the level of force that individuals could command. This gave the military personnel the moral authority to oust political structures and install themselves as the putative leaders promising the restoration of peace in different African countries.

These promises of peace and stability from the African military juntas were empty. The execution of articulating interests—bridging social inequity in ways defined by the selfish interests of the select bourgeois class, establishing lines of communication between the government and the governed, creating the independent institutions needed in a democratic environment, and bringing technocrats into the system to employ their tactical knowledge to begin distributing leadership to civilians—was not forthcoming. Instead, all these were substituted with unprecedented greed by the emerging military groups, and they ruled with emboldened impunity that greatly contributed to the emasculation of their systems and their eventual paralysis.

In governance, precedence takes an important position in determining the future trajectory. No matter how disastrous, whatever happens in the corridor of governance automatically becomes established and provides the motivations defining the reactions to similar experiences encountered in the future. Still, while the military rule in some African countries set abysmal precedence for others on the continent, the unsettled political atmosphere under democratic leadership gave the moral impetus to these military interventions.

It is imperative to lay bare these situations to better understand what truly inflamed the already explosive situations and weakened African political systems and institutions. The first coup on the continent that led to the ousting of a democratically elected African President, Sylvanus Olympio of Togo, a then-popular politician who defeated the colonial structures, was triggered by a wide-ranging conspiracy. Olympio was elected in 1958, immediately after Togo's independence, beating a candidate that was fully supported by the French political blocs. His victory triggered urgent aggression by France's bureaucrats who envisioned Olympio's victory as a scary signal for the termination of France's influence over their ex-colonies, and this was not going to be allowed without them putting up a fight. While Olympio[8] was developing his political plans to ensure that the country was rid of France's influence, the French government plotted a totalitarian overthrow to take down their targeted enemies. Olympio's victory became a rallying cry for many African countries to begin full-scale pursuit of their independence, unsettling French powerbrokers and fueling their desire for vengeance. It was, therefore, no surprise that the success of the first African coup in 1963 had the moral backing of the French government.

Barely three years after the military takeover of the Togolese political system, two successive coups happened in Nigeria within a year. In January 1966, General Kaduna Nzeogwu and Major Emmanuel Ifeajuna, among other high-ranking Nigerian military officers, masterminded a coup to oust the president and install a military officer as the de facto president of the country. Another coup, popularly called the Nigerian counter-coup, happened in July of the same year and saw Major-General Yakubu Gowon succeed the first military president, General Aguiyi Ironsi.

Without understanding the internal conflicts and unsettled feuds carried over from the colonial experience, one might believe that the ascension of the military into the political corridor of the country was wholly related to the issues identified by functionalist analysts like Almond. It was a necessary transitional experience needed by a society with weak political knowledge in order to attain modernization and civilization. Conclusions such as Almond's are off-target, failing to properly account for the true situation of the country. It is difficult to confidently judge a people as a failure if they have spent only about six years as independent entities. Even in countries with neoliberal economies and advanced political structures, achieving stable development requires consistency and planning due to evolutionary experience.

Some experts have claimed that ethnic politics was the primary motivation for the military interventions in Nigeria in 1966. Some intellectuals even call the first coup, led by Nzeogwu and Ifeajuna, "the Igbo Coup," a name tied to the ethnic identity that constituted a majority of those who perpetrated the coup. However, those who staged the counter-coup represented another ethnic group, which shows that the emergence of these coups was not related to the underwhelming performances of the ruling political class and instead was borne from the desire to stem internal expansionism threatening the growth of other ethnic nationalities that make up the country.

As previously stated, these complicated issues in African postcolonial politics are due to colonialism and then the imposition of a haphazard national identity. There would have been less instability if the creation of countries by the Europeans had factored in ethnic differences, existing political structures filled with contradictions, and economic systems riddled with inequality. The escalation of political tension occasioned by the emergence of military regimes in African countries was the only motivation needed for the dissolution of the countries into instability and conflict.

There are too many examples of military interventions on the continent during the postcolonial era to be included in this chapter, but we are exposing the characteristic internal shortcomings that gave room for future chaos. Under different military presidents in Africa, the new atmosphere was expected to bring about observable differences, even if Nigerians accepted that their freedom would be the necessary sacrifice. The self-designated mandate of these military officers to ensure that peace would be restored and appropriate institutions would be installed to attract promised development made their elevation justifiable. Regrettably, the result of military governance showed them in a different light. Just as the democratically elected African presidents showed weakness in overseeing the affairs of their respective countries, the military leaders ruled with impunity in places where others were being carefully diplomatic to try and transition back to democratic rule. As such, the handover of power to democratically elected officials was not certain, and, in situations where it occurred, it was either delayed or administered wrongly, another phenomenon brought about due to postcolonial contrivances.

In some situations, there were occasions of coups and counter-coups happening simultaneously. Countries like Nigeria (as already indicated), Congo, Ethiopia, Sudan, Dahomey (Benin Republic), Somalia, Togo, Kenya, Sierra Leone, and Algeria have all experienced military interventions at one point or another, obviously creating unstable environments that could hatch violence and make situations more complicated. Again, we should be careful in accepting the functionalist rhetoric because it is reductionist and carelessly evasive of the contexts. To ascribe the prevalence of wars and hostilities in the postcolonial African environment to a lack of appropriate institutions in actuality indicts the European governments that ruled the continent for hundreds of years. The availability of the institutions serving as preventive measures against the destabilization of their polity proposed by these political scientists would mean the absence of infractions and contradictions. As such, if instability immediately gripped African countries after the termination of European politics, does that not suggest that their long stay produced no functional institutions that could outlast their stay?

Due to the instability imposed by the alternating regimes of democratic and military governance, the continent became an incubator for violence and hostility, divided among groups claiming their own political mandate. The atmosphere was unfavorable for political socialization and development, birthing secessionist movements in most African countries. For example, as Nigeria experienced two occasions of military coups in 1966, separatist agitation for the Biafra region was launched, creating another breeding ground for tension and security threats. The emergence of groups such as the Movement for the Emancipation of Niger Delta (MEND) in Nigeria, the Rwanda Hutu Militia in Rwanda, the Movement of Democratic Forces of Casamance (MFDC) in Senegal, the Al-Shabaab Somali Islamist group in Somalia, the Sudan Liberation Army in Sudan, the Lord's Resistance Army in Uganda, the Ogaden National Liberation Front in Ethiopia, and many others was geared toward getting political advantages by fomenting disorder that would trouble the peace of the people and advance the power of the select few.

Democracy in Postcolonial Africa

To talk about democracy in Africa without laying down its foundations and all the conditions and circumstances that prompted it, is counterproductive. Democracy in Africa—or the local adaptation of any other foreign political philosophy, for that matter—presupposes colonization or other forms of conquest. Many authors, especially of Eurocentric or supremacist leaning, are usually evasive when discussing how Africa has coped with democracy in the relatively recent history of its arrival on the continent for understandable reasons. By avoiding the underlying imperialism and undemocratic nature of the Eurocentric bias in the administration of the colonial system in Africa, these scholars partake in image or reputation management. In most of their academic work addressing the conflicts that are rife in Africa in the contemporary world, the contributions of the erstwhile imperialists in creating the divisive atmosphere engendering political breakdown, social disunity, and ideological clashes have been creatively elided, resulting in succeeding generations lacking insight into the involvement and complicity of these expansionists.

Democratic leadership had been accepted in European countries centuries before their colonial (mis)adventures, yet the visitation of imperialists in Africa began with the introduction of human trading to improve their Euro-American economies by dredging the human resources of Africa for their exploitation. Hardly had this abusive practice ended that they introduced another form of occupation strategy of the African continent by forcibly overtaking the territories of indigenous societies and dividing them into arbitrary units to ease control of the economic systems and political structures within them. Was the system of ruling Africa introduced by these colonialists consistent with those adopted in various European countries for their own use? If the conventional definition of democracy follows the maxim that "it is the government of the people, by the people and for the people," were the government systems imposed on these Africans during colonialism representative of that ideal? Even if we concede that the imposed systems were necessary to aid their expansionism and ensure that their African colonies were submissive and humble, to what extent could that justify how the Europeans extended their undemocratic rule in the countries before introducing democracy?

All these are legitimate questions begging objective responses to contextualize democracy in Africa and see how it affected African collective development. Apart from the complicated nature of the end of the relationship between the colonizers and the colonized, which led to the independence of many African countries, including Ghana, Angola, Kenya, Guinea-Bissau, and Madagascar, some European countries refused to bow to pressure and cede independence to their African colonies despite the spread of independence elsewhere and the insistence of other European countries. In particular, those countries colonized by the French suffered extreme political and economic despoliation. During these experiences, those who would become the future leaders after independence were internalizing the governing and ruling strategies of these despots, naturally demonstrating these characteristics when offered the opportunity to rule.

No fewer than 14 African countries were in the grip of France and were ruled inhumanly during the colonial period. Indeed, the gravity of France's totalitarianism in these countries is revealed by how they were all compelled to make financial commitments to France and concede a great deal of ground to them as the condition for their independence. To the present, these countries continue to make these cutthroat contributions to France, honoring their contractual agreements before independence. One must ask how these countries are held down by these mind-boggling conditions and expected to attain a sudden transformation in their postcolonial life.

Alternatively, democracy can be considered a political philosophy designed not for universal application but only for civilizations that buy into the system. Different African identities and nationalities had their respective political systems, views, and philosophies before the arrival of the Europeans, while the way that the new colonial identities imposed on these people could be a deterrent for functional democracy has always been swept under the carpet. Immediately as colonization ended, the different nationalities making up these countries began to compete for dominance, contending for political power so that their interests would be protected and their identities would flourish.

The ambition to dominate a people is common, but having multiple parties with this ambition in the same territory is a potential disaster, leading to people fighting for what they believe to be a just cause, irrespective of the danger it poses to others. While it appeared that these newly independent countries were operating as democracies on the surface, internally, mutual suspicion was rife and transformed their societies into hotbeds of crisis and hostility. Political analysts focus solely on this and make (vain) projections about the whole of Africa, its history, and its political prospects.

A suitable example that illustrates our argument that colonialism and identity imposition were crucial background reasons for the explosion of conflicts that made democratic stability impossible—even impractical—is the Nigerian experience. Nigerian society is made up of many different ethnic nationalities, each with different numerical strengths. While the beauty of democracy lies in the elevation of majority preferences to leadership, Nigeria's composition makes democracy unique. The major ethnic groups in the country are the Yoruba, Hausa-Fulani, and the Igbo (with countless numbers of other smaller groups) and, by their numerical power, a particular shared identity among these three has benefited from the majoritarian weakness of democracy.

As the system favored the majority group over the numerous minority communities, it reduced the ability of the country to gain the progress it should have through the practice of democracy. Perhaps the situation might have been prevented if the erstwhile imperialists had adopted a truly democratic approach to governance in their regime of domination and subjugation, but Nigeria's system is a far cry from what democracy should represent. Those who found themselves in the minority among these emerging African countries in their postcolonial environment have suffered from government abandonment, project irregularities, and a lack of sociopolitical integration.

Even if we agree that democracy is a valid political philosophy, as it has proven successful in some other civilizations, we must address the cultural and economic peculiarities of Africa and how they have affected its acceptance and success. African economies managed by the emerging post-independence African political elites faced the challenges of mismanagement and philosophical deficits hampering their immediate transformation, as the focus was instead to create a bourgeoisie group from those who succeeded the colonialists. The fundamental consequence is that progress and development have experienced vivid downturns that inevitably made the economic systems weak, a potential reason for the failures on the political front as citizens face economic hardships that are received with aggression and grievance. A major contribution to the fast decline of the economic growth of postcolonial African countries is that leaders have treated the ascension to political office as an opportunity to corner the commonwealth's resources, making life difficult for the common people and halting the transformation of African societies for all. Even when they experienced a surge in income tax revenue, African leaders struggled to develop their economies and infrastructure.

For those African countries transitioning into democratic governments, their experience has been marked by electoral fraud, such as vote-rigging and manipulation. To sabotage postcolonial African democracies, various African leaders have deliberately weakened the institutions under their control by placing people into offices for reciprocal altruism.[9] The refusal to allow institutions to have full independence often threatens the practice of democracy and comes with foreboding consequences for the people's general progress, worsening societal problems. The elites are aware of how their political practices impede the revolutionary turnaround of the status quo but dread the possibility of the proletariat taking control. To ensure that the masses are kept in perpetual indigence, they use the systems they run to repress them and keep them from relevance. These underlying issues give African democracies the identity they possess, with their elections being not about choosing the best to run their countries but rather the preservation of power and the interests of the bourgeoisie.

The challenge of democracy in Africa cannot end without providing solutions to the problems of colonial identity. When there are cohesive national identities, there is a commitment toward national unity, which, in turn, influences the management of the economy for collective advantage. This ensures the creation of strong national infra-structures and institutions to provide an environment suitable for the enablement of true transformation. Even when they encounter challenges that test this national identity, they most likely come to a common ground that allows a peaceful resolution of their differences for national progress. A vibrant economy has the potential to create a mid-dle class that embraces its responsibility for the development of the society. The reasons countries like Ghana, Benin Republic, Mauritius, Namibia, and Botswana have made considerable progress in Africa are connected to their unified identities. The escalation of disruptive activities elsewhere on the continent is because issues around identity for-mation continue to challenge their general development.

Transforming Politics: Strengthening Their Democracies

The transformation of African political systems will be based on specific factors, natural drivers for political sensitization, and transformation. The first is the strengthening of their democracies, as democracy has shown its capacity to be amenable to the dictates of the people. Although it is difficult to imagine a perfect democracy, it thrives in general because it allows for modifications and corrections in policy, representing the opinion of the popular majority. Many countries in the West African region have experienced alternating democratic and military governance within their short times of independ-ence. Challenging their democratic growth occasionally enabled canny leaders to care-fully mastermind a form of quasi-democracy where the democratic elements outlined in their constitutions do not prevent them from serving as pseudo-democratic leaders in practice alone. This also disrupts the level of development recorded in the region because despotic leaders always come to haunt their countries' social, economic, and political lives, causing institutions to crumble under their leadership and making it continually difficult to embark on reasonable and transformative projects.

These democracies can be strengthened by allowing individuals to be well-represented within their political systems, and electoral reform is necessary to enhance this. Where a country is experiencing the quasi-democracy identified above, other countries in the region should have the right to intervene and prevent totalitarianism. Their interest is necessary and should be protected because the failure of one country among them signals a possible threat to the others and may cause a decline in their economies and politics. Without it affecting their sovereign integrity, African countries should weave together political systems where individuals have the freedom to vote and have their votes counted accurately and without manipulation. The voice of the people is important in any strong democracy; they must be represented in the electoral decisions they make and in their collective yearnings. When the larger part of the people collectively seeks social changes, every attempt to repress the people amounts to a miscarriage of justice that undermines their political efficacy. In a country conscious of only developing the bourgeois class, to the detriment of the proletariat, it is difficult to progress democrati-cally as the majority of the people have been denied active participation in the process.

Transparent Leadership Recruitment

It is difficult for individuals prepared for public service to enter into the political struc-tures and practices currently featured in West Africa and on the continent generally.

Political parties glorify those with financial muscle to keep the electorates' attention riveted on them during the electioneering period without questioning the sources of their wealth. The situation is worsened when those who have benefited from diabolical leadership and crooked political cultures decide to use their ill-gotten wealth to run for political office, gaining partisan support because of the understanding that they would generate financial profits for the parties. Thus, the process of selecting political representatives is muddled and tends to favor individuals with questionable moral and financial character. Even when contemporary elections appear free and fair on the surface, the underlying factors usually impede the political growth of the countries, and since their political structures are not built on a strong foundation, it reduces the ability of the people to grow either economically or socially.

For West African politics to become a cynosure for all observers and a beacon of hope for the people, it is compulsory that their leadership recruitment systems and processes are clear and transparent. A transparent process and system would allow individuals to remedy the perpetual challenges confronting the region by gathering those ready for serious developmental projects without having to contend with conflict from party leaders or money-infested politicians. Individuals representing a political interest should be chosen based on the content of their character, their political philosophy and economic plans, rather than ethnic or religious sentiment. When people are considered for political office because of these group identities, they are indirectly endangering their country's political future, deliberately or otherwise. To graduate from their level of political inconsistency, these countries need to be transparent in their political organization.

Youth Participation

Throughout the world, there is now an understanding that the agility and vibrancy of the youth is a great addition to the political life of a people. Apart from their skills for innovation and the power of creativity, youths have the zeal and drive to move any society to a better condition, and all efforts to marginalize them in the political activities of a country come with devastating consequences. As such, youth in West African countries should be consciously factored in and progressively incorporated when considering the development of the region. The economic system must feature a high percentage of, and the presence of, youths because the economic system of the world, in general, is evolving. With the transformation of the global economy from analog to digital, the world has continued to make accelerating progress in the digital economy, and young people are the important drivers of these aspects of modern economics. With their competence in technology and their widened curiosity, they have masterminded revolutionary moves in all sectors. Their involvement in political activities would similarly be additive.

DEEP DIVE

Assignment 1

Objective

The objective of this assignment is to ensure that students complete the reading of Chapter 20 and to encourage them to explore the concept of democracy and the question of whether it can truly be applicable and successful in the African continent.

Method

Students will be expected to write a short note in response to the question.

Reading Comprehension

What was the state of democracy in the early years of post-independence Africa? Consider the ethnic and cultural diversity of the continent and how that may influence democracy in practice.

Assignment 2

Discussion

Given the lingering impact of European imperialism, can Africa ever be free of Western domination?

Objective

The objective of this assignment is to encourage students to examine the definition of "post-colonial" and whether it is possible for African countries to avoid Western domination.

Method

Students will be expected to have a group discussion (either in person or on the online discussion forum) to talk to their peers about the discussion question. Each student would be expected to create a post and respond to at least one other student. If this were to take place in person, then it would simply be a class-wide discussion.

Notes

1 Nasrullah Mambrol, "Postcolonial Novels and Novelists," *Literary Theory and Criticism*, March 8, 2019, https://literariness.org/2019/03/08/postcolonial-novels-and-novelists/.
2 Ato Quayson, "What is Postcolonial Literature?" *The British Academy*, January 2, 2020, https://www.thebritishacademy.ac.uk/blog/what-is-postcolonial-literature/.
3 Edward Said, *Culture and Imperialism* (New York: Vintage Books, 1993).
4 Donald Molosi, "On Decolonizing the Postcolonial African Classroom," *Literary Hub*, February 28, 2019, https://lithub.com/on-decolonizing-the-postcolonial-african-classroom/.
5 Ruth First, *The Barrel of a Gun: Political Power in Africa and the Coup d'Etat* (London: Penguin African Library, 1972).

6 Samuel Huntington, *Political Order in Changing Society* (New Haven: Yale University Press, 1968).
7 Gabriel Almond, "Introduction: A Functional Approach to Comparative Politics," in *The Politics of the Developing Areas*, eds. Gabriel Almond and James S. Coleman (Princeton: Princeton University Press, 1960), 3–64.
8 Howe Warren, "Men of the Century," *Transition* 86 (2000): 36–50.
9 Francis Fukuyama, *Political Order and Political Decay: From the Industrial Revolution to the Globalisation of Democracy* (London: Profile Books, 2014).

21
ECONOMIES AND DEVELOPMENT

Introduction

Even though recent discoveries have established the close relationship between postcolonialism and economics,[1] incorporating postcolonial criticism into economics demands a cautious re-territorializing in order to appropriately reflect the history of subjugation from the time of colonization to the present. Doing so would allow the roles of colonial power structures and underlying systems of discoloration in ex-colonies' economic systems to be reflected and focus on the interlocking connections between postcolonial political pressures and the economic trajectory of the ex-colonized people. An economy is developed based on two crucial factors, the absence of which signals outright problems: human resources and natural resources. The characteristic rationalization of the colonizers for their political occupation of Africa was a mission to "civilize" Africans, justifying the subjection of the African economy to the brutal exploitation of its human and natural resources as part of their determination to "improve" it. For this reason, there is a close affinity between the political occupation of the continent and the encroachment of its economy.

African human capital was severely damaged by enslavement and then extortion that continued over centuries, leaving it dispossessed of the human capital that could be responsible for the economic rejuvenation of the continent. Natural resources also became a victim of perpetual displacement, theft, and exploitation in the service of the interests of the West. It is no coincidence that the supposed sacrifice these African countries were forced to make to access civilization and development were their own natural and human resources. What has been discovered late in the protracted and painful experience of postcolonial politics is that the international organizations and multilateral corporations that have an imposing presence in many of these ex-colonies continue the economic exploitation established during colonial times.

Even when postcolonial theory refuses to consider the continuity of the African economy after the termination of colonialism, the relationship between the two is obvious.

DOI: 10.4324/9781003198260-26

While our focus here is on the economic systems of African countries and how they have been influenced by the unseen but ever-present hands of colonialism, we will also interrogate the motivations and aspirations of the external systems of colonizers to better map their contribution to postcolonial Africa's perennial dysfunctionality. Creating distance between the African economy and its postcolonial politics gives a false impression that the two domains are disconnected, but postcolonialism affects the totality of the ex-colonies' experiences, including their social structures, cultures, and national psychological and emotional makeups, so it is eminently reasonable to expect that it would also continue to influence their economic trajectories.

To facilitate a better understanding of postcolonial economics and development, this chapter will look broadly at the events that have shaped the contemporary African political outlook. According to Adegoke, the precarious financial state of most African countries reflects their increased interest in seeking funding alternatives to established international institutions.[2] In 2018, the accumulation of African debt to both the International Monetary Fund (IMF) and the World Bank skyrocketed to $583 billion from $236 billion in 2008.[3] This exponential increase signals something unusual about these ex-colonies because a functional economic structure would not attract such a huge obligation from institutions designed to further deplete their economies through debt servicing. These loans continue to be issued, creating further increases in debt, indicating the ongoing conspiracy of the supremacists to continue despoiling their ex-colonies' economies.[4]

Given that successful debt servicing requires a strong economic base, Africa's ongoing relationship with these international organizations has been a strong contributor to the hobbling of their economic systems. The West understands this relationship and prefers to maintain colonialism in this form into the present. These organizations routinely provide opportunities to countries with weak political systems, calculating on overtaking their economic structures through infiltration by introducing multinational corporations, among other tactics. Their postcolonial motivation springs from the conviction that the global economic space is homogeneous, with all efforts from the players geared toward the predation of others through economic policies of exploitation, making it clear that offering relief funds to these ex-colonies' struggling economies is a planned endeavor. The West invests heavily in the international financial system, deliberately weakening the economic structures of these ex-colonies through direct involvement or by proxy and then waiting on them to come seeking further financial rescue.

On this basis, the cycle of debt in most ex-colonies keeps growing. Are these allegations contrived or actually legitimate? The Western perspective that sees economic systems as homogeneous confers on them the perceived responsibility and right to establish the nature of economic relations, as seen in the behavior of the international organizations toward Africa and the humongous debt packages awarded to them. Therefore, it is no coincidence that the debt behavior of African countries changed radically from bad to worse within a decade after the late 1970s.[5] Even when some African countries defy the predictions of doomsday economic analysts by making incredible progress in their economic trajectories, most are languishing in dysfunctional economic systems and conditions that keep hampering their efforts toward effective development.

Exacerbated by the challenges of poverty and disease, the role played by external corporations in holding back development in Africa is unbearable. The resources extracted by these multinational organizations have come without reasonable improvements to these indigenous peoples' economic systems. The history of these resource extractions dates back to the beginning of colonialism, marked by the large-scale encroachment on indigenous peoples' human and natural resources. As victims of these efforts, many of these countries have lost substantial control of their natural and human resources to the West, which continues into the contemporary era. Before we invoke examples of countries having their resources drained, we will establish that the economic emancipation of ex-colonies lies in their internal commitment to reform and fix the problems of their participation in the external economic systems. If that is not forthcoming, it is an omen of imminent doom.

Ciku Kimeria reveals the mind-boggling level of encroachment of the Europeans on artifacts and authors that have African roots, explaining how the French government in the colonial period staged a bloody siege on the Segou Royal Palace in modern-day Guinea.[6] After succeeding in capturing the target, they carted away several artifacts, which today remain locked up far away in the museums of Europe. The substantial economic income accrued by European countries from these cultural treasures justifies their appropriation according to the West's postcolonial perspective of their ex-colonies, especially the African countries. Other examples are the many adorned bronzes taken from the Benin Kingdom, well-prized in British museums, or carved elephant tusks and ivory masks found in Western museums, known for their prestige or income generation to the museums without directing any benefits to their original owners. They serve as markers of the economic despoliation perpetrated by the colonizers that continue to haunt the economies of the African people.

There have been some attempts at restitution. In 2018, President Emmanuel Macron announced the intention of the French government to return 26 artifacts originally stolen by France from Benin,[7] and the British government has made some efforts to return artifacts unjustifiably stolen from African countries. But beyond these gestures lies the reality of the economic rewards for those who benefited, and continue to benefit, from the looting of Africa's cultural treasures through tourism or other related reasons. We consider the British and the French museums as shining exemplars of the broader phenomenon of the long-lasting gains of colonial resource looting. After colonization, the West continued to believe, as they did during its heyday, that they should control the economic reins of the world by maintaining a master–subordinate relationship with their ex-colonies, dominating Africa's trade to prevent its growth. Within this context, it makes sense that international organizations, after making sufficient economic gains from materials generated from Africa, would then offer them debt-loading financing to make it easier for them to forget the compounding economic pressures.

The early nineteenth-century European scramble for Africa was partly based on the understanding that Africa was home to the largest deposit of some natural resources in the world, which, if properly exploited by the expansionists, could bring radical development to Europe within a limited amount of time. The 1880s scramble saw different European countries contesting to gain control of African countries so that their respective resources could be extracted for selfish advantage. With abundant oil, timber, gas, diamond, gold, coltan, and bauxite, Africa saw a swift invasion of the continent by European settlers drawn by the promise of quick wealth. Countries like Ghana, for example, had sufficient deposits of gold carted away by the Europeans, contributing significantly to the marginalization of the Ghanaian economy to the benefit of the colonizers and making Ghanaian economic growth difficult. The systemic exploitation of the period has been termed "international trade arrangements," and a closer inspection reveals their one-sided nature. European companies derived maximum benefits from shipping arrangements, import and export trade in the most valuable goods, and monopolies that gave them extractive rights.

As Walter Rodney suggests, African economic systems were further wrecked by European-owned multinational companies using their understanding of the depth of African resources to mastermind different types of internal contradictions, which could justify the need for a Western military presence. With the eruption of wars and hostilities, African countries would be consumed by a slow pace of development while external businesses owned and operated by the European bodies would continue their encroachment. On this basis, the abundance of natural resources deposited in Africa does not always translate into concrete results for the continent because their economy is controlled remotely by these foreign interests. As such, the postcolonial economics of Africa are circumscribed within layers of interlocking complexities centered on the efforts of the erstwhile imperialists to keep them perpetually under their influence. This exploitation perpetrated by the United States of America, the United Kingdom, Australia, Canada, and France, among other states, continues to bring massive economic benefits to the West while the African people are left out.

Economic Imperialism in Africa and its Postcolonial Impact

Having established the various socioeconomic exchanges between Africa and the colonial world, we will further illustrate the link between colonial economic activities and the African postcolonial economic conditions. This is necessary because there is no disconnection between the past and the present; rather, the present is a reflection of history and not a departure from it. An assurance of the success of resource exploitation and the understanding of the economic potential of the African countries encouraged explorers to seek to exploit Africa. The nineteenth century was a period of radical industrialization in Europe, generally known as the Industrial Revolution. The creation of new factories necessitated a ready supply of raw materials for manufacture, and the deposited resources of Africa were an attractive target.

Trade in African resources required the Europeans to bring manufactured goods as the needed articles of exchange, making Africa the new market for their goods as well as the source of their resource extractions. Closely related to these economic motives were the political factors that fueled the entry of Europeans into the African world. The Europeans had developed a philosophy of patriotism that gave them pride in directing and protecting their civilization. Patriotism was a nationalist impulse used to enhance the promulgation of identity, business, politics, and other connections between a group of people, and it fueled the desire among European nations—particularly Great Britain, France, and Germany—to have colonies in their control that resulted in the scramble for Africa. Paired with the belief that the rise in European civilization rested on its ability and tenacity to have control over African countries, the political drive of colonialism was intrinsically economic.

The significance of the scramble for Africa notwithstanding, the economic strangulation of Africa by Europeans preceded this time. Rodney reveals how European countries like Portugal perfected the act of seizing some African seaports to take control of the trade passing through them,[8] displacing the influence of both India and the Arab world. Contrary to the generally held misconception that Europeans were the sole custodians of civilizational and architects of modern technology, the Spanish and Portuguese relied on trade with India in the seventeenth century, purchasing goods from them, which later were sold to the African people in exchange for slaves that would mine gold for them in Central and South America. They increased their grip on these African countries by dominating the purchasing market of goods that were already used in virtually all European countries, including iron, linen, wine, brandy, glass beads, and muskets. The Europeans needed buyers for these goods purchased from India or manufactured in Europe, and there was ample demand from Africans.

The European monopoly of international regulation of business began during this period. Even when Africans provided substantial raw materials to the world economy, they were left out of the development of the economic rules of the game, forced to accept the terms of the West in a manner that continues in today's market. In economic politics, the control of borders, trade, or slavery enables the opportunity to accrue economic gains at the expense of the controlled or enslaved. This dynamic has long persisted, and the African countries that have been delegitimized and seen their economic growth constrained have conceded defeat and begun to seek financial assistance from the same establishment responsible for Africa's denigration and degeneration. This search for economic assistance from multinational companies and international organizations is ultimately ineffective as a way out of the economic turmoil of African countries, in most cases creating havoc rather than solutions. The international laws and regulations surrounding borrowing, economic policy, and debt servicing, created exclusively by the West, have, in the long run, crushed Africans' economies and made them ever more indebted.

The combination of increased American and Chinese interest in African resources attests to the substantial deposits of natural resources and is a warning signal as to the long-term survival chances of African economies. While the investments of these giant civilizations are expected to generate massive amounts of financial returns for them, the continued dominance of external players in Africa constitutes a further challenge to the continent's economic future. Due to its oil reserves, Africa has attracted more than 50 percent of all global foreign direct investment,[9] with half of that going to a combination of Nigeria, Chad, Egypt, Equatorial Guinea, Sudan, and Algeria. Despite the competitive business environment in which these international corporations operate in Africa, they are still collectively committed to seizing total control of these countries' resources for their monopolistic economic advantage. This determination has led directly to the imposition of an American military presence in most of these African countries. The United States of America has successfully signed bilateral agreements with some African countries, including Ghana, Mali, Gabon, and Senegal, and has demonstrated an intention to include more.[10]

These imperialistic tendencies continue the postcolonial challenges to African economic growth, creating an unstable environment with their presence and the prolonged imperialism it represents. We should also consider the emergence of China as a new and important player in the African economy as another form of re-colonization, or pseudo-colonization, even if it does not manifest through such forceful engagements as those with the previous colonizers. But as with the earlier experiences, China today looks eagerly to mineral and precious metal exchanges with South Africa and Congo, timber from Gabon and Cameroon, and oil from Nigeria, Angola, and Sudan, explaining their massive extension of financial rescue funding as loans given to Nigeria, for example, and other related investments in other African countries. Understanding the influential position they occupy, China continues to deepen its engagement with Africa, doling out debt and shaping the necessary atmosphere needed for a smooth business union with the region.

Contemporary global economic powers like the United States and China have contributed largely to the recent weakening of the African economy. One tactic they employ is offering monetary support—driving the burgeoning debt levels on the continent—to the African countries that seek their assistance while simultaneously selling arms to these same governments, diverting them from making concrete use of the borrowed money for development, and limiting their reasonable methods of offsetting it. Instead, their resources become the collateral for servicing these debts built off military purchases. For example, while Sudan attracts Chinese oil investment, they also receive arms worth $100 million,[11] directed to terror groups who target civilians with their acquired weapons. For a country like this, challenged by security pressures, economic development is challenging, and this serves as an invitation for foreign economies like China to take over.

Importantly, the hobbling of the African economy is a conscious decision by the European world, which invests heavily and makes concerted efforts to sabotage Africa. For example, the French government holds their 14 ex-colonies in Africa by the jugular, continuing to mop up their economic resources even decades after the formal end of colonialism by holding them to payments negotiated as a condition for their independence. It is improbable that the African countries caught within a perpetual cage under these unfriendly circumstances could suddenly make reasonable transformations economically or politically.

Many scholars, including Rodney, have concluded that the contemporary economic destiny of African countries remains tied to the apron strings of the Europeans, who are the primary beneficiaries of their dysfunctionality and, as such, are not inclined to reform the dynamic. Unless the resources of Africa and the rules of economic engagement related to them are determined by Africans, as opposed to the existing first-world control, the African economy will continue to suffer from the same pangs of imperialism and colonialism that have damaged the people's identity and impeded their growth for so long.

(Under)Development in Postcolonial Africa

Some scholars conceive African underdevelopment as a purely internal challenge, believing that Africa has receded into the abyss of retrograde dysfunctionality that cannot be linked to their colonial experience as many countries of the world were also colonized but are today economically competitive with the established world powers. Underlying this argument is the European bias that Africans are primitive, savage, and incapable of thinking their way out of their consuming challenges. Conversely, others believe that Africa's underdevelopment cannot be divorced from the totality of the European destruction of their systems and institutions in favor of replacements built on European models, in addition to the harsh consequences of the perpetual extraction of African human and natural resources.

The people who hold this analytical position understand that the more-than-500-year history of slavery and cultural and economic predation of Africa did not automatically stop influencing Africa's present and future with independence. Instead, their past experiences still manifest in enduring pain and the scars of destitution. Restitution from those who masterminded these conditions would require the total dissolution of their activities, but this has forever remained elusive. In all fairness, many countries that were once subjected to some kind of temporary domination are doing comfortably well today, including China, Canada, Japan, Australia, and even the almighty United States of America.

However, there is something unique about the African people and their colonizing experience. There is no other place on earth that has the magnitude of some natural resources that are in Africa. As previously mentioned, Africa has been blessed with a surplus of all the natural resources conceivable to humanity, attracting the Europeans, who immediately fixated their attention on further exploitation. Their initial focus was the expropriation of African men and women from their homes to be carted off across the Atlantic as part of the slave trade, but as their presence in Africa grew, they discovered the natural resources Africa is blessed with and realized their immense economic potential. In fact, this discovery ultimately led to the abolition of the slave trade and the introduction of colonialism. As such, while it is possible to argue that there are no longer chains limiting the economic and political progress of the continent because its countries have all been granted independence, colonization has only become redefined in Africa rather than removed, manifesting in the form of international debt financing and new methods of resource extraction midwifed by the same Europeans and other emerging world powers. The institutionalization of American military bases in Africa allows subtle monitoring of African political activities so that their economic systems do not take a turn unfavorable to America.

Civil unrest is masterminded, and internal conflicts are deliberately triggered by selling arms to ferocious and offensive groups and offering support to known despots, providing the opportunity for the United States to intervene and assume a Big Brother position under the auspices of preserving peace. Simultaneously, diplomacy with established, corrupt African leaders provides them with necessary alliances to maintain their hold on power, often through loans and other services, despite full awareness of their records of mismanagement and entrenched corruption. Under the rationale that these countries are helped out from their economic strangulation, the West subjects them to the anguish of debt servicing or defrayment.

To criticize development in these countries, particularly those challenged by neocolonialism, is to ridicule their humanity and be insensitive to their plight, ignoring how the Global North is fixated on what economic opportunities are available to seize in their relationship with African countries. Nigeria, for example, once faced sanctions from the United States, still has the presence of Total, the French national oil company, in the country to provide sufficient economic gains. Apart from this, the United States and Nigeria have a bilateral economic treaty signed in 2017, which led to the importation of

$9 billion in goods from the United States.[12] But while the relationship is a two-way business agreement that stands to benefit both parties, there can be no contention that the United States stands to profit far more than Nigeria ever will. The United States will not encourage a country from which it derives massive financial gain to create unfavorable trade and monetary advantages. Just as the Global North decided the rules of engagement during the colonial period, so too is the case in the present day.

Recently, there has been an escalation of secessionist agitation in some countries blessed with natural resources such as oil, gas, solar energy, iron, zinc, lead, silicone, and helium. This call for separation has prevented the country from maximizing this potential and developing standards expected of countries with its quantity of resources. Countries such as Liberia and Sierra Leone dissolved into civil war and rampant violence. Arms are carried freely by groups with conflicting beliefs about the right to control resources, sparking frequent and widespread fights. The development of places like this is prevented because of the legacy of colonial identities. The mergers of multiple ethnic and social groups within borders drawn by the colonial powers have continued to become an albatross to their collective peace. Because of the presence of these natural resources, powerful countries have benefited from these internal divisions, becoming complicit in exacerbating them by selling arms and taking positions against parties that would object to their dominance. Their economy is sabotaged by an environment wracked by violence, where development cannot be sustained.

In countries such as Nigeria, Chad and Cameroun, there are substantial national resources that attracted the attention of colonial adventurers and brought about secessionist agitation by minority ethnic groups. This recent upsurge of insurgent activities in the Sahel points to dissatisfaction with the colonial identity imposed on them despite the obvious cleavages in cultural identity and moral perceptions within the population. The West is positioned to benefit immensely from those internal conflicts in many ways. It gives them the opportunity to interfere in Kenya's political system—and those of similarly situated ex-colonies featuring sectarian violence—under the excuse that they are keeping the peace, opening up economic opportunities for Western countries through resource extraction.

Despite the world moving away from physical colonization, the Francophone African countries are still swept under colonial structures and will face significant difficulties in reaching their desired level of development. Their economies have been sabotaged, and their currency weakened, subjected to economic strangulation. They remain committed to economic ties with their former colonizers, even as successive presidents in these former French colonies had unsuccessfully attempted to untangle their political destinies from France by pulling out of the cutthroat economic conditions that were enacted when they left. The control France holds over their economies and politics cripples their efforts.

Transforming West African Economies

Regional Integration

West African economies have followed the wrong trajectory recently, casting doubt on the management ability of their regional leadership. Without strong economic foundations made possible by the presence of effective policies, it is impossible to revive their economic systems, having a domino effect on their financial, political, and social institutions and ability to take full advantage of their ample resources. One of the most important things to do is to regionally integrate their economies in order to build their global competitiveness. Although there have been various economic groups created within the region to enhance their shared economic system, much work remains to enhance their integration. Trade opportunities in West Africa must be eased, with the countries within the region granted unfettered access to each other and to the rest of the world to market their goods, as well as ensure that the political and economic conditions for economic rejuvenation are present.

The creation of effective policies that can factor in the different social and political conditions of the people is essential in order to successfully attain economic independence. Economic integration comes when there are infrastructural linkages providing increased access and flow for cross-border trade. There are models available for West African countries ready for true, modern transformations of their economic systems. For example, the European Union has a network of pliable and good infrastructure that makes the conduct of regional business less complicated and would rejuvenate West Africa if copied.

The Development of Agriculture

Along the lines of regional integration is the development of the West African agricultural system. Although natural resources like crude oil are becoming less important in the evolution of society every day, their importance has still not entirely eroded and may not be diminished any time soon. Regardless, the agricultural sector will always prove important and useful, no matter the direction of social or economic evolution. West African countries could cash in on this by investing heavily in agricultural businesses, as they have ample fertile land that can reliably produce tremendously for the region, the continent, and the world. Economic integration through enabling infrastructural connections in the region requires increased agricultural output, and these are the goods that can most easily be transported within countries to remake their economic systems.

As such, the governments of these countries are encouraged to invest heavily in a revolution of their agriculture systems to provide alternative sources of income if some of the natural resources they have relied on are frustrated by a lack of outside patronage. An explosion of the agricultural industry would bring massive employment opportunities for Africans within the region, and the youth would particularly benefit because their energy invested in agricultural activities would allow them to take control of their economic systems themselves. As important as it is to ensure working road and rail connections to link the countries together, it is also crucial that they embark on agricultural production to take advantage of goods moving freely across the region.

Industrial Revolution

No one can cast doubt on the importance and significance of the Industrial Revolution in transforming European countries. The upsurge in European economic growth in the eighteenth, nineteenth, and early twentieth centuries illustrates the boons that rapid technological development can bring. Ever since then, industrialization has become an instrument of economic progress for European countries. For West African countries to make similar gains, they must increase their investment in industrialization to propel their economies and, in turn, revolutionize their political systems.

West African agriculture has been chiefly subsistent, so a considerable part of their economies is dependent on handicrafts. With the advent of a local industrial revolution, this could be transformed into a large-scale industry with a renewed factory system and modern mechanized manufacturing. These would grow the economy of the region and make it the preferred destination of international investors, whose presence would also add significantly to the growing economy. An industrial revolution would ensure the arrival of different systems of working and organization and make the business atmosphere conducive to uncommon growth. Rather than the old system of relying on human capacity, productivity would leap forward because of the transference of duty to machines, driving efficiency.

West African countries have a strong chance to take full advantage of industrialization as it is generally accepted that the success of industrialization depends on, among other factors, the availability of iron and steel. These are natural materials that are abundant in the region and can be leveraged to improve and increase the industrial presence in the region. With a focus on transforming the region's economy, manufacturing could be easily facilitated, which would drive productivity in unimaginable proportions. Virtually all the other ingredients that can fast-track industrialization in West Africa are readily available, including ample energy sources.

What is truly required is the political will of the leaders because the transformation of the region through industrial development requires collaboration and mutual support. Understanding this would encourage the atmosphere necessary to engage in negotiation, make policies, and consolidate what has already been achieved. It is a reality that the region comes under occasional attacks from hoodlums, bandits, and terrorist groups, so their cooperation is needed to jointly address crucial issues in the region capable of threatening the survival of their economic systems. These different elements must work in consonance with the enhancement of West African success.

Women's Empowerment

As the population of West Africa has exponentially surged, the female demographic has risen to a new height. Due to their high number, they must be factored in for every major decision. Women tend to be the primary agents of socialization, reinforcing their crucial importance in building human society. They control the power to determine the economic direction of the people, as well as influence the political trajectory of their countries. It behooves policymakers and political heavyweights in the region to immediately consider empowering women beyond what they have ever experienced. Undoubtedly, the social respect accorded to women would be different, among other things, thereby reducing the economic pressures they are subjected to that can expose them to dangerous situations. Women's empowerment would increase their access to decision-making, granting them power over the issues that affect them personally. Gender inequity in society is an expression of unequal power positions and relations between men and women, which would change if the latter were gainfully empowered.

Women who are given proper education would understand the value of their identity and contribute to society by exploring and employing their talents. Education limits the possibility of a person being misled, and the assurance that education provides via the information they receive would give women a strong foundation to enable them to be independent and make their own choices about their lives. They would also be empowered politically; in fact, the proportion of women in the population holds more value than just providing numerical strength during elections. They should also be enfranchised because the foundation of a solid society lies in the freedom of the people to pursue their political interests without experiencing oppression based on their gender. When they are allowed the opportunity to be elected to office, women can directly make contributions to the advancement of African societies. This also would be a path to economic empowerment.

Conclusion

The chapter has stated the various circumstances surrounding postcolonial African economies and their development, and their response to the pressure and efforts toward the rejuvenation of their contemporary economic systems. The chapter has documented how the economy-wrecking policies of the West from the time of slavery to the postcolonial era have been the reason for the continuous hobbling of their economic systems, showing that the quest for globalization began during the period of the early expansionist agendas of the Europeans over the African people. The creation of trade routes has been to facilitate smooth business relationships in which they stand to gain the most from business engagement.

After slavery and "legitimate trade," the Europeans imposed colonialism as a comprehensive framework for the exploitation of African resources. The installation of this system meant that after forcibly having taken human resources from the continent for centuries, they started another mode of exploitation by seizing their natural resources. Even when African countries were largely awarded formal independence in the 1960s, colonialism did not stop; it was only redefined. This redefinition has continued to impede African development by undermining their economic policies and imposing Western alternatives. Some African countries are doing well regardless of exploitation, but many of them are still lagging, pointing to the dangers of postcolonial economies.

DEEP DIVE

Assignment 1

Objective

The objective of this assignment is to ensure that students complete the reading of Chapter 21 and to encourage them to question why African economies are seen as entirely dependent on European aid and how they have struggled to develop significantly since independence.

Method

Students will be expected to write a short note in response to the question.

Reading Comprehension

Why are African economies unsustainable, and how can they be made durable?

Assignment 2

Discussion

Why and how are African countries participating in a neocolonial economic system? Is full economic emancipation possible?

Objective

The objective of this assignment is to encourage students to consider the extent to which African countries still act as colonial entities that produce goods for Western consumption and benefit. Additionally, students will have to decide if the African economy of the future can sustain itself without European intervention.

Method

Students will be expected to have a group discussion (either in person or on the online discussion forum) to talk to their peers about the discussion question. Each student would be expected to create a post and respond to at least one other student. If this were to take place in person, then it would simply be a class-wide discussion.

Notes

1 Eiman O. Zein-Elabdin and S. Charusheela, eds., *Postcolonialism Meets Economics* (New York: Routledge, 2004); and Callari Antonio, *Postmodern Materialism and the Future of Marxist Theory: Chapters in the Althisserian Tradition* (New England: Wesleyan University Press, 1996).
2 Yinka Adegoke, "Africa's Rising 'Unsustainable' Debt is Driving a Wedge Between the World Bank and Other Lenders," *Quartz Africa*, February 16, 2020, https://qz.com/africa/1803280/world-bank-imf-worry-on-africa-raising-debt-to-china-afdb/.
3 Adegoke, "Africa's Rising."
4 Antonio, *Postmodern Materialism*, 113.
5 Antonio, *Postmodern Materialism*, 113.
6 Ciku Kimeria, "The Battle to Get Europe to Return Thousands of Africa's Stolen Artifacts Is Getting Complicated," *Quartz Africa*, November 29, 2019, https://qz.com/africa/1758619/europes-museums-are-fighting-to-keep-africas-stolen-artifacts/.
7 Theodora Aidoo, "Check Out Some of Africa's Most Prized Artifacts That Were Stolen by Colonizers but Now Returned," *Face 2 Face Africa*, September 30, 2019, https://face2faceafrica.com/article/check-out-some-of-africas-most-prized-artifacts-that-were-stolen-bycolonisers-but-now-returned.
8 Walter Rodney, *How Europe Underdeveloped Africa* (London: Bogle-L'Ouverture Publications, 1972).
9 Mandy Turner, "Scramble for Africa," *The Guardian*, May 2, 2007.
10 Turner, "Scramble for Africa."
11 Turner, "Scramble for Africa."
12 Turner, "Scramble for Africa."

22

POSTCOLONIAL CULTURES

Introduction

Beyond what Walter Benjamin referred to as "the tradition of the oppressed,"[1] post-colonialism affects the totality of life in former colonies far above a physical manifestation. Colonialism has laid the foundation for the exploitation of colonized people, and various academic theories have been created to address the different dimensions of oppression and their devastating consequences on the general life of the colonized people. For example, the Marxist school of thought specifically addresses the power of capitalism and its inconsiderate exploitations of the working class, where the colonialists occupy the position of oppressors, milking people of their economic resources and, thus, increasing their pain. Invariably, the colonized are those oppressed. In equal measure, feminism emphasizes the power of patriarchal political systems that objectify women, exploit them, and subject them to economic and political marginalization of some sort. Exploring postcolonial culture is not restricted by boundaries constructed by physical geography because even countries that did not colonize others in the past centuries have now, deliberately or otherwise, joined the race for the continuation of contemporary globalization.

Postcolonialism addresses a broad span of concerns ranging from the evaluation of those institutions that emerge from colonialism. In this chapter, the interrogation of bequeathed political philosophies and structures handed to emerging African elites at the near termination of colonial rule and the examination of the various ways through which these institutions and philosophies stand and continue to stand in the way of African reclamation of their precolonial identity, among others, will be captured. Many of the indices of colonialism identified here are made possible because of a very strong factor—language and culture. A quick observation of the majority of African countries will reveal the use of European languages as the official ones.

Countries in Africa adopt the languages and cultures of their colonizers in differing manners that reflect the exigencies of colonialism. In the 1880s, the "scramble for

DOI: 10.4324/9781003198260-27

Africa" saw the haphazard European struggles for African human resources, and as a result, each of the European countries who attended the meeting at Berlin scrambled to allocate to themselves land and people whom they were able to conquer. Because of the potency of language in determining the epistemological and ontological reality of a people, however, a number of these African countries continue to act in accordance with those colonial plans, which are: the centralization of European values at the expense of others; the reinstatement of the colonial institutions even after independence; and the subjugation of the colonized people.

Linguistic and Cultural Imperialism

Colonialism was a historical experience with two opposing ends. On the one hand, there were the colonial imperialists who conceived the act of colonization as a mere expedition of altruism where they "civilized" lower individuals they called uncivilized, "educate" a people who had no education, and offered them a religion to save them from themselves. On the other hand, there were the people at the receiving end of colonialism whose cultures had been carelessly infringed upon, whose religions were mercilessly maligned, whose political systems and structures were uprooted and substituted with contextually alienating ones, and whose epistemic roots were deracinated.

Therefore, these two opposing ends create different intellectual spectrums that address the situation of colonialism through dissimilar perspectives. Obviously, those who benefit from colonization, that is, those whose economies flourished, have predictably gravitated toward the rationalization of colonialism, while those who were exposed to insufferable conditions because of the experience have always addressed it differently. Thus, the colonizer–colonized dichotomy remains constant.

Postcolonialists are undivided in their conviction that the imposition, or adoption, for that matter, of the language and culture of the oppressor signals a confusing situation about ex-colonies and their identity. More than anything, to live the culture, to speak the language of the colonizers and use it as a medium of instruction in African schools, for example, is an expression of defeat and the affirmation of the European sentiments that Africans were desolate in thinking and stagnant in development. More inflicting is the fact that it also suggests that these colonized people accept and acquiesce to the power of the erstwhile imperialists, despite the termination of their colonial dominance over them.

Even when there have been numerous debates about the conscientious continuation of colonialism by the ex-colonized people through the use of colonial culture and languages, the fact remains that there are aspects of colonized culture that are automatically pushed to the background because of the use of alien languages. In the past, the probable consequences of this adoption have created two opposing intellectual blocks of scholars where those who support its use comfortably state all the potential advantages of using foreign languages, among which are the expansion of communication coverage; and those who are against it argue that it will ultimately help in the subjugation of the people's identity and cultural traditions. On one side of the adoption of European languages are Chinua Achebe, Wole Soyinka, and others, while on the opposing side are scholars such as Ngũgĩ wa Thiong'o and Obi Wali.

Before we address the question of circulation and coverage, we must look at the possible reinstitutionalization of European biases that were strengthened predominantly because of the adoption of European languages. Accepting these foreign languages compels the ex-colonized people to conceive themselves as citizens of a global community who have important contributions to make for global advancement. Whereas coming to this conclusion or making the decision is necessary to project the ideas and perspectives of African people who were once colonized, there is an underlying deceit covered by such superficial acknowledgment of colonialism.

The adoption of European languages exposes many of the adopters to a Western way of thinking, making them vulnerable, not because they may at any time soon become potential victims of physical conquest but because they are brought to an unfamiliar space with limited instruments available with which to wrestle or resist temptations. In what would soon be revealed, the appropriation of the colonial languages leads to what we have identified as linguistic imperialism, which ultimately endangers some aspects of Africa's existence. Although Achebe and his intellectual disciples have argued that it is possible to tame colonial languages to one's cultural framework,[2] the use of language spans beyond communication; it is an instrument of identity design.

We are reminded that the use of a language, a foreign one for that matter, in education systems, commerce, and cultural exchange signals to the introducers of these languages their dominance and domineering status, apart from serving as a potential threat to the survival of the people's cumulated cultural identity. When a people whose culture was dominated for many years think that the physical termination of colonial rule in their spaces (which came into existence partly as a result of concerted pressure from such epochal events like World War II and Black insistence on the abolition of colonization in the Third-World countries) would automatically translate to the end of domination, they would predictably be exposed to challenges that would render them vulnerable.

Here is where the concerns and issues of postcolonial discourse create an important concern to address peripheral issues. Most African countries continuously suffer from colonialism-related dangers and effects because they believe that the attainment of independence automatically translates to an abrupt end of their existential challenges against the imperial systems. For emphasis, colonization was not terminated in the wake of African independence; rather, it was redefined. The thought that they were free from the shackles of domination once colonization ended ultimately created the illusion of freedom in their minds, giving them false confidence in their ability to compete with the countries of the Global North, who have historically benefited and continue to benefit from systems of oppression. Therefore, some Africans accept these languages erroneously, thinking that language is an innocent phenomenon in determining a people's identity, sustaining their culture and survival. The superficiality of this thinking and mindset is reflected in the reality that it is continuously difficult for virtually all African countries to attain a level of development even after spending six decades in the post-independence era.

Unlike some Asian countries, Africans have been unable to transform their countries into developed nations. Even after independence, Africans are still educated in European fashion, eventually resulting in de-emphasizing the use of their languages. They, therefore, are the physical manifestation of pseudo-Europeans, and their minds continue to experience Western thinking, philosophy, and ideologies. Through these languages, they have been taught a history that is not their own, and they have been introduced to the political philosophies that works in the West. Equally, they are offered cultural traditions and systems that are counterproductive to indigenous ones. The vast examples of Africans that immediately run to cite and identify with Western-centric ideologies validate this conclusion. Even intellectuals who are naturally expected to be arduous researchers usually suggest Western alternatives, unconscious of how their leaning toward Western culture is a product of their cultural immersion in it.

When we identify that the adoption of European languages is reductionist to the African cultural legacies, what we mean partly is that indigenous languages are already disfavored by the nature of the colonial encounter that makes them abandon their language in preference to the colonial ones because they would make little contribution to the agenda of globalization. Let us consider these situations in a different light. Through political lens, the Global North prefers the political philosophy of democracy. With this political ideology in mind, it continues to measure a country's political functionality by its vested standards. This means that those countries that decide to operate on a political system that contradicts democracy would be considered primitive and uncivilized.

These Western judgments can be observed throughout history. The fact that the Global North has accepted itself as the global standard for measuring the level of civilization dates back in time, as this was precisely the foundational reason justifying colonization in the first place. Therefore, to be considered civilized in Western eyes, these African countries, using their erstwhile imperialist languages, must accede to the existential pressure and accept democracy as the scaffold of their political infrastructure. Africans were not contributors to the design of such political philosophy; therefore, they had to rely on the knowledge and information provided by the Europeans, who were accepted as the generators of philosophy.

For the most part, this manifests both internal confusion and complicated contradictions. Let us imagine, for example, that Britain or the United States suddenly updates their democracies in a particular fashion; many Anglophone African countries that still retain the English language and culture would be under pressure to follow suit. This explains why an ex-colony like Nigeria is considered a space for complex political systems. While they were attracted to the bicameral legislature system of the United States of America, they took Britain's parliamentary system of government at independence. Perhaps to make its federalism work, Nigeria now operates the presidential system of the United States, leaving aside its Electoral College system.

All these, therefore, are manifestations of confusion, contradictions, and inconsistencies that come up because the countries adopt foreign ideas and, invariably, political systems. In relation to the self-deceit that comes with seeing themselves as stakeholders in the determination of global systems and as contributors to the general ideas where, coincidentally, their conquerors were also present, Africans would not generate a model of democratic leadership or system that can be adopted by countries of the First-World. This does not signal their inability; instead, it confirms how they are still perceived and would always occupy the base level because they are consumers and not producers of the ideas and systems.

With the appropriation of democracy as the dominant political system in these former colonies, there comes an additional yet inevitable condition: the application of the colonial educational systems, whose very import is the disarticulation of the indigenous knowledge systems for the reconstruction of new identities. Colonialism, we should always remember, sets out to achieve a provincial mandate in the beginning, and that is the globalist thinking that humans of diverse cultural permutations are, or can be, homogeneous, in which case their education system would be tailored toward a common end.

While the probability of cultural syncretism suggested by such orientation remains constant, its target and focus are to eclipse the contributions of these former colonies under the assumption that it was incompatible with civilized thinking or impractical for collective development. Africans who have been introduced to Western education during colonialism are usually not aware of the immeasurable ways that the ideas of colonization have impacted their psyche. Their situation was compounded by the twin problems of cultural deracination and colonial configurations. For the first one, they were the first generation of Africans to divorce themselves from African epistemology and systems in order to reduce their understanding of it while eventually campaigning against it.

These people perfectly fit Frantz Fanon's *Black Skin, White Masks*[3] in that they were the physical definition of African people but the psychological description by the West. In essence, the education system that Africans inherited foregrounds the perspective of Western imperialists on knowledge systems by carefully delegitimizing African perspectives. Thus, they were introduced to the thinking of imperialists, which was carefully reflected in different ways in the lives and activities of the former colonies. European histories were introduced to students whose discipline was History. As a corollary of this, the European experience and history in Africa were adopted as African History.

In medical science, all the expanse of indigenous African medical history and research was dubbed unscientific, occultic, and even primitive, while those in the legal profession were taught about European legal systems that were philosophically different from Africa's. For these neocolonialist Africans, education, which naturally should be used as an instrument of liberation, emancipation, or freedom, became a very potent tool for re-colonization and reconstruction. Since they were educated in the Western way, they were not supportive of their indigenous educational system and epistemological base, which denied them the opportunity to expand their intellectual horizon in consonance with the dictates of their social surroundings. This particular challenge continues into contemporary times.

Perhaps this is what individuals like Ngũgĩ wa Thiong'o projected that prompted his suggestion about abolishing the English Department at the University of Nairobi.[4] The central question was, "How can a colonial language be useful in the creation of nationalist citizens whose moral ethos and social ethics would reflect that of their ancestral legacies?"[5] This results from the consensus that language should be used as the instrument for creating responsible and responsive citizens. Therefore, the alienation of an individual from their indigenous language would have a profound impact on their perception and understanding of the world. As a preventive measure to this, he consistently maintained a position in support of the African language to use it as a medium of cultural rejuvenation. To demonstrate his commitment to this ambition, Ngũgĩ produced a number of intellectual materials in his Gikuyu language, and his revolutionary works register a succinct impression—coloniality is a defeatable opponent.

Once again, using colonial languages erects a wall of distance between the people and their history. Since the history of Europeans was imposed on these unassuming

Africans, making unsubstantiated claims about their history, Africans would always remain in an existential crisis. Africans' understanding of their history will be limited by European timelines in Africa; therefore, their minds will negate perspectives that offer alternative histories, especially those that counter the positions of the colonizers' revisionism. In fact, the consequences of this will manifest at a deeper level. For example, a student introduced to the Western medical system would most likely conceive the African system as contrived and unnecessary.

Ngũgĩ's position is informed by several factors, all of which are not unconnected to familiar racist prejudices that characterize Western education. The first factor is related to the history of Western philosophy. During the early period of slavery and colonization, Western philosophers like Immanuel Kant and David Hume, among others, insisted that Africans did not have any history of philosophy from which they could exhume ideas and philosophies to use for their development or advancement. This bias was complemented by a scientist who distributed and contrived a scientific conclusion that Africans possessed shrinking human skulls that made their brain size observably smaller than that of the Europeans, which invariably determines their capacity and ability.

These biases, construed as scientific fact, in actuality were the racial tenets used to rationalize the expedition of slavery and their corresponding economic expropriation. It was the necessary behavioral sentiment to be achieved to justify the act of cultural predation that Europeans masterminded, as well as clear themselves of any potential guilt. Cultural arrogance was a tool of domination. Even though those Africans who attended school during this period understood the underlying imperialism and permutations of narratives, they had no power or instruments to challenge the system.

Another reason that prompted Ngũgĩ's proposition about the abolition of the Department of English from the University of Nairobi was that, contrary to the termination of the colonizer–colonized dichotomy that Africans expected with the end of colonialism, was the continuity in the thinking of such scholars as Hugh Trevor-Roper in the twentieth century and the baseless arguments against African achievements. Like his predecessors, Trevor-Roper asserted that African history was nonexistent because of the absence of writing. The underlying imperialism in such a conclusion is that there is no coincidence in the proliferation of Western epistemic violence against African identity. This is because scholarly and scientific efforts of intellectuals that established that Africans had history, education, medical system, philosophy, and epistemic background before the incursion of the Europeans, did not influence Europeans to change their perception of Africa. Thus, the consumption of their education models constructed in their language and developed with their philosophical insights portend great danger to the cultural survival of the African people in the colonial and postcolonial environment.

Culture and Postcolonialism in Africa

Postcolonialism addresses a wide range of ideas that are not disconnected from the deliberations on imperialism, colonialism, and their corresponding consequences on the ex-colonies' cultural frameworks and designs. While some scholars believe that postcolonial discourse should address the history of the subjugated cultures under imperialism and reclaim this historical order, others believe that it should specifically examine the long-lasting consequences of colonialism. Having this in mind, we identify that postcolonialism, therefore, needs to answer some questions that would help in understanding the cultural situations of the ex-colonized people.

For example, is the cultural life of Africans in the aftermath of colonialism reflective of histories of long-lasting suppression and despoliation before the disengagement of European expansionism in Africa? If European culture has significantly impacted the indigenous cultural spectrums, what foundation is their coping strategy built on, such as hybridity or outright rejection of colonialist structures? There are many questions to be asked in order to understand the postcolonial culture of the ex-colonized people.

Frantz Fanon, a Martiniquan philosopher, offered a transparent analysis of what ex-colonized people are confronted with, especially in their postcolonial environment. In *The Wretched of the Earth*,[6] he argues that postcolonialism alters the people's cultural history because their relationship with the imperialists has enforced an eruption of contradictory thoughts that make them immediately question their cultural traditions and, therefore, distance themselves from them. Through this relationship, the colonized people become psychologically imbalanced and oscillate between their indigenous identity and the newly imposed one from their colonizers. Unlike the colonizers, they do not always possess a mind of their own, as their world is framed between binary structures. Apart from the political battleground where the French colonialists used excessive violence, the domestic environment became another atmosphere for contention and contradictions around culture as to what to choose and privilege between the European and African. This collision occurred in their minds, prompting the rebuilding of their cultural identity and allowing for different perspectives. This perspective represented by the European cultural identity does not in itself appear dangerous. However, the fact that it was meant to challenge the indigenous identity created postcolonial dialectics that laid the foundation for debate and polemics.

Since it is important, we should reiterate the deep-rootedness of the European capture of African culture. During the early years of imperialism, Europeans who came as traders and missionaries manifested the underlying forces that maintained the business of colonialism. Creating the impression that they were superior to Africans, at least as demonstrated in their superior ideas and technology, they equally maintained that they were better in every other aspect of human experience, including but not limited to their culture, education, politics, and religion. Therefore, it was necessary that Europeans export their culture into these former colonies' cultural spaces using education as the medium.

It was not until discerning Africans understood the potential setback that excessive Eurocentrism could mean for Africa that they began the decolonization project in earnest. This attempt complemented Fanon's position that the formerly colonized people should react not necessarily in a violent language but with the demonstration of organicity that will reflect in the philosophy and strategy that would enhance the reconstruction of their lost identity. Without this, there would be some measure of difficulty in upstaging the colonial systems and structures that have been carefully established. The colonized are greatly affected by the institutionalization of the Western epistemic perception, which has imposed alien structures and beliefs that continue to manifest in their sociopolitical life.

To challenge the imperial order and systems, therefore, springs from the conviction that the cultural life of the formerly colonized people has seen drastic changes in the aftermath of colonial relationships. Perhaps the best way to understand this is to discuss the relationship between African culture and some of its institutions. Africa is home to massive cultural institutions used to govern social existence. One such is the group of political institutions responsible for leadership and social administration, which covers the expanse of security, social regulations, and the economy. Before the advent of the Europeans, a large part of these African nation-states operated a political system that was managed by appropriate cultural institutions.

This structure was gradually dissolved at the inception of colonial conquests, creating the passageway for the alterations of African cultures and traditions subsumed under the colonial system. The marginalization of the indigenous leadership structure creates a parallel one that, however, does not have a contextual valuation in the African world. Setting this precedence created the atmosphere for the continuation of such systems after the attainment of independence, not minding those angles where the indigenous structures are crushed as a result. In what Edward Said's *Orientalism* addresses,[7] the subtle marginalization of the existing leadership structure creates a sense of Otherness and, as such, becomes another reason for postcolonial cultural identity.

The interconnection between the African political and social institutions is undebatable, although one might argue that the imposition of the imperialist structures does not automatically demean the indigenous systems. However, the fact that they were rendered powerless as a result of their collision should not be overlooked when making contributions to the debate. The leadership institutions responsible for such subcategories, such as security institutions, would not experience any relegation without foreboding consequences reflective of the people's lives. Added to this structural redefinition is the fact that the indigenous structures have difficulty surviving in the new system designed to cater predominantly to the colonial identity. Except for ceremonial purposes, they have been weakened and dismembered, which is reflected in their current systems in many ways. When the security architecture installed by the colonial regimes encounters internal contradictions, they are usually ineffective in addressing the issues, and in situations where they do, they do so by setting off additional struggles to compound the existing challenges. When there are numerous security agencies, for example, the record of security challenges skyrockets. The implication of this is that the colonial structures, which have, for example, affected the security culture of the people, do not exclusively appear functional as it is devoid of the social and cultural traditions that could improve the polity.

As a corollary of the same colonial structures that continued long into postcolonial African life, the culture of the Global North has been brandished as the benchmark for any cultural civilization. This mindset is not new, as the establishment of Eurocentric bias was basically founded on this orientation. However, the implosion of indigenous African culture springs from access to alternative cultural traditions in the internet age, and since many individuals are victims of colonization, even mostly unaware, they are caught in the web of multiple identities that make issues more complicated. These are the individuals that Homi Bhabha referred to as *unhomed*[8] because of their struggling conditions.

They are presented with multiple pieces of information, all of which create a psychological eruption in their minds. Apart from the fact that approaching their local or indigenous cultures could be problematic, they are also faced with the possibility of adopting the Western knowledge systems that once again continue to condition their thoughts, reconfigure their mindsets and reconstruct a new set of identities for them. Ever since its inception in the fifteenth century, when the early expansionists extended their economic ambition to cover people and civilizations from other places than Europe, the force of globalization has always continued in different realizations until modern history.

Once the peculiar aspects of their culture bear the marks of colonialism as explicated by the substitution of the African leadership system, educational structures and social institutions are shortchanged, and the less peculiar aspects of their culture are equally brought to unspoken ruination. For instance, the media industry is guilty of cultural alienation by producing materials that glorify European identities as opposed to African identities. Cultural productions that demean Africans were not uncommon because the individuals involved did not consider their African heritage worthy.

The education system became complicit as it was used to further advance the superiority campaigns of those who lean toward European values. The rejection of the African language as vernacular in favor of the European languages and the adoption of old-style European uniforms was the norm, not minding its impracticality with African weather. This alone ridicules the African culture that addresses situations such as this. According to Donald Molosi, "the school systems all over Africa remain thus troublingly nostalgic for colonial rule, seeking to defeat the African child by all means necessary."[9] Marriage culture in the modern African world is predominantly Western, in practice and law.

Because of the situation resulting from the experiences of colonialism, some postcolonial African scholars have suggested various methods to contain the spread of Eurocentric narratives and structures from determining the African postcolonial cultural conditions. Some have suggested acute decolonization over the assumption that it would inspire radical development by consciously disregarding and disengaging with the Western epistemic structures that have dominated African lives for eons. Scholars such as Molefi Asante, Cheikh Anta Diop, and others have published works to provide the structural steps to be followed to enhance this agenda. Other scholars from different fields have performed similar tasks to ensure that the system is changed to favor African independence.

On the other hand, however, some scholars believe that hybridization would work in an attempt to rejuvenate African culture for contemporary advantages. Some have expressed optimism about the workability of this approach because of the understanding that Africans would continue to take the heat from the international community without it. Hybridity suggests the possibility of merging cultures. What remains unchallenged is that the relationship between the colonizers and the colonized has continued to influence the formerly colonized people's cultural trajectories. What, therefore, are the potential outcomes of these two different lines of thought between hybridity and decolonization?

Total decolonization is inherently impossible because of the reality that many contemporary Africans are not fully connected to their past African cultural traditions. Therefore, calling for the reintroduction of those systems could be another potential ground for reinstalling some structures that are unhealthy for cultural transformation. Even when anthropologists conduct research that establishes the greatness of past Africans in history, it cannot bring forth their cultural traditions and behavior. If this happens perchance, we are aware that one of the constant attributes of the culture is that it evolves. The survival of all cultures is underpinned by its ability to accommodate new ideas and philosophies and update itself to align with contemporary requirements.

As such, precolonial African cultures are not meant to be stable entities that would be unreceptive to change and evolution. However, the suggestion of system collaboration that would bring hybridity also has two opposing aspects. For example, the call for hybridization must factor in the collocational relationship between the two opposing cultures. This is because a culture easily attracts others who share similar ideas and philosophies. Again, Africans are not unfamiliar with such a plea for globalization or universalization and are comfortably aware of their limitations in contributing to these ideas of globalization and universalism, which requires a balanced relationship.

Contemporary West African Culture

With the advent of postcolonial life comes the reasons for the update of one's cultural traditions and leanings because of the enhancement of multiculturalism brought about by contemporary progress in virtually all human societies. Having access to various people's cultural traditions gives one the necessary motivation to update one's cultural viewpoints, in which case the idea of hybridization of values cannot be overridden. During missionary exploration of West African countries, there was an establishment of the marital philosophy of monogamy associated with the Christian religion. The missionaries considered polygamy as against the Christian tradition and, therefore, denounced association with it. Anyone interested in the Christian faith would thus be encouraged to consider dropping their polygamous intentions. Whereas the system was designed by the African countries to contain sexual immoralities, the introduction of the colonizers into the West African cultural space encouraged the gradual but very steady dissolution of the polygamy system of marriage in preference for monogamy. Today, a lot of West African homes prefer the Western marriage structure even if it does not have maximum advantages for the social reality of the people. Thus, the dominance of monogamous marital structures in the postcolonial is a colonial legacy.

Although there are various social issues arising from the prevalence of the monogamous marriage system in the region, there are other social structures, such as the commodification of sexual exchange, which have become ingrained into the cultures of contemporary West African life. Because people's perception has been modified, they consider sex, marriage, and relationships a topic of personal preference that cannot be regulated by existing social regulations, whether written or conventionally internalized. With the acceptance of the monogamous marriage structures came expanding social and economic challenges that significantly altered West African situations. Added to this social (mal)adjustment is the reality of globalization. Although the project of globalization, as some scholars have argued, goes back to the beginning of the slave trade that marked the initial Western contact with the African people, it has reached an unprecedented peak in recent times.

Globalization, apart from ensuring a multicultural environment, has necessitated that people have access to remote or otherwise distant cultures and systems, and the inventions that come with it provide a golden opportunity to make choices from the vast majority available. Now that individuals in a different sociopolitical environment understand and find comfort in different cultures, it increases their chances of cultural integration and cross-cultural relationships. The West African countries continue to create and embrace opportunities from globalization projects because it allows for the exchange of cultural traditions with and without attendant worries. Therefore, global citizenship is facilitated in various ways through the project, and the underlying advantages of this span from the ability to make one's voice heard, regardless of distance. Through it, regional bonds and integration among the countries of the West African region have been dramatically improved. As such, globalization remains an active force in changing traditional methods and indigenous systems to enable foreign approaches to problem-solving situations. Contemporary West African countries have identical cultural systems because of globalization.

Another important area of drastic change in West African cultural traditions is in the area of popular culture. Before postcolonial times, each country in the region had indigenous cultural practices that were popular and located within their cultural spaces. In the current West African reality, however, there has been an exponential increase in the patronage of pop culture, as that appears to be the major content demand of the new generation. Having access to the cultural practices of others that include but are not limited to their music, drama, art, artifacts, and others, specifically, has a compelling influence on a people's taste and preferences. Nearly all of the younger generation of West African countries are sold on pop culture, and they demonstrate their loyalty to it by their increased interest in artistic productions that are pop-culture specific.

It is relatively easy for many of these countries to make the instant switch from their indigenous cultural systems and traditions to pop culture because there is a semblance of that system in West African history. It is understandable that the acceptability of pop culture among the younger generations in the region aligns with existing foreign cultural systems. Many music artists from the region today have made a global impact by creating awareness of their musical artistry and carving a niche for themselves.[10] Among the world-renowned music artists from the West African region excelling in pop culture are Wizkid, Burna Boy, Davido, Oma Lay, Yemi Alade, Shatta Wale, and Stone Boy. These pop-culture artists have commanded maximum global attention, and they continue to use the medium to promote African identity and cultural traditions in the postcolonial world. Their success is a direct outcome of cultural change encouraged by the globalization agenda and the forces of development resulting from it. Globalization has provided them with the opportunity to redefine their cultural systems and, as a result, market them to the rest of the world. As a result of the unhindered access they have to other cultures of the world, these music artists have been able to magnetize the pop cultures of others and also made the most effective use of them.

Virtually all these improvements would be impossible without the internet. Although access to the international community predated the internet, it happened manually in the past. However, there can be no contention about the complicity of the internet in making access to different cultures easy. Through the internet, people are able to infiltrate different cultures without visibly changing their location. They critically examine these cultures and make changes to their own when convinced of an item of culture to import. In fact, the freedom that comes with people's choices in the Internet age cannot be overemphasized. One can choose to embrace a marital philosophy or culture of a target civilization without taking their name or other customs.

It is possible to embrace the collective data system of a particular country without taking its democratic system. Borrowing and adaptations are possible under the cultural system dictated by the introduction of the internet. The changes, however, alter the various ways of thinking, analyzing, and passing judgment. This creates a long cultural distance between the older generations in the region and the current ones. The age difference and technological accomplishments sometimes lead to some differences in their perception and evaluation strategy. Irrespective of their cultural differences, however, the internet continues to affect postcolonial West African countries.

It seems the change in concrete cultural traditions in postcolonial times does not necessarily border on the improvement of the virtual culture alone. It goes on in the choices of settlement. In contemporary times, the taste for rural–urban mobility is notably high, and this comes from the deliberate decision of the colonizers to create an environment convenient for them during the colonial experience. By creating an urban system where employment opportunities increase and social amenities are significantly provided, people's tastes about settlement began to change as individuals intended to improve their socioeconomic conditions and enjoy the amenities that come with city life.

The economic prosperity offered in the urban centers is the basic centrifugal force that brings people there. The fact that these need to be replicated in many other forms has encouraged different government establishments to create more urban areas so that people from rural communities can always relocate for more economic opportunities. There is a consensus that staying in urban centers has the additional benefit of experiencing government projects and programs first-hand. Given the fact that government officials choose to reside within the urban community, this is undebatable.

Quality education systems, reliable infrastructural networks, and better medical system, among others, characterize urban life in the postcolonial time, and this has triggered the rush into the cities. Added to this is that urban life can expose individuals to a timely evaluation of personal growth and cultural orientations because of the diversity of these places. For all these reasons, there have been notable developments in the city life of many West African countries as people seek easier access to better urban communities with many more opportunities for them. Urban preference in contemporary times is accelerated because there are promises of securing better economic growth and financial freedom necessary to improve life. Therefore, because of the assurance that all these are readily available, the interest in living in urban areas has equally increased drastically. Even though this has come with a level of reduction in rural development, urban preference is one of the entrenched results of postcolonial West African life.

Added to the change that happens to the West African countries in postcolonial situations is the decline of their indigenous worship systems. The introduction of colonialism meant the violent displacement of some established cultural traditions in the region. At the beginning of colonialism, there was a ferocious campaign against the African worship systems as cultural colonizers addressed them very negatively in degenerating terms. They associated indigenous worship with primitivism and fetishist groups. Their ignorance of the operational process of the religion led to their hurried and haphazard evaluation, which produced a not-too-friendly result.

After carefully distancing people from the system, the postcolonial environment reinforced the distance by placing less attention on these worships and contributing to their destruction in some situations. This brought insufferable consequences on the indigenous worship systems, and eventually, they bowed down to the religious practices of foreign countries. This was reinforced by the globalization mantra coupled with the narrative of multiculturalism. People who now have a flair for religion in postcolonial times are ridiculed socially, discouraged diplomatically, and rejected politically, all of which combine to wage untold havoc on indigenous systems.

Conclusion

The appropriation of a people's language over another is one of the foundations for cultural alienation or colonization. When an oppressing group's language is adopted for official purposes such as education and commerce, it gives adequate information about the two civilizations whose language is adopted and those who adopted it. For Africans, their adoption of European languages has been a testament to their age-long imperialist relationship, which subjected Africans to protracted suppression and despoliation of their cultural traditions. The adoption of a language does not end at that positional boundary. It continues in other aspects of their existence, including but not limited to the acceptance of their political philosophy, the reception of their culture, and the eventual cultural deracination that enervates their whole existence in the process.

All of these are carefully manifested in the postcolonial world as African cultures are steadily undermined, creating for people an illusion of freedom or being an active member in the globalized world. Therefore, this thinking continues to cripple the African mentality and expose Africans to more dangerous treatments that further affect their chances of political and cultural revitalization. Asante, Fanon, Bhabha, Rodney, and a host of others, have suggested different alternatives to contain the situation. Africa needs to carefully consider these proposed solutions to prevent further loss, which would come as a result of an unplanned escapist philosophy toward the postcolonial challenges.

DEEP DIVE

Assignment 1

Objective

The objective of this assignment is to ensure that students complete the reading of Chapter 22 and encourage them to use Fanon's theory to explore the extent to which African culture was and continues to be influenced by European values and ideas. Additionally, students will be expected to address the internal cultural conflicts that the colonized people struggle with.

Method

Students will be expected to write a short note in response to the question.

Reading Comprehension

What are some elements of African culture that can be seen as remnants of colonial intervention? How do these make evident the "psychological imbalance" of colonized peoples that Fanon references?

Assignment 2

Discussion

How does the inevitability of globalization and multiculturalism affect African cultures and their attempts to disconnect themselves from both European and Western cultural influences?

Objective

The objective of this assignment is for students to consider the extent to which globalization has also infiltrated African societies and cultures and whether its influences are comparable to those of European colonization.

Method

Students will be expected to have a group discussion (either in person or on the online discussion forum) to talk to their peers about the discussion question. Each student would be expected to create a post and respond to at least one other student. If this were to take place in person, then it would simply be a class-wide discussion.

Notes

1 Howard Eiland and Michael Jennings, eds., *Walter Benjamin: Selected Writings, Vol. 4, 1938–1940* (Cambridge: Belknap Press, 2003).
2 Chinua Achebe, *Morning Yet on Creation Day* (London: Heinemann, 1975).
3 Frantz Fanon, *Black Skin, White Masks* (New York: Grove Press Inc., 1967).
4 Ngũgĩ wa Thiong'o, Henry Owuor-Anyumba, and Taban Lo Liyong, "On the Abolition of the English Department," in *Homecoming: Essays on African and Caribbean Literature, Culture and Politics*, ed. Ngũgĩ wa Thiong'o (Brooklyn: Lawrence Hill Books, 1972), 145–150.
5 Wa Thiong'o, Owuor-Anyumba, and Liyong, "On the Abolition of the English Department."
6 Frantz Fanon, *The Wretched of the Earth* (New York: Grove Press, 1963).
7 Edward Said, *Orientalism* (New York: Pantheon Books, 1978).
8 Homi Bhabha, *The Location of Culture* (New York: Routledge, 1994).
9 Donald Molosi, "On Decolonizing the Postcolonial African Classroom," *Literary Hub*, February 28, 2019, https://lithub.com/on-decolonizing-the-postcolonial-afican-classroom/.
10 Christine Ochefu, "The World is Now Coming to Africa: Why Madonna and Ed Sheeran want a Piece of Afrobeats," *The Guardian*, March 4, 2023.

23

CULTURAL CHANGES AND POPULAR CULTURES

Introduction

The concept of culture is so complicated that there are as many definitions as the number of viewpoints available, which explains why anthropologists Kroeber and Kluckhohn came up with 165 different definitions after considering different approaches to culture.[1] Culture can be defined as a uniform pattern of behavior, systems, engagement, and structure that distinguishes a set of people from others.[2] It is a generally accepted set of attitudes that could be conscious or subconscious. Every culture has its own set of symbols, which could be material, non-material, verbal, or nonverbal.[3] Language, norms, rituals, values, ethics, and artifacts are all common elements of culture.[4] In most cases, these elements are different in every culture or have few similarities.

In the scope of this discussion, popular culture includes generally observed beliefs, practices, and lifestyles that have traveled through time and evolved into a new set of practices or newly adopted concepts widely accepted by a set of people.[5] With time, certain traits in a society tend to disappear or become scarcely practiced, while some persist over the years without being affected or with little or no changes. In some other instances, some new traits are acquired. Those traits or beliefs generally sustained through history or in contemporary society are referred to as popular culture.

West African cultures are unique in their manner of growth and are somewhat related due to their shared situations and histories. If one does not understand the dynamics of cultural uniqueness, one might fall into ethnocentrism, that is, the debacle of false cultural superiority. However, as rightly established by different sociologists, anthropologists, and historians, the cultural state of every society only marks its uniqueness. Accepting this will help one understand why some values are respected and observed in some other parts of the world while they are not treated the same in Africa or vice versa.

DOI: 10.4324/9781003198260-28

Ancient Cultures

Older cultures still exist in the contemporary world, and it is necessary to remember this so as not to see everything as new and recent. The prestige of African history is embedded in the long and unique experiences that make it stand out among other societies. History has explained why West Africans can be described as people of culture. It was never a "dark continent" with no history, literature, politics, or systems, as exemplified by some racial apologists.[6] The West African culture had developed into constructing notable items and buildings toward the end of the Stone Age.[7] The discoveries at Iwo Eleru in southwest Nigeria traced the existence of early cultures to about 13,000 years ago.[8] The scientific proof of a long-existing culture in West Africa has positioned it in an enviable state that needs to be studied and has removed the fogs of inferiority in the classification of African culture.

Agriculture was one of the sectors of African society that outlined the historical relevance of West African culture. For instance, plant domestication had been developed early in West Africa, and through time, the region had developed its own cultivation method. Yam cultivation has been traced to about 11,000 years ago.[9] The cultivation of yam and oil palm was one of the oldest agricultural activities in the region, serving as a pointer to the ancient cultural heritage of the region. The palm tree maintained its significance up till the present as a result of its diverse use for many products, as practically every part of the palm tree is useful for one thing or the other. The earliest cultivation of the crop was traced to about 5,000 years ago by associating the use of oil palm fruit with pottery and early tools in that era.[10] The sap of oil palm was used in the production of palm wine; the shell and fiber from its pericarps were used as fuel and fishing lines; the trunks were used for some construction works; and the other parts had their different functions, including palm oil and soap production. This product was a source of attraction for the invasion of the European countries and their interests in the domination of the region. More comprehensive research into the origin of oil palm shows that the fruit is particular to West Africa, and its pollen was discovered in the Niger Delta area as early as 35,000 to 2,800 years ago (Figure 23.1).[11]

Other culturally specific practices in prehistoric West African agriculture were animal husbandry and pastoralism. These practices were responsible for the establishment and cultural construction of many West African countries. The rearing of animals in West Africa was location-specific, with different strategies that went to the root of some societies. Early husbandry history can be traced to the Early Holocene period of the Late Stone Age, with evidence in Tagalagal, Adrar Bous, and Tamaya Mellet in present-day Niger Republic.[12] Other evidence was found in the desert areas of Erg Jmeya, Erg-in-Sakane, and Hassi el Abiod in Mali.[13] Archaeological excavations have shown proof of these practices in other parts of the region.

West African societies were also distinguished for their early discovery of iron technologies, which placed them among the very early societies to discover this type of technology. Early iron technology and culture were traced to sites in Ghana and Nigeria. The Ghanaian Hani site with furnaces was associated with the period between 180 to 75 AD.[14] In Nigeria, the Nok culture was discovered in about 30 different sites, over 300 miles long and 100 miles wide.[15] With such overwhelming excavations and discoveries, the sites suggest a compact culture of a permanent society with defined industrial

THE FIRST DAY OF THE YAM CUSTOM.

FIGURE 23.1 Yam ceremony, Asante https://en.wikipedia.org/wiki/File:Ashanti_Yam_ Ceremony_1817.jpg.

activities, similar to the Taruga site of the Taruga legacy.[16] Nok culture was put at no earlier than 500 BC.[17] Some sources placed it as far back as 1500 BC.[18] These technologies prove that West Africa had developed sophisticated and comprehensive societies as early as the first millennium BC. There is also the possibility that the people around this region have been in existence since that time.[19] The iron technologies and iron smelting practices discovered in this old era made their way to contemporary times (Figure 23.2).

The discussion on how far West African culture has developed itself through history was strengthened by the practice of pottery and the production of terracotta in the deep history of the region. As early as 500 BC, the sophisticated Nok culture had started sourcing for its own immediate collective needs, including cooking oil, millet, and ceramic pots, and by 800 BC, the culture was associated with terracotta and the use of iron.[20] A more developed use and construction of clay, pottery, and terracotta existed in the old Ile-Ife around 1000–1500 AD. Earthworks were used in advanced constructions, including inner and outer elitist designs of dignitaries' houses.[21] This development and culture are similar to those in Benin City, where the use of earthwork was overwhelmingly common such that they were always 17.4 meters in average height.[22] In addition, the advancement and existence of beads and other items in Igbo-Ukwu in Nigeria and Gao in Eastern Mali have also lent credence to the advancement in the early African culture.[23]

These and several other cultures, most of which predated the advent of colonialism, have been modified or adapted in the contemporary era. Essentially, the political arrangements of the people were built on their cultures. One of the historically remarkable

FIGURE 23.2   Nok sculpture https://commons.wikimedia.org/wiki/File:Nok_sculpture_Louvre
_70-1998-11-1.jpg.

political arrangements was the Empire of Tekrur which spread into the middle and lower Senegal, the desert, and The Gambia. The empire had trade interaction with the North African people as early as the tenth century and had an army that preserved its territory.[24] Others included the empire of Ghana, the Mansa Musa's Mali, the Songhai Empire, the Hausa and Kanuri Empires, the Oyo Empire, the Dahomey Kingdom, and so on.[25]

Several cultural conditions and orientations have shaped the kind of people living in the region. To a great extent, this cultural heritage influences the new norms of contemporary West Africa. For instance, the collectivist societal orientation of Africans, although significantly influenced by contemporary individualism, still thrives in many communities and in the minds of others.[26]

Cultural Changes

No matter how compact, seemingly perfect, and fundamental a culture is, it will always be susceptible to change. Cultural change is a popular phenomenon that includes the transformation of social psychology and the general behaviors of people. The main elements of cultural change and the emergence of a new culture are innovations and cultural diffusion.[27] Invention and innovation in a society include new cultural discoveries and the advancement of preexisting cultures within the society itself. For instance, the development of Kente fabric only morphed into colorful designs after a long period of the black-and-white pattern. Later on, new techniques were developed that allowed for a more refined way of producing Ghanaian cloth.[28] And as new cultures gradually displaced the old belief systems, new designs gradually replaced the old patterns.

Another factor in cultural change is cultural diffusion. Cultural diffusion refers to the conscious or unconscious adoption of other cultures through societal interaction with foreign cultures. Cultural diffusion can be intranational or international. With the advent of globalization and the civilization process, the world is gradually becoming a global village because of the continuing exchange of systemic and behavioral patterns.[29] Cultural diffusion in West Africa has been a result of different change agencies. The first example of massive cultural change came with the early contact with the Europeans (including the early Portuguese traders) and the Arabic world. Migration, education, and new religion are a few outcomes of these contacts that resulted in the displacement or transformation of many cultures.[30] The cultural impacts of the slave trade, as well as the trans-Saharan trade, have also been evident in contemporary society.[31] Also, colonial experience and the participation of West Africans in the two world wars are responsible for many of the popular cultures in contemporary West Africa.[32]

The trans-Saharan trade formed a commercial relationship between the Arab Peninsula, North Africa, and West Africa through the Sahara in the seventh century. The routes that linked West Africa with North Africa are claimed to have been discovered by the Carthaginians of North Africa.[33] Products like gold, ivory, slaves, kola nuts, leather products, dyed cloths, and animal skin, among others, were transported in large quantities from West Africa to North Africa and the Arabian Peninsula, while salt, guns, horses, beads, Manchester cotton, Arabian cloths, glasses, French silk, etc., were transported to West Africa.[34] The trans-Saharan trade brought about great cultural diffusion in West African societies as they started imbibing North African cultural values, with their cultural materials gaining popularity across West Africa.[35]

One of the prominent attributes of the trans-Saharan trade is the importation of the Islamic religion into West Africa and its radical adoption by some societies such that it became the state religion in their early stages and the most practiced in their contemporary societies. The first spread of Islam was through peaceful persuasion and conquests targeted for different purposes depending on the type of society. The conversion of the Soninke/Mandingo people and traders was solely for establishing reliable missionaries among the people, but the conversion of the rulers or kings was to achieve an automatic imposition of Islam on the citizens as a state religion.[36]

By the ninth century, there were already Islamic practices in Kanem, Tekrur, ancient Ghana, and Kumbi, among others.[37] Though there was wide Islamization in Western Sudan in this period, it only assumed total Islamic identity under the rule of Mansa Musa of Mali. Although Islam practice in all those areas, including Kano and other parts of Nigerian societies, was already taking a cultural diversion over a long period, different revivals and jihads were carried out in some areas of West Africa to purify it. For instance, Ahmad Lobo was responsible for the jihad and Islamic revival that institutionalized Islamic theocracy and purity in Futa Jallon in 1725.[38] Similarly, Usman Dan Fodio carried out jihad for the purification of Islam, the creation of the Sokoto Caliphate after conquering several other empires, and the spread of Islam, especially in Northern Nigeria.[39]

In large parts of West Africa, where such beliefs were rampant, the spread of Islam introduced monotheism and non-interference of the dead in matters involving the living. It was also responsible for the displacement of the majority of the cultural values in some areas like the Hausa/Fulani region. Islam also brought about early writing cultures in West Africa, including the *Kano Chronicles* and other Islamic scholarship.[40] In West Africa, almost half of the population now practices Islam instead of the traditional religion that had characterized them before Islam. Many of these people have, in many respects, forgotten their traditional religions. Apart from Islam, Christianity is another agent of cultural change in West Africa. With its positioning in the coastal area, West Africa attracted many European states to trade and spread their ideologies. However, the history of West Africa's contact with Christianity is connected to the European exploration of the region and might not be taken independently.

One of the first properly documented European interactions with the West African coasts was the exploration of Prince Henry, the Navigator of Portugal, to fortify Portuguese power, wealth, and the spread of the empire in many places in the fifteenth century.[41] While strengthening Portuguese dominance in the West African coastal regions, their culture and religion were presented as superior.[42] In the north of Cape Verde and other parts of the region, the Portuguese carried out different trading activities that led to the initial transfusion of European cultures, especially in the Wolof states, Warri, and the old Benin Empire, among others.[43] This marked the initial introduction of Christianity in West Africa, although the influence of the religion subsided before the eighteenth century.

In the eighteenth and nineteenth centuries, Christian missionaries returned to West Africa after the unfortunate history of the slave trade that drained West Africa of both resources and labor. The second phase of the Christian missionary projects in West Africa brought about a new culture. It served as one of the foundations of colonialism and, to some extent, prepared the minds of the people for a new system of government aside from their native political systems. Christianity also brought about Western education as different schools were built across the regions with missionaries as their teachers.[44]

These Islamic and Christian expansions are gradually wiping out the traditional African religions, which were the direct foundation of the West African cultures. In Mauritania, The Gambia, Mali, Niger, Côte d'Ivoire, Burkina Faso, Nigeria, Guinea Bissau, Guinea, and Senegal, about 50 to 100 percent of the population are now Muslims, while the remaining part of the population are either Christians or traditional worshippers while the majority of Ghana, Benin, and Cape Verde are Christians.[45] However, it is important to note that traditional religions are practiced by minorities in the region, but some of the traditional beliefs have been adapted to Christian and Islamic practices.

One historical experience that West Africa cannot forget is colonialism and its attendant European imperialism. After the Berlin Conference of 1885–1886, West Africa was divided primarily between the French and British colonial governments for economic gains.[46] The colonial government established its authority and culture across West Africa for approximately 100 years, and as such, there was a heavy Western cultural influence on the region.[47] The cultural impacts of colonialism first manifested in the change of political orientation from a traditional system rooted in the people's history to indirect rule and democracy. The basic traditional political institutions in West Africa were significantly changed or adjusted to fit in with the new system of government. Colonialism also opened trade routes for the sale of European products and the exploitation and exportation of West African products. This created huge cultural diffusion and brought about the popular cultural makeup of present West Africa in literature, lifestyle, entertainment, communication, military, religion, economics and commerce, professions, and health.[48]

During the colonial era, the two world wars further increased global cultural diffusion, and West Africa was not left out. The British and French colonial governments deployed hundreds of thousands of West Africans to the fronts of the First and Second World Wars. In Nigeria, the British colonial government was said to have deployed between 55,000 and 121,652 Nigerians to the wars.[49] These African soldiers mingled with their counterparts from other countries, especially the Europeans. The returnees adopted different European principles, which greatly impacted West African society. New forms of entertainment, lifestyles, and healthcare started emerging. Some of the returnees also took up various professions different from the traditional agricultural systems.

Furthermore, the advent of the Western educational system in West Africa became one of the major factors of cultural change in the region. In addition to evangelism, the Christian missionaries took it as a point of duty to impact Western values through education. The missionaries were credited for the first set of educational institutions across West Africa. The colonial governments in British West Africa were not much interested in educating indigenes of their colonies at the inception of colonialism until around 1877, especially in Nigeria where the British took the back seat until they had solidified their colonial authority.[50] The missionaries, on their part, only saw education as a tool for attracting people with the sole purpose of teaching the gospel.

Aside from schools created by the Europeans for primary education, which included how to read and write in English and the corresponding languages, a more advanced educational system was also introduced. In 1827, the Fourah Bay College was established in Freetown, Sierra Leone, by Anglican missionaries and was notably the first higher institution of learning in the region.[51] The college became a symbol of civilization and Westernization of the region as many Africans, including Samuel Ajayi Crowther, were enrolled in the institution.[52] Similar institutions were later built across the region for advanced and more technical education for Africans.

In 1932, the British government in Nigeria founded Yaba College at the King's College in Lagos for advanced learning and technical training that could allow more Nigerians to be employed in the service of the colonial government.[53] Graduates of this college were required to travel to England for a more advanced and sophisticated curriculum in different professions. After their studies in England, these individuals returned to West Africa to influence the cultural orientation of the people. More advanced education was later introduced with the establishment of the University College of the Gold Coast (currently the University of Ghana) and the University College Ibadan (presently the University of Ibadan) in 1948 after the Asquith and Elliot Commissions.[54]

In West Africa, Western education has become a basic societal requirement that an average citizen must achieve. It has defined the social culture and relevance by which a new order of stratification is created. Popular culture in West Africa is defined basically by this system of formal education. All other sectors and cultural elements have been created and instituted in Western education.

Contemporary Cultures

After years of contact with other cultures of the world and the evolvement of some of the original cultures, it seems there are now noticeable new ways of life that explain the new West African society. Thus, contemporary West Africa is an amalgam of new and old cultures that have transformed the general image of the region. The new West African society can be identified principally by the use of language. After the colonial experience, European languages, especially English and French, became the most recognized languages in the region. Despite Africa and, most importantly, West Africa's multi-linguistic traits, they succumbed to the domination of foreign languages.[55] Today, three things happen in the West African language space: the speaking of European languages, the Africanization of European languages, and the use of the West African indigenous languages in their original or adapted forms.

One common feature in most colonized countries is that the colonialists left their languages behind. In contemporary West Africa, some of these languages are being adapted to original West African languages and cultures. For instance, the English language spoken in Ghana and Nigeria has been significantly affected by the linguistic features of their indigenous languages. This could be seen in the pronunciation, semantics, and syntactic structure of this English language form.[56] One such remarkable adaptation is Pidgin English, mostly used among Nigerians and Ghanaians. As a Creole language, Pidgin English is blended in a way that makes it easy for many West Africans to learn and speak.[57] Pidgin has been quite instrumental in mitigating linguistic barriers in Nigeria and Ghana as local speakers adapt more quickly to speaking it than the proper English language.

Another evidence of contemporary West African societies is the advancement of the movie industry, which has formed an important part of this region. The movie industry has been a prominent agent in the spread and exhibition of both foreign and local cultures. West Africa has one of the most powerful movie industries in the world. As of 2010, Nigeria's Nollywood was the second-highest movie-producing industry in the world after Indian Bollywood, despite being founded only in 1992.[58] The industry is prominent in Africa, next only to Hollywood in the drive to take over the global market. Nollywood movies represent the common and popular culture of the country as they depict the people's daily experiences and reenact current trends of culture, which leads to subconscious cultural change.[59] Their productions have also served as a means of maintaining social values, controlling social vices, and a platform for the expression of specific experiences for learning purposes.[60] The movie industry has also been a dissenting voice against the common misrepresentation of African culture, since it shows African culture at its best and diffuses it into other parts of the world. The success of the industry as a primary medium of showing African culture informs its predominance in many African countries, including Ethiopia, Kenya, South Africa, and other parts of the world.[61]

According to Abah, three factors distinguish the industry as an agent and evidence of social change in contemporary West Africa.[62] Firstly, the industry is free from ideological blocs and government restrictions. As a result, the ideological explorations of the screenwriters and filmmakers have contributed to the reconstruction of Nigerian society. Secondly, although the ideology behind filmmaking and its processing might have been Western and born out of economic and social interests, the ideas and concepts were initially original to the African community.[63] The industry has been able to reposition African culture and showcase the current cultural trends without the superimposition of Western culture. With its diverse blocs based on different ethnic specifications, it has also been able to promote local languages in a society adjusting speedily to English and French. Thirdly, the average West African movie industry, especially Nollywood, has moralization as the primary endgame of all its production and largely tries to portray a sane society.[64] The Ghanaian movie industry, popularly known as Ghallywood, has exhibited similar characteristics, and it is becoming more developed and widely accessible.[65]

In many other ways, the movie industry qualifies as popular culture in contemporary West Africa. The industry provides a cultural alternative to the indigenous modes of relaxation and fun. African society is known for its subscription to long-surviving folktales and folklore, which were often some of the instruments of social construction and the impartation of social values in West African society. Folktales and folklore were told to children at an early age to help them imbibe good morals and cultural values.[66] While these old cultures served as entertainment and education mediums, the movie industry has virtually taken over. The use of folktales and folklore is now often incorporated into movies with a more realistic and imaginative representation of those values.[67] Unlike traditional means of relaxation, movies and films have become more popular in contemporary West African society.[68]

Music and entertainment systems provide insight into society and its culture. Music is an important cultural material that tells the course of beliefs of a society as they relate to every aspect of its life. Hence, it is one of the foremost pieces of evidence and proof of cultural change, forming a reference point for the dominant cultures of contemporary society.[69] The West African history of music does not have a definitive answer to when music culture started in the region; however, there was evidence of music in sub-Saharan Africa as far back as 2,500 years ago when exploratory expeditions were carried out from the old Carthage region of North Africa to the coastal areas of Africa.[70] This predates the contact of African societies with the first Portuguese traders around the twelfth and thirteenth centuries. It is also important to note that the evidence of the existence of music in West Africa in the second half of the last century BC does not mean it started at that point. Music is etched into West African culture and cannot be separated from it. Drumming, singing, and dancing, as practiced by the *jelilu* and *jalolu* of the Maninka and Mandinka people of Mande origin, are a core aspect of West African society, culture, tradition, and religion (Figure 23.3).[71]

Initially, African music had a traditional purpose, especially if it was portraying morals. It was basically for rituals, societal criticism, appraisal, historical reenactment, and transmission of historical knowledge. Contemporary African music has changed in purpose and manners.[72] However, music is still a veritable means of criticizing society and its institutions. Many musical productions and performances in contemporary West Africa have been critical of the political class and the actions and inactions of the government. Fela Anikulapo Kuti and his commitment to the criticism of the government

FIGURE 23.3   Mandinka dancer   https://commons.wikimedia.org/wiki/File:DC_-_Foto_Serra
_No_100_-_Dan%C3%A7arino_mandinga_(Farim).jpg.

and military rule in Nigeria come to the fore in this discourse.[73] In addition, music has been a reliable way of teaching morals, the same way it was done in ancient African societies. These musicians expose social vices and criticize them publicly, making people see why they should be done away with. There are also instances where music is used to explain or change unwanted narratives and resolve societal conflicts. An example is the role of music toward the end of the 1967 Nigerian Civil War and how it helped people adjust to the aftermath of the war.[74]

Although the old traditional musical styles and instruments are still used considerably in many parts of the region, there are new adjustments to mainly Western styles of music. Music like Juju, Fuji, Apala, and highlife, like that of the *konkomba* in Ghana, Sierra Leone, and Nigeria, originated from West Africa.[75] New types of music have surfaced, especially with the advent of globalization and the introduction of new instruments.[76] This is evident in the contemporary trends that include hip-hop, jazz, blues, Afro-calypso, and the like, and it has created a new class of celebrities who now enjoy global recognition. The new musical styles in the region are a result of the long-standing interaction and interrelationship with other cultures. An example is a blend of the African style of music and that of West Germany by the Ghanaian musician, George Darko.[77]

Before contemporary Francophone West African music attained its current identity, it passed through three stages of reformation. The first of such phases was the era of French colonial music domination between 1940 and 1960. After that, French West African music started seeking a distinct identity from 1960 to 1980. This was followed by the period where local music took into cognizance the local culture and global musical tendencies from 1980 to 2000. In contemporary Senegal, although people recognize who a musician is, they would rather have specific words for different musicians based on their type of music. Examples of this include *wolof* for a singer and *woykat* for instrumentalists. The different type of instrument also suggests the designation given to different musicians, and such names include *xalamkat* and *tamakat*, among others.[78] In all, the music culture across West Africa has moved largely toward European culture and abridged cultures.

Cultural change in West Africa has given birth to some common dress and fashion styles in the region. After different contacts with European cultures and various other cultures, the traditional fashion sense and dress styles in the region have changed considerably. The most common dress in West Africa was not shirts, trousers, or skirts, as adopted from the colonial experiences of the people.[79] However, in contemporary West Africa, the definition of formal dress tends toward Western dress, and basic African dress is mainly worn on Fridays.[80] The workplace dress cultures at different establishments and the compulsion of workers to abide by these dress codes have proven to be a basic driving force behind the continuing adoption of Western dress. For instance, professionals like lawyers, medical doctors, pharmacists, as well as all corporate "white collar" workers are compulsorily attached to Western dress, and any other dress, including traditional African dress, might not be tolerated or admissible at work. This new cultural trend of attachment to Western dress and fashion has its foundation in the dress codes of primary and secondary schools in West Africa.

As stated, the basic regular dress in West Africa is gradually becoming Western, while traditional dress, mostly worn on weekends and traditional occasions, has been adapted to Western styles. One type of West African dress that is still widely worn in the region and elsewhere is *Kente*. This traditional Asante dress has been a symbol of African culture and the vivid creativity of the region. *Kente* started as a royal fabric adopted based on the tradition of learning *Ananse*'s spider web. Initially, the royal dress was woven in white and black until the era of Asantehene Nana Agyeman Prempeh, who made colored yarns accessible to the people.[81] From this point, the Ghanaians developed more sophisticated technology around cloth production to increase the quality and meet contemporary demands. *Kente* has been a global commodity and style as people throughout different countries find it comfortable to wear (Figure 23.4).

Another West African fabric with prestige similar to *Kente* is the Yoruba *Aso Oke*. *Aso Oke* is a cultural and prestigious wear among the Nigerian Yoruba society. *Aso Oke* is distinct for the skills of the weavers, the yarns used, the techniques, and the introduction of different designs while weaving it. Initially, the unique patterns were drawn using *iket*, holes, and side inlay floats.[82] The introduction of machines for easier production and design has helped in the large production of these materials. Consumers can now describe or dictate the kind of designs they want.[83] *Aso Oke* is not as fondly worn as it was in the precolonial and early colonial Nigerian society. It is now worn on rare traditional occasions and during celebrations like weddings and the funeral of aged people to showcase African culture.

In Côte d'Ivoire, there is still the widespread use of *pagnes*—colorful traditional blouses with matching head wears and wrappers—among Abidjan women. In addition, Baule loincloths are also largely in use in Côte d'Ivoire and have also been adapted

Nana Otumfoe Sir Oasei Agymang Prembeh II., König von Asante.

FIGURE 23.4 Asante King Prempeh II wearing *kente* https://commons.wikimedia.org/wiki/File :PrempehII.jpg.

to contemporary Western culture.[84] Baule loincloths were often used in ceremonies and traditional events but are now popularly used for different styles and occasions in contemporary Côte d'Ivoire.[85] The clothes were originally made from barks and strips of trees that are finely made for easy construction of the fabrics. Later, weaving techniques were introduced, and the clothing attained more designs and patterns that made it outstanding.

In addition to the cultural evidential specification of West African society, the naming culture in the region is worthy of note. The ceremony is part of the cultural rite of passage in African society, starting from the conception of a child, adulthood, major events in life, and death. It is a belief system that defines the societal construction and adoption of individuals. The naming ceremony culture persists in contemporary West Africa with different varieties based on individual societies. In Yoruba Nigerian society, it is called *"Isomo l'oruko,"* and the ceremony is performed eight days after the birth of the child.[86] A naming ceremony is important in African societies as it is significant to society as a way of incorporating the child into the community and socializing with them. The celebration is often held at the father's family house, as West African societies are largely patriarchal.[87] It is often presided over by the oldest member of the family, using cultural items such as honey, kola nut, and bitter kola, all of which have significant meanings and roles. Honey (*oyin*) signifies the desire for happiness. Kola nut (*obi*) is used to pray against ill luck and evil events, while bitter kola (*orogbo*) and water depict long life. The use of salt (*iyo*) symbolizes relevance in life, and alligator pepper (*ataare*) signifies fulfillment of purpose and having many children. Palm oil, fish, liquor, money, and white cloth are also symbolic in the naming ceremony.[88] This practice is common in West African societies but with specific differences across the region.

The traditional naming ceremony and rites have been influenced considerably by Christianity and Islam, or whichever foreign religion the child's parents practice. These religions and their beliefs have heralded a new form of naming culture that takes place either at home or in religious buildings. Traditional prayers are gradually replaced by religious prayers, depending on the religion. The traditional systems and processes are only adopted in a few cases, either fully or in part. Many Nigerian societies still practice the traditional seven to eight days interval between the date of birth and the child's naming ceremony. West African names are symbolic and still carry the cultural sampling prevalent before Westernization and globalization in West Africa. However, it is presently a popular practice to adopt a Western or Islamic name for children due to the overbearing Western culture's interference and globalization.[89] This explains why a West African would be given the names "Jack," "Arthur," or any other Western name.[90]

African names have specific meanings based on religious beliefs or the parents' experience before or during the birth of the child. For instance, among Cameroon's Bakossi people, names are given along gender attributes and the qualities positively attributable to the two genders.[91] In some other instances, the Bakossi society could name a child after a midwife, especially when the midwife is a Bakossi indigene, and when they are not, the adopted name would be temporary until another name or an equivalent Bakossi name is given to the child.[92] Many of these traditional names are not often used, and even where children are given those names, they are hardly taken as their first names. West Africans still use some of them and widely adopt the mentality and rationale behind many of the names. In this sense, the situation and religious beliefs of the parents determine the name of the child. Religious names are also often adopted into their local language interpretation.

Furthermore, the general social orientation of West African society before colonialism was collectivist in that every individual had a feeling of social responsibility toward the other. This was evident in how child-raising was approached. The moral upbringing of a child was seen as a social responsibility, starting with the extended family. Communal and individual issues were often tackled collectively, using division of labor rather than leaving the affected individuals to them.[93] This orientation could be seen in all sectors of society as businesses, commerce, and vocations were seen as collective or family duties rather than those of the individual.[94] This communal orientation allowed quick social incorporation and unity toward confronting collective or individual challenges.

However, these social values and orientations assumed individualistic approaches after various contacts with Western and other foreign cultures and values.[95] This is because West African cultures are associated continuously with foreign cultures built on individualistic foundations; as a result, the principles of "self" became paramount in the social constructs. In contemporary West Africa, collectivism is no longer the basic societal orientation. In these societies, the closest to it is the coexistence of the two principles—individualism and collectivism.[96] Political and economic systems are entirely founded on individualistic orientation, while most people's lifestyles are largely mixed orientation. An average West African society and family are still hospitable and tolerant as in the precolonial era.

Furthermore, the transformation in the role of women in West Africa has brought about a new and popular culture about how women should be treated in these societies. The precolonial, colonial, and early postcolonial West Africa considered women as second-class citizens due to the patriarchal social construction of most parts of the region. Women were expected to be modest and live according to the will of their father, brother, or husband. For instance, the purdah system practiced in the Hausa/Fulani parts of Northern Nigeria and Southern Niger subjects women to different social limitations.[97] The system is meant to restrict the movement of married women, conceal their faces, and limit their interaction with other men until they attain menopause.

Women could be ill-treated when they lost their husbands and were considered the first suspects, no matter the circumstances in which the men died. More so, the political construction of society was largely discriminatory in favor of its male members. Women only earned political relevance on rare occasions. Only a few societies like Igbo and Ijaw in Nigeria, Balobedu, Asante, and Wolof kingdoms reserved chieftaincy roles for women. However, in some of these societies, leadership and kingship were always conferred on male children based on patrilineal lines.[98] Today, this trend is fading gradually. Special attention has been given to girls' education to achieve gender equality in areas where girls have been subjected to educational discrimination.[99]

Countries like Ghana and Nigeria have been able to get more girls into school, which has become a popular practice in these areas. Also, as various constitutional developments put women's rights into perspective, more women are assuming political positions to the extent that some women have attained major and sensitive leadership positions in the region. There is an emerging popular economic reformation that has created space for women-owned mega-companies. As more people become conscious of women's rights, gender equality has become popular culture.

Festivals

Cultural festivals exhibit the values, prestige, customs, and belief systems of any society. In West Africa, festivals are used to either worship a particular god or celebrate the beginning of an agricultural season. Every year or season, these activities were originally used to praise, worship, and lay demands before the corresponding deity. Although the original organizers of these festivals still hold the religious values attributed to the festivals, they have turned into major tourist attractions all over the world.[100] Some of these notable festivals will be discussed below in detail as major evidence of popular cultures in West Africa.

Gerewol Festival

The festival is organized annually by the Wodaabe Nomads, who rear cattle in the Niger villages. The male nomads dress in adorned apparel and sophisticated ornaments to attract female counterparts at the festival. The festival is held for a week, often after the rainy season. The Fula traditional music is sung while the men gather together to perform traditional line dancing. Women are often camped at the venue while men visit them to display their attractiveness and strength to convince the most beautiful women in the form of competition.[101] For sustenance and the stamina to dance and perform for a whole week, the men are made to drink concoctions that will energize them. In recent times, the tradition has attracted tourists across the world because of its uniqueness. International media, including magazines, documentaries, filmmakers, and cultural enthusiasts, visit the festival sites for cultural appreciation, content creation, and publicity for the interest of the international community (Figure 23.5).

Argungu Fishing Festival

The Argungu Fishing Festival is a unique cultural symbol that exhibits the agricultural disposition of West Africans in Sokoto and Kebbi in northwestern Nigeria. Although the origin of the festival is disputed, it is often assumed that it was used to end the inter-settlement rivalry between Sokoto and Kebbi residents. It was supposed to be an appreciation of the visit of Hassan Dan Mu'azu, the then Sultan of Sokoto, to Argungu to mark the end of rivalry in 1934. Another account states that the festival marks Sarkin Kebbi Muhammadu II's permission for the Kebbawas to fish in rivers belonging to Sokoto

FIGURE 23.5   Wodaabe ethnic group sing and dance during the Gerewol festival https://commons.wikimedia.org/wiki/File:1997_274-29_Gerewol.jpg.

around the same period.[102] In another narration, the festival was linked to the Su Festival of the sixteenth century, marking the fishing profession of Kebbi indigenes.[103]

Most importantly, the festival was designed to carry out fertility rituals, a tradition that has persisted throughout history. The Huma, who was the head of the fishermen and a priest of the river, goes with some other chiefs to the middle of the river to perform a rice-flour ball and honey ritual with the Sarkin Ruwa and the Jirgi. Other items like hens, goats, and some vegetables are added to the ritual. It is also believed that the ritual would preserve the fish and prevent them from migrating to other rivers. The festival is done about one mile upstream into the river, where fishing activities are prohibited to avoid unsettling the fish. The fishermen are put on alert with music and songs, and they charge into the river at the sound of a signal. They are allowed to enjoy themselves until the fishing period is over. After this, the area is conserved, and no one is allowed to fish there till the following year.

The festival receives a lot of publicity since it has become a major tourist activity that attracts people all over the world. As a result, many people attend the festival for entertainment, while the religious organizers focus on the ritual. Without a doubt, the Argungu festival has attained a popular social status (Figure 23.6).[104]

The Calabar Festival

The Calabar Festival in Nigeria is a mixture of tradition and Christianity and has become a basic culture of the people. It started as a Christmas festival and, as such, has close similarity with the Christmas celebration. The festival is filled with performances,

FIGURE 23.6 Argungu fishing festival https://www.shutterstock.com/image-photo/argungu -kebbi-state-nigeria-march-2020-1787785844.

FIGURE 23.7   A Burundian performer at the Carnival Calabar in Calabar, Nigeria https://commons.wikimedia.org/wiki/File:Burundian_performers.jpg.

displays, and dances of masquerades around the city, traditional dance, and food-sharing in abundance. It takes higher intensity from December 24 to 26, but it is often held for 32 days, from December 1 to January 1 of the following year. The festival has become a national heritage, and the state has been committed to its annual commemoration. It has also been used to address important issues in society. For instance, the first day is often used to commemorate the campaign against HIV/AIDS through a walk of about 12km. The culture is widely associated with colorful, fun-filled, and entertaining programs (Figure 23.7).[105]

Conclusion

Culture is the core identity of every society and an attribute that determines the mindset of its average members. It is susceptible to change depending on the changes that members of the society may experience and their interaction with other cultures. Such other cultures, whether imported or evolved, spread gradually among members of the society until they became popular culture. This is the situation in West Africa, where previously widely practiced cultures have changed with time and are now scarcely observed. People's various experiences have brought about a new order that dictates the new mode of habits, values, and psychology that have distinguished the region from other parts of the world.

While change and cultural shifts are inevitable in West Africa, as they are everywhere else, it is important to ensure that the heritage is not lost, as there must be concerted efforts to preserve institutions that reenact West African cultural values and allow cultural retention and mixture in cases where those new cultures cannot be excused. It is not bad to speak English or French or wear Western apparel; it would, however, amount to hopeless submission to neocolonialism and disregard for history if those acts were not mixed with local alternatives in their styles and frequencies. West Africa must focus on the effective coexistence of the dominant foreign and indigenous cultures. This is the only way to preserve local cultures while also allowing an opportunity for cultural growth and diversity that would engender development and sustainability.

DEEP DIVE

Assignment 1

Objective

The objective of this assignment is to ensure that students complete the reading of Chapter 23 and get them to consider the different developmental phases of popular culture in West Africa.

Method

Students will be expected to write a short note in response to the question.

Reading Comprehension

Identify the main elements of cultural change and factors that created the emergence of a new culture in West Africa.

Assignment 2

Discussion

How can society and its culture be understood from the music and entertainment systems?

Objective

The objective of this assignment is to get students to consider how culture can be understood through the framework of West African music and entertainment.

Methods

Students will be expected to participate in a group conversation (either in person or on the online discussion forum) to talk to their peers about the discussion question. Each student will be expected to create a post and respond to at least one other student. If this were to take place in person, it would simply be a class-wide discussion.

Notes

1 Alfred L. Kroeber and Clyde Kluckhohn, *Culture: A Critical Review of Concepts and Definitions* (Massachusetts: Peabody Museum, 1952).

2 Allan Hanson F., *Meaning in Culture* (Oxfordshire: Routledge, 2004).

3 Roger E. Axtell, *Gestures: The Do's and Taboos of Body Language around the World* (New York: Wiley, 1991).

4 Susan Tyler, "Human Behavior and the Social Environment," accessed April 20, 2022, https://open.umn.edu/opentextbooks/textbooks/880.

5 Chandra Mukerji and Michael Schudson, "Popular Culture," *Annual Review of Sociology* 12, no. 1 (1986): 47–66.

6 Henry Morton Stanley, *Through the Dark Continent* (London: Sampson Low, 1889).

7 Eleanor Scerri, "The Stone Age Archaeology of West Africa," *Oxford Research Encyclopedia of African History* (2017).

8 Anders Bergström, Chris Stringer, Mateja Hajdinjak, Eleanor ML Scerri and Pontus Skoglund, "Origins of Modern Human Ancestry," *Nature* 590, no. 7845 (2021): 229–237.

9 David R. Harris, "Traditional Systems of Plant Food Production and the Origins of Agriculture in West Africa," in *Origins of African Plant Domestication*, eds. Jack R. Harlan, Jan M. J. de Wet and Anmn B. L. Stemler (Mouton: The Hague, 1976), 311–156.

10 Thurstan Shaw, "Early Crops in Africa: A Review of the Evidence," *Origins of African Plant Domestication*, eds. Jack R. Harlan, Jan M. J. De Wet and Ann B. L. Stemler (Berlin: De Gruyter Mouton, 1976), 107-154.

11 Anton C. Zeven, "On the Origin of the Oil Palm (Elaeis Guineensis Jacq.)," *Grana Palynologica* 5, no. 1 (1964): 121–123.

12 Desmond Clark, Martin A. J. Williams, and Andrew B. Smith, "The Geomorphology and Archaeology of Adrar Bous, Central Sahara: A Preliminary Report," *Quaternaria* 17 (1973): 245–297.

13 Augustin F. C. Holl, "Livestock Husbandry, Pastoralisms, and Territoriality: The West African Record," *Journal of Anthropological Archaeology* 17, no. 2 (1998): 143–165.

14 Merrick Posnansky and Roderick McIntosh, "New Radiocarbon Dates for Northern and Western Africa," *The Journal of African History* 17, no. 2 (1976): 161–195.

15 Benjamin Kinsell Swartz and Raymond Dumett, eds., *West African Culture Dynamics: Archaeological and Historical Perspectives* (Berlin: Walter de Gruyter, 2011).

16 Bernard Fagg, "Recent Work in West Africa: New Light on the Nok Culture," *World Archaeology* 1, no. 1 (1969): 41–50.

17 Gabriele Franke, "A Chronology of the Central Nigerian Nok Culture–1500 BC to the Beginning of the Common Era," *Journal of African Archaeology* 14, no. 3 (2016): 257–289.

18 Stephen Dueppen, "The Archaeology of West Africa, 800 BCE to 1500 CE," *History Compass* 14, no. 6 (2016): 247–263.

19 Swartz and Dumett, *West African Culture Dynamics*.

20 Dueppen, "The Archaeology of West Africa," 247–263.

21 Chapurukha Kusimba, Sibel Barut Kusimba and Babatunde Agbaje-Williams, "Precolonial African Cities," in *Urbanism in the Preindustrial World: Cross-Cultural Approaches*, ed. Glenn R. Storey (Alabama: The University of Alabama Press, 2006), 145.

22 Graham Connah, "Archaeology in Benin," *The Journal of African History* 13, no. 1 (1972): 25–38.

23 Timothy Insoll and Thurstan Shaw, "Gao and Igbo-Ukwu: Beads, Interregional Trade, and Beyond," *African Archaeological Review* 14, no. 1 (1997): 9–23.

24 George T. Stride and Caroline Ifeka, *Peoples and Empires of West Africa: West Africa in History, 1000–1800* (New York: Africana Publishing Corporation, 1971).

25 Stride and Ifeka, *Peoples and Empires of West Africa*.

26 Heejung S. Kim, David K. Sherman and John A. Updegraff, "Fear of Ebola: The Influence of Collectivism on Xenophobic Threat Responses," *Psychological Science* 27, no. 7 (2016): 935–944.

27 Susan Andreatta and Gary Ferraro, *Elements of Culture: An Applied Perspective* (California: Cengage Learning, 2012).

28 Shea Clark Smith, "Kente Cloth Motifs," *African Arts* 9, no. 1 (1975): 36–39.

29 Jan Nederveen Pieterse, *Globalization and Culture: Global Mélange* (Maryland: Rowman and Littlefield, 2019).

30 Stephen Castles, "Migration and Community Formation under Conditions of Globalization," *International Migration Review* 36, no. 4 (2002): 1143–1168.

31 Pier Larson, "African Slave Trades in Global Perspective," *The Oxford Handbook of Modern African History* 55 (2013): 56.
32 Peter P. Ekeh, "Colonialism and Social Structure," Inaugural Lecture, University of Ibadan (1983): 11.
33 Eric Ross, "A Historical Geography of the Trans-Saharan Trade," in *The Trans-Saharan Book Trade: Manuscript Culture, Arabic Literacy and Intellectual History in Muslim Africa*, eds. Graziano Krätli and Ghislaine Lydon (Netherland: Brill, 2011), 1–34.
34 Ross, "A Historical Geography," 1–34.
35 Cordelia O. Osasona, "Transformed Culture, Transforming Builtscape: Experiences from Nigeria," *International Journal of Sustainable Development and Planning* 7, no. 1 (2012): 69–100.
36 John Trimingham, *Islam in West Africa* (Oxford: Clarendon Press, 1964).
37 Stride and Ifeka, *Peoples and Empires of West Africa*.
38 Ralph A. Austen, *Trans-Saharan Africa in World History* (Oxford: Oxford University Press, 2010).
39 Nsemba Edward Lenshie and F. E. F. Ayokhai, "Rethinking Pre-Colonial State Formation and Ethno-Religious Identity Transformation in Hausa Land under the Sokoto Caliphate," *Global Journal of Human Social Science Political Science* 13, no. 4 (2013): 1–10.
40 John Hunwick, "A Historical Whodunit: The So-Called 'Kano Chronicle' and Its Place in the Historiography of Kano," *History in Africa* 21 (1994): 127–146.
41 Malyn Newitt, *A History of Portuguese Overseas Expansion 1400–1668* (London: Routledge, 2004).
42 Joao De Barros, *Da Asia de João de Barros e de Diogo de Couto Vol. B* (Lisbon: Na Regia Officina Typografica, 1777).
43 Ivana Elbl, "Cross-Cultural Trade and Diplomacy: Portuguese Relations with West Africa, 1441–1521," *Journal of World History* 3, no. 2 (1992): 165–204.
44 Lamin Sanneh, *West African Christianity: The Religious Impact* (New York: Orbis Books, 2015).
45 Fatou Kiné Camara, *States and Religions in West Africa: Problems and Perspectives* (London: Routledge, 2016).
46 Muriel Evelyn Chamberlain, *The Scramble for Africa* (London: Routledge, 2014).
47 Stephen Ocheni and Basil C. Nwankwo, "Analysis of Colonialism and Its Impact in Africa," *Cross-Cultural Communication* 8, no. 3 (2012): 46–54.
48 Dare Arowolo, "The Effects of Western Civilisation and Culture on Africa," *Afro Asian Journal of Social Sciences* 1, no. 1 (2010): 1–13.
49 Samson Ukpabi, "The Changing Role of the Military in Nigeria, 1900–1970," *Africa Spectrum* 11, no. 1 (1976): 61–77.
50 Immaculata Nnenna Enwo–Irem, "Colonialism and Education: The Challenges for Sustainable Development in Nigeria," *Mediterranean Journal of Social Sciences* 4, no. 5 (2013): 163.
51 Daniel J. Paracka Jr., *The Athens of West Africa: A History of International Education at Fourah Bay College, Freetown, Sierra Leone* (London: Routledge, 2004).
52 Daniel F. McCall, "Review of 'A Preface to Modern Nigeria: The 'Sierra Leonians' in Yoruba, 1830–1890' by Jean Herskovits Kopytoff," *The Historian* 28, no. 4 (1966): 712.
53 Ade Fajana, "Colonial Control and Education: The Development of Higher Education in Nigeria 1900–1950," *Journal of the Historical Society of Nigeria* 6, no. 3 (1972): 323–340.
54 Kenneth Mellanby, *The Birth of Nigeria's University* (London: Methuen and Company Limited, 1958), 25–27.
55 Braj B. Kachru, ed., *The Other Tongue: English Across Cultures* (Illinois: University of Illinois Press, 1992).
56 Kachru, *The Other Tongue*.
57 Pieter Muysken and Norval Smith, "The Study of Pidgin and Creole Languages," in *Pidgins and Creoles: An Introduction*, eds. Jacques Arends, Pieter Muysken and Norval Smith (Amsterdam: J. Benjamins,1995), 3–14.
58 Jade Miller, "Global Nollywood: The Nigerian Movie Industry and Alternative Global Networks in Production and Distribution," *Global Media and Communication* 8, no. 2 (2012): 117–133.

59 T. L. Lester, "Beyond Popular Entertainment: Citizenship Articulation within Nigerian Video," Paper Presented at the Aegis Conference on African Studies, African Studies Centre, Leiden, The Netherlands, July 11–14, 2007.
60 Adedayo Ladigbolu Abah, "Popular Culture and Social Change in Africa: The Case of the Nigerian Video Industry," *Media, Culture and Society* 31, no. 5 (2009): 731–748.
61 Abah, "Popular Culture and Social Change in Africa."
62 Abah, "Popular Culture and Social Change in Africa."
63 Jonathan Haynes and Onookome Okome, "Evolving Popular Media: Nigerian Video Films," *Research in African Literatures* 29, no. 3 (1998): 106–128.
64 Emmanuel Obiechina and Chinua Achebe, *An African Popular Literature: A Study of Onitsha Market Pamphlets* (Cambridge: Cambridge University Press Archive, 1973).
65 Araba Sey, "New Media Practices in Ghana," *International Journal of Communication* 5 (2011): 380–405.
66 Felix Boateng, "African Traditional Education: A Method of Disseminating Cultural Values," *Journal of Black Studies* 13, no. 3 (1983): 321–336.
67 Usman Joshua, Ohwovoriole Felicia, Owoicho I. Odihi, Dik Ali Joshua and Torutein Richaard Walson, "Folktale as Material Resources for Movie Production in Selected Nollywood Movies," *International Journal of English and Literature* 4, no. 5 (2013): 236–241.
68 Jonathan Haynes, "Nigerian Cinema: Structural Adjustments," *Research in African Literatures* 26, no. 3 (1995): 97–119.
69 Joseph A. Kotarba, *Understanding Society through Popular Music* (London: Routledge, 2013).
70 Simon Byl, "Jerker Blomqvist, The Date and Origin of the Greek Version of Hanno's Periplus," *L'Antiquité Classique* 51, no. 1 (1982): 392–393.
71 Eric Charry, *Mande Music: Traditional and Modern Music of the Maninka and Mandinka of Western Africa* (Chicago: University of Chicago Press, 2000).
72 Ruth M. Stone, ed., *The Garland Handbook of African Music* (New York: Routledge, 2008).
73 Tejumola Olaniyan, *Arrest the Music: Fela and His Rebel Art and Politics* (Indiana: Indiana University Press, 2004).
74 Chioma Oruh, *Music and Liberation During the Biafran War (1967–1970)* (Washington: Howard University, 2009).
75 Edna M. Smith, "Popular Music in West Africa," *African Music: Journal of the International Library of African Music* 3, no. 1 (1962): 11–17.
76 Ikenna Emmanuel Onwuegbuna, "Urbanization and African Pop Music: The Nigerian Experience," *Awka Journal of Research in Music and the Arts (AJRMA)* 7 (2010): 161–173.
77 Kwabena Fosu-Mensah, Lucy Duran and Chris Stapleton, "On Music in Contemporary West Africa," *African Affairs* 86, no. 343 (1987): 227–240.
78 Jenny Fatou Mbaye, "Reconsidering Cultural Entrepreneurship: Hip hop Music Economy and Social Change in Senegal, Francophone West Africa," PhD diss., The London School of Economics and Political Science (LSE), 2011.
79 Jean Marie Allman, ed., *Fashioning Africa: Power and the Politics of Dress* (Indiana: Indiana University Press, 2004).
80 Fatou Diop and Dwight Merunka, "African Tradition and Global Consumer Culture: Understanding Attachment to Traditional Dress Style in West Africa," *International Business Research* 6, no. 11 (2013): 1.
81 Smith, "Kente Cloth Motifs," 36–39.
82 A. B. Agbadudu and F. O. Ogunrin, "Aso-Oke: A Nigerian Classic Style and Fashion Fabric," *Journal of Fashion Marketing and Management: An International Journal* 10, no. 1 (2006): 97–113.
83 Agbadudu and Ogunrin, "Changing a Craft to an Industry through Technological Innovation: The Case of Hand-Woven Aso-Oke Fabric," *Benin Journal of Social Sciences* 10/11, no. 1 (2002): 122–131.
84 Bernhard Gardi, "Africa Interweave—Textile Diasporas," *African Arts* 44, no. 4 (2011): 84–87.
85 Susan Mullin Vogel, *Baule Art as the Expression of a World View* (New York: New York University, 1977).

86 Ikechukwu Anthony Kanu, "An Igwebuike Approach to the Study of African Traditional Naming Ceremony and Baptism," *Journal of Religion and Human Relations* 11, no. 1 (2019): 25–52.

87 T. N. O. Quarcoopome, *West African Traditional Medicine* (Ibadan: African Universities Press, 1987).

88 Kanu, "An Igwebuike Approach," 25–52.

89 Liseli A. Fitzpatrick, "African Names and Naming Practices: The Impact Slavery and European Domination had on the African Psyche, Identity and Protest" Ph.D diss., The Ohio State University, 2012.

90 Emma Umana Clasberry, *Culture of Names in Africa: A Search for Cultural Identity* (Indiana: Xlibris Corporation, 2012).

91 Kathryn Woodward, ed., *Identity and Difference*, Vol. 3 (California: Sage, 1997).

92 Ivo Ngade, "Bakossi Names, Naming Culture and Identity," *Journal of African Cultural Studies* 23, no. 2 (2011): 111–120.

93 Drew Westen, *Self and Society: Narcissism, Collectivism, and the Development of Morals* (Cambridge: Cambridge University Press, 1985).

94 Otonti Nduka, "Moral Education in the Changing Traditional Societies of Sub-Saharan Africa," *International Review of Education* 26, no. 2 (1980): 153–170.

95 C. Triandis Harry, Xiao Ping Chen and Darius K. S. Chan, "Scenarios for the Measurement of Collectivism and Individualism," *Journal of Cross-Cultural Psychology* 29, no. 2 (1998): 275–289.

96 Jüri Allik and Anu Realo, "Individualism-Collectivism and Social Capital," *Journal of Cross-Cultural Psychology* 35, no. 1 (2004): 29–49.

97 Barbara M. Cooper, "Gender, Movement, and History: Social and Spatial Transformations in 20th Century Maradi, Niger," *Environment and Planning D: Society and Space* 15, no. 2 (1997): 195–221.

98 Robert Kofi Koomson, "A Spirituality of Unity and Hospitality among the Akans in Ghana and Chicago and the Challenges of the Matrilineal Inheritance Kinship Structure" Ph.D diss., Garrett-Evangelical Theological Seminary, 2010.

99 Joseph I. Uduji, Elda N. Okolo-Obasi and Simplice A. Asongu, "The Impact of Corporate Social Responsibility Interventions on Female Education Development in the Rural Niger Delta Region of Nigeria," *Progress in Development Studies* 20, no. 1 (2020): 45–64.

100 Carol Xiaoyue Zhang Lawrence Hoc Nang Fong and Tuan Phong Ly, "National Identity and Cultural Festivals in Postcolonial Destinations," *Tourism Management* 73 (2019): 94–104.

101 Bo Winegard, Ben Winegard and David C. Geary, "The Status Competition Model of Cultural Production," *Evolutionary Psychological Science* 4, no. 4 (2018): 351–371.

102 Frank Aig-Imoukhuede., *A Handbook of Nigerian Culture* (Lagos: Department of Culture, Federal Ministry of Information and Culture, 1991).

103 Folarin Shyllon, "Argungu Fishing Festival in Northwestern Nigeria: Promoting the Idea of a Sustainable Cultural Fest," *International Journal of Cultural Property* 14, no. 3 (2007): 329–337.

104 Shyllon, "Argungu Fishing Festival in Northwestern Nigeria."

105 Esekong H. Andrew and Ibok Ekpenyong, "Promoting Culture and Tourism in Nigeria through Calabar Festival and Carnival Calabar," *Mediterranean Journal of Social Sciences* 3, no. 3 (2012): 287–287.

24

RELIGIONS AND RELIGIOUS CHANGES

Introduction

Throughout history, religion has been a lens through which people make sense of the world, events, and their lives.[1] In his attempt to define religion, Emile Durkheim believes that it is "a unified system of beliefs and practices relative to sacred things, that is to say, things set apart and forbidden … beliefs and practices which unite into one single moral community called a Church all those who adhere to them."[2] Although Durkheim might have referred to "church," his definition refers to a rather captivating definition of religion, which, to some extent, explains most of its contexts. It underscores what Edward B. Tylor refers to as "a belief in spiritual things."[3] As a body of beliefs, religion tends to give the right explanation of a force that is in charge of things or some things.[4]

Out of the many theories about understanding religion, some classifications are worthy of examination, especially in the West African context.[5] One such classification is that of "wishful-thinking," where religion is explained as a form of comfort and compensation acquired from holding supernatural beliefs.[6] This emphasizes that religion, as a means of hope, is a better ending and explains the supernatural intervention in issues that individually or collectively plague people. Another such classification is that of symbolism. Some scholars believe that religion is a symbol of social purpose and control.[7] It is believed that religion is not just the understanding of the world or events that occur within it but the greater compensation that waits for loyal observers or an unending love with a supernatural being alone.

Despite displaying all of these characteristics on the surface, religion is seen by some scholars as more of a concealed essence of social purpose directed toward societal control and orderliness. One such scholar is Emile Durkheim, who tried to view religion through a sociological lens. In addition, another set of scholars believes that religion should rather be viewed from the vantage point of intellectualism and posits that religion is an explanation of the world and a means of controlling it.[8] It positions religion as a means of affirming uncertainty, matter, the universe, society, and a means to control it

DOI: 10.4324/9781003198260-29

that draws from those beliefs. The purpose of explaining the above classification is to fit the role and explanation of what religion does in contemporary West Africa. It is obvious, upon observation, that contemporary African religions serve all three purposes, which explains why religion has been fundamental to West African societies throughout history and contemporary societies.[9]

Traditional Religions

Scholars and people often refer to the African religion with singular noun references, alluding to one religion. This has been prevalent, although there exist different ethnic groups and societies with almost no ties in West Africa. In some instances, this has been defended based on the similarities that they all have. Some scholars have also posited that African traditional religions share a similarity in divination, the concept of God, ancestral cults, and *Africanness*, among others.[10] While this argument might be reasonable, it underestimates the diversity of the religions in the subregion.

The different African religions have never been the same and are not the same, even in contemporary West Africa. This is because many families and societies have pledged their allegiance to the worship of some gods to the exclusion of others. For example, while there might be cross-concepts of beliefs between the Igbo traditional religion and that of the Yoruba in Nigeria, their traditions and religions are different in some ways. More so, the fact that there are common elements in Islam and Christianity, including some that were "attributed" to African traditional religions, does not make the two religions the same. Hence, the African religions might be similar in some of their attributes, but they are different. However, they could be classified together only based on their commonalities.

West African religion stands as the hallmark of African religion.[11] Like every religion, African religion grew out of the sacredness attached to a particular culture of a particular society. This is also evident in Islam and Christianity and the manner of practice in their respective places of origin. West African traditional religions heavily rely on sacrifices, rituals, and festivals, among other physical commitments. In some instances, these sacrifices could take the form of animals, although many of these practices have been outlawed by recent legal developments in contemporary society. The intentions of these religions were communally oriented and they promoted collectivism.

Religious activities were performed to appease the gods and to ward off evil. Where issues affected society, the people had a religious obligation to react together toward resolving those issues. The sins of an individual are often regarded as a predicament for all people in society. Religion was a societal belief and not basically toward the redemption of individuals, as seen in Christianity and Islam.[12]

The religions of West African society are intertwined with culture to the extent that the two are almost interchangeable. Religion overshadows the reasoning process of any given West African society such that the whole structure of the society is built on it. This is evident in the lifestyles of Africans, including how they dress, dance, and their opinions toward issues.[13] Their rituals, festivals, ceremonies, and other cultural duties are closely linked to society's religious values.[14] The African traditional religion is directly linked to all aspects of society, and there is always a religious implication to every action and inaction of the members of the society. This underscores how important the religions were to the Africans practicing them and their relevance to the people.

As stated earlier, African traditional religions influenced all aspects of society. Their role in agricultural practices, for instance, which served as the major source of survival in precolonial West Africa, cannot be underestimated. Many agricultural products and cultivations had religious connections, and their seasons alluded to gods they believed were in charge. In some instances, there had to be festivals before crops like yam could be consumed or harvested. The community was expected to wait until the appropriate season before consuming it. The new yam festival is a common phenomenon in West Africa and cuts across different countries. In Ghana, the Fante society marks the yam festival with prayers and a form of sacrifice that includes using chicken or lamb mixed with the new yams to start the new season.

Also, the Krobos in Ghana use the festival to worship the spirit of *Likpotfu*, whom they invoke and offer sacrifices to in exchange for its protection against any sicknesses that may arise from the consumption of the crop. This festival is also prominent in Asante society. Similar practices could be found among the Fon and Holli of Benin Republic (Dahomey), the Yoruba, Tiv, Igala, and Igbo of Nigeria, and the Bubi society of the Fernanda Po, among others across West Africa.[15] In addition, some areas and trees are kept separate from others for religious purposes and serve as a harboring against some evil or good spirits.[16] If agriculture is a major part of the lives of Africans, as well as a primary source of income for most Africans, then the uniqueness of religious significance, which cannot be separated from agriculture, can truly not be underestimated.

African traditional religion also had an influence and relationship with the political systems of the people who practiced these religions. The manner of selection and appointment of kings and chiefs in various centralized precolonial African societies demonstrated this relationship. Through divination, the gods were often consulted to determine whether or not a candidate was the right person for chieftaincy or kingship. At the coronation of a new chief or king, rituals and sacrifices made to the gods constituted a major part of the ceremony. Even after these ceremonies and throughout the reign of a chief or king, he was expected to carry out religious duties and partake in religious activities in consultation with the gods and their representatives, the traditional priests. The gods gave the king relevance and blessed his reign with glory and goodwill. However, when he was no longer favored, it constituted a bad omen for society.

The authority of the king was also obtained from the gods. For instance, in the traditional system of the Nigerian Yoruba society, the king's power was derived largely from the gods and the people. Therefore, he was often referred to as *Alase Ikeji Orisa*, meaning second only to the gods. Among the Akan people of Ghana, the chief was the connection between the ancestors, gods, and society. As such, he was the source and embodiment of all traditional powers and references.[17] Hence, aside from the fact that the chief was a descendant of a royal family and kinship, he was often selected by the *Ohemaa* after sacrifices had been offered to the gods and the relevant rituals had been completed.[18]

Furthermore, the place of traditional religions also extended to the individual roles in communities and the incorporation of children into society. These were often handled through the rite of passage and via child-naming ceremony processes.[19] Toward the maintenance of peaceful coexistence in West African societies, religion served another role as the provider of law and order, with different moral codes that demanded strict compliance. Breaching any of these codes amounted to either individual or collective punishments.[20] The shrines and other religious materials associated with the gods were often used in oath-taking to assert the truth and enter into contracts. Also, in the determination of cases brought for adjudication, many were subjected to different traditional religious tests, such as the drinking of the *Ayelala* water among the Yoruba in the Ondo State region of Nigeria.[21] Punishments were also meted out according to religious precepts laid down by the gods.

Popular aspects of the traditional religions in West Africa are their practices of medicine and magic. Often, the gods are seen as the beholders of solutions to several health challenges faced by Africans. Children and sick people are taken to shrines and rivers, among other significant places, for healing and diversion of sickness through rituals and sacrifices. These religions have a comprehensive body of knowledge for treating illnesses through herbs, and, in extreme circumstances, the gods are consulted.[22] Where the sickness is beyond the efficacy of basic herbal knowledge, the infirm are often brought before the shrines of the gods, where sacrifices and appeasement are made for healing.[23]

It is widely believed that the West African traditional religions are polytheistic.[24] While this might be true in many cases, it would be erroneous to assume that such beliefs are general. Although there might exist many gods, there is always a Supreme God or Being that is not of the same rank as other gods. The Igbo's *Chukwu*, Benin's *Osanobuwa*, Yoruba's *Olodumare* or *Olorun*, the Nupe's *Soko*, and the Ewe's *Nana Buluku* are Supreme Beings that rank higher than any other gods in these societies. This implies that forms of monotheism and polytheism exist in the same system. The "small" gods have specific duties and areas of influence yet are often answerable to the Supreme Being who created them.[25]

Christianity and Islam

The preeminence and uniqueness of the African traditional religions, to which the people subscribed before African society welcomed beliefs and practices from the outside world, were challenged, limited, and ultimately reduced in relevance. Introduced into West Africa through trade, missionary activities, colonialism, and migration, the advent of Christianity and Islam on the continent changed the way of life of the people and fundamentally altered and hijacked the significance of traditional religion in every aspect of society where it previously held sway. The first recorded contact of Christianity with West African society was through Prince Henry, the Portuguese Navigator's expeditions toward the western coastal areas of Africa.[26] Aside from the political and economic interests of the Portuguese explorers, the evangelization of these areas was also a primary duty for the missionaries at that time.

After the "Padroado" agreement between the Roman Catholic Church and Portugal, Portuguese missionaries were encouraged to come to West Africa, and the first church was built at Elmina in 1482.[27] The first attempt to spread Christianity in West Africa was focused on the chiefs, as they believed that the conversion of these chiefs would amount to the conversion of their respective communities. From this point, Christianity spread to other parts of the region, like Benin, Warri, and Sierra Leone. The diffusion of Christian religious values was further enhanced by the abolition of the slave trade in

West Africa and the resettlement of the returnees. Liberia and Sierra Leone became two of the most active missionary areas for the resettlement of ex-slaves and the operation of new sets of missionaries. After that, Christianity continued to re-penetrate the West African areas for evangelism (Figure 24.1).[28]

The spread of Islam in West Africa witnessed a gradual but slow growth from the eleventh to the seventeenth century. The trans-Saharan trade with North Africa and the Arabic countries was instrumental in spreading Islam. The religion started as classist with elites from the clerical class, royalty, and traders.[29] This was obvious in the conversion of the Soninke/Mandingo society, as rulers were converted to achieve the state religion, and the traders in the community became Muslims too.[30] The religion spread around the region with empires like Kumbi, Ancient Ghana, Tekrur, and Kanem, which had already defined Islamic practices by the ninth century.[31] The religion was further institutionalized by the various jihads that occurred in West Africa, such as Usman Dan Fodio's jihad[32] that created the Islamic Sokoto caliphate and Ahmad Lobo's jihad in Futa Jallon in the seventeenth and eighteenth centuries, respectively.[33]

During these early periods when Christianity, Islam, and traditional religions co-existed within the African continent, the religions were practiced together in many instances as the traditional religion, which formed the cultural values of the people, continued to do so in many instances. For example, the belief in divination on issues and events that had happened or were yet to happen still existed and traditional priests were still contacted, although the priests or religious heads in other religions were also consulted to explain the mysteries behind several things. In the wake of "civilization" and globalization across Africa, especially West Africa, religious practices changed from

FIGURE 24.1   Basilique de l'Immaculée Conception, Ouidah, Benin https://commons.wikimedia.org/wiki/File:Ouida_cathedral_(46594927815).jpg.

how they were received or developed in the region. Time and cultural diffusion rubbed off on these religions, and as such, it is important to look into the current state of religion in contemporary West Africa and the new practices that exist.

Contemporary Religious Practices

In the wake of increased interaction between West African societies and other parts of the world through globalization and other processes of transformation, the religious life of the region has changed drastically. Traditional religion is fast becoming extinct because only a few people today are convinced and true believers of these religions. Many have either "paganized" it or only practice it in a more concealed or mixed manner. Also, the nature of the Christianity received, especially in the seventeenth century in West Africa, has changed periodically along the lines of beliefs and manner of practice. New Christian movements have sprouted across West Africa, and denominations with specific creeds and dogmas are increasing daily. Although Islam has groups of believers in West Africa, the beliefs and practices have changed too.

The overall change and conversion in contemporary West Africa are radical and intensive religious revolutions that are becoming uncontrollable within African societies.[34] The practice of traditional African religions is currently one of the social values West Africa is losing rapidly. Science and technology have posed significant challenges to many of the traditional beliefs, as these beliefs were said to lack logic and scientific ascertainment and, as such, were proclaimed to be, at best, superstitious. This is pushed boldly even though many Christian and Islamic beliefs are being embellished with similar religious beliefs that do not scale the logic and scientific ascertainment hurdle.

At the beginning of the prominence of Christianity on the African continent, the missionaries referred to traditional beliefs as paganism and an offense toward God, believed to be adequately punished after death. The Islamic religion has a similar belief system that warranted many adherents carrying out jihads in a final attempt to destroy traditional religion. The antagonistic beliefs of these religions have all the resources and support they need to convince the people and poison or change the minds of the indigenous African traditional religious practitioners toward conversion; the number of those who abandon traditional religion has continued to increase. With more Christian colonial officials, colonialism played a major role in the enactment of Christianity and encouragement of the practice, as many available values and platforms created by the officials had Christian undertones. The different humanitarian services, including education, healthcare services, and the provision of basic societal needs, also helped neutralize traditional religion that influenced these sectors in West Africa.[35]

The African traditional religion had always been a way of social orientation among individuals and an avenue for the impact of social values through rituals and practices. The presence of different institutions, such as a school in contemporary Africa, served as the new medium of social impact and orientation. Practices like the rites of passage that were often used to incorporate individuals into society through traditional religious institutions and processes have either been stopped, are practiced in part, or mixed with other religious beliefs.[36] An example is the current practice of naming ceremonies in West Africa. Before the contemporary period, rituals such as the naming ceremony were carried out according to the traditional beliefs of society. In the current dispensation, only a few people practice this ceremony in such a manner. However, there is a little retention of the old practice as people in some Nigerian societies incorporate traditional items like honey, fish, salt, kola nuts, alligator pepper, and other ingredients while prayers are offered for the child. This practice, although traditional, is observed by some Christian and Muslim believers in contemporary West Africa. The whole practice of the naming ceremony is African, and it has been turned into a usual religious practice among the Christian and Muslim faithful.

A similar instance is seen in the burial ceremony of Africans. There is an evident adoption of traditional practices in the conduct of a ceremony on the seventh day and other time-spacing practices like that after 41 days. The Nigerian communities in Yoruba regions still commonly fry *Akara* (bean cakes) for distribution among the people of the community and scatter them around the compound to appease the dead and pray for their good rest. Furthermore, the widespread belief in the interference of the spirits of deceased community members and ancestors in society exists throughout West Africa.[37] Traditional worshippers in West Africa had the common belief that dead persons came back to society or visited their families. Their visits were good or bad for the community, depending on the circumstances of their death. Some communities in West Africa immortalized some of these ancestors and consulted them on issues affecting society.[38] The existence of these ancestors affected the thinking process and orientation of the people, who deferred to them in their daily activities.[39] Although this belief is scarcely regarded in contemporary West Africa, it is still held.[40] One of the reasons for the subsistence of this practice is the belief in spirituality and post-human life, which is not dissimilar from the concept of the soul leaving the body in the contemporary belief of spirituality and spiritual activities of the Christian and Islamic religions (Figure 24.2).

As stated earlier, the influence of traditional religions does not allow its total extinction. The development of syncretic ideologies, consciously or subconsciously, holds on to traditional religion and other contemporary religions in West Africa. One of the geneses of this was the gleeful acceptance of the Christian missionaries in Abeokuta and the traditional activities that followed. A report stated that the missionaries who arrived from Sierra Leone with some ex-slaves that initially resided there brought with them the technology of the corn mills and Bibles, among other things, as gifts for the *Alake* and his subordinates. After witnessing the effectiveness of the corn mill in making the process less laborious, the people wanted to make sacrifices of worship to the corn mill.[41] Another illustration of the above includes the retention of the traditional funeral rites, where the children and the deceased siblings are expected to perform their traditional duties so that the ancestors' anger will not be provoked. More so, extended family members and relatives still show up to mourn with the deceased family as a show of solidarity (Figure 24.3).[42]

Modern African traditional movements in West Africa hold to the tenets of African traditional religions and conform to the present civilizations and orientations by adopting sophisticated and comprehensive developments in their manner of worship and activities. For instance, the Ogboni Aborigine and Reformed Ogboni Fraternity still carry out cultic doctrines from African traditional religions in Nigeria but have adopted social functions, among other values, to their modes of operation. The Atinga and Babalawo Onisegun are more particular about healing processes with the use of traditional, medical, and religious knowledge coupled with modern knowledge, while the Awo Opa,

FIGURE 24.2   The Cathedral Church of St. Peters Abeokuta Ogun State, Nigeria https://commons.wikimedia.org/wiki/File:The_Cathedral_Church_of_St._Peters_Abeokuta_Ogun_State,_Nigeria.jpg.

Opa Amukala, and Osugbo groups perform sociopolitical functions that involve reputable individuals in West Africa. The bodies that carry out Egungun, Igunuko, Eyo, and Gelede use traditional mysteries to parade these masquerades with newly adapted modern knowledge and entertainment due to their position as sociocultural groups.[43] One feature common to these groups, and other similar groups scattered across West Africa, is the oath of secrecy their members swear while they seek both traditional and modern relevance and knowledge to keep them important in the current society.

African traditional religions experienced a radical change that refocused all their systems, and Christianity and Islam have also been subjected to change in contemporary West Africa. The Christianity received in West Africa targeted every segment of society, from politics, healthcare, education, and other developmental engagements. Positions in the colonial governments across West Africa were filled majorly by Christian officials, who complemented the evangelistic missions of the missionaries. Hence, the ideology of the modern governmental foundation in West Africa was infused with Christian values. Secularism, at the time of colonization, was not as pronounced as it is today.

Missionaries were so committed to developing the healthcare sectors that they were practically the first to start attending to the healthcare needs of the people in society and used it as a medium to evangelize. For instance, British colonial Nigeria was not totally in support of the spread of Christianity to northern Nigeria because of its Islamic background and history. Lord Lugard had already made a promise to the Sultan that they would not do anything that would ridicule their Islamic practices. The Christian

FIGURE 24.3   The Cathedral Church of St. Peters Abeokuta Ogun State, Nigeria https://commons.wikimedia.org/wiki/File:IMG-20180617-WA0024.jpg.

missionaries then decided to carry out societal developmental projects, including healthcare services. This allowed them to talk and evangelize to people while they were being attended to. The missionaries also pioneered the establishment of modern educational facilities, teaching the ability to read and write and providing early advanced education, as seen in Sierra Leone.

Many of these remarkable contributions continued in the recent dispensation, with many churches and congregations engaged in societal development projects around them, even though the government has taken over many of the institutions built by the missionaries. However, these facilities built by religious bodies, especially for healthcare and educational services, were often expensive and, therefore, primarily only available to rich individuals and families. Essentially, this began a new trend as religious bodies, more than before, were inclined toward privatization across different sectors in West Africa, a shift from what was obtained in the initial religious practices.[44]

The first set of the circulation of the Christian faith was based on missionaries' evangelism, with the majority of the early churches being the Catholic, Orthodox, and Protestant churches.[45] In French West African states, the first set of faith circulated and the churches built were those of the predominantly Roman Catholic missionaries. This was a result of the dominance of the Catholic faith in France and its wide practice among colonial officials. In The Gambia, although the majority of the citizens were Muslims,[46] the spread of Christianity was initiated firstly by the Roman Catholic missionaries and the Church Missionary Society in 1821. The operation of the Anglican Reverends in Cape Coast in 1752, as well as Basel missionaries, the Wesleyans, and the Roman Catholic, set the pace for Christianity in Ghana.[47] Similarly, the orthodox churches laid the foundation for Christianity in Sierra Leone, Nigeria, and other West African countries (Figure 24.4).

The recent practice of Pentecostalism has greatly influenced the practice of Christianity in contemporary West Africa. The African Pentecostal churches project a new faith with an emphasis on the operation of the spirit in the church, characterized by speaking in tongues, healing, prophecy, exorcism, and many other practices that were not seen in the orthodox churches.[48] The contemporary models of Christian practitioners differentiate themselves by large crowds, ultra-modern church buildings, and heavy sound systems that distinguish them from the old style of worship. These new sets of churches organize open-air healing services across megacities.[49]

A remarkable part of the history and establishment of African Pentecostal churches was the creation and operation of the Faith Tabernacle, although the religious body and its faithful adherents did not regard themselves as Pentecostals at first. The church was a breakout faction from John Alexander Dowie's Christian Catholic Church. In 1897, John Wesley Ankins, one of Dowie's many followers, left the Christian Catholic Church to found his Christian denomination, which he named Faith Tabernacle.[50] By 1907, the Faith Tabernacle had developed into a force to be reckoned with, with a strong

FIGURE 24.4 The Basilica of Our Lady of Peace of Yamoussoukro, Côte d'Ivoire https://en .wikipedia.org/wiki/File:Notre_dame_de_la_paix_yamoussoukro_by_felix _krohn.jpg.

following, church buildings, a network of branches, and prayer homes. The first set of branches of the Tabernacle in West Africa was built in Nigeria and Ghana in 1918. Others were built afterward in countries like Togo to add to those two.[51] During the flu that claimed a lot of lives and tested the faiths of many, the population of the worshippers grew as more people joined the Faith Tabernacle, with the likes of J. B. Sadare and David Odubanjo, among others, becoming popular figures with their prayer meetings and revivals.[52]

There was a need to create what was referred to as the Aladura Churches that relied heavily on the powers of prayer, healing, deliverance, and speaking in tongues.[53] Sophia Odunlami,[54] Joseph Ayo Babalola, Moses Tunolase Orimolade, Christiana Abiodun Akinsowon, and some others became distinguished figures of the new radical Christian movement.[55] The movement set the foundation for the creation of many West African Pentecostal and modern churches like the Celestial Church of Christ, Christ Apostolic Church, Church of the Lord, Cherubim and Seraphim, among others. The adoption of many traditional beliefs and orientations in the practice of modern forms of Christianity was witnessed during this period as these beliefs were copiously embedded into the practices of Aladura Christians despite their decision to do away with the African traditional religious practices.[56]

West African Pentecostalism has grown to the extent that its members now have their system of beliefs, which are somewhat different from others, and they have codified it with core values that they expect from their members. By 1995, the number of denominations of African origin was already about 11,000, with over 500,000 congregations that will have increased drastically by now.[57] The existence of Pentecostalism in West Africa has given rise to cross-faith traffic between Christianity and traditional religions. This gave the traditional worshippers the impetus to modernize the religions and give them more acceptable attributes, bearing in mind the new social order in the societies in which they found themselves. The new groups of traditional worshippers who adopted Christian values still carry out traditional activities, including sacrifices, rituals, and the recognition of the ancestors.[58] Many African independent churches, including the Aladura Churches, have been found to carry out these practices while still following the same principles of Christianity.[59] As of 2014, about 152,021,000 Christians in West Africa were scattered across all the countries despite the high number of Islamic faithful in the subregion.[60]

Changes in the people's belief structure also affected Muslims who followed Islam and shared such orientations. There was the establishment of Islamic states, which could be seen in the Sokoto Caliphate and Futa Jallon.[61] Although the practice of Islamic theocracy was an attribute of the religion in the many countries where it is practiced, especially in the Middle East, the introduction of the religion in West Africa only took on a theocratic face in very few societies in the subregion. With the imposition of colonialism, which gave birth to modern forms of democracy, Islam was practiced more as a religion than a state religion. Aside from Ghana, Cape Verde, and the Benin Republic, the population of Muslims in West African countries has increased to between 50 and 100 percent of their population, and Christianity, as well as other minor religions, share the remaining parts of the population.[62] This shows that the Islamic religion in contemporary West African societies has been increasing at a higher magnitude than might be imagined by its pioneers in the region.

An attribute of Islam in West Africa, as anywhere else, is its Quranic educational system, where Islamic values and beliefs, the prophets' messages, and Arabic languages are taught. The knowledge of these beliefs and languages was core to Islamic societies, and many children were often required to attend a Quranic school as early as possible. Furthermore, Arabic was often spoken and read out on many occasions, including in regular conversations between Muslims. However, the advent of colonialism and Western civilization has been responsible for remodeling such an educational system. The new educational systems supersede these Islamic institutions in the current dispensation, but many believers still adopt Quranic studies in Muslim schools or lessons after regular secular school hours.[63]

Before colonialism, Islamic practices in West Africa depended on the operation of Sharia law in the adjudication of issues of Islamic concerns, and living within this legal system in Islamic society was one of the core values of Islam. Therefore, Islamic courts were created to adjudicate issues according to the position of the Quran, as well as the instructions and teachings of the prophets. However, colonialism in Nigeria brought about a new legal system that first reduced the criminal jurisdiction of the Sharia courts and regulated the operation of civil Sharia laws. In recognition of the societal influence of the religion, many societies, like Nigeria, created a Sharia court that listened to Islamic matters in the north and provided a special penal code for criminal law. In the present dispensation, Muslims have the choice to either pursue their matters before Western courts or the Sharia courts.[64]

As a result of ethnic and religious diversity in West Africa, Muslims are liberal in order to promote peaceful coexistence. The propagators of liberal Islam believe that everyone has the right to his or her religion without interference from others. They refer to Verse 6 of Sura 109 in the Quran, where it says, "To you your religion, to me my religion." Also, reference is often made to the "Medina Document," where Prophet Mohammed had a treaty with Jews in Medina on peaceful coexistence without any interference. Due to the importation and spread of many new religions, as well as pre-existing traditional religions, liberal Islam must be encouraged to tolerate people with different beliefs. This is the current trend of Islamic practice in West African states as they move gradually toward secularization.

Islam in West Africa has also been affected by different traditions, religious values, and practices because of the people's backgrounds that cannot be erased. One such adoption and influence was the impact of African respect for the elders and leaders of Sufism. The Sufi system was used to ascribe importance to the Islamic religious leaders, popularly referred to as *shaykh*, who served as religious and spiritual mentors to the people. When these *shaykhs* die, their graves are visited as a form of *ziyarah* to the saint. Examples of these sites include the Shrine of Sidi Boumediene, Bilqis Sungbo of Ijebu (Queen of Sheba),[65] and Muhammad Jimoh, who was considered the Mahdi of Ijebu Ode.[66] Different movements have opposed this practice because of its traditional coloration.

In addition, many people have questioned the rationale behind using the Quran for the healing process in Africa, which they find strange to the Islamic faith. There is the practice of writing Quranic chapters or verses on *walaa*, a slate often in black color with *tadaa* ink and cleaned up with water that would be drunk by and administered to people who require healing. More so, the writing and reading of *Suratu'l-Kafirun* are considered an antidote or solution to madness and other serious sicknesses.[67] In addition, the celebration and observance of *Eid-il-Fitr*, *Eid-il-Kabir* and the addition of *Maulud Nabiyy*, especially in Ghana and Nigeria, have been mixed with cultural practices.[68]

The freedom of religion and association in West Africa, as provided by individual governments, has ensured that Africans have the opportunity to join their religious organizations of preference as long as such bodies are not illegal and restricted by law and other regulations. This has allowed the rise of different religious movements in the region. One such popular religious movement is the Indigenous Faith of Africa, popularly referred to as *Ijo Orunmila*. *Ijo Orunmila Ato* was founded in 1920 by Olorunfumi Oshinga, who received a vision and message from Orunmila, a Yoruba god representing the Supreme Being, to organize an assembly and religious body that would be based on the tenets of the *Ifa* corpus and doctrines. Oshinga, after that, broke from the Anglican Church in Nigeria to establish a church that was supposed to exhibit and uphold the African traditional religious principles.[69] In 1932, Oshinga, along with other followers and supporters, built a temple or worship center in Ebute Metta to allow people access to worship and appreciate the African culture. After Oshinga established his center, similar churches and establishments started coming up. A notable example was Chief James Adeyemi Adeshina's group in Ijebu Ode, which had a similar name after the British officials had refused their first proposed name, *Ijo Akoda*, which means "the first church." Adeshina had to settle for the Indigenous Faith of Africa, *Ijo Orunmila Adulawo*.[70]

Over the years, the Orunmila church grew to about two million members, in Nigeria and the diaspora, following the principles and doctrines of the church. In propagating their faith, the indigenous Faith of Africa engaged in physical and media drives to bring people to their fold. Some of such efforts were the *Odu Ifa* and *Iwure Aro*'s radio programs on Radio Lagos, alongside other publicity activities. The church now has about 21 branches in Nigeria, 18 in the Benin Republic, and many others in London, California, New York, and Florida.[71] The religion is open to Christians and Muslims willing to be members, which explains why worship dates and periods were moved from Sunday to Saturday to allow Christians and Muslims to attend their services, seeing that the Muslims go to the mosque on Friday and Christians go to church on Sunday.[72]

The leadership of the Orunmila church is well-structured and has an established manner of conducting services with the members. The *Oluwo*, who serves as the High Priest, is the highest in rank in the church and has the authority to lead them in their services and many other obligations and activities. He is deputized by other individuals, including the direct voice of the high priest, *Akoda Awo*. The *Aseda Awo* is the next in rank after the *Akoda Awo*, and the *Abese Awo* serves as the churchwarden.[73] Services and their activities are conducted almost similar to those of the Anglican and African churches of the Christian faith, although there is a radical difference. The services are based on the *Ifa* verses, doctrines, and exhortations that impart moral values, as well as teach worshippers how to react to situations. The religion has a standing choir like in the Christian faith and an *Apena*, who functions as the choirmaster. The procession into the auditorium for the commencement of service is accompanied by hymns by the *Apena* and the ministers in charge of the service. Other programs within the service are also supported by hymns till the end of the service. The members are required to approach the *Babalawo* for divination, prayers, and some rituals, such as the breaking of kola nuts and *obi pupa*.[74]

A popular emerging new religion in West Africa is the One Love Family by Sat Guru Maharaji, which was established in 1987. Maharaji claimed to have received instructions from God to salvage the human race from poverty and suffering across the world. They believed nature and natural elements, like the sun, air, and fire, among others, to be instrumental to their faith and humanity. Worshippers are expected to be vegetarians who worship the Guru as a master and god on earth and dress in red and white apparel. The claim by Guru Maharaji as a god on earth has brought the faith continuous criticism.[75]

Aside from the One Love Family, another religious movement that is quite popular in West Africa is the Brotherhood of the Cross and Star, also known as Olumba Olumba, established by Olumba Olumba Obu in 1950 and initially practiced in the Niger Delta region of Nigeria before it started having a wider outreach. Olumba had claimed to have been directed by God to lead all men across the world through faith and healing. The anointing of Olumba at a stream close to his house was seen as holy. People, therefore, went there with the belief of getting solutions to their problems. They endeavored to enter the stream but not earlier than 5 a.m. and not later than 5 p.m., as required.[76] The believers of Olumba were convinced that God had reincarnated in human form seven times and that Olumba was the seventh of that line, according to Genesis 5:24. The church embraced some traditional African systems and a high-level belief in schism. Olumba was believed to have healing powers strong enough to cure all sicknesses, including cancer.[77] A large religious center was built for worship, and the church has since been developing sporadically across the region. It has been able to build 48 branches in Africa, nine in North America, and eight in Europe.[78]

New Ideologies

Modernization, civilization, and globalization have made ideas travel across the world to influence people's conception of different existing institutions through the diffusion of ideologies and inspiration for the adaptation of new ones. Hence, as the trend of change to the essence and beliefs of religious ideologies occur across the world, West Africa is not left behind. An example of such a change in the religious orientation of the people is the shift from salvation-based preaching to prosperity preaching. Among Christians, contemporary churches rely on biblical preaching that encourages financial progress more than salvation. The core ideology of prosperity churches is to make financial and material wants the main essence of Christianity and thereby focus their preaching on how faith can transform one's life materially.[79]

A popular example of this kind of church is the Christian Action Faith Ministries International, established by Nicholas Duncan-Williams in Ghana.[80] Several other churches across West Africa have adapted these messages and put lesser efforts into salvation, good morals, and Christian doctrines while emphasizing the predestination of every Christian to be successful.[81] This preaching has been blamed for the destruction of the moral values of members as it increases unnecessary desperation in the pursuit of wealth and, more so, piles unnecessary pressure on the Christians who subscribe to its core message, which could yield unfavorable consequences. The prosperity churches often pull a larger crowd than the others due to the average person's need for comfort, material things, and financial progress.

An ideology that has affected religious practice and society is religious fundamentalism. Religious extremists believe in the absolutism of the purity of their respective religion and a strict observance of its religious values, teachings, and tenets. This means there is often no room for influencing these practices by believers and current societal values and demands. Most times, these extremists feel a convincing need to control others in ensuring strict adherence to the values and dogmas of their religion and may go to every possible length to see to this adherence.[82] Religious fundamentalism has been a recurring phenomenon in West Africa, as the subregion houses one of the world's most religious populations. As of 2012, Nigeria was claimed to be one of the most religious countries in the world.[83] This puts the continent in a difficult position as religious fanatics and extremists have been militating against the peaceful coexistence of people in West Africa.

Gradually, these sets of believers have been gathering in groups to establish their core beliefs. An example of such extremists is the Jamā'at Ahl as-Sunnah lid-Da'wah wa'l-Jihād, locally known as Boko Haram, who were linked to Al-Qaeda,[84] an international terrorist group led by the late Osama Bin Laden, who claimed responsibility for the September 11, 2001 terrorist attacks in the United States of America.[85] The idea of Boko Haram in Northern Nigeria was the full restoration of pure Islamic practice, agitation against Western civilization, and the full operation of Sharia law without any limitation.[86] To achieve this, they sought to establish an Islamic state over every individual in their areas of operation. This principle ran against the practice of religious diversity as enshrined in the constitution in these areas of West Africa, which were populated by Christians, Muslims, and adherents of other minority religious organizations.[87] The Boko Haram Sect has been responsible for thousands of attacks on Nigerians since 2003, when they first massacred about 30 people in Maiduguri. The primary target of the sect is young people, especially in northern Nigeria and neighboring countries.[88] Religious fanaticism and extremism have been a bane to the developmental goals and targets of West African governments. This has been the cause of major developmental setbacks toward attaining sustainable development in the region.[89]

Another ideological development witnessed by West African communities is the repositioning of women within religious circles. Largely, the traditional religious systems in Nigeria do not have a defined place. In general, women are limited in the roles they can play in religious affairs. Although certain religious activities and groups reserve positions and priesthood for women, they are largely under the religious influence of men. Some gods were known to be female gods, and they often attracted female priestesses to administer their doctrines and maintain their shrines.[90] However, in most communities, women were restricted from participating in some activities. For instance, the *Oro* tradition of the Yoruba societies in southwestern Nigeria forbids the presence of women during their ceremonies. It was also an abomination for a woman to see the *Oro*, no matter how far away she was.[91]

A similar practice was observed among the Muslims in West Africa. The institution of the purdah in several communities where Islam was widely practiced, such as in southern Niger and northern Nigeria, limited the freedom of women to go out and restricted them to reserved areas in their husbands' houses.[92] The purdah system was targeted at married women, from the point of their wedding ceremony to menopause. The Islamic religion in West Africa had a limited space for female religious leadership in mosques and for major religious activities. Women were often made to sit at the back of the pews during prayers and programs.

Among the Christian believers, the role of women, from the time of the Christian missionaries, was restricted to social development, provision of healthcare services, education, as well as assistance in the church. The African churches were also initially against women's active roles in the church because of their social orientation. For instance, in the Akan communities, women had disadvantageous social relevancies and, as such, the belief in the restriction of women meant they could not take up important roles in church.[93] The position of women in the church in contemporary West Africa is becoming more pronounced as they have started gaining more roles in the church than in any other religion in West Africa. The new movement for the involvement of women in the church is encouraged by the social consciousness of society toward the role of women, feminism movements, the principle of equality, and the belief that God has showered his gift on all humans without reserve.[94]

Many women in West Africa have established churches with millions of worshippers across the region and with branches beyond the continent. The new Christianity in West Africa has largely accommodated women on the pulpit rather than at the back of the pews.[95]

Secularism

Secularism is the belief in the disengagement of society and social functions from any religious ties and attribution.[96] Every secular governmental body is expected to create an atmosphere that does not suggest any religious preference or activities that promote religious diversity in society. This is to ensure the observance of freedom of religion and discourage the promotion of one religious practice over the other.[97] Secular society is important in West Africa due to religious diversity. This step has been taken by most of the countries in the subregion upon independence and is reflected in their constitutions. As a result, every individual is free to associate or disassociate from any religious practice in society without unfavorable consequences. The maintenance of secular principles in society is not the duty of the government alone; it is the responsibility of everyone, religious or otherwise, to observe and respect the religious principles of every member of society.

Conclusion

Notably, religion in contemporary West Africa has been responsible for many developmental projects, as followers of these religions are often encouraged to judiciously observe their civil responsibilities and philanthropic activities. Many religious organizations in West Africa have taken up social responsibilities in their immediate communities, sometimes extending them beyond the confines of their geographical areas. Contemporary religious bodies construct roads, feed citizens, help orphans and widows, and provide water or boreholes for communities. These social responsibilities are also a means of evangelism by the church to preach the gospel and get new converts.

While religion has made undeniable contributions to the progress of society, it has also been a means of social discrimination and destruction. As previously stated, West Africa has been a major victim of the untoward activities of religious bigots, fanatics, and extremists who wrongly uphold the belief of terrorizing society in the name of religion. Despite all these, it is important to note that the current practice of religion in contemporary West Africa can be harnessed to make religious adherents, and even the fanatics among them, elements of peaceful coexistence and development. The duty to ensure this rests partly on the shoulders of various religious leaders, who must instill in their members a sense of responsibility for the common good and the love of the other as oneself.

DEEP DIVE

Assignment 1

Objective

The objective of this assignment is to ensure that students complete the reading of Chapter 24 and get them to consider the different religions that make up West African society from its early beginnings up to the emergence of colonial rule in the twentieth century.

Method

Students will be expected to write a short note in response to the question.

Reading Comprehension

How is religion in West Africa intertwined with the people's diverse cultures?

Assignment 2

Objective

The objective of this assignment is to get students to consider the different phases and processes through which Islam and Christianity made entry into West Africa, eroding the powers enjoyed for many centuries by African traditional religion.

Methods

Students will be expected to have a group discussion (either in person or on the online discussion forum) to talk to their peers about the discussion question. Each student would be expected to create a post and respond to at least one other student. If this were to take place in person, then it would simply be a class-wide discussion.

Reading Comprehension

Identify some of the major changes in West African religious practices.

Notes

1 Richard L. Corliss, *Making Sense of Religion: A Study of World Religions and Theology* (Oregon: Wipf & Stock, 2014).

2 Alan Aldridge, *Religion in the Contemporary World* (Cambridge: Polity, 2007), 67.
3 Edward B. Tylor, "The Religion of Savages," *Fortnightly* 6, no. 31 (1866): 71–86.
4 Harriet Martineau, *Life in the Sick-Room* (Peterborough: Broadview Press, 2003).
5 Stewart Elliott Guthrie, "'Religion': What is it?" *Journal for the Scientific Study of Religion* 35, no. 4 (1996): 412–419.
6 Rodney Stark and William Sims Bainbridge, *A Theory of Religions*, Vol. 2 (New York: Peter Lang, 1987).
7 James Ballantyne Hannay, *Symbolism in Relation to Religion: Or, Christianity: The Sources of Its Teaching and Symbolism* (New York: Kennikat Press, 1971).
8 Robin Horton, *Patterns of Thought in Africa and the West: Essays on Magic, Religion and Science* (Cambridge: Cambridge University Press, 1997).
9 Edward Geoffrey Parrinder, *West African Religion: A Study of the Beliefs and Practices of Akan, Ewe, Yoruba, Ibo, and Kindred Peoples* (London: Epworth Press, 1978).
10 John S. Mbiti, *African Religions and Philosophy* (London: Heinemann, 1969), 1.
11 Douglas E. Thomas, *African Traditional Religion in the Modern World* (North Carolina: McFarland, 2015), 17.
12 Thomas, *African Traditional Religion*, 19.
13 Raphael Chijioke Njoku, *West African Masking Traditions and Diaspora Masquerade Carnivals: History, Memory, and Transnationalism* (New York: University of Rochester Press, 2020).
14 Thomas, *African Traditional Religion*, 17.
15 Donald Gilbert and Cecilia K. Coursey, "The New Yam Festivals of West Africa," *Anthropos* H. 3/4 (1971): 444–484.
16 Kenneth Swindell, "Faith, Work, Farming and Business: The Role of the Spiritual in West African Livelihoods," *Journal of Asian and African Studies* 54, no. 6 (2019): 819–837.
17 Kwesi Yanka, *Speaking for the Chief: Okyeame and the Politics of Akan Royal Oratory* (Bloomington & Indianapolis: Indiana University Press, 1995).
18 Samuel Awuah-Nyamekye, "The Role of Religion in the Institution of Chieftaincy: The Case of the Akan of Ghana," *Lumina* 20, no. 2 (2009): 1–1.
19 John S. Pobee and Emmanuel H. Mends, "Social Change and African Traditional Religion," *Sociological Analysis* 38, no. 1 (1977): 1–12.
20 Oluwafunminiyi Raheem and Mike Famiyesin, "Controlling the Boundaries of Morality: The History and Powers of Ayelala Deity," *Yorùbá Studies Review* 2, no. 1 (2017): 231–247.
21 Dada Ojo and Matthias Olufemi, "Incorporation of Ayelala Traditional Religion into Nigerian Criminal Justice System: An Opinion Survey of Igbesa Community People in Ogun State, Nigeria," *Issues in Ethnology Anthropology* 9, no. 4 (2014): 1025–1044.
22 Alexander Zizka, Adjima Thiombiano, Stefan Dressler, Blandine MI Nacoulma, Amadé Ouédraogo, Issaka Ouédraogo, Oumarou Ouédraogo, Georg Zizka, Karen Hahn and Marco Schmidt, "Traditional Plant use in Burkina Faso (West Africa): A National-scale Analysis with Focus on Traditional Medicine," *Journal of Ethnobiology and Ethnomedicine* 11, no. 1 (2015): 1–10.
23 Lee M. Pachter, "Culture and Clinical Care: Folk Illness Beliefs and Behaviors and their Implications for Health Care Delivery," *Jama* 271, no. 9 (1994): 690–694.
24 Edward G. Parrinder, *African Traditional Religion* (London: Sheldon Press, 1965).
25 Joseph Omosade Awolalu, "What is African Traditional Religion," *Studies in Comparative Religion* 10, no. 2 (1976): 1–10.
26 Malyn Newitt, *A History of Portuguese Overseas Expansion, 1400–1668* (London: Routledge, 2004).
27 Samson A. Fatokun, "Christianity in Africa: A Historical Appraisal," *Verbum Et Ecclesia* 26, no. 2 (2005): 357–368.
28 Fatokun, "Christianity in Africa," 357–368.
29 John Spencer Trimingham, *Islam in West Africa* (London: Oxford University Press, 1959).
30 George T. Stride and Caroline Ifeka, *Peoples and Empires of West Africa: 1000–1800* (New York: Africana Publishing Corporation, 1971).
31 Stride and Ifeka, *Peoples and Empires of West Africa*.

32 Edward Lenshie Nsemba and F. E. F. Ayokhai, "Rethinking Pre-Colonial State Formation and Ethno-Religious Identity Transformation in Hausaland Under the Sokoto Caliphate," *Global Journal of Human Social Science Political Science* 13, no. 4 (2013): 1–10.

33 Ralph A. Austen, *Trans-Saharan Africa in World History* (Oxford: Oxford University Press, 2010).

34 John S. Mbiti, *African Religions and Philosophy* (London: Heinemann, 1990), 216.

35 Vincent A. Nwosu, *The Catholic Church in Onitsha: people, places and events;* (Onitsha: EPL, 1985), 16–41.

36 Kane C. Anyanwu, "Alien Religious Influence on African Religion and Social Change," *Ufahamu: A Journal of African Studies* 6, no. 3 (1976): 119–134.

37 William H. Newell, "Good and Bad Ancestors," in *Ancestors*, ed. William H. Newell (The Hague: Mouton, 1976), 17–29.

38 Victor C. Uchendu, "Ancestorcide! Are African Ancestors Dead?" in *Ancestors*, ed. William H. Newell (The Hague: Mouton, 1976), 283–296.

39 Olaniyi Bojuwoye, "Integrating Principles Underlying Ancestral Spirits Belief in Counseling and Psychotherapy," *IFE Psychologia: An International Journal* 21, no. 1 (2013): 74–89.

40 Bojuwoye, "Integrating Principles Underlying Ancestral Spirits."

41 John D. Y. Peel, "Syncretism and Religious Change," *Comparative Studies in Society and History* 10, no. 2 (1968): 121–141.

42 John S. Pobee and Emmanuel H. Mends, "Social Change and African Traditional Religion," *Sociological Analysis* 38, no. 1 (1977): 1–12.

43 Ibigbolade Aderibigbe and Carolyn M. Jones Medine, eds., *Contemporary Perspectives on Religions in Africa and the African Diaspora* (New York: Palgrave Macmillan, 2015).

44 Olalekan A. Dairo, "Privatization and Commercialization of Christian Message," in *Creativity and Change in Nigerian Christianity*, eds. David O. Ogungbile and Akintunde E. Akinade (Lagos: Malthouse Press, 2010), 193–200.

45 Byron Rushing, "A Note on the Origin of the African Orthodox Church," *The Journal of Negro History* 57, no. 1 (1972): 37–39.

46 Martha T. Frederiks, "Methodists and Muslims in the Gambia," in *Critical Readings in the History of Christian Mission*, eds. Martha Frederiks and Dorottya Nagy (Netherland: Brill, 2021), 1370–1385.

47 Paul Jenkins, "The Anglican Church in Ghana, 1905–24 (II)," *Transactions of the Historical Society of Ghana* 15, no. 2 (1974): 177–200.

48 Allan Anderson, "Pentecostalism in Africa: An Overview," *ORITA: Ibadan Journal of Religious Studies* 36, no. 1–2 (2004): 38–56.

49 Charles Piot, "Pentecostal and Development Imaginaries in West Africa," in *Pentecostalism and Development: Churches, NGOs and Social Change in Africa*, eds. Dena Freeman (London: Palgrave Macmillan), 111–133.

50 Adam Mohr, "Out of Zion into Philadelphia and West Africa: Faith Tabernacle Congregation, 1897–1925," *Pneuma* 32, no. 1 (2010): 56–79.

51 Benjamin Nicholas Lawrance, *Locality, Mobility, and "Nation": Periurban Colonialism in Togo's Eweland, 1900–1960*, Vol. 31 (New York: University of Rochester Press, 2007).

52 Adam Mohr, "Faith Tabernacle Congregation, the 1918–19 Influenza Pandemic and Classical Pentecostalism in Colonial West Africa," *Studies in World Christianity* 26, no. 3 (2020): 219–238.

53 John D. Y. Peel, *Aladura: A Religious Movement among the Yoruba* (Oxford: Oxford University Press, 1968), 60–62.

54 Samson A Fatokun, "'I Will Pour Out My Spirit upon All Flesh': The Origin, Growth and Development of the Precious Stone Church–The Pioneering African Indigenous Pentecostal Denomination in Southwest Nigeria," *Cyber Journal for Pentecostal-Charismatic Research* 19, accessed June 12, 2022, http://www.pctii.org/cyberj/cyberj19/fatokun.html.

55 Allan Anderson, *African Reformation: African Initiated Christianity in the 20th Century* (New Jersey: Africa World Press, 2001).

56 Benjamin C. Ray, "Aladura Christianity: A Yoruba Religion," *Journal of Religion in Africa* 23, no. 3 (1993): 266–291.

57 Isaac Phiri and Joe Maxwell, "Gospel Riches: Africa's Rapid Embrace of Prosperity Pentecostalism Provokes Concern—and Hope," *Christianity Today* 51, no. 7 (2007): 22–29.

58 Allan Anderson, "African Pentecostalism and the Ancestor Cult: Confrontation or Compromise," *Missionalia: Southern African Journal of Mission Studies* 21, no. 1 (1993): 26–39.
59 Ogbu U. Kalu, *Testing the Spirit: A Typology of Christianity in Igboland Revisited* (London: International Institute of African Studies, 1990), 4.
60 Aderibigbe and Jones Medine, Contemporary Perspectives on Religions
61 Ralph A. Austen, *Trans-Saharan Africa in World History* (Oxford: Oxford University Press, 2010).
62 Fatou Kiné Camara, *States and Religions in West Africa: Problems and Perspectives* (London: Routledge, 2016).
63 Rudolph T. Ware, *The Walking Qur'an: Islamic Education, Embodied Knowledge, and History in West Africa* (Chapple Hill: University of North Carolina, 2014).
64 Philip Ostien and Albert Dekker, "Sharia and National Law in Nigeria," in *Sharia Incorporated: A Comparative Overview of the Legal Systems of Twelve Muslim Countries in Past and Present*, ed. Jan Michiel Otto (Leiden: Leiden University Press, 2010), 553–612.
65 Abdur Rahman I. Doi, *Islam in Nigeria* (Zaria: Gaskiya Corporation, 1984).
66 Doi, *Islam in Nigeria*, 217.
67 Muhib O. Opeloye and S. L. Jimoh, "The Yoruba Muslims of Nigeria and the Glorious Qur'an," *NATAIS: Journal of Nigeria Association of Teachers of Arabic and Islamic Studies* 7 (2004): 65–83.
68 Doi, *Islam in Nigeria*, 151–152.
69 Danoye Oguntola-Laguda, "Pentecostalism and African Religious Movements in the 21st Century: A Case Study of Indigenous Faith of Africa, Ijo Orunmila," *Journal of Oriental and African Studies* 19 (2010): 191–205.
70 Aderibigbe and Jones Medine, Contemporary Perspectives on Religions
71 Danoye Oguntola-Laguda, "African Religious Movements and Pentecostalism: The Model of Ijo-Orunmila, Ato," in *Contemporary Perspectives on Religions in Africa and the African Diaspora*, eds. Ibigbolade S. Aderibigbe and Carolyn M. Jones Medine (New York: Palgrave Macmillan, 2015), 49–59.
72 Aderibigbe and Jones Medine, *Contemporary Perspectives on Religions*.
73 Aderibigbe and Jones Medine, *Contemporary Perspectives on Religions*.
74 Aderibigbe and Jones Medine, *Contemporary Perspectives on Religions*.
75 Nereus I. Nwosu, "Religion and the Crisis of National Unity in Nigeria," *African Study Monographs* 7, no. 3 (1996): 141–152.
76 G. I. S. Amadi, "Healing in 'the Brotherhood of the Cross and Star'," *Studies in Church History* 19 (1982): 367–383.
77 Rosalind J. Hackett, *Religion in Calabar: The Religious Life and History of a Nigerian Town* (Berlin: Mouton de Gruyter, 1989).
78 Galia Sabar and Atalia Shragai, "Olumba in Israel: Struggling on all Fronts," *African Identities* 6, no. 3 (2008): 201–225.
79 Eric Z. M. Gbote and Selaelo T. Kgatla, "Prosperity Gospel: A Missiological Assessment," *HTS: Theological Studies* 70, no. 1 (2014): 1–10.
80 Nicholas Duncan-Williams, *You are Destined to Succeed* (Accra: Action Faith Publications, 1990).
81 Gbote and Kgatla, "Prosperity Gospel," 1–10.
82 Austin O. Omomia, "Religious Fanaticism and 'Boko Haram' Insurgency in Nigeria: Implications for National Security," *Journal of Advocacy, Research and Education* 2, no. 1 (2015): 58–73.
83 Omomia, "Religious Fanaticism and "Boko Haram.'"
84 Sean M. Gourley, "Linkages between Boko Haram and al Qaeda: A Potential Deadly Synergy," *Global Security Studies* 3, no. 3 (2012): 1–14.
85 Karen Tracy and Sarah J. Tracy, "Rudeness at 911: Reconceptualizing Face and Face Attack," *Human Communication Research* 25, no. 2 (1998): 225–251.
86 Dogara. J. Gwamna, "Interrogating the Nexus of Religion and Terrorism in the Jos Crisis in Central Nigeria," *Insight: Journal of Religious Studies* 7 (2011): 1–18.
87 Irene N. Osemeka, "The Management of Religious Diversity in West Africa: The Exceptionalism of the Wolof and Yoruba in the Post-independence Period," *Historia Actual Online* 33 (2014): 61–75.

88 Freedom C. Onuoha, "The Audacity of the Boko Haram: Background, Analysis and Emerging Trend," *Security Journal* 25, no. 2 (2012): 134–151.

89 Horvath Henriet, "Boko Haram–Terrorism against the Leadership in Nigeria," *St Andrews Africa Summit Review* 1 (2017): 1–3.

90 Karin Barber, "How Man makes God in West Africa: Yoruba Attitudes towards the Orisa," *Africa* 51, no. 3 (1981): 724–745.

91 Oyeronke Olajubu, *Women in the Yoruba Religious Sphere* (New York: Suny Press, 2012).

92 Barbara M. Cooper, "Gender, Movement, and History: Social and Spatial Transformations in 20th Century Maradi, Niger," *Environment and Planning D: Society and Space* 15, no. 2 (1997): 195–221.

93 Daniel Kasomo, "The Role of Women in the Church in Africa," *International Journal of Sociology and Anthropology* 2, no. 6 (2010): 126–139.

94 Francis J. Moloney, *Women First among Faithful* (London: Longman and Todd, 1984), 27–96.

95 Kasomo, "The Role of Women in the Church," 126–139.

96 Jim Harries, *Secularism and Africa: In the Light of the Intercultural Christ* (Oregon: Wipf and Stock Publishers, 2015).

97 Donald Eugene Smith, *India as a Secular State* (Princeton: Princeton University Press, 2015).

25
CONTEMPORARY IDENTITIES

Introduction

On the continent, divided into "tribes" and by "tribal" sentiments, Africans have continued to contend with identity-based crises as one major bane to positive development in the region. The crises, which take the forms of violent ethnic conflicts, as well as a litany of other sociopolitical maladies—marginalization, corruption, political instability, human rights abuses, poverty, hunger—are by-products of the expressions of a combination of primordial allegiances and modern ambitions in competition for limited resources within colonially created multi-ethnic nation-states.[1] The analyses of the origins of the identity predicament of peoples of African origin (Blacks) can be split into two broad but related positions: the external disruption hypothesis and the internal complicity hypothesis. The former (external disruption) identifies racialism, slavery, colonialism, and "tribalism," which developed from Africa's "tragic" contact with the West,[2] tainting African identity perception and formation processes. It also faults the intrusion of this foreign (Western) culture, which not only relegated Africans (Blacks) to an inferior status by denigrating everything indigenous to Africa but also introduced systems of economic and political organization that accentuated "tribal"/ethnic fault lines that have continued to undermine African unity.

Nevertheless, the internal complicity angle faults the role Africans played in their own enslavement—as enablers. It also highlights the enthusiasm with which Africans have embraced Western culture, evident in the deference to African names, tongues, religion, and other indigenous cultural norms, especially in contrast to other erstwhile Western colonials like the Indians, who after that experience have endeavored to uphold their "indigenous" culture and traditions as the basis of their identity.[3] Incidentally, the argument is also made that "it is all this, this racialism, the slavery and the oppression of colonialism, the ambiguities of attitudes on the part of both whites and blacks which gave rise to the psychological and cultural alienation to the loss of collective identity of the Africans."[4]

DOI: 10.4324/9781003198260-30

The Western-orchestrated debasement of the African person provided the excuse for the inhumanities of slavery, colonialism, and apartheid, creating a universally dented African (Black) identity. Feelings of a common struggle for peoples of African descent arose from a shared history of oppression and a common aspiration for dignity and self-determination (including from the diaspora). Armed with the conviction that the fortunes of people of African ancestry—both on and off the continent—were inextricably linked, an affirmation of their personhood was the first step in the right direction toward their political and economic emancipation and recovery. Efforts were made by Black elites/intelligentsia to bridge the ethnic and geographical divides and unite African energies in a common struggle to redeem the African person from an undesirable position in the Western fabricated hierarchy of peoples. To achieve this aim, it was necessary to disabuse the African mind of mental slavery (notions of inferiority indoctrinated during years of propagating servile and colonialist ideologies), reinstate pride in African culture, and establish the capacity of African agency for development. Hence, the African mind was to be liberated from all racial, class, "tribal"/language, and geographical hierarchies that could stand in the way of a sociopolitical awakening necessary to reclaim African agencies from the chokehold of Western imperialist machinations.

However, Pan-Africanism and Négritude and Negrista, as avenues of African unity and emancipation, were not immune from the Western-dominated stream of conventional thought on Africa in the nineteenth and twentieth centuries. In line with Kanneh's postulation that "the subjectivities we inhabit and the times in which we live, makes dramatically apparent the ways in which 'race' has become the founding illusion of our identities,"[5] these movements were developed around racial themes, a factor that had dire consequences on their development. Although relatively successful initially, racialism proved an inadequate ideology for sustaining Pan-African sentiments, especially after the "demise of colonialism, segregation, and apartheid."[6] Incorporating "within itself conflicting tendencies and imaginaries of Africa, premised on racial, spatial, and ideological constructs,"[7] Pan-Africanism gradually gave way to continentalism, nationalism, and regionalism with the establishment of the Organization of African Unity (OAU) in 1963, doubling as "a triumph for continental Pan Africanism and a setback for trans-Atlantic Pan-Africanism."[8]

Postcolonial Africa in the twenty-first century witnessed the relegation of Pan-African sentiment, replaced by a focus on continental, regional, subregional, and intranational coalitions—identity formations. This localization in the articulation of political and economic interests resulted from the inadequacies of the founding ideologies of earlier transcontinental approaches and the result of particular historical developments—the Westphalian nation-state and globalization. The Westphalian nation-state paradigm introduced to Africa and its neoliberal systems proved inadequate in deemphasizing inherent contradictions like racial, ethnic, ethnolinguistic, and religious variables, posing significant challenges to the development of a united front;[9] while globalization—under a capitalist-oriented global political economy, including a tendency for cultural imperialism—progressively "subverts Africa's autonomy and powers of self-determination."[10]

Understanding Identity

To attempt a conceptualization of what an African identity connotes, it is pertinent to begin by providing an understanding of what identity is, particularly its (social) delineations and implications. In its definition of "identity," the Merriam-Webster dictionary provides explanations that effectively unbundle what has become a multifaceted social application. It explains identity as follows:

- The distinguishing character or personality of an individual—Individuality
- The relation established by psychological identification
- The condition of being the same with something described or asserted
- The sameness of essential or generic character in different instances.[11]

Each preceding explanation conveys a defining component of identity as a distinguishing attribute, a socially constructed label, a tool for individual and collective placement, and a medium of universal recognizability.

Other attempts to provide a functional meaning of identity have resulted in a surfeit of definitions on the subject, with a common conclusion that it is an attempt to answer the questions: "Who am I (are we)?" and "What is it?"[12] The point is also made that contemporary definitions (should) suggest a move from the idea of identity as a fixed, unitary, and fundamental social phenomenon to perceptions of identity as a manifold, polymorphic social invention whose structures are subject to sociohistorical development.[13] Hence, as a socially constructed and contextual conception, "The intuitive notion that identity is 'natural', is thus misleading and even dangerous."[14] As a concept, identity is generally associated with social identity: individual or personal, ethnic, state, national, transnational, and the like.

What is African Identity?

Two issues are central to the controversial subject of the meaning of an African identity, who an African is or should be: the meaning of "Africa" to Africans—inferring the external origins of that label—and Africa's cultural heterogeneity as a challenge to a cohesive identity. The naming of Africa, like some other important aspects of its being—cartographic representation, national compositions, politico-economic structures, identity, ontology, ethnology, and agency—was unduly influenced by an external culture whose apparent goal is to undermine, conquer, and subject "Africa" to a relationship of perpetual disadvantage. As a result, this has informed a widely shared conviction that Africa needs a new way of thinking. Without such a rethink, achieving unity of purpose under one cohesive African identity, especially in light of Africa's racial, cultural, linguistic, and religious diversity, as well as the cultural outcome of its encounter with Europe, is not feasible.[15] According to Kwame Appiah:

To speak of an African identity in the nineteenth century—if an identity is a coalescence of mutually responsive (if sometimes conflicting) modes of conduct, habits of thought, and patterns of evaluation; in short, a coherent kind of human social psychology—would have been "to give to aery nothing a local habitation and a name." ... there is no doubt that now, a century later, an African identity is coming into being.[16]

This activity of the pursuit of an African identity, which Paul Zeleza describes as a twenty-first-century reconfiguration egged on "by both the processes of contemporary globalization and the projects of African integration,"[17] is credited to the outcome of Africa's "unhealthy" contact with Europe. According to Dukor, "Africans of the first half of this century have begun to search for their identity because they had the feeling that they had lost it. The three factors which led to this feeling were; slavery, colonialism and racialism."[18] However, Appiah warns that "the bases through which so far it has largely been theorized—race, a common historical experience, a shared metaphysics—presuppose falsehoods too serious for us to ignore."[19]

West African Identities

As asserted earlier, identities are fluid and contextual social inventions, and their denotations are subject to historical development. Certain historical developments have shaped the nature of contemporary West African identities—agriculture and human settlement, trans-Saharan trade, Islam, slavery, colonialism/Westernization, Christianity, and globalization—some of which date back to as early as the Late Stone Age (between 4000 and 1000 BCE).[20] In the course of these historical developments and social changes, identities were developed, some of which—like the Muslim identity—have remained till the contemporary era. Taking stock of the identities of West Africans in contemporary times would reveal multiple levels of social identification representative of varying social and political contexts/periods.

For example, a female from the southwestern region of present-day Nigeria might identify as an Ijebu and a woman—the two central aspects of her social identity—given a particular social and political context, say Egbaland, before colonialism. However, in colonial Nigeria, she becomes a Yoruba Christian/Muslim class teacher from the Ijebu people. Going further outside the shores of Africa, the same person becomes a Black African woman from the Yoruba ethnic group in Nigeria, somewhere in West Africa. This demonstrates the fluidity and contextuality of identity, depicting different social and political contexts. In our modern era of limited spaces and resources, the significance of identity as a medium of allocation of limited social goods—security, sustenance, rights/liberties—has grown to necessitate the existence and ownership of multiple identities. This way, an individual can be Black, American, African, West African, Nigerian, Yoruba, Christian or Muslim male, upper-class, and educated, all of which are identities that come with certain privileges depending on the given social and political context.

Sources of Identities

Before tracing the origins of contemporary West African identities and how they have become so multi-layered, it is pertinent to understand the concept of "West Africa" as conceptualized in this chapter. West Africa is deployed in the conventional sense of an assigned label bequeathed on a cartographically and geographically demarcated section of African territory. Geographically, this designation covers the westernmost regions of the African continent, including present-day Nigeria, Ghana, Benin, Niger, Togo, Côte d'Ivoire, the Gambia, Mali, Burkina Faso, Senegal, Guinea-Bissau, Mauritania, Sierra Leone, Liberia, and Cabo Verde. Hence, to be "West African" is understood as being a citizen—either by birth or registration—of any of these countries/areas.

The western corner of the African continent (West Africa) is home to numerous people, spread around different regions, with diverse cultures, physiological characteristics, outlooks, and aspirations. Even before the continent ever came to be known as "Africa" or its peoples called "Africans," "West Africans," "sub-Saharan Africans," or any other such geographical and political delineation, the inhabitants of this region had—in reaction to their varied environments and interaction with neighbors—either developed or exhibited peculiar cultural characteristics by which they were identified. Also, as an outcome of social evolution, they had successfully established family, kinship, lineage, and kingship structures that served the purposes of sociopolitical organization and internal identity formation.

Indigenous Identities

Having a relatively conducive topography, the West African subregion was a locus of human activity, hosting numerous groups of people who adapted regions stretching from the coast through the forested and savannah areas to the Sahel, establishing thriving dominions and cultures. With archaeological remains that prove the presence of humans in the area before at least 9000 BCE,[21] the transformation began in these societies with the use of metals and stone tools, which allowed for a switch from migratory hunting and gathering existence to an agrarian and settled one. Such settlements were originally organized into a decentralized system of "small villages or village groups or units."[22] Each village comprised groups of families that combined to form lineages and groups of lineages that combined into clans, all making for a complex network of kinship ties. As Toyin Falola and M. M. Heaton explain societies in the Nigerian area:

> Each lineage was based on the idea of a common ancestry, in which each person in the lineage could trace his or her roots back to the founder of the lineage. Relationships between lineages could be strengthened through intermarriage, thereby linking the lineages and expanding the kinship group. Individuals' identities were primarily centred on kinship links.[23]

Such kinship links are known to grow quite extensively, transcending cultural borders, given the cultural/linguistic heterogeneity of the West African social environment that provided for intercultural exchanges through trade and intermarriage. Intermarriage was a common practice, considering the social checks instituted to prevent the problems of inbreeding and the factor of marriage as a popular medium of establishing intercommunal alliances for peaceful coexistence and defense. Thus, individuals enjoyed some considerable social relevance/identities across cultural borders based on kinship ties through marriage. Zain Abdullahi explains how these complex and multifaceted identities are reflected within the family unit. He posits that:

> Even within a single family, however, members often hold identities designated by multiple linguistic ties. Unlike the Western sense of family, in which there is the assumption of cultural conformity, in the West African family, cross-cultural marriages between people from mutually unintelligible ethnolinguistic groups are not uncommon. In the West African context, belonging to a clan or a "tribe" does not suggest homogeneity at all. On the contrary, it indicates tremendous heterogeneity and an environment in which identities are constantly negotiated.[24]

This way, an average individual in precolonial West Africa carries multiple identities that come alive in different social instances and have benefits and obligations. For example, a man from a patrilineal society inherits his father's family, lineage, clan, and village identity, and if his mother hails from a different village or culture, he assumes some rights and obligations determined by that village or culture's traditions. In any case, the individual inherits the son status (however far removed) and some part of the village or culture's identity.

Apart from trade and marriages, other traditional institutions such as age-grade groups and secret societies also provided levels of identity that transcended individual community lines.[25] In the case of the former, it was a common feature among decentralized societies like the Igbo in present-day Nigeria's southeastern region. Among the Igbo, political authority "tended to be founded on an age-based hierarchy at the village level: that is, elders, defined as the heads of patrilineal lines, were responsible for the most important decisions of a community."[26] Other age-grade levels, such as the youths, were responsible for maintaining thoroughfares, law and order, and matters of external security.

With economic diversification and specialization came new social identities in the form of artisans (blacksmithing, crafts), traders, and hunters' guilds, some of which were exclusive in certain societies. Metalworking also aided agricultural development and social expansion by facilitating the provision of surplus for trade, talents for hire, weapons for expansionary wars, and overall intensifying interaction between societies. These interactions, as Abdullahi elaborates, involved "a continuous flow of people, goods, and knowledge resulted in extensive journeys and the growth of elaborate trade routes."[27] And:

> While most West African peoples still lived in communities ranging from "stateless" (egalitarian) societies to hierarchical chiefdoms, the movement of goods and people produced complex political and economic systems, changing many villages into powerful city-states, which later formed federations made up of kingdoms and empires.[28]

Islamic and Indigenous (State) Identities

The development of intensive trans-Saharan trade between West African subregion societies and those of North Africa and the Middle East brought great wealth and development to the former, especially those principalities who supplied its chief commodities (gold and slaves) or were situated along its established routes. Thus, "As early as the fourth century CE, Black kingdoms of western Sudan built vibrant urban centers of wealth and learning by controlling the trans-Saharan trade routes linking North Africa, southern Europe, and the forests of the southern coast."[29] One such entity was ancient Ghana, benefitting from its strategic location along trade routes between what is today southeastern Mauritania and southwestern Mali,[30] along the trade routes and the possession of a key commodity (gold), which it had in considerable amounts.

By the tenth century, Ghana had grown into a major empire,[31] attracting other West Africans and Berbers from North Africa and Arab merchants from the Middle East. Traveling in huge camel caravans, the northern contingent (Berber and Arabs) brought textiles, salt, and utensils to be exchanged for slaves, gold, and kola nuts from the south.

Alongside these trade items came religion and cultural practices. Consequently, a thriving Muslim settlement was established close to the empire's capital, which housed both religious and legal scholars, some of whom were taken into the employ of the Ghanaian court, working for the king as interpreters, advisers, and treasurers. Attempts by the Ghanian court to fend off Almoravid attacks, like the one it suffered in 1076,[32] by solidifying its alliances with Arab merchants, saw the Ghanian king converting to Islam. That notwithstanding, Islam remained an "imperial cult and the religion of state elites and trading people, but the agricultural populations maintained their traditional beliefs."[33]

Other kingdoms of Western Sudan, notably the Malinke of the succeeding Mali empire and its subject, the Wolof[34] confederacy—both one-time vassal states of the ancient Ghana empire—also came under some influence of Islam from Ghana. Though this influence continued under the Mali Empire, the majority of the Malinke and Wolof maintained their traditional beliefs for a considerable length of time, only gradually adopting Islamic governing principles and social values. This transformation among the Malinke and Wolof identities replaced traditional positions with Islamic ones in the existing social order—a hierarchy of hereditary castes. Whereas the nobility—which usually included the founders and wealthiest members of the community—retained their positions atop the social ladder, Muslim scholars and clerics were elevated to ranks next to them.

Describing this gradual adaptive process, especially the insistence on indigenous practices, which in most cases led to a fusion of traditions, Abdullahi makes the following clarification:

> The Islamization of the Malinke gradually introduced different positions and a new set of responsibilities. In pre-Islamic times, for example, Malinke *mansas* (kings) were expected to appeal to a number of deities and spirits to ensure a plentiful harvest or to ward off calamity. Under the Islamic rule of the Mali empire, *mansas* substituted their belief in animistic spirits for a worldview that included the *jinns* (evil or virtuous beings Muslims believe inhabit the world of the unseen). Moreover, nobility based strictly on ancestry and tribute gave way to high status based on Islamic learning and mastery of the Qur'an, Islam's sacred text. The initiates of age grades, for instance, were no longer inducted into puberty according to the old social customs. Rather, coming of age necessitated a certain level of Islamic maturity too. This does not mean that these changes occurred all at once or without resulting in some sort of syncretism. Changes were usually gradual and more often than not involved a fusion of traditional practices with Islamic tenets, frequently retaining the supremacy of Islam's godhead and the legitimacy of the Prophet.[35]

It took the jihadist reformist movements of the eighteenth century to achieve large-scale conversions among the general population.

The cohabitation of these identities (Islamic and state identities) in Malinke society is perhaps best captured by the celebration—in the Malinke identity formation story—of an extensive Islamic tradition symbolized by the exploits of legendary figure Mansa Musa and those of Sundiata, which "links them to an African tradition that predates their conversion to Islam."[36] This also played a major role in the development of "Black

Islam," which stood as resistance to "both French assimilatory practices and the cultural hegemony of Arab reform movements out of North Africa and the Middle East."[37] The scenario in the western Sudanic states in the fourteenth and fifteenth centuries was not very different from what transpired in the Hausa states of the Nigerian savannah and Sahel regions from the fifteenth century.[38]

Like their predecessors from whom they inherited the shifting trans-Saharan trade routes, the trade brought wealth and cultural and religious influences into Hausa territories, contributing to their transformation into reputed city-states and empires. Islam and the trans-Saharan trade ignited more interactions and important relations between the Hausa states and their neighbors both to the south (lower regions of Nigeria from whence they acquired and sold items of trade) and northwards in North Africa, the Middle East, and Europe. Also, like their counterparts in the collapsed Ghana, Mali, and Songhai empires, Islam was largely restricted to the ruling class, with most of the population keeping with their traditional religious practices. As for the Hausa aristocracy, adopting Islam was an opportunity to fully exploit their interaction with the Islamic world. Thus, Islam and traditional practices ran concurrently until the Uthman Dan Fodio Jihadist reformist movements of the nineteenth century, celebrated as a successful proselytization campaign. Though these Hausa states adopted many of its tenets and developed Muslim identities due to their interaction with Islam, they never abandoned their state identities[39] as they continued to identify with titles like Kanawa/Bakaon, Gobirawa, Katsinawa, and Zagzagawa.

The Uthman Dan Fodio Islamic reformist movements of the nineteenth century also expanded the Muslim identity into the southwestern region of Yorubaland. Ilorin was captured and converted, and became the base for the launch of proselytization campaigns in the interior of the Yoruba cultural centers. However, unlike in the northern regions, trans-Saharan trade, not Islam, may have contributed to the expansion and fame of Ile-Ife, Oyo, and Benin political cultural centers. The argument can be made that Islam added to the existing division, as it came when the region was embroiled in a series of internecine conflicts. Nevertheless, this period planted the seeds of Muslim identity in the region, and unlike other places in the greater Nigerian region where Islam was introduced, it made the least progress in displacing the traditional belief systems here.

Slave and Colonial Identities

The appearance of European trading ships on the coast of West Africa marked a turning point in the social, economic, and political lives of both the peoples of that region and the continent at large. "The first Europeans to arrive on the West African coast were the Portuguese, who had established trading post with the Benin Kingdom at Gwarto (Ughoton) by 1480."[40] The articles of this trade came to increasingly include humans, and less than a century later, with the discovery of the West Indies, other nations, including Britain, Netherlands, and France, came to share in it. As the demand for slaves across the Atlantic increased, trade spread along the coast, drawing in the societies in the interior. More than two centuries later, millions were enslaved, and political and economic conditions in Europe changed enough to warrant abolition, beginning with Britain in 1807.

Through imperialist historiography, the Europeans demonized and debased Africans to justify the sale of Africans. They reduced Africans to subhuman status. Theories were fabricated to explain the limitations foisted on their person. Even physiological characteristics were weaponized against them. They are "Black"—devilish, evil, bad—undeveloped, childlike, and in need of civilizing. They are from a dark continent with no history and wander about without aim or purpose. Academic disciplines—anthropology, ethnography, sociology—were developed to convince their home populations and anyone who cared to look that the "Black" person was from a race inferior to others; therefore, any sign of intellectual activity in their vicinity was the work of a "White," superior neighbor. On account of these, they neither own nor deserve any rights except that given to them by their superiors, in whose shadows they must walk in perpetuity. This doctrine of slavery and imperialism produced the Black racial identity of West Africa.

Among the ex-slaves and freeborn who either opted to or were compelled to return to Africa, two particular countries—America and Britain—supplied the highest figures.[41] Split between Liberia (for returnees from America) and Sierra Leone (for returnees from Britain), these groups arrived to meet indigenous populations in these territories, among whom they constituted another identity, separate from their racialized titles as "Blacks" and that of their historical experience/titles as ex-slaves. This contact between Africa and Europe also led to the creation of the Creole[42] identity. In the case of British Sierra Leone, a Creole identity also developed. A component of this Creole community, including returnees from Portugal, Brazil, and the Caribbeans, also made its way to Nigeria, settling in Lagos, where they set up businesses and represented a distinct class of returnees for a time.

In pursuit of administrative expedience for economic appropriation, European colonialism in West Africa reorganized the existing (precolonial) social and political structures, thereby lumping diverse peoples and cultures into arbitrary borders—in heterogeneous nation-states. Overnight, people from diverse cultures and identities fell under the title of newly established nation-states, with their cultural kith and kin scattered into two or three separate states. The choice of administration—the indirect rule system in British territories and the assimilation strategy in French territories—all have identity consequences in these varied cultures hatched via the machinations of the European empire. In British West Africa, indirect rule created rulers from the non-elite. While the French assimilation policy made French citizens out of its African subjects, other colonialism-induced changes, such as the development of Christianity, mission schools, administrative departments, and new urban centers, introduced new identity forms to colonial West African society. New identity dichotomies might be seen among adherents of various church missions and non-Christians, between urban and rural dwellers, a new urban elite and proletariat, European educated and non-educated, civil servants, and private-sector workers.

While all these were developing, the colonial governments carried out some identity manipulations, which became obvious from the obstacles they had become to unity and cohesion in the region. Whereas the colonial dictionary, which was developed and operated at the time, classified Africans into ethnolinguistic, religious, and racial enclaves, while tagging them with "racial" and "tribal" labels, the colonial administration did its best to make these labels a reality by promoting the idea of their perpetual antagonism.

This activity redefined identity perceptions and emphasized identity dichotomy along religious and "ethnic" fault lines. The role played by the colonial government in encouraging social fragmentation is best captured by Falola and Heaton's position on Lugard's decision to limit missionary activities to the south. They explain that unlike the southern protectorate where colonial officials were disposed to favoring the expansion of education and social services:

> in the name of preserving traditional cultures, Lugard and his successors severely restricted the access of Christian missionaries to the Muslim areas of northern Nigeria. As a result, the inhabitants of northern Nigeria did not have the access to European education that southerners had. By the time the Colonial Office decided to amalgamate the northern and southern provinces of Nigeria into a single administrative unit in 1912, the two regions were already on very different paths.[43]

Therefore, at Nigeria's independence in 1960, it could hardly be expected that the other regions that did not enjoy as much colonial developmental attention as the south would ignore the contrast and commit to building on unequal footing. Such sentiment and feelings of mutual distrust greeted the politics of independent Nigeria.

Independence in West Africa crystallized cultural, ethnolinguistic, and historical variations into enduring identities. At Liberia's independence in 1847, the American returnees separated themselves from the local population to form a group of "Americo-Liberians" with exclusive rights to the political edifice. In Nigeria, there was also the crystallization of analogous ethnolinguistic groups into cultural identities in an attempt to secure regional interests in a multinational state. These produced the politicized Yoruba, Igbo, and Hausa/Fulani identities which were non-existent before 1960. Around West Africa, the stories were similar: divisions between ethnolinguistic pools, north–south dichotomies, and indigene/settler contestations.

Globalization and West African Identities

Among the many definitions of globalization are the conquest of capital over the world and the enthronement of money and status over values and humanity. While some have insisted that the focus should be on the advantages globalization has brought to the world—dual citizenship, multiple identities, expanded opportunities, increased scope and speed of economic transactions and social exchange, and technological proliferation—others argue about the threat of cultural homogeneity and loss of autonomy. In particular, the focus of capitalism (individualism) as the proper economic ideology for Africa is still in question. Indeed, all these accolades and concerns find expression in globalization. It has been described as one of "the most challenging development in the movement of world history."[44] The most important question we try to answer here is, what is the place of West Africa in the scheme of things (globalization)?

Unfortunately, West Africa does not enjoy an enviable place in this increasingly globalizing world. Its intermittent glorification for having "one of the fastest" or "the fastest" growing economies globally does not come with tremendous progress. It has been plagued by social ills, from a difficult historical experience to a contemporary history of bad governance, coups in the Sahel, protracted devastating and reoccurring identity conflicts, health issues, militant insurgency, poor infrastructure, millions of out-of-school children, and internet fraud. It is so bad that except for the exceptional cases of brilliance and individual cases of personal agency, there would be no West African identity to reference beyond the geographical delineation, age-old traditions of glory, and other fixed categories. As it stands, to speak of a West African identity in this era of globalization is to paint a picture of disadvantage, disunity, and strife.

Conclusion

Being one of the most densely populated regions of the world, with cultural and linguistic groups in their hundreds that have been in constant interaction for thousands of years, West Africa is a kaleidoscope of identities. Hence, it is common for its people to possess multiple identities at the continental, subcontinental, national, intranational, biological, and professional levels. Some of these identities that the people inhabit in contemporary times date back generations, but as a people conscious and proud of their history, these identities have been maintained, even though severally modified. For a people so different and yet so similar, the cultures and identities of West Africa hold the potential for unity in diversity and all the grandeur it promises. But that has not been the case, mostly because the region has not moved as a collective.

In its contact and interactions with the outside world, West Africa has not been so well served. Undoubtedly, people's destinies are in their own hands; however, when such a people have been pillaged, oppressed, misled, and actively plotted against for so long, sometimes with the participation of people they call brethren, it is understandable that community feelings are relegated. As experience has proven, great feats are possible when people stand above their differences, as West Africans did with Pan-Africanism in the days of nationalist struggles. The region can appreciate that identities are relevant only how and when the bearers want them to be. And as such, people should endeavor to commit their identities to the benefit of all in their society, connected as they are.

DEEP DIVE

Assignment 1

Objective

The objective of this assignment is to ensure that students complete the reading of Chapter 25 and to encourage them to understand the concept of identity and examine what constitutes West African Identities.

Method

Students will be expected to write a short note in response to the question.

Reading Comprehension

How did the cohabitation of Islamic and indigenous identities combine to form the development of "Black Islam" in West Africa?

Assignment 2

Objective

The objective of this assignment is to ensure that students complete the reading of Chapter 25 and to encourage them to consider how colonial rule enforced a redefinition of West African identity along religious and ethnic fault lines.

Method

Students will be expected to write a short note in response to the question.

Reading Comprehension

What role did globalization play in creating the view that West Africa is a subregion of disunity and strife?

Notes

1 Vigdis Broch-Due, "Violence and Belonging: Analytical Reflections," in *Violence and Belonging: The Quest for Identity in Post-Colonial Africa*, ed. Vigdis Broch-Due (London: Routledge, 2005), 2.
2 Frank O. Ndubisi, "The Philosophical Paradigm of African Identity and Development," *Open Journal of Philosophy* 3, no. 1A (2013): 222–230.
3 Araoye Oyebola, *The Black Man's Dilemma* (Ibadan: Board Publications, 1982).
4 A. E. Ruch and K. Chukwulozie Anyanwu, *Africa Philosophical Trend in Contemporary Africa* (Rome: Catholic Book Agency, 1981), 168, quoted in Ndubisi, "The Philosophical Paradigm," 223.
5 Kadiatu Kanneh, *African Identities: Race, Nation and Culture in Ethnocentrism, Pan-Africanism and Black Literatures* (London: Routledge, 1998), 1.
6 Toyin Falola and Kwame Essien, "Introduction," in *Pan Africanism and the Politics of African Citizenship and Identity*, eds. Toyin Falola and Kwame Essien (New York: Routledge, 2014), 1.
7 Paul Tiyambe Zeleza, "The Inventions of African Identities and Languages: The Discursive and Developmental Implications," in *Selected Proceedings of the 36th Annual Conference on African Linguistics*, eds. Olaoba F. Arasanyin and Michael A. Pemberton (2006), 14–26; and Richard A. A. Enoh, "The Global Implications of Pan Africanism and the Establishment of 'New Communities' in Africa: The Case of Victoria in Southwest Cameroon," in *Pan Africanism and the Politics of African Citizenship and Identity*, eds. Toyin Falola and Kwame Essien (New York: Routledge, 2014), 85.
8 Zeleza, "The Inventions of African Identities," 18.
9 Richard A. Griggs, *Boundaries, Borders and Peace-building in Southern Africa: The Spatial Implications of the 'African Renaissance'* (Durham: International Boundaries Research Unit, 2000), 14.
10 Ikechukwu A. Kanu, "African Identity and the Emergence of Globalization," *American International Journal of Contemporary Research* 3, no. 6 (2013): 34–42.
11 Merriam Webster Dictionary, "Identity," accessed April 5, 2022, https://www.merriam-webster.com/dictionary/identity.
12 Kanu, "African Identity"; and Anton du Plessis, "Exploring the Concept of Identity in World Politics," Paper Presented at a Conference on "Politics and Identity and Exclusion in Africa:

From Violent Confrontation to Peaceful Cooperation" at the University of Pretoria on July 25–26, 2001, 14.
13 Du Plessis, "Exploring the Concept of Identity"; and Kristin Loftsdottir, *The Bush is Sweet: Identity, Power and Development Among the WoDaaBe Fulani in Niger* (Uppsala: Nordiska Afrikainstitutet, 2008), 18.
14 Du Plessis, "Exploring the Concept of Identity," 14.
15 Maduabuchi Dukor, *African Freedom: The Freedom of Philosophy* (Germany: LAP LAMBERT Publications, 2010), 160.
16 Kwame Appiah, *In My Father's House: Africa in the Philosophy of Culture* (New York: Oxford University Press, 1992), 174.
17 Zeleza, "The Inventions of African Identities," 14.
18 Dukor, *African Freedom*, 159.
19 Appiah, *In My Father's House*, 174.
20 Toyin Falola and Matthew M. Heaton, eds., *A History of Nigeria* (New York: Cambridge University Press, 2008), 18.
21 Falola and Heaton, *A History of Nigeria*, 18.
22 Falola and Heaton, *A History of Nigeria*, 16.
23 Falola and Heaton, *A History of Nigeria*, 41.
24 Zain Abdullahi, "Negotiating Identities: A History of Islamization in Black West Africa," *Journal of Islamic Law and Culture* 10, no. 1 (2008): 5–18.
25 Falola and Heaton, *A History of Nigeria*, 36.
26 Falola and Heaton, *A History of Nigeria*, 22.
27 Abdullahi, "Negotiating Identities," 11.
28 Abdullahi, "Negotiating Identities," 11.
29 Abdullahi, "Negotiating Identities," 11.
30 Abdullahi, "Negotiating Identities," 11.
31 It is pertinent to point out that the Sudanese empires of Ghana, Mali, and Songhai did not owe their emergence solely to the northern trade influence. These states grew out of their own environments and as a result of the agency of their populations. The trade was a booster of social and economic activity. Walter Rodney, *How Europe Underdeveloped Africa* (London: Bogle-L'Ouverture Publications, 1972); and Falola and Heaton, *A History of Nigeria*, 34.
32 Falola and Heaton, *A History of Nigeria*, 12.
33 Ira M. Lapidus, *A History of Islamic Societies* (New York: Cambridge University Press, 2002), 401.
34 The Wolof in this period were settled in an area north of Senegal, present-day Mauritania. Today, those who share that identity are spread into Senegal, The Gambia, and Mauritania. See Abdullahi, "Negotiating Identities;" and Tijan M. Sallah, *Wolof* (New York: Rosen, 1996).
35 Abdullahi, "Negotiating Identities," 16.
36 Abdullahi, "Negotiating Identities," 17.
37 Abdullahi, "Negotiating Identities," 14.
38 This period, according to Falola and Heaton, was when the Hausa states began their ascendancy. See Falola and Heaton, eds. *A History of Nigeria*, 16.
39 Falola and Heaton, *A History of Nigeria*, 31.
40 Falola and Heaton, *A History of Nigeria*, 53; and Colin W. Newbury, *The Western Slave Coast and Its Rulers: European Trade and Administration Among the Yoruba and Adja-Speaking Peoples of South-Western Nigeria, Southern Dahomey and Togo* (London: Oxford University Press, 1961), 17.
41 America alone is given as exporting about 13,000 Africans to Liberia in the nineteenth century, with Britain depositing thousands in Sierra Leone. See Lawrence Aje, "'Africa, the Land of Our Fathers:' The Emigration of Charlestonians to Liberia in the Nineteenth Century," in *Pan Africanism and the Politics of African Citizenship and Identity*, eds. Toyin Falola and Kwame Essien (New York: Routledge, 2014), 51.
42 Consisting mostly of a mixture of African and European stock, these became a common sight among the coastal communities of West Africa. Colin W. Newbury made several mentions of them in his book, *The Western Slave Coast and its Rulers*.
43 Falola and Heaton, *A History of Nigeria*, 116.
44 Anthony, "African Identity," 38.

26

WEST AFRICA AND THE WIDER WORLD

Introduction

During the 1980s, African countries, especially those in the West African region, were hit with a sudden economic recession that challenged their economic and political systems as it exposed them to threatening conditions. The future was bleak, following the realization that the resuscitation of their economic systems would demand a radical approach amidst their continued weakness and uncertainty to breathe life into their entire existence. Although the immediate challenge was the economy, there were potential reasons to exercise fear, given the understanding that other aspects of their livelihoods would be severely affected if the economy suffered. It was, therefore, necessary that these African countries opened their arms to the international community for rescue by accepting their policies, initiatives, and other approaches that can help salvage the people from the ensuing complicated economic equation in which they were embroiled.

The postcolonial West African economy reacted to the economic threat by embracing collaboration from the international community. At the tail end of the 1980s, the World Bank organized a study that would stimulate intellectual evaluation of the emerging conditions and decide how to contain the challenges for regional growth.[1] Titled *Sub-Saharan Africa: From Crisis to Sustainable Growth: A Long-Term Perspective Study*, the report enhances intellectual thinking on development strategy, and its success automatically encourages similar expeditions at the regional level so that prompt solutions could be offered to their enduring challenges. Such collaboration would assist in taking an expert view of situations in the countries of the region within specific periods of their recent history. For example, it would encourage a demographic study and how economic systems, political structures, and security issues have been affected. If these issues have significant consequences on people's progress generally, there would be measures to arrest the situations. Looking into the West African situation during the postcolonial environment would thus feature changes in a spatial settlement, the market dynamics, as well as changes in population within a specific period.

DOI: 10.4324/9781003198260-31

The Formation of ECOWAS

The Economic Community of West African States (ECOWAS) was created in 1975 to promote regional integration and the establishment of cooperation that would facilitate economic and monetary union to reinforce the economic growth of the states. The postcolonial African political outlook requires collaboration. Therefore, it is essential that countries within the same region come together to devise strategies to manage and mitigate situations of probable economic inflammation. Although African economic problems continue to surge because of the absence of a clear-cut economic agenda and the lasting legacy of structures made available during colonialism, their conditions are increasingly clouded by the exponential increase in their population.

According to some data, the West African population experienced an expansion from the 1960s to 2015,[2] which might become a problem if corrective economic systems are not appropriately created. In order to address the already complex situations that could erupt at a moment's notice, such an economic system requires the collaboration of countries within the region so that their plans, and the approach to achieving them, would have a profound impact in the long run. Without a strategic means of containing the epidemic spread of economic strangulation in the region, the tendency that the region would engage in meaningful economic competition is regrettably low.

The problems of West Africa began from the imposition of imperialist expansionism that started because of the intention for political and economic exploitation of the people. Prior to this time, even if not deeply aware of the global economic system, the region predominantly conducted economic exchange horizontally. However, the happenstance of that colonial experience and the reality of population increases further exposed them to the global economy, and because of their unpreparedness, they were exposed to situations that challenged their thinking politically, economically, and even culturally. Therefore, this postcolonial time has necessitated that countries forge a Pan-African identity that will help attend to challenges while retaining their sovereignty and the human dignity that comes with it. The realization that doing the opposite would most likely expose them to danger and risk compelled them to create united fronts, such as ECOWAS, to have a clear understanding of their present economic situation and how they can leverage their current resources to obtain optimum results in contemporary times. Their inability to erect good economic infrastructures that will structure their growth in the postcolonial period is connected to the exploitation that West Africans have experienced from their erstwhile imperialists and the emerging neocolonialists.

The need for West African collaboration is prompted more by the region's growing population, as demographic shift usually puts pressure on people to devise better ways toward collective development. As we have identified, the population of the West African countries surged between the years of independence to date, and the projection that it would continue to do so justifies the reason for the creation of ECOWAS. Experts predict that the region's population will increase to 500 million before 2030,[3] which puts the responsibility on the policy developers and stakeholders to deliberate on the possible way out from the impending economic crisis that may result if the necessary methods are not put in place. Without such preventive measures, an increase in population would certainly attract more challenges, given the fact that the pressure to cope with society's needs would increase exponentially.

Population growth places pressure on governments in various ways. Firstly, there would be the need to provide shelters for the projected 500 million individuals; secondly, there is the political necessity to provide gainful employment to the adults, who would provide food and basic needs to children. Thirdly, the need for upgraded security measures would arise due to increased security challenges that basic provisions cannot cover. All these are indices of conflicts and wars, as their continued existence would lead people to depression, frustration, and resignation. There is, however, the problem of revenue generation that improved only when these countries came together under the banner of common interest.

ECOWAS was created to address the enormous challenges facing West Africa because of issues closely connected to colonial economic structures. Because the imperialists were only interested in extracting natural resources from the people, they developed an economic model solely dependent on the Global North. This means that the financial success of these West African countries is dependent on the volume of resource exports they could make to first-world countries, among which are European countries and the United States specifically. As such, Africa was not encouraged to embark on technological investment that could provoke sudden and everlasting transformation, as it did in Europe, for example, in the eighteenth and nineteenth centuries. Instead, they mandated these West African countries to produce agricultural products and mineral commodities for exportation needed mainly for the transformation of the Global North's economy.

We should always be reminded that part of the claims of the European imperialists for the activation of colonization was their "altruistic" intention to "civilize" and "modernize" Africa and Africans under the assumption that they were below all necessary standards associated with being human. Nevertheless, this intention to civilize included discouraging West African countries from embarking on technological investment, which contradicts such unsubstantiated claims. Actively encouraging agricultural production and export, along with an education system focused on basic literacy and numeracy without gearing the people up to concentrate on the radical development of their technological capabilities, was an attempt to make West Africans serve Western interests.

Incidentally, one of the notorious challenges that comes from such biases is that technological success in the Global North automatically makes its countries less dependent on agricultural and commodity products, as was significantly demanded from Africa. In fact, West Africa's problem was compounded by the realization that Asian countries joined in the competition, and they became willing product suppliers to the same West. Therefore, West African countries are compelled to come together to address their unveiling economic crisis in postcolonial times. The creation of the forum became important in the negotiation of their future economic positions in the comity of nations.

Because globalization has mandated that the people's plans must be coherent and have a common focus, the coming together of the West African countries was necessary so that they would plan their economic agenda in such a way that any change in the global market would be attended to by the established systems, which the union would have ascertained. ECOWAS, thus, becomes a necessary economic union that engages in long-term plans for bringing the region out of the mess of economic degeneration. In the eventuality that the countries that demand agricultural and commodity products from West Africa turn to rely on their internal capacity or become overwhelmed by competitive offerings from other economic blocs, say in North Africa, East Africa, or in Asian countries, what would happen to West African countries and their economies?

It is on this basis that the foundation for such a strong economic group was established. The ECOWAS is geared toward the provision of regional solutions to rising issues such as population increases. The West African countries are confronted with a population surge that strictly demands higher consumption and, expectedly, employment. However, the postcolonial African political system encourages an urban economy, which further increases people's attraction to the city. To save the region from the potential threat of sanctions by the West, countries could produce what they consume and consume only those things they produce.

One of the most reliable ways to attend to this is to ensure that the region provides its citizens with the opportunity for social mobility without experiencing significant difficulties. Upward and horizontal mobility would expose people to different economic opportunities and cultures, enabling them to improve their financial fortunes. Immigrants are expected to increase, especially in the postcolonial world, where they are supposed to be well-connected to the people to whom they are responsible for their well-being. Consequently, the attraction becomes more compelling as immigrants with better financial opportunities in the urban centers encourage more immigration. However, during the period these countries recorded quick economic transformation, urbanization experienced rapid growth, which also increased the mobility of these immigrants.

As part of the reasons for collaboration, the ECOWAS is saddled with paying increased attention to the educational issues facing the region. It is often identified that one of the enduring problems of the region is education. This region has a large underage demographic that does not have access to education, but it pays discouragingly little attention to its education system. For this reason, the ECOWAS has also concentrated on the development of the people's educational systems because of an understanding that greater economic growth is ensured through education. When people are well educated, they dedicate their intellectual resources to the rejuvenation of their economic systems so that they can experience a rapid turnaround. Therefore, the rehabilitation of schools is necessary because not only does it increase people's intellectual development, but it also contributes to higher economic performance. The long-term failure of the region to achieve integration comes from its failure to provide good education systems for the people. In fact, the awareness that the region should maintain a unified identity and structure springs from the understanding that it is the best approach to confront the bigger economic challenges facing them collectively.

ECOWAS understands again that the transformation of the region is also dependent on shared information generally. Most of the time, policymaking relies on knowledge about the people, which means that a policy is liable to be updated once there is a demographic change. Therefore, countries within the region must have a clear knowledge of those changes that happen within a member state to make necessary adjustments in their policies. This means that communication is vital to enable a strengthened bond, and consistent population censuses are needed to consolidate progressive decisions. Following this is the fact that knowledge about the production of each member country is needed, including their consumption behavior. Budgetary calculations of households, then of states and of countries, are needed to effectively draw the policies needed to strengthen transregional relationships and allow intraregional understanding. Therefore, the knowledge of all these would contribute to the awareness of the required economic information, leading to the decentralization of information networks in the region. As has been identified, this requires the strengthening of the education systems within the region.

West African Relations With the World

West Africa is important to the world. With regard to the question of political structures, West Africa has demonstrated a reasonable level of decorum with an amazing ability to coordinate, integrate, and accommodate change flexibly. For this, the region has continued to show its strength politically, thus creating the impression that its political maturity is a catalyst for international collaboration with countries, especially in the European world and their Global North counterparts. Therefore, it is understandable that this level of consciousness of its importance should provoke policy awareness from Western European countries, the United States of America, China, and Russia.

After considerable progress in managing the piles of colonialist challenges that stifled their growth in the post-independence era, African leaders now consider building an image for themselves in the international community so that their political and economic growth can experience a sudden and steady development. In different ways, they have shown their intention to join the community of nations with global regard and respect so that their status would become more receptive to the economic and technological transformation they usually imagine. For example, several West African nations' decisions to join the United Nations illustrate their readiness for this development.

For a long time, West African countries have encountered troubling challenges that determined their political and economic affairs, which signals the fact that they are only enjoying reductionist independence or quasi-freedom. This awareness has mandated them to rethink by joining the United Nations so that they can coordinate their efforts on issues that are closely related to self-determination, reduction, or total erasure of policies riddled with prejudices both racially and status-motivated.[4] It will also ensure that the former colonial structures are truly dismantled to the extent that the countries can become ideologically and culturally independent like the majority of developing nations.

Achieving all of these needs more than a verbal declaration. It demands rapid development of these countries as that would serve as the physical evidence for their readiness. Additionally, it requires economic growth that would register an impression that they have the required parameters for growth and that their technological improvement can be relied upon to improve the shape of their economies. Surprisingly, all these metrics of development are carefully checked off by these West African countries as they continue to demonstrate their invincible character and the ability to take control of their future economic and political trajectories. On this basis, they increasingly attract the interest of the Global North and other important allies, provoking international integration that promises success.

What must be understood is that the international relationship between first-world countries, especially the United States and European countries, has taken its roots from the time of their independence. Having attained independence and demonstrated their readiness to control their own economic and political systems, these countries should now encourage their ex-colonies to have policy freedoms that correspond to their free status as members of the Free World.

Unlike the colonial experience when regional integration was not achievable, particularly because of the realization of colonialism, which was encouraged by partitioned geographical space, the international community agreed that these countries would strike free relations among the countries within the same region and out of it, without restrictions occasioned by different languages and unequal political structures. Apart from this, the United States would also grant them an unrestricted relationship so that all the necessary economic exchange expected of such collaboration would not be restricted, and neither would it be hindered. Again, because of this relationship with the West, all forms and examples of internal expansions were discouraged, and xenophobic ideas were not encouraged because they were potential barricades against the realization of a people's economic and political potential in postcolonial times.

Following the resolution for the invigoration of the West African countries' economies, there have been other diplomatic relationships with the international community and organizations. For example, the European Union (EU) entered into an economic agreement (Economic Partnership Agreement (EPA)) with the West African countries, which caters for all economic engagements that would go on between the European and the West African countries.[5] According to the agreement,

> non-originating materials which at importation to the European Union are free of customs duties by means of application of conventional rates of the most-favored nation (MFN) tariff in accordance with its Common Customs Tariff shall be considered as materials originating in a West African State when incorporated into a product obtained there, provided that they have undergone working or processing there which goes beyond the operations referred to in Article 5(1) of this Protocol.

An agreement like this would invariably mean that the countries have a reserved right to obtain maximum gains from materials and commodity products that are produced in the region to gain easy access to European countries where they would make sufficient economic outputs in the long run. By relaxing the customs policy and rules that guide the exportation of goods from the West African countries, the international relationship between them is solidified to promote free trade.

The core reason for enabling this stress-relieving economic policy is to ensure that the West African countries are integrated into the global trading system, as this would facilitate the regional economic growth of the beneficiaries. However, the underlying benefit is that it would increase the percentage of exports to European countries, which will boost the survival of their economies. With the smooth economic exchange enhanced by this, EU investment would be stimulated simultaneously, bringing speed to the productive capacity of West African countries and, in the long run, would reduce their unemployment rates. These initiatives represent the postcolonial efforts set at a pace so that West African countries can experience reduced economic frustration. The general interest of the European Union and the West African states is the facilitation of an environmental system where trade relations would be used as the instrument for the economic and political integration of the countries of the world so that challenges can be considered from a holistic perspective and countries offered a better approach. The engagement with West Africa reflects the global recognition that every country's economic surplus, stability, and productivity are dependent on the amount of interdependent assistance that can be attracted from other countries. All these factors contribute to the anticipated collaborations.

Even in other important aspects, West African countries are integrated into a union where pushing for a common agenda remains their political objective. Apart from organizations that address all market-oriented issues and, therefore, improve the economies of these countries, West African countries have another interesting union. For example, the West African College of Physicians is a professional society created to allow medical experts to jointly contribute toward the provision of safe medical services and research, primarily for West African coverage.[6] It was inaugurated in 1967 after the experts realized that the uniqueness of medical systems lies in their appreciation of geographical differences and cultural factors in the determination of people's medical conditions. Although the topic of medical challenges remains a global one, they understand that approaches to these challenges are usually different because of the fact that biology or body systems are, to a large extent, conditioned by environmental factors. This, therefore, compelled them to create an atmosphere where the medical-related challenges confronting the countries within the West African region are addressed and looked into by experts familiar with the social and cultural environment.

One of the primary ambitions of the group is to offer professional support for specialist training in postgraduate studies, develop the corresponding curriculum, which would be used as a compass for the in-training students, and provide certification for successful candidates across medical fields such as community health, internal medicine, laboratory medicine, psychiatry, family medicine, and pediatrics, among others. As a result of their specific interests and expert knowledge, they usually provide policy advice to the governments of member countries within the West African region to enable strong and better medical systems in preparation for the health emergencies of the collective.

At the point of creation, this professional organization limited its membership to all ex-colonized countries under Britain in West Africa; however, this was eventually updated to accommodate others regardless of their colonial or linguistic heritage. Because of the nature of its emergence, the union has the capacity to collaborate with medical professionals outside of the continent, especially those within Britain, for the consolidation of knowledge and collaboration of ideas. For example, on many occasions, they have collaborated with Britain's Royal Medical Colleges and the American College of Physicians and also had a history with the South Africa Medical College.[7]

Due to the understanding that the postcolonial environment requires creativity in dealing with emerging challenges, the West African countries decided to rely on their ingenuity in solving their existential problems, especially within the medical territory. The common history of colonialism inspired this collaboration, and it has brought about maximum development and discovery to the people. Necessary information was shared by experts within different places, and, as a result, this has forged a stronger bond that would be useful for strengthening West Africa's information and knowledge infrastructure. For the success of the group, it has experienced a strong will from professional physicians from the West African region who continue to make immense contributions toward preserving the group, with the desire to always make an impact in the medical industry. This means that the relationship forged in the political and economic trajectory extends to this aspect so that West African countries become immediately competitive in every domain.

West Africa's Involvement in International Organizations

Apart from the active involvement of West African countries in the organizations of the United Nations, starting with Liberia in 1945, there has been conscious participation of member countries from the same region whose involvement in the UN has not only been globally recognized but has also made a remarkable impact. The credibility of these nations is measured by their efforts and political decisions that have enhanced global peace and the restoration of African respect. From Nkrumah to Dr. Davidson Nicole and other ambassadors who have occupied one or another position in the organization, the commonality of their objective is reflected in their demands from the United Nations. On different occasions, their involvement has led to the invitation of the UN security arm for intervention in the secessionist agitations in Katanga (Southern DRC), which was instigated by their ex-colonial imperialists.[8] Beyond this, however, there are other international organizations that West African countries have become a decisive part of because of their growing members.

For example, the West African region has been an active player in the Organization of African Unity (OAU), formed in 1963, and later replaced by the African Union (AU) in 2002. The organization is a continental one with an international mandate geared toward repudiating colonial oppression and resuscitating Africa's dignity and image. The formation of this platform was inspired by a cringing neocolonial experience that became constant in the postcolonial African environment. It has now been commonly acknowledged that the relationship between some ex-colonies and their colonial imperialists remains the union of strange bedfellows that produces discomfort and supports maximum conflict. Such an instance can be seen in the apartheid regime in South Africa that continued long after many African countries gained independence. The result of this regime was increased racial discrimination and prejudice that remained strong in the country even though Africa had the illusion of independence.

In the 1960s and 70s, French colonies remained tied to the apron strings of their ex-colonial imperialists economically and politically. There was still dominant rule from the white minority in Rhodesia, while Portugal continued its colonial rule into 1974. It was, therefore, considered a blemish that these countries remained under the bondage of all colonial structures and faced squarely the challenges that came with them. This realization led to the creation of the OAU, which was primarily concerned with the critical engagement of the colonial institutions for their freedom. The impact of the West African countries on this cannot be overemphasized. Not only did the platform come in a timely manner, but its purpose was noble as it promoted African unification. Instead of forming a united front to combat the existential challenges that would consume them on the occasion of disunity after their independence, many African countries engaged in avoidable conflicts for dominance of regional power. However, this became an impediment to the collective growth of the people as the onerous relationship of the newly independent African countries has always been an advantage to the colonial administrators, who were always ready to exploit this to unleash their parochial interests on the countries once again. Whereas these countries needed to develop a union capable of creating a counterforce to the neocolonialists, their inability to recognize the potency of their unity served as an advantage to their international detractors.

Immediately, they were able to identify this, and they became united with the creation of the OAU and the internal efforts of West African countries to ensure the countries in the continent became respected and could pursue a common agenda using this medium. During the early periods of African independence, there were occasions of European-induced internal rivalries in Africa, which had a severe impact on their politics as a number of them were almost consumed by conflicts. As soon as many of these countries became aware of the immeasurable contributions of their erstwhile imperialists toward the unabated conflicts, they saw the reason for unity and forged it through the OAU. Several other factors, including but not limited to the increased segregation in South Africa and the diplomatic moves from Emperor Haile Selassie of Ethiopia, helped to bring about the OAU.[9]

In addition to this, several West African countries have obtained strong memberships in the Commonwealth Group. Sierra Leone, The Gambia, Nigeria, and Ghana are members of the Commonwealth Group formulated by British ex-colonies globally, and the group continues to register a compelling and resounding impact in contemporary times. Regardless of their geographical capacity, members of the union have equal rights and are given equal respect in the system. Their economic and political stature has not been used as an instrument for measuring their importance. Everyone is given an equal chance to participate and make other decisions directed toward the progress of their country, regardless of their economic standing. This union maintains that respect for human rights and the observation of democratic principles are the core tenets of their platform. If any country fails to acknowledge the importance of individual human rights, it will lose its membership and automatically fall short of the diplomatic assistance offered to countries that fall within the ambit of that forum. They generate policies that would be used as a guide for all their internal activities and convene once every two years. They constantly utilize their platform to address critical issues in member nations and those around the globe that may pose a danger to the global community.

Furthermore, there is another group called the Non-Aligned Movement (NAM), of which West African countries are active members. The group appeals to virtually all African countries, excluding South Sudan. After the group was founded in Yugoslavia in 1961,[10] it substantially contributed to the member countries by improving their political and economic status. Certain individuals were instrumental in its creation and sustenance. When Kwame Nkrumah was the President of Ghana and Sékou Touré was the President of Guinea, their personal efforts toward the creation of the platform continued to have an impact. Popular with every group, their specific focus was that the territorial integrity of all member countries is protected and that they continue to decide their political destiny without interference from foreign governments. Their philosophy is foregrounded by the support offered to member countries whenever there are ensuing challenges. The history of the platform's creation is associated with the Cold War, which pitted the West against the Soviet Communist bloc. To avoid labeling, the countries that did not play a part in this struggle formed the union, and as the name suggests, they are the ones who do not align with any of these two powers having a political score to settle. One of the cardinal functions of the platform was the reneging of every act of colonialism on member countries and the resistance to all forms of oppression.

Dependence on World Powers

Despite the commendable feats accomplished by the West African countries in the postcolonial environment, they also have areas where they depend on world powers for intervention and rescue. The reason for this is apparent—there is no particular ex-colonized country that would not require a level of freedom to establish itself completely. This is because the nature of the world in the period after colonization was altered. Globalization necessitates that people conduct different businesses either jointly or individually just so that the economy and politics of these countries can run smoothly. The need for West African countries to be interdependent on the world was more pressing, as these countries have suffered resource exploitation that weakened their economic systems and exposed them to dangerous situations that could be detrimental. This realization brings a number of ex-colonial countries in Africa to the mercy of a number of world power countries, including those in the Global North and all that qualify to be called first-world countries. For example, the World Bank established the Regional Power Trade in West Africa with the purpose of ensuring that people have access to dependable energy.[11] Still in programs, the project allows for the horizontal and vertical importation of cheaper electricity sources among countries within the region that stands to reduce costs by \$5–8 billion on an annual basis.

The reason behind this World Bank–West African integration in this respect is because of the unstable power supply that has persisted in the region for a long time, which weakens their economic system in the long run. In contemporary times, the lack of electricity results in a decline in potential investors, as they would not find the economies of these nations attractive. Not only will the investment opportunity be reduced, but the unemployment rate will remain high. Whereas the region has the potential in its rich natural resources that can translate to immediate economic and financial greatness for them, it is bewildering that they would miss out on such opportunities because of the challenges of electricity.

Efforts toward restoring this economic potential can be determined by the amount of electricity provided in the region, as that would simultaneously attract business and investments that would immediately transform the people exponentially. The World Bank is thus partnering to improve access to reliable electricity in the West African region so that it would reduce their cost of power production. With the backing of these international powers, the West Africa Power Pool (WAPP) promises to create an atmosphere where notable West African countries can possibly transmit electricity, which will create a regional power market.

Conclusion

In this chapter, we have x-rayed the relationship of West Africa with the world since the beginning of postcolonial times. Colonization and the eventual struggle for independence have inevitably educated a majority of African countries to see that the cords binding them together are far greater and stronger than the ones dividing them. From the observation that their collective economic interest is under serious threat in the absence of a unifying economic force, West African countries created the ECOWAS so that their exclusive economic systems are taken care of using policies that encourage general development. ECOWAS is charged with providing useful information for the countries within the region so that they can make proper decisions that could have maximum impact on their political and economic trajectory.

West Africa established a relationship with the European Union because of the impression that such would enable mutual benefits for the parties involved. To reinforce their collaboration and consolidate their shared advantages, the West African College of Physicians was also created with the intention of ensuring that they independently gather necessary data and information that will help improve the medical knowledge of the experts in the region, allowing them to offer expert advice to different government administrators in the region for comparative advantage. In all, postcolonial West African life has been an admixture of challenges and progress, and it is impossible to conclude that they have stopped in their quest for development, knowing how committed they have been to ensuring regional and continental integration.

DEEP DIVE

Assignment 1

Objective

The objective of this assignment is to ensure that students complete the reading of Chapter 26 and to encourage them to use Pan-Africanist ideas to understand how West African countries have united to generate relevance. Students will be expected to address the extent to which they believe these efforts have been successful.

Method

Students will be expected to write a short note in response to the question.

Reading Comprehension

How are ECOWAS, the West African College of Physicians, and the Organization of African Unity projecting the interest of West Africa?

Assignment 2

Discussion

Is it possible for postcolonial West African countries to fix and develop their economies by attempting to gain power in the same global economies that exploit them?

Objective

The objective of this assignment is for students to decide whether it is possible for West African countries to fully participate and thrive in a Western-dominated economy.

Method

Students will be expected to have a group discussion (either in person or on the online discussion forum) to talk to their peers about the discussion question. Each student would be expected to create a post and respond to at least one other student. If this were to take place in person, then it would simply be a class-wide discussion.

Notes

1 World Bank, *Sub-Saharan Africa: From Crisis to Sustainable Growth: A Long-Term Perspective Study* (Washington, DC: World Bank, 1989).
2 Jean-Marie Cour and Serge Snrech, eds. *Preparing for the Future: A Vision of West Africa in the Year 2020: West Africa Long-Term Perspective Study* (Paris: OECD Publications, 1998).
3 John English, *Does Population Growth Inevitably Lead to Land Degradation?* (Paris: Club Du Sahel, 1993).
4 English, *Does Population Growth Inevitably Lead to Land Degradation?*
5 European Commission, *Economic Partnership Agreement Between the West African States, the Economic Community of West African States (ECOWAS) and the West African Economic and Monetary Union (UEMOA), of the One Part, and the European Union and Its Member States, of the other Part* (Brussels: Council of the European Union, 2014).
6 "West African Journal of Medicine," accessed November 13, 2021, https://www.scimagojr .com/journalsearch.php?q=20854&tip=sid&clean=0.
7 "West African Journal of Medicine."
8 Office of the Historian, "27. National Security Council Report[0] NSC 6005/1 April 9, 1960: Statement of U.U. Policy Toward West Africa," accessed November 13, 2021, https://history .state.gov/historicaldocuments/frus1958-60v14/d27.
9 Office of the Historian, "27. National Security."
10 Office of the Historian, "27. National Security."
11 Office of the Historian, "27. National Security."

27

THE FUTURE OF WEST AFRICA

Introduction

West Africa comprises 16 countries in the western part of the African continent and the island country of Cape Verde. With a total population of about 500 million people, accounting for nearly 40 percent of the population of the entire African continent, West Africa is easily the most populous African subregion. Beyond these amazing facts, West Africa also has a certain additional historical significance. The region is home to Africa's most populous country (Nigeria) and Africa's oldest republic (Liberia). It is also home to Ghana, the first West African country to gain independence from European colonial powers in 1957. According to Adebayo Olukoshi, the success of Ghana's nationalist agitations, culminating in the erstwhile British colony gaining independence in 1957, inspired other countries, most notably Guinea-Conakry.[1] The citizens protested the lingering European colonial domination of their country, making Guinea-Conakry the first of all Francophone African countries to gain independence.

The Western African subregion is distinguished by tropical rainforest and savannah climatic zones. This natural phenomenon causes mosquito infestation in the region. On the bright side, however, the region has abundant natural resources, including agricultural resources such as cocoa, cotton, sorghum, sugar, millet, groundnuts, palm oil, and minerals like petroleum, dolomite, gold, iron ore, and coal. European powers were drawn to the region because of their interest in exploring and exploiting these resources, marking one of the most significant eras in the region's and continent's history.

The political history of West African colonial states is distinct from those of countries in other subregions in Africa. Historians and scholars observed that while European colonial powers in other African subregions undertook settler forms of colonialism, these colonialists did not settle in any of their colonies in West Africa. This is perhaps because of the frustration and discomfort associated with malaria outbreaks in the mosquito-infested rainforest and savannah climate regions in the subregion. Similarly, while certain countries in the eastern, northern, and southern regions of Africa engaged in

DOI: 10.4324/9781003198260-32

extensive armed conflicts to gain independence from the colonialists, there was scarcely any instance of armed struggles in anti-colonial nationalist agitations in most parts of the West African subregion. Guinea-Bissau and Cape Verde, both Lusophone countries, were the only two West African countries to participate in military liberation movements to actualize political independence. Despite the absence of armed liberation efforts in the region, anti-colonial nationalist efforts in West Africa were intense and vibrant. Educated elites in countries like Nigeria, Ghana, Liberia, and The Gambia spearheaded several national and cross-national nationalist agendas that would have long-lasting impacts on the region's political history.

The postcolonial history of West Africa portrays a subregion that has undergone a series of political upheavals and crises. Within the first decade after the independence of most West African states, the first military coup in Africa was staged in Togo, toppling a few years of democracy.[2] Following the Togolese coup d'état of 1963, a series of military incursions into politics happened in almost all West African states, such that the subregion soon gained the reputation of the coup d'état belt of the African continent.[3] While military coups have become a trend in Africa, their predominance is more apparent in West Africa. Scholars have associated prolonged military rule in West Africa with human rights abuses, poor leadership quality, corruption, and a range of political crises, including increased ethnoreligious conflicts and criminal activities.[4] The combined effect of these phenomena is the underdevelopment of the political and economic climates in respective West African states.[5] However, the most remarkable form of development that has taken place on the African continent is sociocultural development.[6] This refers

FIGURE 27.1   Sylvanus Olympio, the first president of Togo, was assassinated by military officers in the 1963 coup https://commons.wikimedia.org/wiki/File:Sylvanus _Olympio.jpg.

to the continuous change in beliefs, values, attitudes, and practices among individuals, families, groups, and communities in West Africa (Figure 27.1).

Present Trajectories of Development in West Africa

The history of West Africa is replete with evidence of its multifaceted sociocultural leanings. Foreigners and, in much later times, scholars have marveled at the remarkable diversity of the region as far back as the fifteenth century when the Portuguese landed in the region in their pioneering colonial enterprise in the Cape Verde Islands.[7] One such scholar was Jack Berry, who once commented on the unexplainable nature of linguistic diversity in the region. For Berry, "Why Africa should be the most multilingual area in the world is a challenging question which can only be answered by conjecture."[8] Another scholar, Daniel Nettle, has sought answers from ecological and other factors (trade, political organizations, and geography) to explain the linguistic diversity of the western parts of the African continent, but he found no convincing rationale for the region's diversity.[9] With over 700 distinct languages, the region is arguably one of the most diverse in the world.[10] However, the region's several hundred languages are often classified under three specific categories—the Niger-Congo group, which comprises all the Bantu languages of east and central Africa and most of the languages of West Africa; the Nilo-Saharan group comprising Songhai and Kanuri languages; and the trans-Saharan Afro-Asiatic group, a leading example of which is the Hausa language of Northern Nigeria.[11]

While linguistic diversity may be the most apparent manifestation of the diversity of West Africa, scholars have also observed instances of cultural diversity in the region's ethnic, religious, and cultural attributions. In Nigeria, for instance, there are at least 250 ethnic groups.[12] Religious diversity was more pronounced in precolonial times. Due to the expansion of Christianity from European imperial states and the rise of Islam a few centuries back, Christianity and Islam have become the two most dominant religions in the region, leaving only a minority professing religious affiliation with African traditional religions, agnosticism, atheism, and certain other less pronounced religious views.[13] The impacts of the region's cultural diversity on religious affiliations are noticeable in the distinct nature of each of the several hundred African traditional religions and their multifarious spiritual practices, beliefs, and values. Despite the breakthrough of foreigners with their proselytization of the region, cultural perspectives continue to shape the moral and religious views of the peoples of West Africa.[14]

As with every other cultural area in the world, West Africa has several symbols that either reflect the diversity of the ethnolinguistic groups in the region or some of their shared beliefs, values, and experiences. Most traditional West African communities place primacy on family institutions and respectable conduct. Children are required to show respect and discipline in their interactions with their parents and the elderly; wives should be submissive to their husbands and be meticulous in housekeeping, while older men are expected to be responsible for managing the affairs of their respective households. They are also expected to make significant contributions to their local communities and teach their sons masculine traits such as bravery, strength, responsibility, and the ability to command respect and lead others.[15] Despite the current trend of disintegration of families in Europe and the Americas, especially with adult children leaving their parents' homes in their late teenage years or early adulthood and keeping their aged parents or grandparents in nursing homes, there seems to be resistance among West Africans against this disposition.[16]

Undoubtedly, nineteenth-century West African colonialism and the rise of neocolonialism in recent decades have impacted the social and cultural life of the people of West Africa.[17] Several scholars have underlined overwhelming European and American influences on the present trajectories of sociocultural development in West Africa. Cultural symbols such as food, music, and economic and religious activities have succumbed to external influences. For instance, most cultures in West Africa were previously known for their predispositions toward starchy, tuberous foods, and seafood. In present times, however, a wider range of food choices has emerged, with rice becoming the most consumed food in the region.[18]

Regarding music and entertainment, West African countries continue to use modern technology and other tools to promote their traditional music and means of entertainment. Leading music genres such as Afropop, Afrobeat, Juju, and Fuji are a blend of traditional music forms and other genres borrowed from Europe and America.[19] Recently, the region's home-grown music genres gained international recognition, with artists such as Burna Boy, Angelique Kidjo, and Wizkid winning several accolades and gaining recognition in the United States, the United Kingdom, and a few other Western countries.[20]

Perhaps the most significant aspect of West African culture is the position of women in society. Traditionally, women are subordinate in roles, functions, and significance to the male gender.[21] The traditionalists expect wives to be respectful and submissive to their husbands and other male members of their husbands' families. Society also regards marriage as an important social institution that ought to be desired and celebrated extravagantly in the presence of the extended families of both partners and members of their immediate communities. Due to the high regard accorded to marriage and the societal expectations of women, mothers are expected to informally train their daughters on the norms, attitudes, and behaviors expected of married women. The premium placed on marriage implies that society frowns upon spinsterhood in middle age, regarding it as a sign of infertility.[22] Unfortunately, women's plight is worsened by harmful cultural practices such as female genital mutilation, widowhood rituals, and female inheritance. For instance, about 97 percent of young girls in Guinea are at risk of being subjected to genital cutting/mutilation based on the assumption that the practice would prevent them from sexual promiscuity.[23]

Due to the rise of Christianity, colonialism, and postcolonial civilization brought about by formal education, cultural exchange, and modern technology, women's positions in most West African communities have improved significantly. Contrary to premodern traditional beliefs that treat women as second-class members of society, there is now an increasing wave of women's participation in household management, sports, politics, and economic activities.[24] Despite the significant breakthroughs in improving women's social conditions and status in some parts of West Africa, there have been little to no breakthroughs in some other parts. For instance, in most parts of Northern Nigeria and other Muslim-dominated communities, there is a scant enrolment of young girls in schools. Even when educated, the level of education they get is considerably lower than that of the male gender, despite activist agendas for the promotion of girl-child education.[25] Observably, current sociocultural beliefs and attitudes in West Africa are a product of an interchange between traditional, religious, and foreign beliefs and atti-tudes, as well as the extent to which any family, community, or ethnic group has moved from traditional to modern cultural beliefs and attitudes based on education, religion, and culture.[26]

In premodern West African communities, culture had a great impact on religion, eco-nomic activities, and education. However, as present trajectories of sociocultural devel-opment suggest, there is a decades-long trend toward the deculturalization of economic, religious, and educational activities. Educational systems in West African countries have become increasingly formalized, technology-enhanced, and inclusive.[27] Major economic activities in most premodern West African communities were agriculture, fishing, and pottery. Though some of these economic activities still have major impacts on the econ-omies of modern West African states (agriculture and agro-allied business activities contributed to about 24.17 percent of Nigeria's GDP in the year 2021),[28] the economies of these modern states are becoming more varied and separate from sociocultural fac-tors.[29] There is, however, a greater deculturalization of religious activities. The modern West African person or family has a religious affiliation with any of the two dominant religions in the world, presently Islam and Christianity, with minimal attention paid to traditional religious activities.[30]

Furthermore, the present formal education system in most modern West African states is perhaps the single most significant indicator of the trajectories of sociocultural development in the region. As earlier stated, education is also a major influence on the present and future trajectories of sociocultural, political, and economic development. As Clifford Sibani observed, the development in the education systems of West African states was due mainly to cultural changes resulting from any of, or a combination of, four factors: invention, discovery, diffusion, and environment. In traditional West African societies, informal education systems such as family farming methods, home training for boys and girls, and apprenticeship prevailed. However, following colonial-ism, Christian missionaries introduced formal education based on Prussian schooling systems, and the colonial administrations later institutionalized this formalized style.[31]

Beyond cultural changes, education systems in West Africa are undergoing a techno-logical revolution. The relevance of technology in education programs in West Africa became more apparent following the outbreak of the COVID-19 pandemic, which saw the region, like other parts of the world, resort to online teaching. In an investigation conducted by René F. Kizilcec et al. on the effectiveness of mobile learning in sub-Saha-ran Africa, they found that mobile learning was an effective tool for formal and informal schooling and with equivalent or higher intensity compared to traditional schooling.[32] Another scholar noted that the continued adoption of mobile technology for teaching and learning will help reduce inequalities or non-inclusiveness in the education systems, particularly regarding persons with disabilities.[33] Notwithstanding the preceding, the adoption of mobile technology is not without some negative effects on the region's devel-opment trajectory. As Sibani pointed out, the Westernized form of technology adopted by West African education systems undermines the development of local technology in the region.

Observable facts agree that modern-day West Africa is culturally diverse. In the pre-colonial period, cultural differences dictated social and historical experiences peculiar to each ethnic group or community, but in modern times, other non-traditional cultural factors influence traditional cultural predispositions. These factors can include family traditions, ethnicity, national laws and policies, education level, and assimilation of foreign cultural practices. Hence, sociocultural development varies between families, societies, ethnic groups, and countries. Contrary to this trajectory, there is a certain degree of formalization and integration of political development in most parts of West Africa. Throughout the subregion, democratic institutions have replaced traditional kingdoms, chiefdoms, and city-states.

In a political sense, West Africa comprises 16 sovereign republics. The political organization of West African communities into republics in the present day is due to the direct influence of colonialism and certain exchanges with foreign states, particularly in Europe and the Americas. The current political map of Africa shows that the western region comprises 16 countries, namely, Mauritania, Senegal, The Gambia, Cape Verde, Guinea-Bissau, Guinea, Sierra Leone, Liberia, Côte d'Ivoire, Mali, Burkina Faso, Ghana, Togo, Benin, Niger, and Nigeria. The extent of political development that has taken place in the region within the past century reflects vividly in the nature of state formation in these countries.

Before the colonial era, the region now known as West Africa consisted of empires, kingdoms, chiefdoms, and city-states. Some of the most powerful political states in the region included the Hausa-Fulani caliphate and the Oyo Empire in present-day Nigeria, the Kanem-Borno in the areas of Northern Nigeria and Niger, the Dahomey, Benin, and Asante empires along the Gulf of Guinea. However, these monarchies have yielded political relevance and dominance to modern democratic republics in present-day West Africa. This trend, which is more or less a relic of colonial invasion and administration in Africa, has become pervasive across Africa. Of the 54 sovereign states in the continent, only three—Morocco, Lesotho, and Eswatini—are still governed by monarchs.

Despite the present trajectory of political development in the region, novel challenges confront the democratization process in the region. Between August 2020 and February 2022, armed forces staged four successful coups in three West African states—Mali, Niger, and Burkina Faso.[34] The Guinea-Bissau military initiated another coup, albeit unsuccessfully, against the country's elected government.[35] While coup leaders often claim corruption, poor leadership, and mismanagement of resources by democratic governments as motivating factors for military intervention in politics, the long history of coups d'état in the region shows that military governments also fail to deliver on their promises to reform the political and economic systems of their countries when they intervene.[36] Imposing harsh measures on countries under military dictatorships by international and regional organizations, such as the Economic Community of West Africa States (ECOWAS), also worsens the economic conditions of such countries. For instance, critics have strongly condemned ECOWAS for its sanctions against countries like Mali, Burkina Faso and Niger for their adverse consequences on the poorest class of people, who are often on the receiving end of such economic sanctions.

Most West African countries are dealing with varying degrees of political instability, democracy, and human rights issues, as well as other political issues. Notably, the surge in pro-democracy political development in West Africa, as in other regions in Africa and the world, occurred in the post–Cold War period of the 1980s and the 1990s. Political liberalization efforts commenced in Benin in 1990, when the populace took to the streets en masse to demand the holding of a sovereign national conference. The Benin National Conference of 1990 precipitated the establishment of constitutional democratic frameworks for the administration of the country's government, including the guarantee of human rights, the establishment of political parties, and the promotion of press freedom. This spark in democratization in Benin later spread to other West African countries within the next decades, with military dictatorships giving in to the establishment of democratic republics. According to a report published by the Kofi Annan Foundation, the wave of political liberalization that swept through the region during this period easily established West Africa as the de facto leading region for Africa's transition to democracy.[37]

Following the political liberalization era of the 1990s was a short-lived period of political stability, protection of human rights and liberties, peace, and security. West Africa was on the verge of collapse on several political grounds. Instances of human rights abuses, ethnolinguistic conflicts, kidnappings, and terrorism shaped the present political climate in the West African region. Some violent activities in different countries in West Africa are attributable to the Boko Haram terrorist organization, particularly in the northern region of Nigeria, where it sprung up initially.[38] Other militant groups have emerged to pursue secessionist agendas or promote radical religious views. There is the Indigenous People of Biafra (IPOB) in the southeastern region of Nigeria, protesting over the federal government's possession of oil resources in the area and clamoring for secession.[39] There are also certain jihadist organizations with cross-national terrorist and other organized criminal operations in the region. For instance, al-Murabitun conducted a terrorist attack in Bamako, Mali, in March 2015 and claimed responsibility for kidnapping a Romanian citizen in Burkina Faso two months later.[40]

Unpalatable political conditions such as election rigging and other electoral malpractices, corruption, and other economic crimes and leadership crises continue to cripple the development of democratic institutions in the region. There are still some residues of autocratic governments in West Africa. However, in present times, the region has witnessed a significant rise in democratic practices compared to about five decades ago. As Gyimah-Boadi observed, an ever-expansive network of media outlets has helped reduce the monopoly erstwhile assumed by governments in the dissemination of information and these outlets seek to promote transparency and accountability.[41] Efforts of regional organizations such as ECOWAS and the African Union (AU) have also helped to advocate the promotion of peace and security in the region.

Undoubtedly, ECOWAS is an active player in the politics of respective individual West African states. An association of 15 member states agreed to the founding of the regional organization with the signing of the Treaty of Lagos in 1975.[42] The last West African country to join the organization was Cape Verde, which became a member in 1977. However, the membership of the organization would later shrink back to 15, following the departure of Mauritania in December 2000. The founding objective was for ECOWAS to serve as a medium for political and economic cooperation between countries in the West Africa subregion. The organization has spearheaded significant developments in terms of economic performance in the region and the region's political economy, politics, peace, and security.[43]

As West Africa's leading political organization, ECOWAS has significantly contributed to political development over the years by preventing political crises that threaten peace and security in the region. Political emergencies in West Africa usually occur post-election. The greed of African leaders to hold on to power, even after losing the people's mandate to govern, is a recurring problem that has slowed the pace of political development. In 2017, ECOWAS constituted ECOMOG—ECOWAS Military Intervention in The Gambia—to coordinate Operation Restore Democracy. This operation, which extended to 2021, was to de-escalate the situation that arose in The Gambia after the incumbent President, Yahya Jammeh, disputed the victory of Adama Barrow in the 2016 presidential election.[44] In the wake of Jammeh's refusal to hand over power, The Gambia witnessed military intervention by ECOWAS. It took the ECOWAS troops' presence within the territory to maintain law and order while ensuring that the democratically elected candidate, Adama Barrow, took over the country's reins of power. This situation underscores the laudable efforts of ECOWAS in promoting democratic political development in the region.

Also, political development in the West Africa region is strengthened by the existence of the ECOWAS judicial organ.[45] It is only reasonable that a dictator-leader will frustrate justice within his territory and further deny citizens the opportunity to seek redress in court. With the establishment of the ECOWAS Court of Justice, member states can settle interstate disputes. Also, individual citizens of a member state can approach the court for redress, subject to the fulfillment of certain preliminary conditions. Since its inception in 2001, the court has served as a potent tool for checking the excesses of political leaders in West Africa.[46]

The current wave of political crises in the West African subregion portends that West African countries still have a long way to go in preserving peace and security in the region. Despite the massive efforts undertaken by ECOWAS to harmonize member states in the region, promote democracy, and guarantee greater economic performance, political uprisings in the region have continued. Decades-old democratic institutions in countries like Niger, Burkina Faso, and The Gambia suffer from the effects of military dictatorships, while other West African countries experience multiple political crises and different degrees of autocratic leadership. The efforts by ECOWAS need to be aided by other international organizations and the internal political agendas of respective member states. According to Taiwo Olaiya, the youth-led ethnic movements in ECOWAS member states are largely responsible for manipulating party politics and promoting ethnic violence in the region.[47] Hence, to completely nip the region's security challenges in the bud, these movements' concerns and agitations must be ascertained and resolved. The corruption of the political class in West African states has also been linked with political instability and economic underdevelopment.[48]

As mentioned previously, the economies of West African states in present times have become more diversified and separate from traditional sociocultural leanings. Although traditional economic activities such as farming, fishing, pottery, and painting, among others, continue to take up significant portions of the economic systems of most of these countries, other types of activities are gaining ground. Generally, there are three categories in the classification of economic activities: agriculture and natural resources, manufacturing, and services. The trend in modern states is a gradual shift from primarily agricultural and natural resources extraction economies toward manufacturing and service-based economies.

There is an observable trend in West Africa, where most West African countries are now showing significant improvements in developing their secondary (manufacturing or industries) and tertiary (services) economic sectors. Official economic statistics for the subregion suggest that the service sector has continued to dominate the economy, contributing about 42 percent to the Gross Domestic Product (GDP) since the 2000s. Agriculture, which provides the largest share of the region's labor force (60 percent), contributes about 36 percent to the region's GDP, while the industrial sector trails last with only about 22 percent. This contrasts sharply with West African countries' high dependence on agriculture and manufacturing a few decades ago.[49]

One of the most noticeable features of advanced economies is their reliance on service industries and manufacturing as opposed to mining and agriculture. Service industries often account for the highest share in terms of GDP and employment in most of these developed countries.[50] This is an observable trend in high-income countries such as the United States, the United Kingdom, France, Germany, Japan, and Canada, and emerging economies such as China, India, and South Africa, among others. Thus, the growth of the manufacturing and service sectors in West Africa portends massive growth opportunities in the economies of respective West African states. As recorded by the African Development Bank Group, the progressive growth in the region's total economy for the last decade shows an annual average growth rate of about 3.3 percent in 2018 alone. Domestic growth statistics varied significantly between as low as 1.9 percent for the region's economic giant, Nigeria, and as high as 7 percent for Côte d'Ivoire, Ghana, and Guinea. The total gross domestic product for the region is about US$700 billion, with Nigeria, the most populous and largest economy, accounting for nearly two-thirds of the GDP. West Africa's GDP accounts for nearly one-third of Africa's entire GDP. However, the region's economic growth is considerably below global expectations and trends in other developing countries outside of Africa, particularly in Latin America.[51]

The economy of West Africa has been thriving in the last few decades. However, the rate of development is not adequate to prepare the region to compete in the global markets. Some authors have linked the low economic performance of most West African countries to a low level of exploration and poor utilization of natural resources, overdependence on a single or few resources, public corruption, political crises, and the aftereffects of colonial exploitation. Understandably, these are phenomena that are general to the African continent. On the bright side, most West African countries are charting the path toward robust economic growth in the next few decades. For instance, the government of Nigeria has been working on reducing the country's overdependence on the oil sector, a factor responsible for the country's volatile inflationary trends.[52] Regional and international organizations such as the ECOWAS, West Africa Economic and Monetary Union, and the World Bank are collaborating with economies in the regions to promote trade development and business growth, with programs such as Trade Facilitation West Africa, and West Africa Trade and Investment Hub.[53] Hence, the region has recorded increased foreign direct investments within the last decades, especially in its financial technology services industry.

Several scholars have ascribed the economic growth of the West African subregion to the activities of ECOWAS. As the leading international organization in West Africa, ECOWAS is charged with the responsibility of fostering political and economic cooperation. Since its inception, ECOWAS has fostered smooth interstate economic activity, especially between the Anglophone and Francophone countries. To ease the burden of doing business, ECOWAS is equally addressing road network issues.[54] Hence, it has embarked on road construction to connect some major cities. Also, one of ECOWAS significant efforts in promoting economic development in the region is the free movement of products and people supported by the reception of the ECOWAS biometric identity card, which facilitates mobility and advanced security in the region.[55]

ECOWAS' most important endeavor is its attempt toward regional economic integration of its member states. At the signing of the Treaty of Lagos that established ECOWAS by the 15 founding member states, political cohesion, economic cooperation and integration of member states were clearly outlined as objectives of the organization. However, while the organization has been making significant breakthroughs in political cohesion and economic cooperation, there is still much to be achieved in terms of economic integration. Scholars, critics, and policymakers have been particularly interested in the economic integration objectives of the organization. Jakob Hegel and Marie-Agnès Jouanjean, in their research on the activities of ECOWAS, linked several political and economic factors constraining the organization's economic integration process.[56] The political and economic constraints identified by the authors include structural and foundational factors, formal and informal institutions, actors and agencies, sector characteristics, and the involvement or noninvolvement of regional and international drivers.

Without a doubt, the West African subregion possesses abundant natural wealth. With vast deposits of agricultural resources such as cocoa, palm oil, groundnuts, sugar, and minerals such as natural gas, bitumen, petroleum, gold, and dolomite, the region has sufficient wealth to provide an economic environment that will guarantee the prosperity of the majority of Africans. The abundant natural wealth of the region, nonetheless, is still home to one of the highest numbers of poverty-stricken classes of people in the world. Although some scholars and critics have traced this tendency to a general phenomenon in Africa,[57] it is pertinent to state that West African nations are more privileged than some other regions in the African continent due to the combined efforts of government policies, ECOWAS and other regional and international organizations that have developed an interest in the region. However, as one of the most ethnolinguistic subregions in the world, West Africa is still encumbered by ethnic-based violence, sabotage of natural resources, public corruption, and military coups. These political challenges have hindered not only the political development but also the economic advancement of the region.

Future Projections of Development in West Africa

Since there are no generally accepted and scientifically accurate methods of analyzing future developmental trajectories, the breadth of the research work done in this part of the chapter will focus on the general perspectives of scholars, analysts, critics, and other authors on possibilities. The three main development areas that present West Africa's trajectories were examined in the preceding section—political landscape, economy, and social culture—and will be considered again in this section. As observed from the thought-provoking article by Olukoshi, there are opposing views on the possible development trajectories in West Africa. Olukoshi notes that on the polar sides of the debate on the region's development are pessimists and optimists.[58] Robert Kaplan's 1994 work, *The Coming Anarchy*, loudly echoes the pessimists' view. This view holds that the region's present trajectories of development suggest a retrogression that may stretch into the distant future.[59] Then there are the optimistic analysts, who suggest that there are abundant opportunities for growth in the region and that present endeavors, however minimal, suggest a trend to maximize these growth opportunities in the near future.

While they may have different views on the future of West Africa, almost all scholars and analysts who have considered the future trajectories of development in West Africa often consider them in the three fundamental aspects of development: political landscape, economy, and social culture. However, when stratified along the polar sides of pessimism and optimism, it is difficult to say whether the views of these authors cover all the three aspects. Notably, while national laws and policies can predetermine the political economy, the overall growth of any economy will depend on the productivity of its population, and social culture is determined informally by the majority of the population. As a result, it is important to consider the future projections of development in the subregion along each of the major aspects of development.

In this chapter, upon a review of a breadth of literature, analytic reports, and other works, it seems rather profound to take a mediating approach to the question of the future of development in Africa. Thus, in subsequent paragraphs, there is a synthesis of the research and analyses conducted by a plethora of authors on the future trajectories of development in the political arena, economy, and social culture, allowing for a multidimensional viewpoints.

The aspect of development that has garnered the most attention from scholars, analysts, and critics is the political economy. Olukoshi has suggested that, as far back as the 1990s, the subject of the future of the political economy of the West African subregion has sparked significant interest among scholars across different fields. In his widely cited 1994 article, Robert Kaplan pioneers the pessimistic orientation of the subregion:

> West Africa is becoming the symbol of worldwide demographic, environmental, and societal stress ... Disease, overpopulation, unprovoked crime, scarcity of resources, refugee migrations, the increasing erosion of nation-states and international borders, and the empowerment of private armies, security firms, and international drug cartels are now most tellingly demonstrated through a West African prism.[60]

Nearly three decades after this article was published, the lamented politico-economic challenges continue to confront the region. Despite these challenges, some other authors, mostly of West African origin, have suggested progressive trajectories of development.[61]

Among the breadth of literature evaluated for this research, two works predicate their theses on the political economy of the West African subregion, "West Africa's Political Economy in the Next Millennium" by Adebayo Olukoshi and *Preparing for the Future: A Vision of West Africa in the Year 2020* edited by Jean-Marie Cour and Serge Snrech. Although both research works are outdated, they lay a foundation for research, analysis, and thought for subsequent works. Meanwhile, we find certain challenges and opportunities in the African continent, which are experienced to a greater degree in the West African subregion, in a variety of works on the political economy of Africa. Hence, due to the lack of sufficient recent literature on the trajectories of political-economic development in West Africa, we rely on both past literature, specifically on West Africa, and present literature on the African political economy. We find the former equally valuable since a majority of the projections made in past literature are yet to be reached.

There are overwhelmingly optimistic views about the future of the African political economy. Most of the authors who hold this view believe that the most significant growth in the continent will be recorded by the eastern and western subregions. This perspective is likely based on East Africa's current growth trajectory, which is the highest in the continent, as well as the abundance of untapped natural, human, and technological opportunities in West Africa that present trajectories suggest are taking significant leaps in overall involvement in the region. In their review of economic progressions in Africa, Acha Leke and Dominic Barton observed three trends that may suggest faster growth in the next few decades. The first trend is the continent's young labor force. Secondly, there are immense opportunities for urbanization in most parts of Africa, and as urbanization increases, there are prospects for increased economic activities. Thirdly, there are rapid technological developments in Africa, and while they may not match the level of development in advanced economies, African economies are well-positioned to benefit from growth opportunities offered by new technology ventures.[62]

The economic outlook for the African region portrays a mixed picture of the future,[63] and many factors may be responsible for this. For one, the present development trajectories take different turns across different countries and subregions in the continent. Thus, it is difficult to suggest a trajectory that will dominate in the future. Also, whether the future of the economy of Africa as a whole or West Africa as a subregion will be progressive or regressive requires drastic action by governments on the continent, and it is yet unclear whether political leaders in respective African countries will muster the political will to lead the economies of their respective countries toward the projected future destination. Also, the recent outbreak of the COVID-19 pandemic, riots, and political violence in Africa (and West Africa in particular) have suggested that even with the political will and cross-national political actions, the trajectories of development may take unexpected turns because of crises and unprecedented events. Thus, while different analysts have suggested skyrocketing growth rates for Africa's poor $1.2 billion GDP, it is important to note that the rate of growth on the continent will depend on the interplay of some factors, a few of which present conflicting views.

A majority of scholars, analysts, and authors who present an optimistic view of the future of Africa's economy also rely on the changing economic structures on the continent. As mentioned in the previous part of this chapter, while advanced economies rely on secondary and tertiary economic structures, namely industry and services, most underdeveloped economies, West African economies inclusive, rely on the primary economic structures of agriculture and mining natural resources. Despite its overdependence on primary economic structures, West Africa has not fully developed its agricultural and mining sectors. In a 2015 report by the United Nations' Food and Agriculture Organization and the African Development Bank on agricultural growth in West Africa, they opined that there are immense global opportunities for agricultural products from emerging markets, which West Africa, whose economy is largely based on agricultural and extractive resources, can provide.[64] Similarly, while natural resources are abundant in West Africa, most of the countries in the region have yet to explore and exploit a vast deposit of these resources.[65]

Aside from the agricultural and mining sectors, which are predicted to contribute significantly to the GDP and overall economic growth in West Africa, one other economic sector that may have the largest impact is the digital economy. Africa is undergoing one of the most massive technological transformations in its history, especially with the growth of financial technology and digital economies on the continent. Although East Africa has had the largest growth in the sector in recent times,[66] it is safe to conclude that the West African region may have a robust digital economy soon, considering the growing technological consumer base in the latter[67] and its place as one of the largest digital economies in Africa. In a research article by Edna Solomon and Aaron Klyton, they established that digitalization leads to economic growth.[68] The prospects of economic growth championed by digitalization will be significant in West Africa, where there is presently greater dependence on the informal sectors of the economy.

Although some scholars have hailed the advent and growth of digital technology in West Africa as springboards to promote economic growth in the region, some also predicted that its impacts on another aspect of development, the social culture, will be negative. As far back as 1998, scholars had raised questions about foreign contacts in West Africa and the impacts of such contacts on cultural change in the region.[69] As explained in the previous part of this chapter, the effects of culture on technology in West Africa can be observed in the present transformations of the region's music, dress, and family life, among others. Digital technology has been responsible for some of the most significant cultural changes in the region. According to Abanyam, digital technology exposes young children to adult issues, violence, and other social issues that are immoral and contrary to African cultural values.[70] Scholars have also suggested that without intervention, the importation of Western culture through digital technology will displace beneficial local customs and values.[71] The rising rape and violence culture among teens in several West African countries is a direct consequence of the waning effects of local cultural values due to the pervasive influence of Western technology.[72] Thus, while the future of West Africa's economy may look bright, there are gloomy forecasts of its sociocultural climate.

As mentioned earlier, there are many political challenges militating against most West African countries, chief among which are transnational insurgencies in the region. Expectedly, the activities of insurgent groups such as Boko Haram in Nigeria and Al-Murabitun in Mali, and the Islamic State in West Africa, parts of Nigeria and the Sahel, have posed serious threats to peace and security in the region. However, what certain scholars have reckoned as perhaps the most debilitating political challenge in Africa's future is the rise of coups in West Africa and its threats to democracy, good governance, and human rights. With terrorism confronting peace and security on the one hand, and military coups interfering with democracy, on the other hand, it is difficult to paint a bright picture of the subregion's political landscape or even its economy. As scholars have observed in many research works, where political crises are not squarely addressed, all sectors and structures of national development suffer immensely.[73] Even with a full democracy devoid of terrorist activities and political crises, the political landscapes of most West African states will still require deliberate action to reach expected levels of development. The current prevalence of corruption, bureaucracy, and non-inclusiveness of political structures undermine a prospective bright political climate in

West Africa.[74] Therefore, individual countries in the region must draw up action plans to combat these challenges.

As we round up the discussion on the present trajectories and future projections of development in West Africa, it is important to mention climate change, a global issue that has become drastically important to the West African subregion and the entire African continent. The United Nations has defined climate change as changing patterns in temperature and weather conditions.[75] Currently, climate change is one of the important global issues, garnering the serious attention of scholars, policymakers, and well-informed ordinary people. Different regions of the world are already observing the effects of climate change, West Africa included. According to Sylla et al., the West African climate has been changing in recent decades due to high anthropogenic greenhouse gas (GHG).[76] Without deliberate action by policymakers in individual countries and international organizations, researchers have suggested that climate change will threaten agricultural yield in West Africa.[77] Whereas reduced agricultural yield may seem a tough and immediate consequence of climate change, its long-term effects may be adverse. It could bring about adverse conditions like drought, resulting in hunger and poverty and the unsustainability of life on the planet.

Conclusion

Undoubtedly, West Africa has immense growth opportunities, but reaching the bright prospective future envisaged for the subregion requires policymaking and drastic action. On the bright side, the social culture of the region is already changing, helping to promote globalization and eliminate harmful traditional practices in the region; on the flip side, however, introducing Western culture and technology has led to the suppression of moral values. The region's economy is also becoming gradually digitalized, and with immense opportunities for both the primary and secondary sectors of the economy, the future may present vast economic opportunities for West Africa. However, the most worrisome issues in the subregion are the rise of terrorism, political crises, and military coups, all of which pose significant threats to democracy.

Therefore, to lead their respective countries to their projected future destinations, political leaders and policymakers in respective West African states need to formulate and enforce policies that will promote the diversification of their economies, encourage entrepreneurship and innovation, allow rising digital economies to flourish, and maximize the potentials of their young populations through human development. Crucially, governments in the subregion must address political crises and establish effective institutions to curtail corruption and promote inclusive and responsible governance. Finally, it is pertinent that West Africa joins the global discourse on climate change and takes drastic actions as other global actors are doing.[78] Otherwise, there may not be West Africa, Africa, or even planet Earth in the next millennium, should the adverse effects of climate change take their toll on the region and the world.

DEEP DIVE

Assignment 1

Objective

The objective of this assignment is to ensure that students complete the reading of Chapter 27 and to encourage them to have a strong grasp of West Africa's historical trajectory before colonial rule. They also need to show a significant level of knowledge about the process that created West Africa's steady progress and decline since independence in the 1950s and 1960s.

Method

Students will be expected to write a short note in response to the question.

Reading Comprehension

What are some areas of West Africa's present trajectories of development?

Assignment 2

Objective

The objective of this assignment is to ensure that students complete the reading of Chapter 27 and to encourage them to examine how ECOWAS has promoted the art of governance, leadership, and economic security in West Africa.

Method

Students will be expected to write a short note in response to the question.

Reading Comprehension

What role can digital technology play in driving West Africa's technological developmental trajectory? How can the problems posed by climate change be addressed as West Africa takes the path of industrialization?

Notes

1 Adebayo Olukoshi, "West Africa's Political Economy in the Next Millennium: Retrospect and Prospect," Senegal: CODESRIA Monograph Series, (2001): 1–33.
2 Samuel Decalo, "Military Coups and Military Regimes in Africa," *The Journal of Modern African Studies* 11, no. 1 (1973): 105–127.
3 Samuel Decalo, *Coups and Army Rule in Africa: Motivations & Constraint* (New Haven: Yale University Press, 1990).
4 Carlson Anyangwe, *Revolutionary Overthrow of Constitutional Orders in Africa* (Bamenda: Langaa RPCIG, 2012).
5 Patrick J. McGowan, "African Military Coups D'état, 1956–2001: Frequency, Trends and Distribution," *The Journal of Modern African Studies* 41, no. 3 (2003): 339–370.

6 Emmanuel Akyeampong, ed. *Themes in West Africa's History* (Oxford: James Currey 2006).

7 Trevor Paul Hall, "The Role of Cape Verde Islanders in Organizing and Operating Maritim Trade Between West Africa and Iberian Territories," Ph.D. diss., The John Hopkins University 1993.

8 Jack Berry, "Language Systems and Literature," in *The African Experience* 2, eds. John N Paden and E. W. Soja (London: Heinemann Education, 1970), 80–88.

9 Daniel Nettle, "Language Diversity in West Africa: An Ecological Approach," *Journal o Anthropological Archaeology* 15, no. 4 (1996): 403–438.

10 Christopher Moseley and Ronald E. Ashley, *Atlas of the World's Languages* (London Routledge, 1994).

11 Nettle, "Language Diversity in West Africa," 404.

12 Richard Bourne, *Nigeria: A New History of a Turbulent Century* (London: Zed Books 2015).

13 Hyacinth Kalu, *Together as One: Interfaith Relationships Between African Traditiona Religion, Islam, and Christianity in Nigeria* (Indiana: iUniverse, 2011).

14 Dare Arowolo, "The Effects of Western Civilization and Culture on Africa," *Afro Asia Journal of Social Sciences* 1, no. 1 (2010): 1–13.

15 Nathaniel A. Fadipẹ, *The Sociology of the Yoruba* (Ibadan: Ibadan University Press, 1970).

16 June Ellis, *West African Families in Britain: A Meeting of Two Cultures* (London: Routledg and Kegan Paul Ltd., 1978).

17 Alfred Abioseh Jarrett, *The Under-development of Africa: Colonialism, Neo-colonialism and Socialism* (London: University Press of America, 1996).

18 Franck Cachia, "Changes in Food Diets in West Africa and their Implications for Domesti Producers," *Stateco* 110 (2016): 53–70.

19 Oluwafunminiyi Raheem, "From the Sublime to the Ridiculous?: Contemporary Nigeria Hip-Hop, Music Consumption and the Search for Meaning (1999–2015)," in *Yoruba Arts Culture, Entertainment & Tourism in the Age of Globalization & Uncertainty*, eds. Feli Ayoh'Omidire, Shina Alimi and Akin Adejuwon (Ile-Ife: Institute of Cultural Studies, OAU 2020), 42–63.

20 Arowolo, "The Effects of Western Civilization," 1–13.

21 Oluwafunminiyi Raheem, "UN Women and the Pitfalls of Gender Equality and Representatio in Nigeria," in *Negotiating Patriarchy and Gender in Africa: Discourses, Practices and Policies*, eds. Egodi Uchendu and Ngozi Edeagu (Lanham: Lexington Books, 2021), 257–272

22 Rozenn Hotte, "Marriage and Wife Welfare in West Africa," Ph.D. diss., Université Pari Sciences et Lettres, 2019.

23 Mamadou Dioulde Balde, Sarah O'Neill, Alpha Oumar Sall, Mamadou Bailo Balde, Anne Marie Soumah, Boubacar Alpha Diallo, and Christina Catherine Pallitto, "Attitudes of Health Care Providers Regarding Female Genital Mutilation and its Medicalization in Guinea," *PLoS One* 16, no. 5 (2021): 1–18.

24 Beniamino Cislaghi, "The Story of the 'Now-Women': Changing Gender Norms in Rura West Africa," *Development in Practice* 28, no. 2 (2018): 257–268.

25 Grace Nmadu, Solomon Avidime, Olugbenga Oguntunde, Vehcit Dashe, Binta Abdulkarim and Mairo Mandara, "Girl Child Education: Rising to the Challenge," *African Journal o Reproductive Health* 14, no. 3 (2010): 107–112.

26 Arowolo, "The Effects of Western Civilization," 1–13.

27 Clifford Meesua Sibani, "Impact of Western Culture on Traditional African Society: Problems and Prospects," *Journal of Religion and Human Relations* 10, no. 1 (2018): 56–72.

28 National Bureau of Statistics, "National Gross Domestic Product Q4 2021," accessed April 2, 2022, https://nigerianstat.gov.ng/elibrary?queries=GDP%202021.

29 Sibani, "Impact of Western Culture," 56–72.

30 Andrew McKinnon, "Christians, Muslims and Traditional Worshippers in Nigeria: Estimating the Relative Proportions from Eleven Nationally Representative Social Surveys," *Review o Religious Research* 63 (2021): 303–315.

31 Romain Tiquet, "Education through Labor: From the Deuxième Portion du Contingent to the Youth Civic Service in West Africa (Senegal/Mali, 1920s–1960s)," in *Education and Development in Colonial and Postcolonial Africa: Policies, Paradigms, and Entanglements*,

1890s–1980s, eds. Damiano Matasci, Miguel Bandeira, Jerónimo Hugo and Gonçalves Dores (Cham: Palgrave Macmillan, 2020), 83–105.

32 René F. Kizilcec, Maximillian Chen, Kaja K. Jasińska, Michael Madaio and Amy Ogan, "Mobile Learning During School Disruptions in Sub-Saharan Africa," *AERA Open* 7, no. 1 (2021): 1–18.

33 Damian Maher and Kristy Young, "The Use of Mobile Devices to Support Young People with Disabilities," in *Advances in Communications and Media Research*, ed. Anthony V. Stavros (New York: Nova Science Publishers, 2017), 101–125.

34 Emmanuel Akinwotu, "Contagious Coups: What is Fuelling Military Takeovers across West Africa?" *The Guardian*, February 7, 2020.

35 Elliot Smith, "West Africa's Political System could see 'Complete Shakeup' as Coups Spike," *CNBC*, February 10, 2022, accessed April 10, 2022, https://www.cnbc.com/2022/02/10/west-africas-political-system-could-see-complete-shakeup-as-coups-spike.html.

36 William Gutteridge, "The Military in African Politics: Success or Failure?" *Journal of Contemporary African Studies* 1, no. 2 (1982): 241–252.

37 Emmanuel Gyimah-Boadi, *Democratic Backsliding in West Africa: Nature, Causes, Remedies* (Geneva: Kofi Annan Foundation, 2021).

38 United Nations Office on Drugs and Crime, *Transnational Organised Crime in the West African Region* (New York: United Nations, 2005).

39 Charles E. Ekpo and Cletus A. Agorye, "A (Un)just and (Un)holy War? The Theme of Imagery and Symbolism in the IPOB Secessionist Struggle," *International Journal in Management and Social Science* 6, no. 6 (2018): 28–55.

40 Office of the Director of National Intelligence, "Terrorism in North and West Africa," *Counter Terrorism Guide*, https://www.dni.gov/nctc/groups/north_and_west_africa.html.

41 Gyimah-Boadi, *Democratic Backsliding*, 6.

42 Francis Etim Nyong, "Nigeria and ECOWAS: The Prospects for Nigeria's Role in ECOWAS: Objectives, Opportunities, Leadership and Policies," Ph.D. diss., Claremont Graduate School, 1983.

43 Emmanuel Balogun, *Region-building in West Africa: Convergence and Agency in ECOWAS* (New York: Routledge, 2022).

44 Ismaila Ceesay, *The Role of the Regional Forces in Gambia and what their Presence will Mean in 2021 Elections* (Dakar-Fann: Friedrich-Ebert-Stiftung Peace and Security Centre of Competence Sub-Saharan Africa, 2020), 1–3.

45 Adewale Banjo, "The ECOWAS Court and the Politics of Access Justice in West Africa," *Africa Development* 32, no. 1 (2007): 69–87.

46 Frederick Cowell, "The Impact of the ECOWAS Protocol on Good Governance and Democracy," *African Journal of International and Comparative Law* 19, no. 2 (2011): 331–342.

47 Taiwo Olaiya, "Youth and Ethnic Movements and their Impacts on Party Politics in ECOWAS Member States," *SAGE Open* 4, no. 1 (2014): 1–12.

48 Nurudeen Abu, Mohd Zaini Abd Karim, and Mukhriz Izraf Azman Aziz, "Corruption, Political Instability and Economic Development in the Economic Community of West African States (ECOWAS): Is there a Causal Relationship?" *Contemporary Economics* 9, no. 11 (2015): 45–60.

49 African Development Bank Group, *West African Economic Outlook*, AFDB, https://www.afdb.org/fileadmin/uploads/afdb/Documents/Publications/2019AEO/REO_2019_-_West_africa.pdf.

50 Juan R. Cuadrado-Roura, "Service Industries and Regional Analysis: New Directions and Challenges," *Investigaciones Regionales – Journal of Regional Research*, no. 36 (2016): 107–127.

51 African Development Bank Group, *West African Economic Outlook*.

52 Ngozi Okonjo-Iweala and Philip Osafo-Kwaako, *Nigeria's Economic Reforms: Progress and Challenges* (Washington, DC: Brookings Global Economy & Development, 2007).

53 United States Agency for International Development, "Economic Growth and Trade," https://www.usaid.gov/west-africa-regiona/economic-growth-and-trade, *USAID*, April 3, 2019, http://www.efaidnbmnnnibpcajpcglclefindmkaj/https://www.afdb.org/fileadmin/uploads/afdb/Documents/Publications/2019AEO/REO_2019_-_West_africa.pdf.

54 Robin Carruthers, Ranga Rajan Krishnamani and Siobhan Murray, *Improving Connectivity: Investing in Transport Infrastructure in Sub-Saharan Africa* (Washington, DC: World Bank AICD Background Paper 7, 2009).

55 Franca Attoh and Ebenezer Ishola, "Migration and Regional Cooperation for Development: ECOWAS in Perspective," *Africa Review* 13, no. 2 (2021): 139–154.

56 Jakob Engel and Marie-Agnès Jouanjean, "Political and Economic Constraints to the ECOWAS Regional Economic Integration Process and Opportunities for Donor Engagement," *EPS Peaks*, February 2015, http://www.efaidnbmnnnibpcajpcglclefindmkaj/https://assets.publishing.service.gov.uk/media/57a08997e5274a31e000017a/Political_and_Economic_Constraints_to_the_ECOWAS.pdf.

57 Greg Mills, *Why Africa is Poor: And What Africans Can Do About It* (South Africa: Penguin Books, 2011).

58 Olukoshi, "West Africa's Political Economy," 1–33.

59 Robert Kaplan, "The Coming Anarchy," *The Atlantic*, February 1, 1994, https://www.theatlantic.com/magazine/archive/1994/02/the-coming-anarchy/304670/.

60 Kaplan, "The Coming Anarchy."

61 Jean-Marie Cour and Serge Snrech, eds. *Preparing for the Future: A Vision of West Africa in the Year 2020* (Paris: Organization for Economic Co-operation and Development, 1998).

62 Acha Leke and Dominic Barton, "3 Reasons things are Looking up for African Economies," *World Economic Forum*, May 5, 2016, https://www.weforum.org/agenda/2016/05/what-s-the-future-of-economic-growth-in-africa on April 20, 2022.

63 International Monetary Fund, *Regional Economic Outlook: Sub-Saharan Africa* (Washington: IMF Publication Services, 2021).

64 Frank Hollinger and John M. Staatz, *Agricultural Growth in West Africa* (Rome: Food and Agriculture Organization and African Development Bank, 2015).

65 Hammed Oluwaseyi Musibau, Waliu Olawale Shittu and Maria Yanotti, "Natural Resources Endowment: What More Does West Africa Need in Order to Grow?" *Resources Policy* 7 (2022): 102669.

66 Priya Sippy, "Digital Platforms are Disrupting East Africa's Traditional Gig Industries," *Tech Cabal*, October 21, 2021, https://techcabal.com/2021/10/21/digital-platforms-are-disrupting-east-africas-traditional-gig-industries/.

67 Titilayo Adewumi, "Through the Looking Glass: An Optimist's View of West Africa's Ten-Year Prospects," *The Guardian*, June 15, 2021.

68 Edna Solomon and Aaron Klyton, "The Impact of Digital Technology Usage on Economic Growth in Africa," *Utilities Policy* 67 (2020): 1–12.

69 Christopher R. DeCorse, "The Europeans in West Africa: Culture Contact, Continuity and Change," in *Transformations in Africa: Essays on Africa's Later Past*, ed. Graham Connah (London: Cassells, 1998), 219–244.

70 Noah Lumun Abanyam, "The Effects of Western Technology on African Cultural Values," *IOSR Journal of Humanities and Social Science (IOSR-JHSS)* 8, no. 4 (2013): 26–28.

71 Kehinde Olatunji, "Don Says Western Culture Infiltrating Africa through Technology, Seeks Intervention," *The Guardian*, March 17, 2022.

72 Damilola Ogunsakin, "Chrisland Scandal: Social Media goes Haywire with Minors' S3x Videos," *Vanguard*, April 19, 2022.

73 Alhaji Ahmadu Ibrahim and Lawan Cheri, "Democracy, Political Instability and the African Crisis of Underdevelopment," *Journal of Power, Politics & Governance* 1, no. 1 (2013): 59–67.

74 Joseph Nye, "Corruption and Political Development: A Cost-Benefit Analysis," *American Political Science Review* 61, no. 2 (1967): 417–427.

75 United Nations Organisation, "Climate Change," *United Nations*, https://www.un.org/en/climatechange/what-is-climate-change.

76 Mouhamadou Bamba Sylla, Pinghouinde Michel Nikiema, Peter Gibba, Ibourahima Kebe and Nana Ama Browne Klutse, "Climate Change over West Africa: Recent Trends and Future Projections," in *Adaptation to Climate Change and Variability in Rural West Africa*, eds. Joseph A. Yaro and Jan Hesselberg (Chams: Springer, 2016), 25–40.

77 Benjamin Sultan and Marco Gaetani, "Agriculture in West Africa in the Twenty-First Century: Climate Change and Impact Scenarios, and Potential for Adaptation," *Frontiers in Plant Science* 7 (2016): 1262.
78 Walter Leal Filho, Belay Simane, Jokasha Kalangu, Menas Wuta, Pantaleo Munishi, and Kumbirai Musiyiwa, eds., *Climate Change Adaptation in Africa: Fostering Resilience and Capacity to Adapt* (Cham: Springer, 2017).

WEST AFRICA TIMELINE

Date	Events
200,000 BC	Homo erectus, the predecessor of Homo sapiens, occupies much of West Africa, as suggested by the tools and other artefacts found in Senegal, Guinea, Mali, Mauritania, and elsewhere.
5000 BC	The Sahara begins to become a desert. Most of West Africa's people forsake transient life and settle around waterholes, begin to rely on agriculture, and start to move south.
2000 BC	Africa south of the equatorial forests is largely inhabited by the Khoisan, of whom the San and the Hottentots are the modern survivors.
500 BC	Nok terracotta figures, found in modern Nigeria, stand at the beginning of the rich tradition of African sculpture.
450 BC	The appearance of ironworking in central Nigeria enables the clearing of forests, which expands agricultural land and commences the process of denuding West Africa's landscape.
300 BC	Jenné-Jeno is founded in what is now Mali and is recognized as West Africa's first-known urban settlement. By CE 800, Jenné-Jeno is home to an estimated 27,000 people.
AD 300	The Empire of Ghana is founded in what is now the Western Sahel. As the first of the great West African empires, it holds sway over the region for 800 years.
900	Islam first reaches the Sahel, almost 250 years after it crossed the Sahara. It arrives as part of the trans-Saharan caravan trade and later becomes West Africa's predominant religion.
Around 1000	Timbuktu is founded, near where the Niger River enters the Sahara, as a seasonal encampment for Tuareg nomads. It later becomes a great center of scholarship and wealth and home to 100,000 people.
1050	Ife emerges as a powerful kingdom in the equatorial forest of the lower Niger.

DOI: 10.4324/9781003198260-33

Date	Events
Late 11th century	One of West Africa's Sahelian kingdoms is overthrown by armies crossing the Sahara, as Berber armies destroy the Empire of Ghana.
1200	Terracotta heads and figures are buried in graves in the region of Djenné in modern Mali.
1240	Sundiata Keita founds the Empire of Mali with its capital at Niani. The empire rules the Sahel for two centuries and presides over West Africa's golden age.
1250	The Yoruba people of Ife create extraordinary sculptures in brass.
1351	Ibn Battuta leaves Fez to cross the Sahara, whereafter he travels extensively throughout the Empire of Mali. His later book is one of the earliest accounts of life in the region.
1375	Mali's King Kankan Musa is depicted on a 1375 European map of Africa holding a gold nugget. The caption reads: "So abundant is the gold found in his country that he is the richest and most noble king in all the land."
1390	The Kingdom of Kongo, one of West and Central Africa's most successful kingdoms, is founded, with its sphere of influence extending across the Congo River basin.
1434	Portuguese ships become the first to round Cape Bojador in almost two millennia, beginning the era of European trade along West Africa's coast. Nine years later, they reach the Senegal River.
1446	Portugal claims ownership of the region of Guinea, which subsequently became the center of their slave trade on the West African coast.
1450	A warrior king, Ewuare, establishes the forest kingdom of Benin.
1466	The Portuguese settlers on the Cape Verde islands are granted a monopoly on the new slave trade.
1480	An increase in trade through the Central Sahara benefits the Songhay, with their capital at Gao, at the expense of Mali.
1482	Portugal constructs the first European structure on West African soil, the warehouse fortress of Sao Jorge de la Mina in what is now Ghana, symbolizing increasingly prosperous trade between Portugal and West Africa.
1492	A French privateer off the west coast of Ghana is the first to plunder a Portuguese vessel carrying home African gold.
1500	The people of Benin begin a lasting tradition of sculpture in brass, melted down from objects brought by traders.
Late 15th century	The Kingdom of Benin helps Portugal to capture and export enslaved people, transforming human trafficking from a small-scale African concern to a much larger global trade.
1512	Leo Africanus visits West Africa and writes that "The rich king of Tombuto keeps a splendid and well-furnished court ... a great store of doctors, judges, priests and other learned men, that are bountifully maintained at the king's expense."
1550	Africans, bought in the Portuguese trading posts of West Africa, are shipped across the Atlantic as slaves.
1570	The Asante establish a powerful kingdom in present-day Ghana, with their capital at Kumasi.
1591	The Empire of Songhai, the last and most extensive of the Sahel's empires, falls to al-Mansur, ruler of Marrakesh, who seizes the Songhai political capital, Gao, and its commercial and cultural capital, Timbuktu.

Date	Events
1600	The Yoruba develop an extensive empire centered on Oyo in southern Nigeria.
1625	Three brothers among the Dahomey people establish a long-lasting kingdom in the Bight of Benin.
1638	The French build a trading station on the estuary of the Senegal River in West Africa.
1659	The British find a base at the mouth of the Gambia River.
1770	The triangular trade, controlled from Liverpool, ships millions of Africans across the Atlantic as slaves.
1787	A British ship lands a party of freed slaves as the first modern settlers in Sierra Leone, on the west coast of Africa.
1795	Mungo Park sets off on his first expedition to explore the Niger on behalf of the African Association.
1796	The Scottish explorer, Mungo Park, arrives at the Niger River near Ségou and solves one of the great unanswered questions Europeans had of African geography: the Niger flows east, not west.
1804	Sokoto Jihad is carried out by Uthman Dan Fodio.
1808	The British government uses Freetown, in Sierra Leone, as a base in the fight against the slave trade.
1809	The Fulani establish a capital at Sokoto, from where they dominate the Hausa kingdoms of northern Nigeria.
1816	The British establish Bathurst (now Banjul) at the mouth of the Gambia as a base against the slave trade.
1821	The Yoruba civil war commences.
	The American Colonization Society buys the area later known as Liberia to settle freed slaves.
1822	The first shipload of freed slaves reaches Cape Mesurado (in the region soon called Liberia) from the USA.
1830	Richard Lander and his brother, John, explore the lower reaches of the Niger, proving that the great river is navigable.
1832	The paddle steamer, *Alburkah*, becomes the first ocean-going iron ship, completing the journey from England to the Niger.
1841	Britain sends four naval ships up the River Niger to make anti-slavery treaties with local kings.
1847	Liberia wins independence and international recognition as a republic.
1850	The British government buys the Danish fortresses on the Gold Coast, including Christiansburg Castle in Accra.
1851	British naval forces bombard Lagos.
1854	William Baikie, on an expedition up the Niger, protects his men from malaria by administering quinine.
1861	On the coast of Nigeria, Lagos is annexed as a British colony when the royal family seem unable or unwilling to end the slave trade.
1862	Richard Burton, visiting Dahomey, provides reports of the kingdom's celebrated Amazons preparing for war.
1870	The trade of enslaved people is officially abolished, but not before up to 20 million enslaved Africans were transported to the Americas, never to return. Around half of them died en route.
1874	The southern region of present-day Ghana becomes a British colony, to be known as the Gold Coast.

Date	Events
1879	George Goldie and British traders on the Niger form the United African Company (later the Royal Niger Company) to consolidate their interests.
1884–85	The Berlin Conference divides Africa between European powers without consulting the African people. France is awarded one-third of the continent and ten West African countries in what becomes known as Afrique Occidentale Française (French West Africa).
1889	France and Britain agree on colonial boundaries for Senegal and Gambia in West Africa.
1892	The French establish a protectorate in part of the ancient kingdom of Dahomey in West Africa.
1893	France claims the Ivory Coast (or Côte d'Ivoire) in West Africa as a French colony.
	The Yoruba civil war comes to an end.
1897	The British burn Benin City in a punitive expedition after members of a British delegation are murdered.
1900	The British government assumes direct responsibility for the entire region of Nigeria, part of which is previously entrusted to a commercial company.
1904	The German, General Lothar von Trotha, drives 8,000 Herrero people to slow death in the Kalahari desert.
1913	Albert Schweitzer and his wife become missionaries at Lambaréné in Western Gabon.
1914	British rule is consolidated in Nigeria by the merging of the north and south as a single colony.
	World War I begins.
	British and French forces invade the German colony of Togoland.
1916	British and French forces win full control of the German colonies of Togoland and Cameroon.
1918	World War I ends.
1922	The League of Nations gives France and Britain mandates to govern separate areas of the German colony of Cameroon.
	France and Britain are given a League of Nations mandate to govern separate areas of the German colony of Togoland.
1939	World War II begins.
1943	William Tubman begins a 28-year spell as president of Liberia.
1945	World War II ends.
1952	Kwame Nkrumah, recently released from jail, becomes prime minister of the British colony of the Gold Coast.
1956	After a plebiscite, British Togo is merged with the neighboring colony of the Gold Coast.
1957	Ghana gains independence after a long campaign entitled "Self Government Now." The campaign's leader, Kwame Nkrumah, becomes Ghana's post-independence leader and hero to millions of West Africans.
1958	Guinea opts to go it alone, rejecting ongoing French rule in favor of immediate independence. France takes revenge by withdrawing all assistance to the country.

Date	Events
1960	French Togo becomes independent as the Republic of Togo, with Sylvanus Olympio as president.
	French Sudan becomes independent as the Republic of Mali, with Modibo Keita as president.
	The French colony of Dahomey (known from 1975 as Benin) becomes independent but suffers six military coups in its first twelve years.
	Niger becomes independent, with Hamani Diori as the new nation's first president.
	The French colony of Upper Volta becomes independent as Burkina Faso, with Maurice Yaméogo as president.
	Félix Houphouët-Boigny, first president of the newly independent Ivory Coast, begins thirty-three years of relatively peaceful rule.
	The French colony of Senegal becomes independent, with Léopold Senghor as the new nation's first president.
	Nigeria wins independence, with Abubakar Tafawa Balewa as prime minister, but its stability is threatened by ethnic and regional factions.
	The French colony of Mauritania becomes independent, with Moktar Ould Daddah as president.
1961	Former British colony, Sierra Leone, becomes an independent state within the Commonwealth.
	The southern part of the British Cameroons votes to merge with Cameroon, becoming the federal republic of Cameroon.
1965	The Gambia becomes an independent member of the Commonwealth, with Dawda Jawara as prime minister.
1966	Kwame Nkrumah, the founding father of Ghana, is toppled in a coup while away on a state visit to China.
	The First Festival of Negro Arts (later known as FESTAC) was held in Dakar, Senegal.
1967	The Igbo of eastern Nigeria claim independence for their region—as the Republic of Biafra.
1970	The breakaway Republic of Biafra surrenders after three years of devastating civil war in Nigeria.
1974	Portuguese Guinea becomes independent as Guinea-Bissau, with Luís Cabral as president.
1975	The Republic of Dahomey changes its name to Benin, an already famous name in African history.
	Yakubu Gowon, who united Nigeria after the Biafran war, is ousted in a military coup.
	The Cape Verde islands, off the west coast of Africa, become independent as the Republic of Cape Verde.
1977	The Second World African Festival of Arts and Culture takes place in Lagos.
1979	Young officers, led by a flight lieutenant, Jerry Rawlings, take power in a coup in Ghana.
1982	Senegal and the Gambia partially merge as Senegambia in a confederation that lasts seven years.
1984	The name of Upper Volta is changed to Burkina Faso, meaning "land of incorruptible people."
1989	The Liberian civil war begins in December.
1990	The aged president, Félix Houphouët-Boigny, wins Ivory Coast's first democratic elections.

Date	Events
1991	A Tuareg uprising in Mali results in some 120,000 refugees fleeing the country.
	The incumbent president, Mathieu Kérékou, loses in Benin's first democratic election.
	The Revolutionary United Front, led by Foday Sankoh, attacks Sierra Leone from bases in Liberia.
1993	Nigerian military dictator, General Ibrahim Babangida, annuls the country's presidential election regarded as the freest and fairest in the country's history.
	Guinea's first democratic election is won by the incumbent president, Lansana Conté.
1995	Ken Saro-Wiwa, playwright and pro-democracy campaigner in Nigeria, is among a group hanged by the ruling junta.
1996	Jerry Rawlings has a convincing electoral victory after seventeen years in power in Ghana.
1997	Ghanaian diplomat, Kofi Annan, is appointed Secretary-General of the United Nations, becoming the first black African in the post.
	The civilian president of Sierra Leone, Ahmad Kabbah, is ousted in a military coup led by Johnny Koroma.
1998	Nigerian military dictator, General Sanni Abacha, dies in office.
	Alleged winner of the June 12, 1993, Nigerian presidential election, Chief M.K.O Abiola, dies in prison.
	Nigerian forces expel Johnny Koroma from Freetown and reinstate Sierra Leone's elected civilian president, Ahmad Kabbah.
1999	Nigeria returns to democratic rule and elects President Olusegun Obasanjo.
	President Kabbah and the guerrilla leader, Foday Sankoh, arrange for shared government in Sierra Leone.
	The UN commits 6,000 troops to a peace-keeping role in war-torn Sierra Leone.
2000	Africans from West Africa living in Libya complain of racial discrimination by Arabs, and hundreds of them return to their countries. The crisis has implications for continental solidarity and reopened old wounds in regional conflicts.
2001	The Africa Union is created to replace the Organization of African Unity.
2002	The terrorist organization, Boko Haram, is founded by Muslim preacher, Mohammed Yusuf.
2003	Liberian president, Charles Taylor, is granted asylum in Nigeria.
2006	Ellen Johnson Sirleaf, the first female president of Liberia, is elected.
2009	Abubakar Shekau takes over the leadership of Boko Haram.
2010	Nigeria's president, Umaru Musa Yar'Adua, dies in office.
	Goodluck Jonathan is sworn in as the substantive President of Nigeria through a controversial doctrine of necessity.
2011	The civil war in Ivory Coast is possibly ended by the capture of the former president and recently defeated presidential candidate, Laurent Gbagbo.
2012	Occupy Nigeria protests after a controversial plan to end fuel subsidies.
2013	Largest Ebola virus disease outbreak in West Africa.
2014	Boko Haram kidnaps Christian female students in Chibok, Borno State, Nigeria.
	#BringBackOurGirls movement and protests rock the country.

Date	Events
2015	Muhammadu Buhari becomes the first opposition leader to win elections in Nigeria.
	Boko Haram aligns with the Islamic State of Iraq and the Levant.
	Multinational Joint Task Force is formed by Lake Chad Basin states to tackle Boko Haram.
	A coup attempt in Burkina Faso leads to the detention of the transitional government of Michel Kafando.
2016	In Cameroon's anglophone regions, protests against President Paul Biya's rule and his government policies favoring francophone areas become more frequent.
2018	CAF strips Cameroon from hosting the 2019 African Cup of Nations due to poor infrastructure, insecurity, and the anglophone crisis.
2020	COVID-19 pandemic.
	A coup in Mali removes President Ibrahim Boubacar Keita and Prime Minister, Boubou Cisse.
	#EndSARS protests rock several cities across Nigeria.
2021	ECOWAS suspends Mali from the regional group.
	Chadian President, Idriss Deby, is killed in combat.
	Guinea President, Alpha Conde, is toppled in a military coup.
2022	Nigeria's inflation rate hit a 17-year-high of 21.47 percent. People living in poverty rose to 133 million, or 63 percent of the population.
	Economic woes in Sierra Leone led to street protesters demanding President Julius Bio step down.
	Ghana's cedi becomes the worst-performing currency against the dollar, leading to the International Monetary fund (IMF) granting it a $3bn loan bailout.
	West African states witnessed the return of artefacts looted by former colonial powers starting with the United States, Germany, and the UK.
	Coup is thwarted in Mali. Attempted coups in Guinea-Bissau and The Gambia.
	Private armies (Wagner Group) make inroads into the region, especially in Mali.
	Nigeria ends its seven-month ban on Twitter.
2023	A coup in Niger on 26 July, 2023 removedfrom power President Mohammed Bazoum.
	Bola Ahmed Tinubu emerged as the President of Nigeria after a bitterly contested election.

Sources

Falola, Toyin. *Key Events in African History: A Reference Guide.* Westport, Greenwood Press, 2002.

Lonely Planet. "West Africa in Detail: Timeline," accessed October 13, 2021, https://www.lonelyplanet.com/west-africa/background/history/timeline/a/nar/2e501fa1-294d48ff-85a9-a0e72a440c2e/1333574

Oxford Reference. Timeline: West Africa (Years: c. 2000 BCE - 2011), accessed October 13, 2021, https://www.oxfordreference.com/view/10.1093/acref/9780191735851.timeline.0001.

INDEX